A Modern Approach to Wills, Administration and Estate Planning (with Precedents)

Third Edition

A Modern Approach to Wills, Administration and Estate Planning (with Precedents)

Third Edition

Christopher Whitehouse and Professor Lesley King

JORDAN
PUBLISHING

Published by Jordan Publishing Limited
21 St Thomas Street
Bristol BS1 6JS

British Library Cataloguing-in-Publication Data

A catalogue record for this book is available from the British Library.

ISBN 978 1 78473 054 3

Typeset by Letterpart Limited, Caterham on the Hill, Surrey CR3 5XL

Printed in Great Britain by CPI Group (UK) Ltd, Croydon, CR0 4YY

PREFACE

The third edition of this work has been updated to take into account recent case and statutory law and, in addition, three new chapters have been included in a new Section D. These deal with the rules of intestacy (taking into account the 2014 changes); the arcane sounding *donatio mortis causa* (and some recent cases) and claims under the 1975 Act (which generates voluminous case-law each year).

Real difficulties, however, have arisen from the activities of HMRC in first looking to simplify the IHT treatment of relevant property trusts and then in striving to make the rules fairer (to HMRC). The result has been chaos and the relevant sections in Chapters 3 and 8 have been endlessly rewritten as one proposed change has been swiftly followed by a u-turn and further proposals. The end result is that the significant changes intended to take effect on 6 April 2015 (with some backdating – in modern jargon 'anti-forestalling' – to 10 December 2014) failed to get into FA 2015 in the last days of the Coalition Government. We are told that these changes will be introduced in a future Finance Bill although it is unclear how HMRC can bind the next Government to do this. Accordingly, at the time of writing, whether the proposed changes will be introduced and, if so, from what date remains a matter of uncertainty. For this reason a card is included in the book which should be completed and returned to the publishers. As and when the position is clarified, an email will be sent to those who have returned the card setting out the position and updating the appropriate sections of the book.

This whole episode raises a number of interesting issues: for instance, how a consultation designed to simplify the legislation was hijacked to remove the IHT benefits of multiple settlements! And why the draft legislation was not included in the large Finance Act that was rushed through all of its Parliamentary stages in a single day. In itself, this is perhaps the most striking event of all. Is Parliament not supposed to scrutinize legislation imposing taxation, and indeed were not rebellions and wars fought in the past to establish the principle that there should be no tax without representation? Nowhere is the decline in the role of Parliament more striking than in the passage of FA 2015.

Through all this Elouise Dale has dealt in her inimitable way with the rewrites, and Jordan Publishing, and especially the long suffering Tony Hawitt, have been models of restraint.

The law is stated at 1 April 2015.

CJW/LK
London

CONTENTS

Section C
Administering the Estate (Including Establishing and Running Will Trusts)

Chapter 11
Obtaining the Grant

Section D
Miscellaneous

Chapter 15
The Intestacy Rules

Contents

Appendices

TABLE OF CASES

References are to paragraph numbers.

TABLE OF STATUTES

References are to paragraph numbers.

TABLE OF STATUTORY INSTRUMENTS

References are to paragraph numbers.

TABLE OF ABBREVIATIONS

AEA 1925	Administration of Estates Act 1925
CGTM	Capital Gains Tax Manual
CTA 2010	Corporation Tax Act 2010
FA (year)	Finance Act
IHTA 1984	Inheritance Tax Act 1984
IHTM	Inheritance Tax Manual
ITA 2007	Income Tax Act 2007
ITTOIA 2005	Income Tax (Trading and Other Income) Act 2005
LPA 1925	Law of Property Act 1925
PAA (year)	Perpetuities and Accumulations Act
SLA 1925	Settled Land Act 1925
TA (year)	Trustee Act
TCGA 1992	Taxation of Chargeable Gains Act 1992
WA 1837	Wills Act 1837

Section A

THE BACKGROUND LAW

CHAPTER 1

THE ESSENTIAL WILLS LAW

1.01 This book is intended to assist those planning the tax efficient disposition of property on death and the precedents provided are selected with that in mind. However, it goes without saying that the clauses provided have to be included in a valid will and that most testators will want to include gifts to individuals which are supplementary to the main tax planning.

A complete will is included at **Precedent 4.1.**

This chapter does three things:

(1) it explains what a will is and what it does;
(2) it deals in outline with the various elements required for a valid will; and
(3) it looks at some elements of a will which cause problems when planning and drafting.

The rules that apply on an intestacy are considered in Chapter 15.

1. WHAT IS A WILL?

1.02 A will is a document, normally in writing, which deals with the testator's wishes for the disposition of his property after death. To be valid, it must comply with certain formalities and, if valid, it will be subject to probate after the testator's death. As well as dealing with the disposition of property, it can appoint executors, trustees and guardians. It will normally revoke earlier wills and may include statements of the testator's wishes for funeral and donation of organs although it is generally preferable for a testator to make family members aware of such wishes independently of the will.

1.03 A codicil is a document executed in the same way as a will which makes minor alterations to the will. The will and any supporting codicils are construed together as one testamentary disposition. A codicil normally[1] republishes a will so that the will and any codicils are construed as if written at the date of the last codicil. In all but the simplest cases it is preferable to prepare a new will as there is scope for error in amending part only of a will. It is all too easy to fail to spot unwanted 'knock-on' effects.

---

[1]   Unless there is any contrary intention shown.

1.04 It is possible to avoid the need for a will and probate by transferring property to a grantor trust under which the settlor retains a right to income and access to capital. The trustees of such a trust will have the legal title to assets and will deal with them in accordance with the terms of the trust after the settlor's death without need for a grant of probate. However, for those domiciled in England and Wales the inheritance tax consequences of transferring property to a settlement may make this an unattractive option.[2]

How does a will differ from a living will or advance decision?

1.05 'Living wills' or 'advance decisions' are documents intended to allow individuals to specify the extent and nature of the medical treatment they would or would not find acceptable should they lose capacity in the future. The term 'living will' is confusing since such documents have no connection with ordinary wills. The Mental Capacity Act 2005 uses the term 'advance decision' and this is becoming more usual.

Competent patients can authorise or refuse consent to treatment, both at the time it is offered and in advance. They cannot make legally enforceable demands about specific treatment they wish to receive. *R (on the application of Burke) v General Medical Council*[3] confirmed that medical practitioners are under no obligation to provide a specific treatment requested by the patient if, in their view, it is clinically inappropriate.

Refusals, however, are a different matter. In *Re B (Consent to Treatment: Capacity)*[4] Dame Butler-Sloss reviewed the authorities and stated that a mentally competent patient has an absolute right to refuse consent to medical treatment for any reason, rational or irrational, or for no reason at all.

1.06 The right to refuse treatment was put onto a statutory footing by the Mental Capacity Act 2005. Section 24 of that Act provides that a person who is 18 or over and who has capacity can make an advance decision to refuse specified treatment at a later date in specified circumstances. If in the future the person loses capacity their decision will remain valid provided it has not been withdrawn or altered.

The advance decision can be expressed in layman's terms. It does not need to be in writing unless (as, in fact, will usually be the case) it relates to life-sustaining treatment. Where it does relate to life-sustaining treatment s 25(5) provides that the decision must be made in writing and include a statement that it is to apply to that treatment even if life is at risk; further:

---

2   As a result of FA 2006 changes in the inheritance tax treatment of settlements, the creation of the grantor trust will be an immediately chargeable transfer giving rise to a charge at 20% once the settlor's nil rate band (£325,000 for tax year 2015–16) is exhausted.

3   [2005] EWCA Civ 1003.

4   [2002] EWHC 429 (Fam).

(a) it must be signed by the person making it (P) or by someone else in P's presence and by P's direction;

(b) the signature must be made or acknowledged by P in the presence of a witness; and

(c) the witness must sign it, or acknowledge his signature, in P's presence.

An advance decision can be withdrawn at any time when P has capacity to do so and a withdrawal need not be in writing. An alteration of an advance decision need not be in writing (unless s 25(5) applies in relation to the decision resulting from the alteration).

An advance decision will only be effective if it is applicable to the treatment in question. Section 25(4) provides that it is not applicable if:

(a) the treatment is not the treatment specified in the advance decision;

(b) any circumstances specified in the advance decision are absent; or

(c) there are reasonable grounds for believing that circumstances exist which P did not anticipate at the time of the advance decision and which would have affected his decision had he anticipated them.

There may be cases where it is unclear whether or not the decision is applicable. The Mental Capacity Act 2005, s 26 allows application to the court to determine such questions. There is no set form for advance decisions, because the contents will inevitably vary, depending on the person's wishes and situation.[5]

1.07 The difficulty of drafting an advance decision to cover all future possibilities means that many people will choose the alternative of a health and personal welfare lasting power of attorney. This can authorise the attorney to give or refuse consent to the carrying out or continuation of life-sustaining treatment; the power must contain an express provision to that effect. An advance decision ceases to be valid if a lasting power of attorney created after the advance decision was made authorises the attorney(s) to give or refuse consent to the treatment to which the advance decision relates or if the donor revokes the advance decision or does anything else clearly inconsistent with the advance decision continuing.[6] A lasting power is 'created' for this purpose when registered not when executed.[7]

---

5   See *X Primary Care Trust v XB (By the Official Solicitor as Litigation Friend) and YB* [2012] EWHC 1390 (Fam); [2012] WTLR 1621 for a discussion of some of issues involved.

6   MCA 2005, s 25(2).

7   *Re E* [2014] EWCOP 27. The case is interesting because the attorneys appointed disclaimed to allow a deputy to be appointed. The creation of the power of attorney had revoked the advance decision and so there was a danger that the treatment preferences expressed in the donor's advance decision (and repeated in the lasting power) would be lost. To remedy that, the court made a declaration under MCA 2005, s 26(4) that, 'the advance decisions made by E in the Living Will and set out in the Schedule to this declaration continue to exist and to be valid and to be applicable to her treatment'.

Individuals who are concerned about their future treatment should consider either an advance decision or a properly drafted lasting power of attorney. Living wills or advance directives which pre-date the Mental Capacity Act 2005 and which deal with the refusal of life-sustaining treatment should be reviewed as they may not comply with the requirements of s 25(5) of the Act. In *NHS Trust v D*,[8] D's very clear letter of wishes authorising his sister-in-law to make medical decisions on his behalf and refusing any medical treatment which would merely extend a reduced quality of life was not binding as it did not comply with the s 25 requirements. An application was, therefore, made to the Court of Protection for a decision as to whether the withdrawal of nutrition would be in D's best interests. The court decided that it would be but the need for the application meant that there was a 9-month delay before D's wishes could be put into effect.

Practitioners need to be alert to a client's full needs. Estate planning may be just one element of a full service. Clients may require a will and two lasting powers of attorney to authorise attorneys to make decisions on their behalf if they lose the capacity to make their own decisions: one power will deal with property and financial affairs and one with health and personal welfare.

2. VALIDITY OF A WILL

1.08   To be valid a will must be made:

(a)   in accordance with the formal requirements of the Wills Act 1837, s 9;[9]
(b)   by a person who:
    (i)   has capacity; and
    (ii)   knows and approves the contents of the will,

and it must not have been subsequently revoked.

Formal requirements of Wills Act 1837, s 9

1.09   Section 9 provides that:

'No will shall be valid unless—

(a)   it is in writing, and signed by the testator, or by some other person in his presence and by his direction; and
(b)   it appears that the testator intended by his signature to give effect to the will; and
(c)   the signature is made or acknowledged by the testator in the presence of two or more witnesses present at the same time; and

---

8   [2012] EWHC 886 (Fam).
9   Unless at the time the will was made the testator had privileged status under the Wills Act 1837, s 11 as a soldier on actual military service or a sailor or mariner at sea. Such cases are rare but for a modern example see *Re Servoz-Gavin* [2009] EWHC 3168.

(d)   each witness either—
        (i)   attests and signs the will; or
        (ii)   acknowledges his signature,
        in the presence of the testator (but not necessarily in the presence of any other witness),

but no form of attestation shall be necessary.'

Writing includes handwriting, typing and word processing and may be on any material.[10]

Signature includes anything which the testator intends as a signature.[11]

Where another person signs for the testator, something in the nature of an instruction is required to demonstrate that there has been a direction. Mere acquiescence or passivity on the part of the testator is insufficient. There must be 'positive and discernible communication (which may be verbal or non-verbal) by the testator that he wishes the will to be signed on his behalf by the third party'.[12]

Writing and signature do not normally present problems in the case of a professionally drafted will. However, in *Marley v Rawlings* a solicitor who was supervising execution failed to notice that a husband and wife who were making wills in identical terms had signed the will of the other. Both signatures were attested by the solicitor and his secretary. The mistake was not picked up on the death of Mrs Rawlings[13] and did not come to light until Mr Rawlings died. The Court of Appeal held[14] that the will signed by Mr Rawlings was invalid. While he undoubtedly intended to give effect to *a* will when he signed the document placed in front of him, he did not intend to sign *the* will that was in front of him. In the Court of Appeal's view it was not possible to rectify the will under Administration of Justice Act 1982, s 20 as rectification requires there to be a valid will in the first place.

On appeal, however, the Supreme Court held[15] that, although there was a problem with knowledge and approval, the will was properly executed in accordance with Wills Act 1837, s 9 as Mr Rawlings had clearly signed the will and he had done so with the intention of giving effect to the will in front of him at that moment. Admittedly, he had made a mistake as to the will he was signing but that mistake did not mean that the s 9 requirements had not been

---

[10]   See Interpretation Act 1978, Sch 1; *Re Barnes Goods* (1926) 343 TLR 71 (will written on an egg shell).
[11]   'Your loving mother': *In the Estate of Cook* [1960] 1 WLR 353; Part of a name: *Re Chalcraft* [1948] P 222.
[12]   *Barratt v Bem* [2012] EWCA Civ 52, per Lewison LJ at [36].
[13]   Presumably all assets were jointly owned so that it was unnecessary to obtain a grant of probate.
[14]   [2012] EWCA Civ 61.
[15]   [2014] UKSC 2.

complied with. The finding that the will was validly executed was significant as it enabled the Supreme Court to rectify it.[16]

The elements which normally present problems are the requirement that the testator signs in the joint presence of two witnesses who afterwards sign in the presence of the testator. Testators often have a rather cavalier attitude to the need to comply with the formal requirements[17] and it is frequently a fruitful line of attack for those unhappy with the contents of a will.

1.10 Those who draft wills for clients should offer the opportunity of supervised execution. There are two reasons for this:

(a) supervised execution is the safest course, avoiding future arguments as to whether or not the formalities were complied with; and

(b) a practitioner who does not offer such an opportunity may be held to have been negligent.[18]

Clients may not wish to take up the offer in which case when the will is sent out for execution, the practitioner must provide clear instructions for execution.[19] Ideally the client should return the will to the practitioner for checking. When a will is returned for checking, it is important that this is done carefully; if a practitioner (or employee of the firm) fails to notice an obvious error, there will be liability in negligence.[20]

When there is a dispute after death as to whether or not the formal requirements of the Wills Act 1837, s 9 were complied with, the presence of a properly drafted attestation clause reciting that these requirements were complied with raises a presumption of due execution which can only be rebutted by the clearest possible evidence to the contrary.[21]

---

16 For rectification see **1.30**.

17 See, for example, *Humblestone v Martin Tolhurst Partnership* [2004] EWHC 151 (Ch) where the testator's in-laws signed the will as witnesses 'ready' for the testator to sign when he got home from work.

18 In *Esterhuizen v Allied Dunbar* [1998] 2 FLR 668 a will writer who had not offered such an opportunity was found negligent when after the testator's death the will was found to have been signed by only one witness.

19 The instructions should also explain that the witnesses must not be beneficiaries of the will or spouses or civil partners of beneficiaries as, if they are, although the will is valid, the gift to the beneficiary will fail: see Wills Act 1837, s 15.

20 See *Humblestone v Martin Tolhurst Partnership* [2004] EWHC 151 (Ch) (failure to notice that testator had forgotten to sign); *Ross v Caunters* [1980] Ch 297 (failure to notice that witness had same surname as a beneficiary – and was in fact married to the beneficiary).

21 See *Sherrington v Sherrington* [2005] EWCA Civ 326 applied in *Olins v Walters* [2007] EWHC 3060 (Ch). An assertion by the witnesses that they did not witness the signature or that there was no other witness present at the time of the signature is not sufficient: see *Re Wright* [2010] EWHC 1607 (Ch). Proof that the witnesses were elsewhere on the date in question would be sufficient; see *Channon v Perkins* [2005] EWCA Civ 1808. For an unusual case of a successful challenge despite an attestation clause, see *Ahluwalia v Singh* [2011] All ER (D) 113 (Sep). For standard attestation clauses see **Precedent 4.3**.

Incorporation of unexecuted documents

1.11 Because of the requirements of the Wills Act 1837, s 9 it is not permissible to change a testamentary disposition by an unexecuted document. However, unexecuted documents can be incorporated into a will provided the document is:

(a) referred to and sufficiently identified in the will;[22]

(b) in existence at the date of the will;[23] and

(c) referred to as being in existence.[24]

The document referred to becomes testamentary and must be construed with the will. Therefore anything in the document which would be invalid in the will is inoperative.

It may be convenient to leave property onto trusts already created (see Chapter 8, Pilot Trusts) and this gives rise to a different problem. The trust must be already in existence and referred to as such in the will and, in addition, the terms of the trust must not be altered before the death of the testator.[25]

Capacity to make a will

1.12 There are two elements to capacity: age and mental capacity.

Age

1.13 Unless the testator has privileged status under the Wills Act 1837, s 11,[26] a testator must be at least 18 at the time the will is made.[27]

Test of mental capacity

1.14 The test of mental capacity for a will is set out in *Banks v Goodfellow*.[28] To have testamentary capacity it is essential that a testator:

---

[22] *Smart v Prujean* (1801) 6 Ves 560; *Croker v Marquis of Hertford* (1844) 4 Moo PCC 339.

[23] *Re Keen* [1937] 1 All ER 452.

[24] *Re Truro's (Lady) Goods* (1866) LR 1 P & D 201.

[25] Because of the prohibition on unwitnessed dispositions. In *Re Edwards' Will Trusts* [1948] Ch 440 (legacy to a settlement where capital was to be held 'for such persons as the settlor should by a memorandum direct'; that clause of the settlement was held to be invalid as an attempt to nominate future beneficiaries by unexecuted writing but the rest of the settlement took effect). The inclusion of powers of appointment or discretionary trusts in a will is permitted. See, for example, *Re Beatty's Will Trusts* [1990] 3 All ER 844 where Hoffmann J said that there was no rule of law that a testator could not delegate the making of his will to his trustees since that would prevent the use of wide powers of appointment in wills. (There was, however, a rule that a gift which was expressed in language too vague to be enforced could not be rescued by giving the executor a power of choice.)

[26] See footnote 9 above.

[27] See Wills Act 1837, s 7.

[28] (1869–70) LR 5 QB 549.

(a)   shall understand the nature of the act and its effects;

(b)   shall understand the extent of the property of which he is disposing;

(c)   shall be able to comprehend and appreciate the claims to which he ought to give effect; and

(d)   with a view to the latter object that no disorder of the mind shall poison his affections, pervert his sense of right, or prevent the exercise of his natural faculties – that no insane delusion shall influence his will in disposing of his property and bring about a disposal of it which, if the mind had been sound, would not have been made.

1.15 In *Key v Key*[29] Briggs J said that he was willing to extend the elements of the test to cover a situation where the severe effects of a sudden bereavement had left the testator in a condition identical to that associated with severe depression. The testator who was in his eighties made a will which substantially changed the disposition of his estate at a time when he was devastated by the sudden death of his wife after a 65-year marriage. Both medical experts in the case agreed that depression may lead to an increased suggestibility in the mind of the patient, so that he simply assents to suggestions from others, for example as to what is or is not fair, not caring to form his own view on the subject. The distress caused by bereavement may make the sufferer suggestible, and may make him say anything to put an end to emotional pressure. A severe reaction to bereavement may, like depression caused by other factors, impair attention and concentration, and the ability of the sufferer to take things in and remember them. Depression could itself cause cognitive impairment with symptoms similar to dementia, from which, unlike true dementia, the patient might recover once the factors causing the depression had passed.

Taking the evidence as a whole, it was clear that Mr Key was unable to exercise the decision-making powers required of a testator – or, at least, that those seeking to uphold the will had not proved that he was:

> 'To the extent that such a conclusion involves a slight development of the *Banks v Goodfellow* test, taking into account decision-making powers rather than just comprehension, I consider that it is necessitated by the greater understanding of the mind now available from modern psychiatric medicine, in particular in relation to affective disorder.'

Impact of the Mental Capacity Act 2005

1.16 *Scammell v Farmer*[30] was the first case involving testamentary capacity to be considered after the Mental Capacity Act came into force. Although Stephen Smith QC, sitting as a deputy judge decided that, because of the date of death, it was appropriate to base his decision on the old law, the judgment contains helpful comments on the differences between the two. He started with s 3 of the Act:

---

29   [2010] EWHC 408 (Ch).
30   [2008] EWHC 1100 (Ch).

'(1) For the purposes of section 2, a person is unable to make a decision for himself if he is unable—

(a) to understand the information relevant to the decision,
(b) to retain that information,
(c) to use or weigh that information as part of the process of making the decision, or
(d) to communicate his decision (whether by talking, using sign language or any other means).

(2) A person is not to be regarded as unable to understand the information relevant to a decision if he is able to understand an explanation of it given to him in a way that is appropriate to his circumstances (using simple language, visual aids or any other means).

(3) The fact that a person is able to retain the information relevant to a decision for a short period only does not prevent him from being regarded as able to make the decision.

(4) The information relevant to a decision includes information about the reasonably foreseeable consequences of—

(a) deciding one way or another, or
(b) failing to make the decision.'

which he said largely restates the *Banks v Goodfellow* test.

However, he pointed out one obvious difference between the position at common law and the position under the 2005 Act as a result of s 1 which provides that:

'(1) The following principles apply for the purposes of this Act.

(2) A person must be assumed to have capacity unless it is established that he lacks capacity.'

As Stephen Smith put it under s 1(2) 'the onus of proof of incapacity under the 2005 Act is from the outset, and remains, on the complainant'. At common law, on the other hand, the persons putting forward a will must prove that it is valid. They are assisted by the presumption of capacity where the will is rational and there is nothing to cast doubt on capacity.

However, he said that s 1 does not appear to apply to testamentary capacity. Section 1(1) says that the principles set out in s 1 apply *for the purposes of this Act.* The making of a will is not within the purposes of the 2005 Act. The only provisions relating to wills are in ss 16–18 and concern the power of the court to make or authorise the making of wills on behalf of persons who lack capacity, not 'the ascertainment of whether a particular testator had capacity when a Will was made'.

1.17 Stephen Smith was also referred to the Mental Capacity Act Code of Practice on the basis that parts of the Code suggest that the Act was intended to apply to testamentary capacity. He said:

> 'Even if that was a correct reading of the Code of Practice, it would not change my interpretation of the 2005 Act. But I do not think that it is a correct reading of the Code of Practice at all.'

Paragraph 4.33 states expressly that there are existing common law tests of capacity for certain tasks, including making a will and that when cases come before the court involving those tests, judges can adopt the new definition if they think it is appropriate. Munby J clarified the meaning of 'if they think it is appropriate' in *Local Authority X v MM (by her litigation friend, the Official Solicitor)*,[31] KM saying that, while judges sitting in the Court of Protection and exercising the statutory jurisdiction under the Mental Capacity Act are obviously bound to apply the statutory principles contained in that Act, judges sitting elsewhere and deciding cases for which there is an existing test can adopt the formulation from the Mental Capacity Act if it corresponds to the existing common law test, having regard to the existing principles of the common law.

Some later cases[32] suggested that the *Banks v Goodfellow* test may have been superseded by the Mental Capacity Act. However, in *Kicks v Leigh*[33] Judge Stephen Morris QC reviewed all the cases and said that he preferred the analysis in *Scammell*. In his opinion the MCA test of capacity (and presumption as to capacity) is relevant only for decisions made by the Court of Protection under the MCA itself. In *Walker v Badmin*[34] Judge Nicholas Strauss QC also reviewed the case-law and concluded that the *Banks v Goodfellow* test for testamentary capacity applied rather than the MCA test. His reasoning did not affect the result of the case since, on the facts, the two tests gave the same result. Nevertheless, it is important for the future that the legal basis for the correct test has been spelled out even though it would be preferable to have a Court of Appeal decision on the point.

Uncertain testamentary capacity

1.18 Cases of uncertain testamentary capacity pose problems for practitioners both at the time they take instructions and later, if capacity becomes the subject of litigation. Not only may a great deal of time be wasted dealing with the case, but a practitioner who allows a client to make a will which is bound to give rise

---

[31]   [2007] EWHC 2003 (Fam), at para [67].
[32]   See *Re Perrins* [2009] EWHC 1945 (Ch) where Lewison J observed at para 40 that the *Banks v Goodfellow* test is 'now superseded' by the MCA 2005, but without further comment (as the events in the case in question took place before the Act came into force with the result that he used common law principles). In *Fischer v Diffley* [2013] EWHC 4567 (Ch) HHJ Dight took the MCA as his starting point. Similarly in *Bray v Pearce* (unreported) 6 March 2015, Judge Murray Rosen QC held that the MCA test can and should be applied in some way either as supplementing, or alongside, the common law.
[33]   [2014] EWHC 3926 Ch.
[34]   (Unreported) 20 November 2014.

to litigation will be at risk of liability for the costs of the unnecessary litigation.[35] In *Corbett v Bond Pearce*, Sir Christopher Slade commented on *Worby v Rosser* as follows:

> 'the significance of this case lies in the fact that the Court of Appeal accepted that in a case where a solicitor's negligence in regard to the preparation or execution of a will was the cause of expensive probate proceedings after the testator's death, this could give rise to a claim for damages against the solicitors at the suit of the testator's personal representatives for the benefit of the estate generally.'

1.19 So what should a practitioner do? A series of cases starting in 1975 with *Kenward v Adams*[36] set out the so-called 'Golden Rule' which solicitors should aim to follow in cases where there may later be questions as to capacity. In that case Templeman J stated that:

> 'in the case of an aged testator or a testator who has suffered a serious illness, there is one golden rule which should always be observed, however straightforward matters may appear, and however difficult or tactless it may be to suggest that precautions be taken. The making of a will by such a testator ought to be witnessed or approved by a medical practitioner who satisfies himself of the capacity and understanding of the testator, and records and preserves his examination and findings.
>
> There are other precautions which should be taken. If the testator has made an earlier will this should be considered by the legal and medical advisers of the testator and, if appropriate, discussed with the testator.
>
> The instructions of the testator should be taken in the absence of anyone who may stand to benefit, or who may have influence over the testator. These are not counsels of perfection. If proper precautions are not taken injustice may result or be imagined, and great expense and misery may be unnecessarily caused.'

It is important to note that even if the rule is complied with, there is no guarantee that the court will agree that the testator had capacity. Compliance with the Golden Rule does not guarantee the validity of a will, nor does non-compliance demonstrate its invalidity. What compliance does do, is to provide contemporaneous medical evidence which 'may assist in the avoidance of disputes, or at least in the minimisation of their scope'. Conversely failing to comply with the rule does not mean that the will is invalid.

There are a string of cases making this point. For example, *Allen v Emery*[37] where Sonia Proudman QC, sitting as a deputy judge of the High Court, said:

> 'It is undoubtedly a desirable precaution, and one which can save a great deal of trouble in the future, for a solicitor to observe the golden rule where there is the possibility of dispute as to testamentary capacity. Failure to do so, however, is not

[35] See *Worby v Rosser* [1999] Lloyds Rep PN 972; *William H J Corbett v Bond Pearce* [2001] 3 All ER 769 and *Sifri v Clough & Willis* [2007] WTLR 1453.
[36] 1975 CLY 3591.
[37] [2005] All ER D 175.

in my judgment determinative; the rule is no more than prudent guidance for a solicitor; see the observations of Peter Gibson LJ on the golden rule in the context of want of knowledge and approval in *Hoff and Others v Atherton* [2004] EWCA Civ 1554. Ultimately capacity is a question of fact like any other which the Court must decide on the evidence as a whole.'

However, failure to follow the rule may lay a practitioner open to judicial criticism and the danger of an adverse costs order. In *Key v Key*[38] Briggs J criticised a solicitor for failing to comply with the Golden Rule on the basis that the failure had 'greatly increased the difficulties to which this dispute has given rise'. On the other hand in *Wharton v Bancroft*[39] Norris J was sympathetic to the plight of those called to a death bed to prepare a will in circumstances of urgency. He said that the solicitor involved was not 'to be criticised for deciding to make his own assessment (accepted as correct) and to get on with the job of drawing a will'.[40]

Criticism of the Golden Rule

1.20 Norris J writing in *Association of Contentious Trusts and Probate Specialists Newsletter*[41] made the point that the opinion of a medical practitioner is not always reliable. General practitioners and geriatricians have widely varying views as to what is required to satisfy the legal test; even when they share the same understanding of the test there is a legitimate divergence of view amongst specialists in any given case and general practitioners do not have the technical knowledge to assess the degree to which a particular condition or drug therapy impairs cognitive function.

In a later article[42] Stephen Lawson suggested that it is often impractical to follow the Golden Rule and that doing so will serve only to increase delay and cost without producing a proportionate benefit. He suggests that the preferable course is for a practitioner to explain the Golden Rule to a client, offer the client the option of obtaining a medical opinion and, if the client declines, to make the will. This echoes the advice of Nicholas Strauss QC sitting as a Deputy High Court Judge who addressed the question of what a practitioner should do if uncertain as to a person's capacity in *Sharp v Adam*.[43] In that case the solicitor had done her best to ascertain capacity in difficult circumstances where a seriously ill father with limited means of communication had expressed a wish to make a will disinheriting his daughters and leaving his estate to employees of his stud farm. Both the solicitor (and the GP who was in attendance) were satisfied that the testator satisfied the first three elements of the *Banks v Goodfellow* test but they could not understand his reasons for

---

[38]   [2010] EWHC 408 (Ch).
[39]   [2011] EWHC 3250 (Ch).
[40]   [2011] EWHC 3250 (Ch) at [110].
[41]   January 2007.
[42]   'The Golden Rule – time to move on?' (2010) Volume 8(3) *Trust Quarterly Review* 10.
[43]   [2005] EWHC 1806 (Ch) at [161].

excluding his daughters entirely from the will; nor had they any practical means of finding out because of the communication difficulties.

Nicholas Strauss QC said that in such circumstances, the solicitor's duty 'was to warn her client that the will might be challenged and, if he ignored the warning, implement his instructions without further delay, both of which she very properly did. To have acted otherwise would have risked depriving her client right to make a will, when he might well have had testamentary capacity.' He concluded 'That a situation of this kind may lead to litigation is regrettable, but that is what the courts are for. The will drafter who has acted correctly is not to be blamed if litigation ensues.'

However, it is important in such cases to ask the client questions designed to explore testamentary capacity,[44] if possible cross-check the accuracy of the answers[45] and record the results in a detailed attendance note.

Time at which capacity has to be proved

1.21 Normally the testator must have capacity at the time when the will is executed; however, under the rule in *Parker v Felgate* a will may be valid even though a testator lacks capacity at that time provided he:

(a) had capacity when giving instructions;

(b) believes the will is prepared in accordance with those instructions;

(c) retains the same testamentary wishes.

Modern examples of the application of the rule are *Clancy v Clancy*[46] and *Re Perrins*.[47] The rule has been extended to the execution of lifetime documents.[48]

Knowledge and approval

1.22 A testator must know and approve the contents of a will. This is normally presumed when a testator signs a will. If someone signs on behalf of the testator, there is no such presumption and the attestation clause should be amended to recite that the testator having had the will read over to him knew and approved the contents and was happy for it to be signed on his behalf.

---

[44] 'What are you seeking to achieve by making a will? What is the approximate value of your estate and how is it made up? Who would be likely to have a moral claim against, or expectation of benefit from your estate?'

[45] For a case where a testatrix appeared to have capacity but had forgotten the existence of family members and friends, see *Charles v Fraser* [2010] EWHC 2154 (Ch). Looking at earlier wills is helpful as a cross check for forgotten family members.

[46] [2003] EWHC 1885 (Ch).

[47] [2010] EWCA Civ 840.

[48] See *Singellos v Singellos* and 1.15 in the authors' *A Modern Approach to Lifetime Tax Planning*.

The presumption can be rebutted by suspicious circumstances. See, for example, *Franks v Sinclair*[49] where a solicitor prepared a will for his mother which excluded the previous main beneficiary, the testatrix's grandson, and substituted the solicitor who had not been included in the earlier will. The case is interesting for the comments of the judge that simply reading a will over to a testator is not sufficient where the wording is complex; the effect of the will must be explained in simple language. Where it is not clear that a testator was given an opportunity to read through the will before execution, the presumption will not arise.[50]

Fraud and undue influence

1.23   A will is invalid if it is procured by fraud or undue influence. Fraud in a testamentary context is referred to as fraudulent calumny. The basic idea is that if A poisons the testator's mind against B, who would otherwise be a natural beneficiary of the testator's bounty, by casting dishonest aspersions on his character, then the will is liable to be set aside. It is a difficult allegation to establish. According to Lewison J in *Re Edwards*[51] (where unusually the allegation was upheld) it is necessary for the person making the allegation to prove that the person alleged to have been poisoning the testator's mind knew that the aspersions were false or did not care whether they were true or false. If a person believes that he is telling the truth about a potential beneficiary then even if what he tells the testator is objectively untrue, the will is not liable to be set aside on that ground alone.[52]

There have been a number of cases recently of people impersonating others in order to make wills in their own favour.[53] It is, therefore, important to check the identity of new clients carefully.

To invalidate a will influence must amount to coercion. A testator must have been forced into making a will in a particular form without wanting to do so. Persuasion is not enough.[54] Undue influence must be proved by the person alleging it. There are no situations in which a presumption of undue influence arises in relation to the making of a will.[55] This is unlike the position in relation to lifetime gifts where a presumption arises if there is a relationship of trust and confidence between donor and donee and a transaction which requires

---

[49]   [2006] EWHC 3365 (Ch).
[50]   *Hawes v Burgess* [2013] EWCA 94; *Gill v Woodall* [2009] EWHC 3778 (Ch).
[51]   [2007] EWHC 1119 (Ch) at [47].
[52]   For an unsuccessful attempt to prove fraudulent calumny see *Re Boye, Nesbitt v Nicholsons* [2013] EWHC 4027 (Ch), [2014] All ER (D) 102 (Jan).
[53]   For a recent example see *Re Willis Estate* [2010] WTLR 169.
[54]   See *Scammell v Farmer* [2008] EWHC 1100 (Ch); *Hubbard v Scott* [2011] EWHC 2750 (Ch); *Cowderoy v Cranfield* [2011] EWHC 1616 (Ch); *Re Devillebichot (deceased) Brennan v Prior* [2013] EWHC 2867 (Ch) for illustrations of mere persuasion. See *Schomberg v Taylor* [2013] All ER (D) 74 (Jan); *Schrader v Schrader* [2013] EWHC 466 (Ch) for illustrations of undue influence.
[55]   For recent confirmation and contrast with the position in relation to lifetime gifts, see *Hubbard v Scott* [2011] EWHC 2750 (Ch).

explanation.[56] The result is that it is extremely difficult to prove a case of undue influence as there is normally insufficient evidence. Modern examples of wills declared invalid on the basis of undue influence are *Killick v Pountney*[57] and *Gill v Woodall*.[58]

Practitioners should be alert for signs of undue influence. Two of the elements of the Golden Rule are helpful in this context:

(a) considering any earlier will of the testator;
(b) taking instructions in the absence of anyone who may stand to benefit, or who may have influence over the testator.

Will must not have been revoked

1.24 Wills can be revoked in three ways:

(1) by destruction;
(2) by subsequent will;
(3) by subsequent marriage or the formation of a subsequent civil partnership.

Destruction

1.25 A will is only revoked by destruction if the destruction is carried out by the testator with the intention of revoking it or by someone else in the presence of the testator and by the testator's direction. In other cases, for example accidental destruction, it is possible to obtain probate of a draft, copy or reconstruction of the destroyed will.[59]

There is a presumption that a will, known to have been in the testator's possession which cannot be found after death, was destroyed by the testator with the intention of revoking it. However, the strength of the presumption is weakened if the testator habitually kept his papers in disorder.[60]

Subsequent will

1.26 A later will always revokes an earlier will to the extent that they are inconsistent. However, it is usual (and good practice) to commence a will with a clause which expressly revokes any earlier will or codicil.

---

[56] See *Royal Bank of Scotland v Etridge* [2002] 2 AC 773; *Pesticcio v Huet* [2004] EWCA Civ 372. See further the authors' *A Modern Approach to Lifetime Tax Planning*, Chapter 3.
[57] [1999] All ER (D) 365.
[58] [2009] EWHC 3778 (Ch). However, in the Court of Appeal the question of undue influence was not considered, as the court decided that the will was invalid on the basis of lack of knowledge and approval; see [2010] EWCA Civ 1430.
[59] Non-Contentious Probate Rules 1987, SI 1987/2024, r 54.
[60] *Rowe v Clarke* [2005] EWHC 3068 (Ch). See also *Nichols v Hudson* [2006] EWHC 3006 (Ch); *Wren v Wren* [2006] EWHC 2243 (Ch).

Probably the only case in which a will should not start with a general revocation clause is where a testator owns property abroad and has made a will in that jurisdiction dealing with the foreign property. The revocation clause should state that it is limited to wills dealing with property in England and Wales and is not intended to revoke any will dealing with assets elsewhere.[61]

Subsequent marriage or formation of subsequent civil partnership

1.27 With two exceptions, wills are automatically revoked if the testator subsequently marries or forms a civil partnership. This is a trap as many people are not aware of it. It is particularly important to explain the effect of marriage or formation of a civil partnership to clients who are cohabiting. The intestacy rules will apply if the will is revoked and may not accord with the deceased's wishes.

The exceptions are where it appears from the will that the testator is expecting:

(a)   to marry;[62] or

(b)   to form a civil partnership with[63]

a particular person and does not want the will to be revoked by the subsequent marriage or formation of the civil partnership.

See **Precedent 4.7.**

Section 9 of the Marriage (Same Sex Couples) Act 2014 provides for the conversion of a civil partnership into a marriage under a procedure to be established by regulations made by the Secretary of State.[64] Sub-section 6 provides that where this is done, the civil partnership ends on the conversion, and the resulting marriage is to be treated as having subsisted from the date when the civil partnership was formed.

Civil partners have been able to convert civil partnerships into same sex marriages from 10 December 2014. There was uncertainty as to whether such a conversion would revoke an existing will but this has been resolved by a

---

[61]   See *Perdoni v Curati* [2011] EWHC 3442 (Ch) for a typical illustration of the problems that can arise in relation to revocation clauses – and also in relation to domicile. It may be helpful to include a statement as to the law which the testator wishes to govern the construction of his will. See *Halsbury's Laws of England*, Fifth Edition, Volume 19, 2011, at para 750 and *Curati v Perdoni* [2012] EWCA Civ 1381 at [23].

[62]   Wills Act 1837, s 18(3) and (4).

[63]   Wills Act 1837, s 18B(3) and (4).

[64]   The regulations permit such conversions from 10 December 2014.

statutory instrument[65] which amends s 18 of Wills Act 1837 and inserts a new s 18D. These amendments provide that, where a civil partnership is converted to a marriage and a party to the civil partnership has an existing will:

- conversion will not revoke the will nor affect any disposition in the will following the conversion, subject to any contrary intention appearing from the will;

- following the conversion, subject to any contrary intention appearing from the will, any reference in the will to a civil partnership or civil partners (however expressed) will be read as referring to the marriage or the married couple, as appropriate.

Effect of divorce or dissolution of civil partnership

1.28   A divorce or dissolution of a civil partnership does not revoke an earlier will. However, it will revoke a gift to the former spouse or civil partner and any appointment of the former spouse or civil partner as executor will fail.[66] The former spouse or civil partner is treated as having predeceased which means that any substitutional gift expressed to take effect if the spouse or civil partner predeceases or fails to survive by a stated period will apply. However, it is only once the decree absolute is obtained that the spouse or civil partner is treated as having predeceased and so it is important to advise clients who are seeking a divorce or dissolution that they should make new wills.

Alteration of wills

1.29   Alterations made to a will after execution are invalid, unless executed like a will[67] and unexecuted alterations are presumed to have been made after execution.[68] A codicil made after the date of the alteration will normally republish the will and, therefore, saves the alteration. If the alteration completely obliterates the will so that it is impossible to read the original wording it will be treated as a partial revocation by destruction and the obliterated words will not be admitted to probate.[69]

The interpretation and rectification of wills[70]

1.30   If the court is satisfied that a will fails to carry out the testator's intentions, because of either a clerical error or a failure on the part of the

---

[65]   The Marriage (Same Sex Couples) Act 2013 (Consequential and Contrary Provisions and Scotland) and Marriage and Civil Partnership (Scotland) Act 2014 (Consequential Provisions) Order 2014/3168, Sch 1, para 1.

[66]   Wills Act 1837, ss 18A and 18C.

[67]   Wills Act 1837, s 21.

[68]   *Cooper v Bockett* (1846) 4 Moo PCC 419.

[69]   If the obliteration is accompanied by substituted words and it can be demonstrated that the intention to obliterate was conditional on the substituted words being admissible to probate, extrinsic evidence of the original wording will be admitted: *Brooke v Kent* (1841) 3 Moo PCC 334.

[70]   For equitable rectification of instruments of variation, see **12.47**.

draftsman to understand the testator's instructions, it may under s 20(1) of the Administration of Justice Act 1982 order the will to be rectified to carry out those instructions. Rectification may be granted either by the Chancery Division during contentious proceedings (CPR, Part 57) or, where no contentious proceedings have been brought, by the Family Division (Non-Contentious Probate Rules 1987, r 55). Applications for rectification must be made within 6 months of the original grant, although the court has power to allow an application after the end of that period.

It had been thought that a clerical error in s 20(1)(a) was confined to typos and errors in cut and pasting. Blackburne J said:[71]

> 'The essence of the matter is that a clerical error occurs when someone, who may be the testator himself, or his solicitor, or a clerk or a typist, writes something which he did not intend to insert or omits something which he intended to insert ... The remedy is only available if it can be established not only that the will fails to carry out the testator's instructions but also what those instructions were.'[72]

However, the Supreme Court has said[73] that the expression should be given a wide, rather than a narrow, meaning. According to Lord Neuberger the expression can extend to a mistake arising out of office work of a relatively routine nature, such as preparing, filing, sending, organising the execution of, a document (save, possibly, to the extent that the activity involves some special expertise). In *Marley v Rawlings*[74] the Supreme Court was asked to rectify a will signed by Mr Rawlings which was actually that of his wife (the terms were identical as the couple had made mirror wills). Lord Neuberger made the following points:

(1)   The fact that the claimed correction would effectively involve transposing the whole text of the wife's Will into the Will did not prevent it from being 'rectification' of each of the Wills. As a general proposition, there might be force in the point that the greater the extent of the correction sought, the steeper the task for a claimant who is seeking rectification. However, there was no reason in principle why a wholesale correction should be ruled out as a permissible exercise of the court's power to rectify.

(2)   The Court of Appeal had refused to allow rectification on the basis that the will was invalid because it had not been signed in accordance with the requirements of Wills Act 1837, s 9 and only a valid will could be rectified. Lord Neuberger said that this was not correct. While it was clear that something had gone 'seriously wrong', Mr Rawlings had signed the will, and had done so intending to give effect to his will. Therefore the will

---

71   In *Bell v Georgiou* [2002] EWHC 1080 (Ch) at [8].

72   *Wordingham v Royal Exchange Trust Co* [1992] Ch 412, [1992] 3 All ER 204, at 419, 211 per Evans-Lombe QC sitting as a deputy judge. A solicitor failed to include in a testator's new will the exercise of a power of appointment already in the testator's current will, even though he was so instructed.

73   In *Marley v Rawlings* [2014] UKSC 2 at [76].

74   [2014] UKSC 2.

was properly executed. It was true that there would be an issue of lack of knowledge and approval but consideration of that came at a later point and once the will was rectified that issue would drop away.[75]

1.31 Such errors extend to cases where the person drafting the will introduces, or fails to delete, a provision because he has not applied his mind to its significance or effect, ie an inadvertent error. There is a distinction between mere inadvertence, where rectification is available, and the situation where the person drafting the will has deliberately selected words but has misunderstood their effect where rectification is not possible.[76]

1.32 If rectification is to be allowed, first instance decisions suggest that the evidence of error must be very clear. As Chadwick J said:[77]

'although the standard of proof required in a claim for rectification made under section 20(1) of the 1982 Act is that the court should be satisfied on the balance of probabilities, the probability that a will which a testator has executed in circumstances of some formality reflects his intentions is usually of such weight that convincing evidence to the contrary is necessary.'

The court will not speculate as to the testator's intentions.[78]

1.33 The modern approach to interpretation of wills may make applications for rectification unnecessary. In the past courts approached the interpretation of wills in a rigid manner applying fixed 'rules' of construction. However, the modern approach to the interpretation of lifetime documents has been much more flexible focusing on establishing the intention of the parties. In *Marley v Rawlings*[79] Lord Neuberger confirmed that this is also the correct approach to the interpretation of wills, saying:

'[18] During the past forty years, the House of Lords and Supreme Court have laid down the correct approach to the interpretation, or construction, of commercial contracts in a number of cases starting with *Prenn v Simmonds* [1971] 3 All ER 237, [1971] 1 WLR 1381 and culminating in *Rainy Sky SA v Kookmin Bank* [2011] UKSC 50, [2012] 1 All ER 1137, [2011] 1 WLR 2900.

[19] When interpreting a contract, the court is concerned to find the intention of the party or parties, and it does this by identifying the meaning of the relevant words:

---

[75] Lord Neuberger went further at [60] saying 'it does not appear to me that a document has to satisfy the formal requirements of s 9, or of having the testator's knowledge and approval, before it can be treated as a 'will' which is capable of being rectified pursuant to s 20'.

[76] *Re Segelman* [1996] Ch 171, at 185. See also *Kell v Jones* [2013] All ER (D) 153 (Jan) and *Joshi v Mahida* [2013] EWHC 486 (Ch).

[77] *Re Segelman* [1996] Ch 171, at 184.

[78] See *Bell v Georgiou* [2002] EWHC 1080 (Ch), [2002] WTLR 1105, where an application was refused for lack of clear evidence. For recent cases where rectification was granted see *Sprackling v Sprackling* [2008] EWHC 2696 (Ch), [2008] All ER (D) 55 (Nov), [2009] WTLR 897 and *Clarke v Brothwood* [2006] EWHC 2939 (Ch), [2006] All ER (D) 207 (Nov).

[79] [2014] UKSC 2.

(a)   in the light of:
    (i)   the natural and ordinary meaning of those words,
    (ii)   the overall purpose of the document,
    (iii)   any other provisions of the document,
    (iv)   the facts known or assumed by the parties at the time that the document was executed, and
    (v)   common sense, but
(b)   ignoring subjective evidence of any party's intentions.

In this connection, see *Prenn* at 1384 – 1386 and *Reardon Smith Line Ltd v Yngvar Hansen-Tangen* [1976] 3 All ER 570, [1976] 1 WLR 989, [1976] 2 Lloyd's Rep 621, per Lord Wilberforce, *Bank of Credit and Commerce International SA v Ali* [2001] UKHL 8, [2002] 1 AC 251, para 8, [2001] 1 All ER 961, per Lord Bingham, and the survey of more recent authorities in *Rainy Sky*, per Lord Clarke at paras 21 – 30.

[20] When it comes to interpreting wills, it seems to me that the approach should be the same. Whether the document in question is a commercial contract or a will, the aim is to identify the intention of the party or parties to the document by interpreting the words used in their documentary, factual and commercial context.'

This section of the judgment is proving to be most significant. The comments on the correct approach to interpretation of wills have already been applied in two first instance decisions.[80] At first sight, it might seem to be a rather dry question whether a particular approach is one of interpretation or rectification. However, it is not simply an academic issue of categorisation. If it is a question of interpretation, then the document in question has, and has always had, the meaning and effect as determined by the court, and that is the end of the matter. On the other hand, if it is a question of rectification, then the document, as rectified, has a different meaning from that which it appears to have on its face, and the court has jurisdiction to refuse rectification or to grant it on terms (eg. if there had been delay, change of position, or third party reliance). There is also a time constraint as applications for rectification (like applications under I(PFD)A 1975) must be made within 6 months from the date of the grant or by obtaining leave to apply out of time.

3. APPOINTMENT OF EXECUTORS AND TRUSTEES

1.34   The most important decision for a testator in relation to the appointment of executors and trustees is whether to appoint professionals or lay persons or a combination of the two.

When an estate is substantial and a will trust is expected to continue for some time there is normally an advantage in appointing a professional. This is particularly important where the client recognises that close family members do

---

[80]   See *Brooke v Purton* [2014] EWHC 547 (Ch) and *Burnard v Burnard* [2014] EWHC 340 (Ch). Wills which clearly did not give effect to the intentions of the testators were rewritten so that there was no need to consider the availability of rectification.

not get on. Squabbling siblings are a recipe for a disastrous administration. Further, selecting only some from a group of brothers and sisters or children may lead to arguments and, in a worst case scenario, expensive applications to court to remove one or more of the executors.[81] Similarly there may be difficulties where beneficiaries are appointed as trustees as there conflicts of interest may arise.[82] In such cases appointing a dispassionate professional is likely to be the best option.

1.35 However, it is important that the client is fully aware that there is no necessity to appoint a professional and is given the clearest explanation of the likely basis for charging. The Solicitors Regulation Authority ('SRA') in its 'Ethics Guidance'[83] makes these points, emphasising that those regulated by the SRA have a duty to act in the client's best interests and must not exploit a client's lack of knowledge for their own advantage. Hence when discussing the appointment of executors it is necessary to:

(a) explain the options available to the client;

(b) ensure the client understands that the executor(s) do not have to be professionals; that they may be a family member or a beneficiary under the will; and that lay executors can choose to instruct a solicitor to act for them if this proves necessary and will be indemnified out of the estate for the solicitor's fees;

(c) document the advice given concerning appointment of executors and the clients decision on the file.

When appointing executors the points set out below should be borne in mind.

1.36 *Self-dealing*: it is common to appoint the principal beneficiary – often the spouse or civil partner – as one of the executors and trustees. For the avoidance of doubt it is important to provide that a trustee may exercise a discretion even though deriving a benefit from that exercise:[84] see **Precedent 4.1, clause 13.**

1.37 *Appointment should take immediate effect*: the beneficiary's entitlement may be made contingent on surviving for a stated period; however, it is not

---

[81] Under the Administration of Justice Act 1985, s 50. See, for example, *Kershaw v Micklethwaite* [2010] EWHC 506 (Ch).

[82] See *Berger v Berger* [2013] EWCA Civ 1305 where the testator created a life interest trust for his second wife and appointed the remainder beneficiaries (who were the sons of his first marriage) as trustees. The result was not happy.

[83] '*Ethics Guidance on Drafting and preparation of wills*' issued on 6 May 2014 (updated 11 July 2014) and available on SRA website. See also the Law Society's Practice Note: *Executorships*.

[84] A trust instrument may authorise trustees to act in ways benefiting themselves. The onus is then on those attacking the exercise of the trustees' function to impeach it (eg, by showing that they acted perversely). The authorisation may (and should preferably) be express but it can also be necessarily implied from the circumstances (eg, when the testator selects a beneficiary as trustee). See *Sargeant v National Westminster Bank* (1990) 61 P & CR 518, CA; *Edge v Pensions Ombudsman* [2000] Ch 602 and *Brudenell-Bruce, Earl of Cardigan v Moore* [2012] EWHC 1024 (Ch).

usually advisable to make the office of executor/trustee similarly contingent in case there is a need for action in the period immediately following the death.

1.38   *Power to charge*: executors and trustees cannot normally[85] charge unless the trust instrument authorises them to do so yet the office of executor/trustee can be both time consuming and troublesome.[86] Particularly where the proposed appointee is not a principal beneficiary, the testator should consider including a power to charge. Although the court has jurisdiction to award remuneration, this 'should only be exercised sparingly and in exceptional cases',[87] for example where trustees have to spend time and effort on a specific project which was unforeseen at the date of appointment.[88]

If the testator does wish to give a power to charge, it is important that the clause included is appropriate. Many clauses authorise a person engaged in a profession or business to charge for professional or business services. This does not authorise the executor/trustee to charge for time spent nor for anything other than services of a strictly professional nature. Hence an estate agent could charge for selling a house and an accountant for preparing accounts but neither could charge for time spent on general administration. Arguably such a clause would not allow a company director to charge as a company director is an officer or employee of the company rather than a person engaged in a business.[89] There is also a difficulty in fixing the level of remuneration; if the power is to charge a 'reasonable' rate, how is what is reasonable to be ascertained?

1.39   In *Pullan v Wilson*[90] an accountant was a trustee of 10 family trusts. The drafting of the trusts varied but it was agreed that the effect was that he could charge 'reasonable' remuneration in relation to all mothers. He charged £400 an hour for his services and his assistants charged £250 an hour. One of the beneficiaries later objected to the fees charged.

A joint expert produced a report which concluded that the rates charged by the accountant and his assistants were excessive. He said that a fair hourly rate for the trustee would have been £275 and for his assistants £165, and that a 7.5 per cent discount should be applied to those fees to reflect excessive administration time.

Judge Hodge held that the fees charged went beyond what was reasonable. In his judgment £330 per hour was appropriate for the trustee and £165 for the

---

85   TA 2000, s 29 gives professional trustees power to charge in limited circumstances.
86   See *Brudenell-Bruce v Moore* [2014] EWHC 3679 (Ch) for an illustration of a very time consuming and troublesome trusteeship.
87   *Re Worthington* [1954] 1 WLR 526 at 528.
88   *Foster v Spencer* [1996] 2 All ER 672.
89   But see Kessler, *Drafting Trusts & Will Trusts* (11th edn, 2012) at 6.48. See **Precedent 4.1**, **clause 10**.
90   [2014] EWHC 126 (Ch).

work of the assistants. It was appropriate to apply a 7.5 per cent discount to those rates to account for excessive administration time.

However, the trustee contended that the beneficiary had initially agreed to his hourly rate of £400. Although the evidence was far from clear the judge was prepared to accept that the beneficiary had known that the trustee had initially charged £400 per hour and his failure to contest it amounted to acquiescence and debarred him from challenging its reasonableness.

The significant point about the case is that it makes clear that, in the absence of agreement, a professional trustee cannot charge at his usual rates. It is, therefore, important to have a clear record of any agreement. As Hodge J said:

> 'Much time and effort in this litigation could have been avoided had the applicable hourly rates to be charged by the first defendant and his assistants been identified to the other trustees, and to the principal beneficiaries, before the first defendant accepted the position of trustee. At the very least, those hourly rates should have been recorded in terms in the engagement letter. If this unhappy litigation serves no other useful purpose, I trust that it will serve as a warning to trustees, to those appointing them, and (where appropriate, as it would have been in the present case, given the background of disputes and ongoing litigation between the trustees and their beneficiaries) to the principal beneficiaries to clarify the precise basis of a trustee's charges and remuneration in advance.'

Partners in a firm of solicitors

1.40 Where the testator wants to appoint a professional, the choice is often a solicitor. It may not be desirable to appoint a named individual as that individual may predecease, retire or change firms or practice areas before the testator dies. It is not possible to appoint a partnership as a partnership has no legal identity. However, it is possible to appoint the partners in a firm at the date of death expressing the wish that no more than two take the grant and act initially in its trusts. It is important that the clause refers to the date of death as, if it does not, it will be construed as referring to partners at the date the will is made. It is also important that provision is made for the firm changing its name or amalgamating.

The introduction of limited partnerships and incorporated practices caused problems as the probate registries took the view that the members of these business structures were not partners. In *Re Rogers*[91] Lightman J held that 'the court can and should take a practical and commonsense view in eliciting and giving effect to the intention manifested by the testatrix'. In his view an appointment of 'the partners' could extend to the profit-sharing members of the LLP (the equivalent of partners in the previous partnership). However, he went on to say that:

---

[91]   [2006] 2 All ER 792.

'even as the "partner in the partnership" means in the case of a partnership a profit sharing partner and not merely a salaried partner or a person merely held out (but not in fact) a partner, so when transposed to a limited liability partnership the member must mean a profit sharing member.'

The decision did not refer to incorporated practices but the registries have taken the view that the spirit of the decision requires profit-sharing members (the shareholders) to be regarded as partners for this purpose.

The statement that only those who share profits can be regarded as partners caused some difficulties for conventional partnerships where salaried partners took grants. The solution is for the will to declare that for the purposes of the will 'partner' includes salaried partner.

See **Precedent 4.5.**

Replacement trustees

1.41 Although there are statutory provisions to deal with the appointment of new trustees, it is helpful to state expressly how this is to occur. The power of appointment can be given to the continuing trustees or it can be given to a named individual. It is important to make the provision as clear as possible as it is common for mistakes to be made as to who has the power. Where an appointment is made by the wrong person, the subsequent actions of the appointee (and hence of the trustee body of which he had acted as a member) are invalid and it can be extremely difficult to unscramble.[92]

See **Precedent 4.1, clause 14.**

Exemption clauses

1.42 Many wills and trust instruments contain clauses which seek to limit the liability of a solicitor or other professional trustee, when acting as an executor or trustee, to loss or damage through fraud or dishonesty and to exclude liability for negligence. There are clearly special cases where it would be reasonable for the trust document to exclude or restrict liability for negligence (for example, estates or trusts involving assets held overseas in countries with unreliable legal systems, long-running and serious family or other disputes, or continuing litigation), but clients may feel that a professional is being paid a sufficient amount to justify shouldering the cost of making good a negligent error. Solicitors should in any event be fully insured against their own negligence.

---

[92] See *Yudt v Ross Craig* [1998] 1 ITELR 531; *Jasmine Trustees v Wells & Hind* [2007] EWHC 38 (Ch).

1.43 In *Armitage v Nurse*[93] and *Bogg v Raper*,[94] the Court of Appeal stated that clauses limiting liability for negligence were not contrary to public policy nor to the essential nature of a trust. Millett LJ commented that, although many people felt such clauses had gone too far, it would require legislation to change their validity.

1.44 Subsequently, the Law Commission published a report (No 301) on trustee exemption clauses recommending that professional and regulatory bodies should adopt rules or guidance to the effect that any paid trustee, who causes a settlor to include a trustee exemption clause in a trust instrument which has the effect of excluding or limiting liability for negligence, must before the creation of the trust take steps to ensure that the settlor is aware of the meaning and effect of the clause. Both STEP and the Law Society were consulted by the Law Commission prior to publication of the report and supported this approach.

Principles 2 and 4 of the Solicitors' Regulatory Authority ('SRA') Code of Conduct 2011 require those regulated by the SRA to act with integrity and in the best interests of each client. Outcome 1 requires clients to be treated fairly and Outcome 1.2 requires that services are provided to clients in a manner which protects their interests in their matter subject to the proper administration of justice. The Principles and Outcomes are mandatory. Indicative Behaviour 1.8 suggests that acting in the following way may tend to show that the relevant Outcome has been achieved and, therefore, that Principles have been complied with:

'If you seek to limit your liability to your client to a level above the minimum required by the SRA Indemnity Insurance Rules, ensuring that this limitation is in writing and is brought to the client's attention.'

On 14 September 2010 in a written ministerial statement the Parliamentary Under-Secretary of State for Justice (Mr Jonathan Djanogly) announced the Government's acceptance of the recommendations made by the Law Commission. Referring to the fact that the leading regulatory and professional bodies had already adopted the recommendations, he said that the Government would be promoting further uptake by writing directly to the relevant regulatory and professional bodies.

A professional preparing a will or trust instrument for a client which limits liability in negligence, should take reasonable steps before the trust is created to ensure that the client is aware of the meaning and effect of the clause. Extra care is needed if the professional, or anyone in or associated with the firm, is a paid trustee of the trust. It is prudent to ensure that there is evidence that the appropriate steps were taken and that the evidence is retained for as long as the trust exists and for a suitable period afterwards.

---

[93] [1997] 3 WLR 1046, CA.
[94] (1998) *The Times*, April 22; [1998] CLY 4592.

The same requirements do not apply to lay trustees where it will often be appropriate to limit liability.

4. PERSONAL CHATTELS

1.45   When planning a tax-efficient will, the bulk of the estate may be left on trust. However, it will rarely, if ever, be appropriate to allow personal chattels to pass as part of the property held on the trust. They should normally be dealt with in a separate disposition. Testators will often want to give particular items to named individuals.

It is easiest to deal with such gifts by means of a gift to an individual (or often the executors) with a request in the will that the individual gives effect to the testator's wishes as set out in an accompanying document. This allows the testator to change the wishes without having to execute a codicil or re-execute the will. From a drafting point of view be careful of the following:

(a)   Do not impose an obligation on the individual; draft the clause as a mere request, a so-called 'precatory trust'.

(b)   Do not refer to the letter of wishes in the will as a document already in existence at the date of execution as this will incorporate it into the will by reference and make it impossible to change the wishes without a codicil or re-execution of the will.

(c)   It is common to define personal chattels by reference to the definition contained in the Administration of Estates Act 1925, s 55(1)(x). Originally the definition was:

> 'carriages, horses, stable furniture and effects (not used for business purposes), motor cars and accessories (not used for business purposes), garden effects, domestic animals, plate, plated articles, linen, china, glass, books, pictures, prints, furniture, jewellery, articles of household or personal use or ornament, musical and scientific instruments and apparatus, wines, liquors and consumable stores, but do not include any chattels used at the death of the intestate for business purposes nor money or securities for money.'

The exclusion of any chattels used for business purposes meant that amendments were necessary if the gift was to include chattels used partly for business purposes.

The Inheritance and Trustees' Powers Act 2014, s 3(1) substituted a new definition for deaths on or after 1 October 2014:

> '"Personal chattels" means tangible movable property, other than any such property which—
>
> – consists of money or securities for money, or
> – was used at the death of the intestate solely or mainly for business purposes, or

> – was held at the death of the intestate solely as an investment.'

Inheritance and Trustees' Powers Act 2014, s 3(2) provides that a will or codicil containing a reference to personal chattels defined (in whatever form of words) by reference to s 55(1)(x) of the Administration of Estates Act 1925 executed before the Act came into force,[95] will be interpreted as referring to the old definition unless there is a contrary intention.

1.46 Disputes over personal chattels can be disproportionately expensive and bitter so warn the client to be careful of the following:

(a) items need to be clearly identified to avoid confusion and argument;

(b) any list needs to be kept up to date to deal with disposals of particular items and the birth of later family members;

(c) when a new list is produced either destroy the old one or make it clear whether the second list supplements or replaces the first;

(d) it is preferable to deal with particularly valuable items specifically rather than including them in a general gift.

The inheritance tax of a precatory trust is governed by IHTA 1984, s 143 which provides that where dispositions are made in accordance with an expression of wishes within 2 years of death, the estate will be taxed as if the property had been left in that way on death.[96] There is no corresponding provision for capital gains tax so the chattels will be treated as left to the person named in the will, who will then be treated as making a lifetime gift. However, it will be rare for a chattel to have risen substantially in value in the period between death and the disposition; any increase is likely to fall within the chattels exemption[97] or the annual exemption[98] of the person named in the will. In a case where the CGT result is not satisfactory, the person named in the will could make a post-death variation and elect that the disposition be treated as the deceased's for CGT purposes.[99]

1.47 An alternative approach is to allow named individuals to select items. Such a clause should include a time-limit within which the selection must be made and a mechanism for dealing with disputes. It is common to provide that the personal representatives are to resolve any disputes.

---

[95] On 1 October 2014.
[96] *Harding (Loveday's Exors) v IRC* [1997] STC (SCD) 321.
[97] TCGA 1992, s 262.
[98] TCGA 1992, s 3.
[99] TCGA 1992, s 62(6).

5. SPECIFIC GIFTS

1.48   Clauses making specific gifts need to deal with the following matters:

(a)   The asset should be carefully identified. For example, does a gift of 'my flat' include the freehold reversion?[100]

(b)   Specific gifts are free of inheritance tax unless the will provides otherwise. It is good practice to refer expressly to the fact that inheritance tax is to be paid from residue for the avoidance of doubt.

(c)   Where a debt is charged on an item specifically given, the beneficiary takes the item subject to the charge unless the will provides otherwise.[101] In the case of a mortgage there will often be a life insurance policy which is intended to provide funds to pay off the mortgage in the event of death; it is always advisable to make clear in the gift that the mortgage is to be discharged from the proceeds of the policy. A court may presume this to be the case[102] but it is preferable to avoid a possible argument.

(d)   Specific gifts will adeem if the subject matter of the gift is no longer owned at the date of death or has changed substantially in nature. Company shares are particularly vulnerable as companies may amalgamate, change their name or be taken over. The clause used should make provision for such possibilities. Houses present similar problems. A gift of a house can be worded as a gift of 'any property in which I am living at the date of my death' but this is no help if the testator has gone into residential accommodation. In cases where an unfair distribution of the estate would result from ademption, it is desirable to discuss this with the client and consider the inclusion of a substitutional gift to cover the possibility.[103] See **Precedent 4.6.**

(e)   Income produced by the asset. In the absence of express provision to the contrary the effect of the Trusts (Capital and Income) Act 2013, s 1 is that the legatee will be entitled to income paid after the date of death irrespective of when it arose. No income will be apportioned to the residuary beneficiary. Section 1 disapplies the Apportionment Act 1870 in relation to trusts created or arising on or after 1 October 2013 (this includes a trust created or arising on or after that day under a power conferred before that day). For clarity it may be helpful to state expressly that there is no need to apportion income. See **Precedent 4.1, clause 7.**

(f)   The cost of delivery and insurance after death. In the absence of express provision the cost of transfer of title falls on the estate. However, the executors are merely required to make the asset available to the legatee so the costs of delivery fall on the legatee. In the case of an item where delivery charges are going to be substantial (for example, a grand piano) it is important to make express provision in the will for the cost of delivery.

---

[100]   See *Re Ross* [2004] EWHC 2559 (Ch) for a dispute on this point.
[101]   Administration of Estates Act 1925, s 35.
[102]   See *Re Ross* [2004] EWHC 2559 (Ch).
[103]   As to problems arising from sales under a lasting power of attorney, see **1.49.**

(g) Disputed ownership of an item specifically given. The decision in *Coutts & Co v Banks*[104] was that executors are not under an obligation to conduct litigation to recover an asset which had been specifically given. Their only obligation was to assign such rights as they had to the disputed item to the beneficiary. It was then for the beneficiary to pursue the litigation. Only if a testator is already aware of a dispute in relation to an item is it likely to be appropriate to include a provision dealing with such a possibility.

Ademption and sales under a lasting (or enduring) power of attorney

1.49 Although there is a statutory provision designed to preserve benefits for legatees where receivers or deputies sell assets specifically given by will,[105] there are no corresponding provisions for sales by attorneys. There is a danger that an attorney who is in ignorance of the contents of a will may sell an asset which has been specifically given, producing an unfair result which is contrary to the wishes of the testator. There is case-law to the effect that ademption does not occur where a third party deals with an asset without the knowledge of the testator.[106] However, in *Banks v National Westminster Bank plc*[107] the court held that a sale by an attorney is not a sale by a third party and therefore does give rise to ademption.

In *Re Dorman*[108] the court was willing to find that ademption had not occurred where an attorney closed one account and reinvested the proceeds in another account carrying a higher rate of interest.

The new account was said to represent the original account so that there had not been a change of substance. However, such a result is entirely dependent on the particular facts and there will be many cases where ademption occurs.

In *Re DP (Revocation of Lasting Power of Attorney)*[109] Senior Judge Lush J described the law regarding ademption caused by an attorney as 'a minefield' saying that over the last twenty years there had been a number of conflicting judgments in different common law jurisdictions.

The best solution is to address the problem when the lasting power of attorney is prepared. Ideally the testator should give a copy of the will to the attorney at that time and include a request in the guidance section of the power that the attorney should avoid disposing of items which have been specifically given. Many testators, however, are unwilling to disclose the contents of their will

---

[104] [2002] EWHC 2460 (Ch).
[105] See the Mental Capacity Act 2005, Sch 2, para 8.
[106] *Jenkins v Jones* (1866) LR 2 Eq 323 and see *Turner (Exor Coutts Gordon) v Turner* [2012] CSOH 41.
[107] [2005] EWHC 3479.
[108] [1994] 1 WLR 282.
[109] [2014] EWHC B4 (COP).

unless and until they lose capacity. This puts a solicitor in a difficult position. A solicitor who has prepared a will for a client is under a duty of confidentiality to the client and cannot reveal the contents before death without the client's instructions. After death the duty of confidentiality is owed to the personal representatives.

The client could give the solicitor written instructions to disclose the contents to the attorney once he has lost capacity but the problem is that the authority becomes ineffective once the client loses capacity. The instruction could be worded as an irrevocable authority to the solicitor. Alternatively the client could expand the request in the lasting power that the attorney should try to avoid making sales which will result in ademption to include an authorisation for the attorney to request a copy of the will from the solicitor. It is difficult to see that a solicitor could be criticised for making the will available in such circumstances,

Of course, there will be cases where assets specifically given have to be sold to provide funds for the testator's care. When this will produce an unfair result, the attorney should apply to the Court of Protection for a statutory will to be made on behalf of the donor.[110]

6. ABSOLUTE PECUNIARY LEGACIES

1.50 Pecuniary legacies are often used to make provision for a class of beneficiaries such as grandchildren. As is so often the case they can produce problems out of all proportion to their value. If gifts of substantial amounts are intended it will always be more appropriate to use a trust.

Class gifts

1.51 A class gift is one where the amount that each class member receives varies according to the number of members the class has. Without special rules it would be impossible to distribute anything until the final size of the class had been ascertained. There are, therefore, a number of rules of construction, designed to allow early distribution, which apply to such gifts. Although the rules are generally sensible, it is preferable to make express provision in the will so that the testator is aware of what will happen. The most common situations are set out below. There are also rules of construction which apply in more complicated situations, for example, where a class gift follows a life interest but as such gifts should always be made by way of a properly drafted trust, these rules have not been set out.

---

[110] Under Mental Capacity Act 2005, s 18(1). The court must exercise its powers in the best interests of the person who has lost capacity. For a discussion of the principles to be applied; see *NT v FS and others* [2013] EWHC 684 (COP).

'£1,000 to each of my grandchildren'

This is not strictly speaking a class gift as the amount each grandchild receives is fixed from the start but the personal representatives will not know how much to retain to fulfill the terms of the gift unless there is express or implied guidance. Such a gift is construed as a gift only to the class members living at the date of the testator's death as it will otherwise be impossible to distribute the estate. Children who are *en ventre sa mere* at the date of death will be 'living' for this purpose.[111] If drafting such a gift, the will should state expressly that the gift is to the class members 'living at my death'.

'£10,000 to be divided amongst my grandchildren'

A gift of a fund to be divided amongst a class will be construed as a gift to those members living at the date of death to the exclusion of those born later. If there are no class members at the date of death, the class remains open until all possible members are ascertained. If drafting such a gift, the will should state expressly that the gift is to the class members 'living at my death'. What is to happen if there are no class members living at the date of death will depend on the wishes of the testator but the best solution may be to say that the gift fails.

Interest on absolute pecuniary legacies[112]

1.52 In the case of absolute pecuniary legacies the rule, in the absence of express provision, is that interest is paid to compensate the legatee for late payment. Unless the will provides that the legacy is to be paid earlier, personal representatives are not required to pay pecuniary legacies until 12 months after the date of death (the executor's year). Interest is, therefore, not normally payable until that date. The rate of interest may be prescribed in the will. If it is not, it is thought to be the rate that the court would order if it ordered an account and this is the basic rate payable on money in court.[113] The rate varies from time to time and a table of rates can be obtained from the website of the Court Funds Office.[114] Legatees can disclaim interest and, if they do, are not assessable to income tax on the interest foregone.[115]

Receipts for pecuniary legacies

1.53 It is usual to provide that the parent or guardian of a minor can give a good receipt on the child's behalf and this is good practice. However, since the Children Act 1989 it is probably unnecessary. Section 3 of that Act defines parental responsibility as including the right 'to receive or recover in his own

---

[111] *Elliott v Joicey* [1935] AC 209.

[112] The rules for interest on contingent pecuniary legacies are dealt with at **1.56**.

[113] CPR Part 40, PD40A, para 15.

[114] See http://www.justice.gov.uk/downloads/guidance/protecting-the-vulnerable/court-funds-office/investments-and-interest-rates/rate_changes2009.doc. For the rates from 1965 to 2009 see **Appendix I**.

[115] *Dewar v IRC* [1935] 2 KB 351.

name, for the benefit of the child, property of whatever description and wherever situated which the child is entitled to receive or recover'. If the testator is not happy for the surviving parent to have this power, the legacy should be left to a trustee to hold for the benefit of the minor.

7. CONTINGENT PECUNIARY LEGACIES

1.54   For the reasons set out at **1.56–1.59** below, it is not desirable to draft a will including contingent pecuniary legacies unless the amounts involved are very small and the period of any contingency is likely to be short. It is preferable to deal with the gifts through a trust.

Class gifts

'£20,000 to be divided amongst such of my grandchildren as reach 25'

1.55   A gift of a fixed amount to the members of a class contingent on the fulfilment of a stated event is construed as a gift to the class members living at the date of the testator's death who fulfil the contingency plus any others born before the first class member fulfils the contingency so long as they also fulfil the contingency. Any born after the first child fulfils the contingency are excluded.

An alternative

An alternative way of drafting such a legacy, which will appeal to some testators, is to provide that each class member who reaches the specified age receives a share the size of which depends on the number of class members at that date. However, while the fund continues, later members are added so that the shares are reduced but all take something until the fund is exhausted.

> *Example 1.1*
>
> Grace leaves £30,000 to be divided amongst such of her grandchildren as reach 21 and she includes the clause described above. At the date of her death there are three grandchildren, Ann, Ben and Charlie. Ann reaches 21 and receives £10,000. The following year two further grandchildren, David and Edwin, are born and join the class. The year after that Ben reaches 21 and takes a one quarter share of the remaining £20,000. If no further grandchildren are born, Charlie, David and Edwin will each take £5,000 on reaching 21.

See **Precedent 4.8.**

Interest on contingent pecuniary legacies

1.56 Unless the will makes express provision for the payment of interest, the position is governed by LPA 1925, s 175 which provides that contingent pecuniary legacies do not carry intermediate income. There are certain limited exceptions:

(a) if the will directs for the purposes of the administration that the legacy fund is severed from the rest of the estate and set aside;[116]

(b) if the legacy is to the testator's minor child (or child to whom the testator is *in loco parentis*) in which case there is a presumption that it was intended for the child's maintenance;[117]

(c) if the legacy is to any child and the testator indicates that it is for the purposes of maintenance.[118]

Where a gift does not carry the right to interest, any income produced by assets in the hands of the personal representatives/trustees will be paid to the person(s) entitled to the residue of the estate who, therefore, have a right to the income in the period between the testator's death and the fulfilment of the contingency. In the meantime the child is entitled to nothing. Section 31 of the Trustee Act 1925 does not give the personal representatives power to apply income for the maintenance, education or benefit of the child as the section applies only where a gift carries the right to intermediate income. The fact that the residuary beneficiaries are entitled to the income produced has important tax consequences.

Tax position if gift does not carry intermediate income

1.57 For income tax purposes the trust rate of tax is not payable because the residuary beneficiaries have a right to income from the gift. For inheritance tax purposes the residuary beneficiaries will have immediate post death interests (IPDIs) (see Chapter 6), so there will be a charge to tax if a residuary beneficiary dies before the contingent beneficiary acquires a vested interest and a PET by the residuary beneficiary when the contingency is fulfilled and the IPDI terminates.

Although the PET is deemed to be made by the residuary beneficiary, any inheritance tax liability will fall on the trustees of the estate who should, therefore, reserve funds or insure the life of the residuary beneficiary for 7 years.

---

[116] *Kidman v Kidman* (1871) 40 LJ Ch 359. See also *Re Eyre, Johnson v Williams* [1917] 1 Ch 351.

[117] *Re Breed's WT* (1875) 1 Ch D 226. It is more difficult, but not impossible, to find such an intention if the contingency is attaining an age greater than 18. See *Re Jones, Meacock v Jones* [1932] 1 Ch 642.

[118] *Re Churchill, Hiscock v Lodder* [1909] 2 Ch 431.

Power to advance capital

1.58 The Trustee Act 1925, s 32 will apply to the contingent legacy so the executors will be able to advance capital for the benefit of a beneficiary with a vested or presumptive entitlement. However, any beneficiary with a prior interest must consent. Therefore, if the residuary beneficiaries are entitled to intermediate income, they must give their consent to any advancement of capital.

What does the beneficiary get when the contingency is fulfilled?

1.59 Assuming that the gift is simply a gift of a specified amount on the fulfilment of a contingency, for example 'the sum of £100,000 to my granddaughter on attaining age 25', the legatee is entitled to nothing other than the specified sum of money on that date. The income and any appreciation of capital value will belong to residue (or those entitled should she fail to attain age 25).

This is significant in so far as the investment obligations of the trustees are concerned. Their job is to make sure that they can pay the required sum at the relevant time. If they invest in assets capable of producing capital growth, there is normally a corresponding risk of capital loss. Hence they should only invest in something that is guaranteed to provide the required sum, even if that means reducing or removing the possibility of capital growth.

1.60 It will be apparent from **1.57–1.59** above that contingent pecuniary legacies are not advisable. If the consequences were explained, most testators would not be happy that the legatees would receive only the initial amount with any income and capital growth being paid to the residuary beneficiaries. Most would prefer, especially in the case of younger legatees, that the particular sum they have in mind should be put aside as at the date of their death, and then invested for the benefit of the legatee, with a view to his inheriting 'the pot' (whatever it may then be worth) on his attaining the qualifying age.

If the problem is not appreciated at the will drafting stage, it may be possible to deal with it during the administration by a post-death variation. The residuary beneficiaries who are entitled to the intermediate income could enter into a deed of variation to settle the amount of the legacy on trust for the legatees contingent on them reaching the specified age. Income and capital growth will then be available to the contingent legatees. If the residuary beneficiaries are the parents of the legatees, any income applied for their benefit while they are minors will be treated as the parents' for income tax purposes under the settlor-interested trust provisions.[119] This will not be the case for income accumulated although it will suffer the 45% rate of tax on income in excess of £1,000. However, it may be possible to invest for capital growth, for example in Treasury bonds so that there is no income to attract tax.

---

[119] ITTOIA 2005, s 629. For variations, see Chapter 12.

Alternatively it is possible to apply to the court to authorise a change to the terms of the legacy under the Variation of Trusts Act 1958.[120]

8. NIL RATE BAND LEGACIES[121]

1.61 Individuals whose main concern is to leave their property in such a way as to avoid the payment of inheritance tax (IHT) will sometimes want to give a pecuniary legacy of the maximum amount that they can give without triggering a charge to inheritance tax to non-exempt beneficiaries, and the rest of their estate to exempt beneficiaries. This is often referred to as a nil rate band legacy.

> *Example 1.2*
>
> Molly who is a successful business woman and very much dislikes paying tax tells you that she wants to leave as much as possible without incurring an inheritance tax liability to her goddaughter, Grace, and everything else to charity.

As no one can know what the level of the IHT nil rate band will be at the date of their death nor whether they will have a whole band available at that date, it is necessary to use a formula to give an amount equal to the available portion of the nil rate band. The simplest form of words is 'the maximum amount that can be given without giving rise to any liability to IHT on my death'.[122]

Since the introduction of the transferable nil rate band, it is important to use wording which makes clear whether or not the gift is intended to extend to any transferred nil rate. Given the costs that can be incurred where wording is unclear, it is also advisable to include an express direction to personal representatives to claim the transferred nil rate band.[123]

9. RESIDUARY GIFTS

1.62 Although it is possible to leave the residue of the estate to an individual or organisation absolutely without using a trust, it is normal drafting practice to use a trust in all but the simplest case (for example, where the residue is left to one adult beneficiary absolutely). Even then, there will be default provisions for substitutional beneficiaries so a trust is still likely to be required. The assumption in this book therefore is that the residue of the estate will be left on trust and the trustees will be furnished with the widest administrative powers: see **Precedent 4.1, clause 6.**

---

[120] *Bernstein v Jacobson* [2010] WTLR 559.
[121] See further **4.10ff**. For a consideration of the position when the personal representatives are entitled to claim an additional nil rate band see **5.12ff**. It should be made clear in this case whether or not it is intended to give away this additional nil rate band.
[122] See further **4.10** *et seq* and **Precedents 4.4** and **4.9**.
[123] For an example of wording which gave rise to litigation see *Loring v Woodland Trust* [2013] EWHC 4400 Ch; *aff'd* [2015] STC 598.

The clause dealing with residue should define it and give it to the trustees to hold on trust. It is normal to direct the trustees to pay debts, IHT and administration expenses from residue before directing them to hold the balance on the desired trusts.[124]

Direction to pay debts

1.63 A direction to pay 'debts' from residue will not include debts charged on an asset specifically given in the will. For this to happen, there must be either a direction in the specific gift that debts charged on the asset are to be paid from residue or a direction in the residuary gift to pay debts including those charged on assets specifically given.

Direction to pay inheritance tax

1.64 There are many different forms of direction to pay IHT. Some are wider than others and it is important to consider which is suitable.[125] The most limited form is a direction to pay IHT 'on property passing by will'. This will not include IHT payable on property:

(a)   passing by survivorship;
(b)   transferred by a lifetime disposition in the 7 years before death (a 'failed PET').

If IHT on property passing by survivorship is to be paid from residue, it is necessary to use a wider form such as IHT 'on property passing as a result of my death'.

If IHT payable on lifetime gifts is to be paid from residue, an even wider form of direction is required either referring expressly to IHT 'payable on lifetime gifts' or IHT 'resulting from my death'. Because such a liability is primarily the responsibility of the donee of the lifetime gift,[126] the direction is treated as a pecuniary legacy to that person of an amount equal to the tax payable.

1.65 Where an estate is to be divided between exempt and non-exempt beneficiaries, there are statutory rules concerning the burden of IHT which cannot be varied. IHTA 1984, s 41 provides that the tax attributable to the non-exempt share must be borne by the non-exempt share. A direction that it is to be borne by the exempt share or paid from the residue before division into shares so that the exempt and non-exempt beneficiaries will take the same amount is ineffective.[127]

---

[124] See **Precedent 4.1**, clause 6.
[125] See also **3.36** and **3.37**.
[126] IHTA 1984, s 41.
[127] See **3.38** *et seq.*

Example 1.3

T, who has exhausted his IHT nil rate band, leaves the residue of his estate to be divided equally between his nephew and a charity. The nephew's share will be reduced by IHT with the result that he will receive less than the charity. A direction by T that the IHT be paid from the residue before division into shares is ineffective.

It is, however, possible for a testator to direct that the residue is to be divided into shares in such proportions that, after the payment of IHT, the exempt and non-exempt beneficiaries end up with the same amounts. In *Re Benham's Will Trusts*[128] the court decided that this was the effect of the words used. The calculations involved are far from easy since grossing up is required! There was some concern after this decision that the common direction used in wills that 'after payment of debts and inheritance tax the residue be divided equally' might be construed as directing such an unequal distribution. However, in *Re Ratcliffe*,[129] Blackburne J said that much clearer words would have to be used to achieve this result.[130]

Grossing up

1.66 Where tax-free legacies are left to non-exempt beneficiaries and the residue is left to an exempt beneficiary, the legacies have to be grossed up to the extent that they exceed the nil rate band. If not foreseen, this can result in a substantially increased IHT liability.[131]

10. MISCELLANEOUS MATTERS

Perpetuities and accumulations

1.67 The rules relating to perpetuity and accumulations were substantially changed by the Perpetuities and Accumulations Act 2009: see Chapter 2.

Administrative powers

1.68 The Trustee Act 2000 greatly extended the statutory powers implied into wills and trusts. Under the Act trustees and personal representatives have the same powers to invest as an absolute beneficial owner;[132] power to acquire land;[133] power to insure trust property;[134] and power to use agents, nominees and custodians.[135] Even so, many practitioners feel that there are additional powers that may be useful. Some practitioners choose to adopt the STEP

---

[128] [1995] STC 210.
[129] *Re Ratcliffe, Holmes v McMullan* [1999] STC 262.
[130] For a detailed discussion see **3.39**.
[131] For a detailed discussion see **3.41** *et seq*.
[132] TA 2000, s 3.
[133] TA 2000, s 8.
[134] TA 2000, s 34.
[135] TA 2000, ss 11, 16, 17.

Standard Provisions by stating in the will or trust instrument that 'The standard provisions of the *Society of Trust and Estate Practitioners* (2nd edn) shall apply'.[136] Others prefer to include their own. **Precedent 4.1** includes a full annotated set of administrative provisions.

Foreign property

1.69   The standard advice for individuals with assets outside the UK is that they should consult a local lawyer with a view to making a will in the relevant jurisdiction to deal with those assets. This facilitates the administration of those assets on death as there will be a document which is in familiar form. The local lawyer can advise on problems arising from local inheritance law. For example, some jurisdictions have forced heirship provisions; in some the office of executor is not recognised and property left to executors to hold on trust will be treated as passing to the executors personally. This will be significant if higher rates of tax on death are charged when property is not left to close relatives.

However, there may be problems arising from the use of local lawyers. The local will may revoke all wills (including, therefore, the carefully drafted 'home' will). It may be possible to avoid forced heirship provisions by putting assets into a company but a local lawyer may not volunteer this information unless specifically asked. It will, therefore, be helpful to provide clients with a list of points to raise with the local lawyer.

Where there is a dispute in relation to the effect of competing wills the UK party may wish to apply in England and Wales for an anti-suit order restraining the other party from litigating in another jurisdiction because England and Wales is the correct jurisdiction.[137] A clause can be included in the UK will making it clear that that the Will is governed by the law of England and Wales. This was discussed in *Perdoni v Curati* where Tomlinson LJ said at [16]:

> 'It is trite that that the construction of a will is governed by the law intended by the testator.'

Secret and Half Secret Trusts

1.70   Sometimes testators wish to keep the way in which they are leaving their property private. One possibility is the use of a discretionary trust with a letter of wishes but another method is the use of half secret or fully secret trusts.

Secret trusts hit the headlines in 2014 because the artist, Lucien Freud, who had a substantial estate and a large number of children left a will allegedly

---

[136]   For a consideration of the STEP Standard Provisions see **4.22**.
[137]   For recent examples of decisions in the probate context see *Tadros v Barratt* [2014] EWHC 2860 Ch and *Morris v Davies* [2011] EWHC 1272 (Ch).

containing a secret trust. Litigation followed[138] in the course of which the principles governing these trusts and the differences between the two were discussed.

1.71 In a fully secret trust property is given to a legatee apparently beneficially without words imposing a trust. However, the legatee agrees with the testator that he will hold it on certain trusts. The trust fails if the terms of the trust are not communicated to the legatee during the testator's lifetime and then takes effect as a beneficial gift to the legatee.

In a half secret trust the terms of the will make it clear that the legatee is to hold on trust but the terms of the trusts are not disclosed. Such a trust fails if the details are not communicated to the trustee before the Will is executed (the distinction is odd, but is well established in case law). If a half secret trust fails for lack of communication, the trustees hold the property for those entitled to residue or on intestacy. The trustees cannot hold beneficially as the will makes it clear that they are taking as trustees.

The Lucien Freud case

1.72 Lucien Freud's last will made in 2006 replaced an earlier will made in 2004. Both wills were professionally drawn by the same solicitor. The 2004 will appointed his solicitor and one of his many children as executors and gave the residue to the executors by name on half secret trusts; the 2006 Will appointed the same individuals as executors and gave the residue to them but this time without any reference to a half secret trust.

The defendant (who would have been entitled to a share of the residue under the intestacy rules) claimed that on a proper construction of the Will, the executors took the residue on trusts which were not set out in the Will, ie on half secret trusts. Had the court found in his favour, he would then have questioned whether the half secret trust was valid, or whether there was a partial intestacy.[139]

The judge applied the dictum of Lord Neuberger in *Marley v Rawlings*[140] that unless extrinsic evidence is admissible under Administration of Justice Act 1982, s 21, the interpretation of a Will should be approached in the same way as the interpretation of a commercial contract, that is:

> 'the court is concerned to find the intention of the party or parties, and it does this by identifying the meaning of the relevant words, (a) in the light of (i) the natural and ordinary meaning of those words, (ii) the overall purpose of the document, (iii) any other provisions of the document, (iv) the facts known or assumed by the

---

[138] *Executors of Lucien Freud v Paul McAdam Freud* [2014] EWHC 2577 (Ch).

[139] In fact, the PRs' evidence was that, even if the defendant's construction of the Will was correct, the half secret trust attaching to the gift would be valid, as its terms were communicated before the Will was executed which made the defendant's position fairly hopeless.

[140] *Marley v Rawlings* [2014] UKSC 2 at [18]–[19].

parties at the time that the document was executed, and (v) common sense, but (b) ignoring subjective evidence of any party's intentions.'

All parties agreed that s 21 was not relevant so the court had to establish the intention of the testator.

While the defendant made some valid points (for example that Clause 7 set out extensive trust administration provisions which were not required unless the gift of residue was intended to be held on trust; clause 8 contained a charging clause, which was inconsistent with an intention that the executors were to receive the residue for their joint absolute benefit), in the opinion of Richard Spearman QC sitting as a deputy judge, these did not outweigh the essential point that the gift in clause 6 was expressed as a simple gift of residue and contained no mention of a trust.

Looking beyond clause 6, and seeking to find the testator's intention from the words used in the entirety of the Will, he considered that the fact that the testator referred to the executors as 'Trustees' in clauses 3 and 4 but referred to them by their names in clause 6 was more consistent with the construction that, under clause 6, he intended them to take personally and absolutely rather than as trustees.

There was a further point of interest. Because one of the individuals taking under clause 6 was the testator's solicitor, who had prepared the Will, public interest considerations required the court to be vigilant before accepting that clause 6 meant that the executors took as beneficial legatees. However, the law recognises that in secret trusts, it is common place for solicitors to be appointed as trustees, and one reasonable explanation for a clause which confers a beneficial gift on a solicitor is that the testator intended to impose a fully secret trust

1.73

The Succession Regulation (EU)

This Regulation[141] ('the SR') came into force on 17 August 2012, although most of it does not apply until 17 August 2015. The Irish and UK Governments exercised their right not to opt in. However, it will apply to assets situated in most EU Member States and to the succession of persons dying habitually resident in the SR Zone (all EU Member States other than Denmark, Ireland and the United Kingdom).

By contrast, Art 21.1 of the SR, unless otherwise provided, the law applicable to the succession is the habitual residence of the deceased at the time of death and is to apply to the whole of the succession. This applies whether or not the applicable law is the law of a SR Zone state.

---

[141] EU Reg 650/2012.

Article 22 provides that a person may choose the law of their nationality as the law to govern their succession as a whole. The substantive validity of the choice is to be governed by the chosen national law (Art 22.3). The choice may be explicit or implicit.

The SR does not apply to property passing by survivorship nor to revenue, customs or administrative matters. Any issue relating to tax is therefore excluded and is governed by the existing rules.

The effect of the SR would seem to be that in the case of a British testator resident in Italy who dies after August 2015, the EU Regulation will apply. The law of his place of habitual residence will be the default succession law, unless he has made an 'express choice' of his national law in his will.

CHAPTER 2

THE ESSENTIAL TRUSTS LAW

This chapter considers three main areas of trust law which can pose problems for the estate planner who is either dealing with or thinking of creating a trust. It does not provide a general summary of trust law. Other aspects of trusts and settlements are mentioned in other chapters, for instance in Chapter 8 (Pilot Trusts) the importance of a trust being constituted (albeit with a nominal value) is discussed. Other chapters also consider practical applications of the dispositive powers of trustees. In Chapter 13, for instance, the use of a power of appointment to achieve tax savings by rearranging the estate under IHTA 1984, s 144 is considered.

1. PERPETUITIES AND ACCUMULATIONS

2.01 The development of the law of trusts was accompanied by a fear of tying up property for long periods. As a result rules designed to limit the life of trusts and the period during which income could be accumulated were developed. These rules were substantially changed by the Perpetuities and Accumulations Act 2009. The new rules apply to wills executed and trusts coming into force on or after 6 April 2010.

Perpetuities

2.02 Except in the case of charitable trusts, interests must vest within the perpetuity period or they are void.

The old rules

2.03 Before the PAA 2009 the perpetuity period at common law was a life or lives in being plus 21 years. The lives could be expressly selected, for example, '21 years from the death of the last grandchild of Queen Elizabeth II living at my death'. If no lives were selected, the relevant lives were identified from the particular disposition: in the case of a gift 'to the first child of Tom to reach 21', for example, Tom is the relevant life in being.[1]

2.04 The PAA 1964 had allowed those drafting settlements to select a fixed period of anything up to 80 years. The trust instrument had to state the period

---

[1]   See further a consideration of relevant lives in the case of spousal by-pass trust in footnote 15 below.

selected or the common law rules applied. This Act relaxed the common law rules in a number of other ways, for example, by introducing 'wait and see' and age reduction provisions.

The new rules

2.05   The PAA 2009 came into force on 6 April 2010. Section 5 provides a mandatory perpetuity period of 125 years which applies to trusts taking effect and wills executed after 5 April 2010. The 125-year period applies automatically and takes precedence over any provisions contained in the trust instrument. In the interests of clarity it is advisable to state the perpetuity period in the settlement's definitions clause and usually this will also be the period chosen as the 'trust period' (the period within which the trustees must exercise their dispositive powers, eg of appointment and advancement). For instance:

> 'The "Trust Period" shall mean the period ending on the last day of the period of 125 years from the date of my death which period (and no other) shall be the perpetuity period for dispositions made by this will.'

2.06   Trusts already in existence and trusts created in wills executed before 6 April 2010 are not generally affected by the new rules and will continue under the old rules. For the meaning of 'wills executed', see **2.13**.

2.07   Section 12, however, allows trustees of existing trusts and will trusts to opt for a fixed period of 100 years from the commencement of the trust where the perpetuity period is defined by reference to a life or lives in being and it is difficult, or not reasonably practicable, to ascertain whether the lives have ended. Trustees must execute a deed stating that they believe there is such a difficulty and that the instrument is to be treated as if it specified a period of 100 years (no other period is possible) from the commencement of the trust.[2]

Special powers of appointment

2.08   Section 6(2) provides that the perpetuity period for an instrument created in the exercise of a special power of appointment will begin on the date on which the instrument creating the power took effect. 'Special' for this purpose includes hybrid or intermediate powers.[3]

> *Example 2.1*
>
> A trust created on 1 July 1980 with an 80-year perpetuity period from that date includes a special power of appointment which is exercised after PAA 2009 came into force. The perpetuity period for any trusts created by the power remains 80 years starting on 1 July 1980.

---

[2]   See **Precedent 13.2**.
[3]   See **2.54**.

2.09 The rule is different for trusts created under a *general* power of appointment which is exercised after commencement of the Act. In this case, the perpetuity period will be 125 years beginning on the date on which the power is exercised, not the date on which it was created.[4]

Accumulations of income

2.10 There were fears that allowing income to be accumulated for lengthy periods would result in such a concentration of wealth in private hands that the economic independence of the nation might be compromised. Whilst there was no common law rule restricting accumulations, there have therefore been a number of statutory provisions limiting the period for which trustees can accumulate income.

The old rules

2.11 The Law of Property Act 1925 and the PAA 1964 set out a choice of maximum periods for which income could be accumulated. The period most commonly selected was 21 years from the creation of the settlement or, in the case of will trusts, the date of death. Once the relevant period expires, trustees have no further power to accumulate income and have to pay it out unless the beneficiary is a minor.[5]

The new rules

2.12 The statutory rules against excessive accumulations were abolished in the case of trusts created after 5 April 2010 and wills executed after that date.[6] Existing trusts remain subject to the old law. The PAA 2009 makes it possible to accumulate throughout the lifetime of a settlement or will trust but it does not override provisions in trust documents. Hence, the unrestricted power to accumulate is subject to any contrary provisions in the trust instrument.[7]

If the trust instrument is silent, on the basis that there are no restrictions on the trustees' power to accumulate, trustees will be able to accumulate throughout the perpetuity period. While it is possible to define the accumulation period, for example:

'The accumulation period shall be the perpetuity period',

---

[4] This is because a general power is considered, for some purposes, to be the equivalent to absolute ownership of the property. For the use of general powers to create IPDIs, see **6.33** *et seq.*

[5] When TA 1925, s 31 applies to a trust, the trustees have a separate statutory power to accumulate during the minority of beneficiaries. See **2.70**.

[6] PAA 2009, s 13.

[7] It may be possible for trustees to remove any such restriction by the exercise of a dispositive power.

in the interests of simplifying trust instruments it may be better to say nothing.[8]

Meaning of 'wills executed'

2.13   The PAA 2009 states that:

(a)   it applies only to wills executed after commencement (s 15(1)(a)); and

(b)   a reference to a will includes a reference to a codicil (s 20(7)).

It is unclear whether the Act applies where a will executed before commencement is republished after commencement by a codicil. The Act will apply to the contents of the codicil itself, but it may not apply to the contents of the original will if these are not expressly restated in the codicil. *In Re Heath's Will Trusts*,[9] which considered the effect of a statute using similar language, suggests that it may not.

Post-death variations

2.14   A beneficiary of a will of a testator executed before 6 April 2010 may wish to vary the terms of the will after that date to create a trust. Does the Act apply to the trust created by the variation? It will, provided that the variation creating the trust is made on or after 6 April 2010. The date of execution of the will is irrelevant. Although a post-death variation can be treated as the deceased's disposition for the purposes of inheritance tax and capital gains tax, the reading-back takes effect only for those limited tax purposes. For other purposes the person making the variation is making a lifetime disposition.[10]

> *Example 2.2*
>
> Aaron made a will on 6 August 2009 leaving his estate to his wife, Frida, absolutely. He died on 6 August 2010. Frida executes a deed of variation on 6 July 2012 by which she settles the estate on a life interest trust (IPDI) for herself, remainder on discretionary trusts for her issue. Note:
>
> 1.   the variation may be read back for IHT purposes: ie. it is as if Aaron had set up the trust in his will;
>
> 2.   but, otherwise, Frida creates the trust on 6 July 2012 and so the 125-year perpetuity period applies;
>
> 3.   contrast the position if the will had set up a trust which was varied (eg. by one beneficiary assigning his interest to another): in this case the date of the will determines the relevant perpetuity period (on these facts the old law applies).

---

8   See **Precedent 4.1**, clause 6(5)(i).
9   [1949] Ch 170.
10   See Chapter 12.

Trusts of death benefits (spousal by-pass trusts)

2.15 Members of pension schemes often request the trustees of the pension scheme to pay any lump sum to which they are entitled on death to a trust created by the member during his lifetime.[11] The pension scheme itself normally involves a trust and so this is a situation where trustees of one trust are exercising a power to make payments to another trust.[12] Section 6(2) of PAA 2009 means that the perpetuity period will be that of the original pension trust. It is, therefore, necessary to know when the pension trust was created.

2.16 It was held in *Privy Council in Air Jamaica Ltd v Charlton*[13] that as each member joins a pension scheme, a new settlement is created for that member irrespective of when the scheme itself began:

> 'Every time an employee joins the scheme, a new settlement is created. The settlement comprises the contributions made in respect of the employee whether by him or by the company. The rule against perpetuities must be applied separately to each individual settlement, and each employee must be treated as a life in being in relation to his own settlement.'[14]

2.17 As a result, if the trustees of a discretionary pension scheme are asked to appoint the benefits on trust, this will involve the transfer of property from a trust created when the member joined the scheme. Hence the new perpetuity period will only apply to the property appointed where the member joins on or after 6 April 2010.

If the member joined before that date, the old rules apply which means that if the trustees exercise a power to transfer funds to a trust, created by the member during his lifetime the perpetuity period applicable to those funds will normally be 21 years.[15]

2.18 However, if the member creates a lifetime trust on or after 6 April 2010, that trust must have a 125-year perpetuity period. There is, therefore, a mismatch between the two periods. The transfer from the pension trust is not automatically void for perpetuity. The 'wait and see' provisions will apply[16] and so long as interests vest within the shorter perpetuity period there will be no problem.

---

[11] This will be set up as a pilot trust: see generally Chapter 8. For a consideration of whether there is any advantage in having a multiplicity of such trusts, see **8.26**.

[12] Contrast contract-based arrangements such as retirement annuity contracts. For the IHT treatment of transfers from one (relevant property) trust to another trust, see IHTA 1984, s 81 (discussed at **8.12**).

[13] [1999] 1 WLR 1399, at 1409.

[14] If pension funds are transferred to a new pension scheme it appears that they are still attributed to the original trust for, eg. IHT 10 yearly charges: see generally the ABI Technical Guidance available at http://wingatefp.com/uploads/2011.06.20_abi_pensions_q_and_a_paper_2.pdf.

[15] The perpetuity period for the pension trust being member's life plus 21 years but of course the member will be dead at the time of the transfer. Consider, however, whether there will be other 'relevant lives' at the time when he enters into the pension: eg. spouse and children.

[16] PAA 2009, s 7.

2.19 If the problem is recognised when the member creates the lifetime trust, steps can be taken to solve the difficulty. The lifetime trust must have the new perpetuity period of 125 years but the 'trust period'[17] can be set at any period the settlor chooses. Hence, when drafting the lifetime trust, either:

(a)   give the trustees power to limit the trust period in the future so that the pilot trust can be made to coincide with the perpetuity period for funds transferred; or

(b)   limit the trust period from the outset to the settlor's life plus 21 years.[18]

Using the Variation of Trusts Act 1958 to obtain a new perpetuity period

2.20 In cases where the amounts involved are sufficient to justify the costs, it is possible to apply to court under the Variation of Trusts Act 1958 for a new perpetuity period. In *Wyndham v Egremont*,[19] substantial funds were held on trust. The perpetuity period was 20 years from the death of the last survivor of the issue, whether children or more remote, of His late Majesty King George V living on 20 May 1940. Given the ages of the remaining Royal Lives in being, the youngest of whom (HRH Princess Alexandra) was 72, the period would expire in the not too distant future and as the current life tenant was only 26, in his lifetime. This would deprive the life tenant's eldest son of an interest in the fund and would trigger a substantial CGT charge on the deemed disposal.[20] Blackburne J approved a variation which inserted a new perpetuity period (the last survivor of the legitimate issue, whether children or more remote, living on 24 July 2009 of His late Majesty King George V and the Fifth Baron Leconfield) which significantly postponed the deemed disposal.

Does the variation involve a tax charge – specifically a CGT charge – if the original settlement has been replaced by a new trust? Section 1(1) of the 1958 Act authorises the court to approve an arrangement varying (or revoking) all or any of the trusts of a will, settlement or other disposition. It does not authorise the court to approve a resettlement. There is no bright-line test for determining what is or is not a resettlement. In *Re Ball's Settlement Trusts*[21] Megarry J stated that:

> 'If an arrangement, while leaving the substratum effectuates the purpose of the original trusts by other means, it may still be possible to regard that arrangement as merely varying the original trusts, even though the means employed are wholly different and even though the form is completely changed.'

---

17   For the meaning of 'Trust Period' see **2.05**.
18   See footnote 15 above for other 'relevant lives'.
19   [2009] EWHC 2076 (Ch).
20   For CGT deemed disposals, see **3.105** *et seq*.
21   [1968] 2 All ER 438.

Useful guidance for determining whether what is proposed is a modification rather than a resettlement is to be found in *Roome v Edwards (Inspector of Taxes).*[22]

2. DISPOSITIVE AND ADMINISTRATIVE POWERS

2.21 None of us have the gift of clairvoyance so it is attractive when drafting trusts and will trusts to give trustees as much flexibility as possible to enable them to deal with changes in the law or in the circumstances of beneficiaries in the best possible way.[23] When drafting, it is important to understand the nature of the various powers that may be included in a trust instrument. And when using the powers given to them, trustees need to choose the correct power and exercise it in the appropriate way to achieve the desired result.

What is meant by a 'dispositive power'?

2.22 In general, a dispositive power is a power which relates to the distribution of trust property for the benefit of the objects (or beneficiaries) of the trust, whether in the form of income or capital or both. For instance, the statutory power of maintenance is a dispositive power over income, whereas the power of advancement is a dispositive power over capital. An administrative power relates to the administration of the trust (eg. a power of investment). Other powers (eg. to remunerate trustees) may best be considered to be 'hybrid' or *sui generis*.

The types of dispositive powers

2.23 The classic division of dispositive powers is into:

(a) powers of appointment giving trustees power to appoint income and capital to one or more beneficiaries (the objects of the power); and

(b) powers of advancement, often derived from the Trustee Act 1925, s 32 as modified by the terms of the trust instrument (eg. to allow the advancement of 100% rather than 50% of the beneficiary's presumptive share[24]). Express clauses frequently confer a power 'to pay apply or transfer' property comprised in the settlement.

Although sometimes considered an administrative power, the power of appropriation is used to allocate particular property for a beneficiary and is therefore thought to be dispositive in nature.

---

[22] [1981] STC 96, [1982] AC 279: see **2.60** *et seq.*

[23] This is not to say that there are not dangers in creating flexible trusts: the trustees will have wide powers to be exercised as they see fit and this makes the choice of trustees especially important.

[24] See **2.46** for the changes to s 32 made by the Inheritance and Trustees' Powers Act 2014.

The exercise of dispositive powers

2.24 When exercising dispositive powers trustees 'must act in good faith, responsibly and reasonably ... [and] must inform themselves, before making a decision, of matters which are relevant to the decision'.[25] This requires the trustee to make 'such a survey of the range of objects or possible beneficiaries' as will enable him to carry out his fiduciary duties.[26] A trustee must find out the 'permissible area of selection and then consider responsibly, in individual cases, whether a contemplated beneficiary was within the power and whether, in relation to the possible claimants, a particular grant was appropriate'.[27]

In making the decision, the trustee is not subject to the rules of natural justice, that is, he is not obliged to hear the person affected by his decision.[28] Of course, the trustees must obey the trust instrument and cannot make an appointment that is not authorised by it.

Challenging the exercise of a dispositive power

2.25 The decisions of trustees may be challenged on the following grounds:

(a)   if it can be shown that they did not act in good faith having properly informed themselves;[29]

(b)   if it is shown that the trustee did not 'consider' the appointment but acted on the direction of another, for example, the settlor.[30] Similarly the trustee may have failed to appreciate that he had any discretion in the matter;[31]

(c)   the exercise may be excessive: for example, because it is intended to benefit a non-object of the trust or involves a breach of the perpetuity rules;

(d)   it may be a fraud on a power;

---

[25]   *Scott v National Trust for Places of Historic Interest and Natural Beauty* [1998] 2 All ER 705, at 717 per Robert Walker J.

[26]   See *Re Hay's Settlement Trusts* [1981] 3 All ER 786 at 792, [1982] 1 WLR 202, at 209 per Sir Robert Megarry V-C, quoting Lord Wilberforce in *McPhail v Doulton* [1971] AC 424, [1970] 2 All ER 228, HL.

[27]   See footnote 25 above.

[28]   The trustees 'are not a court or an administrative tribunal. They are not under any general duty to give a hearing to both sides': *Scott v National Trust for Places of Historic Interest and Natural Beauty* [1998] 2 All ER 705, at 718. See also *R v Charity Comrs ex p Baldwin* [2001] WTLR 137.

[29]   *Klug v Klug* [1918] 2 Ch 67. On the giving of reasons by trustees see *Re Beloved Wilkes' Charity* (1851) 20 LJ Ch 588, 3 Mac & G 440; *Dundee General Hospitals Board of Management v Walker* [1952] 1 All ER 896, HL and Robert Walker J in *Scott v National Trust for Places of Historic Interest and Natural Beauty* [1998] 2 All ER 705, [1998] 1 WLR 226.

[30]   For instance, in *Turner v Turner* [1984] Ch 100, [1983] 2 All ER 745 the appointments were held to be void.

[31]   This may be seen as the equivalent to non est factum: see *Judge (personal representatives of Walden, dec'd) v RCC* [2005] STC (SCD) 863 in which the trustees erroneously believed that the deceased's surviving spouse had an interest in possession in the matrimonial home and so by writing to confirm that she could occupy the property were not exercising their discretionary powers.

(e) there may be a formal or procedural defect, for example, failure to exercise the power by deed or to obtain a requisite consent.

These grounds for challenging indicate that powers can never be 'absolute' or 'uncontrolled' and clauses which seek to allow trustees to act in their 'absolute and uncontrolled discretion' serve little purpose. By contrast, a provision that in exercising, say, a power to apply capital for a particular beneficiary (typically an interest in possession beneficiary) the trustees are required only to consider the interest of that beneficiary and do not have to balance the 'competing' interest of the other beneficiaries, has a value in limiting the factors to be taken into account in exercising the power.

Hastings-Bass and mistake

2.26 The complexity of UK tax law has led to trustees making mistakes in exercising their dispositive powers. Similarly settlements may be created without appreciating that the settlor will incur a substantial tax liability. In recent years a large body of case law developed with trustees seeking to escape from decisions that they regretted by invoking the so-called rule in *Hastings-Bass* and using the doctrine of mistake to set aside the unwanted gift or settlement.

Virtually all the decisions on *Hastings-Bass* and mistake were at first instance. In the early cases HMRC were not represented but it soon became apparent that the effect of the line of decisions was to deprive HMRC of substantial tax revenue. HMRC, therefore, started to appear and argued that the line of cases was wrong in allowing professional advisers to escape from the consequences of their mistakes in an unjustifiable way. The response from the courts to these arguments was that they were too late in the day. The case-law at first instance was too well settled to overturn; only the Court of Appeal could change it. Finally in two appeals heard together, *Pitt v Holt* and *Futter v Futter*,[32] the Court of Appeal got its chance and declared that in the *Hastings-Bass* line of cases the law had taken 'a wrong turn'. The Supreme Court confirmed this although it took a different view from the Court of Appeal on mistake.[33]

What was thought to be the *ratio decidendi* of *Hastings-Bass*[34]

2.27 The following statement by Buckley LJ[35] had been regarded as the *ratio decidendi* of the *Hastings-Bass* case:

'To sum up the preceding observations, in our judgment, where by the terms of a trust (as under section 32)[36] a trustee is given a discretion as to some matter under which he acts in good faith, the court should not interfere with his action

---

[32] [2011] EWCA Civ 197.
[33] [2013] UKSC 26.
[34] [1975] Ch 25.
[35] At 41F–H.
[36] Ie TA 1925, s 32 (power of advancement).

notwithstanding that it does not have the full effect which he intended, unless (1) what he has achieved is unauthorised by the power conferred upon him, or (2) it is clear that he would not have acted as he did (a) had he not taken into account considerations which he should not have taken into account, or (b) had he not failed to take into account considerations which he ought to have taken into account.'

In the subsequent case of *Mettoy Pension Trustees v Evans* Warner J said:[37]

'I have come to the conclusion that there is a principle which may be labelled "the rule in *Hastings-Bass*". I do not think that the application of that principle is confined ... to cases where an exercise by trustees of a discretion vested in them is partially ineffective because of some rule of law or because of some limit on their discretion which they overlooked. If, as I believe, the reason for the application of the principle is the failure by the trustees to take into account considerations that they ought to have taken into account, it cannot matter whether that failure is due to their having overlooked (or to their legal advisers having overlooked) some relevant rule of law or limit on their discretion, or is due to some other cause.

It is not enough, however, for the principle to apply, that it should be shown that the trustees did not have a proper understanding of the effect of their act. It must also be clear that, had they had a proper understanding of it, they would not have acted as they did.'

2.28   The Court of Appeal concluded that the true ratio of *Hastings-Bass* was more limited. On Warner J's decision in *Mettoy* Lloyd LJ said at para 72:

'The principle on the basis of which the judge decided this aspect of the case cannot, in my judgment, be found in the decision in *Re Hastings-Bass* itself. What the trustees did in relation to the Mettoy pension scheme was within their powers.'

Mummery LJ said at para 227:

'these appeals provide examples of that comparatively rare instance of the law taking a seriously wrong turn.'

The correct *ratio decidendi* of *Hastings-Bass*

2.29   According to Lloyd LJ the true ratio of the *Hastings-Bass* case was set out at 40H–41C of Buckley LJ's judgment and is as follows:

'Trustees considering an advancement by way of sub-settlement must apply their minds to the question whether the sub-settlement as a whole will operate for the benefit of the person to be advanced. If one or more aspects of the provisions intended to be created cannot take effect, it does not follow that those which can take effect should not be regarded as having been brought into being by an exercise of the discretion. That fact, and the misapprehension on the part of the trustees as to the effect that it would have, is not by itself fatal to the effectiveness of the advancement ... If the provisions that can and would take effect cannot reasonably

---

[37]   [1990] 1 WLR 1587, at 1624B.

be regarded as being for the benefit of the person to be advanced, then the exercise fails as not being within the scope of the power of advancement. Otherwise it takes effect to the extent that it can.'

Lord Walker giving the judgment of the Supreme Court agreed with Lloyd LJ's conclusion.

When can the exercise by trustees of a dispositive power be set aside?

2.30 Lloyd LJ concluded that Lightman J had been correct when he said in *Abacus v Barr*[38] that to challenge the exercise of a discretion successfully there must have been a breach of duty by the trustees. He identified two types of case in which the exercise of discretions can be challenged. In one the exercise is void; in the other voidable.

(i) If what is done is not within the scope of the power, it will be void. For instance:

  - a procedural defect, such as the use of the wrong kind of document; the failure to obtain a necessary prior consent, or the wrong people executing the document;[39]
  - a substantive defect, such as an unauthorised delegation, or an appointment to someone who is not within the class of objects (cases of a fraud on a power are similar);[40]
  - a defect under the general law, such as the rule against perpetuities, the impact and significance of which will depend on the extent of the invalidity.

(ii) If what is done is within the terms of the power, but the trustees have in some way breached their duties in respect of that exercise, then (unless it is a case of a fraud on the power) the act is not void but it may be voidable at the instance of a beneficiary who is adversely affected (subject to equitable defences and the court's discretion). If a third party purchaser has acquired trust property as a result, he may have an indefeasible title if he gave value without notice of the breach of fiduciary duty but in such a case the beneficiary's interest would attach to the proceeds of the sale.[41]

Lord Walker agreed saying that Lloyd LJ's judgment correctly spelled out the important distinction between an error by trustees in going beyond the scope of a power (for which Lord Walker used the traditional term 'excessive execution') and an error in failing to give proper consideration to relevant matters in making a decision which is within the scope of the relevant power (which he

---

[38] [2003] EWHC 114 (Ch).

[39] For example in the case of *Jasmine Trustees Ltd v Wells & Hind* [2007] EWHC 38 (Ch), [2008] Ch 194, [2007] STC 660 many documents were invalid because they had been executed by people who were not the trustees!

[40] See the striking case of *Turner v Turner* [1984] Ch 100, where the trustees executed documents prepared on the instructions of the settlor without considering the exercise of their discretion.

[41] See *Foskett v McKeown* [2001] 1 AC 102, at 127F–G (Lord Millett).

termed 'inadequate deliberation'). In the latter case, breach of duty is essential (in the full sense of that word) because it is only a breach of duty on the part of the trustees that entitles the court to intervene: generally, the inadequate deliberation on the part of the trustees must be sufficiently serious as to amount to a breach of fiduciary duty. It is not enough to show that the trustees' deliberations have fallen short of the highest possible standards, or that the court would, on a surrender of discretion by the trustees, have acted in a different way. Apart from exceptional circumstances (such as an impasse reached by honest and reasonable trustees) only breach of fiduciary duty justifies judicial intervention.

What are the duties of a trustee?

2.31   Trustees are under a duty of care, obliging them to exercise such skill and care as is reasonable in the circumstances. They have to weigh benefits and take into account relevant factors when exercising a discretionary power. It is not possible to lay down any absolute rule as to the matters which trustees ought to take into account when considering the exercise of a power of advancement or other dispositive power. Circumstances will differ from one trust to another, and even within one trust they may change from time to time or according to the nature of the particular exercise under consideration. Lord Walker and Lloyd LJ agreed that in many cases fiscal consequences will be relevant considerations which the trustees ought to take into account.

Professional advice

2.32   Where tax matters are relevant it will usually be the duty of the trustees to take proper advice. But where trustees have taken advice from appropriate and reputable advisers on how to proceed in a tax efficient manner which they follow, they will not be in breach of duty if that advice turns out to be wrong. Hence, in the absence of any other basis for a challenge, the trustees will not be in breach of their fiduciary duty to have regard to relevant matters. Accordingly in such a case the trustees' act is not voidable. Lloyd LJ accepted:

> 'that this distinction makes potentially vulnerable an act done by trustees who fail to take any advice, whereas the same act done in the same circumstances by trustees who take advice which proves to be incorrect is not vulnerable. That is said to reduce significantly the protection afforded to beneficiaries by the *Hastings-Bass* rule. I accept that the point of the principle is to protect beneficiaries rather than trustees. I also accept that a claim by beneficiaries against the trustees themselves may often be precluded by an exoneration clause in the trust deed. It may also be ... that a claim against the professional advisers of the trustees would face problems even if liability can be established, because different loss may be suffered by different people, not all of whom may have a claim against the advisers. Recognising those points, nevertheless I see no anomaly in the distinction that I have drawn. It arises from the need to find a breach of trust in order to set aside an act of the trustees which is within their powers ... One practical consequence, if I am right, is that if in future it is desired to challenge an exercise by trustees of a discretionary power on this basis, it will be necessary for

one or more beneficiaries to grasp the nettle of alleging and proving a breach of fiduciary duty on the part of the trustees. Only rarely would it be appropriate for the trustees to take the initiative in the proceedings.'

Lord Walker agreed with this statement adding that trustees should not regard such applications 'as uncontroversial proceedings in which they can confidently expect to recover their costs out of the trust fund'.

Was relief available in the cases being appealed?

2.33 Applying the principles set out above as the trustees in both *Futter* and *Pitt v Holt* had acted within their powers and taken and relied on proper advice, the exercise of their discretion was not voidable.[42]

2.34 A number of the offshore jurisdictions which follow the law of England and Wales were unhappy at the demise of what they regarded as the useful *Hastings-Bass* jurisdiction. As a result they have introduced statutory equivalents.[43]

The equitable jurisdiction to set aside a voluntary transaction for mistake

2.35 In *Pitt v Holt* application had been made to set aside the transaction on the basis of mistake as well as *Hastings-Bass*. The decision of the Supreme Court has extended the scope for obtaining relief on the basis of mistake. As relief for mistake is available both to individuals and trustees, it may be of assistance in cases where trustees would previously have made *Hastings-Bass* applications.

---

[42] Many of the decided first instance cases would be decided differently as a result of the Supreme Court decision. For instance, *Green v Cobham* [2002] STC 820; *Abacus Trust Co v NSPCC* [2001] STC 1344 and *Sieff v Fox* [2005] EWHC 1312 (Ch), all of which involved mistakes as to the impact of CGT, and *Burrell v Burrell* [2005] STC 569 involving a mistake as to IHT.

[43] For example Jersey and Guernsey. Typical is Art 47H inserted into the Trusts (Jersey) Law 1984:

'(2) The court may on the application of any person specified in Article 47I(2), and in the circumstances set out in paragraph (3), declare that the exercise of a power by a trustee or a person exercising a power over, or in relation to a trust, or trust property, is voidable and –
(a) has such effect as the court may determine; or
(b) is of no effect from the time of its exercise.
(3) The circumstances are where, in relation to the exercise of his or her power, the trustee or person exercising a power –
(a) failed to take into account any relevant considerations or took into account irrelevant considerations; and
(b) would not have exercised the power, or would not have exercised the power in the way it was so exercised, but for that failure to take into account relevant considerations, or that taking into account of irrelevant considerations.
(4) It does not matter whether or not the circumstances set out in paragraph (3) occurred as a result of any lack of care or other fault on the part of the trustee or person exercising a power, or on the part of any person giving advice in relation to the exercise of the power.'

The facts in *Pitt v Holt*

2.36 Mr Pitt was left brain damaged after a road accident and received £1.2m in agreed damages. His wife was appointed his receiver. Acting on the advice of financial advisers she transferred the lump sum into a discretionary settlement. The settlement did not qualify as a trust for the disabled under IHTA 1984, s 89 and so IHT was payable both on creation and on 10-yearly anniversaries. No one ever considered the impact of inheritance tax.

She applied for relief both on the basis of *Hastings-Bass* (where she was successful at first instance but failed in the Court of Appeal and Supreme Court because there was no breach of duty) and on the basis of mistake (where she failed at first instance and in the Court of Appeal but won in the Supreme Court).[44]

2.37 There is a long standing equitable jurisdiction to set aside voluntary dispositions which are vitiated by fraud, undue influence, unconscionable bargains and mistake. There had been significant case law differences as to the type of mistake required.

An early case was the Court of Appeal and House of Lords decisions in *Ogilvie v Littleboy*[45] and *Ogilvie v Allen*[46] dismissing an application to set aside voluntary dispositions to charity which a wealthy widow had come to regret. In the Court of Appeal Lindley LJ said:

> 'Gifts cannot be revoked, nor can deeds of gift be set aside, simply because the donors wish they had not made them and would like to have back the property given. Where there is no fraud, no undue influence, no fiduciary relation between donor and donee, no mistake induced by those who derive any benefit by it, a gift, whether by mere delivery or by deed, is binding on the donor ... In the absence of all circumstances of suspicion a donor can only obtain back property which he has given away by showing that he was under some mistake of so serious a character as to render it unjust on the part of the donee to retain the property given to him.'

Lord Halsbury LC in the House of Lords referred to setting aside transactions where 'misunderstanding on both sides may render it unjust to the giver that the gift should be retained'.

2.38 Another case decided in 1909 illustrates a different basis for the jurisdiction. In *Lady Hood of Avalon v Mackinnon*,[47] Lady Hood had power under her marriage settlement to appoint capital to her two daughters. In 1888 she appointed half the fund to her elder daughter. In 1902 and 1904 she appointed sums to her younger daughter. Having forgotten the appointment to her elder daughter, Lady Hood made a further appointment to her in an

---

[44] In *Futter v Futter* the claim was based on *Hastings-Bass* alone at first instance and in the Court of Appeal. Leave to argue mistake before the Supreme Court was refused.
[45] (1897) 13 TLR 399.
[46] (1899) 15 TLR 294.
[47] [1909] 1 Ch 476.

attempt to achieve equality between the two. When she discovered the duplication of gifts she applied to have the gift set aside. Eve J said that forgetting the earlier disposition was equivalent to a mistake:

> 'It seems to me that when a person has forgotten the existence of a pre-existing fact, and assumes that such fact did not pre-exist, he is labouring under a mistake, and he acts on the footing that the fact really did not pre-exist.'

On that basis, and satisfied that the last appointment was made under a mistake with regard to the existing facts, he held that she was entitled to have the appointment set aside.

2.39 In *Gibbon v Mitchell*[48] the plaintiff had a protected life interest under a settlement, and a limited power to appoint an annuity to a surviving spouse, and subject to that the capital was held on trust for his children. For tax planning reasons he wished his children's interest in the fund to be accelerated and was advised that he could achieve this by surrendering his life interest. However, because the life interest was protected, a discretionary trust came into being.[49] The beneficiaries of this discretionary trust included all his children, whenever born, and not, as he wished, his present children.

Millett J referred to a number of cases where voluntary dispositions were set aside for mistake which he summarised as follows:[50]

> 'In my judgment, these cases show that, wherever there is a voluntary transaction by which one party intends to confer a bounty on another, the deed will be set aside if the court is satisfied that the disponor did not intend the transaction to have the effect which it did. It will be set aside for mistake whether the mistake is a mistake of law or of fact, so long as the mistake is as to the effect of the transaction itself and not merely as to its consequences or the advantages to be gained by entering into it.'

He held that the plaintiff was mistaken as to the effect of the deed of surrender in that he believed that the effect of surrendering his life interest would be that his two children would become entitled to the fund immediately and absolutely.

This formulation substantially limited the number of cases in which equitable relief for mistake was available. Also the line between a mistake as to effect and a mistake as to consequences was sometimes surprisingly difficult to draw.

2.40 There had been suggestions that *Ogilvie* and *Gibbon* propounded different tests but in the Court of Appeal Lloyd LJ said there was no incompatibility. In his opinion the correct test as a matter of authority and principle was a combination of *Gibbon v Mitchell, Lady Hood* and *Ogilvie v Littleboy*:

---

[48]   [1990] 1 WLR 1304.
[49]   For protective trusts, see TA 1925, s 33.
[50]   At 1309D–F.

- There must be a mistake on the part of the donor either as to the legal effect of the disposition (*Gibbon*) or as to an existing fact which is basic to the transaction (*Lady Hood*).
- The mistake must be of sufficient gravity as to satisfy the *Ogilvie v Littleboy* test, which provides protection to the recipient against too ready an ability of the donor to seek to recall his gift.
- The fact that the transaction gives rise to unforeseen fiscal liabilities is a consequence, not an effect, for this purpose, and is not sufficient to bring the jurisdiction into play.

The result of this formulation (requiring a mistake as to affect not merely the consequences) was that the Court of Appeal held that no relief was available in *Pitt v Holt*. Mrs Pitt had understood the effect of what she was doing (settling her husband's personal injury payment on trust) and was merely mistaken about the fiscal consequences. However, the Supreme Court disagreed.

The correct test for mistake

2.41   Lord Walker stated that the distinction between effect and consequences was too difficult to apply. Continuing to require courts to apply it would create uncertainty. It was also contrary to the general disinclination of equity to insist on rigid classifications expressed in abstract terms.

In the view of the Supreme Court the true requirement is simply for there to have been a causative mistake of sufficient gravity that it would be unconscionable for the court to leave the error uncorrected. As guidance to judges in finding and evaluating the facts of any particular case, he said that the test will normally be satisfied only when there is a mistake either as to the legal character or nature of a transaction, or as to some matter of fact or law which is basic to the transaction.

The injustice (or unconscionableness) of leaving a mistaken disposition uncorrected must be evaluated objectively, but with 'an intense focus' on the facts of the particular case.

What is a mistake?

2.42   Despite 'simplifying' the law Lord Walker spent a considerable amount of time discussing what amounts to a 'mistake'. He said:

> 'a mistake must be distinguished from mere ignorance or inadvertence, and also from what scholars in the field of unjust enrichment refer to as misprediction ... These distinctions are reasonably clear in a general sort of way, but they tend to get blurred when it comes to facts of particular cases. The editors of *Goff and Jones, The Law of Unjust Enrichment*, 8th edn (2011) para 9-11 comment that the distinction between mistake and misprediction can lead to "some uncomfortably fine distinctions", and the same is true of the distinction between mistake and ignorance.

> Forgetfulness, inadvertence or ignorance is not, as such, a mistake, but it can lead
> to a false belief or assumption which the law will recognise as a mistake.'

The distinctions are far from academic. In *Pitt* at first instance the trial judge
found that there was no mistake: 'If someone does not apply his mind to a
point at all, it is difficult to say that there has been some real mistake about it.'
The Court of Appeal adopted a different view of the facts, treating the case
(para 216) as one of an incorrect conscious belief on the part of Mrs Pitt that
the discretionary trust had no adverse tax consequences. The editors of *Goff &*
Jones had argued in favour of treating mere causative ignorance as sufficient.

Lord Walker rejected this and said that 'mere ignorance, even if causative, is
insufficient, but that the court, in carrying out its task of finding the facts,
should not shrink from drawing the inference of conscious belief or tacit
assumption when there is evidence to support such an inference'. He was
willing to do this in the case of *Pitt*.

A misprediction relates to some possible future event, whereas a legally
significant mistake normally relates to some past or present matter of fact or
law. In relation to misprediction Lord Walker considered *In re Griffiths, decd*[51]
(a potentially exempt transfer made shortly before the transferor's death from
cancer). The medical evidence was inconclusive and the case was uncontested.
The trial judge accepted, despite the unsatisfactory evidence, that at the date of
the gift Mr Griffiths was suffering from lung cancer about which he was
unaware. He had therefore made a mistake about his state of health. He
thought he had a reasonable chance of surviving 7 years but in fact had no
chance at all.

In Lord Walker's view, had the judge not made that finding about the presence
of cancer at the date of the gift, it would have been a case of misprediction, no
different from a failure to predict a fatal road accident. Even with that finding
there must be a query as to whether it was an error of a type which would make
it unconscionable for the court not to intervene.

Tax Consequences and Unconscionability

2.43 Before the Supreme Court HMRC was given leave to argue a new point
which was that a mistake which relates exclusively to tax cannot in any
circumstances be relieved. Mistake of law is not a defence, it submitted, to tax
lawfully due and payable.

Lord Walker rejected this as much too wide and unsupported by principle or
authority. But, he said, it is still necessary to consider whether there are some
types of mistake about tax which should not attract relief. Tax mitigation or
tax avoidance was the motive behind almost all of the *Hastings-Bass* cases that
were concerned with family trusts (as opposed to pension trusts). On the test

---

[51] [2009] Ch 162.

proposed above, consequences (including tax consequences) are relevant to the gravity of a mistake, whether or not they were basic to the transaction.

In *Pitt v Holt* the mistake made related to tax but there was clearly nothing unconscionable about granting Mrs Pitt relief. It was recognised that a person in receipt of a personal injury award would often want those funds to be settled and that it would be inappropriate to demand an entry charge. It was for that reason that trusts for disabled persons existed. The mistake lay in not selecting the appropriate settlement vehicle.

Had the Supreme Court allowed mistake to be argued before it for the first time in *Futter*, there would have been a real issue as to whether the court should assist in extricating claimants from a tax-avoidance scheme which had gone wrong. Lord Walker said at para 135:

> 'The scheme adopted by Mr Futter was by no means at the extreme of artificiality (compare for instance, that in *Abacus Trust Co (Isle of Man) v NSPCC* [2001] STC 1344) but it was hardly an exercise in good citizenship. In some cases of artificial tax avoidance the court might think it right to refuse relief, either on the ground that such claimants, acting on supposedly expert advice, must be taken to have accepted the risk that the scheme would prove ineffective, or on the ground that discretionary relief should be refused on grounds of public policy. Since the seminal decision of the House of Lords in *WT Ramsay Ltd v IRC* [1982] AC 300 there has been an increasingly strong and general recognition that artificial tax avoidance is a social evil which puts an unfair burden on the shoulders of those who do not adopt such measures.'[52]

3. POWERS OF ADVANCEMENT AND TO PAY OR APPLY CAPITAL

The statutory power

2.44 Section 32 of the Trustee Act 1925 applies to all settlements unless excluded and allows trustees to pay or apply capital for the advancement or benefit of any person with a vested or presumptive interest in capital. As originally drawn the amount advanced under the section could not exceed one-half of that interest.[53] Any beneficiary with a prior interest who would be prejudiced by the advancement must consent and the advance must be brought into account on final distribution.

Express powers

2.45 Trust instruments and wills often contain express powers modelled on s 32 which usually extend the statutory power to permit the advancement of 100% of the presumptive share of a beneficiary. For instance:

---

[52] The test for mistake laid down in the Supreme Court was applied in *Kennedy v Kennedy* [2014] EWHC 4129.

[53] See **2.46** for amendments to the section made by Inheritance and Trustees' Powers Act 2014.

'The Trustees may pay or apply any Trust Property for the advancement or benefit of any Beneficiary.'

Further amendments are also commonly made. The other two limitations noted above may be removed and the trustees may be given power to use capital for the benefit of beneficiaries who only have a right to income.[54]

Inheritance and Trustees' Powers Act 2014

2.46   The Act came into force on 1 October 2014. It amended s 32 to remove the limit on advancements of one half of vested or presumptive entitlement for trusts 'created or arising after the Act comes into force' subject to amendment or exclusion of the power by the terms of the will. According to Explanatory Note 51 trusts created by will arise at the date of death not the date of execution.

The section was also amended to make clear that:

(1)   advances can be of assets not merely cash;

(2)   trustees may advance assets on the basis (express or implied) that the advance represents a proportionate part of a beneficiary's future entitlement for the purpose of taking it into account at the time when the beneficiary becomes entitled rather than at its nominal value at the time of the advance.[55]

These two amendments (which basically reflect the old law) apply to all trusts whenever established.

Meaning of 'advancement or benefit'

2.47   An important question for trustees is what the words 'advancement or benefit' mean. According to Lord Radcliffe in *Pilkington v IRC*[56] the word 'advancement' originally meant the establishment in life of the beneficiary who was the object of the power. In the nineteenth century this meant buying an apprenticeship or the purchase of a commission in the army or an interest in business. In the case of women there could be advancement on marriage. In *Pilkington*, Lord Radcliffe made the important point that the word 'advancement' does not carry with it the idea of paying money to a beneficiary early. That will often be the result since the funds advanced come from property

---

[54]   This is commonly done in the case of IPDI trusts: see **6.17**.

[55]   The amendment (which applies to all trusts whenever created) does not change the previous position which, according to *Re Leigh's Settlement Trusts* [1981] CLY 2453, [2006] WTLR 485 was that trustees could choose the basis on which they make an advance. Per Blackett-Ord J: '... the court is not restricted to the traditional method of valuing appropriations or advances if the trustees give their mind to the matter and decide to make an appropriation or advance on some different basis.'

[56]   [1964] AC 612.

to which the beneficiary does not yet have an absolute entitlement but in some cases the advancement might actually defer the vesting of the beneficiary's absolute entitlement.[57]

Advancement was thought to have a limited range of meaning since it conveyed the idea of some step in life of permanent significance. It, therefore, became common for those drafting trusts to add words such as 'or otherwise for his or her benefit'. It was always recognised that these added words were 'large words' (see Jessel MR in *In Re Breeds' Will*).[58] The expression 'advancement or benefit' according to Lord Radcliffe means 'any use of the money which will improve the material situation of the beneficiary'.[59]

2.48   Some examples of benefit are as follows:

(a)   payments for maintenance: *Re Breeds' Will*;[60]

(b)   discharge of debts: *Lowther v Bentinck*;[61]

(c)   loan for setting up beneficiary's husband in business: *Re Kershaw's Trusts*;[62]

(d)   making settlements on beneficiaries in no particular need to save estate duty: *Re Ropner's Settlement Trusts*[63] and *Re C L*;[64]

(e)   making charitable donations in discharge of a moral obligation felt by a wealthy beneficiary: *Re Clore's Settlement Trust*[65] (but contrast *X v A*, see 2.48).

2.49   In *Re Hampden's Settlement Trusts*[66] a settlement on the beneficiary's children was held to be for his 'benefit' as it relieved him of the 'considerable obligation in respect of making provision for their future' which he would otherwise have owed. The case contains a useful summary of the decided cases:

(a)   a power to apply capital for the *benefit* of somebody is the widest possible formulation of such power;

(b)   under such a power the trustees can deal with capital in any way if:
   (i)   viewed objectively, it can fairly be regarded as being to the benefit of the object of the power; and
   (ii)   subjectively, they believe to be so;

---

[57]   As was the case with the proposed advance in Pilkington. The beneficiary's entitlement would have been deferred from 21 to 30.

[58]   (1875) 1 Ch D 226 at 228. See also Jessel MR in *Lowther v Bentinck* [1874–75] LR 19 Eq 166 where he said that preferment and advancement were 'both large words' but that 'benefit' was the 'largest of all'.

[59]   At 635.

[60]   (1875) 1 Ch D 226.

[61]   (1874) LR 19 Eq 166.

[62]   (1868) LR 6 Eq 322.

[63]   [1956] 1 WLR 902.

[64]   [1969] 1 Ch 587.

[65]   [1966] 1 WLR 955.

[66]   [2001] WTLR 195.

(c)   such benefit need not consist of a direct financial advantage to the person who is being benefited. It may be that he is benefited by provision for a near relation or by relieving him of moral responsibilities.

The use of the words 'material situation' in *Pilkington* might be regarded as imposing a limitation. However, in *Re Clore's Settlement Trust*,[67] Pennycuick J held that:

> 'A. the improvement of the material situation of the beneficiary is not confined to his direct financial situation but can include the discharge of moral or social obligations particularly in relation to provision for family and dependants;
>
> B. that the court has always recognised that a wealthy person has a moral obligation to make appropriate charitable donations.'

Limitations on 'benefit'

2.50   In *X v A*[68] the court refused to direct that an advance of the whole of the trust fund to charity was for the 'benefit' of a beneficiary with a life interest (who was opposed to inherited wealth), since:

(a)   the proposed advance did not relieve the beneficiary of an obligation she would otherwise have had to discharge out of her own resources because the amount proposed to be advanced exceeded the amount of her resources;

(b)   in any event, the court had no reason to suppose that, in relation to her free assets, she would regard the advance as having discharged her moral obligation;

(c)   none of the decided cases went anywhere near recognising the existence of a moral obligation of the extent of the proposed transaction.

2.51   In *Wright v Gater*,[69] Norris J refused to consent to the variation of the terms of a trust which would have deferred the age at which a 3-year-old boy became entitled to capital from 18 to 30:

> 'While a deferment of vesting is capable of constituting "benefit" for the purposes of the Variation of Trusts Act 1958, none of the cases justified the conclusion that the postponement of vesting beyond the age of majority was, in principle, "beneficial". In each case the Court must be persuaded that a variation incorporating a deferral is justified on the facts of the particular case; perhaps because the proven personal characteristics of the beneficiary, or the size of the fund, the circumstance in life of the beneficiary, the family context in which the existing trusts will be implemented or some similar feature (the list is not exhaustive) give rise to risks which any reasonable person would regard as real, and to which the proposed variation provides a sufficient and proportionate

---

[67]   [1966] 1 WLR 955.
[68]   [2005] EWHC 2706 (Ch).
[69]   [2011] EWHC 2881 (Ch).

response. There was nothing in the character or circumstances of this 3-year-old toddler to suggest that that was a real risk that he would be incapable of dealing with any income or capital inherited from his grandfather without supervision before he attained 30.'

2.52   The exercise of both the power of advancement and of trustees' powers of appointment is circumscribed by the terms of the power so, for example, a power cannot be used with the intention of benefiting non-objects as this would amount to a fraud on the power. However, it is not objectionable for non-objects to benefit incidentally by an exercise of the power of advancement and as in *Re Hampden* (above) it may be possible to argue successfully that providing for a beneficiary's children is for the beneficiary's benefit as it relieves him of the cost.

Uses of the power to advance capital

2.53   The power to advance capital is commonly used to give capital to a beneficiary absolutely. There are no formalities required for the exercise of the statutory power.[70] However, the power is increasingly used to postpone a beneficiary's entitlement to capital if that is considered to be for his benefit. Normally this will be by the making of a 'settled advance';[71] see *Lord Inglewood v IRC*[72] where Fox LJ said:

> 'It will thus be possible, by an exercise of the statutory power, to advance half the fund to the trustees of a new settlement under which the beneficiary's interest is postponed to an age later than 25 or, indeed, under which he took no interest at all (see *Re Hampden Settlement Trusts* [1977] TR 177). The sole criterion is the benefit of the beneficiary. If it is for his benefit, for example for fiscal or family reasons, to make such an advance as I have mentioned there would be power to do so.'

2.54   In *Pilkington v IRC*[73] the Revenue objected that such a settled advance was 'nothing less than a resettlement' and argued that a power of advancement cannot be used so as to alter or vary the trusts created by the settlement from which it is derived. Lord Radcliffe agreed that it was a resettlement but did not see this as a problem. Trustees who have been given a power to pay money for the benefit of a beneficiary, have the power to settle it on new trusts and this is inevitably a resettlement. The issue is simply one of construction: are the powers conferred on the trustees sufficient to allow them to do what they want to do? Note that powers of appointment by contrast with powers of advancement are construed more restrictively.[74]

---

[70]   Hence the power may be exercised by trustee resolution or simply by the payment or transfer being recorded in the trust accounts. If, however, it is important to fix the date when the property is advanced (for instance, for capital gains tax purposes) then a deed should be used declaring that the beneficiary is absolutely entitled to the property: see **Precedent 13.6**.

[71]   See *Pilkington v IRC* [1964] AC 612, at 637.

[72]   [1983] STC 133.

[73]   [1964] AC 612.

[74]   See **2.55–2.57**.

Example 2.3

Under the Bloggs Family Trust, Sid is entitled to a substantial slice of the capital at age 30. He is currently aged 28 and, as a result of the operation of the Trustee Act 1925, s 31 in receipt of income as of right.[75] The trustees have a widened power of advancement which enables them to apply Sid's share of the capital for his benefit. It is clear that Sid is unsuitable to receive capital at 30.

Accordingly the trustees exercise their widened s 32 power to give Sid a right to income for life with a reserved power to give him capital at any time in their discretion and, subject to that, declare trusts for Sid's wife and young children.[76] Notice that the other persons can benefit under the exercise of the power: in this case Sid's wife and young children. The test is always in this exercise for the benefit of Sid (being the beneficiary in whose favour the power is exercisable).

The power of advancement is particularly useful in the case of trusts for bereaved minors or bereaved young people[77] where beneficiaries must become entitled to capital at or before the age of 18 or 25. However, the terms of ss 71A and 71D allow the trusts to include an extended power to advance the whole of a beneficiary's entitlement for his benefit. The power can, therefore, be used to settle the capital on continuing trusts before the beneficiary becomes entitled to it. For IHT purposes the property will leave the ss 71A/71D trust and become comprised in the relevant property regime.[78]

Can the trusts created by a settled advance be discretionary?

2.55 There is some uncertainty as to whether the power of advancement is sufficiently wide to allow trustees to make a settled advance on discretionary trusts. In *Re Wills Will Trusts*,[79] Upjohn J (as he then was) said that:

> 'any settlement made by way of advancement upon an object of the power by trustees must not conflict with the principle of *delegatus non potest delegare*. Thus, unless upon its proper construction the power of advancement permits delegation of powers and discretions, a settlement created in exercise of the power of advancement cannot in general delegate any powers or discretions, at any rate in relation to beneficial interests, to any trustees or other persons.'

The cases he cited in support of this statement were all cases on the exercise of powers of appointment where different principles apply. However he said in *Re Pilkington's Will Trust*[80] in the Court of Appeal that the principle applies 'not only to a person exercising a power of appointment but to a person exercising a power of advancement'.

When *Pilkington* went to the House of Lords, Lord Radcliffe said that the issue of improper delegation was beside the mark:

[75] For the 'vesting effect' of s 31 see **2.70**.
[76] See **Precedent 13.3**.
[77] IHTA 1984, ss 71A and 71D.
[78] See further **Example 7.3**.
[79] [1959] Ch 1 at 12–13.
[80] [1961] Ch 466.

'The law is not that trustees cannot delegate: it is that trustees cannot delegate unless they have authority to do so.'

The issue was how the power of advancement should be construed. Sadly that is of little assistance to a trustee trying to decide what he is able to do under a standard power of advancement. Given the scope of 'benefit' it is thought that there can be no absolute bar on establishing discretionary trusts by exercise of advancement type powers. As in other cases, the only question is whether it is for the benefit of the beneficiary being advanced.[81] For the avoidance of doubt, when drafting a will trust or settlement, it is desirable to give trustees express authority to advance on discretionary trusts.

4. POWERS OF APPOINTMENT[82]

Distinction between special and general powers

2.56 Special powers of appointment are those which can be exercised only in favour or for the benefit of a defined class. The choice of appointee is restricted by the terms of the power and it is classified as special even where the appointor is a member of the restricted class.[83] Special powers can be fiduciary (when exercisable by trustees or non-fiduciary (where, for example, a life tenant can appoint capital to his or her issue); they can be overriding (so that appointments may break in and terminate an existing interest or discretionary trust which would otherwise continue) or non-overriding (so that the appointments take effect only upon some natural break in the existing trust provisions).

They differ from general powers which are exercisable in favour of anyone in the world including the appointor who can, therefore, appoint the property to himself and become absolutely entitled. A power is general even if only exercisable by will despite the fact that the owner of the power cannot then appoint to himself (he can, of course, appoint to his personal representatives). A general power is in most cases treated as equivalent to outright ownership.[84]

Where the donee is given power to appoint to anyone except certain people or classes, the power is a hybrid or intermediate power.[85] Hybrid powers are classified as special for some purposes[86] and general for others.[87]

---

[81] The leading textbooks now take this view.
[82] See Richard Oerton in (1995) Private Client Business 317–327; 402–409 contrasting powers of appointment and powers of advancement.
[83] *Re Gestetner* [1953] Ch 672.
[84] See eg, IHTA 1984, s 5(2) and Inheritance (Provision for Family and Dependants) Act 1975, s 25(1). For the use of a general power to create an IPDI, see **6.33** and **Precedent 6.5**.
[85] *Re Manisty's Settlement* [1974] Ch 17; *Re Hay's Settlement Trusts* [1982] 1 WLR 202; *Re Beatty's Will Trusts* [1990] 1 WLR 1503.
[86] WA 1837, s 27.
[87] PAA 2009, s 11.

The use of special powers of appointment

2.57 These powers enable the original trusts of the settlement to be modified. They can be used to alter administrative as well as beneficial provisions. Many settlements contain powers to appoint a part or proportion of the trust property to beneficiaries and may contain power to appoint separate trustees of the property so appointed. It is an important principle that the trusts declared by the exercise of a special power of appointment are read back into the original settlement.

It goes without saying that, when exercising a power of appointment, trustees can do only what the power authorises them to do. The courts will ascertain the intention of the settlor as expressed in the instrument. Typically such powers are used to vary the rights of beneficiaries to income and capital.

2.58 In general, a power of appointment cannot be used to transfer funds out of the settlement freed from the original trusts (because this is not a modification of the existing settlement). It is a power 'in the narrower form'. However, some powers expressly authorise this and are often referred to as powers 'in the wider form'.[88]

2.59 However, even a power to transfer property out of the settlement will not authorise the trustees to transfer on new discretionary trusts,[89] unless clear words have been used because of the principle of *delegatus non potest delegare*.

See **Precedent 4.13**; and see **Precedents 13.4** and **13.5**.

5. DOES THE EXERCISE OF A POWER CONSTITUTE A RESETTLEMENT?

2.60 It is important to know whether or not the exercise of a power of advancement or power of appointment creates a new settlement. The creation of a new settlement will have CGT consequences[90] because the trustees of the new settlement become absolutely entitled as against the trustees of the original settlement (albeit that they may be the same persons). The entitlement does not need to be beneficial.[91] A line of CGT cases has explored when a 'new' settlement arises; see, for example, *Hoare Trustees v Gardner;*[92] *Roome v Edwards;*[93] *Bond v Pickford;*[94] *Swires v Renton.*[95]

---

[88] For this distinction between powers in the wider and narrower form, see *Bond v Pickford* [1983] STC 517, CA.

[89] *Re Hay's Settlement Trusts* [1982] 1 WLR 202.

[90] Because a deemed disposal of all the assets then in the settlement at market value will result, although hold-over relief may be available under TCGA 1992, s 165 or s 260.

[91] TCGA 1992, s 71.

[92] [1979] Ch 10, [1978] 1 All ER 791.

[93] [1982] AC 279, [1981] 1 All ER 736, HL.

[94] [1983] STC 517, CA.

[95] [1991] STC 490.

2.61 In *Roome v Edwards*, Lord Wilberforce drew a distinction between trustees using a special power of appointment to modify the existing trusts of a settlement (no new settlement) and the exercise of a wider form of power where property is removed from the original settlement and subjected to other trusts (resettlement). He identified the following indicia[96] to decide whether a new settlement had been created:

(a)   separate and defined property;

(b)   separate trusts;

(c)   the appointment of separate trustees;

(d)   a separate disposition bringing the separate settlement into existence.

These indicia he described as helpful but not decisive!

2.62 The approach of Lord Wilberforce was refined and developed in *Bond v Pickford*[97] in which Slade LJ stressed that the exercise of a power of appointment or advancement cannot create a new settlement unless the trustees have express or implied authority to remove assets altogether from the trusts of the original settlement and bring them within the trusts of a different settlement. It is only where they have this authority that the trustees can free themselves completely from responsibility (in their capacity as trustees of the original settlement) for the property appointed or advanced. He drew a distinction[98] between 'powers in the wider form' and 'powers in the narrower form' which has subsequently been widely adopted.

Powers in the wider form were:

> 'powers to alter the presently operative trusts of a settlement which expressly or by necessary implication authorise the trustees to remove assets altogether from the original settlement (without rendering any person absolutely beneficially entitled to them).'

Powers in the narrower form were 'powers of this nature which do not confer on the trustees such authority'.

2.63 In *Swires v Renton*,[99] Hoffmann J (as he then was) made the important point that where a settlement contains a special power of appointment drawn in the wider form, trustees do not have to use it to take the assets out of the settlement; they could choose to use it in a narrower way keeping the property within the settlement and simply modifying the trusts on which it is held.[100]

---

[96]   At 292.

[97]   [1983] STC 517, CA.

[98]   At 523.

[99]   [1991] STC 490.

[100] This will commonly be the goal of the draftsman of a settled advance who will not wish to trigger a CGT charge by creating a new settlement.

2.64 The consequence of these decisions is that when drafting settlements, a selection of powers should be included so that trustees are free to transfer property out of the settlement onto whatever kind of trusts they wish but can also use narrower powers to modify the existing trusts.

When exercising the powers given to them trustees should indicate the way in which they are exercising their powers: for instance 'by way of resettlement' or 'in modification of the existing trusts'.[101]

HMRC interpretation

2.65 This is set out in SP 7/84 and at CGTM para 37841.

(a) In deciding whether or not a new settlement has been created, each case must be considered on its own facts and by applying established legal doctrine to the facts in a common sense manner. The consideration of the facts must include examination of the powers which the trustees purported to exercise and determination of the intention of the parties, viewed objectively.

(b) A deemed disposal under TCGA 1992, s 71(1) cannot arise unless the power exercised by the trustees confers on the trustees expressly or by necessary implication authority to remove assets from the original settlement by subjecting them to the trusts of a different settlement – such a power was referred to by the Court of Appeal in *Bond v Pickford* as being 'in the wider form'.

(c) When a power 'in the wider form' is exercised, a deemed disposal under s 71(1) cannot arise if the appointment is revocable or the trusts declared in exercise of the power are not exhaustive (eg. where there is a possibility of reversion to the original trusts on the failure of a contingent interest).

(d) When a power 'in the wider form' is exercised, a deemed disposal under s 71(1) is unlikely if duties in regard to the appointed assets still fall to the trustees of the original settlement in their capacity as trustees of that settlement.[102]

(e) The guidelines above should be followed whether the appointment etc extends to the whole or only to part of the settled property.

---

[101] See **Precedent 13.3**.

[102] A single settlement can have more than one set of trustees but TCGA 1992, s 69(3) requires them to be treated as a single body, see CGTM33340. On the other hand, if there is a separate settlement, TCGA 1992, s 69(1) requires the trustees to be treated as a separate body. It is possible for separate CGT settlements to be created by a sub-fund election: see TCGA 1992, Sch 4ZA.

Powers must not be used to benefit non-objects (fraud on the power)

2.66   The exercise of both the power of advancement and of trustee powers of appointment is circumscribed by the terms of the power (eg. it cannot be used to benefit non-objects). Using a power in such a way will amount to a fraud on the power.

However, it is not objectionable for non-objects to benefit incidentally from powers of advancement and as in *Re Hampden*[103] it will usually be possible to say that providing for a beneficiary's children is for their benefit as it relieves them of the cost.

6. POWERS OF APPROPRIATION

2.67   These powers allow trustees to appropriate assets in or towards satisfaction of a beneficiary's entitlement. They are often used to allocate assets to particular beneficiaries so as to facilitate accounting. For example a trust fund is settled on four minor grandchildren contingent on them reaching 25. The trustees expect to apply income and advance capital to the grandchildren during the life of the trust. It may make life easier if they allocate the assets into four 'shares'.

2.68   The statutory power of appropriation enjoyed by personal representatives administering an estate requires the consent of the person to whom the asset is being appropriated.[104] It is, therefore, equivalent to a sale. This has important implications:

(a)   in the case of land or qualifying investments the appropriation can be used to trigger a claim for IHT loss relief under IHTA 1984, Chapters III and IV;[105]

(b)   if a personal representative appropriates property (other than cash) to himself without authority in the will, this breaches the rule against self dealing. Such an appropriation is voidable[106] by beneficiaries interested in the estate unless the personal representative obtains the consent of the relevant beneficiaries or the consent of the court to the appropriation.

Case law requires the appropriation to be on the basis of the market value of the property at the date of the appropriation (not the date of death).[107] It is, however, possible for the will to authorise personal representatives to

---

[103]   [2001] WTLR 195.

[104]   AEA 1925, s 41.

[105]   See 14.29.

[106]   See *Kane v Radley-Kane* [1999] Ch 274. The court said that the self-dealing problem would not arise if the property appropriated was 'equivalent' to cash, such as quoted shares or government stocks.

[107]   *E Collins (deceased)* [1975] 1 WLR 309; [1975] 1 ALL ER 321.

appropriate at death value. An example is the STEP Standard Provisions (2nd edn Special Provision clause 22) which give the personal representatives a power to appropriate at the value at the date of death provided that the appropriation occurs within 3 years of death. HMRC is believed to accept the alternative basis of valuation.[108]

2.69 In the case of settlements it is standard practice to include an express power for trustees to appropriate. Such a power is normally treated as an administrative power but it determines 'who gets what' and should be considered a species of dispositive power.

2.70 There are cases where the court has regarded a power of appropriation as being dispositive. In *Re Freeston*[109] at first instance Fox J said that the division of one fund into two separate funds was not 'mere administration':

> 'it was an alteration of the beneficial interests. The right to one moiety of the income of a fund is quite a different thing from the right to the income of a severed moiety of the fund. And the difference is not just a technicality. The advantages from the point of view of investment and administration in keeping a large fund intact may be substantial.'

In the Court of Appeal,[110] Goff LJ agreed saying:

> 'It is manifest that an interest in half the income of an undivided fund is quite different from the whole income of a divided half of that fund.'

2.71 In *Sutton v England*[111] trustees made an application under Trustee Act 1925, s 57 asking Mann J to introduce a power of partition and appropriation to allow them to create a separate sub-fund for American beneficiaries of the settlement. This would have allowed the appointment of US resident trustees and eased the tax burden on the assets held for the US beneficiaries. He refused on the basis that s 57 only allows the court where it is expedient to grant trustees powers of 'management or administration'. It does not allow the court to vary beneficial interests which can only be done under the Variation of Trusts Act 1958. He was satisfied that an appropriation would be expedient. However, he was not satisfied that the appropriation would be an act of management or administration. He accepted that there are cases which have treated the conferring or exercise of a power of appropriation as administrative and managerial, but these were cases where any effect on the

---

[108] See further **14.03**.
[109] [1978] 1 WLR 120 at 127–8. And see *Hughes v Bourne* [2012] EWHC 2232 (Ch) where the trustees, by an appropriation, created separate funds.
[110] [1978] 1 WLR 741 at 752.
[111] [2009] EWHC 3270 (Ch).

beneficial interests was merely incidental.[112] In his opinion, like *Freeston*, the appropriation in this case would be altering the very nature of the beneficial interest.[113]

However, on appeal[114] Mummery LJ granted the application. While agreeing that the court should be cautious in exercising its jurisdiction under s 57(1), *Freeston* did not require Mann J to reach the decision that he did. The partition of a trust fund is not necessarily a variation or re-arrangement of the beneficial interests. Here the impact on the beneficial interests was incidental only, there was no legal obstacle to granting the application and the proposed transaction was clearly expedient in the interests of the trust as a whole.

7. MAINTENANCE: SECTION 31 OF THE TRUSTEE ACT 1925

2.72 Section 31 is implied into all settlements and will trusts unless excluded and affects the rights of beneficiaries to income. As the tax treatment of settlements often depends on whether or not beneficiaries have a right to income, the section has important tax implications.[115]

Subject to prior interests, s 31 applies: (1) where a contingent gift carries with it the right to intermediate income; and (2) where a minor has a vested interest in income. Where the section applies, the trustees have a discretion until the child's 18th birthday to apply income for the maintenance, education or benefit of the child and, to the extent that they do not, must accumulate it. Income which is accumulated is available for maintenance of the child in subsequent years. On the child's 18th birthday, if the interest is still contingent, the discretion ceases and the trustees must pay the income to the child. Trust instruments may remove the right to income at 18 allowing the trustees' discretion to continue. Section 31(2) provides that income which is accumulated will be paid to the child at 18 if he becomes entitled to the capital at that age[116] or if he has a vested interest in income. In other cases the accumulations are added to capital.

Example 2.4

1.   Trustees hold property on life interest trusts for Adam who is aged 12. As he has a vested interest in income, normally he would be entitled to receive each year's income but the effect of s 31 is that the trustees can accumulate the

---

[112]   *Hornsby v Playoust* [2005] VSC 107 (a scheme to change the assets of the trust, and distribute in specie to beneficiaries who were entitled to the trust assets).

[113]   See Chapter 14 for a consideration of appropriations during the administration of an estate which can alter (significantly) the CGT charge on a subsequent disposal of an asset.

[114]   *Southgate v Sutton* [2011] EWCA Civ 637, [2012] 1 WLR 326, [2011] WTLR 1235.

[115]   See *Fine v Fine* [2012] EWHC 1811 (Ch) where a failure to exclude TA 1925, s 31(2)(ii) prevented an infant having an interest in possession for IHT purposes. The relevant deed of appointment was rectified by the court.

[116]   Or on marriage or formation of a civil partnership, if earlier.

income. If the trustees accumulate income, the accumulations will be paid to him at 18 (s 31, in this case, therefore has a divesting effect).[117]

2. Trustees hold property for Ben contingent on reaching 25. Ben is aged 12 and, therefore, has no right to income. The trustees may choose to apply it for his maintenance, education or benefit and, if they do not must accumulate it. Accumulated income will be added to capital so Ben will not get the accumulations unless and until he reaches 25. When Ben reaches 18, the trustees must pay him the income until his 25th birthday so that Ben acquires a right to income (s 31, in this situation, has a vesting effect).

3. Trustees hold property for Caitlin for life remainder to Danny. Caitlin is 70 and Danny is 14. While Caitlin is alive she is entitled to the income and s 31 is of no significance.

2.73 The proviso to s 31(1) as originally drawn provides that trustees may apply such income 'as may, in all the circumstances, be reasonable' which imposes an objective test. It sets out various matters that the trustees must consider when exercising their discretion to pay maintenance or accumulate income: they must have regard to the minor's age, his requirements and generally to the circumstances of the case, in particular what other income, if any, is applicable for the same purposes. Where trustees have notice that the income of more than one fund is applicable for those purposes, then, so far as practicable, unless the entire income of the funds is paid or applied for the minor or the court otherwise directs, a proportionate part only of the income of each fund should be so paid or applied.

Trust instruments commonly remove these requirements leaving the trustees with an unfettered discretion.[118] For changes introduced by the Inheritance and Trustees' Powers Act 2014, see **2.74**.

Inheritance and Trustees' Powers Act 2014

2.74 Section 8 of the Act amends s 31 to remove the objective requirement and give trustees an unfettered discretion when deciding on whether and how much income to apply. The amendment will apply for trusts 'created or arising after the Act comes into force' subject to amendment or exclusion of the power by the terms of the will.

According to Explanatory Note 51 a will trust is created at the date of death not execution.

Income tax implications of s 31

2.75 While the trustees have a discretion as to what they do with income, the trust will be subject to the trust rate of income tax on everything in excess of

---

[117] See *Fine v Fine* (footnote 115 above).
[118] See **Precedent 4.1, clause 8**.

the first £1,000 which is taxed at 10% on dividends and 20% on other income. For the tax year 2014–15 the trust rate is 37.5% on dividends and 45% on other income.

All income paid to or applied for the beneficiary at the discretion of the trustees will be received by the beneficiary with a 45% tax credit (irrespective of the rate of tax actually paid on it); and the child will be able to reclaim tax if, as will usually be the case, the child is not liable for 45% tax. However, the trustees may have a further liability to income tax under the Income Tax Act 2007, s 496, on any income which suffered tax at less than 45% (eg. the first £1,000 and any dividend income). If the trustees' discretion ceases when the beneficiary reaches 18 (as it will unless the terms of s 31 have been amended by the instrument), the income tax rules change and the trust will be taxed under the simpler rules which apply to trusts where a beneficiary has a right to income.

Inheritance tax implications

2.76   The effect of s 31 may be to convert what would otherwise be a s 71D trust into an immediate post-death interest. See **Example 7.5**.

CHAPTER 3

THE ESSENTIAL TAX LAW

This chapter summarises the parts of inheritance tax (IHT), capital gains tax (CGT) and income tax which are important to estate planning. It does not attempt to provide a comprehensive explanation of the three taxes.

1. CALCULATING IHT ON DEATH

Basic principles

3.01 IHT is charged not only on the assets in an estate at the time of a person's death, but also on some lifetime transfers.[1] The rate of tax charged depends on the 'cumulative total' of the transferor at the time of the transfer.[2] When calculating the tax due on a transfer, chargeable transfers made in the previous 7 years are aggregated and the final transfer is taxed as the highest part of that aggregate. There is a nil rate band, and transfers which fall within that band are taxed at zero per cent. Above that, tax is charged at 40%. The nil rate band is frozen at £325,000 until the end of tax year 2017–18.

The transfer of value

3.02 IHT is charged on transfers of value which is defined in IHTA 1984, s 3(1):

> 'A transfer of value is a disposition made by a person (the transferor) as a result of which the value of his estate immediately after the disposition is less than it would be but for the disposition.'

'Disposition' is not defined. The term includes an omission to exercise a right[3] and a disposition effected by 'associated operations'.[4] Section 3(3) of IHTA 1984 provides that where the value of a person's (A's) estate is diminished and that of another person or settled property is increased by A's omission to

---

[1]   Some lifetime transfers are immediately chargeable (notably the creation of most settlements) whilst others are PETs (potentially exempt transfers) and only taxable if the taxpayer dies within 7 years.

[2]   IHTA 1984, s 7.

[3]   IHTA 1984, s 3(3).

[4]   IHTA 1984, s 272 although note the limitations imposed on the concept of 'associated operations' in cases such as *Rysaffe v IRC* [2003] EWCA Civ 356 and *Macpherson v IRC* [1988] STC 362.

exercise a right, A is treated as having made a disposition at the latest time when he could have exercised that right, unless it can be shown that the omission was not deliberate.[5]

A disposition is not a transfer of value if it was not intended to confer a gratuitous benefit and either it was an arm's length transaction between persons not connected with each other or it was such as might be expected to be made in such a transaction.[6]

3.03 Certain events, for example, death and the termination of a qualifying interest in possession, are 'deemed' to be transfers of value.[7] In the case of settled property a beneficiary entitled to certain types of interest in possession in settled property is treated for IHT purposes as beneficially entitled to the property in which he has the interest (see s 49(1)). Such interests are referred to as 'qualifying' interests in possession.

On death, a person is deemed to make a transfer of value equal to the value of his estate immediately before death (see s 4(1)).

3.04 Property which is subject to a reservation of benefit is included in the estate of the donor when he dies.[8] Property is subject to a reservation of benefit where an individual makes a gift of property on or after 18 March 1986 and either:

(a)   the donee does not assume possession and enjoyment of the property, or

(b)   the property is not enjoyed to the entire, or virtually entire, exclusion of the donor and of any benefit to him by contract or otherwise.[9]

So, for example, if a mother gives her daughter a seaside cottage and continues to take holidays there herself, the cottage will be treated as part of her estate on death for IHT purposes. However, the property is not included in the estate for any other purpose so there will be no tax-free uplift on death for CGT purposes.[10] There are various exemptions from the reservation of benefit rules, for example where the donor pays full consideration for his occupation of land or use of a chattel that he has given away.[11]

---

[5]   See *Fryer (PRs of Arnold dec'd) v RCC* [2010] UK FTT 87 (TC) and see *Perry and others (PRs of Staveley dec'd) v RCC* [2014] TC/2012/7106.

[6]   IHTA 1984, s 10.

[7]   IHTA 1984, ss 3(4), 4. For the meaning of a qualifying interest in possession, see Chapter 6.

[8]   FA 1986, s 102(3).

[9]   FA 1986, s 102(1). See *Revenue Interpretation 55* for guidance on 'virtual exclusion'.

[10]   See **3.105** for CGT and death.

[11]   FA 1986, Sch 20, para 6(1)(a) and s 102(5).

Estate

3.05 IHTA 1984, s 5(1) defines a person's estate as 'the aggregate of all the property to which he is beneficially entitled' other than excluded property[12] whilst s 5(3) confirms that 'in determining the value of a person's estate at any time his liabilities at that time shall be taken into account except as otherwise provided by this Act'.[13]

'Property' includes all rights and interests of any description.[14]

Note the following:

(a) property over which the transferor has a general power of appointment is included in his 'estate' unless it is held in a settlement;[15]

(b) property owned by the deceased in a fiduciary capacity, for instance as a trustee or as an informal 'treasurer' for his family, is not included;[16]

(c) the estate includes property in which the deceased had reserved a benefit at the time of his death;[17]

(d) the estate includes property which the deceased is deemed to own by virtue of enjoying a qualifying interest in possession;[18]

(e) as the transfer is deemed to occur immediately before the death,[19] the estate includes a share of the deceased in jointly owned property that passes by operation of law (*jus accrescendi*) to the surviving joint tenants at the moment of death.[20] The estate also includes a gift made before death in anticipation of death and conditional upon it occurring (a '*donatio mortis causa*'). Accordingly although dominion over the property has been handed over it is still included in the donor's estate.[21]

3.06 Although the general rule is that the estate must be valued immediately before death, funeral expenses can be deducted (including a reasonable sum for a 'wake' and the cost of a gravestone: SP 7/87). Further, IHTA 1984, Part VI permits values to be amended in certain circumstances: see Chapter 14 for loss on sale relief.

---

[12] Excluded property is defined in IHTA 1984, ss 6 and 48 and includes reversionary interests.

[13] See **3.07** for the deduction of liabilities.

[14] IHTA 1984, s 272.

[15] IHTA 1984, s 5(2).

[16] *Anand v IRC* [1997] STC (SCD) 58.

[17] FA 1986, s 102(3).

[18] IHTA 1984, s 49(1).

[19] IHTA 1984, s 4(1) provides that 'on the death of any person tax shall be charged as if, immediately before his death, he had made a transfer of value and the value transferred by it had been equal to the value of his estate immediately before death'.

[20] For the 'severance' of a joint tenancy by deed of variation, see Chapter 12.

[21] See further Chapter 16.

3.07 Liabilities are only deductible if incurred for consideration in money or moneys worth.[22] Personal debts of the deceased can only be deducted from his personal estate, and so surplus liabilities cannot be set against property which is deemed to be part of the estate such as property subject to a reservation or property in which the deceased had a qualifying interest in possession.[23] Once the personal estate is reduced to zero, there can be no further deductions.

Non-deductible debts

3.08 Finance Act 1986, s 103 makes so called 'artificial' debts non-deductible. The section provides that, when determining the value of a deceased person's estate, a debt incurred by him or incumbrance created by him is not deductible for IHT purposes to the extent that the consideration given for the debt or incumbrance consisted of property derived from the deceased. Property 'derived from the deceased' means any property which was the subject matter of a disposition by the deceased other than a disposition[24] which does not amount to a transfer of value.[25] The operation of the section can be illustrated by the following example.

> *Example 3.1*
>
> Dad gives £100,000 to son and subsequently borrows the money back. The £100,000 debt is not deductible when Dad dies.

Finance Act 2013 changes

3.09 Finance Act 2013 inserted new sections into IHTA 1984 which created three new types of non-deductible debt.[26]

3.10 *IHTA 1984, s 162A: Liabilities attributable to financing excluded property*: for example, Arturo, a non-UK domiciliary, raises a loan on his Mayfair home to acquire non-UK situs property which will be excluded property and so outside the UK tax net. The liability charged against the UK property will be ignored in calculating the IHT liability of Arturo. The legislation applies to direct and indirect financing (so raising a loan on Mayfair to discharge an existing offshore loan taken out to purchase excluded property is caught) and, apart from loans to *acquire* excluded property, the section also catches loans for 'the maintenance, or an enhancement, of the value of any such property'.

There are three exceptions to this general rule. These are where the excluded property:

---

[22] IHTA 1984, s 5(5).
[23] *St Barbe Green v IRC* [2005] EWHC 14 (Ch).
[24] FA 1986, s 103(3).
[25] FA 1986, s 103(4). Examples of dispositions which are not transfers of value are those within IHTA 1984, s 10 (no gratuitous intent) and s 11 (dispositions for family maintenance).
[26] For detailed guidance, see IHT Manual 28010-28031. FA 2014 corrected an error in the original legislation.

(1) has been sold (for full consideration) and the proceeds are chargeable assets in the deceased's estate (s 162A(2)),

(2) is no longer excluded property (s 162A(3)), or

(3) has fallen in value (s 162A(4)) unless the conditions set out in ss 7 are met. These are:

    (a) arrangements the main purpose, or one of the main purposes, of which is to secure a tax advantage,

    (b) an increase in the amount of the liability (whether due to the accrual of interest or otherwise), or

    (c) a disposal, in whole or in part, of the property.

The date the liability was incurred is irrelevant. The new rules apply where death (or other chargeable event) occurs on or after 17 July 2013.

3.11 *IHTA 1984, s 162AA: Liabilities attributable to financing non-residents' foreign currency accounts*: the new s 162AA, introduced by FA 2014, extended the non-deductibility rule to UK bank accounts denominated in a foreign currency held by individuals who are neither domiciled nor resident in the UK. Such accounts are not excluded property yet are not taken into account in determining the value of a person's estate on death. They were therefore not affected by the provisions in s 162A.

3.12 *IHTA 1984, s 162B: Liabilities attributable to financing property eligible for business or agricultural property relief or woodlands relief*: for example an elderly taxpayer raises a mortgage on (say) his main residence using the monies to purchase an AIM portfolio which will, after two years, qualify for 100% business property relief.[27] In the case of liabilities incurred on or after 6 April 2013 the liability is treated as reducing the value of the relievable property (in effect it becomes a charge on that property) so that it is only the excess value (if any) which is deducted against other assets. These rules apply to liabilities incurred on and after 6 April 2013 although to stop a tax-saving manoeuvre if an existing loan agreement is varied on or after that date to make additional funds available, the additional liability is treated as having been incurred on the date the agreement was varied.

3.13 *IHTA 1984, s 175A*: in valuing the estate on death, a liability is deductible if 'it is discharged on or after death, out of the estate, in money or money's worth'.

In other cases when the liability is not discharged it is only deductible where 'there is a real commercial reason for the liability or the part not being discharged' and it must not be left outstanding 'as part of arrangements for the main purpose, or one of the main purposes, of which is to secure a tax advantage'.[28]

---

[27] See further the authors' *A Modern Approach to Lifetime Tax Planning*, Chapter 33.

[28] 'Tax' includes income tax and CGT.

Discharging 'out of the estate' includes the situation where the personal representatives borrow money to discharge the liability. The date the liability was incurred is irrelevant. The restriction applies where death (or other chargeable event) occurs occur on or after 17 July 2013.

There was concern as to how the s 175A restriction would operate in practice: in completing the IHT 400 would a deduction only be allowed for a liability which has then been discharged? But until a grant has been obtained it is usually not possible to pay off the deceased's debts. Did that mean that it would be impossible to deduct utility bills and similar mundane liabilities until after payment?

HMRC Guidance[29] says that the starting assumption is that all commercial liabilities (such as utility bills, credit card bills, council tax, payments due to HMRC, outstanding care fees, professional fees to the date of death, overpaid pension, payments for goods and services) will be repaid and will make no enquiries as to their payment. So, unless the personal representatives are aware that a liability is not going to be repaid, the IHT 400 Notes allow the personal representatives to include all the deceased's liabilities when completing the form.

Where non-arms' length liabilities are deducted, HMRC will ask for evidence that the money has been repaid out of the estate. Where the personal representatives do not repay a liability during the normal administration of the estate and the 'commercial' exception does not apply, HMRC will disallow the deduction and ask for the tax to be paid. If the liability is subsequently repaid, the deduction may then be allowed and the tax repaid, provided the claim for repayment is made within the 4-year period set out in IHTA 1984, s 241.

HMRC accepts[30] that 'there may be good reasons why a liability should not discharged and will be taken over by the beneficiaries of the estate. This may be the case where a business is being taken over by the beneficiaries and the bank is prepared to allow any lending and overdraft facilities to continue'.

Example 3.2

Harvey dies leaving a nil-rate band (NRB) discretionary trust under his Will with the residue of the estate passing to his wife, Wendy. The executors of the estate exercise their powers to pass the whole of the Harvey's estate to Wendy in return for her agreeing to repay an amount equal to the NRB (£325,000) to the trust. Interest is charged on the debt at 3% per annum, compounded annually.

On Wendy's death four years later, interest has increased the liability by £40,000 from £325,000 to £365,000. The liability can be taken into account to the extent that it is actually repaid out of the estate.

Of course, the interest received by the NRB trustees will be income of the trust and will be taxed accordingly at 45%.

---

[29] See IHT Manual 28030.
[30] See IHT Manual 28029.

In these circumstances, the trustees of the NRB trust may conclude that taking the interest of £40,000 is unattractive as it creates a liability to income tax.[31] They may, therefore, choose to disclaim the £40,000 of interest.[32] The result is that only £325,000 can be deducted from Wendy's estate for inheritance tax purposes.

Value

3.14 The value of property comprised in the estate is the price which the property might reasonably be expected to fetch if sold on the open market at that time, provided that such price is not assumed to be reduced on the ground that the whole property is to be placed on the market at the same time.[33] In other words, the value will be the open market value of the property immediately before the death. There are special rules for taking into account changes in value which occur by reason of the death, for example to life policies,[34] for valuing related property[35] and for sale of land and qualifying investments for less than probate value.[36]

3.15 A number of valuation principles have been developed in case-law in respect of the open market value test:

(a) *The sale on the open market is a hypothetical one between a vendor and purchaser*

The hypothetical parties are assumed to be reasonable and prudent. It is assumed that the hypothetical purchaser would make the proper enquiries but is not too eager to buy; he embodies the demand at the particular time for the property concerned.[37] No allowance is made for the costs of the hypothetical sale.[38]

(b) *The buyer is not a speculator*

The hypothetical vendor and purchaser are serious prudent men of business of the kind who buy and sell the asset in question. If in the real world there are no buyers of the kind of asset under consideration, it is not permissible to invent 'a hypothetical willing speculator'.[39]

(c) *Effect of restrictions on sale attached to the particular asset*

Restrictions on sale are ignored and the asset is deemed capable of being freely sold. However, the restrictions on a future sale must be taken into account in determining the price which that purchaser would be likely to pay. For instance, where shares in a private company are subject to restrictions on sale by reason of provisions in the company's articles of

---

[31] See **3.134**.
[32] They can safely do this if the beneficiaries of Harvey's estate are the same as those of Wendy's estate or if they all agree. This will normally be the case as these arrangements typically arise in family trust situations.
[33] IHTA 1984, s 160.
[34] IHTA 1984, s 171.
[35] IHTA 1984, s 161.
[36] IHTA 1984, ss 178–198: see **14.25** *et seq*.
[37] *IRC v Gray (surviving executor of Lady Fox)* [1994] STC 360, at 372.
[38] *Duke of Buccleuch v IRC* [1967] 1 AC 506; see also *Price v RCC* [2010] UKFTT 474 (TC).
[39] *Bower v RCC* [2008] EWHC 3105 (Ch).

association, the value of the shares for IHT purposes is the price they would fetch if sold on the open market on terms that the purchaser is entitled to be registered and to become the holder of the shares but will take subject to the provisions of the articles of association including those relating to alienation and transfer of shares.[40] In other words the question is: 'What would a purchaser have paid to enjoy the rights attached to the property at the relevant date?'

(d)   *The hypothetical vendor acts to get the best price possible*
      Accordingly the estate may be divided into units for the purposes of sale or items of property may be lotted together for sale provided that such splitting or joining does not entail undue expenditure of time and effort.[41]

(e)   *Price which any 'special' purchaser may be prepared to pay should be taken into account*
      A special purchaser is a person for whom the property has special value and is therefore willing to pay more than an ordinary purchaser. Of course, although there may be a potential special purchaser it is a question of fact whether he would be interested in buying the property.

It is important that assets are valued correctly as HMRC will impose penalties where there are careless or deliberate errors in accounts resulting in underpaid tax.[42] For instance, when valuing land it is important that any development or 'hope' value is included.

Related property rules

3.16   IHTA 1984, s 161 provides that:

'(1) Where the value of any property comprised in a person's estate would be less than the appropriate portion of the value of the aggregate of that and any related property, it shall be the appropriate portion of the value of that aggregate.

(2) For the purposes of this section, property is related to the property comprised in a person's estate if:

(a)   it is comprised in the estate of his spouse [or civil partner]; or
(b)   it is or has within the preceding five years been:
      (i)   the property of a charity, or held on trust for charitable purposes only, or
      (ii)   the property of a body mentioned in section 24, [24A,] [or 25] above,

and became so on a transfer of value which was made by him or his spouse [or civil partner] after 15th April 1976 and was exempt to the extent that the value transferred was attributable to the property.

---

40   *IRC v Crossman* [1937] AC 26.
41   *IRC v Gray (surviving executor of Lady Fox)* [1994] STC 360, at 372.
42   See **11.82** *et seq.*

(3) The appropriate portion of the value of the aggregate mentioned in subsection (1) above is such portion thereof as would be attributable to the value of the first-mentioned property if the value of that aggregate were equal to the sums of the values of that and any related property, the value of each property being determined as if it did not form part of that aggregate.

(4) For the purposes of subsection (3) above the proportion which the value of a smaller number of shares of any class bears to the value of a greater number shall be taken to be that which the smaller number bears to the greater; and similarly with stock, debentures and units of any other description of property.'

3.17 HMRC have always been of the view that where the co-owners of real property are husband and wife no discount is available because the deceased's interest in the property is to be valued as a mathematical proportion of the whole under s 161(4).

3.18 However, in *Arkwright v IRC*[43] the taxpayer argued that in the case of related property other than shares (where the valuation is governed by s 161(4)), the procedure is governed by s 161(1) and (3). The effect of these sections is that first the aggregate is valued; then each party's interest is valued separately to establish a ratio; that ratio is applied to the aggregate and if the deceased's share of the aggregate is greater than the value of his separate interest, the value of his interest for IHT is taken to be his share of the aggregate. Where the value of each party's interest is equal, the value of their interest will be a 'straight' mathematical proportion of the whole. In *Arkwright* the taxpayers argued that the value of the interest of a seriously ill co-owner will always be less than the interest of a healthy party. This is because pursuant to the Trusts of Land and Appointment of Trustees Act 1996, each spouse enjoys a right of occupation and that right reduces the open market value of the other's share. The hypothetical willing purchaser would, therefore, discount the value of the sick co-owner's share to take account of the fact that the purchaser of that interest would be unable to benefit from it until the death of the survivor. If correct, a deceased co-owner's share will only be an exact half of the total where the values of the deceased's property and the related property are identical. Otherwise the value of the deceased's interest will always be more or less than half of the aggregate.

The Special Commissioner agreed with the taxpayer, concluding that the value of the deceased's interest 'was less than a mathematical one-half of the vacant possession value'. HMRC did not pursue this point when its appeal was heard by the High Court,[44] arguing instead that the question of open market valuation was, in the absence of agreement, a matter for the Lands Tribunal. On appeal Gloster J agreed.

3.19 However, in the course of seeking to reach agreement with the taxpayers in *Arkwright*, HMRC apparently received legal advice that in some

---

[43] [2004] STC (SCD) 89.
[44] [2004] EWHC 1720 (Ch), [2004] STC 1323.

circumstances s 161(4) may, in fact, apply to fractional shares of a single unit. In *Revenue & Customs Brief* 71/07, HMRC announced that as a result of that advice it will:

> 'apply section 161(4) when valuing shares of land as related property in any inheritance tax case where the account is received by HMRC after the publication date of this Brief.'

3.20   Section 161 was revisited in *Price v RCC*[45] where HMRC accepted that s 161(4) did not apply to the valuation of land and that the correct approach was as set out in *Arkwright*. The First-tier Tribunal agreed with HMRC that the two interests in land which are to be valued, should be valued on the basis that they are offered for sale at the same time.[46]

Lifetime transfers

3.21   IHT is charged on chargeable lifetime transfers, and on potentially exempt transfers if they are made within the 7 years preceding the transferor's death. Such transfers affect tax on the estate on death as they are cumulated with the value of the estate at death and so may increase the rate of tax payable.

3.22   To be a potentially exempt transfer, the gift must be made on or after 18 March 1986, by an individual, to another individual or into a disabled person's trust.[47] After 7 years a potentially exempt transfer becomes fully exempt and will not be included in the individual's cumulative total of lifetime gifts.[48]

3.23   Transfers made before 22 March 2006 to certain types of settlement were also potentially exempt transfers. Since that date, however, all lifetime transfers to settlements are chargeable transfers, unless the settlement is for the benefit of a person who is disabled within the meaning of IHTA 1984, s 89 or created for the settlor's own benefit at a time when the settlor is suffering from a condition that it is reasonable to expect will lead to his becoming disabled within the meaning of s 89.[49] Lifetime chargeable transfers are taxed at half the death rates at the time they are made and become chargeable at the full death rates if the transferor dies within 7 years.

3.24   Once a transferor survives for 3 years from his transfer, taper relief reduces the rate of tax[50] charged on that transfer as follows:

(a)   transfer 3 to 4 years before death: 80% of tax is payable;

---

45   [2010] UKFTT 474 (TC).
46   The question of the appropriate portion of the valuation which was to be attributed to the deceased's interest was referred to the Lands Tribunal.
47   IHTA 1984, s 3A. For disabled trusts, see **3.58** *et seq*.
48   IHTA 1984, s 7(4) as amended by FA 1986, Sch 19, para 2(4).
49   IHTA 1984, s 89A.
50   Note that there is no reduction in the cumulative total of transfers made by the taxpayer. Hence a transfer may exhaust the nil rate band without the benefit of taper relief given that no tax is payable (ie there is nothing to taper).

(b)   transfer 4 to 5 years before death: 60% of tax is payable;

(c)   transfer 5 to 6 years before death: 40% of tax is payable;

(d)   transfer 6 to 7 years before death: 20% of tax is payable.

Example 3.3

1. Don, who is divorced, dies in 2014 with an estate of £300,000 having made no lifetime transfers. He leaves his entire estate to his daughter. No IHT is payable as the estate is within his nil rate band.

2. In June 2014 Sid transferred £400,000 to a lifetime settlement for the benefit of his two grandchildren. The transfer is chargeable at the date made. Tax at 20% is payable on the portion in excess of Sid's nil rate band (£75,000 × 20% = £15,000).[51]

If Sid dies in August 2016 the lifetime transfer is then chargeable at the full death rates (£75,000 × 40% = £30,000). The trustees are liable for the extra tax due. Credit is given for the tax already paid so that the trustees will only have to make up the difference between the tax due and the tax already paid. It is important that trustees are aware of the potential additional liability to tax and do not distribute the trust assets without making provision for it.

If Sid had made the transfer to the settlement 5 years and three months before his death, only 40% of tax at the full death rates would have been payable, ie £30,000 × 40% = £12,000. As the trustees have already paid £15,000, they are not required to pay any more, but are not entitled to a refund.

No nil rate band will be available on Sid's death estate so tax at 40% will be payable on the whole value of his free estate.

3. Jake, having already used his annual exemption, gifted £400,000 to his two grandchildren 2 years before his death in 2014. The transfer was potentially exempt at the date made. As he has died within 7 years the transfer is now chargeable at the full death rates. The portion in excess of the nil rate band is chargeable at 40% (£75,000 × 40% = £30,000). The donees will be primarily liable for the tax although the personal representatives will become liable if tax remains unpaid 12 months after the end of the month of death.[52] If Jake had made the transfer to his grandchildren 3 years and three months before death, only 80% of tax at the full death rates would be payable, ie. £30,000 × 80% = £24,000.

No nil rate band will be available to Jake's death estate so tax at 40% will be payable on the whole estate.

Exemptions and reliefs

3.25   A number of exemptions and reliefs are available only in the case of lifetime transfers:

(a)   Section 11: gifts made for the care or maintenance of dependent relatives or the maintenance, education or training of children and stepchildren of

---

[51]   Assuming there is no need to gross up and that the transfer is not reduced by Sid's annual exemption.

[52]   IHTA 1984, s 204(8)(b).

the donee are not transfers of value. In the case of dependent relatives the gifts must be reasonable and in the case of children the gift must be for a period ending no later than age 18 or the completion of full-time education.[53]

(b)   Section 19: the annual exemption. An individual may make lifetime transfers of up to £3,000 in any tax year without liability to tax. The exemption may be carried forward for one year only in so far as it is not used.

(c)   Section 20: outright gifts of up to £250 to any number of persons are exempt from tax.

(d)   Section 21: lifetime gifts out of income which forms part of the donor's normal expenditure are exempt provided the donor is left with sufficient income to maintain his usual standard of living.

(e)   Section 22: certain gifts made in consideration of marriage or formation of a civil partnership are exempt. The amount varies depending on the relationship of donor and donee but the maximum is £5,000. Gifts which are exempt under s 22 can be combined with gifts which are exempt under s 19.

3.26   The most important exemptions available for both lifetime and death transfers are as follows:

(a)   Section 18: transfers between spouses and civil partners are exempt. If, however, the donee spouse or civil partner is not domiciled in the UK, the exemption was limited to £55,000 in the case of transfers made before 6 April 2013 and to the level of the nil rate band for transfers made on or after that date (currently £325,000).[54]

(b)   Sections 22 and 24: gifts to charities[55] and political parties are exempt.

(c)   Sections 102–114: business property relief.

(d)   Sections 115–124: agricultural property relief (available on lifetime and death transfers). Business and agricultural reliefs are considered in detail in Chapter 10.

(e)   Sections 30–35: there is a conditional exemption for transfers of assets designated as heritage property. To qualify, property must be designated by the Treasury as falling into one of the categories set out in s 31(1):
    Category 1: items of pre-eminent national, scientific, historic or artistic interest; or
    Category 2: land of outstanding scenic, historic or scientific interest; or
    Category 3: buildings of outstanding or architectural interest and their amenity land and chattels historically associated with such buildings.

---

[53]   For an illustration of the operation of s 11(3), see *McKelvey v RCC* [2008] STC (SCD) 944.

[54]   This change was introduced by the Finance Act 2013 which also introduced an election for non-domiciled spouses/civil partners to be UK domiciled. These changes were dictated by the requirements of EU law. See generally the authors' *A Modern Approach to Lifetime Tax Planning*, Chapter 25.

[55]   See the authors' *A Modern Approach to Lifetime Tax Planning*, Chapter 39.

Undertakings must be given to take reasonable steps for the preservation of the property, to secure reasonable access by the public and, in the case of category 1 items to keep the property in the UK. FA 1998 inserted new subsections[56] into s 31 to ensure extended access for the public and for greater disclosure of information. Undertakings must be given by such person as the Treasury thinks appropriate. In practice this will be the lifetime donee or person inheriting on death. Where relief is given the item is conditionally exempt, which means that so long as the undertakings are observed and the property is not further transferred IHT liability will be postponed. The deferral can be renewed on transfer if further undertakings are given. The deferred tax will become payable on sale, breach of an undertaking or failure to give undertakings on a subsequent transfer. Where IHT is deferred there is also a deferral of CGT.

Heritage property can be given for national purposes or for the public benefit without any IHT charge (s 23). Alternatively the property can be sold by private treaty to heritage bodies listed in IHTA 1984, s 25(1) and Sch 3. Such a sale does not lead to an IHT charge nor is there any liability to CGT.[57]

3.27 The following reliefs are available only on death:

(a) Section 141: *quick succession relief*. This relief is designed to mitigate the effect of a double charge to IHT where property passes through two estates due to the death of a donee shortly after the death of the original donor. The relief is based on a sliding scale depending on the time between the two deaths. A percentage of the tax charged on the property on the first occasion is deducted from the amount payable on the same property on the subsequent death.

(b) Section 154: *death on active service*. No IHT was chargeable on the death of a person from a wound inflicted or a disease contracted while a member of the armed forces if that person was on active service at the time, or on service of a warlike nature or involving the same risks.[58] From 19 March 2014 the scope of this exemption has been significantly widened to:
    (i) include emergency service personnel and police officers in certain circumstances;
    (ii) exclude an IHT charge not just on death but in respect of failed PETs and extra IHT otherwise payable on death resulting from an immediately chargeable lifetime transfer.[59]

---

[56] Section 31(4FA) and (4FB).

[57] See TCGA 1992, s 258.

[58] See *Barty-King v Ministry of Defence* [1979] 2 All ER 80, [1979] STC 218 (QBD). The injury or disease does not have to be the only cause. It is sufficient if it is one of several operative causes. See further **5.17**.

[59] See generally **5.19** *et seq*.

Liability for inheritance tax

3.28 The rules on liability are statutory and cannot be overridden by express provision in the will. In many cases on death it is the personal representatives who are liable for inheritance tax.

The primary liability of personal representatives for IHT on death is for the inheritance tax attributable to any 'free estate' of the deceased.[60] Free estate for this purpose includes property passing by survivorship, *donatio mortis causa* or nomination.

This liability can be troublesome for personal representatives as they have no control over property passing by survivorship, etc. However, where personal representatives pay tax on jointly owned property etc, they have a right of recovery from the person in whom the property becomes vested.[61]

3.29 In addition to their primary liability for tax on the estate of the deceased, personal representatives have a secondary liability[62] for any tax chargeable in respect of lifetime transfers;[63] that is, on the value of any potentially exempt transfer (PET) which has become chargeable, or of any other chargeable transfer made within 7 years of the transferor's death, and which would not have been payable if the transferor had not died within 7 years after the transfer. This secondary liability arises if tax remains unpaid 12 months after the death. It can obviously cause problems for the personal representatives who may have no information about lifetime transfers made by the testator. There is no statutory right to recover from the lifetime donees although such a right may exist as a matter of general law.[64]

3.30 A further secondary liability arises in respect of unpaid tax chargeable under FA 1986, s 102 on a gift with reservation,[65] although the personal representatives have a statutory right to recover any tax from the donee.[66] This liability can be even more problematic for personal representatives than their secondary liability for tax on lifetime gifts. They may not be aware that a gift was made at all or of the possibility of a reservation, the existence of which may involve a difficult question of law. The deceased may have made an election to bring property which would otherwise have been caught by the pre-owned assets charge into the reservation of benefit regime.[67] Neither the donee nor the personal representatives may know anything about the election.

---

[60]   IHTA 1984, s 200.
[61]   IHTA 1984, s 211(3).
[62]   IHTA 1984, s 204(6) (as amended).
[63]   IHTA 1984, s 199(1) (as amended).
[64]   See (1998) *Private Client Business* 58.
[65]   IHTA 1984, s 204(9).
[66]   IHTA 1984, s 211(3).
[67]   FA 2004, Sch 15, para 21. Taxpayers who are liable to pay the pre-owned assets charge can opt out of the income tax charge and into the IHT reservation of benefit provisions within the relevant time limit. The election must be made, using Form IHT 500, on or before the relevant filing date which is 31 January of the year of assessment that immediately follows the first year

The personal representative's liability for inheritance tax is a personal liability, to which distribution of the estate is no answer. Their liability to tax is limited to the value of the estate but is not affected by a certificate of discharge.

Example 3.4

Dan dies leaving an estate (fully taxed) of £650,000. The personal representatives are unaware of any lifetime gifts and therefore pay inheritance tax of £130,000 (tax year 2014–15 with a full nil rate band of £325,000 being available) and distribute the remainder of the estate.

1. After some years a lifetime gift by Dan of £300,000, which had been made 6 years before his death and was potentially exempt when made, is discovered. Although no inheritance tax was chargeable on that gift (which benefits from the deceased's nil rate band) the personal representatives are accountable for extra inheritance tax on the death estate of £120,000; or

2. A gift of £1,000,000 made one year before Dan's death is discovered. In this case not only are the personal representatives accountable for extra inheritance tax of £120,000 as above, but in addition if the donee fails to pay inheritance tax on the £1,000,000 gift, the personal representatives are liable to pay that inheritance tax (limited to the net assets in the estate which have passed through their hands).

3.31 These potential liabilities present major problems for personal representatives and the following matters should be noted:

(a) Their liability may arise long after the estate has been fully administered and distributed (for example a potentially exempt transfer may be discovered which is not only itself taxable, but also affects the charge on subsequent lifetime chargeable transfers and on the death estate). It may therefore be desirable for personal representatives to obtain suitable indemnities from the residuary beneficiary before distributing the estate, although simple personal indemnities are of course always vulnerable (for example in the event of the bankruptcy of that beneficiary).

(b) Although personal representatives have no statutory right of recovery from lifetime donees,[68] there is, of course, nothing to stop a donor taking an indemnity from a donee to pay any future inheritance tax as a condition of making the potentially exempt transfer. Such an arrangement would be expressed as an indemnity in favour of the donor's estate and does not involve any reservation of benefit in the gifted property. As noted at (a) above, personal indemnities are, however, vulnerable in the event of the bankruptcy or emigration of the donee.

(c) It is not satisfactory for personal representatives to retain estate assets to cover the danger of a future tax liability. Apart from being unpopular with beneficiaries, there is no guarantee that personal representatives will retain an adequate sum to cover the tax liability on a potentially exempt transfer

---

in which the taxpayer would otherwise be subject to a POA charge (unless the taxpayer can show a reasonable excuse for missing the deadline – Sch 15, para 23(3)).

[68] Except in the case of reservation of benefit property: IHTA 1984, s 211(3).

which they did not know had been made: only by retaining all the assets in the estate would they be wholly protected.

(d)   Insurance would seem to be the obvious answer to these problems. Personal representatives should give full information on matters within their knowledge and then seek cover (up to the limit of their liability) in respect of an unforeseen inheritance tax liability arising. It would seem reasonable for testators to give a power in the will for their personal representatives to insure against these risks. It is believed that cover can be arranged on an individual basis in such cases with the premium payable ranging from 0.2% up to 2% of the amount of indemnity required.

3.32   Limited comfort to personal representatives is afforded by a letter from the Revenue to the Law Society dated 11 February 1991. The Revenue says that they will not 'usually' pursue PRs for IHT who:

‘a.   after making the fullest enquiries that are reasonably practicable in the circumstances to discover lifetime transfers, and so

b.   having done all in their power to make full disclosure of them to the Board of Inland Revenue

c.   have obtained a certificate of discharge and distributed the estate before a chargeable lifetime transfer comes to light.’

Note, however, that the reference to the 'fullest' enquiries that are 'reasonably practicable' suggests a high test. Certainly in the IHT 400 Toolkit issued by HMRC there are references to the importance of following up enquiries to discover whether gifts were made.

The burden of tax on transfers chargeable because of death

3.33   There are statutory rules for determining where the burden of inheritance tax falls. In most cases these can be varied by the testator.

3.34   The burden of inheritance tax on lifetime transfers (ie on failed PETs and in respect of the supplementary charge on immediately chargeable transfers) falls on the transferee.[69] If the testator directs in his will that the tax on lifetime gifts is to be paid from the estate, the direction will be treated as a pecuniary legacy.

3.35   In the case of gifts by will, testators are generally free to allocate the burden of tax as they wish. The one exception is IHTA 1984, s 41 which provides that, notwithstanding the terms of any disposition:

(a)   none of the tax on the value transferred shall fall on any specific gift if, or to the extent that, the transfer is exempt with respect to the gift; and

---

[69]   IHTA 1984, s 199(1)(a), (2). The same position applies to reservation of benefit property with the burden falling on the donee.

(b) none of the tax attributable to the value of the property comprised in residue shall fall on any gift of a share of residue if or to the extent that the transfer is exempt with respect to the gift.

3.36 If the will is silent, IHTA 1984, s 211 provides that the burden of tax will be a testamentary expense and therefore payable from residue if it is attributable to UK property which vests in the personal representatives and which is not immediately before death comprised in a settlement. In the following cases IHT is not a testamentary expense:

(a) foreign property;

(b) property passing by survivorship, *donatio mortis causa* or nomination (that is, property which does not vest in the personal representatives);

(c) property comprised in a settlement immediately before the testator's death (eg. when the deceased had enjoyed a qualifying interest in possession);

(d) additional IHT on lifetime gifts chargeable as a result of the testator's death;

(e) property treated as part of the testator's estate as a result of the reservation of benefit rules (as in (b) above, the property does not vest in the personal representatives);

(f) works of art and the like, where tax becomes payable as a result of sale or breach of an undertaking.

So, for example, if a will dealing with UK property is silent, the burden of tax on specific and pecuniary legacies will fall on residue but the burden of tax on property passing by survivorship will fall on the surviving joint tenant.

3.37 A gift of residue usually includes an express direction that IHT is to be paid from residue. It is important to consider whether the testator wishes merely to restate the statutory position for the avoidance of doubt, or to change it.[70] For example, a direction that 'inheritance tax payable on property passing under my will' is to be paid from residue merely restates the statutory position, whereas a direction to pay 'all inheritance tax resulting from my death' is much wider and throws the burden of tax onto residue. Consider the following clause dealing with the payment of tax out of residue:

> 'My trustees shall pay my funeral and testamentary expenses and my debts together with inheritance tax payable [and any death duties payable outside the United Kingdom][71] [in respect of any property passing under this will][72] *or* [in respect of any property passing as a result of my death][73] [and in respect of any gift or other transaction given or effected in my lifetime giving rise to a claim for

---

[70] See **Precedent 4.1, clause 6(1).**

[71] This brings in as an expense of the estate tax on foreign property.

[72] This will only affect the tax on property passing by will, so will not affect, for example, the tax on property passing by survivorship, held in trust or given by lifetime transfer.

[73] This is wider but would still not affect the tax on property given by lifetime transfer.

inheritance tax or additional inheritance tax][74] and any legacies given by this will or any codicil to it out of such property or its proceeds of sale.'

Residue shared by exempt and non-exempt beneficiaries

3.38 As noted at **3.35**, no matter what the will says, none of the tax on non-exempt residue can fall on exempt residue.[75] The residue must be divided into shares and the tax attributable to the non-exempt shares must be borne by those beneficiaries.

> *Example 3.5*
>
> Ted leaves his £1m estate to be divided equally between his son, Sam, and his wife, Wendy. Ted has made no lifetime chargeable transfers and has not been married before so there is no transferred nil rate band.[76] The nil rate band at the date of his death is £325,000. Wendy will take £500,000. Sam's share suffers tax at 40% on £175,000 which amounts to £70,000 so he will only receive £430,000.

3.39 If this result is explained to Ted when he is making his will, he may object on the basis that he wants his wife and son to receive the same amount. A direction in the will to pay the tax first and divide the net residue equally is of no effect because of s 41. It is, however, permissible to direct that the residue is to be divided unequally between the beneficiaries in such proportions that (after tax on the chargeable share) they each end up with the same amount.[77] For example:

> 'I declare that the shares of my estate of any beneficiaries who do not qualify for exemption from inheritance tax shall be deemed to be of amounts such that the amounts received, after payment of inheritance tax due, shall be the same for all the beneficiaries named in clause ...'

The calculation is mathematically challenging although there is a calculator available on the HMRC website at http://www.hmrc.gov.uk/cto/g_up.pdf.

3.40 Most taxpayers will not want the complexity of such a result. *Re Ratcliffe*[78] confirmed that a gift which merely directs an 'equal' division between exempt and non-exempt beneficiaries will not be construed as requiring an unequal division into pre-tax shares unless there is clear evidence of such a wish. To make it clear that a testator accepts that the non-exempt and exempt beneficiaries will receive different amounts after tax, the following clause may be used:

---

[74] This will include the tax on property given by a lifetime transfer.
[75] IHTA 1984, s 41(b).
[76] For the transferred unused nil rate band, see Chapter 5.
[77] See *Re Benham's Will Trusts* [1995] STC 210 for an example although the wording in that case was obscure.
[78] [1999] STC 262.

'I declare that if the share in my estate of any beneficiary named in clause ... does not qualify for exemption from inheritance tax, that share shall bear its own tax so that the amount received by each beneficiary named in that clause is the same before the payment of inheritance tax.'

When is it necessary to gross up?

3.41 IHT is charged on the loss to the estate. Hence if £500,000 is settled by lifetime transfer and the transferor agrees to pay the IHT, the transferor is losing more than £500,000 and the tax must be calculated on the total loss. It is therefore necessary to gross up the £500,000 to calculate the amount on which tax is payable. This involves multiplying the amount to be grossed up by 100/100 less the rate of tax.[79]

Example 3.6

Sam who has already used up his nil rate band settles £500,000 and pays the tax. The rate of tax is 20% so the £500,000 must be grossed up.

1. Gross up the amount transferred using the grossing up formula:

$$£500,000 \times \frac{100}{100 - 20} = £625,000$$

2. IHT is calculated on a total transfer of £625,000:

$$£625,000 \times 20\% = £125,000$$

3.42 On death it is rarely necessary to gross up. It is only required if non-exempt beneficiaries receive an amount in excess of the testator's nil rate band and the tax is being paid from residue which is passing to an exempt beneficiary. Hence there is no need to gross up if:

(a) the whole estate is passing to non-exempt beneficiaries, eg. 'to my children';

(b) the whole estate is passing to exempt beneficiaries, eg. 'to be divided between the following charities';

(c) an amount within the deceased's available nil rate band is passing to non-exempt beneficiaries and the rest to exempt beneficiaries, eg. 'a legacy equal to the amount that can pass without payment of inheritance tax to my children, the rest to my wife';

(d) an amount in excess of the nil rate band is left to non-exempt beneficiaries subject to the beneficiaries paying the tax, the rest to exempt beneficiaries, eg. 'legacies of £1m each to my two daughters subject to tax, residue to my husband';

---

[79] When there is a gift to charity in the will, grossing up is at the 36% rate to determine whether the IHT reduced rate applies: see **9.16.**

(e)   residue is divided between exempt and non-exempt beneficiaries.[80]

Examples of grossing up

3.43   The common situation where grossing up is required is where a will leaves legacies in excess of the available nil rate band to non-exempt beneficiaries, residue to exempt beneficiaries and the tax on the legacies is to be paid from residue. This may arise either because the legacies are expressed to be 'free of tax' or because the will is silent.[81]

> *Example 3.7*
>
> T who has only £100,000 of his nil rate band remaining, gives £400,000 free of tax to his daughter and the rest of his £1m estate to his wife. He dies when the rate of IHT is 40% on all transfers in excess of the nil rate band. £300,000 of the legacy needs to be grossed up as follows:
>
> £300,000 × 100/60 = £500,000
>
> The IHT is, therefore £200,000 and the wife's share of the estate is reduced from £600,000 to £400,000. This is fine if all concerned were expecting this result but may be an unpleasant shock for the spouse. If the daughter is an adult and the family united, a variation may be used to reduce the daughter's legacy and achieve a substantial IHT saving although care is needed.[82]

Life becomes more exciting if, in addition to a tax free legacy, the residue is divided between exempt and non-exempt beneficiaries. Double grossing up is then required.

> *Example 3.8*
>
> The facts are as in the previous example save that T left the residue equally between his wife and sister. The tax on the legacy has to be paid from the residue before division into shares and the sister's share of residue must bear its own tax. The mathematical complication is that the size of the sister's share cannot be known until the IHT attributable to the legacy is known and the IHT attributable to the legacy cannot be calculated until the size of the sister's share is known. The solution to this conundrum is set out in IHTA 1984, ss 36–42.
>
> First the legacy is grossed up as if it was the only taxable part of the estate; the result is then added to any tax bearing legacies and to the taxable share of residue to calculate the hypothetical chargeable value of the estate for IHT purposes. The hypothetical chargeable value of the estate is then used to calculate an assumed estate rate of tax. The specific legacy is then grossed up at this assumed estate rate. Finally the re-grossed up legacy and the taxable share of residue are added together to give the taxable estate and tax is calculated on that figure.
>
> In summary the stages are therefore:

---

[80]   This can present problems of construction. See **3.39** *et seq*; IHTA 1984, s 41, *Re Benham's Will Trust* [1995] STC 210 and *Re Ratcliffe Deceased* [1999] STC 262.

[81]   Where the will is silent the burden of tax in such a case falls on residue: see IHTA 1984, s 211 and **3.36**.

[82]   For post-death variations generally see Chapter 12.

Stage 1

Gross up tax free legacies

Stage 2

Calculate assumed tax by adding
- Grossed up legacies, to
- Tax bearing legacies, plus
- Chargeable share of residue

This is the **'hypothetical chargeable estate'**. Then calculate IHT on that hypothetical chargeable estate

Stage 3

Use assumed tax to calculate an assumed rate

<u>Assumed tax</u> = **Assumed rate**

Hypothetical chargeable
estate

Stage 4

Grossed up Net tax-free legacies at assumed rate

The four stages are illustrated as follows:

Stage 1

Gross up tax free legacies

Stage 2

(Hypothetical chargeable estate)

Other legacies plus chargeable residue

Grossed up

Grossed up

Tax-free legacies

Tax-free legacies

Stage 3

Assumed rate = assumed tax divided by hypothetical chargeable estate

Stage 4

Grossed up at assumed rate

Net tax-free legacies

Example 3.9

Ted leaves a legacy of £328,000 to his daughter (free of tax), land (worth £50,000) to a friend (subject to tax), and residue to be divided equally between his widow and his son (tax year 2012–13): the share of residue passing to the son is not grossed up. Estate value £625,000.

1.   **Gross up tax-free legacy as if it were the only legacy:**

     (£328,000 − £325,000) x 5/3rds = £5,000 + £325,000 = £330,000

2.   **Calculate assumed tax:**

     Work out hypothetical chargeable estate by adding subject-to-tax legacy and half the residue remaining:

     Residue remaining £625,000 − (£330,000 + £50,000) = £245,000.

     Hypothetical chargeable estate £330,000 + £50,000 + (1/2 x £245,000) = £502,500.

Calculate inheritance tax on hypothetical chargeable estate:

(£502,500 – £325,000) x 40% = £71,000.

3. **Calculate assumed rate (estate rate on hypothetical chargeable estate):**

$$\frac{71,000}{502,500} = 0.1412935$$

4. **Gross up £328,000 legacy again, using assumed rate:**

$$\frac{£328,000}{1 - 0.141935} = £381,969.85$$

5. **Calculate chargeable estate** by adding subject-to-tax legacy to regrossed tax-free legacy and chargeable part of residue (1/2):

Residue £625,000 – (£381,969.85 + £50,000.00) = £193,030.15

Chargeable share of residue: £193,030.15 ÷ 2 = £96,515.075

Chargeable estate:

£381,969.85 + £96,515.075 + £50,000.00 = £528,484.92

6. **Calculate inheritance tax on chargeable estate:**

(£528,484.92 – £325,000.00) x 40% = £81,393.968

7. **Gross up tax-free legacy as if it were the only legacy:**

8. **Allocate tax:**

Tax on tax-free legacy (paid by estate)

$$£381,969.85 \; x \; \frac{81,393.968}{528,484.92} = £58,828.59$$

Tax on land paid by friend

$$£50,000.00 \; x \; \frac{81,393.968}{528,484.92} = £7,700.68$$

Tax on chargeable part of residue

$$£96,515.075 \; x \; \frac{81,393.968}{528,484.92} = £14,864.64$$

Total tax   £81,393.91

9. **Distribute the estate:**

Daughter receives tax-free legacy in full: £328,000.00

Friend receives £50,000.00 land less £7,700.68 inheritance tax:	£42,299.32
Widow receives half residue: residue is £625,000.00 − (£328,000.00 + £50,000.00 + £58,828.59 [tax on tax-free legacy]) = £188,171.41 x 1/2:	£94,085.705
Son receives half residue (£94,085.705) less inheritance tax (£14,864.64):	£79,221.065
Inheritance tax	£81,393.91
	£625,000.00

This double grossing up calculation is decidedly challenging (though the HMRC calculator is helpful)[83] and those planning the disposition of an estate are advised to avoid the necessity wherever possible.

Estate duty hangover

3.44 Until 13 March 1975 the estate duty regime operated. The various transitional provisions for estate duty are beyond the scope of this book although mention should be made of IHTA 1984, Sch 6, para 2 which preserves for IHT purposes the estate duty surviving spouse exemption. This exemption provided that where property was left to a surviving spouse in such circumstances that the spouse was not competent to dispose of it (for instance, was given a life interest) estate duty would be charged on the first death but not again on the death of the survivor. This exemption was continued into the CTT (and now IHT) era by IHTA 1984, Sch 6, para 2 which excludes such property from charge whether the limited interest is terminated *inter vivos* or by the death of the surviving spouse. All too often this valuable exemption may be overlooked and an over-emphasis on the attractions of making PETs may have unfortunate results.

> *Example 3.10*
>
> 1. On his death in 1973, Samson left his wife Delilah a life interest in his share portfolio. She is still alive and in robust health and the trustees have a power to advance capital to her. Estate duty was charged on Samson's death but because of IHTA 1984, Sch 6, para 2 there will be no charge to IHT when Delilah's interest comes to an end. At first sight, there appear to be advantages if the trustees advance capital to Delilah which she then transfers by means of a PET. However, this arrangement carries with it the risk of that capital being subject to an IHT charge if Delilah dies within 7 years of her gift. Accordingly, an interest which is tax free is being replaced by a potentially chargeable transfer.
>
> 2. Terminating Delilah's interest during her life may, however, have other attractions. In particular, the exemption from charge in IHTA 1984, Sch 6, para 2 is limited to the value of the property in which the limited interest subsists but that property may, by forming part of Delilah's estate, affect the value of other assets in

---

[83]   See **3.39**.

that estate. Assume, for instance, that Delilah owns 30% of the shares in a private company (Galilee Ltd) in her own name and that a further 30% are subject to the life interest trust and that the shares are not eligible for business property relief. When she dies she will be treated as owning 60% of the shares: a controlling holding which will be valued as such. Although one-half of the value of that holding will be free from charge under para 2, the remaining portion will be taxed. Accordingly, it may be better in such cases for her life interest to be surrendered *inter vivos* even if that operation is only carried out on her deathbed.

2. THE IHT TREATMENT OF SETTLEMENTS

3.45 FA 2006 introduced significant changes to the IHT treatment of settlements and will trusts created on or after 22 March 2006. As this is a planning book the focus is on the regime applying to post-22 March 2006 settlements with only a brief mention of the previous rules.[84]

Settlements created before 22 March 2006

3.46 Before 22 March 2006 there were two different IHT taxing regimes: one for settlements with an interest in possession[85] and one for those without.

Pre-22 March 2006 Settlements

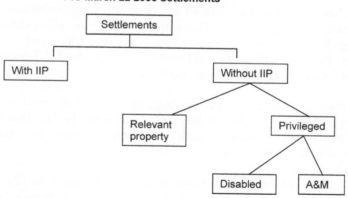

Pre-March 22 2006 Settlements

3.47 An interest in possession is not defined in the legislation but the House of Lords in *Pearson v IRC*[86] considered that it was 'a present right to present enjoyment' of the trust property. In most cases it is clear whether or not such a right exists. A beneficiary who has an immediate right to receive income or to use and enjoy trust property has an interest in possession. A beneficiary whose right to capital is contingent on reaching a specified age may obtain an interest

---

[84] See also the authors' *A Modern Approach to Lifetime Tax Planning* Chapter 13.
[85] See **3.47** and **6.12** *et seq* for the meaning of 'interest in possession'.
[86] [1981] AC 753.

in possession earlier if the settlement deed or Trustee Act 1925, s 31[87] gives him a right to income at an earlier age. Beneficiaries of a discretionary trust do not have interests in possession as they have no right to receive income unless, of course, the trustees choose to exercise their powers to give them such a right.[88]

3.48 There are marginal cases where the position is less clear. In *Pearson* a trust fund was held for three beneficiaries (all adult) who were entitled to the income subject to the trustees' powers to appoint the income elsewhere or to accumulate it. The House of Lords held by a majority of three to two that there was no interest in possession. The beneficiaries did not have a present right to receive income because the trustees were free to accumulate it.[89]

3.49 Before 22 March 2006 lifetime transfers into settlements with an interest in possession were potentially exempt transfers.[90] Whether the settlement was created by lifetime transfer or on death, the beneficiary with the interest in possession was treated as beneficially entitled to the underlying capital.[91] Any termination of the interest in possession (including its termination on the death of the beneficiary) was a transfer of value by that beneficiary. The transfer could be exempt, potentially exempt or chargeable depending on where the property passed after the termination and on what terms. Pre-March 2006 interests in possession continue as 'qualifying' interests with the IHT treatment of the relevant beneficiary being the same: ie. under IHTA 1984, s 49(1) he is still treated as beneficially entitled to the capital in the settlement.

3.50 Settlements without an interest in possession were subdivided into those which qualified for privileged IHT treatment and those which did not. Those qualifying for privileged treatment were accumulation and maintenance settlements ('A&M settlements') and trusts for the disabled.[92] Transfers to such settlements were potentially exempt transfers.

3.51 In the case of trusts for the disabled, the value of the trust property was treated as included in the beneficiary's estate, despite the fact that he did not have an interest in possession. Such settlements continue to attract special treatment after 22 March 2006.[93]

3.52 In the case of A&M settlements there were normally no charges during the lifetime of the settlement nor exit charges when a beneficiary became

---

[87]   See **2.72**.
[88]   See **Precedent 13.4**.
[89]   See further for the meaning of an 'interest in possession' **6.12** *et seq.*
[90]   IHTA 1984, s 3. If the settlor was the interest in possession beneficiary, it was a 'nothing' since the value of his IHT estate was not reduced.
[91]   IHTA 1984, s 49.
[92]   IHTA 1984, s 71 (A&M trusts) and s 89 (disabled trusts).
[93]   A new s 89A was inserted into IHTA 1984 by FA 2006, s 156 and Sch 20 which provides for a settlement to be treated as a disabled person's settlement where a person transfers property to a settlement for their own benefit at a time when he is suffering from a condition that it is reasonable to expect will lead to the settlor becoming 'disabled' within the meaning of s 89. These trusts are 'qualifying' interest in possession trusts: see **3.58**.

entitled to capital. No new A&M settlements can be created on or after 22 March 2006. Existing settlements continued unchanged until 6 April 2008 on which date they lost their privileged status and entered the relevant property regime (or s 71D) unless they fulfilled the much more stringent requirements of the amended IHTA 1984, s 71, *viz*:

(a) the beneficiaries will, on or before attaining a specified age not exceeding 18, become beneficially entitled to the trust property; and

(b) there must be no interest in possession in the trust property and the income from it is to be accumulated so far as not applied for the maintenance, education or benefit of a beneficiary.

(c) Either

   (i) not more than 25 years have elapsed since the commencement of the settlement or, if it was later, since the time (or latest time) when the previous two conditions stated in paragraphs (a) and (b) above became satisfied; or

   (ii) all the persons who are or have been beneficiaries are or were either grandchildren of a common grandparent, or children, widows, widowers or surviving civil partners of such grandchildren who were themselves beneficiaries but died before becoming entitled as in (a) above.

Where the conditions are met no IHT is charged when a beneficiary becomes beneficially entitled to settled property on or before attaining the specified age, nor if the beneficiary dies before attaining the specified age.

Many former A&M settlements continue to exist but will now be taxed under the relevant property regime. In some cases a beneficiary had become entitled to an interest in possession before 22 March 2006 with the result that the settlement was an interest in possession settlement on that date.

3.53 Non-interest in possession settlements not qualifying for privileged treatment (broadly, discretionary trusts and accumulation trusts not qualifying as A&M settlements) were subject to the relevant property regime under which there are three main charges to IHT:

(a) the lifetime creation of a settlement is a lifetime chargeable transfer (not a PET) and liable to tax at half the death rates;

(b) a periodic charge at 10-yearly intervals on the anniversary of creation of the settlement;

(c) a proportionate periodic charge when property left the settlement between anniversaries or an interest in possession arose in it (an 'exit' charge).[94]

---

[94] From 22 March 2006 there will not generally be an exit charge when an interest in possession arises since it will not be 'qualifying'.

The 'relevant property' regime, continues after FA 2006 for settlements created before the Act came into force and, as will be seen, has been extended to catch most lifetime settlements created after that date.

Settlements created on and after 22 March 2006

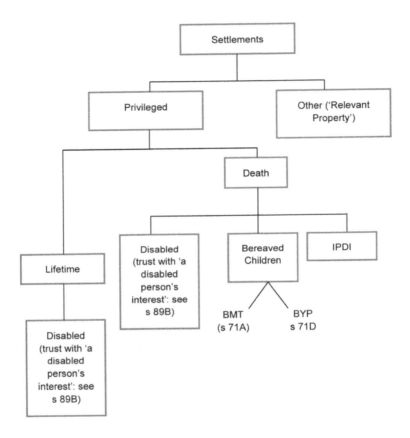

3.54 All settlements created by lifetime transfer are now within the relevant property regime unless they qualify as a settlement for the disabled.

Will trusts are also all within the relevant property regime unless they qualify as:

(a)   a settlement for the disabled;[95]

(b)   a bereaved minor's trust;[96]

(c)   a bereaved young person's trust;[97]

(d)   a settlement with an immediate post-death interest.[98]

Trusts for bereaved minors and bereaved young people are dealt with in Chapter 7. Settlements with an immediate post death interest are dealt with in Chapter 6.

This major change in the IHT treatment of settlements was achieved by:

(a)   amending the definition of a qualifying interest in possession in IHTA 1984, s 59 to exclude interests in possession arising on or after 22 March 2006 with only three exceptions (trusts for the disabled,[99] immediate post-death interests[100] and transitional serial interests);[101]

(b)   amending IHTA 1984, s 49(1) to exclude interests in possession arising on or after 22 March 2006 with the same three exceptions;

(c)   amending the definition of estate in IHTA 1984, s 5 to exclude the value of interests in possession arising on or after 22 March 2006 with the same three exceptions;[102]

(d)   amending the definition of potentially exempt transfer in IHTA 1984, s 3A for transfers of value made on or after 22 March 2006. Transfers which arise on the ending of an existing interest in possession are potentially exempt transfers provided that either the settlement then ends; or the property becomes held on disabled trusts.

Practical results

3.55 The result of the changes is that the lifetime creation of a settlement will, unless the trust is one for a disabled person, be a chargeable transfer. Further, the settlement may be subject to IHT anniversary and exit charges. Creating lifetime trusts without an immediate payment of IHT is limited to:

---

[95]   Within IHTA 1984, s 89B.
[96]   Within IHTA 1984, s 71A: see Chapter 7.
[97]   Within IHTA 1984, s 71D: see Chapter 7.
[98]   Within IHTA 1984, s 49A: see Chapter 6.
[99]   See **3.58**.
[100]   See Chapter 6.
[101]   See **3.59**.
[102]   But note amendments in FA 2010 to counter the effect of *Melville* type schemes: see IHTA 1984, s 49A(1B).

(a)   gifts up to the amount of the settlor's available IHT nil rate band. Both spouses (or civil partners) can establish nil rate band trusts and gifts *inter se* (eg. to enable both to set up such trusts) are spouse exempt;

(b)   gifts into trust of property attracting 100% relief (businesses and farms) so that no IHT is payable on the creation of the trust;[103]

(c)   gifts into a bare trust which will still take effect as a potentially exempt transfer;[104]

(d)   settled gifts falling within the normal expenditure out of income exemption (IHTA 1984, s 21).[105]

The DOTAS regime[106]

3.56   Finding ways of getting property into settlements without attracting the 20% entry charge has been a major preoccupation of estate planners since the 2006 changes. Apart from the above, there was renewed interest in '*Melville* schemes'. This prompted the government to close down the latest variant ('Melville III') in FA 2010 and to extend DOTAS to catch IHT schemes which seek to transfer property into relevant property trusts without incurring the 20% entry charge.[107] New proposals[108] will extend DOTAS in relation to inheritance tax still further. There are three proposed changes:

(1)   To include all arrangements designed to avoid or reduce an immediate charge to IHT, rather than, as now, those designed to avoid or reduce the entry charge for transfers into relevant property trusts.

(2)   To introduce a requirement to disclose arrangements which, although not giving rise to an immediate charge to IHT, are intended to reduce or avoid that tax on death. This would include, for example, arrangements that sought to circumvent the reservation of benefit rules, or the rules for deducting liabilities introduced by the Finance Act 2013.

(3)   To extend the application of some of the general DOTAS hallmarks, such as the confidentiality and premium fee hallmarks, to include IHT. This would ensure that anything particularly innovative or where a promoter seeks to design their way around the detail of the extended IHT hallmark would also fall to be disclosed. But this is not intended to catch arrangements that fall outside of the IHT hallmark where they involve the straightforward use of reliefs and exemptions.

'Arrangements' are defined for DOTAS as including any scheme, transaction or series of transactions. However, the Government says that it recognises that

---

[103]   See Chapter 10.

[104]   See Chapter 7. This is because bare trusts are not settled property for IHT purposes.

[105]   See **3.25** and Chapter 38 of the authors' *A Modern Approach to Lifetime Tax Planning*.

[106]   On DOTAS generally, see the authors' *A Modern Approach to Lifetime Tax Planning*, Chapter 17.

[107]   The Disclosure of Tax Avoidance Schemes (DOTAS) legislation had not hitherto applied to IHT. The change was effective from 6 April 2011.

[108]   See *Strengthening the Tax Avoidance Disclosure Regimes*, published 31 July 2014.

reliefs and exemptions are used legitimately in many arrangements by the vast majority of people. It wants to ensure that the hallmark is appropriately targeted without inadvertently putting an information requirement under DOTAS on situations where a relief is being used in the way that the legislation intended it to work, or for normal family arrangements that take place after death.

So that the application of DOTAS to IHT does not pick up what would be regarded as acceptable tax planning, only arrangements which an informed observer could reasonably conclude are an IHT avoidance scheme or arrangement would be disclosable. 'Straightforward' use of the existing IHT reliefs and exemptions would not be disclosable.

Accelerated Payment notices can be given where there is an open enquiry or appeal in respect of the tax advantage purported to arise through implementation of a scheme disclosed under DOTAS. For IHT there will be differences for lifetime charges and charges following death:

i.   For lifetime IHT charges an Accelerated Payment notice may be given during the scheme user's lifetime where a chargeable event has occurred in relation to a scheme and an IHT return has been delivered to HMRC so bringing the case within the rules for giving an Accelerated Payment notice.

ii.   For IHT chargeable following death no Accelerated Payment notice can be issued until after the person had died and an IHT account had been delivered, irrespective of when the scheme was made available by the promoter or implemented by the user.

Drafting settlements today

3.57 Because the type of settlement no longer affects its IHT treatment, the decision as to the form of the settlement may be governed by non-tax considerations. The choice is:

(a)   to select a discretionary trust for maximum flexibility; or

(b)   to limit the beneficiaries, for example to grandchildren, with a view to the trust fund being used to pay school fees and give the trustees powers to use the income and accumulate any surplus; or

(c)   to provide a person with a right to income (which may be beneficial for income tax purposes).[109] There will, of course, be no CGT uplift on the death of that beneficiary (since, after FA 2006, he no longer has a qualifying interest in possession for IHT purposes) but nor will the assets of the trust be aggregated with his free estate on death.

---

[109] Because the 45% trust rate will not apply to the trustees: see **3.133**.

It is also possible for trustees to give and take away rights to income without the nature of the settlement changing for IHT purposes: ie. there is no longer an exit charge on such an event.[110]

Disabled trusts[111]

3.58   Disabled trusts are not subject to the relevant property regime. The scope of a disabled trust was extended in FA 2006 so that it includes:

(a)   an old-style IHTA 1984, s 89 trust;

(b)   under IHTA 1984, s 89A a self-settlement made on or after 22 March 2006 by a person with a condition expected to lead to disability;

(c)   in addition, s 89B defines a 'disabled person's interest' widely to include an interest in possession to which a disabled person becomes entitled after 21 March 2006 and an interest in possession trust set up by a person whose condition makes it likely that he will become disabled (both involve actual rather than deemed interests in possession).

The lifetime creation of a disabled trust is a potentially exempt transfer. After creation (whether by a lifetime transfer or transfer on death) the disabled person is then treated, under IHTA 1984, s 49(1), as the beneficial owner of the settled property so that tax may be payable on his death but 10-year anniversary and exit charges are avoided. Finance Act 2014 amended TCGA 1992, s 72 in respect of deaths from 5 December 2013 to provide that the usual CGT uplift occurs on the death of the disabled beneficiary.[112] Previously, if there was a disposal of the settled property following the death because of no uplift there was a potential tax liability.

Transitional serial interests (TSI)

3.59   Transitional serial interests were introduced by FA 2006 and allowed a brief window to re-organise existing interests in possession. There are three types of transitional serial interest:

(a)   An interest in possession created in the transitional period between 22 March 2006 and 5 October 2008[113] and replacing an interest in possession in existence on 22 March 2006. (The interest must not qualify as a s 71A settlement or as a disabled person's interest.) The requirements are that:

(i)   the settlement commenced before 22 March 2006;

---

[110]   And without CGT consequences: see **Precedents 13.4** and **13.5**.

[111]   See further **7.36** *et seq.*

[112]   See **3.144**. The lack of an uplift before this date was because, under IHTA 1984 s 89, the beneficiary had a deemed but not an actual interest in possession. The CGT legislation had required the beneficiary to have an interest in possession as a matter of trust law.

[113]   IHTA 1984, s 49C.

(ii) immediately before that date, someone was beneficially entitled to an interest in possession ('the prior interest');

(iii) the prior interest came to an end at a time on or after 22 March 2006 but before 6 October 2008;

(iv) the new beneficiary became beneficially entitled to the current interest at that time.

Example 3.11

Dan had a life interest in a valuable trust fund created by his father in 2004.

In 2007 the trustees used their powers to terminate Dan's interest and appoint the property to his son, Sam, on a terminable life interest. Sam's interest is a transitional serial interest so that Sam will be treated as owning the underlying trust property.

With the general ending of the TSI 'window' on 6 October 2008 it is important that no steps are taken which might have the effect of replacing an 'old' qualifying interest in possession with a 'new' interest which will not be qualifying. The problem arises especially in connection with the making of settled advances when the risk is that a beneficiary who had obtained an interest in possession at 18 as a result of TA 1925, s 31[114] has that interest replaced by the settled advance of a life interest. Were this to happen he would be treated as making a chargeable transfer with the continuing trusts being taxed under the relevant property regime.[115]

(b) An interest in possession replacing an interest in possession of a spouse or civil partner which was in existence on 22 March 2006.[116] The replacement must occur on the death of the spouse or civil partner. A lifetime replacement will not create a transitional serial interest. (The interest must not qualify as a s 71A settlement or as a disabled person's interest.) The requirements are that:

(i) the settlement commenced before 22 March 2006;

(ii) immediately before that date, there was an interest in possession ('the previous interest');

(iii) the previous interest came to an end on or after 6 October 2008 on the death of the person with that interest ('the previous beneficiary');

(iv) the previous beneficiary's spouse or civil partner becomes immediately entitled on the death to an interest in possession.

Example 3.12

In 1990 Damian's father settled property on Damian for life, remainder to Damian's wife, Candice for life. Damian dies in 2014 and Candice takes her life

---

[114] See **2.72**.

[115] For settled advances see **2.53** and **Precedent 13.3**.

[116] IHTA 1984, s 49D.

interest. Candice's interest is a transitional serial interest and she will be treated as owning the underlying trust property. The effect is that on Damian's death the spouse exemption will apply.[117]

(c)   An interest in possession in settled property where the settled property consists of, or includes, rights under a contract of life insurance entered into before 22 March 2006 will be a transitional serial interest if the conditions set out in IHTA 1984, s 49E are satisfied.

3. THE TAXATION OF RELEVANT PROPERTY SETTLEMENTS

3.60   There are three occasions on which IHT may be payable in the case of a relevant property settlement:

(a)   creation;

(b)   10-yearly anniversaries;

(c)   exits.

Creation

3.61   If the creation is by lifetime transfer there is an immediate charge to IHT at half the death rates so tax is at 0% on the portion within the settlor's available nil rate band and thereafter at 20%. If the trust is created on death IHT is calculated in the normal way on the death estate and the property then passes to the trustees.

> *Example 3.13*
>
> George and Grace are well-off and want to set up a discretionary trust for their grandchildren. Neither has made any previous lifetime transfers. How much can they transfer without payment of IHT?
>
> Each can transfer an amount equal to:
>
> 1. the nil rate band, currently £325,000;
>
> 2. two annual exemptions, £6,000;
>
> 3. any property qualifying for 100% business or agricultural property relief.
>
> After 7 years a full nil rate band will be restored to them which they can use to create a further settlement.
>
> Note that:

---

[117] It does not matter that the marriage occurred after 22 March 2006: for instance, the settlement might have given Damian a power to appoint a life interest in favour of his wife which after his marriage in 2009 he exercised. On his death in 2014 the spouse exemption will apply.

(a) the couple can be joint settlors of a single settlement without there being any IHT 'downside' (see IHTA 1984, s 44(2) which provides that in a case such as this each will be treated as creating a separate settlement for the purposes of the tax charge);

(b) the trust for the grandchildren can provide whatever the couple want: eg, it may vest capital at 25, 30 or any age or no age! If it is discretionary it should be supplemented with a letter of wishes.

Anniversary charges[118]

3.62 The method of calculation set out in IHTA 1984, s 66 was to be amended from 6 April 2015: however this change will now be introduced in a future Finance Bill.[119] The maximum rate of tax is 6% (the rate charged on exits is a proportion of the anniversary rate). Careful planning can keep the rate lower than 6%.[120] Section 66 provided as follows:

(a) The rate charged on the value of the relevant property in the settlement on each 10-year anniversary is 30% of an average rate calculated at half the death rates on a 'hypothetical chargeable transfer'.

(b) The table of rates is joined at the point reached by the settlor's chargeable transfers in the 7 years before the creation of the settlement plus any transfers from the settlement in the previous 10 years. It is, therefore, always beneficial for the future taxation of relevant property settlements for the settlor to create them at a time when his cumulative total is zero.

3.63 The 'hypothetical chargeable transfer' ('HCT') is found by adding:

(a) the relevant property in the settlement immediately before the anniversary;

(b) the value, immediately after creation of the settlement, of property in any related settlement (one created on the same day);[121]

(c) the value at the date when the settlement was created, of any non-relevant property in the settlement which has not subsequently become relevant property.

Step 1

Calculate the hypothetical chargeable transfer (HCT).

Step 2

Calculate tax at half death rates on HCT.

Step 3

---

[118] The charge is imposed at 10-yearly intervals from the date of creation of the settlement.
[119] See **3.72** *et seq.*
[120] See **3.67.**
[121] IHTA 1984, s 62.

Turn the tax calculated at Step 2 into an average rate and take 30%.

Step 4

Apply that 30% rate to the relevant property in the settlement.

> *Example 3.14*
>
> Ted died in 2014 with a large estate. He is divorced and although he has not used up his nil rate band he has no transferable nil rate band. His will creates two relevant property settlements each of £300,000. He has made no previous lifetime settlements. 10 years later the nil rate band is £500,000, both settlements have increased in value to £500,000 and there have been no payments out of either settlement. The anniversary charge on Settlement A is calculated as follows:
>
> *Step 1*
>
> Calculate the hypothetical chargeable transfer (HCT)
>
> HCT is £500,000 + £300,000 (value of property in related settlement at time created) = £800,000
>
> *Step 2*
>
> Calculate tax at half death rates on HCT
>
> First £500,000 is taxed at 0% = nil
>
> Next £300,000 is taxed at 20% = £60,000
>
> *Step 3*
>
> Turn the tax calculated at Step 2 into an average rate and take 30%
>
> $$\frac{60{,}000}{800{,}000} \; x \; 100 = 7.5\%$$
>
> 7.5 × 30% = 2.25%
>
> *Step 4*
>
> Apply that rate to the relevant property
>
> £500,000 × 2.25% = £11,250

The treatment of income

3.64 What is meant by 'relevant property' for the purpose of calculating anniversary (and exit) charges? Before changes in FA 2014, IHT was payable only on the capital of the settlement not on undistributed income.[122] Only if it was accumulated by the trustees did the income become relevant property and so subject to the charge.[123]

---

[122] SP 8/86.
[123] There is a discount to reflect the fact that the accumulated income has not been relevant property throughout the previous 10 years.

Although, in practical terms, trustees of discretionary trusts commonly have a free choice between either distributing or accumulating income, in trust law terms their powers are framed in different ways. There may either be a trust to distribute and a power to accumulate or a trust to accumulate with a power to distribute. In both cases the power will lapse if not exercised within a reasonable time, but what is a reasonable period will depend on the context. HMRC became concerned that in some cases income was being retained for many years and reinvested within the income account, yet on the 10-year anniversary the trustees would maintain that they had not yet decided whether to accumulate.

3.65 In 2013 HMRC proposed[124] a deeming rule to provide certainty about the IHT position in these situations and avoid long running disputes between the taxpayer and HMRC. Their initial proposal was that income would be deemed capitalised for all inheritance tax charges after 2 years. This proposal was unpopular. Those responding to the consultation paper made a number of points including the following:

(a) The proposed period of 2 years was insufficient for trustees to be able to consider the beneficiaries' requirements. Trustees often retain income for the future needs of their income beneficiaries knowing that it will be required for use within a set period of time, for example to pay school or university fees.

(b) Most importantly, there would be a mismatch between the trust law position and the tax law position – that is income which was still income for trust purposes would be capital for IHT (but not other) tax purposes. Tax treatment should follow trust law and where there is a power to accumulate but a trust to distribute, a deemed accumulation in a tax statute cannot change the character of the income. Income received by trustees which is not accumulated has not lost its character of income and will frequently be distributed as income to beneficiaries in a later year.

(c) There would be an element of double taxation – the concern being that income would be taxed as capital but later distributions would be taxed as income with no credit for any IHT paid.

(d) There would be an added administrative burden on trustees and practitioners to keep track of income generated each year and how payments were to be matched – would there be set rules and, if so, would it be first in first out or last in first out?

HMRC took on board some of the responses made to the consultation paper.

3.66 As a result, the provisions introduced by the Finance Act 2014 provide for deemed accumulation after five years instead of two and only for the purposes of the anniversary charge. HMRC considered that, framed in this way, issues of double taxation would not arise. This is because the income retains its

---

[124] In the Consultation Paper '*Inheritance Tax: Simplifying Charges on Trusts – the next stage*' issued on 31 May 2013.

nature as income and is only treated as capital for the purposes of the 10-year anniversary charge. If this income is later paid out of the trust, it will not be subject to an exit charge because it will be income in the hands of the beneficiary and subject to income tax.

To avoid the need for trustees to keep detailed records, tax will be charged on the 10-year anniversary at the full rate on any undistributed income without any proportionate reduction to reflect the period during which the income has been retained. While simplifying matters, it is clear that this effectively imposes a tax penalty upon those trusts where income is retained.

The provision applies to 10-year charges arising on or after 6 April 2014. This is therefore effectively a retroactive tax charge, as it will include income that was not previously liable to charge at a time where the trustee is unable to take any properly considered actions to manage the potential inheritance tax charge.

The legislation contains no provisions dealing with how payments are to be matched although HMRC have stated that they will apply a 'first in first out' ('FIFO') rule. New section 64(1A) was inserted into IHT 1984:

'(1A) For the purposes of subsection (1) above, property held by the trustees of a settlement immediately before a ten-year anniversary is to be regarded as relevant property comprised in the settlement at that time if—

(a)   it is income of the settlement,
(b)   the income arose before the start of the five years ending immediately before the ten-year anniversary,
(c)   the income arose (directly or indirectly) from property comprised in the settlement that, when the income arose, was relevant property, and
(d)   when the income arose, no person was beneficially entitled to an interest in possession in the property from which the income arose.'

Rather unfairly a new section 66(2A) provides that the normal reduction to the rate of tax which applies where property has not been relevant property in the settlement for the whole 10-year period[125] does not apply in relation to the deeming provision for undistributed income. This is said to be in the interests of simplicity. Trustees should consider the position in the run up to a 10-year anniversary. It may actually prove cheaper to make a decision to accumulate undistributed income thereby benefitting from the normal discount.

Example 3.15

The periodic charge for the Jenkins Settlement falls on 1 April 2015. On reviewing the position on 30 March 2015, the trustees discover:

(a)   that they have undistributed income from before 1 April 2010 totalling £100,000; and

(b)   after that date, a further £75,000.

---

[125] See **3.68** below.

If they do nothing, the £100,000 will be deemed relevant property at the time of the anniversary and may therefore suffer a tax charge of £6,000.

But if the trustees resolve on 30 March to accumulate that £100,000 of income then, although it will suffer a periodic charge, there will be a discount for the 29 quarters during which it was not relevant property so that the tax charge is reduced to £150.

Also bear in mind that if there is the usual power to distribute accumulations as income, the £100,000 can still be distributed without an IHT exit charge if subject to income tax in the hands of the beneficiary.

Planning

3.67 To keep the rate for anniversary charges low, it is desirable:

(a)   to create the settlement when the settlor has a nil cumulative total; and

(b)   not to increase the hypothetical chargeable transfer by:
   (i)   related settlements (two or more settlements created on the same day), or
   (ii) non-relevant property included in the same settlement (eg. one settlement, part of which is a relevant property settlement and part of which is a bereaved minor's trust);

(c)   to consider distributing or accumulating retained income before 10-year anniversaries.

Where a settlor wants to settle substantial amounts without incurring anniversary charges, the use of pilot trusts has been beneficial. The Revenue proposed to remove the advantages of using multiple trusts from 6 April 2015 with anti-forestalling measures applying from 10 December 2014. In the event, this legislation was not passed in FA 2015 but will be included in a future Finance Bill.[126]

There are other ways of reducing the periodic charge. For instance, with advance planning the trust fund could be invested in 100% relievable property, ie business and agricultural property (this must be done at least 2 years before the anniversary).[127] Note also:

(a)   that 'nil rate band discretionary trusts' (*viz* trusts set up with property worth no more than £325,000) will suffer no IHT exit charges on distributions out of the trust in the first 10 years but may suffer a 10-year charge if the value of property in the settlement has increased in value by more than rises in the IHT nil rate band;

---

[126] See **3.72** *et seq* and generally Chapter 8.

[127] This property may then be sold but distributions in the 10 years following the anniversary will still be taxed on the basis that there was 100% relievable property at the time of the anniversary.

(b) distributions in the first 10 years are taken into account when calculating the anniversary charge (they are on the settlement's cumulative total) so that reducing the value of the settled property shortly before the 10-year anniversary to the then nil rate band will not prevent an anniversary charge arising.

Exit charges

3.68 There is a charge on the fall in value of the trust fund resulting from capital distributions of the trustees. The rate of charge is a proportion of the rate charged on the previous anniversary. The proportion is one-fortieth of the number of complete quarters which have elapsed since the previous anniversary.[128] There is no charge if property ceases to be comprised in the settlement in the first 3 months.[129] So, if we continued **Example 3.14**, where we calculated that the rate of the tax on the first 10-year anniversary was 2.25% and assume that £50,000 leaves the trust 18 months and 1 day after the first 10-year anniversary, six complete quarters have elapsed so the tax charge will be:

$$\frac{6}{40} \; x \; 2.25\% \; x \; £50,000 = £168.75$$

When asset values are increasing, it will be tax efficient to appoint property out just before an anniversary rather than just afterwards to get the benefit of a rate calculated on a lower value.

Where the whole or part of the value of the trust fund is attributable to property which was not relevant property, or was not comprised in the settlement, throughout the whole of the 10-year period ending immediately before the relevant 10-year anniversary, the rate at which tax is charged on that value or part is reduced by one-fortieth for each of the successive quarters in that period which expired before the property became, or last became, relevant property comprised in the settlement.

3.69 In the first 10 years there is no previous anniversary and the rate has to be calculated from scratch. This is done by taking the value of the property settled immediately *after* the settlement commenced and the settlor's cumulative total immediately before creation.[130] Any previous transfers from the settlement are ignored. This means that if the value of the property settled was within the settlor's nil rate band, the rate will be nil for the first 10 years no matter how much the value of the property increases. For example, if £300,000 is settled in 2010 by a settlor with a full nil rate band and by 2019 the value of the assets

---

[128] IHTA 1984, s 69.
[129] This is significant in considering the use of IHTA 1984, s 144 to achieve 'reading-back' and was the reason for the (to be removed) *Frankland* trap: see **13.13**.
[130] IHTA 1984, s 68.

has increased to £1m, they can be appointed out without any charge to tax until the first 10-year anniversary. At that point they will be revalued.

With one exception it is always desirable to consider making appointments within the first 10 years in case the value of the settled property has increased beyond the level of the nil rate band at death.

3.70 The one exception is where the property settled qualifies for business or agricultural property relief. If property leaves the settlement in the first 10 years, the value of the property exiting will be reduced by relief (assuming it is still available) but the rate charged will be calculated by reference to the value of the property settled immediately *after* the settlement commenced. Assume that in June 2010 property worth £600,000 qualifying for 50% relief is settled. The value settled is reduced by the relief to £300,000 so no IHT is payable on creation. If the property leaves the settlement in the first 10 years the rate is calculated by reference to the value of the property settled immediately after creation of the settlement and so relief is not taken into account and the property settled will be valued at £600,000.[131]

Additions to a settlement

3.71 The addition of further property to a relevant property trust by a chargeable transfer made by the settlor can affect the IHT charged on the settlement: this matter is considered further at **8.10** and is the reason such additions are normally avoided.[132] Note three other points:

(a)   there is no doubt that the addition will form part of the original relevant property settlement, it will not create a new relevant property settlement.[133]

(b)   HMRC consider, however, that the position is different if property is added to a qualifying interest in possession settlement and that the addition will result in the creation of a relevant property trust with the settlor therefore making a chargeable transfer. It is far from certain that this analysis is correct, since it is hard to see that s 43 (which defines what is a settlement) gives rise to a new trust of the addition (it certainly does not in the case of relevant property trusts). It may, however, be the case that there cannot be a qualifying interest in possession in the property added because the definition in s 49(1) refers to the property in which that interest (ie pre-22 March 2006 interest) subsisted. HMRC may therefore be right for the wrong reason![134]

---

[131]   Of course 50% relief may still be available when the property leaves the settlement to reduce the amount taxed. This trap is particularly dangerous when the business property has been sold and it is proposed to distribute the cash.

[132]   For these purposes there may be a distinction between adding property and adding value to a settlement.

[133]   IHTA 1984, s 67.

[134]   Often the added property is spent so that there can, in any event, be no continuing settlement of it.

(c)   if property is added by someone other than the original settlor that person will be treated, for IHT purposes, as having created a separate settlement.[135]

Proposed new rules for taxation of relevant property settlements

3.72   In his 2012 Budget, the Chancellor announced a consultation exercise aimed at simplifying the calculation of IHT charges on relevant property trusts ('RPTs'). The first consultation lasted from 13 July to 5 October 2012[136] and a second from 31 May to 23 August 2013.[137] This resulted in two changes in FA 2014: first, rules deeming income to be relevant property after it has been in the trust for more than 5 years, and second the introduction of a standard date for filing an account and paying tax, being 6 months after the end of the month in which the taxable event (whether a 10-year anniversary or exit charge) occurred. While the latter offers a measure of simplification,[138] it is difficult to believe that retained income was a major problem in practice and the new rules are hardly a model of simplicity!

By the time the third Consultation was reached (it ran from 6 June to 29 August 2014), the emphasis had switched to creating 'fairness' in the system involving an attack on the use of pilot trusts to mitigate future Chapter III charges.[139] The key proposal involved the idea of a settlement nil rate band ('SNRB') to be divided between all settlements/will trusts created by a single settlor. There were to be anti-forestalling provisions to 6 June 2014. In his Autumn Statement of 3 December 2014, however, the Chancellor announced that these proposals had been wholly abandoned and instead draft clauses published on 10 December 2014 contained new provisions directed at pilot trusts.

3.73   It was envisaged that these new rules would be introduced on 6 April 2015 with anti-forestalling rules applying from 10 December 2014. In the event, however, the necessary legislation was not included in FA 2015 although the Revenue say that it will be in a future Finance Bill. The result is something approaching chaos and it is difficult to see how the original implementation dates can apply. Not only is there no legislation on the statute book but the Revenue have confirmed that the original draft clauses will be significantly amended. The following discussion is based on the draft clauses published in December 2014, together with the changes which the authors believe will be made to these. The cornerstone of the new rules is the concept of a same day addition to more than one settlement.

---

[135]   IHTA 1984, s 44(2).

[136]   '*IHT – Simplifying charges on trusts.*' FA 2013 corrected an anomaly in the treatment of AUTs and OEICs held in a relevant property trust created by a non-UK domiciliary.

[137]   '*IHT – Simplifying charges on trusts: the next stage.*'

[138]   But note that the new filing / payment dates only apply to the Chapter III charges arising on or after 6 April 2014. They do not apply to entry charges when the trust is created, nor to the additional charge if the settlor dies within seven years of having created his trust. For the income deeming rules, see **3.64**.

[139]   The Consultation was entitled "*IHT – a fairer way of calculating trust charges*".

Same day addition ('SDA')

3.74 If value is added to a relevant property settlement ('Settlement A') and on the same day the same settlor adds value to one or more other settlements ('Settlement B' – presumably this can include more than one settlement) then in taxing Settlement A include the value of the addition to Settlement B (and if not already included by reference to the related settlements rule, add the original value of Settlement B).

Proposed changes in the calculation of the 10-year charge

3.75 So to calculate the 10-year anniversary charge on a relevant property trust ("RPT"), first take the value of settled property immediately before the 10-year anniversary; then add the value of property in a related settlement (when set up); and if there has been a SDA to the Settlement then include the value of the addition to any other settlement(s) and (if necessary) the original sum settled in those settlements.

Example 3.16

Calculating the anniversary charge under the new rules.

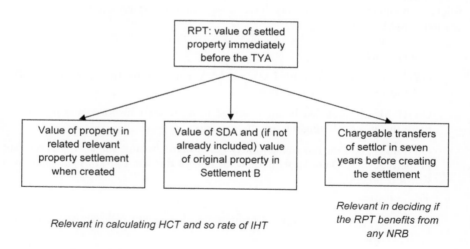

Features of SDA

3.76 In the draft legislation, the 'other' settlement (Settlement B) did not need to be a RPT: ie it could have been a disabled trust with a qualifying interest in possession! This would have had startling results.

Example 3.17

In 2015 Xandra set up a disabled trust for her grandchild Chloe settling £500,000 (a PET). In 2016 she added £10,000 to the disabled trust and established a RPT with £325,000. In taxing this RPT in the future, the value of the SDA (£10,000) and of the property originally in the disabled trust (£500,000) would be included in the HCT as the result of the SDA.

In the event, it is understood that the draft legislation will be revised to require the other settlement (Settlement B) to be a relevant property trust. Consistent with this approach, the definition of a 'related settlement' will be limited to other relevant property trusts created on the same day. Further, the SDA rules will not apply if the addition is below £5,000 (a *de minimis* exemption).

A SDA can involve a lifetime transfer by the settlor or an addition by will (including the creation of a new RPT in the will).

Example 3.18

In 2014 Janus set up a discretionary trust of £300,000. On his death in 2022, he added £50,000 to the existing trust and set up a will trust (also a RPT) of £350,000. This involves a SDA.

3.77   It will no longer be necessary to aggregate the value of property held in any non-relevant property part of the settlement for the purpose of calculating the hypothetical chargeable transfer. This change will be a genuine measure of simplification and is consistent with limiting SDAs and related settlements to relevant property trusts. It may have a significant impact on the taxation of former A&M trusts.

Example 3.19

On 6 April 2000, Pluto settled £1m on A&M trusts for his two grandchildren (Sid and Sad): this was a PET by Pluto.

On 21 March 2006 Sid became entitled to an interest in possession in half the fund: this is a qualifying interest in possession.

On 6 April 2008 the remaining moiety (Sad's share) became subject to the relevant property regime. On 6 April 2010 (at the time of the first TYA) this half share was worth £700,000.

The old rules

1)   The HCT is £700,000 + £500,000 (value of Sid's share when settled) = £1.2m.

2)   The tax rate is £1.2m – £325,000 = £875,000 x 20% = £175,000 giving a rate of 14.58 x 30% = 4.37%.

3)   Tax on Sad's share = £30,590 (less an 8-year discount when the A&M rules applied = £6,118).

The proposed new rules

If we ignore Sid's share, the HCT is £700,000 so that the tax rate is £700,000 – £325,000 =- £375,000 x 20% = £75,000 giving a rate of 10.72% x 30% which is 3.22%. As a result the tax on Sad's share is £22,540 (after discount £4,508).

Anti-forestalling (protected settlements)

3.78   The rules on SDA will not apply to *protected settlements*. A settlement is protected if there have been no transfers of value into it by the settlor on or after a prescribed date, which in the draft legislation was 10 December 2014.

Example 3.20

1) Jake established four pilot trusts (each of £10) on consecutive days in October 2014, and on 9 December 2014 added substantial funds to each. *The settlements are protected and the benefits of the IHT planning using multiple trusts not removed.*

2) As above but Jake made the additions on 10 December 2014. The proposed new rules may apply so that the SDA must be included in the computation.

3) As in para 1 except that an addition is made in January 2015 to only one of the pilot trusts. The proposed new rules do not apply since there is no SDA to another settlement.

Protected settlements and additions by will

3.79   Property can be added to an existing settlement after 10 December 2014 (or whatever is the implementation date) without the proposed new rules applying if:

1. the addition is by a disposition made in the settlor's will and those provisions '*are in substance the same as they were immediately before [10 December 2014]*';

2. the taxpayer must die before 6 April 2016 (it is understood that the draft legislation will be amended to push this date back to 6 April 2017).

Example 3.21

Jan set up four pilot trusts in 2013 and in her will (made the same year) she leaves her residue to be divided equally between them. She dies on 5 April 2016. The settlements are protected and any savings from the use of pilot trusts are retained.

Consider:

1) In 2015 Jan makes a new will because she wishes to change her executors but the residue is still left to the pilot trusts (*still protected*).

2) In 2015 she makes a new will to leave a pecuniary legacy to her godchild. The residue is reduced but still left to the pilot trusts: *still protected?*

3) In 2015 she makes a codicil which removes a legacy thereby increasing the amount of residue passing to the settlements (*still protected?*). Contrast the position if she does not make a codicil but a legacy in the will is adeemed and so, again, residue is increased.

It is therefore thought that:

1. making a new will/codicil is not fatal to there being a protected settlement provided that the disposition to the settlement remains in substance the same;

2. if the settlor does not die before 6 April 2016 (2017) so that the new rules apply to the additions, it will be possible to redirect the additions (eg onto IPDI trusts) by an appointment falling within s 144;

3. ideally, clients should review wills in these cases and consider making a new will to take effect if they survive to 6 April 2016 (2017).

CONCLUSIONS

3.80   The following example contrasts the effect of the old and proposed new rules.

Example 3.22

A comparison of the tax results under the current rules and under HMRC's proposed alternative is set out below. The illustration looks at a 10-year anniversary charge and assumes that the present IHT rates and nil rate band remain in place.

Illustration

Christopher, whose cumulative total of chargeable transfers stood at £10,000, set up Pilot Trust A with £10 on 1 June 2015 and Pilot Trust B with another £10 on 2 June 2015. They are both discretionary settlements.

Christopher died on 1 January 2016 and his will instructed that £250,000 should be added to each trust.

When the first 10-year anniversary charge arrived in June 2025, the value of the property in each trust was:

Trust A (1 June 2025)	£340,000
Trust B (2 June 2025)	£340,000

There have been no exit charges.

Current rules

The IHT payable in connection with the 10-year anniversary charge on Trust A is calculated as follows:

	£
Christopher's chargeable transfers prior to Trust A	10,000
Add: Value of Trust A property on 1 June 2025	340,000
	350,000

IHT at lifetime rates on the value of Trust A's property is:

	£
On 10,000 – 325,000 = 315,000 @ 0%	–

On 325,000 – 350,000 = 25,000 @ 20% <u>5,000</u>

5,000

Thus:

5,000/340,000 x 100 = 1.471%

On the assumption that the 10-year anniversary charge is wholly ascribable to the addition on 1 January 2016 (ie the initial value settled is ignored), the number of quarters taken is 40 less the number of complete successive quarters prior to the addition – this comes to two, and so the fraction becomes 38/40ths.

The rate of IHT actually charged is:

1.471% x 30% x 38/40 = 0.419%

Therefore, the trustees of Trust A must settle a liability of 0.419% x £340,000 = £1,425.

The 10-year anniversary tax calculation for Trust B is taken to be the same, ie another £1,425.

Proposed alternative

The IHT payable in connection with the 10-year anniversary charge on Trust A is calculated as follows:

	£	£
Christopher's chargeable transfers prior to Trust A		10,000
Add: Value of Trust A property on 1 June 2025	340,000	
Value of same-day addition to Trust B	250,000	
Initial value of Trust B	10	
		<u>590,010</u>
		600,010

IHT at lifetime rates on the chargeable value for Trust A is:

	£
On 10,000 – 325,000 = 315,000 @ 0%	–
On 325,000 – 600,010 = 275,010 @ 20%	<u>55,002</u>
	55,002

Thus:

55,002/590,010 x 100 = 9.322%

Making a similar assumption to the previous calculation, the rate of IHT actually charged is:

9.322% x 30% x 38/40 = 2.657%

Therefore, the revised liability for the trustees of Trust A is 2.657% x £340,000 = £9,034, with the same sum being due from the trustees of Trust B, ie a more than six-fold increase.

Note that if Christopher had set up a single settlement then under the new rules the charge on the TYA would be:

	£
Total value of relevant property	680,000
IHT at lifetime rates:	
0 – £325,000	nil
excess £355,000 @ 20%	71,000

So the average rate is 71,000 / 680,000 = 10.44

And the rate charged is 10.44 x 30% = 3.13%

So that the tax payable is £680,000 x 3.13% = £21,284.

There may therefore still be an advantage in using more than one settlement (in this example, the saving is £21,284 – £18,068 = £3,216). The saving arises because under the SDA rules the two settlements are not aggregated: what happens is that the value of the property in Settlement B is taken at two different times (when set up and on the SDA) but increases in value are ignored.

The scope of section 81

3.81   When property is transferred from one settlement to another IHTA 1984, s 81 provides that it is to be treated for the purposes of the relevant property regime as remaining in the initial settlement.

Example 3.23

Sid puts property into a life interest trust (Trust 1) for his children in 2011 but the trustees have power to transfer all or any part of the trust fund into a qualifying settlement (defined as any settlement in which the children can benefit). In 2013 the trustees exercise this power to transfer the entire trust fund into a family discretionary trust (Trust 2) which Sid had set up in 2000.

The property is treated – for IHT purposes – as remaining comprised in the 2011 settlement. Hence the first 10-year charge will be in 2021, etc. Note that there is no such rule for other taxes so that the transfer may give rise to a CGT charge[140] whilst as a matter of trust law the assets will normally merge with whatever property is already in the 2000 settlement.

---

[140]   Hold-over relief will only be available if the property is a business asset within TCGA 1992 s 165. Hold-over relief is not available under s 260 because there is no IHT payable – the property is treated as remaining in the first settlement for IHT purposes.

4. BASIC PRINCIPLES OF CGT

3.82 CGT is charged on individuals resident in the UK, personal representatives and trustees who make a disposal of a chargeable asset.[141] 'Assets' are defined[142] as:

> 'All forms of property ... whether situated in the United Kingdom or not, including—
>
> (a)   options, debts and incorporeal property generally, and
> (b)   any currency other than sterling, and
>
> any form of property created by the person disposing of it, or otherwise coming to be owned without being acquired.'

Certain assets are not chargeable, including sterling,[143] National Savings Certificates, Premium Bonds, Save as You Earn deposits[144] and private motor vehicles.[145] Gains and losses on the disposal of PEPs and ISAs are disregarded. Certain gains are exempt from CGT.[146]

3.83   A 'disposal' is commonly the sale of an asset, but the term has a wide meaning and includes gifts and transfers into settlements[147] as well as part disposals. The Act extends the term to include situations where a capital sum is derived from assets,[148] the total loss or destruction of an asset,[149] and certain deemed disposals under settlements.[150] It therefore includes any transfer of a beneficial interest in property by one party to another, whether gratuitous or for value.

3.84   The chargeable gain is generally the difference between the sale price and the acquisition cost. Also deducted is expenditure on improvements to the asset and disposal expenses. Where, however, the sale is not for full market value or the transfer is by way of a gift, the chargeable gain is calculated with reference to the market value of the asset at the time of the gift and there is deemed to be a disposal at the price on that date. Conversely, the deemed disposal price is used as the acquisition cost when calculating the gains on a subsequent disposal of the asset by the donee.

Sales at an undervalue are gifts of the difference between the sale price and the market value. In the case of a sale at an undervalue, market value is substituted

---

[141]   TCGA 1992, s 1. FA 2015 has extended the charge to non-residents who dispose of UK residential property.
[142]   TCGA 1992, s 21.
[143]   TCGA 1992, s 21.
[144]   TCGA 1992, s 121.
[145]   TCGA 1992, s 263.
[146]   See 3.87.
[147]   TCGA 1992, s 70.
[148]   TCGA 1992, s 22.
[149]   TCGA 1992, s 24(1).
[150]   TCGA 1992, ss 71 and 72.

for the consideration on disposal. This is especially relevant in the case of disposals between 'connected persons'[151] which are presumed not to be at arm's length so that the onus is on the taxpayer to prove that the sale was for full market value. 'Connected persons' include spouses, civil partners, relatives and partners.[152]

Rates of tax

3.85 Unless entrepreneurs' relief was available[153] the rate of tax for tax year 2009–10 was 18% for individuals, personal representatives and trustees no matter how great the gain.[154] In tax year 2010–11 the rate remained at 18% for gains realised before 23 June 2010. For gains realised on or after that date, however, F(No 2)A 2010 introduced the following changes:

(a)   personal representatives and trustees pay CGT at 28%;

(b)   for individuals the rate remains 18% where total taxable gains *and income* are less than the upper limit of the income tax basic rate band (which is £31,786 for 2015–16). However, a 28% rate applies to gains or any part of a gain above that limit.

The 2010 changes involved using the taxpayer's income to fix the rate of CGT: for instance, a taxpayer with taxable income in excess of £34,370 in that year suffered CGT at 28% whereas one with no taxable income paid CGT at only 18% on the first £34,370 of chargeable gains.

Example 3.24

In 2014–15 Baffled has:

1. taxable income of £21,865 (after all deductions and personal allowances);

2. disposed of an asset in November 2014 with a gain of £26,000.

The CGT annual exemption is £11,000 and Baffled is not entitled to entrepreneurs' relief.[155]

Baffled should calculate his CGT liability as follows:

(i) Deduct the annual exemption against the gain (*viz* £26,000 – £11,000) leaving £15,000.

(ii) Tax the remaining gain:

1. as to £10,000 at 18%;[156]

2. as to £5,000 at 28%.

---

151   For definition see TCGA 1992, s 286.
152   See TCGA 1992, s 286.
153   See **3.86**.
154   Taper relief was abolished from 6 April 2008.
155   See **3.88**.
156   The basic rate threshold for 2014–15 is £31,865.

£5,000 excess gain	Limit of basic rate in 2014–15 £31,865
£10,000 gain	
Income £21,865	

Entrepreneurs' relief

3.86 This relief was introduced by FA 2008, s 9 and is contained in TCGA 1992, ss 169H–169R. When it applies, it reduces the rate of tax to 10%. Originally only the first £1m of gains made by individuals on the disposal of certain business assets (including shares in the family trading company) was eligible but this was extended to £2m by FA 2010; to £5m by F(No 2)A 2010 and to £10m by FA 2011. It is a lifetime limit. However, the effect of the changes is that a person who had used up his limit can find himself with relief available again. Note the timing of the increases:

(a) disposals before 6 June 2010, limit £1m;

(b) disposals after 5 April 2010, limit £2m (less any of the previous limit used up);

(c) disposals after 22 June 2010, limit £5m (less any of the previous limits used up);

(d) disposals after 5 April 2011, limit £10m (less any of the previous limits used up).

The relief has to be claimed and a person may decide not to claim it for a particular disposal (this is less relevant now that the relief has been increased to gains of up to £10m). It is not available to personal representatives but is available to trustees if there is a qualifying beneficiary (one who has an interest in possession in the whole of the settled property or the part of it which includes the business assets being disposed of) and who agrees to his relief being used by the trustees.

5. CGT EXEMPTIONS AND RELIEFS

3.87 Gains on the disposal of certain assets are exempt including:

(a) decorations for valour unless acquired for money or money's worth;[157]

(b) gilt-edged securities;[158]

---

[157] TCGA 1992, s 268.
[158] TCGA 1992, s 115.

(c)   ordinary shares in Venture Capital Trusts[159] and shares acquired under the Enterprise Investment Scheme.[160]

When heritage property is given or sold by private treaty to a charity or other national institution any gain will be exempt from CGT provided the Treasury so directs.[161] As in the case of IHT, gains on gifts of heritage property will be conditionally exempt provided the requisite undertakings are given as to maintenance, preservation and access.[162] Gains on any property accepted by the Treasury in satisfaction of IHT ('acceptance in lieu') are exempt from CGT.[163]

Annual exemption

3.88   Each tax year gains made by an individual up to a specified figure are exempt from tax.[164] For tax year 2014–15 the annual exemption is £11,000 and for 2015–16 £11,100. Personal representatives have the same exemption for the year of assessment which includes the date of death, and for the following 2 tax years. Thereafter personal representatives have no annual exemption. They should, therefore, claim time disposals so as to take advantage of the annual exemptions available in the first 3 tax years of the administration. Trustees have an annual exemption which is half that of an individual (unless the trust is for a vulnerable beneficiary when a full exemption is available or the settlor created more than one settlement, in which case the half annual exemption is divided among the trusts with a minimum of one-tenth of the full annual exemption per trust).

Chattels disposed of for £6,000 or less

3.89   If the amount or value of the consideration for an article or a set of articles is equal to or less than £6,000 at the time of disposal then, provided the asset being disposed of is tangible, movable property, no CGT is payable on any gain accruing on the disposal.[165]

Charities

3.90   Disposals to charities and by charities and certain national institutions are exempt from CGT.[166]

---

[159]   Now contained in ITA 2007, Part 6.
[160]   Now contained in ITA 2007, Part 5.
[161]   TCGA 1992, s 258(2).
[162]   TCGA 1992, s 258(3), (4).
[163]   TCGA 1992, s 258(2)(b).
[164]   TCGA 1992, s 3.
[165]   TCGA 1992, s 262.
[166]   TCGA 1992, s 257. When charities benefit under a will, PRs ought to consider vesting any asset to be sold in the charity rather than selling themselves and distributing the proceeds to the charity: see Chapter 14.

Life policies

3.91 Gains from the disposal of life insurance policies are exempt if the disposal is made by the original beneficial owner.[167] But if the person making the disposal is not the original beneficial owner and acquired the policy for value, the gain is chargeable.

Private dwelling houses[168]

3.92 The exemption in respect of a private dwelling house is one of the most important. It provides that a person's only or main residence may be disposed of, and the whole of any gain arising is exempt from CGT. The exemption includes the garden and grounds of up to 0.5 hectares or such larger area as is required for the reasonable enjoyment of the dwelling house. Provided that the dwelling house is covered by the exemption, a gain made on the disposal of part of the grounds or garden is also exempt from CGT where the house itself is retained. If a dwelling house is to be sold separately from part of its grounds, the grounds should always be sold first to take advantage of the exemption.[169]

Qualifying residence

3.93 For relief to be available, the dwelling house in question must have been the individual's only or main residence throughout the period of ownership, except that a final period may be disregarded. For tax years 2013–14 and earlier this was 3 years but the Finance Act 2014 reduced this to 18 months.[170]

While it is usually apparent whether particular property has been used as the main dwelling house of the individual, or forms part of it, this is not always the case. When there is more than one residence, the taxpayer should nominate his main residence.[171]

Where a dwelling house has been occupied as a main residence for part only of the individual's ownership (after March 1982) then only a corresponding proportion of any gain is exempt. The taxpayer is entitled to have periods of absence disregarded if the absence was necessitated by employment – provided the house was his main residence before and after each such period of absence.

Where the whole or part of the property has been let as residential accommodation, this may result in a partial loss of the exemption. However, the gain attributable to the letting (calculated according to how much was let and for how long) is exempt up to the lesser of £40,000 and the exemption attributable to the owner's occupation. This relief does not apply if the let

---

[167] TCGA 1992, s 210.
[168] See also the authors' *A Modern Approach to Lifetime Tax Planning*, Chapter 31.
[169] See *Varty v Lynes* [1976] 1 WLR 1091.
[170] Except in the case of a taxpayer who is in a nursing home, where the period remains 3 years.
[171] See **3.94**.

portion forms a separate dwelling.[172] HMRC have stated that taking in a lodger does not result in loss of the exemption provided the lodger lives as part of the family and shares living accommodation.[173]

Nomination of main residence

3.94 Where a taxpayer has more than one residence, he may nominate which is to be his main residence for CGT purposes. Spouses and civil partners who live together may only nominate one residence between them.[174] The nomination must be made within 2 years of acquiring a further residence and can be backdated for up to 2 years to the date when the further residence was acquired. Once made, it can be varied at any time and the variation backdated for up to 2 years.[175] An election is frequently varied when a second home to be sold to gain the benefit of the exemption for the last 3 years (now 18 months) of ownership.

> *Example 3.25*
>
> Devious purchases a buy to let flat in Putney on 1 January 2011. After 2 years he occupies the property himself as his residence and elects for it to be his main residence. After a further 6 months he sells. The gain is wholly covered by PPR relief. See CGTM 64510:
>
> > 'Two or more residences: Variation of a notice [May 2010]
> >
> > A notice given under TCGA 1992/222(5) can be varied by a further notice at any time. The further notice can be backdated to be effective from up to two years from the date that it was given.
> >
> > A variation will often be made when a disposal of a residence is in prospect or the disposal has already been made and the individual making the disposal wishes to secure the final period exemption. See CG64985+.
> >
> > For example, where an individual with two residences validly nominates house A, they may vary that nomination to house B at any time. The variation can then be varied back to house A within a short space of time. This will enable the individual to obtain the benefit of the final period exemption on house B with a loss of only a small proportion of relief of on house A.'

FA 2015 changes to the nomination

3.95 In the 2013 Autumn Statement the Chancellor announced that he would charge capital gains tax on gains made by non-residents disposing of UK

---

[172] TCGA 1992, s 223(4).
[173] SP14/80 and CGTM, para 64702.
[174] TCGA 1992, s 222(6).
[175] TCGA 1992, s 222(5) and see *Griffin v Craig-Harvey* [1994] STC 54.

residential property. In March 2014 he published a Consultation Paper[176] on possible ways of achieving this. The following appeared at 3.3 of the Consultation Paper:

> 'Under the current system an individual with more than one residence can choose, for any given period, which of those properties they would like to qualify for PRR. They do this by notifying HMRC of their election. CGT is then due on gains relating to the other residences they own, irrespective of whether it is their main residence. Bringing non-residents into CGT without any changes could mean that non-residents invariably chose to nominate their UK residence as their main residence and obtain tax relief on gains made on that property, even where it was not in fact their main residence, yet not pay any UK CGT on gains relating to their other residences outside of the UK. This would undermine the extension of CGT to non-residents.'

With this in mind, the government considered removing the nomination rules to allow the relief only on a property which could be demonstrated to be the taxpayer's main residence.

3.96 In the event, it remains possible to make a nomination after 5 April 2015 but a residence will only be eligible for relief if:

(a) the person making the disposal was tax resident in the same territory as the property for that tax year; *or*

(b) if not resident in the territory, the person spent at least 90 midnights in the property (or in other properties in the same territory) in that tax year.

The change will affect UK residents with a holiday home abroad but not with a number of properties only in the UK.

Trustees

3.97 Section 225 extends the private residence exemption to trustees disposing of a dwelling house which has been the only or main residence of a person entitled to occupy it under the terms of the settlement during the trustees' period of ownership.

The exemption applies to life tenants, and in *Sansom v Peay*[177] the court held that it was also available where a beneficiary occupied a property held on discretionary trusts even though occupation was a matter for the trustees' discretion. The width of this exemption means that it does not matter that the beneficiary occupies by virtue of a lease with the freehold interest being held on separate trusts: see **5.29**.

---

[176] *Implementing a capital gains tax charge on non-residents.* The relevant legislation is in FA 2015.

[177] [1976] 1 WLR 1073, [1976] 3 All ER 375.

Spouses and civil partners

3.98 Husbands and wives and civil partners are each entitled to a full annual exemption, and are taxed separately on their own gains. Where assets are transferred from one party to a marriage or civil partnership to the other, they are treated as disposed of for a consideration which produces neither a gain nor a loss.[178] Thus the exemption cannot be used to 'uplift' the acquisition cost, but if the 'donee' spouse receives the property by reason of the death of the other, there is the usual 'uplift' on death. Assets can therefore be freely transferred between spouses and civil partners without any charge to CGT. When the donee spouse or civil partner sells the asset, the entire gain since the asset was acquired by the donor spouse or civil partner becomes chargeable.

3.99 The special treatment of disposals between spouses and civil partners applies only where the parties were living together in the year of assessment in which the disposal was made. If the parties have separated and the disposal is made in the following tax year, the no gain/no loss rule does not apply. Transfers between cohabitees do not benefit from the no gain/no loss provision.

Hold-over relief

3.100 Hold-over relief allows an election to be made not to pay CGT at the time of making a gift but instead to 'hold over' the gain, ie to defer payment of the tax. The effect is that the donee is deemed to acquire the property at the acquisition cost of the donor, and is therefore liable for tax, when he sells the property, on the whole gain from the date when the donor acquired the property. If the donee makes a disposal by way of a gift, a further election to hold over the gain may be made. If the donee dies still owning the property, the uplift on death means that the tax held-over never becomes payable. The election must be made jointly by the transferor and transferee except in the case of a transfer into settlement where the transferor alone elects.

3.101 There are two provisions which allow hold-over relief:

(a) *under TCGA 1992, s 165*: gains can normally be held over on a gift or transfer of business assets to an individual or a trust, but not on a transfer of shares or securities to a company;

(b) *under TCGA 1992, s 260*: gains can normally be held over where the transfer is a chargeable transfer for IHT purposes. Thus, after 22 March 2006, lifetime transfers to settlements other than those for the disabled and disposals from such trusts to beneficiaries can qualify for hold-over relief, as they do not qualify as potentially exempt transfers. Disposals from A&M trusts, bereaved minor trusts and bereaved young person trusts also attract hold-over relief under s 260.

---

[178] TCGA 1992, s 58.

3.102 The relief is not available on a settlement of assets if the settlement is 'settlor-interested', ie if any property is or may become used for the benefit of:

(a)   the settlor;

(b)   the settlor's spouse or civil partner;

(c)   a minor child or stepchild of the settlor who is unmarried and does not have a civil partner.[179]

Note, however, that hold-over relief may be available when property ceases to be comprised in a settlor-interested trust.

Non-residents

3.103 CGT is generally charged only on individuals who are resident in the UK,[180] so it used to be possible for taxpayers to avoid the tax by moving abroad and making the disposal in a tax year in which they were not resident in the UK. However, TCGA 1992, s 10A[181] now provides that an individual who leaves the UK is liable to CGT on subsequently realising assets owned before departure if:

(a)   he has been resident in the UK for any part of at least 4 out of the 7 years before departure; and

(b)   he becomes non-resident for a period of less than 5 years.

An individual who has been resident in the UK for 4 of the previous 7 years would therefore have to be prepared to become non-resident for at least 5 years to take advantage of the exemption. If the individual does move abroad, he should delay the disposal until the tax year following his departure. Although concession D2 provides that the individual will not be charged to CGT on disposals after the day of departure, the concession cannot be relied on for the purposes of tax avoidance.

3.104 The residence status of individuals is now governed by the statutory residence test ('SRT').[182]

6. DEATH AND CGT

3.105 Death is not a disposal by the deceased to his personal representatives and there is therefore no charge to CGT. Instead, the personal representatives are deemed to acquire the deceased's assets at the date of his death at market

---

[179]   TCGA 1992, s 169F(3A), (4A) and (4B). The extension to cover minor children was introduced by FA 2006 and applies to disposals made on or after 6 April 2006.

[180]   FA 2015 introduced a charge on the disposal of UK residential property by a non-resident.

[181]   Added by FA 1998, s 27.

[182]   FA 2013 Schs 45 and 46. For HMRC Guidance, see RDR 3 (December 2013).

value.[183] Where assets have increased in value since their acquisition by the deceased, this 'death uplift' may save a considerable amount of tax. If personal representatives sell property of the estate, the chargeable gain is calculated by deducting from the sale price the deemed acquisition cost at death and any allowable subsequent expenditure and disposal costs incurred by the personal representatives.

3.106   If the personal representatives transfer assets to the beneficiaries, there is no disposal for CGT purposes and the beneficiaries are deemed to acquire the assets at the market value at the date of the deceased's death.[184]

There is no disposal for CGT purposes when property passes under a *donatio mortis causa*, a nomination or by survivorship in the case of joint property, but again the recipient is deemed to have acquired the property at the market value at the time of the deceased's death.

> *Example 3.26*
>
> 1. Included in T's estate on his death in November 2014 is a rare first edition of *Finnegan's Wake* that T had acquired in 1990 for £10,000. It is worth £100,000 at death. The gain of £90,000 is not chargeable on T's death. Instead his PRs acquire the book at a new base value of £100,000.
>
> 2. Alternatively, T was the life tenant of a pre-22 March 2006 interest in possession trust and the book had been given to the trust by his mother in 1989 with the benefit of a hold-over claim. The gain held over was £20,000. On T's death the held-over gain of £20,000 becomes chargeable and only the balance of the gain (70,000) is wiped out on death (see TCGA 1992, s 74). However it is possible to make another hold-over claim to avoid paying tax on the £20,000 gain if T's death results in an IHT chargeable transfer.

3.107   Personal representatives are liable to CGT even if the beneficiaries of the estate would not be; for example, where they are UK charities. In the case of gains realised on or after 23 June 2010 personal representatives pay tax at 28% whereas beneficiaries may pay at 18%. It is, therefore, important that personal representatives consider whether a tax saving can be achieved by transferring assets which have risen in value to beneficiaries rather than making the sale themselves. Rather than transferring legal title, it is possible to assent assets to beneficiaries and then make the sale on their behalf. HMRC requires evidence of the assent and of the approval of the beneficiary for the sale.[185]

See **Precedent 13.7.**

3.108   Capital losses (calculated in the same way as gains) can be set off against gains realised in the same year of assessment, and any excess losses may be carried forward to the following year. Losses realised by personal representatives cannot be transferred to beneficiaries under the will, so there

---

[183]   TCGA 1992, s 62(1).
[184]   TCGA 1992, s 62(4).
[185]   See further **14.07** *et seq.*

will be cases where it is preferable to vest the loss making asset in the beneficiary and let the beneficiary make the disposal. Personal representatives have an annual exemption equal to that of an individual in the tax year of death and the following 2 tax years. After that period, no further exemption is available and gains are charged at the full 28% rate.

Losses of the deceased can be carried back and set against gains realised by him in the 3 tax years preceding the tax year of death taking later years before earlier years.[186]

7. SETTLEMENTS AND CGT

3.109 'Settlement' is not defined in the legislation, but there is the following definition of settled property:[187]

> 'any property held in trust other than property to which section 60 applies and references, however expressed, to property comprised in a settlement, are references to settled property.'

Thus, references to property comprised in a settlement are to be construed as references to settled property.

3.110 Where assets are held by a person or persons as nominee for another, or as bare trustee for another or others, or as trustee for someone who would be absolutely entitled as against the trustee but for infancy or other disability, TCGA 1992, s 60 provides that the property is not settled property and is treated as if belonging to the beneficiary.

Example 3.27

Tim and Tom hold 1,000 shares in DNC Ltd on trust for Bertram, aged 26, absolutely. This is a bare trust since Bertram is solely entitled to the shares and can at any time bring the trust to an end.[188] The shares are treated as belonging to Bertram so that a disposal of those shares by the trustees is treated as being by Bertram and any transfer from the trustees to Bertram is ignored.

Example 3.28

1. Topsy and Tim hold property for Alex absolutely, aged 9. Because of his age Alex cannot demand the property from the trustees and the trust is not simple or bare. Alex is, however, a person who would be absolutely entitled but for his infancy and he is (for CGT purposes) treated as owning the assets in the fund.

---

[186] TCGA 1992, s 62(2). For a negligible value claim made by executors in respect of a period before the deceased's death, see *Drown and Leadley (Exors of Leadley dec'd) v RCC* [2014] UKFTT 892 (TC).

[187] TCGA 1992, s 68 as amended by FA 2006.

[188] See *Saunders v Vautier* (1841) 4 Beav 115. For a recent illustration where beneficiaries together absolutely entitled prevented a sale of a controlling shareholding held by the trustees, see *Hughes v Bourne* [2012] EWHC 2232 (Ch).

2. Teddy and Tiger hold property on trust for Noddy, aged 9, contingent upon his attaining the age of 18. At first sight it would seem that there is no material difference between this settlement and that considered in (1) above since, in both, the beneficiary would be absolutely entitled were it not for his infancy. Noddy, however, is not entitled to claim the fund from the trustees. Unlike (1) above, Noddy's entitlement is contingent upon living to a certain age, so that, were he to ask the trustees to give him the property, they would refuse because he has not satisfied the contingency. This distinction would be more obvious if the settlement provided that the contingency to be satisfied by Noddy was the attaining of (say) 21.[189] The property in Noddy's settlement is, therefore, settled for the purposes of CGT.

Example 3.29

1. Bill and Ben purchase Blackacre as tenants in common in equal shares. The land is held on a trust of land, but for the purposes of CGT the property is not settled and is treated as belonging to Bill and Ben equally.[190]

2. Mr T and his family hold 72% of the issued share capital in T Ltd (their family company). They enter into a written agreement as a result of which the shares are transferred to trustees and detailed restrictions, akin to pre-emption provisions in private company articles, are imposed. The beneficial interests of Mr T and his family are not, however, affected. Subsequently the shares are transferred out again to the various settlors. In such a 'pooling arrangement' the shares will be treated as nominee property with the result that there is no disposal for CGT purposes on the creation of the trust nor on its termination.[191]

3. Thal and Tal hold property on trust for Larry for life, remainder to Renata absolutely. Both are adult. Although Larry and Renata are, in common parlance, jointly entitled to claim the fund from the trustees, they are not 'jointly absolutely entitled' within the meaning of s 60. The property is settled for CGT purposes.

Creation of the settlement

3.111 When a settlement is created by a lifetime transfer, there is a disposal by the settlor/donor to the trustees at market value which may give rise to a charge to CGT. If the trusts are created on death, by will or intestacy, there is no disposal and the trustees are deemed to acquire the settled assets at their market value at the date of the testator's death.

Actual disposals by trustees

3.112 A sale of settled assets by trustees may give rise to a charge on the gain, being the difference between the consideration on sale and the acquisition cost (or deemed acquisition cost), taking into account any allowable costs. Trustees have an annual exemption which is half that of an individual (if the settlor

---

[189]   See *Tomlinson v Glyns Executor and Trustee Co* [1970] Ch 112, [1970] 1 All ER 381.
[190]   *Kidson v MacDonald* [1974] Ch 339, [1974] 1 All ER 849.
[191]   *Booth v Ellard* [1980] 3 All ER 569, [1980] STC 555 and see *Jenkins v Brown* and *Warrington v Sterland* [1989] STC 577 in which a similar result was arrived at in the case of a pooling of family farms.

created more than one settlement, the exemption is divided among the group of settlements, with a minimum of one-tenth of the full annual exemption).

The rate of CGT paid by trustees is 28%.

Deemed disposal when beneficiary becomes absolutely entitled

3.113 When a person becomes absolutely entitled as against the trustees to all or any part of the settled property, there is a deemed disposal of that property by the trustees. The person becoming absolutely entitled will normally be a beneficiary but could be another body of trustees if the property is resettled.[192] CGT is chargeable on any increase in value between the acquisition by the trustees and the deemed disposal.[193]

3.114 When a beneficiary becomes absolutely entitled on the death of a beneficiary with a qualifying interest in possession, there is normally no charge to CGT. Instead the beneficiary is deemed to acquire the property at its market value at the date of becoming absolutely entitled.[194] However, if the settlor held over gains when he transferred property into the settlement, the held over gain is not wiped out on the death of the beneficiary with the interest in possession. It becomes chargeable.[195]

3.115 Where the interest in possession was created on or after 22 March 2006, the tax free death uplift provisions apply only if the interest terminating is 'qualifying' for IHT purposes, ie:

(a)   an immediate post-death interest;[196] or

(b)   a transitional serial interest;[197] or

(c)   somewhat anomalously an interest in possession in a trust for a bereaved minor.[198]

In other cases there is a deemed disposal if a beneficiary becomes absolutely entitled on the ending of the interest in possession, with a consequent charge on any increase in the value of the trust property. If no beneficiary becomes absolutely entitled so that the trusts continue, there is no disposal and no charge.

---

[192] See **2.60** *et seq.*

[193] This is an 'exit charge': TCGA 1992, s 71. Hold-over relief may be available to postpone the charge: see **3.83**.

[194] TCGA 1992, s 72(1). For the meaning of a qualifying interest in possession, see **3.54**.

[195] TCGA 1992, s 74, subject to the possible availability of hold-over relief.

[196] See Chapter 6.

[197] See **3.59**.

[198] See Chapter 7.

When does a person become absolutely entitled?

3.116   Section 60(2) of TCGA 1992 provides that a person is absolutely entitled as against the trustee where that person has:

> 'the exclusive right, subject only to satisfying any outstanding charge, lien or other right of the trustees to resort to the property for payment of duty, taxes, costs or other outgoings, to direct how that asset shall be dealt with.'[199]

Often this is obvious. For example if trustees are holding property for a beneficiary contingent on reaching 25, the beneficiary becomes absolutely entitled on reaching 25. However, there are two situations which can cause difficulties:

(a)   Where trustees exercise a power to settle property on new trusts, it may not be immediately apparent whether there has been a modification of the existing trusts or the creation of a completely different settlement. Ideally the trustees will have carefully considered whether or not a deemed disposal is beneficial and made it clear which power they are using and in what way. For a discussion of advances and appointments see **2.44** *et seq*.

(b)   The effect of the decision in *Crowe v Appleby*[200] can mean that a beneficiary who appears to be absolutely entitled is not. In some cases, a beneficiary cannot claim a share of a trust fund if the effect of distributing one share will be to damage the interests of the other beneficiaries. In *Crowe v Appleby* the principle was applied to land.

Example 3.30

Trustees are holding land for the three children of the settlor contingent on reaching 25 and if more than one in equal shares. The eldest child reaches 25 but cannot call for her one-third share and the settlement of the land will continue until all three children reach 25 or die under that age.

3.117   The principle of *Crowe v Appleby* may apply to other indivisible assets. HMRC say:[201]

> 'In *Stephenson v Barclays Bank Trust Co Ltd*, Walton J said that as regards shares in a private company in very special circumstances, and possibly mortgage debts, the person with a vested interest in a share of the property might have to wait for sale before he could call upon the trustees to account to him for his share. The principle of *Crowe v Appleby* therefore may apply to other indivisible assets. A good example would be an Old Master painting or valuable antique, or indeed a single share in a company.'

---

[199]   See *McLaughlin v RCC* [2012] UKFTT 174 (TC).
[200]   [1975] 3 All ER 529.
[201]   CGTM para 37560.

HMRC's view is that the principle also applies where trustees have an express power to appropriate as this prevents beneficiaries having a right to call for specific assets. The CGT Manual says:[202]

> 'If the trustees have an express power to decide which assets should go to a beneficiary in satisfaction of his or her beneficial interest, no beneficiary should be regarded as having become absolutely entitled to the appropriate share of any such assets until the last contingency is fulfilled. For these purposes the statutory power of appropriation given to personal representatives should be disregarded because it no longer applies once the administration of the estate is completed and they then hold as trustees rather than as personal representatives.'[203]

See **Precedent 13.8** being a resolution to transfer assets to a beneficiary (under an advancement-type power) which creates an immediate bare trust so that even though the assets may not yet have been transferred the beneficiary becomes absolutely entitled.

8. INCOME TAX AND PERSONAL REPRESENTATIVES

3.118 Personal representatives must separate the income of the deceased from the income of the administration period. For 2015–16 individuals pay income tax as follows:

Rate	2015–16	
Starting rate for savings	0%	(basic and higher rate taxpayers only)
Basic rate	20%	Dividends 10%
Higher rate	40%	Dividends 32.5%
Additional rate	45%	Dividends 37.5%

The administration period starts with the day after the date of death and continues until the completion of the administration of the estate.[204] It is generally accepted that completion of the administration occurs on the date when the residue is ascertained for distribution.[205]

3.119 Income which is *due* before the death is part of the deceased's income (for example, a dividend on shares due and payable on a date before death) even if paid after death. Income which is *due* after the death is income of the estate (eg a dividend due and payable after death or interest which becomes due and payable on a date after the death). The Apportionment Act 1870 provided for the apportionment of income on a day-to-day basis for the purposes of

---

[202] CGTM para 37530.
[203] For the power of appropriation, see **2.67** *et seq*. There will be cases where it is desirable to keep the settlement in being so as to avoid the CGT exit charge.
[204] ITTOIA 2005, s 653.
[205] See **13.02**.

distribution[206] did not apply for income tax purposes.[207] Limited income tax relief is available where income received after death has been apportioned for IHT purposes and some of that income has been included as an asset of the estate at death attracting IHT.[208]

3.120   Personal representatives cannot claim personal allowances since these are available only to individuals. They can deduct interest on a loan (but not an overdraft) to pay IHT when calculating the taxable income of the estate but only in so far as the loan is to pay tax on personalty vesting in the personal representatives. Further, this interest is only deducible for 12 months. Other expenses incurred when administering the estate are not deductible.

3.121   The rate of tax paid by personal representatives is determined by the type of income which they receive. They do not pay tax at the higher or additional rates irrespective of the amount of income they receive:

(a)   *Dividends*: they are only liable to tax at 10% and so the tax credit they receive with the dividend discharges their liability.

(b)   *Interest*: they will pay at the basic rate unless the non-dividend income does not exceed the limit of the starting rate band. Interest is normally received net of 20% tax so they will either have no further liability or be entitled to a refund.

(c)   *Other income*: this will be assessed to basic rate tax applying the rules relevant to the particular type of income. So, for example, if the deceased was carrying on a business which the personal representatives continue, the profits during the administration period form part of the assessable income of the personal representatives as trading income.[209]

3.122   The residence status of the personal representatives determines the status of the estate for income tax purposes.[210] The residence status of the deceased is irrelevant. If all the personal representatives are resident in the UK, then the estate is UK-resident. On the other hand, if none of the personal representatives is UK-resident, then the estate is non-UK-resident. If the personal representatives have mixed residence, the residence of the deceased acts as a 'tie-breaker'. If the deceased was UK-resident or domiciled then all of the estate is UK-resident. If not, the estate is non-resident. As with individuals, if the estate is not UK-resident, personal representatives are only assessable on income arising in the UK.[211]

---

[206]   Apportionment Act 1870, s 1. Note that the Trusts (Capital and Income) Act 2013, s 1 removed the statutory apportionment rules (as well as the equitable apportionment rules) for trusts created or arising on or after 1 October 2013.

[207]   *IRC v Henderson's Executors* [1931] SC 681.

[208]   ITTOIA 2005, s 669.

[209]   Under ITTOIA 2005, Part 2.

[210]   Contrast CGT where PRs have the residence and domicile of the deceased.

[211]   ITA 2007, s 834 and ITTOIA 2005, s 651.

Beneficiaries

3.123 Beneficiaries are assessed to income tax on their share of the estate income, grossed up by reference to the rate at which the personal representatives have paid income tax. If requested, personal representatives must provide a written statement of the amount of residuary income paid to residuary beneficiaries in any year of assessment and the tax paid on it.[212]

Non-residuary legatees

3.124 Legatees may be entitled to a specific legacy or to a pecuniary or general legacy.

(a) *Specific legatees*

Income arising from property which is the subject of a specific disposition by the will belongs to the beneficiary from the date of death, subject to anything in the will to the contrary. Any income arising after death will belong to the beneficiary and when it is paid to him will form part of his estate income. The income received must be grossed up at the appropriate rate and included in the beneficiary's tax return for the year of receipt. The beneficiary has a credit for tax paid by the personal representatives.

(b) *Pecuniary and general legatees*

Such legatees may be entitled to be paid interest on the value of their legacies (normally to compensate them for late payment). Generally interest is payable from 12 months after death but this is a general rule which can be varied by the terms of the will. Vested legacies payable at a future date carry interest from that date and not before. The date may be fixed or dependent on an uncertain event.[213] The question of the legatees' liability to income tax on such interest then arises. In the case of interest, tax is only payable on sums actually received. Thus, if a beneficiary disclaims entitlement to interest payable to him on a pecuniary or general legacy or the personal representatives cannot pay it, he is not liable to tax[214] (unless a sum has been specifically set aside to pay the legacy in which case tax must be paid even if the legatee fails to draw the interest).[215] If interest is paid to the beneficiary it is taxed as savings income in his hands.[216] Payment will be made gross (ie without deduction of any tax).

---

[212] ITTOIA 2005, s 682A(1).

[213] The rate of interest is set by CPR, Pt 40, Practice Direction – Accounts, Inquiries etc, para 15 as the basic rate payable on funds in court; a table of rates is available from the website of the Court Funds Office: http://www.justice.gov.uk/downloads/guidance/protecting-the-vulnerable/court-funds-office/investments-and-interest-rates/rate_changes2009.doc; see **Appendix I.**

[214] *Dewar v IRC* [1935] 2 KB 351.

[215] *Spens v IRC* [1970] 1 WLR 1173.

[216] Under ITTOIA 2005, s 369.

Residuary beneficiaries

3.125 The rules relating to residuary beneficiaries are themselves subdivided into those which relate to beneficiaries with:

(a) limited interests;
(b) absolute interests;
(c) discretionary interests;
(d) successive interests,

in the residue of the estate. Where there are different interests in different parts of the residue, each part is treated as a separate estate.[217] Residuary beneficiaries are charged to tax on their share of the residuary income of the estate. Broadly speaking the income on which residuary beneficiaries may be taxed is their share of the 'aggregate income' of the estate less various deductions set out in ITTOIA 2005, s 666 such as:

(a) interest (other than interest on unpaid IHT);
(b) higher rate income tax relief available under ITTOIA 2005, s 669 where income of the estate has been included in the calculation of IHT; and
(c) management expenses which are properly chargeable to income under the general law (as opposed to under a direction in the will).

Aggregate income is income of the estate which is chargeable to income tax less allowable deductions and excluding income to which a specific legatee is entitled.[218]

3.126 Amounts treated as income of the beneficiary are 'grossed up' at the basic rate, savings rate or dividend ordinary rate, as applicable for the tax year of receipt. The estate income is then treated as having borne income tax at that rate or rates. In determining the rate applicable, it is assumed *first* that amounts are paid to beneficiaries out of the different parts of the aggregate income of the estate in such proportions as are just and reasonable for their different interests, and *secondly* that payments are made from those parts bearing tax at the basic rate before they are made from those parts bearing tax at the dividend ordinary rate.[219]

Beneficiary with a limited interest

3.127 A beneficiary who is entitled to income but not to capital has a limited interest[220] (eg a person who has a life interest in residue). All sums received by the beneficiary will be liable to income tax in the year of receipt. In the final tax

---

[217] ITTOIA 2005, s 649(4).
[218] ITTOIA 2005, s 664.
[219] ITTOIA 2005, s 679.
[220] ITTOIA 2005, s 650(3).

year of the administration, the beneficiary is assessed on all receipts before the end of the administration period plus any amounts payable to him at the end of the administration period.[221]

In the case of income received by the personal representatives gross, they will deduct basic rate tax and pay it to HMRC on behalf of the beneficiary. In the case of savings and dividend income the personal representatives will themselves have received the income net of tax or with a tax credit and so will not have to make any further deduction. The beneficiary is liable to tax on income received in each tax year and will gross up the income at the appropriate rate and then deduct the tax credits.

3.128 Because income is taxed in the year in which the beneficiary receives it, personal representatives should ideally ascertain the income tax position of the beneficiary. In the case of a taxpayer who is liable at 45% throughout the administration, the date of the receipt will be irrelevant in terms of the amount of tax paid. However, a basic rate taxpayer, who receives several years' worth of estate income in one lump sum may be pushed into higher rates unnecessarily.

Beneficiary with an absolute interest

3.129 A beneficiary has an absolute interest in residue if the capital is properly payable to him, or would be so payable if the residue had been ascertained.[222] Such a beneficiary is entitled to both income and capital; but income tax is, of course, only payable on income receipts. Therefore, when a beneficiary receives a distribution from the estate it is necessary to distinguish income from capital receipts.

All payments to the beneficiary are treated as income up to the level of his 'assumed income entitlement' for the tax year in question. 'Assumed income entitlement' is the beneficiary's share of the residuary income for all the years of the administration in which he had the interest less income tax at the appropriate rate and any payments already made to him.[223]

For the year in which the administration period ends (the 'final tax year'), income is treated as arising if the beneficiary has an assumed income entitlement for the year (whether or not any payments are made).

Payments to a beneficiary of an estate are deemed to be made out of his share of income bearing tax at the basic rate in priority to his share of income bearing tax at the savings rate.

Again, so far as is practicable, personal representatives should discuss with the residuary beneficiary the strategy for making payments. It may be possible for

---

[221] ITTOIA 2005, s 654(3).
[222] ITTOIA 2005, s 650(2).
[223] ITTOIA 2005, s 665.

the beneficiary to avoid paying higher rate tax on the estate income in certain tax years if payments can be suitably staggered.

Beneficiary with a discretionary interest

3.130　A person has a discretionary interest in all or part of the residue of an estate if a discretion may be exercised in his favour and (if the residue had been ascertained at the beginning of the administration period) on the exercise of the discretion any of the income of the residue would be properly payable to him.[224] The person in whose favour the discretion is exercised is charged to income tax on the total payments made in a tax year in exercise of the discretion, grossed up, where appropriate.[225]

Successive interests

3.131　Special rules apply to the calculation of estate income where there are two or more successive absolute or limited interests during the period of administration.[226]

9. INCOME TAX AND TRUSTEES

Calculating the taxable income

3.132　The income of trustees is calculated in the same way as for an individual.[227] Thus if the trustees are carrying on a trade, the income derived from the trade is assessed in accordance with the provisions of ITTOIA 2005 and they can deduct allowable business expenses. They cannot deduct trust management expenses.[228]

Rates of tax payable by trustees

3.133　Having calculated the income of the trust, the trustees are in general liable to pay income tax at the basic or dividend ordinary rate on the rest of the trust income without the deduction of personal reliefs (which are only available to individuals). Trustees are not liable to higher or additional rate tax regardless of the amount of the income. However, trustees of some types of trust are liable at the trust or dividend trust rate.[229]

Much of the trust income will already have borne tax at basic or dividend ordinary rate and the trustees will, therefore, only have a liability to pay tax on income received gross.

---

[224] ITTOIA 2005, s 650(3).
[225] ITTOIA 2005, s 655.
[226] See ITTOIA 2005, ss 671–676.
[227] By applying the rules set out in Chapter 3 of Part 2 of ITA 2007.
[228] *Aikin v MacDonald's Trustees* (1894) 2 SLT 317, IH (1 Div).
[229] See **3.134**.

The trust and dividend trust rates

3.134 Section 479 of ITA 2007 requires trustees[230] who have income which must be accumulated or which is payable at their discretion or the discretion of some other person to pay tax at the trust or dividend trust rate on trust income in excess of the first £1,000. The section does not apply to income of an estate of a deceased person during the administration of the estate. Once distributed by the personal representatives to the trustees, it is income in their hands and will be subject to the s 479 charge with a tax credit for the tax paid by the personal representatives.

The trust rate is 45% for 2015–16; the dividend trust rate is 37.5%. These rates are payable on all income in excess of £1,000, and are difficult to justify when compared with the levels of income on which individuals pay higher and additional rates. Income which is accumulated suffers the loss of tax but where income is paid to beneficiaries who are basic rate taxpayers (or who do not pay tax), the beneficiaries can recover tax (see **3.138**). Where trustees have power to distribute accumulated income as if it were income of the current year either under TA 1925, s 31 or under an express power in the trust instrument, it is considered that the payment will be treated as an income payment allowing the beneficiary to reclaim tax, if appropriate.

3.135 The trust and dividend trust rates are not payable on income properly used to pay trust expenses. Whether an expense is 'properly' chargeable to income is a question of general law not the terms of the particular trust instrument.[231] Expenses must be set against capital not income to the extent that they are incurred for the benefit of the whole trust fund.[232] In *RCC v Trustees of Peter Clay Discretionary Trust*[233] the taxpayers contended that, where a particular expense of managing the trust related partly to income, that expense could and should be apportioned fairly between income and capital; so that part of the expense was attributed to income. The Court of Appeal said it was 'beyond argument' that an expense is incurred 'for the benefit of the whole estate' when the purpose or object for which that expense is incurred is to confer benefit both on the income beneficiaries and on those entitled to capital on the determination of the income trusts. Earlier authority made it clear that expenses which are of that nature are to be charged against capital only. However, the rule is not all or nothing. Apportionment is possible:

> 'if it can be shown that an identified or identifiable part of an expense is for work carried out for the benefit of the income beneficiaries alone, then that part is properly chargeable to income.'[234]

---

[230] Other than trustees of trusts for charitable purposes.
[231] *Carver v Duncan* [1985] AC 1082.
[232] *Carver v Duncan* [1985] AC 1082.
[233] [2008] EWCA Civ 1441.
[234] Adopted by Sir John Chadwick as a correct statement of the law at para 31.

The onus of showing that an element of an expense relates to income rests on the trustees. In the absence of time, records and minutes of what was considered at each trustees' meetings, it will be almost impossible to establish a basis for apportionment.[235]

Trustees' liability under ITA 2007, s 496

3.136 Section 495 of ITA 2007 provides that trustees who make a discretionary payment to a beneficiary are to be treated as making a payment all of which has borne tax at the trust rate (45% for 2015–16). They will provide beneficiaries with a certificate of deduction of income tax at 45%.[236] To the extent that the beneficiaries are not 45% taxpayers, they can recover tax from HMRC. The trustees, of course, have not paid tax at 45% on the first £1,000 of trust income nor on dividend income, There may, therefore, be a mismatch between the tax treated as paid under s 495 and the tax actually paid.

Section 496 of ITA 2007 provides that when the trustees make a distribution they will be assessed on the difference between the tax treated as paid and the tax actually paid. This may be satisfied by tax credits available in the trust's tax pool. The tax pool consists of tax actually paid by the trustees plus any recoverable tax credits.[237] Trusts which have been in existence for many years and which have accumulated income will have substantial tax pools. Others may have little or nothing in their tax pool in which case they will have to pay the s 496 charge with cash. Accordingly trustees need to consider their liability under s 496 when deciding how much income to distribute.

Beneficiaries with a right to income

3.137 A beneficiary with a right to income (an interest in possession beneficiary) is entitled to receive all the trust income less trust expenses. Expenses are set first against income taxed at the dividend ordinary rate and then against income taxed at basic rate.[238]

The income paid to the beneficiary retains its original nature and is included on the beneficiary's tax return under the appropriate heading grossed up at basic or dividend ordinary rate. The beneficiary receives a certificate of deduction of income tax at basic or dividend ordinary rate. If the beneficiary is liable to higher or additional rate tax, he will have to pay the difference between the rate of tax paid by the trustees and his own rate. If he is a basic rate taxpayer, he will have no further liability.

---

[235] For the views of HMRC, see TSEM 9000.
[236] ITA 2007, s 495.
[237] Prior to 6 April 1999 dividends from UK companies were paid with a recoverable tax credit of 20%. From that date the tax credit was reduced to 10% and was made irrecoverable. Dividend tax credits do not enter the tax pool.
[238] ITA 2007, s 503(2).

If he is not a taxpayer, he will be able to recover the tax paid on all trust income except for dividends where the tax credit is irrecoverable.

Beneficiaries of accumulation and discretionary trusts

3.138 Where trustees exercise a discretion to pay income to a beneficiary, a new source of income comes into existence – trust income. The original source of the income is irrelevant.[239] The beneficiary is treated as having a 45% tax credit and can claim a tax refund if his rate of tax is lower. Where trusts have received dividends which they pay to beneficiaries, there can be a disproportionately high rate of tax on the dividends. This is because:

(a)   the beneficiaries are treated as receiving a new source of income (trust income) not dividends and therefore do not benefit from the lower rates of tax which are charged on dividends;

(b)   the dividend tax credit is irrecoverable and does not enter the trust's tax pool.

Beneficiaries who are not taxpayers at all are in no worse a position than individual taxpayers but basic and higher rate taxpayers suffer because they lose the benefit of the lower rates on dividends.

Example 3.31

This example illustrates the treatment of dividend income received by discretionary trustees.

	£
Dividends received	900.00
Tax credit (1/9th)	100.00
Gross income	1,000.00
Deduct: Tax @ 37.5%	375.00
Income after tax	625.00
Tax due from trustees	375.00
Deduct: Tax credit	100.00
Additional tax due	£275.00
Amount credited to tax pool	£275.00

If the trustees accumulate the net income there is no further income tax to pay and £625 becomes capital. But if the trustees distribute that income the position is as follows:

(1) the non-repayable tax credit cannot be added to the tax pool, and so

(2) if the trustees distribute to a beneficiary the whole of the income after tax, the position is:

---

[239] *Cunard's Trustees v IRC* [1946] 1 All ER 159.

	£
Net income distribution to beneficiary	625.00
Addition for tax @ 45%	375.00
Gross income of beneficiary	1,000.00
Tax due under s 496	375.00
Deduct: Tax credited to tax pool	275.00
Shortfall	£100.00

In this situation, unless there is a balance in the tax pool brought forward which can be used to 'frank' the tax of £375, the shortfall has to be funded from other sources. In such cases the trustees may therefore have to adopt an alternative strategy. For instance, they may take the view that the distribution to the beneficiary and the tax payable under s 496 must be wholly met from the net of tax income received, £625 in the above example. To achieve this, the distribution to the beneficiary must be limited to 45% of the cash dividend received. Continuing the example above, the trustees would disregard the tax credit and limit the distribution to 55% of the £900 actually received. The result would be:

	£
Distribution to beneficiary £900 × 45%	495.00
Addition for tax @ 45%	405.00
Gross income of beneficiary	900.00
Tax due	405.00
Deduct: Tax credited to tax pool	275.00
Balance paid by trustees	£130.00

This is met out of the cash balance held by the trustees of £625 less the net payment to the beneficiary of £495.

This problem can be avoided by giving beneficiaries a right to income as explained in **3.139**.

Giving beneficiaries a revocable right to income

3.139 As discretionary and accumulation trusts pay income tax at 45% on all income in excess of £1,000, it will be attractive to pay out income to beneficiaries who can reclaim tax rather than accumulating the income and suffering the loss of tax. However, as explained above there are problems relating to the rate of tax suffered on dividend income which are not solved by simply paying it out.

Trustees of discretionary and accumulation settlements should therefore consider using their powers to grant one or more beneficiaries a revocable right to the trust income. This has the effect of taking the trust into the simpler income tax regime which applies where beneficiaries are entitled to income. See **Precedents 13.5** and **13.6**.

3.140 Before the changes to the IHT treatment of trusts introduced by FA 2006, this might have been unattractive as it would have given the beneficiary a qualifying interest in possession within IHTA 1984, s 49. The beneficiary would have been treated as beneficially entitled to the trust property so, had the beneficiary died still entitled to the interest in possession, the property would have been included in his estate. Had the trustees terminated the interest, the beneficiary would have been treated as making a transfer of value. Since 22 March 2006, however, it is impossible for trustees to create a qualifying interest in possession within s 49[240] so trustees can give beneficiaries a right to receive income (and terminate it) without IHT consequences.

3.141 There are no CGT consequences as there has been no deemed disposal. No one has become absolutely entitled as against the trustees. There has simply been a modification of the trusts on which the property is held.

3.142 The conversion of the trust means that the tax pool is in abeyance but should the trust, in the future, become discretionary again the trust pool will again become available.

---

[240] The only exceptions are where the trust is a Will Trust and the trustees make the appointment within 2 years of death, when the reading-back effect of IHTA 1984, s 144 will create an IPDI or, if the beneficiary is disabled, a disabled trust (see **3.58**).

Section B

DRAFTING THE WILL

CHAPTER 4

NOTES FOR THE WILL DRAFTSMAN

4.01 As with the drafting of any legal document, it is important that, when drafting a will, you are clear in your objectives and fully informed with all necessary information. It is common to ask the testator to complete a standard questionnaire which is designed to elicit the basic information needed to draft the will. It is then desirable to go through the will in draft form with the client highlighting matters of uncertainty and areas where further detail is needed. For instance, it is important to ensure that the question 'but what happens if X dies before you' is answered. Commonly this requires the appointment of a substitute executor or alternative beneficiary.

1. USE OF PRECEDENTS – STRUCTURE OF THE WILL

4.02 The majority of wills are in standard form and can be prepared from a precedent. The basic structure will be:

First part: declaration of the identity of the testator and revocation of previous wills. Appointment of executors/trustees and (if necessary) guardians. Wishes with regard to burial/cremation.

Second part: dispositive provisions (I) dealing with specific gifts, pecuniary legacies; chattel clauses.

Third part: dispositive provisions (II) dealing with the residue and giving the executors power to sell and reinvest; to pay all liabilities (including IHT) and to hold the balance on trust. In the common family will, residue will be held on trust for the surviving spouse either absolutely or on a life interest (IPDI) trust.

Fourth part: administrative and hybrid provisions including trustee charging, exoneration and self-dealing clauses; and purely administrative powers dealing with those cases where the statutory fall back provisions are inadequate or need supplementing.

Finally, the attestation clause. This is normally standard but in certain cases will require modification. For example, where a testator cannot sign, either because of weakness or injury, there is no presumption of knowledge and approval so the attestation clause should recite that the will was read over to and approved by the testator.

4.03 Precedent 4.1 corresponds to this model with clauses 1–3 comprising the First Part and clause 4 the Second Part (note that the precedent creates a discretionary trust of the whole estate – save for the chattels: it is, of course, open to the trustees to carve-out legacies within 2 years of death).[1] Clauses 5 and 6 comprise the Third Part whilst the remaining clauses 7–15 are the Fourth Part being made up of the hybrid and administrative provisions. The will should end with the standard attestation clause.[2]

2. USE OF TRUSTS

4.04 In the simplest will, no trust is involved: for instance:

'I leave everything to my brother John and appoint him my executor.'

What, however, if John were to predecease the testator? As soon as alternatives have to be considered (as they should!) matters are not so straightforward. The will might then include an alternative executor and substitute beneficiary saying:

'for John but if he shall predecease me for his children in equal shares absolutely.'

4.05 Trusts in wills may be short-lived with the trustees being charged with distributing the property amongst a number of beneficiaries. But they may also be full blown settlements as in the case of the so-called nil rate discretionary will trusts or flexible IPDI. In these cases, the trustee needs all the usual trustees' powers which are set out in the family settlement: see, for instance, **Precedent 4.1** and note that in such cases it may be attractive to include a separate clause of definitions.[3]

4.06 If the trustees are to be given discretionary powers (eg if the trust is fully discretionary or if the IPDI is flexible) it is desirable for the testator to leave a letter of wishes with the will in which he sets out how he would envisage the trusts being administered.[4] Bear in mind that:

(a)   this letter is for guidance only and is not legally binding on the trustees: it should include something along the lines of:

'this letter is intended to offer you guidance in administering the trust but it is not in any way legally binding and all decisions are yours alone to be taken in the light of the then circumstances (which may be quite different from those at the time when I am writing this letter) ...'

---

[1]   For appointments out of discretionary will trusts within 2 years of death with reading-back under IHTA 1984, s 144: see Chapter 13.

[2]   See **Precedent 4.3**.

[3]   **Precedent 4.1, clause 5(1)**. Typically this will define the Beneficiaries; the Trust Period; the Trustees and may, as in this case, give the trustees the power to modify (whether by addition or subtraction) the beneficial class.

[4]   See **Precedent 4.2**.

(b)   the will should not refer to the letter of wishes: this is to avoid any risk of it being incorporated by reference;

(c)   because it is not incorporated by reference, the letter can be revised during the testator's lifetime.[5]

4.07   In addition to **Precedent 4.1**, see also:

(a)   **Precedent 4.4** providing clauses to establish a nil rate band discretionary trust with a flexible IPDI trust of residue. Note that these clauses (numbered 5–9) can be slotted into the basic will in **Precedent 4.1** by the deletion of clauses 5–6 and the renumbering of clause 7 (and following) as 10 etc;

(b)   **Precedent 6.3** – IPDI trust of residue for minor children of the testator with substitution in the case of a predeceasing child leaving issue.

3. CHOICE OF EXECUTORS/TRUSTEES

4.08   Often this presents no difficulties but it can go spectacularly wrong: see generally **1.34** and, for the appointment of firms and limited partnerships, **1.40**.

When drafting the appointment clause, also consider:

(a)   whether to include:
  –   an exculpation clause: see **1.42–1.44**;
  –   a charging clause: see **1.38**;

(b)   whether to exclude the equitable self-dealing rules:[6] see **Precedent 4.1, clause 13**; and

(c)   who should have the power of appointing future trustees.

4. CHATTELS AND LEGACIES

4.09   For a consideration of gifts of chattels, see **1.45–1.47**. In the usual family situation these will be left outright to the surviving spouse/civil partner. The drafting of legacies (including issues concerning ademption and the problem that can be created by contingent pecuniary legacies) have been dealt with at **1.48–1.60**.

---

[5]   For letters of wishes, see the authors' *A Modern Approach to Lifetime Tax Planning*, Chapter 9.

[6]   This is desirable when appointing a beneficiary as a trustee. There is some authority to suggest that where a settlor appoints a beneficiary as trustee this may amount to implied authority to exercise powers in his own favour: see *Sargeant v National Westminster Bank plc* [1990] 61 P & CR 518. However, it is more satisfactory to include express authority which can make clear exactly which powers the beneficiary/trustee can exercise and include safeguards, if desired.

5. NIL RATE BAND LEGACIES

4.10 Because the amount that will ultimately pass under such a legacy cannot be known at the date the will is executed, it is important when discussing the use of such a clause with a client to point this out and to explain the following which will affect the amount passing:

(a) the level of the nil rate band may substantially[7] increase or decrease;

(b) if the client has a spouse or civil partner who dies with unused nil rate band, the unused proportion may be transferred and so may increase the amount that can pass under such a legacy;

(c) if at the date of death the client has property eligible for business or agricultural property relief which passes as part of the residue, the benefit of the relief will be spread through all the estate and will increase the amount of the pecuniary legacy that can pass without payment of IHT;[8]

(d) the amount of the nil rate band pecuniary legacy will reduce to the extent that there are other items which attract a charge to IHT at death. These items are:
   (i)   chargeable lifetime transfers including failed PETs;
   (ii)   other gifts by will to non-exempt beneficiaries;
   (iii) property passing by survivorship to non-exempt beneficiaries;
   (iv) property in which the deceased had a qualifying interest in possession;
   (v)   property in which the deceased had a reservation of benefit.

4.11 Precedent 4.9, Form 1 passes the maximum available without payment of IHT. Some practitioners like to use an expanded form of the precedent which lists the items which have to be taken into account when calculating that amount. Such a formulation adds nothing (other than length and complexity) but may perhaps help avoid argument as to the amount which was intended to pass.[9] For an expanded precedent see **Precedent 4.9, Form 2**. Where the client has (or may have) the benefit of a transferred nil rate band at death, it will avoid doubt if the PRs are directed to claim any nil rate band available for transfer: see **Precedent 4.9, Form 3**.

4.12 A client may be concerned that too much may pass under the terms of such a legacy. It is always possible to include a maximum amount that can pass. This could be a specified amount but it is more common to limit the amount by reference to the IHT threshold at the date of death. This will cap the amount that can pass if the client has the benefit of a transferred nil rate band at the

---

7   In 2007 the then Shadow Chancellor, George Osborne, announced at the Conservative Party Conference that their policy was to increase the nil rate band to £1m. It now appears that the proposal is to increase the nil rate band by £175,000 in respect of the main residence.

8   IHTA 1984, s 39A. See **10.41** *et seq.*

9   For an illustration of the sort of argument that can result from a badly drafted legacy, see *RSPCA v Sharp & Mason* [2010] EWHC 268 (Ch), [2010] STC 975 *reversed* [2011] STC 553 (CA). *Loring v The Woodland Trust* [2014] 2 All ER 836 *aff'd* [2014] EWCA Civ 1314 is a further example of the difficulties that can arise when construing such clauses.

date of death or if the apportioning of business or agricultural property relief would otherwise increase the amount that could pass under the clause. For an example of such a cap, see **Precedent 4.9, Form 4**.

4.13 It will often be attractive to leave the nil rate sum on discretionary trusts rather than to direct its immediate payment to named individuals.[10]

6. GIFTS TO CHARITY

4.14 Wealthy families may have their own charity and family members may therefore wish to leave property to it. Alternatively it may be that the testator wishes to establish a family charity and, whilst this can be done by his will, it is usually preferable for a 'pilot' charity to be set up during his lifetime to which he then adds property by his will.[11]

It is, however, more usual for the will to leave property to existing charities and in this case it is the duty of the will draftsman to ensure that the charity is correctly identified by name, address and its charity registration number.

Sometimes a discretionary will trust includes charities in the class of beneficiaries. In this case, a standard form of words is 'any trust company or other body which is established for charitable purposes only'.

Charities may be used as longstop (or default) beneficiaries in a will trust. For instance, 'to such charity or charities as my trustees shall select'.

Despite the statutory merger provisions discussed below,[12] it is preferable to give the executors a discretion as to what happens in such circumstances. Failure to do so may mean that the legacy has to be paid to a charity which the testator would not have wished to benefit, for example one which goes into insolvent liquidation after death and before payment.[13]

Gifts to unincorporated charities

4.15 Traditionally charities took the form of charitable trusts or unincorporated associations. Every gift by will to an unincorporated charity by name without further qualification must be construed as a gift for a charitable purpose because it cannot be said to be a gift to the trustees or members beneficially.[14] If the named charity ceases to exist in the testator's lifetime, the

---

[10] See the discussion in relation to the use of a transferred nil rate band in Chapter 5.

[11] For the use of pilot trusts generally see Chapter 8. Bear in mind that the trust should be extant when the will is executed. An attraction of establishing the charity in pilot form is that it can obtain registration so that any doubts as to its charitable status can be resolved.

[12] See **4.17** and **4.18**.

[13] This is what happened in *Berry and another v IBS-STL Ltd (in liquidation)* [2012] EWHC 666 (Ch). See **4.17** and **4.18**.

[14] *Re Vernon's Will Trusts* [1971] 3 All ER 1061, at 1064. It is important to include a receipts clause: see **Precedent 4.1, clause 9(11)**.

merger provisions (see **4.17**) may apply but, if they do not, the gift will normally be applicable cy-près unless the testator's intention was to make the gift dependent on the named charitable organisation being available at the time when the gift takes effect.

Gifts to incorporated charities

4.16   It is increasingly common for charities to be constituted as companies. A bequest to an incorporated charity, unlike one to an unincorporated charity, takes effect as a gift to that body beneficially, unless there are circumstances which show that the recipient is to take the gift as a trustee. Without the imposition of a trust a bequest is simply added to the corporate body's general funds and will, therefore, become available to pay its general debts in the case of insolvency.[15]

In the case of substantial legacies it may be advisable to provide that the bequest is to be held on trust although too detailed limitations may make the gift unattractive to the donee. Gifts to a company which has been dissolved can be saved by the merger provisions or by the cy-près rule, although it may be more difficult to find a general charitable intention in the case of a gift to a named corporation.

There is a further problem in relation to incorporated associations concerning the time at which they cease to exist. This is because an incorporated association which is subject to an insolvent winding-up order continues to exist until formally dissolved.[16] The result is that legacies from testators dying after the winding-up order but before formal dissolution will be payable to the liquidator. It is therefore desirable to make provision in the will for the possibility that a charity is subject to a winding up order at the date of death: see **4.19**.

The merger provisions and recent case law

4.17   The merger provisions, originally in s 75F of the Charities Act 1993 (now consolidated into s 311 of the Charities Act 2011), provide that in relation to merged charities:

> 'Any gift which is expressed as a gift to the transferor, and takes effect on or after the date of registration of the merger, takes effect as a gift to the transferee.'

---

[15]   *Wedgewood Museum Trust Ltd (in administration), Young v Attorney General* [2011] EWHC 3782 (Ch) where a museum collection was held to be available to help meet a pension fund shortfall of the group of companies to which it belonged. See also Charity Commission Guidance: Managing Financial Difficulties and Insolvency in Charities – (CC12) which defines 'restricted funds' as 'funds to be used for specific purposes, set out by, for example, the donor, grant maker or the terms of a public appeal' and explains that they are not unavailable for other purposes.

[16]   *Re ARMS (Multiple Sclerosis Research) Ltd* [1997] 2 All ER 679.

4.18 *Berry v IBS-STL Ltd (in liquidation)*[17] considered the relationship
between this provision and the wording used in the will. In this case the will
provided:

> '6.1 I GIVE the residue of my estate ... to my TRUSTEES upon trust to divide in
> equal shares between such of the following charities as shall to the satisfaction of
> my Trustees be in existence at the date of my death namely:
>
> [6 named charities including International Bible Society UK('IBS')]
>
> 6.2 IF any charity or charitable organisation which I have named as a beneficiary
> in this Will is found never to have existed or to have ceased to exist or to have
> become amalgamated with another organisation or to have changed its name
> before my death then the gift contained in this Will for such charity or charitable
> organisation shall be transferred to whatever charitable institution or institutions
> and if more than one in whatever proportions as my Trustees shall in their absolute
> discretion think fit and
>
> 6.3 I EXPRESS THE WISH but without imposing any obligation on my Trustees
> that the gift be given to such charitable institution or institutions whose purpose is
> as close as possible to those of the charity or charitable organisation named by me
> in this Will.'

IBS was at the date of the will an unincorporated registered charity. With effect
from 31 May 2007 it transferred the entirety of its assets to an incorporated
registered charity. The merger was registered on 2 January 2008, and the
register recorded that IBS ceased to exist on 5 February 2008, both dates
preceded the death of the testatrix so, prima facie, s 75F applied. After the
death of the testatrix, the incorporated charity went into insolvent liquidation
and was wound up.

The issue for the executors was whether s 75F *compelled* them to pay to the
merged charity, and so, in effect, to the liquidator for the benefit of the
creditors, or whether they could use their discretion under clause 6.2 to pay the
available funds to a similar charity. They asked the court for guidance.

The court's decision was based on the wording of clause 6.1. David
Donaldson QC, sitting as a Deputy High Court Judge, held that it gave the
property *only* to those organisations which were in existence at the date of the
testatrix's death. As the original charity had already ceased to exist as a result
of the incorporation, there was no gift to it and s 75F was not engaged.

4.19 This result is probably what most testators would want and so the use of
such wording is desirable. However 'being in existence' is a difficult concept
particularly in relation to incorporated charities and it may be difficult to
decide whether or not a charity meets the test at the relevant time.

---

[17] [2012] EWHC 666 (Ch).

In *Re ARMS (Multiple Sclerosis Research) Ltd*[18] an incorporated charity went into liquidation. Several testators had left it legacies. The court decided that if the testator died after the date of the winding up order but before formal dissolution was completed, the charity still existed at the date of the testator's death. Therefore, the legacies had to be paid to the liquidator for the benefit of the creditors and could not be applied cy-près because the charities still existed at the date of death.

In the case of gifts to incorporated charities it is, therefore, desirable to give the executors a discretion to allow them to apply gifts for similar charitable purposes where a legatee is subject to a winding-up order at the date of death but not yet formally dissolved.

4.20   The concept of 'being in existence' also caused problems in *Phillips v Royal Society for the Protection of Birds*.[19] The New Forest Owl Sanctuary ('NFOS'), an incorporated charity, ran into difficulties as a result of which, in August 2006, it was struck off the Register of Charities on the ground that it had ceased to operate and was finally dissolved in February 2007 a few days after the death of a testator who left the charity a share of his residuary estate. The will contained a typical amalgamation clause providing that if:

> 'before my death (or after my death but before my Trustees have given effect to the gift) any charitable or other body to which a gift is made by this will ... has changed its name or amalgamated with any other body or transferred all its assets then my Trustees shall give effect to the gift as if it were a gift to the body in its changed name or to the body which results from the amalgam.'

There was a charity which had received some of the assets of NFOS but Cooke J held that it had not received a sufficiently great proportion to bring it within the clause. He then decided that the legacy could be applied cy-près.

Suggested clauses

4.21   (a) **Gift to named charity**

> 'I GIVE [£] to [name of charity] [on trust][20] for its general charitable purposes and I DIRECT that
>
> EITHER
>
> [my Will shall be construed and take effect as if section 311 of the Charities Act 2011 did not apply to this legacy. If]
>
> OR
>
> [Subject to the provisions of section 311 of the Charities Act 2011, if]

---

[18]   [1997] 2 All ER 679.
[19]   [2012] EWHC 618 (Ch).
[20]   If the charity is incorporated consider inserting these words: see **4.16**.

at the date of my death [name of charity] is no longer in existence or is subject to a winding up order] my Trustees shall pay the legacy to such other charity or charities having the same or similar objects as my Trustees shall select'

(b) Trustees given power to select charities with default provision

A further possibility is to leave the executors a discretion to decide on the amount or share to be given to each of several named charities, and even to select the recipients from a group of named charities.[21] Conscientious executors may consider it necessary however, to make enquiries into the potential recipient charities. This may lead to a delay in the actual distribution of the estate, and a time limit might therefore be reasonably imposed in such cases.

'I GIVE [ ] to my Trustees to hold upon trust for such charities in such shares as the Trustees shall in their absolute discretion appoint.

Any appointment shall be made by my Trustees by deed within the period of [ ] from my death.

In default of any such appointment the legacy shall be held for [ ] for its general charitable purposes.'

(c) Gift to several charities in equal shares

One method of avoiding the problems caused when a charity ceases to exist before the will takes effect is to make a gift to several charities in equal shares, excluding any charity which no longer exists at the date of the testator's death. Such a provision is relatively common where the gift is of residue. The shares need not be equal if the testator's priorities require there to be some differentiation.

The STEP Standard provisions

4.22 Some charities have expressed concern about the wording of standard condition 4.16.2 in the *STEP Standard Provisions* (2nd edn) which is as follows:

'If any charity ceases to exist, changes its name, or enters into insolvent liquidation before the time that a gift to the charity takes effect in possession, the gift shall instead be paid to such charity as the Trustees decide having regard to the objects that were intended to benefit.'

Many people think that the inclusion of a discretion where the charity merely changes its name is too draconian. However, while a name change may be simply that, it may indicate a rebalancing of the charity's priorities. The author of the *Standard Provisions* (James Kessler QC) has commented as follows:

---

[21] See Precedent 4.10, Form 2.

'The power is exercisable in three cases, if the charity (1) ceases to exist, (2) changes its name, or (3) enters into insolvent liquidation. In exercising the power the trustees must have regard to the objects that were intended to benefit. The gift can only be paid to another charity.

It seems to me that a charity may change its name in two circumstances. Sometimes the change reflects a modernisation without any change in the charities objects or activities. An example, perhaps, is Dr Barnardo's which changed its name to Barnardo's. Sometimes the change does reflect a change in objects or activities. For example, when the charity formerly called "the Centre for the Study of Jewish Christian Relations" extended its activities to include Islam, it changed its name to "the Woolf Institute of Abrahamic Faiths".

The object of the standard provisions is to help to carry out the wishes of the testator. In the first case testators would wish the gift to continue to pass to the charity, despite its new name. In the second case, where the change reflects a change of objects or activities, I wonder about that. The testator would want the gift to pass to charity, but perhaps not the same charity. So it seems to me that there is a case for allowing the trustees to reflect on what the testator's wishes would have been. I bear in mind that the trustees are persons chosen by the testator and should be best placed to do that.

In most situations the trustees will be likely to exercise their discretion in favour of the renamed charity. Where the name change is a simple modernisation, it is difficult to see how trustees reasonably could do anything else, given that they must "have regard to the objects that were intended to benefit".

Thus I do not think that the clause goes too far, though those who take another view can of course amend the provisions as they prefer.'

7. GIFTS RELEASING A DEBT

4.23 The right to enforce payment of a debt is an item of property which the testator owns. If he so wishes he can make provision in his will for the release of the debt and in so doing he will make a pecuniary legacy in the debtor's favour.

The testator should be advised that if his debtor dies before him, then the release, just like any other legacy, will lapse. That being so, the testator's executors can still enforce payment against the debtor's estate and if they refuse to do so, may risk a claim of breach of duty from the other beneficiaries. It is therefore necessary to provide expressly that the release extends to the debtor's personal representatives. It is also prudent to make clear that the release extends to all interest owing, as well as the outstanding capital. If the debt is secured, its discharge will also require release of the security and the testator may wish to make clear that any associated costs in achieving this are met as a testamentary expense from residue.

If a testator wishes to release multiple debts, each should be dealt with separately. A general release of 'all debts owing to my estate' could be construed as relieving banks and other financial institutions from an obligation to account for what they owe to the estate!

8. GIFTS IN PRIORITY

4.24 A testator may add provisions to a legacy saying that it is to be paid immediately on death and/or that it will rank in priority to all other legacies in the will. Such a provision is usually added to a legacy in favour of a dependant whom the testator wishes to benefit in preference to anyone else.

> *Example:*
>
> 'I give £20,000 to my husband to be paid immediately after my death and I declare that this legacy shall be paid in priority to all other gifts in my will and shall not abate with them.'

The first part of the clause requires the executors to pay the legacy as soon as sufficient funds are available and interest will be carried from the date of death rather than from the first anniversary of the death.

The second part ensures that the legacy will be paid in priority to other legacies in the event of their being insufficient assets to pay all legacies in full. Without this provision, the legacy would abate proportionately with other legacies of the same kind.

9. GIFTS OF HOUSES

4.25 A dilemma for some testators is that a house or land that they own represents a substantial part of the estate and giving it to one beneficiary means that there is insufficient elsewhere to fund a similar provision (in terms of value) for other beneficiaries. This is typically the case if the testator is a farmer and wants to pass on the farm to one of his children but there is not enough in the rest of the estate to make provision for his other children. An option to buy is sometimes helpful in these circumstances. The price may be fixed at below market value thereby giving the person exercising a benefit and the funds produced can be used to make provision for other family members.

Option to buy

4.26 A testamentary option in favour of one beneficiary to buy the property at an undervalue can produce the necessary liquid funds to provide for other beneficiaries. The difference in price between the full market value and the option price represents a legacy in favour of the grantee and any inheritance tax applicable to it will be paid from residue unless a contrary intention is expressed in the will. Great care is needed, both in determining the terms of the option and then in drafting them in the will.[22] Factors that must be considered include:

(a)   What property is the subject of the option?

(b)   Is the price to be fixed by the testator in the will, by the trustees or by a valuer?

(c)   If the valuation is to be by a named person or made in a specific way, is that to be of the essence? If it is and it fails (as where the named person predeceases), then the option cannot take effect. If not of the essence, the court can always order an appropriate method of fixing the price.

(d)   If the price is to be determined after death, what is the basis for the valuation? Is it to be based on the agreed probate value for inheritance tax purposes (assuming there is one) or on an 'open market valuation' which will not necessarily produce the same figure? For example, a probate valuation will not take account of rights of occupation conferred by the will. It will only take account of facts known at the time of death and not subsequent events such as the giving up of rights of occupation unless the will directs otherwise.[23]

(e)   Within what time period must the option be exercised and in what manner? Any time limit in the will for the exercise of the option must be strictly complied with if time is intended to be one of the terms of the offer.[24] If a time limit is included, it should be carefully worded to ensure that the person with the benefit of the option is not placed in a position where it is impossible to meet the time limit because of factors outside his control. It is not recommended that time starts to run from the date of death because there may be delay in obtaining a grant and the will may be challenged. Ideally, time should not start to run until the price has been determined. It is desirable to provide that the executors must give notice to the grantee of the option to ensure the grantee has the chance to exercise it and that his right to do so does not lapse through ignorance. It may be helpful to separate acceptance of the option in principle, for which it may be appropriate to impose a strict time limit, from the mechanics of the conveyancing process, for which it is less likely to be appropriate. Where there are problems complying with a time limit the court is likely to find that time was not intended to be of the essence where there is no gift over, and no prejudice.[25] If the will does not provide a specific time limit then the option must be exercised within a reasonable time. If the price has to be fixed, the time cannot run until the price has been communicated to the grantee.

---

[22]   See **Precedent 4.11**.
[23]   See *Re Bliss* [2001] 1 WLR 1973.
[24]   See *Allardyce v Roebuck* [2004] EWHC 1538 (Ch).
[25]   See *Re Bowles* [2003] EWHC 253 (Ch).

4.27 Before the coming into force of the Perpetuities and Accumulations Act 2009[26] the date for the exercise of an option had to be within the period allowed by the perpetuity rule.[27] This is still the position for options created before 6 April 2010. It was generally advisable to limit expressly the period during which the option remains exercisable.

In the case of options granted after the 2009 Act came into force the perpetuity rule no longer applies. Section 1 of the Act defines the circumstances in which the rule against perpetuities applies and it only applies to the estates, interests, powers and rights mentioned (broadly trust interests). The rule does not apply, for example, to most future easements, options and rights of pre-emption, which will fall outside these categories. It is, therefore, for those deciding the terms of an option to include such limitations as they see fit as to the period within which the option can be exercised.

Gifts of houses

4.28 A testator may wish a dwelling-house to be retained after his death to provide a residence for a beneficiary. Since 1 January 1997 and the coming into force of the Trusts of Land and Appointment of Trustees Act 1996, this can be achieved without the risk of creating a strict settlement. The testator may wish to give the dwelling-house (or his interest in the dwelling-house) to his trustees upon trust to permit the surviving spouse to use the property during her life or until she remarries, with a gift over on her death. In such a case the title to the property is vested in the trustees of land, who have powers to manage the property. The trustees may, however, delegate to the surviving spouse their functions as trustees which relate to the land.[28]

Trustees of land have all the powers of the absolute owner of the land.[29] They have a power of sale and a power to acquire land.[30] Hence the dwelling-house left on trust to provide a residence may be sold and an alternative dwelling-house purchased if the circumstances of the case so dictate.

Granting a right to occupy creates an immediate post-death interest for inheritance tax purposes[31] which may be undesirable. However, if the occupant is the deceased's spouse, the transfer will benefit from the spouse exemption. The value of the property will be included in the surviving spouse's estate for inheritance tax purposes.

Where the testator does not wish to create an immediate post-death interest in the dwelling-house, then the property may be devised to trustees upon

---

[26] On 6 April 2010.

[27] See PAA 1964, s 9(2).

[28] Trusts of Land and Appointment of Trustees Act 1996, s 9.

[29] Trusts of Land and Appointment of Trustees Act 1996, s 6(1).

[30] Under TA 2000, s 8, which specifically allows land to be acquired for occupation by a beneficiary.

[31] For IPDIs, see generally Chapter 6.

discretionary trusts for a class of persons. No one individual will have a right to occupy under the trust, but the trustees could grant a licence to occupy. This would not create an immediate post-death interest. The terms of the gift should not require beneficiaries to consent to the sale as this may create an unwanted immediate post-death interest.[32]

Occupation by a beneficiary under the terms of a trust will attract the principal private residence exemption on disposal.[33]

See **Precedent 4.12.**

10. ADMINISTRATIVE AND HYBRID PROVISIONS

4.29 The trustees of continuing will trusts should be given the same administrative powers as trustees of a lifetime settlement. Some practitioners will use a standard set of provisions (most commonly the STEP Standard Provisions which have recently been revised; the 2nd edition includes standard clauses which are included automatically, unless expressly excluded, and special provisions which have to be expressly selected). Alternatively, and with very little additional effort, express powers may be included in the will. In the authors' view the attraction of this is that the powers can be tailored to the circumstances of the case. Powers that are unlikely to be needed (eg to run a business) can be deleted.

Tailoring the powers makes it easier to take the testator through their effect to make sure that he understands and is happy with what has been included. This is particularly important in relation to any exculpation clause[34] which should be expressly approved as should a trustee charging clause.

A sensible 'fall back' is to include a provision along the lines of **Precedent 4.1, clause 9(14)** which enables the trustees to give themselves a power 'to effect any transaction which the trustees consider to be expedient'.

4.30 As noted, the second edition of the STEP Provisions includes a category of 'special provisions' which will only be incorporated into a will if expressly referred to: eg 'the Standard Provisions and all the Special Provisions ... shall apply'. It may seem surprising for a set of 'standard' provisions to have add-on extras but it only goes to show that in all but straightforward wills it is necessary to consider what powers the trustees should be given.

Amongst the powers that one would expect to find in any will (or standard set of provisions) are:

---

32 See *IRC v Lloyds Private Banking Ltd* [1998] STC 559, [1999] 1 FLR 147.
33 This is so whether the terms of the settlement give a fixed right or confer powers on trustees to allow occupation at their discretion. See **14.68** and TCGA 1992, s 225.
34 See **1.42.**

(a) a wide power of investment (including a power to acquire in non-income producing assets and in property for occupation or use by a beneficiary);[35]

(b) power for the trustees to retain assets as left to them in the will: typically this will allow the trustees to retain shares in a private company or the family home;[36]

(c) the statutory power of appropriation should be widened:
   (i)   to remove the requirement for consents;
   (ii) to extend it to trustees (it is otherwise limited to PRs);
   (iii) to allow trustees to exercise the power in their own favour.[37]
   The STEP Special Provisions allow trustees to appropriate property (for the period of 3 years from the date of death) at its probate value instead of (as the general law provides) its value at the date of appropriation;[38]

(d) powers in relation to land, eg to sell, lease, mortgage it and to improve or develop it;[39]

(e) powers to delegate (eg the management of an investment portfolio) and to use a nominee;[40]

(f) a receipts clause permitting the trustees to accept the receipt of a parent or guardian of a minor and the relevant charitable officer in respect of a gift to charity (note that if the wording 'permits' the trustees to accept such a receipt, they cannot be required to do so);

(g) powers to lend to a beneficiary and to allow the occupation of trust property provided that, in both cases, this is in conformity with the beneficial trusts.[41]

4.31 Consider including the clauses set out below which are not of a purely administrative nature.

(a) Modification of s 31 of the Trustee Act 1925:
   it was common to vary s 31(1)(i) which required trustees to apply such income as shall 'be reasonable' and to exclude the proviso to s 31(1) which required the trustees to take certain factors into account when deciding what was reasonable. Instead the trustees would be given an unfettered discretion to apply income as they saw fit. As from 1 October 2014 it is no longer necessary to make these changes as the Inheritance and Trustees' Powers Act 2014, s 8 amends the wording of s 31 to achieve this result. These changes to s 31 apply to trusts created or arising after 1 October 2014.[42]

---

[35] Precedent 4.1, clause 9(1): see the STEP Provisions at clause 4 and the special provisions in clause 21.
[36] Precedent 4.1, clause 9(2).
[37] Precedent 4.1, clause 9(3); STEP 4.15.
[38] See further Chapter 14. The authors are not convinced of the merits of this provision.
[39] Precedent 4.1, clauses 9(5) and (6).
[40] Precedent 4.1, clauses 9(8) and (9).
[41] Precedent 4.1, clauses 9(12) and (13).
[42] Explanatory Note 51 says that if a trust is created by will, it is the date of death not execution

Consider deferring the s 31 vesting of income at 18 in the case of contingent gifts. For instance, if the beneficiary is to be entitled to capital if and when he attains the age of 30, is entitlement to income at 18 acceptable or should it also be deferred to 30 with the trustees until then having a power to apply it for the maintenance of the beneficiary and to accumulate the balance?[43] If so, s 31 could be amended by providing that a beneficiary is to be treated as attaining majority at the 'Specified Age' which could then be defined as 30 or such earlier age as the trustees may specify (it is unnecessary to require this to be by deed).

If the testator wishes to create an IPDI for a minor beneficiary,[44] it is necessary to vary s 31(2)(ii) which provides that accumulated income will pass as an accretion to capital if the minor beneficiary fails to reach 18, thus preventing the beneficiary having a right to income. It is necessary to provide that any income retained by the trustees is held for the beneficiary absolutely.[45]

(b) Modification of s 32 of the Trustee Act 1925:

it was common to enlarge s 32 so that the trustees have power to advance 100% (not 50%) of a beneficiary's presumptive share. As from 1 October 2014 it is no longer necessary to make this change as the Inheritance and Trustees' Powers Act 2014, s 9 amends the wording of s 32 to achieve this result. The changes to s 32 will apply to trusts created or arising after 1 October 2014.[46]

It may be appropriate to replace the other two statutory limitations which apply to the power of advancement: (1) the need for consent of any beneficiary with a prior interest and (2) the requirement to bring an advance into account, with a general discretion for the trustees to advance without prior consent and on such terms as they see fit.

(c) Exclusion of apportionments of income and expenses:

For trusts created and arising after 1 October 2013 the Trusts (Capital and Income) Act 2013 makes this unnecessary as it disapplies the apportionment rules.[47] However, it may be helpful for the avoidance of doubt to include a statement that income is to be treated as arising when paid and that no apportionment is required.

(d) a clause allowing trustees to exercise their powers even if the administration of the estate is incomplete;[48]

---

that is significant. Hence, if the death occurs on or after 1 October 2014, the amendments will apply, subject to any amendment or exclusion of the power by the terms of the will.

[43] Giving the right to income may be undesirable if, for example, the amount of income is very substantial. If the right to income arises at the date of death (because the beneficiary is already 18), this will produce an IPDI for IHT purposes which may not be what the testator intended.

[44] Popular with grandparents who wish to settle funds and avoid ongoing IHT anniversary and exit charges. See **7.02** *et seq.*

[45] See *Fine v Fine* [2012] EWHC 1811 Ch and **7.02**.

[46] Explanatory Note 51 says if a trust is created by will, it is the date of death not execution that is significant. Hence, if the death occurs on or after 1 October 2014, the amendments will apply, subject to any amendment or exclusion of the power by the terms of the will.

[47] See **14.62** *et seq.*

[48] Whilst it is considered that the trustees have powers from the date of death, this is a comfort clause and seems to be favoured by HMRC: see Chapter 13.

(e)   clause headings (to aid comprehension) and a provision that these are for informative purposes only may be inserted (although this reflects the position at law, the statement aids clarity).

4.32   As a general matter, it is up to the will draftsman to consider what other provisions may be needed: this will be dictated both by the nature of the assets in the estate and by the beneficial trusts. For instance, if the estate includes business property the trustees should be given power to run the business.[49] It may also be desirable for a separate trustee with business experience to be appointed or for the trustees to allow the intended beneficiary to run the business from the date of death (he could, for instance, be appointed the manager).

Where the assets of a trust include shares in a private company the testator should consider whether so-called anti-*Bartlett* clauses are required.[50]

11. SPECIFIC IHT RELATED PROVISIONS

4.33   Two recent IHT changes may need to be considered:

(a)   *the availability of an additional IHT nil rate band.* If this will be available on the death of the testator, consider how is it being used and inserting a provision requiring it to be claimed by the personal representatives;[51]

(b)   *the reduced IHT rate applying to the chargeable estate where a sufficiently large proportion of the estate is given to charity.* Consider whether charitable gifts should be so drafted as to ensure that the conditions for the relief are met and whether the personal representatives should be given a power to elect for the components of the estate to be merged.[52]

---

[49]   **Precedent 4.1, clause 9(7).**

[50]   *Re Lucking's Will Trusts* [1967] 3 All ER 726 and *Bartlett v Barclays Bank* [1980] Ch 515 both suggest that a shareholding in a private company large enough to confer some measure of control brings special responsibilities. It is not enough to leave the conduct of the business to the directors. Trustees are under a duty to keep themselves informed about the company's affairs and the directors' plans. They must be willing to act on the information and may be liable for a breach of trust if they fail to take steps to prevent the dissipation of the company's assets in a speculative and ill-considered venture. However, unless specially chosen for their expertise, trustees will not normally have the expertise to satisfy themselves that a trading company is being managed prudently. It is, therefore, common to include so-called anti-*Bartlett* clauses. The protection afforded by such clauses will vary depending on how they are drafted. There is a discussion in *Lewin on Trusts* (19th edn) at 34.059 on alternative clauses and their effect.

[51]   See Chapter 5.

[52]   See Chapter 9.

PRECEDENTS

Precedent 4.1: Discretionary will

I [ ] of [ ] hereby revoke all former Wills Codicils and testamentary dispositions made by me and declare this to be my last Will.

Disposal of Body

1. I wish my body to be cremated.

Appointment of Executors[53]

2. I appoint [ ] to be the executors and trustees of this Will (and they or the survivor of them or other the trustee or trustees for the time being hereof are hereinafter called 'my Trustees').

Appointment of Guardians

3. In the event of my husband/wife [ ] predeceasing me I appoint [ ] of [ ] to be the guardian of my minor children.

Gift/Precatory Trust of Chattels[54]

4. I give and bequeath to [ ] for his/her own absolute use and benefit free of any tax or duty arising in respect of my death all my personal chattels as defined in section 55(1)(x) of the Administration of Estates Act 1925 not otherwise specifically disposed of by this Will or any Codicil hereto [but it is my wish without creating any trust or imposing any binding obligation that he/she should dispose of such personal chattels in accordance with any written memorandum or memoranda left with this Will or with my personal papers].

Definition of Terms used in Clause 6

5.

(1)   In clause 6 of this Will where the context so permits the following expressions shall have the following meanings:
   (i)   'the Beneficiaries' shall mean subject to the provisions of clause 5(2)[55] below:
      (a)   my surviving spouse (whether or not remarried);
      (b)   my children and remoter issue;
      (c)   the spouses widows and widowers of the persons mentioned in (b);

---

[53]   See **1.34** *et seq.*
[54]   See **1.45** *et seq.*
[55]   This allows additional beneficiaries to be added and beneficiaries to be excluded (including charities).

and 'beneficiary' shall have a corresponding meaning.

(ii) 'the Trust Period' shall mean the period commencing with the date of my death and ending one hundred and twenty five years thereafter and such period of one hundred and twenty five years shall be the perpetuity period applicable to the dispositions made by my Will.[56]

(iii) 'my Trustees' shall mean the trustees from time to time being of my Trust Fund.

(iv) 'Charitable' means charitable (and exclusively charitable) according to the law for the time being of England and Wales and 'Charity' means a trust corporation association society or other institution established (in any EU country) only for Charitable purposes and 'Charity' has a corresponding meaning.[57]

(v) 'Spouse' shall include a civil partner registered under the Civil Partnership Act 2004 and 'widow' 'widower' and 'remarried' shall be construed accordingly.

(2)

(i) Subject to sub-clause (b) below:

(a) My Trustees (being not less than two in number or a trust corporation) shall have power by any deed or deeds revocable (during the Trust Period) or irrevocable executed during the Trust Period to declare that any individual or individuals whether or not then born or ascertained or any Charity or Charities (other than any individual then a trustee of this Will and other than any individual or Charity previously excluded under the power set out in (b) below) shall from such time and (subject to any future exercise of the power set out in clause 2(i)(b) below) either permanently or for such period or periods as shall be specified in any such deed or deeds be included in the class of Beneficiaries defined in clause 5(1)(i) above; and

(b) My Trustees (being not less than two in number or a trust corporation) shall also have power by any deed or deeds revocable (during the Trust Period) or irrevocable executed during the Trust Period to declare that any individual or individuals whether or not born or ascertained or any Charity or Charities who or which is or are a member or members (or eligible to be added as a member or members) of the class of Beneficiaries immediately prior to the execution of such deed or deeds shall from such time and either permanently or for such period or periods as shall be specified in any such deed or deeds cease to be a member or members (or eligible to become a member or members) of such class;

---

[56] For the 125-year perpetuity period see **2.05** *et seq.*

[57] IHT relief may be available in respect of gifts to charitable organisations in the EU, Norway, Iceland and Liechtenstein: see FA 2010, s 30, Sch 6, SI 2010/1904, SI 2012/736 and SI 2014/1807. See the authors' *A Modern Approach to Lifetime Tax Planning*, Chapter 39.

(ii)   Provided always[58] that no such deed made in exercise of either of the powers conferred by sub-clause (i) shall affect the validity or effect of:

    (a)   any distribution previously made to or for the benefit of any beneficiary under or pursuant to any power or discretion;

    (b)   any transmissible interest (whether vested or contingent) previously conferred on any beneficiary;

    (c)   any future distribution to any beneficiary consequent on the absolute vesting in possession of any such interest as is mentioned in sub-clause (ii)(b); and

    (d)   my Trustees (being not less than two in number or a trust corporation) may at any time or times during the Trust Period by deed or deeds extinguish (or restrict the future exercise of) both or either of the powers (but not any of the restrictions applicable to them) conferred by sub-clause (i) above.

Trusts of Residue

6. I give all my property both movable and immovable of whatever nature and wheresoever situated except property otherwise disposed of by this Will or by any Codicil hereto unto my Trustees upon trust to sell call in and convert the same into money (so far as not already consisting of money) with power to postpone the sale calling in and conversion thereof (even as regards property of a terminable hazardous or wasting nature) in the absolute and uncontrolled discretion of my Trustees without being liable for loss and to hold the net proceeds and my ready money upon the following trusts:

(1)   Upon trust to pay thereout (in exoneration of any property which would otherwise be liable for payment of the same) all my funeral and testamentary expenses and debts and any general legacies given by this Will or any Codicil hereto and any tax or duty arising in respect of my death (even if not a testamentary expense) on all gifts in this Will and any Codicil hereto given free of such tax or duty;[59]

(2)   Upon trust if necessary to invest the remainder after such payment in or upon any investments hereinafter authorised for the investment of trust funds with power to vary and transpose the same;

(3)   Upon trust to stand possessed of such investments and such of my estate as remains for the time being unsold and my ready money and all property from time to time respectively representing the same (hereinafter together called '**my Trust Fund**') and the income thereof upon the following trusts;

(4)   During the Trust Period my Trustees (being at least two in number or a trust corporation) may at any time or times:

---

[58]   This is designed to protect benefits that have already been conferred: for instance, if the trustees have appointed capital outright to a beneficiary that will not be affected by the exercise of the power to exclude that beneficiary.

[59]   See **3.33** *et seq.*

(i)   by deed or deeds revocable (during the Trust Period) or irrevocable appoint[60] that all or any part or parts of the income or capital of my Trust Fund shall be held on such trusts (including discretionary and protective ones) in favour or for the benefit of all or any one or more of the Beneficiaries and with and subject to such powers (including dispositive and administrative ones exercisable by my Trustees or any other person) and other provisions as my Trustees think fit;[61]

(ii)   pay transfer or apply the whole or any part or parts of the capital of my trust Fund for any purpose whatever which the Trustees may think to be for the benefit of any one or more of the Beneficiaries for the time being in existence;[62] and

(iii)   transfer all or any part or parts of the income or capital of my Trust Fund to the trustees of any Settlement or Will Trust wherever established (whose receipt shall be good discharge to them) to be held free from the trusts of my Will and on the trusts and with and subject to the powers and provisions of that Settlement but only if those trusts powers and provisions are such that (at the time of the transfer) they could themselves have created them under (i) above.[63]

(5)   In default of and subject to any exercise of the powers given them by the preceding provisions:

(i)   during the Trust Period my Trustees shall pay or apply the income of my Trust Fund to or for the maintenance education support or otherwise for the benefit of such one or more of the Beneficiaries as my Trustees may in their absolute discretion think fit but with power to accumulate such income or any part or parts of it (with power to apply the accumulations of past years as if they were income of the current year) and with power (during the Trust Period) to resolve to hold the whole or any part or parts of such income as income on trust for any of the Beneficiaries absolutely; and[64]

(ii)   on the expiry of the Trust Period my Trustees shall hold my Trust Fund as to both capital and income on trust absolutely for [*insert default beneficiary*].[65]

(6)   My trustees (being at least two in number) may by deed or deeds (and so as to bind their successors) wholly or partially release or restrict the powers given them by this clause.

---

[60] See **2.56** *et seq* for a consideration of powers of appointment.

[61] Note that this power can be exercised revocably or irrevocably and can be used to create further discretionary trusts (eg for a more restricted class of beneficiaries): see generally **2.55** *et seq*.

[62] For advancement type powers see **2.44** *et seq*. The exercise of the statutory power does not require a deed: it can be by trustee resolution.

[63] For a consideration of powers to transfer property to another settlement see **2.53–2.55** and **2.60** *et seq*. The power in this precedent is relatively restricted (eg it cannot result in 'new' beneficiaries benefiting: see further **Precedent 4.13**).

[64] This clause deals with income: note that income can be accumulated during the 125-year perpetuity period. See **2.12**.

[65] It is not envisaged, given the trustees' wide dispositive powers, that this default trust will take effect. Some testators provide for the property to be held 'for such charities as my trustees shall select'.

(7)   No exercise of the power conferred by sub-clause (4) shall invalidate any prior payment or application of all or any part of the capital or income of my Trust Fund made under any other power conferred by my Will or by law.

Apportionments[66]

7. I direct and declare that all interest dividends and other payments in the nature of income arising from property of mine in respect of any period partly before and partly after my death shall be treated as accruing wholly after my death and shall not be apportioned.[67]

Modification of Trustee Act 1925, ss 31–32

8. The statutory powers of maintenance accumulation and advancement contained in sections 31 and 32 of the Trustee Act 1925 shall apply to the trusts of this Will and any Codicil hereto but with the following variations namely:

(1)   the said section 31 shall apply with the substitution of 'the trustees in their absolute discretion think fit' for 'may in all the circumstances be reasonable' in sub-section (1) and the omission of the proviso to sub-section (1); and

(2)   the said section 32 shall apply with the omission of 'one-half of' from proviso (a) to sub-section (1).[68]

Administrative Provisions

9.

(1)   Monies requiring to be invested under the trusts hereof may be invested or laid out or otherwise applied in the acquisition by purchase or otherwise or upon the security of such stocks funds shares securities or other property movable or immovable of whatsoever nature and wheresoever situate (whether comprised in the word 'investment' as ordinarily understood or not) and whether involving liability or not and whether producing income or not (including property of a wasting character) or upon such personal credit with or without security as my Trustees shall in their absolute discretion think fit including (but without prejudice to the generality of the foregoing) the purchase furnishing redecoration or alteration of property of any tenure in any part of the world as a residence for any beneficiary to the intent that my Trustees shall have the same full

---

[66]   This clause is strictly speaking unnecessary since 1 October 2013 when the Trusts (Capital and Income) Act 2013 became law. See **14.62**.

[67]   For the exclusion of apportionments, see **14.66**.

[68]   For a consideration of the scope of advancement-type powers, see **2.44** *et seq*. This clause is no longer necessary in the case of wills executed from 1 October 2014: see **4.31**.

and unrestricted powers of investing and transposing investments and laying out monies in all respects as if they were absolutely entitled thereto beneficially.[69]

(2) My trustees may retain any assets subject to the trusts declared by this will (including any uninvested money) in their actual state and condition for any period even although the whole or a substantial part of the assets so subject may be producing no or little income or may consist of shares or securities of a single company.[70]

(3) The statutory power of appropriation conferred by section 41 of the Administration of Estates Act 1925 shall be exercisable by my Trustees without any of the consents made requisite by that Section and shall include power to appropriate in favour of any of my Trustees entitled to a share or interest in my estate.[71]

(4) Any property for the time being subject to any of the trusts of this Will or any Codicil hereto may be kept insured against such risks (if any) and for such amount as my Trustees shall in their absolute discretion think fit (but so that my Trustees shall not in any way be obliged to effect any insurance and shall not be liable for any failure to insure) with some insurance office of repute in the names of my Trustees and my Trustees may for such purpose pay all premiums and other costs incurred in connection with such insurance out of any monies held upon the same trusts under this Will or any Codicil hereto as such insured property (and so that the benefit of any such insurance shall be held upon the like trusts).[72]

(5) My trustees shall have power to sell lease let mortgage charge license and generally manage and deal with any property (whether movable or immovable) which or the proceeds of sale of which may for the time being be subject to any of the trusts of this Will or any Codicil hereto as if they were beneficial owners absolutely entitled.[73]

(6) Any land or other immovable property which or the proceeds of sale of which may for the time being be subject to any of the trusts of this Will or any Codicil hereto may be improved or developed in such manner (including the building rebuilding demolishing erecting enlarging or improving of any buildings or other structures thereon) as my Trustees shall in their absolute discretion think fit out of capital money held on the like trusts as such property.[74]

(7) My trustees shall have power from time to time to carry on whether by themselves or in partnership with any other individual or corporation

---

[69] The statutory investment powers of trustees are set out in TA 2000, Part II. This express power (a) allows trustees to invest in land in any part of the world, and (b) allows the purchase of property as a residence for a beneficiary (which is not in law 'an investment').

[70] Many trusts hold a single asset (eg set up to hold shares in the family company) and there is no intention that the asset be sold.

[71] For powers to appropriate, see **2.67** *et seq*.

[72] See TA 1925, s 19 (as substituted by TA 2000, s 34(1)): the express power makes it clear that there is no obligation on trustees to insure.

[73] This general power extends to property anywhere in the world.

[74] See previous footnote.

(whether or not such individual shall be beneficially entitled under the trusts of this settlement) any trade or business which they consider to be for the benefit of the beneficiaries under this settlement and in connection with any such trade or business the Trustees may:

(a)   employ all or any part of the capital of the Trust Fund;

(b)   be indemnified out of the Trust Fund against any liability which they may incur in connection with the setting up carrying on or dissolution of such trade or business;

(c)   use for the purposes of the trade or business any land or buildings which are subject to the trusts of this settlement;

(d)   exercise in relation to any such trade or business and the assets thereof any of the administrative powers conferred on the Trustees by this deed or by law including (but without prejudice to the generality of the foregoing) powers of borrowing and charging and of delegation;

(e)   employ or join in employing on such terms as to remuneration and otherwise as they shall think fit any manager and other employees.[75]

(8)   My trustees shall have power to put or leave any shares stocks securities insurance policies or other property whatsoever (including money) in the name or names of any nominee or nominees for my Trustees and to put or leave any movable chattels and bearer or other securities and certificates for safe keeping in the possession or custody of any person or persons without being responsible for any loss or damage and on such terms and subject to such conditions including remuneration of any such nominee or custodian as my Trustees shall think fit and so that any such nominees or custodians may be or include any one or more of my Trustees.

(9)   My trustees shall have power to delegate all or any of their powers contained in my Will and any administrative power conferred by law (and all or any of the duties and discretions of my Trustees relating to the exercise of such powers) to any person or persons subject to such conditions (if any) as my Trustees shall think fit (without being liable for the acts or defaults of any such delegate) and to revoke or modify any such delegation or conditions.

(10) My trustees shall have power to pay to the parent or guardian of any minor for the intended purpose any sum of money intended to be applied for the maintenance education benefit or advancement of that minor and the receipt of such parent or guardian shall be a sufficient discharge to my Trustees for any such sum of money (and they shall not be bound to see or to inquire into the actual application thereof).[76]

(11) The receipt of the person professing to be the treasurer or other proper officer of any charity to which any capital or income may be payable or transferable shall be a sufficient discharge to my Trustees.

(12) My trustees shall have power (subject as provided below) to permit a Beneficiary or Beneficiaries (either alone or concurrently or successively)

---

[75]   See 10.01.
[76]   See 1.53.

to occupy use or enjoy personally any movable or immovable property which may for the time being be comprised in my Trust Fund upon any terms or conditions whatever which the Trustees may think fit PROVIDED that this power shall not be exercised except in conformity with the beneficial trusts powers and provisions for the time being governing my Trust Fund (or the part of it in which such movable or immovable property is so comprised) and the income from it.[77]

(13) My trustees shall have power (subject as provided below) to lend any money with or without security to a Beneficiary or Beneficiaries with or without payment of interest and upon such terms as to repayment and otherwise in such manner in all respects as the Trustees shall in their absolute discretion think fit PROVIDED that this power shall not be exercised except in conformity with the beneficial trusts powers and provisions for the time being governing my Trust Fund (or the part of it from which such loan is to be made) and the income from it.[78]

(14) If in the course of the management or administration of the assets for the time being subject to the trusts of this Will or any Codicil hereto my Trustees shall consider that any transaction is expedient but the same cannot be effected by reason of the presence or absence of any power for that or any other purpose vested in my Trustees by this Will or any Codicil hereto or by law my Trustees may by any deed revoke vary or confer upon themselves or on their nominees either generally or in any particular instance the necessary power for that purpose and on the execution of such deed my Trustees shall have such power as if it had been expressly conferred on them by my Will.[79]

Charging Clause[80]

10. Any executor or trustee for the time being hereof a solicitor or other person engaged in any profession or business shall be entitled to charge and be paid all usual professional or other reasonable and proper charges for business done or services rendered or time spent by him or his firm in proving my Will and administering my estate and in relation to the trusts hereof or of any Codicil hereto whether in the ordinary course of his profession or business or not and although not of a nature requiring the employment of a solicitor or other professional or business person.

---

[77] This power (along with the similar power to lend in (12) below) is desirable even in the case of a discretionary trust. In the case of land and chattels, occupation should be regulated by a licence granted by the trustees. In the case of loans, an agreement should be drawn up. Commonly loans are interest free, repayable on demand, which will have no tax consequences.

[78] See previous footnote.

[79] A useful 'fall back' power: see **4.29**.

[80] See **1.38–1.39**.

[Exculpation Clause[81]

11. No trustee being an individual shall be liable for any loss or damage which may happen to my estate or any property or the income of any property forming part of my estate or for the time being subject to the trusts of this Will or any Codicil hereto arising from any improper investment or purchase made by such Trustee in good faith or for the negligence or fraud of any agent employed by him or by any other Trustee hereof although such employment was not strictly necessary or expedient or by reason of any mistake or omission made in good faith by any Trustee hereof.]

Administration of Estate incomplete[82]

12. My Trustees may exercise any or all of the powers contained in this Will notwithstanding that the administration of my estate may then be incomplete and my residuary estate not by then established and notwithstanding that probate of this Will may not have been granted.

Exclusion of the self-dealing rule[83]

13.

(1)   Any of my Trustees may join in exercising the powers and discretions conferred on him by this Will notwithstanding that such Trustee may be personally interested as a Beneficiary provided that such powers shall not be exercisable by a sole trustee who is my said husband/wife.

(2)   My Trustees may in their absolute discretion enter into any agreement or transaction with the trustee or trustees of any other will or settlement (being an agreement or transaction which apart from the present provision the Trustees could properly have entered into if one or more of them had not also been a trustee of such other will or settlement) notwithstanding that my Trustees or one or more of them may also be trustees or a trustee or the sole trustee of such other settlement or will and in like manner in all respects as if none of my Trustees were a trustee of such other settlement or will.

---

[81]   See **1.42** *et seq*. This clause should not be included without the express approval of the testator.
[82]   Arguably the trustees do not need this power since the will trust is constituted at death. It does, however, provide reassurance: eg when a s 144 appointment has to be made within 2 years of death (see Chapter 13).
[83]   See **1.36**.

Appointment of New Trustees

14.

(1)   The statutory power of appointing new trustees is applicable hereto [and shall be vested in my said husband/wife during his/her life].[84]

[(2)   The provisions of sections 19 and 20 of the Trusts of Land and Appointment of Trustees Act 1996 shall not apply to this Will or any Codicil hereto.]

Incapacity

15. If any person (hereinafter called 'the Patient') in whom any power in this deed or by law is for the time being vested (whether solely or jointly) is by reason of illness incapable of exercising the power and the same is confirmed in writing to the Trustees by a qualified medical practitioner then during the period of such incapacity the power shall be exercisable as if the Patient had died.

Clause Headings

16. The headings to the clauses of this Will are for the purposes of information only and are not part of and shall not be used in the construction of this Will or of any part of it.

IN WITNESS wherefore etc.

---

[84]   See **1.41.** Consider adding a proviso 'whilst he/she retains mental capacity and subject thereto shall be vested in my trustees'.

Precedent 4.2: Letter of wishes[85]

To the trustees of my discretionary will trust

I am writing this letter to offer you guidance of how I envisage the trusts of my residuary estate being administered. This is only an expression of wishes: it is not binding on you and the decisions that you make will, of course, reflect the circumstances of the time. My thinking behind the trust is that:

1. during her lifetime I wish my wife to be treated as the principal beneficiary and so far as she needs to receive income and capital from the trust;

2. after her death (or to the extent that she does not need to be provided for out of the trust) I wish my children to be the main beneficiaries and, in principle, I would envisage them benefitting equally. However there may well be good reasons to treat the children differently. For instance, my daughter may have no need herself to receive monies from the trust in which case her 'share' might be used to benefit her children. Alternatively, one of my children might have a special need (for instance, as a result of illness or suffering an accident) and this may justify benefitting him to a greater extent than his siblings. I view the trust as an ongoing family asset and wish it to be used for the benefit of the family as a unit.

It follows that I do not envisage the trust being wound up on the death of my wife but would hope that it can be used to benefit not just my children but also grandchildren (it even may be great-grandchildren!).

Of course, a future tax regime may make this unattractive in which case you may wish to use your powers to bring the trust to an end.

I wish this letter to be circulated amongst my family[86] so that they can see what I hope to achieve with this trust and that I am content to rely upon your good sense to administer the trust in the future.

Signed and dated

---

[85] This can be used alongside **Precedent 4.1**. In general, whenever flexible trusts are created it is desirable for the testator to provide some guidance for his trustees. This is the case with **Precedent 4.4** when, apart from the nil rate band discretionary trust, there is also a flexible IPDI in the residuary estate. Some indication of the circumstances in which the surviving spouse's interest in possession might be terminated is desirable.

[86] Whether letters of wishes are confidential documents has given rise to litigation (see, for instance, *Hartigan Nominees Pty Ltd v Rydge* (1992) 29 NSWLR 405). The testator can put the matter beyond doubt by requiring distributions of the letter which, unless it contains sensitive material, is desirable. See the authors' *A Modern Approach to Lifetime Tax Planning*, Chapter 9.

Precedent 4.3: Standard attestation clauses

Form 1: standard clause

Signed by [name of testator/trix] in our joint)
presence and then by us in [his] [hers])

Form 2: clause where another signs for testator

This will was read over to the [testator][testatrix] in our)
presence

and [he][she] appeared thoroughly to understand it and to)
approve

its contents. The will was then signed by [name of person)
signing]

in the presence of the [testator][testatrix] and by [his][her])
direction

and in our joint presence and it was then signed by us in the)
presence of the [testator][testatrix])

Note: This form recites two essential elements:

(a) the testator directed that the will be signed on his behalf;[87]
(b) the testator knew and approved the contents of the will.[88]

---

[87] Positive evidence of direction is required: see *Barratt v Bem* [2012] EWCA Civ 52 and **1.10**.
[88] See **1.22**.

Precedent 4.4: Clauses creating nil rate band discretionary trust and flexible IPDI trust of residue

Definitions

5.

(1) In clause 6 of this Will where the context so permits the following expressions shall have the following meanings:
  (i) 'the Discretionary Beneficiaries' shall mean subject to the provisions of clause 5(2) below:
    (a) my said husband/wife
    (b) my children and remoter issue
    (c) the spouses widows and widowers of the persons mentioned in (b)

    and 'discretionary beneficiary' shall have a corresponding meaning.
  (ii) 'the Trust Period' shall mean the period commencing with the date of my death and ending one hundred and twenty five years thereafter and such period of one hundred and twenty five years shall be the perpetuity period applicable to the dispositions made by my Will PROVIDED THAT my Legacy Fund Trustees may declare by irrevocable deed that the Trust Period (but not the said perpetuity period) shall terminate on such date as they may specify therein (such date of termination to be earlier than the end of the said period of one hundred and twenty five years but the same as or later than the date of such deed)
  (iii) 'the Legacy Fund Trustees' shall mean [insert details of trustees] or other the trustee or trustees for the time being of the Legacy Fund.[89]
    (2)
  (i) SUBJECT to sub-clause (b) below:
    (a) My Legacy Fund Trustees (being not less than two in number or a trust corporation) shall have power by any deed or deeds revocable (during the Trust Period) or irrevocable executed during the Trust Period to declare that any individual or individuals whether or not then born or ascertained or any Charity or Charities (other than any individual then a trustee of the Legacy Fund and other than any individual or Charity previously excluded under the power set out in (b) below) shall from such time and (subject to any future exercise of the power set out in clause 5(2)(i)(b) below) either permanently or for such period or periods as shall be specified in any such deed or deeds be included in the class of Discretionary Beneficiaries defined in Clause 5(1)(i) above and

---

[89] In drafting the will it is helpful to designate 'Legacy Fund Trustees' even if they are the same persons as the trustees of the will.

    (b)   The Legacy Fund Trustees (being not less than two in number or a trust corporation) shall also have power by any deed or deeds revocable (during the Trust Period) or irrevocable executed during the Trust Period to declare that any individual or individuals whether or not born or ascertained or any Charity or Charities who or which is or are a member or members (or eligible to be added as a member or members) of the class of Discretionary Beneficiaries immediately prior to the execution of such deed or deeds shall from such time and either permanently or for such period or periods as shall be specified in any such deed or deeds cease to be a member or members (or eligible to become a member or members) of such class.

  (ii) PROVIDED always that no such deed made in exercise of either of the powers conferred by sub-clause (i) shall affect the validity or effect of:

    (a)   any distribution previously made to or for the benefit of any beneficiary under or pursuant to any power or discretion

    (b)   any transmissible interest (whether vested or contingent) previously conferred on any beneficiary

    (c)   any future distribution to any beneficiary consequent on the absolute vesting in possession of any such interest as is mentioned in sub-clause (ii)(b) and

    (d)   the Legacy Fund Trustees (being not less than two in number or a trust corporation) may at any time or times during the Trust Period by deed or deeds extinguish (or restrict the future exercise of) both or either of the powers (but not any of the restrictions applicable to them) conferred by sub-clause (i) above.

Legacy Fund—Nil rate band discretionary trust (with loan/charge provisions)

6.

(1)   THIS clause shall not take effect unless the gift made to my [husband/wife] by Clause [number] of my Will takes effect (or but for this Clause would do so).

(2)   IN this Clause 'the Nil-Rate Sum' means the largest sum of cash which could be given on the trusts of this Clause without any inheritance tax becoming due in respect of the transfer of the value of my estate which I am deemed to make immediately before my death and that the value of any unused nil rate band to which my estate may be entitled shall be taken into account in arriving at the Nil Rate Sum.[90]

    (3)

---

[90] In the event that an additional nil rate band is available (because the testator had been married before and his spouse had predeceased without making use of the IHT nil rate band), the definition of 'the nil rate sum' will catch both the deceased's and the transferred nil rate band. Amend if this is not desired and delete clause (3)(ii).

(i)   I GIVE the Nil-Rate Sum to my Legacy Fund Trustees on trust to invest it in exercise of the powers of investment given them by my Will and by law and to hold it and the property which currently represents it ('the Legacy Fund') on the trusts and with and subject to the powers and provisions set out in this clause.

(ii)   I REQUIRE and DECLARE that my Executors shall claim the benefit of any unused inheritance tax nil rate band to which my estate may be entitled

(4)   DURING the Trust Period my Legacy Fund Trustees (being at least two in number or a trust corporation) may at any time or times:

(i)   by deed or deeds revocable (during the Trust Period) or irrevocable appoint that all or any part or parts of the income or capital of the Legacy Fund shall be held on such trusts (including discretionary and protective ones) in favour or for the benefit of all or any one or more of the Discretionary Beneficiaries and with and subject to such powers (including dispositive and administrative ones exercisable by my Legacy Fund Trustees or any other person) and other provisions as my Legacy Fund Trustees think fit;

(ii)   transfer all or any part or parts of the income or capital of the Legacy Fund to the trustees of any Settlement wherever established (whose receipt shall be good discharge to them) to be held free from the trusts of my Will and on the trusts and with and subject to the powers and provisions of that Settlement but only if those trusts powers and provisions are such that (at the time of the transfer) they could themselves have created them under (i) above; and

(iii) pay transfer or apply any part of the Legacy Fund to or for the advancement or benefit of any Discretionary Beneficiary.

(5)   IN default of and subject to any exercise of the powers given them by the preceding provisions:

(i)   during the Trust Period my Legacy Fund Trustees shall pay or apply the income of the Legacy Fund to or for the maintenance education support or otherwise for the benefit of such one or more of the Discretionary Beneficiaries as my Legacy Fund Trustees may in their absolute discretion think fit but with power to accumulate such income or any part or parts of it (with power to apply the accumulations of past years as if they were income of the current year) and with power (during the Trust Period) to resolve to hold the whole or any part or parts of such income as income on trust for any of the Beneficiaries absolutely and

(ii)   on the expiry of the Trust Period my Legacy Fund Trustees shall hold the Legacy Fund as to both capital and income on trust absolutely for such of my issue as are then living and if more than one in equal shares through all degrees according to their stocks and so that no issue shall take whose parent is alive and so capable of taking.

(6)   MY Legacy Fund Trustees (being at least two in number) may by deed or deeds (and so as to bind their successors) wholly or partially release or restrict the powers given them by this clause.

(7)   ANY other non-residuary gifts made by my Will or any Codicil to it shall have priority to this one.

(8)   INSTEAD of satisfying the legacy wholly by the payment of cash (or by the appropriation of property) to the Legacy Fund Trustees my Trustees may:

    (i)   require the Legacy Fund Trustees to accept in place of all or any part of the Nil-Rate Sum a binding promise of payment made by my Trustees as trustees of any residuary property given by this Will or any Codicil hereto on trusts under which my [husband/wife] has an interest in possession for the purposes of Inheritance Tax which debt shall be repayable on demand;[91]

    (ii)   charge all or any part of the Nil Rate Sum on any property which is (or but for this clause would be) given by this Will or any Codicil to it on trusts under which my [husband/wife] has an interest in possession for the purposes of Inheritance Tax.[92]

(9)   THE Legacy Fund Trustees may lend money currently held by them to my spouse.

(10)   IN amplification of the foregoing provisions

    (i)   if my Trustees exercise their powers under (8)(i) above they shall be under no further liability to see that the Legacy Fund Trustees receive the sum promised and if they exercise their powers under (8)(ii) they shall be under no further liability to see that the Legacy Fund Trustees receive the sum secured

    (ii)   if my Trustees exercise their powers under (8)(ii) above they may give an assent of the property subject to the charge and no one in whose favour the assent is made shall become personally liable for the sum secured

    (iii)   the Legacy Fund Trustees may require security to be given for any debt to be created by a promise within (8)(i) above or by a loan within (9) and in relation both to such debts (whether or not secured) and to any debt to be secured by a charge within (8)(ii) (all of which shall be debts payable on demand) they

        (1)   may (subject to the foregoing provisions) impose such terms (if any) as they think fit including terms as to interest and the personal liability of the borrower and terms linking the debt to the Index of Retail Prices or otherwise providing for its amount to vary with the passage of time according to a formula and

        (2)   may subsequently leave the debt outstanding for as long as they think fit and refrain from exercising their rights in relation to it and waive the payment of all or any part of it or of any interest due in respect of it

    and they shall not be liable if my Trustees are or become unable to pay the debt or a security is or becomes inadequate or for any other loss which may occur through their exercising or choosing not to exercise any power given by this sub-clause

---

[91]   This enables a simple debt trust to be created: see Chapter 13.
[92]   This envisages the creation of a charge over the deceased's property.

(iv) the powers given by this clause are without prejudice to any other powers given by this Will or any Codicil to it or by the general law and are exercisable even though my Trustees and the Legacy Fund Trustees may be the same persons and my spouse may be among them (but they are not exercisable while my spouse is the sole Legacy Fund Trustee) and any of the Legacy Fund Trustees may exercise or concur in existing all powers and discretions given to him by this clause or by law notwithstanding that he has a direct or other personal interest in the mode or result of any such exercise.

Trust of Residue

7. I GIVE DEVISE AND BEQUEATH all my property both movable and immovable of whatever nature and wheresoever situated except property otherwise disposed of by this Will or by any Codicil hereto unto my Trustees UPON TRUST to sell call in and convert the same into money (so far as not already consisting of money) with power to postpone the sale calling in and conversion thereof (even as regards property of a terminable hazardous or wasting nature) in the absolute and uncontrolled discretion of my Trustees without being liable for loss and to hold the net proceeds and my ready money upon the following trusts:

(1) UPON TRUST to pay thereout (in exoneration of any property which would otherwise be liable for payment of the same) all my funeral and testamentary expenses and debts and any general legacies given by this Will or any Codicil hereto and any tax or duty arising in respect of my death (even if not a testamentary expense) on all gifts in this Will and any Codicil hereto given free of such tax or duty

(2) UPON TRUST if necessary to invest the remainder after such payment in or upon any investments hereinafter authorised for the investment of trust funds with power to vary and transpose the same

(3) UPON TRUST to stand possessed of such investments and such of my estate as remains for the time being unsold and my ready money and all property from time to time respectively representing the same (hereinafter together called 'my Residuary Trust Fund') and the income thereof upon the following trusts.

Trusts for surviving spouse[93] and children

8. THE PROVISIONS of this clause shall apply in default of until and subject to any exercise of the powers conferred by clause 9.

8.1 THE income of my Residuary Trust Fund shall be paid to my [Husband/Wife] during [his/her] lifetime.

---

[93] The remainder trusts apply (a) on the death of the surviving spouse and (b) in the event that she predeceases the testator. Note that in the latter eventuality the nil rate band trust does not take effect (see **clause 6(1)**).

8.2 THE Trustees may, at any time during the Trust Period, pay or apply the whole or any part of the Trust Fund in which my [Husband/Wife] is then entitled to an interest in possession to [him/her] or for [his/her] advancement or otherwise for [his/her] benefit in such manner as the Trustees shall in their discretion think fit. In exercising the powers conferred by this sub-clause, the Trustees shall be entitled to have regard solely to the interests of my [Husband/Wife] and to disregard all other interests or potential interests under my Will.

8.3 Subject thereto the Trustees shall hold the capital and income of my Residuary Trust Fund for such of my children as shall survive me and attain the age of 18 years before the end of the Trust Period, or shall be living and under that age at the end of the Trust Period, and, if more than one, in equal shares absolutely.

8.4 [Consider inserting general power of appointment – see **Precedent 6.5.**]

Overriding powers

9. MY Trustees shall have the following powers exercisable during the Trust Period [and while my spouse is alive]:[94]

9.1 My Trustees shall hold the capital and income of my Residuary Trust Fund in favour or for the benefit of all or such one or more of the Discretionary Beneficiaries (as defined in clause [6]) at such ages or times exclusive of the other or others of them in such shares or proportions if more than one and with and subject to such powers trusts and provisions for their respective maintenance education or other benefit or for the accumulation of income (including administrative powers and provisions and discretionary or protective trusts and powers to be executed or exercised by any person or persons whether or not being or including my Trustees or any of them and including powers or trusts to accumulate the whole or any part of the income of my Residuary Trust Fund during the Trust Period) and in such manner generally as my Trustees (subject to the application (if any) of the rule against perpetuities) by any deed or deeds revocable during the Trust Period or irrevocable and executed during the Trust Period shall appoint PROVIDED ALWAYS that such power may only be exercised by the Trustees during the lifetime of my spouse and provided further that no exercise of this power shall deprive the spouse of any income to which s/he was entitled at the time when it arose or otherwise invalidate any prior payment or application of all or any part or parts of the capital or income of the Residuary Trust Fund made under any other power or powers conferred by my Will or by law.

9.2 For the purpose of giving effect to any such appointment the Trustees shall have power to revoke all or any of the trusts powers and provisions

---

[94] Delete words in square brackets if it is intended that the children should not take outright on the spouse's death. The children would then take only defeasible absolute interests at 18 that can be ended by exercise of the clause 10 powers.

contained in clause 8 including any interest in possession under clause 8 with respect to my Residuary Trust Fund or part or parts thereof to which such appointment relates.

9.3 I declare that provided they are at least two in number or a corporate trustee my Trustees may exercise any or all of the powers contained in this clause whether or not some or all of my Trustees are beneficially interested (either presently or prospectively) in my Residuary Trust Fund and notwithstanding that at the date of such exercise there shall have been no grant of probate or administration in respect of the property over which the said powers shall be executed or that the administration of my estate shall not have been completed.

9.4 The Trustees' powers conferred upon them by the preceding paragraphs of this clause shall include power to transfer pay or apply any part of the capital and income of the Residuary Estate to the trustees for the time being of any settlement wherever established (whose receipt shall be a good discharge to them) to be held free from the trusts of the Will and on the trusts and with and subject to the powers and provisions of that settlement but only if those trusts powers and provisions are such that at the time of the transfer they could themselves have created them under clause 9.1 above.

Precedent 4.5: Appointment of executors/partners

1. I appoint as my executors and trustees the partners at the date of my death in the firm of [AB & Co] (solicitors) of [address] or the firm or incorporated practice which at that date has succeeded to and carries on its practice.

2. In (1) above 'firm' includes an incorporated practice recognised by the Solicitors Regulation Authority and 'partners' includes salaried partners and directors or members of or beneficial owners of shares in an incorporated practice.

3. In my Will the expression 'my Trustees' shall, where relevant, include my executors and the trustees for the time being of any trust arising under my Will.

4. I express the wish that only two of the partners I have appointed shall prove my will and act initially in its trusts.

5. Any of my Trustees who is a solicitor or is engaged in any other profession may charge his usual professional charges for work done by him or his firm (including acts which a layman could have done personally) on the same basis as if he were not one of my Trustees but employed to carry out the work on their behalf.

Precedent 4.6: Specific gift of shares/house to avoid ademption

Gift of shares

(a) I give to [*name of beneficiary*] [provided he/she survives me by 28 days] all my [*identify class of shares*] shares in [ ] Plc.

[(b) Any charge on the shares existing at my death shall be paid out of my Residuary Estate.]

[(c) If any of the shares referred to in the gift in paragraph (a) above are as a result of takeover amalgamation or reconstruction represented by a different holding paragraph (a) above shall take effect as a gift of that holding.]

Gift of house or flat

I give to [*name of beneficiary*] [provided he/she survives me by 28 days] [free of tax] [subject to tax] [free of mortgage] [my house or flat known as [*insert address*] [that property which at my death constitutes my principal private residence and if doubt exists as to which is my principal private residence the decision of my Trustees shall be final and binding] [and I direct that any charge on the house or flat shall be discharged out of my Residuary Estate].

Precedent 4.7: Declaration that will is made in expectation of marriage/entering civil partnership

I make this Will in expectation of [my marriage to [ ]] [forming a civil partnership with [ ]] and I intend that this will is not to be revoked by [my marriage] [the formation of that civil partnership].

Precedent 4.8: Class gifts[95]

My Trustees shall hold the trust fund on trust absolutely for such of my grandchildren living at my death or born afterwards at any time during their parents' lifetime as reach the age of 18 or marry under that age and if more than one in equal shares PROVIDED that the share in the Trust Fund of any grandchild who has attained a vested interest shall not be diminished by the birth or marriage of or the attainment of 18 by any further grandchildren.

---

[95] This clause allows grandchildren born after the date at which the class would normally close to participate. Assume that a testator has three grandchildren, A, B and C, living at the date of death. A reaches 18. After that date, and before B and C have reached 18, D and E are born. Normally the class will close as soon as A reaches 18 but if this clause is included: A takes one-third of the fund immediately; and B, C, D and E take one-quarter of the remaining fund at 18.

Precedent 4.9: Nil rate band legacies

Form 1 – Short form[96]

I give to those of my children who survive me and if more than one in equal shares such sum as at my death equals the maximum amount which could be given to them by this will without inheritance tax becoming payable on my estate.

Form 2 – Expanded form[97]

I give to those of my children who survive me and if more than one in equal shares such sum as at my death equals the maximum amount which could be given to them by this Will without inheritance tax becoming payable on my estate after taking into account the following:

(a)   all or any chargeable transfers (including potentially exempt transfers which have become chargeable as a result of my death) made by me during my lifetime in the cumulation period specified by section 7(1)(a) of the Inheritance Tax Act 1984; and

(b)   all other gifts (if any) taking effect under my Will or any Codicil hereto to the extent that they are not exempt transfers for the purpose of the charge to inheritance tax on my death; and

(c)   all other property (if any) which is treated as property to which I am beneficially entitled immediately before my death (including property subject to a reservation as defined by section 102 of the Finance Act 1986); and

(d)   all or any settled property in which on my death I have a qualifying interest in possession so that section 49 of the Inheritance Tax Act 1984 applies and results in the settled property being chargeable to inheritance tax by reason of my death.

Form 3 – Form to include a transferred nil rate band and which requires it to be claimed by the personal representatives

The Nil Rate Sum shall mean whichever is the lesser of:

(a)   twice the upper limit of the nil rate per cent band in the table of rates of tax applicable on my death in Schedule 1 to the Inheritance Tax Act 1984; and

(b)   the maximum amount which will not give rise to a charge to inheritance tax by reason of my death

---

[96]   This legacy will give the maximum possible without payment of IHT. If the transferor has the benefit of a transferable nil band (see Chapter 5), the size of the legacy will be increased.

[97]   This clause does exactly the same as the short form.

PROVIDED THAT I require my Executors to claim the benefit of any unused inheritance tax nil rate band to which my estate may be entitled and that the value of that unused nil rate band shall be taken into account in arriving at the Nil Rate Sum.

Form 4 – Limited to single nil rate band[98]

I give to [ ] such sum as is equal to the upper limit of the nil per cent band in the table of rates of tax (applicable on my death) in Schedule 1 to the Inheritance Tax Act 1984 less an amount equal to the aggregate of the amount chargeable to inheritance tax of:

(a)   all or any chargeable transfers (including potentially exempt transfers which have become chargeable as a result of my death) made by me during my lifetime in the cumulation period specified by section 7(1)(a) of the Inheritance Tax Act 1984; and

(b)   all other gifts (if any) taking effect under my Will or any Codicil to my Will to the extent that they are not exempt transfers for the purpose of the charge to inheritance tax on my death; and

(c)   all other property (if any) which is treated as property to which I am beneficially entitled immediately before my death (including property subject to a reservation as defined by section 102 of the Finance Act 1986); and

(d)   all or any settled property in which on my death I have a qualifying interest in possession so that section 49(1) of the Inheritance Tax Act 1984 applies and results in the settled property being chargeable to inheritance tax by reason of my death.

---

[98]   This clause limits the amount given to a single nil rate band: for transferable nil rate bands: see Chapter 5.

Precedent 4.10: Charitable legacies

Form 1 – Gift to named charity

I GIVE [£] to [name of charity] [on trust] for its general charitable purposes and I DIRECT that my Will shall be construed and take effect as if section 311 of the Charities Act 2011 did not apply to this legacy. If at the date of my death [name of charity] is no longer in existence or is subject to a winding-up order] my Trustees shall pay the legacy to such other charity or charities having the same or similar objects as my Trustees shall select.

Form 2 – Trustees given power to select charities with default provision

I GIVE [*identify property*] to my Trustees to hold upon trust for such charities in such shares as the Trustees shall in their absolute discretion appoint.

Any appointment shall be made by my Trustees by deed within the period of [ ] from my death.

In default of any such appointment the legacy shall be held for [ ] for its general charitable purposes.

Precedent 4.11: Option to purchase land

(a) I DIRECT my trustees to offer my freehold property situate at [etc] to [name] at the purchase price of £... such offer to be made within six months of the date of the grant of probate or administration to my estate and to be accepted by [name] within one year from the date on which such offer is made by my trustees whereupon the right of the said [name] to exercise the option by accepting such offer shall absolutely cease and I DIRECT that my trustees shall take such steps as may reasonably be required to bring the said offer to the attention of the said [name] as soon as may be practicable.

(b) I FURTHER DIRECT that:
   (i) the option is personal to [name] and may not be exercised by any person save for himself and is not transmissible to his personal representative or otherwise;
   (ii) following the payment of the price as aforesaid the said [name] shall be indemnified out of my residuary estate from and against any inheritance tax and any foreign death duties payable in respect of the said property on or by reason of my death or in the administration of my estate;
   (iii) my trustees may in their absolute and uncontrolled discretion accept payment of the said purchase price in instalments or otherwise and may accept such security as they in their absolute discretion think fit in respect of any sum remaining unpaid and may charge interest on any outstanding sum at such rate as they shall in their absolute discretion determine;
   (iv) upon the said [name] exercising the said option my trustees shall forthwith convey to him the fee simple of the said property free from incumbrances save any mortgage or other security in respect of part or all of the said purchase price for the time being remaining outstanding and any interest due in respect of the same;

(c) I DECLARE that if the said option is not exercised within the said period, then at any time after the expiration of the said period my trustees shall deal with the property in accordance with the trusts hereof and in any deed relating to the said property executed by my trustees any recital or other statement in writing to the effect that the offer to sell the property to [name] hereunder has not been accepted shall be conclusive evidence of the same to anyone dealing with my trustees for money or money's worth; and

(d) MY TRUSTEES SHALL accumulate the income of the said property until the exercise of the said option or the expiry of the time for its exercise whichever is the sooner and hold such accumulations as part of my residuary estate.

Precedent 4.12: Clauses dealing with the residence

Form 1: Clause creating trust to hold a residence for a spouse

I GIVE my freehold property situate at ... to my trustees UPON TRUST to sell the same with power to postpone the sale so long as they see fit and to use the proceeds of such sale for the purpose of acquiring a freehold property to be held on a discretionary trust for my wife [*name*] with power to grant her a right to occupy the said property or any other property acquired in substitution therefore during her lifetime or until she shall remarry.

Form 2: Clause creating trust for spouse of the testator's share as tenant in common of residence, with a full life interest for the spouse and with provision for a substitute dwelling

I GIVE to my trustees UPON TRUST my share held as tenant in common with my wife [*name*] in the freehold property situate at [*insert details*] for her lifetime with power to sell the said share with the consent of my said wife and with power to use the said proceeds of the sale of my said share in or towards the purchase of a further property my share in which to be held UPON TRUST by my trustees for my said wife during her lifetime.

Note: this clause is likely to create an interest in possession (an IPDI) for the wife.

Form 3: Clause leaving (leasehold) residence to trustees and allowing them to grant a licence to the surviving spouse

I GIVE my [leasehold] property situate at ... to my trustees to be held UPON TRUST with power to grant to my wife [name] a licence to occupy the said property upon such terms as my trustees shall in their absolute discretion think fit and provided that she shall pay any rent due in respect of the same and shall observe and perform the lessee's covenants and conditions reserved by and contained in the lease of the said property throughout her period of occupation.

Note: this clause is likely to create an interest in possession (an IDPI).

Form 4: Clause leaving residence to trustees with power to allow unmarried daughter to live there

I GIVE my freehold residence situate at [*etc.*] [free of inheritance tax] [and free of all moneys secured thereon at my death (which moneys shall be paid out of my residuary estate)] to my trustees UPON TRUST AND I DIRECT that my trustees shall permit my daughter [name] if she shall be unmarried at my death to reside there rent free for so long as she shall remain unmarried she keeping the same in good repair and insured to the satisfaction of my trustees throughout the period of her residence and I DECLARE that upon the death or marriage of my said daughter for the time being or if my said daughter after my death shall be unwilling to reside therein my trustees shall stand possessed of the said property upon the following trusts ...

Note: this clause is likely to create an interest in possession (an IPDI).

Precedent 4.13: Power to transfer property to another settlement (drafting note)

Drafting note

The wording of such clauses varies widely. In drafting the will trust or settlement, the draftsman needs to discuss with the testator (settlor):

1. whether he wants to include such a power. Bear in mind that this can be useful as a way of merging settlements for greater efficiency (eg. a number of pilot trusts: see **7.16**);

2. is the power to be limited so that the transferee trust must be one which the trustees could themselves have created? See, for instance, **Precedent 1.1, clause 6(4)(ii)**:

    > 'but only if those trusts powers and provisions are such that (at the time of the transfer) they could themselves have created them under [the power of appointment in the will] above'

3. a wider power enables the trustees to transfer property to any trust if it is for the benefit of any beneficiary despite the fact that the new trusts may be discretionary and that persons (not beneficiaries under the transferor settlement) can benefit. Consider the following:

    > 'power to transfer the Trust Fund or any part of it to the trustees of any other trust or settlement wherever established or existing[99] under which any one or more[100] of the Beneficiaries is or are beneficially interested (whether or not[101] such one or more of the Beneficiaries is or are the only person or persons interested or capable of benefitting under such trust or settlement) [so long as neither the Settlor nor any spouse of the Settlor shall be interested or capable of benefitting under such other trust or settlement].'[102]

---

[99] The settlement may have been set up outside the UK.

[100] It suffices that only *one* of the existing beneficiaries can benefit under the transferee settlement.

[101] Other persons – not beneficiaries in the transferor settlement – may benefit in the transferee settlement.

[102] Include the words in the square brackets if the transferor trust was a lifetime settlement: they are obviously irrelevant to will trusts. For the dangers if they are not included, see *IRC v Botnar* [1999] STC 711, CA.

CHAPTER 5

THE IMPACT OF THE TRANSFERABLE NIL RATE BAND

1. SETTING THE SCENE

5.01 The introduction of a transferable unused nil rate band between spouses and civil partners as from October 2007 revolutionised the drafting of the traditional family will. In this chapter we will consider the position before this change and then look at the rules introduced in 2007 together with their implications for the will draftsman. Finally, we will review the position of wills made before the change where the testator has now died. Before doing so, there are two background points to consider.

The frozen nil rate band

5.02 The nil rate band has been frozen at £325,000 by FA 2014 until the end of tax year 2017–18. Previously one of the advantages of transferring the nil rate band was that what was available on the survivor's death was an additional nil rate band of the amount current at the time of the survivor's death. Accordingly, the benefit of increases in the amount of the nil rate band after the first death was secured. With freezing, however, the amount of the nil rate band will not be rising in line with CPI or rises in property values. Hence, there is an argument for using the nil rate band sooner (ie on the first death) rather than later (on the second death) to ensure that increases in asset values take place outside the estate of the surviving spouse.

> *Example 5.1*
>
> Janet died in July 2013 leaving her entire estate to her husband, Alfred. Included in her estate was an investment property worth £325,000.
>
> Alfred died in 2017 when the nil rate band was still £325,000 and the investment property was worth £400,000. On his death, his estate will be able to claim an additional nil rate band.
>
> 1.   At the time of Janet's death, the investment property fell within her nil rate band but by the time of Alfred's death its value had increased by £75,000, which increase had not been matched by an equivalent increase in the nil rate band. Accordingly, tax at 40% may be charged on the £75,000 increase (a potential tax bill of £30,000).
>
> Contrast the position if:

2.   Janet's will had put the property into a discretionary trust under which Alfred and her children could benefit. This exhausts Janet's nil rate band but on Alfred's death no IHT will be payable on the property.[1] If desired, the trust can be ended at any time during the 10-year period from Janet's death without any IHT exit charge being payable[2] and with the benefit of CGT hold-over relief.[3] If it is decided to keep the trust in being, the charge on the 10-year anniversary will be at 6% on the value of the property in excess of the then nil rate band. For instance, if it is then worth £425,000 and the nil rate band remains frozen at £325,000, the tax will be £6,000.[4]

Future legislative changes

5.03   Some fear that in the future the rules allowing an unused nil rate band to be transferred will be repealed.[5] That might, of course, leave taxpayers who had died without using up their nil rate band worse off. Whilst it is impossible to predict future legislative changes, it is suggested that, out of basic fairness if nothing else, any such change ought to apply only where the first spouse dies after the change, leaving the rules intact if the first spouse had already died.

2. USING THE NIL RATE BAND BEFORE 9 OCTOBER 2007[6]

5.04   Before 9 October 2007 standard IHT planning advice for a married couple (or civil partners) was to ensure that the nil rate band of the first spouse to die was used on his death. Leaving everything to the surviving spouse meant that the first nil rate band was wasted. In tax year 2007–08 using two rather than just one nil rate band was worth £120,000 (£300,000 × 40%). However, using the nil rate band of the first spouse to die was not always straightforward.

First, each spouse had to have enough assets in his estate to make use of his nil rate band. If the first to die (H) only owned assets of (say) £100,000 at his death his nil rate band could only be used to this extent.[7]

---

1   Because it is comprised in a relevant property trust and so only subject to charges every 10 years and when property leaves the trust: see **3.62** *et seq.*

2   Because the settlement has a full nil rate band available and until the first anniversary property is not revalued and previous transfers are not taken into account when calculating the charge to IHT: see **3.67**.

3   For CGT hold-over relief when property ceases to be comprised in a relevant property settlement, see **3.100**.

4   For the calculation of the 10-year charge, see **3.62**.

5   This does seem unlikely given that it was introduced by the then Labour Government in response to the Conservative Party's proposal to increase the nil rate band to £1m (and, a subsequent refinement, to retain the transferable nil rate band)!

6   The rules on the transferable nil rate band apply to both spouses and civil partners. For simplicity the examples below use husband (H) and wife (W) and assume that H dies first.

7   A deed of variation could not change this to 'put assets into' a deceased's estate.

Secondly, unless the couple had a sufficiently large joint estate they would not want assets equal to the nil rate band to pass direct to the children on H's death because this would leave W financially vulnerable.

Thirdly, in many cases the bulk of the family wealth was tied up in the matrimonial home and couples usually disliked the idea of H's share in the home passing outright to the children in case the children tried to force a sale (especially if the children were from H's first marriage).[8] There were two other downsides to leaving the deceased's interest in the matrimonial home to the children:

(a) If a child became bankrupt or divorced, his interest in the property was available for creditors or for provision on divorce.[9]

(b) The children's share in the property did not qualify for CGT principal private residence relief.

5.05 The solution to these problems was for H to set up a discretionary trust in his will to utilise his IHT nil rate band: the discretionary beneficiaries would include W as well as the children/grandchildren and usually it was envisaged that W would be the principal beneficiary. It was important to ensure that nothing was done which could result in W becoming entitled to a qualifying interest in possession since, were that to occur, the value of the trust fund would be aggregated with W's estate and taxed on her death[10] with the result that H's nil rate band would be wasted.

5.06 It was often difficult to find appropriate assets to go into the trust. A simple solution was to put H's share of the matrimonial home (or a proportion of it) into the discretionary trust (assuming that its value[11] was equal to or

---

[8] In fact it seems unlikely that in this situation the children would succeed in persuading the court to order a sale of the property or to force W to pay them a 'rent': note the wide powers of the court under the Trusts of Land and Appointment of Trustees Act 1996, ss 14–15. Of course, the children could seek to sell their beneficial share but even if a purchaser could be found the price received was likely to be heavily discounted.

[9] If a child became bankrupt the normal factors considered by the court on application for an order for sale did not apply. Instead the trustee in bankruptcy could apply to the court having jurisdiction in the bankruptcy where regard was had to the interests of the bankrupt's creditors as well as to all the circumstances of the case. However, 12 months after the bankrupt's assets first vested in the trustee the interests of the creditors were deemed to outweigh all other considerations unless the circumstance of the case were exceptional. At this point it was therefore likely that an order for sale would be made: see Insolvency Act 1986, s 335A.

[10] Before FA 2006 W would obtain a qualifying interest in possession if she obtained a right to income or a right to use trust property at any time during the life of the settlement. After FA 2006 the only qualifying interests in possession which can be created are IPDIs and disabled person's interests. Hence, provided the surviving spouse was not disabled within the meaning of IHTA 1984, s 89, nothing the trustees did would create a qualifying interest in possession. The one exception is where the interest in possession is created within 2 years of H's death when the effect of IHTA 1984, s 144 is that the interest will be treated as arising on death and will therefore be an IPDI. See **13.11** *et seq* for a discussion of s 144.

[11] For the valuation of joint property owned by husband and wife, see the related property rules in IHTA 1984, s 161; *IRC v Arkwright* [2004] STC 1323; R&C Brief 17/07 indicating that the Revenue do not consider this case to be correctly decided, but see *Price v RCC* [2010] UKFTT

exceeded his available IHT nil band). However, there were concerns that by virtue of her continuing occupation of the property W would enjoy an interest in possession in the share of the property held in the discretionary trust. Another problem was the CGT position if the property was sold since the availability of principal private residence relief on the share held by the trust depended on whether W as beneficiary of the trust was entitled to occupy the beneficial share of the property under the terms of the settlement.[12]

Constituting the trust by a debt or charge

5.07 To deal with these concerns it became common to constitute the nil rate band discretionary trust with *either* a debt owed to the trustees by W who then received all the assets of H's estate *or* by a charge being placed over the assets in H's estate by his executors (typically over his share in the house) which were then assented to W. For many couples the practical results of this arrangement were acceptable since W would enjoy the benefit of all the couple's assets whilst H used up his IHT nil rate band on death.

However the debt/charge route had its own problems: for instance, what should be the terms of W's debt or of the charge? It would generally be repayable on demand but should it carry interest (rolled-up and so only payable with the principal on W's death) or be index linked? So far as index linking was concerned – whether by reference to the RPI or to (say) a property index – the tax treatment of the indexed sum in the hands of the trustees was (and remains) far from clear cut.[13] Stamp duty land tax (SDLT) could also apply if a debt rather than charge arrangement was used, on the basis that W was acquiring an interest in land in consideration of the debt.

5.08 Finally, FA 1986, s 103 was capable of operating to disallow the debt on W's death which would nullify all the tax planning. We saw in Chapter 3[14] that s 103 provides that when determining the value of a deceased person's estate a debt incurred by him or incumbrance created by him is not deductible for IHT

---

474 (TC) discussed at **3.18** where they appear to have had a further change of mind! A half share of a jointly owned house where the house is worth £650,000 will not necessarily be half this (ie £325,000) in the hands of the executors. Arguably a discount should be applied, so that in the above case H's share would not fully satisfy the amount due to the discretionary trustees under the terms of his will, since they are entitled to receive £325,000 but have received a half share worth less than this. This point is also relevant if the IOU scheme is adopted. If the house share is the only asset in H's estate the executors will not have security for a debt for more than it is worth. However, bear in mind that when the charge is imposed the share may have risen in value: that increased value may be enough to cover a charge for the full nil rate band.

12 See TCGA 1992, s 225; *Sansom v Peay* [1976] 3 All ER 375 and SP 10/79. It was a balancing exercise to obtain the best of both worlds: ie no IHT charge but CGT relief. There are difficult arguments concerning sub-funds under the Trusts of Land and Appointment of Trustees Act 1996. After some hesitation, it is thought that HMRC now accept that CGT main residence relief will be available on a sale of a settled share in such circumstances.

13 HMRC is adamant that the index linking element is liable to income tax. Many people disagree, but at the time of writing a promised test case has failed to materialise.

14 See 3.08.

purposes to the extent that the consideration given for the debt or incumbrance consisted of property derived from the deceased.[15]

The section could nullify the effect of debt arrangements as the following example shows.

> *Example 5.2*
>
> Wanda gives her husband, Harry £400,000, as part of an equalisation of estates arrangement. He dies first and leaves £300,000 (the amount of the nil rate band in force at his death) to a nil rate band discretionary trust and the residue of his estate to Wanda. Harry's executors transfer all the assets of the estate to Wanda who gives them an IOU for £300,000. The debt is not deductible when Wanda dies. The case of *Phizackerley*[16] showed that HMRC were not slow to take this point.

Note that s 103 applies only to debts incurred and incumbrances created by the deceased. If the executors of the first spouse to die themselves charged the assets with a debt repayable only from the assets and not by the surviving spouse personally (referred to as a 'non-recourse' charge) it was they rather than the surviving spouse who created the incumbrance and the section would have no application.

The *Phizackerley* case

5.09   In this case:

(a)   Mr and Mrs Phizackerley had lived in university accommodation throughout their married life;

(b)   in 1992 Mr Phizackerley retired and jointly purchased a retirement property with his wife;

(c)   Mrs Phizackerley had never worked during the marriage and hence, as the Special Commissioner found, 'the funds must have been provided by (Mr Phizackerley)';

(d)   the joint tenancy in the property was severed in 1996 and Mrs Phizackerley then made a will establishing a nil rate band discretionary trust (NRBDT) and leaving residue to Mr Phizackerley. She died on 26 April 2000;

(e)   Mrs Phizackerley's estate was administered with Mr Phizackerley being assented her share in the property in return for which he promised to pay £150,000 (index linked) to the NRBDT ('the debt');

(f)   Mr Phizackerley died in July 2002 leaving an estate of over £500,000. HMRC argued that the debt was non-deductible as a result of FA 1986, s 103 and the Special Commissioner agreed;

---

[15]   Property 'derived from the deceased' means any property which was the subject matter of a disposition by the deceased other than a disposition which does not amount to a transfer of value: FA 1986, s 103(4). Examples of dispositions which are not transfers of value are those within IHTA 1984, s 10 (no gratuitous intent) or s 11 (dispositions for family maintenance).

[16]   *Phizackerley v RCC* [2007] STC (SCD) 328; see **5.09** *et seq.*

(g)   the taxpayers accepted that Mr Phizackerley had made a gift to his wife in 1992 (as is required if s 103 is to apply). However, they contended that the gift was a disposition for the maintenance of a party to a marriage within IHTA 1984, s 11 and, as such, was not a 'transfer of value'. Hence s 103 did not apply (see s 103(4));[17]

(h)   the Special Commissioner did not accept that the gift of the property interest was 'maintenance' and so was not within s 11;

(i)   the result of the decision was that the debt owed by Mr Phizackerley to the trust was disallowed for IHT purposes as a deduction from his estate. The couple's combined assets were taxable in Mr Phizackerley's estate and Mrs Phizackerley's IHT nil rate band was wasted.

Limited effect of the decision

5.10   Although the decision attracted a lot of press attention, its significance was limited to relatively simple arrangements. Most debt/charge arrangements escaped for the following reasons:

(a)   Mr Phizackerley bought back a share in the very property which he had given to his wife; had they moved and each applied their share of the proceeds to a replacement, it would have been more difficult for the s 103 argument to succeed;

(b)   the couple died in the wrong order: ie the donor spouse survived! There would have been no problem had Mr Phizackerley died first;

(c)   because the s 103 problem had been long debated (and because of SDLT concerns), most practitioners established NRBDTs by using the 'charge route' or by drafting the will to leave the residue to the survivor on interest in possession trusts (rather than outright). If either of these approaches had been adopted in *Phizackerley*, s 103 would not have applied since it requires *the deceased* to either incur a debt or create an incumbrance by way of a disposition made by him.

As explained at **5.08** in the case of the charge route, a non-recourse charge is put on the deceased's share of the property by her executors and that charged share is then assented to the survivor who accordingly incurs no personal liability to repay the sum charged. Given therefore that the survivor neither created the incumbrance nor incurred a debt, s 103 would not have applied.

The charge route was also preferable to avoid a SDLT charge on property acquired by the survivor.

Example 5.3

David died in March 2007 with an estate worth £500,000, the main asset of which was a half share in the family home (with no discount for joint ownership worth

---

17   The transfer was clearly spouse exempt but this did not assist the taxpayers as a spouse exempt transfer is still classified as a transfer of value, albeit an exempt one.

£300,000). His will left the nil rate sum (which was £300,000) on discretionary trusts for beneficiaries who included Deirdre, his wife, and his children. The residue of the estate was left to Deirdre absolutely. *How should the executors establish the trust to avoid tax problems?*

1.   They could put the half share of the house into the trust but that was considered risky by many, who feared that HMRC would attempt to prove that Deirdre's occupation of the property would create an interest in possession in the trust thereby causing David's nil rate band to be wasted.[18]

2.   Alternatively, they could vest all David's assets in Deirdre on the basis that she would enter into a simple debt agreement with the discretionary trustees. Given that there would be no intention to call in the debt until after Deirdre's death, this was attractive but it would be important to check that Deirdre had not made gifts to David, otherwise s 103 would disallow all (or part) of the debt.[19] Further, HMRC took the view that Deirdre was purchasing David's share in the house: ie. she had paid £300,000 for his interest in the property on which SDLT was payable.[20]

3.   Accordingly the most attractive option was for the executors to charge David's interest in the property with the payment of the sum owing to the trust on terms that the charge was only to be satisfied out of the property (a non-recourse charge) and then assent the interest to Deirdre burdened with the charge. Both s 103 and SDLT problems where thereby avoided.

The alternative (but slightly more complicated) way of avoiding s 103 problems was for the will to settle the residue on a life interest trust for the surviving spouse. It would then be the trustees of that residuary trust who would incur the debt and not the surviving spouse. Hence s 103 was again circumvented. However, using a simple debt arrangement would still leave an SDLT problem. Therefore, the 'best buy' was to combine the interest in possession with a non-recourse charge which involved the executors placing a non-recourse charge on the assets and then transferring them charged with the debt to the trustees of the interest in possession settlement. The only difficulty was the practical one of explaining all this to clients and convincing them that two trusts were a good idea.

5.11   If using the charge route, a s 103 problem could still arise if the property was sold by the survivor who then needed the bulk of the proceeds of sale to purchase a replacement property. In this situation:

(a)   the charge would have to be paid off, so that the trustees of the NRBDT would receive part of the proceeds of sale;

(b)   the trustees of the NRBDT could then lend a sum to the surviving spouse but in cases where s 103 was a problem (ie when the surviving spouse was a donor for the purposes of that section) this was not possible since if the trustees lent money representing funds from the estate of the deceased spouse to the survivor, the debt would be non-deductible because of s 103.

---

[18]   See 5.06.
[19]   See 5.08.
[20]   See HMRC Statement of 12 November 2004 ('SDLT and Nil Rate Band Discretionary Trusts').

The solution was for the trustees to acquire an interest in the replacement house (ie becoming co-owners with the survivor). The trustees would allow the surviving spouse to use their share of the house under the terms of the trust giving him a life interest once 2 years had elapsed since death (to avoid IHTA 1984, s 144 applying to 'read back' the interest as an IPDI). Such an appointment would be a 'nothing' for IHT purposes.

3. THE POSITION FROM 9 OCTOBER 2007

5.12 In the light of these difficulties, the pre-Budget announcement on 9 October 2007, introducing a transferable unused nil rate between spouses and civil partners taking effect from that date, was extremely welcome. In most cases these complex manoeuvres became unnecessary.

The necessary legislation in the form of new ss 8A–8C was introduced into IHTA 1984 by FA 2008. These sections allow a claim to be made to transfer any nil rate band unused on the death of an individual to be used against the estate of their deceased surviving spouse or civil partner provided that survivor died on or after 9 October 2007.[21] On the death of the survivor the percentage of the nil rate band unused on the first spouse's death, expressed as a proportion of the nil rate band at the time of the survivor's death is added to the survivor's own nil rate band. Even if the first death took place before 9 October 2007 these provisions enable the percentage of unused nil rate band to be carried forward for use against the survivor's estate.[22]

Example 5.4

1. H died in 1987. On his death none of the then nil rate band was used because his entire estate was left to his wife or to charity. His wife dies in 2015 when the nil rate band is £325,000 having made no lifetime gifts. She can leave up to £650,000 tax free because her nil rate band is increased by H's unused nil rate band which is 100% of £325,000.[23]

2. H died in June 2007 having made chargeable gifts of £120,000 so that 60% of the then nil rate band of £300,000 is unused. If at the time of W's death the nil rate band is £325,000, 60% of that, ie. £195,000 can be claimed so increasing W's nil rate band to £520,000.

---

[21] The nil rate band can only be transferred between spouses and civil partners and does not affect cohabitees: for instance, the elderly sisters in *UK v Burden* [2007] STC 252 could not benefit.

[22] HMRC have produced tables showing what the nil rate band was: (i) for inheritance tax from 18 March 1986 to the present day (and, of course, the rate has been frozen at £325,000 until after the tax year 2017–18); (ii) for capital transfer tax from 13 March 1975 to 17 March 1986; (iii) for estate duty from 16 August 1914 to 12 March 1975. From 1914 to 1946 the nil rate band was £100! Inevitably, there will be difficulties in producing full documentation establishing an entitlement to an unused nil rate band when the death occurred in, say, the 1940s. For HMRC's approach to a claim when full supporting evidence is unavailable, see **5.23** below. For the nil rate band tables, see **Appendix II**.

[23] The mechanism for claiming H's unused nil rate band is considered below.

Position on the first death

5.13   The size of the estate of the first spouse to die is irrelevant: the question is simply what was the then nil rate band and what percentage did that person use up either by making a chargeable transfer on death or by chargeable lifetime transfers which cumulated with his estate on death. The wording of IHTA 1984, s 8A(2), in referring to the maximum ('M') that 'could' be transferred, is making the assumption that the deceased had sufficient assets without requiring that to be the case. Note also that 'M' is defined as 'the maximum that could be transferred by the chargeable transfer made (under s 4) on the person's death' and must be reduced in a case where the deceased had made chargeable lifetime transfers which were included in his cumulative total at death.

There is nothing in the wording of the legislation to require the first spouse to die domiciled or deemed domiciled in the UK.

> *Example 5.5*
>
> Ben and Jen had been domiciled for many years in Hong Kong and owned no UK situs assets. However, on Jen's sudden death Ben returned to the UK resuming his domicile of origin. He died in 2010 owning substantial property. A claim to transfer Jen's unused nil rate band is available to Ben's personal representatives.

5.14   Note two consequences of the introduction of the transferable nil rate band:

(a)   in the past it was standard IHT planning to ensure that the estates of spouses were equalised or at least that both had sufficient assets to take advantage of their nil rate bands. The introduction of the transferable nil rate band means that is no longer necessary;

(b)   there are cases where it is preferable from an IHT point of view not to include a survivorship clause in wills of married couples or civil partners. If the couple die in quick succession and the estate of the first to die exceeds the nil rate band while that of the second is below the nil rate threshold, it is preferable for there to be no survivorship clause.[24]

5.15   In 'Frequently Asked Questions'[25] HMRC comment that on the first death the personal representatives should:[26]

> 'work out what the chargeable amount is and make sure that the surviving spouse is given sufficient documents and information to support the claim that their personal representatives will need to make.'

---

[24]   For an example and a discussion of how to use a post-death variation to solve the problem see **12.37**.

[25]   Available on the HMRC website at www.hmrc.gov.uk.

[26]   Obviously this advice is only relevant to deaths from 9 October 2007 when the changes were announced and to estates of persons dying before that date where the administration of the estate had not then been concluded.

It may, in fact, be difficult to do this given that values will only be agreed with HMRC when tax is at stake: hence if a chargeable transfer falls within the IHT nil rate band of the deceased then its value will not be considered by HMRC (it will not be 'ascertained'). The question of value will, therefore, now have to be considered on the second death since it will affect the size of the unused IHT nil rate band which is capable of transfer. The personal representatives of the first to die should obtain written valuations which are retained for the surviving spouse. HMRC say: 'You should not contact HMRC to establish and agree the transferable amount when the first person dies.'

When the first spouse died before 12 March 1975

5.16   Estate duty was charged until 12 March 1975 when it was replaced by capital transfer tax and then in 1986 by IHT.[27] Where the first spouse died in the days of estate duty, in principle any unused nil rate band can be claimed on the death of the surviving spouse. However, it is relatively unlikely that there will be any unused nil rate band as estate duty did not include a general exemption for gifts between spouses[28] or to charity.[29] It is important to check that nil rate band is available for transfer before putting in a claim, as a wrongful claim is likely to trigger a demand for penalties from HMRC.[30]

> *Example 5.6*
>
> Dot has just died. Her husband died on 1 January 1970 leaving his entire estate worth £25,000 to Dot. This will have been a chargeable gift which used up the husband's nil rate band (which was then £10,000) so that no transferable nil rate band will be available.[31]

Relief for deaths of members of the armed forces/emergency service personnel etc

5.17   The original relief for members of the armed forces whose death was caused or hastened by injury whilst on active service has been substantially extended and the reliefs increased by legislation in FA 2015. These new rules apply to deaths on or after 19 March 2014[32] and are contained in the following sections:

(a)   IHTA 1984 s 154: death on active service (members of the armed forces);

---

27   IHT is largely a watered down version of capital transfer tax (CTT): e g with 7-year cumulation and PETs albeit backed up by the reintroduced reservation of benefit legislation.
28   From 21 March 1972 the first £15,000 of such gifts was exempt.
29   From 21 March 1972 the first £50,000 of such gifts was exempt.
30   Under FA 2007, Sch 24. The IHT400 Toolkit highlights this trap.
31   Under estate duty some relief was due if, for instance, the husband left his estate on a life interest trust for his wife but that relief did not affect the tax charge on the husband's death, it merely prevented a tax charge on the wife in respect of the settled property. Because relief was given on the second death, the husband would still use up his nil rate band. This estate duty exemption has been carried over into the CTT/IHT legislation: see IHTA 1984, Sch 6, para 2.
32   This was the date of the 2014 Budget when the Chancellor announced a consultation on the extension of the existing relief.

(b)   IHTA 1984 s153A: death of emergency service personnel;

(c)   IHTA 1984 s155A: death of constables and service personnel targeted because of their status.

The reliefs

5.18   These sections provide the following reliefs:

(a)   no IHT is chargeable on the death of the individual (IHTA 1984 s 4 is excluded). Note that the exemption applies whoever the estate passes to;

(b)   a potentially exempt transfer made in the 7 years before death is not chargeable;

(c)   extra IHT is not payable in respect of a chargeable transfer made within 7 years of the death.

The old legislation had merely given relief for the death charge.

The death on active service exemption

5.19   This is the oldest exemption in the long history of death duties dating back to the reign of William and Mary and to the Probate Duty introduced in 1694.[33] It applies where the taxpayer died from a wound inflicted, accident occurring or disease contracted while on active service against an enemy or on other service of a warlike nature or involving the same risks.[34] It also applies where death is from a disease contracted at some previous time, but the death is due to or hastened by the aggravation of the disease during a period of such service. The exemption is capable of a wider application than might from its title be imagined. For instance:

(a)   the death does not have to be 'on the battlefield': it suffices that the wound, accident or disease was inflicted, occurred or was contracted at a time when the deceased was on active service (albeit he might have been off duty or absent on leave at the time of the cause of death);

(b)   the wound does not need to be the only or direct pathological cause of death:[35] it simply has to be *a* cause.

In order to claim the exemption it is essential to obtain a certificate from the Ministry of Defence Joint Casualty and Compassionate Centre. IHTM para 11291 deals with the procedure for claiming exemption. There are two forms of certificate: a simplified one for deaths of currently serving people where there is no doubt that s 154 is satisfied, and one for other deaths (see IHTM para 11301).

---

[33]   In estate duty the exemption was in FA 1952, s 71 and it is now in IHTA 1984, s 154.

[34]   By extra-statutory concession F5 the exemption was applied to the estates of members of the Police Service of Northern Ireland (or the previous police authority, the Royal Ulster Constabulary) who die from injuries caused in Northern Ireland by terrorist activity.

[35]   *Barty-King v Ministry of Defence* [1979] 2 All ER 80.

Death of emergency service personnel

5.20   The exemption applies to members of the emergency services: eg police; fire brigade; search and rescue services such as coast guards; medical, ambulance and paramedic services including those transporting organs and medical equipment. In addition, it covers humanitarian aid workers who may be working for a government; state or international organisation.[36] The relief is given if the relevant person died etc while 'responding to emergency circumstances'.[37] As with the armed services exemption, the death may occur later and it suffices that the injury sustained whilst responding to an emergency was one of the causes of death.

On 25 March 2015, guidance on the extended exemption was issued for inclusion in HMRC's inheritance tax manual in due course. This guidance sets out useful information including the evidence that must be produced to show that the exemption is due.

Constables and armed services personnel targeted because of their status

5.21   This exemption is contained in IHTA 1984, s 155A. It is immaterial whether the individual was acting in the course of his duties when attacked. A 'service person' is defined as 'a member of the armed forces of the Crown or a civilian subject to service discipline (within the meaning of the Armed Forces Act 2006)'. The individual must have died/been injured as a result of being deliberately targeted because of his status. The provision extends to 'former' constables and 'former' service persons so the exemption applies to retired constables and service personnel who die in such circumstances

The guidance on the extended exemption referred to at **5.20** above also deals with this extension.

The exemption and transferable nil rate band

5.22   The existence of this exemption can, of course, affect the availability of a transferred nil rate allowance and so should be investigated in any case where there are facts suggesting that it may apply.

Position on the death of the survivor: making the claim

5.23   Section 8B indicates that a claim must be made if the unused nil rate band of the predeceasing spouse is to be transferred. Normally the claim will be made by the survivor's personal representatives and it must be made in the

---

[36]   See IHTA 1984 s 153A(6) for the definition of an 'emergency responder'. This definition may be extended by Treasury regulation.

[37]   For the definition of 'emergency circumstances', see s 153A(3). These include the death or serious injury of a person or animal.

'permitted period'.[38] In the event that they make no claim 'any other person liable to the tax chargeable on the survivor's death within such later period as the Commissioners for HMRC may specify' can make a claim.

The obvious situation where the personal representatives will have no interest in claiming an unused allowance is when any transferred nil rate band will be used to offset the tax on a failed PET for which the donee is primarily liable: see further **Example 5.7** below.

The claim must be made on the claim Form 402 (part of the IHT400). The form requires the production of certain documents: these include the death certificate of the first spouse to die; a copy of the will (and any deed of variation effected under IHTA 1984, s 142(1)); the marriage certificate; a copy of the grant of representation; the valuation of assets that passed on that death by a chargeable transfer and a copy of the IHT return.[39]

In cases where the first death occurred before the introduction of the transferable nil rate band, there was no reason to keep documentation once the estate had been administered and some of these documents will be unavailable. Copies of some of the above documents can be obtained even if the originals have been lost. HMRC may have details of the Form 400 (200) containing contents of the estate. In the 'Frequently Asked Questions'[40] in response to the question:

> 'We did not know about the need to keep records when the first person died and we do not have papers relating to that death – how can we make a claim?'

HMRC say:

> 'The personal representatives will need to make enquiries of those who inherited the first estate to see if they can recall whether or not there may have been other assets that were chargeable on the first death. If values are not known, the personal representatives should complete the claim form to the best of their ability and explain the position to HMRC when they make the claim. If there is no evidence that any other assets were chargeable, the personal representatives can make their claim based on the information which they have.'

Using the transferred nil rate band

5.24 It is important to appreciate that any transferred portion of the nil rate band is used to increase the nil rate band of the survivor 'for the purposes of the

---

[38] 'Permitted period' is defined as the period of 2 years from the end of the month in which the survivor dies or, if later, the period of 3 months beginning with the date on which the personal representatives first act as such. The meaning of the latter words is somewhat imprecise: it might have been expected that the alternative period would run from the date when the grant of representation was obtained.

[39] Form 400 (or Form 200 which was accepted until 9 June 2009) will reveal, inter alia, whether the deceased had made chargeable transfers in the 7 years before his death.

[40] Available on the HMRC website.

charge to tax on the death of the survivor'. This was confirmed in *Loring v Woodland Trust*[41] where Asplin J held that a gift on an amount equal to 'my' nil rate band included nil rate band transferred from the deceased's husband because the effect of the legislation was that the deceased's own nil rate band was increased.

It is therefore not correct to say that a surviving spouse is entitled to two nil rate bands. His estate may be so entitled but he is not. The consequence is that the transferred nil rate band can be used against IHT on the deceased survivor's:

(a)   death estate;

(b)   chargeable lifetime transfers made within 7 years of death;

(c)   reservation of benefit property;[42] and

(d)   settled property in which he had enjoyed a qualifying interest in possession.[43]

Lifetime gifts of the survivor

5.25   How does this affect the position if the survivor has made lifetime gifts? It will be appreciated that a lifetime gift may, when made, be a potentially exempt transfer (such as an outright gift to a child) or an immediately chargeable transfer at lifetime (half) rates (such as a gift into a relevant property settlement).[44]

> *Example 5.7*
>
> Mrs Adam died in 1991 having made no lifetime gifts and leaving everything to her husband Mr Adam. Mr Adam gave away £650,000 in the 7 years prior to his death to his daughter. He died in 2014 and, since he died within 7 years of the gift, it is a failed PET. His remaining estate at death is worth £325,000. The lifetime gift is not chargeable – two nil rate bands are allocated against it. The £325,000 left in his estate at death is fully charged at 40%.[45]
>
> Contrast the position if instead of making an outright gift to his daughter Mr Adam had settled £650,000 on an interest in possession trust for the daughter and her children and died within 7 years. The IHT position would then be as follows:
>
> 1.   The making of the settlement involved an immediately chargeable transfer

---

[41]   *Loring v Woodland Trust* [2013] EWHC 4400 (Ch), *aff'd* [2014] EWCA Civ 1314.

[42]   Property included in his estate as a result of FA 1986, s 102(3).

[43]   So that under IHTA 1984, s 49(1) the capital of the settlement is treated as comprised in his estate at death.

[44]   Since FA 2006 all new inter vivos settlements are taxed under the relevant property regime and so involve an immediately chargeable transfer except only for a trust creating a disabled person's interest falling within IHTA 1984, s 89B(1) which is (usually) created by a PET: see 3.58.

[45]   In this case the daughter and not the personal representatives of Mr A will make the claim.

by Mr Adam. He settled £650,000, he had a nil rate band of £325,000 leaving a tax charge on £325,000 at 20% (£65,000).[46]

2.   On his death within 7 years of creating the settlement additional IHT is payable but because this tax is charged on the death of the survivor the unused nil rate band of Mrs Adam is available and hence no additional tax is charged. There is no refund of the tax charged when the settlement was created.[47]

5.26 In cases where the chargeable lifetime gifts will take the benefit of any transferred unused nil rate band, the personal representatives (PRs) will have no interest in submitting a claim. Instead, it will be the donee of the PET who will benefit from that nil rate band. Section 8B provides for 'any other person liable to the tax chargeable on the survivor's death' to make a claim:

(a)   if no claim has been made by the PRs in the 'permitted period';

(b)   within 'such later period as an officer of Revenue and Customs may in the particular case allow'.

All of which suggests that the donee will have to wait until the end of the permitted period to submit a claim which not only defies common sense but will lead to the absurdity of him paying tax on the failed PET (due 6 months after the end of the month of death).[48] With the co-operation of the PRs, the practical solution will be for the donee to submit a claim at the time when the IHT 400 is returned.

Will trusts of the survivor

5.27 Assume that the surviving spouse died in January 2014 (without having made any PETs and chargeable transfers) and left an estate worth £650,000 on discretionary trusts for her grandchildren. If a full transferable nil rate band allowance is available then tax on the creation of this settlement is nil. However, once created, this relevant property settlement will benefit only from the single nil rate band of the testator (£325,000) with the result that exit and anniversary charges may arise.[49] This is, of course, consistent with the limited use to which a transferred nil rate band is to be put (only against tax arising on the death of the survivor). It has been common to use pilot trusts to avoid

---

[46]   It is assumed in this and the following illustrations that the trustees pay the tax so that grossing up does not apply.

[47]   Note that if Mr Adam had settled £975,000 the immediate tax payable would have been £130,000 (20% × £650,000 being £975,000 − £325,000). On Mr Adam's death the additional tax at 40% would have been chargeable on £325,000 only (because of Mrs Adam's transferred nil rate band) giving tax of £130,000 which is, however, covered by the tax already paid. No extra IHT is therefore payable.

[48]   IHTA 1984, s 226(3A).

[49]   IHTA 1984, s 66(3) which posits a transferor with the chargeable transfers of the settlor in the 7 years before he created the trust and then takes the lifetime rates (see s 7(2)). The rate before the first 10-year anniversary is similarly calculated: see s 68(4): see **3.62** *et seq*.

future charges on the settlement but the proposed legislation (aimed at stopping the use of multiple settlements) makes it unclear whether this can still be done.[50]

The nil rate band maximum

5.28   Section 8A(7) defines the nil rate maximum as the upper portion of the value charged at 0% (for 2012–13 this is £325,00) and this imposes a ceiling on the amount available for transfer under the rules. No matter how many predeceasing spouses the survivor may have had, the maximum value of the unused nil rate bands that can be used against tax on his death is limited to this amount (in effect to one extra nil rate band).

> *Example 5.8*
>
> 1.   Tootsie dies, predeceased by her two husbands Sid and Sad; both of whom had left her everything. Her personal representatives can claim an additional nil rate band of £325,000 only.
>
> 2.   If in (1) above Sid had used up 50% of his nil rate band and Sad 75% of his then Tootsie's PRs would be entitled to claim 75% of an additional nil rate band (£243,750 in 2014–15).

Claiming the unused nil rate band: issues for personal representatives

5.29   These are two problems that may arise. First, a question of construction: does a will which makes a nil rate band gift result in the legatee (or nil rate band trust) receiving a single nil rate band (the testator's) or does it include the benefit of any unused nil rate band from the testator's predeceasing spouse? The answer depends on the terms of the gift. Consider the following gifts:

(a)   'to my trustees the maximum sum that can be given without IHT becoming payable in respect of the transfer of value that I make on my death'

These words are sufficiently wide to catch not just the deceased's nil rate band but also any transferred nil rate band which may be claimed by his personal representatives.

However, given that the benefit of the transferable nil rate band does have to be claimed, it is sensible to put the matter beyond argument by including an express reference to two nil rate bands as in (b) below.

(b)   'The Nil Rate Sum shall mean whichever is the lesser of:
   (i)   twice the upper limit of the nil rate per cent band in the table of rates of tax applicable on my death in Sch 1 to the Inheritance Tax Act 1984; and
   (ii)   the maximum amount which will not give rise to a charge to inheritance tax by reason of my death.'

---

[50]   See **3.72** and generally Chapter 8.

It is also sensible to include a direction making it clear that the PRs must claim the transferred nil rate band:[51]

(c) 'to my trustees an amount equal to the upper limit of the nil per cent rate band in the table of rates in IHTA 1984'

These words simply give the amount from the rate tables: for 2015–16 that figure is £325,000.

(d) 'to my trustees such sum as I could leave immediately before my death without IHT becoming payable'

(e) 'to my trustees an amount equal to the nil rate band in force at my death'

As a result of the *Loring* case, it is thought that the wording in (d) and (e) will include the amount of any transferred nil rate band.

The second problem that may arise is illustrated by the following example.

Example 5.9

Janet dies in 2014 and has not used up her nil rate band. Her husband predeceased her in 2000 leaving her everything so that a transferable nil rate band is available. She appoints her second husband as one of her executors and her will leaves:

1. 'such sum as I can leave without IHT becoming payable in respect of the transfer that I make on my death to my children' (all from her first marriage);

2. residue to her second husband.

The second husband refuses[52] to claim the transferred nil rate band since that will increase the sum passing to the children at the expense of his residue.[53] Can he be compelled to do so since the wishes of Janet, as expressed in her will, are to leave the maximum amount that she can tax free to her children? If the wording is sufficiently plain, it is thought the children may bring an action for breach of trust against the trustees for failure to collect in the assets left to the trust.[54] However, in *Loring v Woodland Trust* the Court of Appeal appeared to accept that a testator, by selecting an individual as an executor, might be regarded as giving him a power to claim or not claim as he saw fit.

However, the Court of Appeal also accepted that it would be possible to provide express guidance for the executors in the will. It is suggested that the will should make it clear that the PRs are required to claim any available transferred nil rate band:

---

[51] See **Example 5.9**.

[52] The personal representatives must act unanimously.

[53] A similar issue may arise if a nil rate band legacy is left to children, residue to charity, when the charity puts pressure on the personal representatives to give only a single nil rate band to the children.

[54] For a contrary view see Kessler, *Drafting Trusts and Will Trusts* (12th edn) at 18.18 where he comments: 'the power of W2 to make (or refuse) a NRB claim should be regarded as a semi-fiduciary power so that other beneficiaries could only challenge a decision not to make a NRB claim where there is bad faith: for W2 to consult her own interests in deciding whether or not to allow a NRB claim to be made is not bad faith.'

'I DECLARE that my Trustees shall, as soon as practicable after my death, make any claim which may be required under the Inheritance Tax Act 1984, s 8A.'

4. IMPACT ON THE DRAFTING OF IHT EFFICIENT WILLS

5.30   Many couples have welcomed the simplicity of leaving everything to the survivor absolutely (so that the entire estate of the first to die is spouse exempt) but still being able to take advantage of two nil rate bands. But this simplicity may be bought at a cost. There are often good reasons for considering a settlement:

(a)   the testator may want to protect capital for children of an earlier marriage in which case a life interest for the survivor will be needed. This will be an immediate post-death interest (IPDI) and so spouse exempt;

(b)   the couple may wish to shield capital against nursing home fees. Again an IPDI for the survivor would be effective: bear in the mind that the interest in possession can be made revocable by the trustees and so bought to an end if future circumstances make this desirable.[55] Of course, protection would also be obtained if assets were put into a discretionary trust but this will only afford protection on assets up to a value of the then nil rate band given that the testator will not wish to incur a tax charge by transferring amounts in excess of the nil rate band to a discretionary trust;

(c)   in the past it was common when the will of the first spouse to die left everything to the survivor for the survivor to use a post-death variation to establish a nil rate band discretionary trust in order to use the deceased's nil rate band. This is normally unnecessary now although there are still situations where the use of a nil rate band discretionary trust is beneficial.[56]

When will it still be attractive to establish a nil rate band discretionary trust[57]

5.31   More generally the question may be put as to when it will be desirable for the first spouse to die to leave property away from the spouse in his will. Consider the following:

(a)   Mr and Mrs A are wealthy. Given that Mrs A does not need all of Mr A's estate he leaves property to a value of his IHT nil rate band to his children/grandchildren;

(b)   if the first spouse to die owns property which is expected to outstrip increases in the nil rate band (frozen until the end of the tax year

---

[55]   For flexible IPDI trusts, see Chapter 6.
[56]   See **6.20** *et seq.*
[57]   For the drafting of nil rate band trusts and gifts see **1.61** *et seq* and **Precedent 4.9.**

2017–18), it will be advantageous to put that property into a nil rate band trust on the first death. This may involve putting a share of the family home into trust;[58]

(c) two separate nil rate band discretionary trusts may have long-term tax advantages if it is intended to keep the property in trust after the surviving spouse's death.

Example 5.10

Mrs A died with an unused nil rate band leaving all her property to Mr A. Mr A dies in January 2012 with an estate of £650,000 which is therefore free of inheritance tax. He leaves this on discretionary trusts for his issue and no tax is payable. However, on the 10-year anniversary there will be inheritance tax payable if the value of the settled property exceeds the value of one nil rate band.[59] By contrast if Mrs A had set up a nil rate band discretionary trust on her death and Mr A's remaining estate was within his nil rate band on his death and left in trust, then on each trust's 10-year anniversary there would be a nil rate band available to set against the value of the property in that trust.[60]

(d) When the deceased spouse owns business or agricultural property attracting 100% relief it may be attractive to provide for this property to be left either to the children/grandchildren or on discretionary trusts.[61] Bear in mind that the trustees may qualify for relief[62] in which case anniversary and exit charges will be avoided so long as the business property remains qualifying. If, however, the trustees were to sell the business for cash then:

  (i) on the next 10-year anniversary a charge will arise given that there is then cash in the settlement;

  (ii) if the sale occurs in the first 10 years of the trust and the cash is distributed an IHT exit charge may arise on the distribution despite the fact that no charge arose when the qualifying business assets were settled;[63]

---

[58] See **Example 5.1**.

[59] See IHTA 1984, s 66(5). Note also that exit charges even before the first 10-year anniversary will also be incurred.

[60] Note the use of pilot trusts to obtain multiple nil rate bands before the changes announced on 10 December 2014: see Chapter 8.

[61] In cases where the availability of the relief is in doubt leaving the property into a relevant property settlement will ensure that HMRC need to consider the position: in the event of relief being denied the property can be appointed out of the trust to the surviving spouse within 2 years on death under IHTA 1984, s 144 with the benefit of the spouse exemption being obtained by reading-back. In the event of the property attracting relief it may be appropriate for it to be sold to the surviving spouse so that provided he or she owns it for 2 further years advantage can again be taken of 100% relief (this is sometimes referred to as having 'two bites of the cherry'!): see further Chapter 10 and particularly 10.50.

[62] Subject, eg, to the usual 2-year ownership period being satisfied.

[63] This is because the rate of tax which applies is calculated by reference to the value of the property originally settled with no allowance being given for 100% relief.

(iii) if, however, the sale occurs after a 10–year anniversary when no tax
has been charged because of the property qualifying for 100% relief,
no exit charge will arise provided that the cash is distributed before
the next 10-year anniversary;

Example 5.11

Suzie has just died, leaving everything on death to her spouse Deirdre. She had not
created any settlements during her life and Deirdre's estate will be entitled to claim
a transferable nil rate band. Deirdre plans to leave all her property on
discretionary trusts for various friends and relatives of herself and Suzie. Her total
estate (including the £400,000 inherited from Suzie) will be worth in the region of
£1m.

1.As matters stand, her estate may be reduced by two nil rate bands but the will
trust can only be allocated Deirdre's settlement nil rate band.

2.If Deirdre amended Suzie's will to leave £325,000 on discretionary trusts which
are 'read-back' under IHTA 1984 s 142[64], then this may benefit from Suzie's
otherwise unused settlement nil rate band.

The widow or widower who remarries[65]

5.32 Particular issues arise for the draftsman asked to produce a will for a
widow (or widower) who has remarried and who wants everything to pass to
the new spouse in the event that he dies first. Before drafting the will in these
terms it is important to check the position regarding transferable nil rate bands.
Where either or both of the couple have the benefit of a transferable nil rate
band, leaving everything to the other will waste at least one nil rate band. This
is because no one can inherit more than one full nil rate band.[66] This is an
occasion for using a nil rate band discretionary trust).

Example 5.12

Fred is a widower with adult children (his wife, Freda, died leaving him everything
a few years ago). He is to marry Flossie (a widow whose husband, Harry, died
leaving her everything last year). The couple own assets worth in the region of
£2m.

Fred wishes to make an IHT efficient will. Fred has a double nil rate band but he
cannot pass this onto Flossie as the maximum that can be transferred is one
additional nil rate band (see IHTA 1984, s 8(5)).

Flossie has already got one additional nil rate band from her first husband so Fred
will waste his double nil rate band if he passes all his assets to Flossie absolutely or
for life. Accordingly, Fred should either leave assets to his children outright or
create a discretionary trust to which he transfers assets to the value of his double
nil rate band. (The same is, of course, true for Flossie.)

---

[64] See further Chapter 12.
[65] Including the situation where a surviving civil partner enters into a new civil partnership.
[66] See **5.28**.

In 2015–16 this will allow £650,000 to be transferred to the trust without any payment of IHT. However, relevant property settlements attract 10-year anniversary charges and exit charges and the settlement will only benefit from a single nil rate band so there will be future IHT charges. Fred might therefore consider creating pilot trusts during his lifetime to which property can be added by will. The advantage of such trusts has been that each trust may benefit from a full nil rate band so that, depending on the value of the property settled, it may be possible to avoid future settlement charges. But is it still worthwhile doing this?[67]

Note that if Flossie only had a single nil rate band, Fred only needs to use up *one* nil rate band since a transferable nil rate band will be available on Flossie's death. In practice, Fred will use up 'his' nil rate band leaving Flossie's PRs to claim Freda's unused nil rate band.

5. POSITION WHERE A TAXPAYER HAS RECENTLY DIED AND HIS WILL CONTAINS AN IHT NIL RATE BAND DISCRETIONARY TRUST WITH RESIDUE PASSING TO THE SURVIVING SPOUSE[68]

5.33 Many testators make wills years before death and never update them. Wills made before 9 October 2007 frequently contain nil rate band discretionary trusts which, when the testator dies, will not be wanted.[69]

If the family wish, the trust can be dismantled by an appointment *within 2 years of death* in favour of the spouse which is 'read back' as a result of IHTA 1984, s 144. The effect will then be that the deceased has not used up any part of his IHT nil rate band which can therefore be used on the survivor's death. Note the following:

(a)   if the appointment is to be absolute, the trustees no longer need to wait more than 3 months from the date of death before making it in order to avoid the 'Frankland Trap';[70]

(b)   can an appointment be made even before the estate has been administered/property vested in the trustees? Some wills expressly provide for this to be done[71] but even in the absence of such a clause it is thought that an appointment can be made since the trust is constituted at death with the trustees being entitled to a *chose in action* (to compel due administration of the estate);

(c)   it does not matter that the trust was set up by a deed of variation made by the surviving spouse; all that is required is that the appointment is made

---

[67]   As a result of the proposed changes to the taxation of relevant property settlements announced on 10 December 2014. See **3.72** and Chapter 8.

[68]   See further **13.11** *et seq.*

[69]   For standard will drafting before the introduction of the transferable nil rate band see **5.04** *et seq.*

[70]   See **13.13**.

[71]   See **Precedent 4.1, clause 12**.

within 2 years of the deceased's death (ie advantage can be taken of 'reading-back' under both IHTA 1984, ss 142 and 144).[72]

5.34 If dismantling an unwanted nil rate band trust, it is important that the matter is properly documented.

Normally the trustees will execute a deed of appointment in favour of the surviving spouse (see **Precedent 13.1**).

Depending on the terms of the will, an alternative might be for the trustees, in reliance on an extended power of advancement, to informally resolve to advance the trust fund to the surviving spouse. If using this method, the trustees should record the resolution in writing so that on the death of the surviving spouse there is proof that a transferable nil rate band is available from the first spouse's death.

When the claim for transferred nil rate band is made on the death of the survivor, it will be necessary to produce the will of the first spouse to die together with an instrument showing that the trust was wound up in favour of the survivor within 2 years of death so that 'reading-back' under s 144 applied.

It sometimes happens that the trust is simply ignored and the surviving spouse takes all the deceased's assets. In this situation, it may be impossible to say that the spouse has been informally advanced the assets and, in any event, because there is no documentary evidence that the trust was ended within the 2-year period required for s 144 reading-back to apply, HMRC will deny the availability of a transferred nil rate band. Given that breach of trust has been committed (by the trustees in allowing the survivor to have all the estate), there is a claim against the survivor's estate for the nil rate sum promised to the trust (and, given that the gift will be a pecuniary legacy) together with interest running from the end of one year from the date of death).[73]

Other issues that may need to be addressed when seeking to take advantage of s 144 are considered at **13.15** *et seq*.

6. ADMINISTERING NRBDTS SET UP BY A SPOUSE WHO DIED MORE THAN 2 YEARS AGO

5.35 It is important to ensure that the trust is administered so that the use of the nil rate band of the first spouse to die is preserved. Hence:

---

[72]   For further considerations see **13.15** and see **Precedent 13.1**.
[73]   For interest on pecuniary legacies see Chapter 1.

(a)   the trustees must not appoint the trust capital to the surviving spouse. The trust capital would become part of the surviving spouse's estate but because there is no reading-back without the benefit of any transferred nil rate band;[74]

(b)   if the trust was established by a debt/charge, check that the documentation is in order: eg has *Phizackerley*[75] caused problems (bear in mind, however, that if there is a *Phizackerley* problem not a great deal can be done about it!);

(c)   if the charge route over the matrimonial home has been used and the property is now to be sold it will be necessary to pay off the charge. If the surviving spouse then needs all/part of those monies to buy a replacement property the trustees may lend it to her (provided there is no s 103 problem) or may buy a share in the property (for her occupation);[76]

(d)   if the trust holds a share in the house occupied by the surviving spouse consider the IHT position (is there any reason to think that the spouse has a qualifying interest in possession)? Also consider what the CGT consequences will be when the property is sold.

---

[74]   Provided the spouse is not a disabled person within the meaning of IHTA 1984, s 89, appointing on an interest in possession once 2 years have elapsed from the date of death does not create IHT problems. The appointment does not create an IPDI and is a 'nothing' for IHT purposes. Such appointments are often beneficial as they improve the income tax position (see **3.137**) and generally save administration costs.

[75]   [2007] STC (SCD) 328.

[76]   See **5.11**.

PRECEDENTS

Precedent 5.1: Clauses to be inserted into a will creating a nil rate band discretionary trust

CL1 *Definitions*

(1) In CL2 of this Will the following expressions shall have the following meanings:

(i)   'the Beneficiaries'[77] shall mean subject to the provisions of CL1(2) below:
    (a)   my said husband/wife
    (b)   my children and remoter issue
    (c)   the spouses widows and widowers of the persons mentioned in (b)
    and 'Beneficiary' shall have a corresponding meaning.

(ii)   'the Trust Period' shall mean the period commencing with the date of my death and ending 125 years thereafter and such period of 125 years shall be the perpetuity period applicable to the dispositions made by my Will PROVIDED THAT my Legacy Fund Trustees may declare by irrevocable deed that the Trust Period (but not the said perpetuity period) shall terminate on such date as they may specify therein (such date of termination to be earlier than the end of the said period of 125 years but the same as or later than the date of such deed).

(iii)   'my Legacy Fund Trustees' shall mean [insert details] or other the trustee or trustees for the time being of the Legacy Fund.[78]

(2)   (i)   SUBJECT to sub-clause (b) below:
    (a)   My Legacy Fund Trustees shall have power by any deed or deeds revocable (during the Trust Period) or irrevocable executed during the Trust Period to declare that any individual or individuals whether or not then born or ascertained or any Charity or Charities (other than any individual then a trustee of the Legacy Fund and other than any individual or Charity previously excluded under the power set out in (b) below) shall from such time and (subject to any future exercise of the power set out in CL1(2)(i)(b) below) either permanently or for such period or periods as shall be specified in any such deed or deeds be included in the class of Beneficiaries defined in CL1(1)(i) above and
    (b)   The Legacy Fund Trustees shall also have power by any deed or deeds revocable (during the Trust Period) or irrevocable executed during the Trust Period to declare that any individual or individuals whether or not born or ascertained or any Charity or Charities who or which is or are a member or members (or eligible to be added as a

---

[77]   Commonly this will comprise surviving spouse and issue: for added flexibility include the power to add/remove beneficiaries: see CL1(2).

[78]   In drafting the Will it is helpful to designate 'my Legacy Fund Trustees' even if they are the same persons as the trustees of the Will.

member or members) of the class of Beneficiaries immediately prior to the execution of such deed or deeds shall from such time and either permanently or for such period or periods as shall be specified in any such deed or deeds cease to be a member or members (or eligible to become a member or members) of such class.

(ii) PROVIDED always that no such deed made in exercise of either of the powers conferred by sub-clause (i) shall affect the validity or effect of:

(a) any distribution previously made to or for the benefit of any beneficiary under or pursuant to any power or discretion

(b) any transmissible interest (whether vested or contingent) previously conferred on any beneficiary.

CL2 *Legacy fund – nil rate band discretionary trust (with loan/charge provisions)*

(1) THIS clause shall not take effect unless the gift made to my [husband/wife] by Clause [insert number] of my Will takes effect (or but for this Clause would do so).[79]

(2) IN this Clause 'the Nil-Rate Sum' means the largest sum of cash which could be given on the trusts of this Clause without any inheritance tax becoming due in respect of the transfer of the value of my estate which I am deemed to make immediately before my death.[80]

(3) I GIVE the Nil-Rate Sum to my Legacy Fund Trustees on trust to invest it in exercise of the powers of investment given them by my Will and by law and to hold it and the property which currently represents it ('the Legacy Fund') on the trusts and with and subject to the powers and provisions set out in this clause.

(4) DURING the Trust Period my Legacy Fund Trustees (being at least two in number or a trust corporation) may at any time or times:

(i) by deed or deeds revocable (during the Trust Period) or irrevocable appoint that all or any part or parts of the income or capital of the Legacy Fund shall be held on such trusts (including discretionary and protective ones) in favour or for the benefit of all or any one or more of the Beneficiaries and with and subject to such powers (including dispositive and administrative ones exercisable by my Legacy Fund Trustees or any other person) and other provisions as my Legacy Fund Trustees think fit and

---

[79] If the spouse predeceased then the nil rate trust is redundant, given that the entire estate is then chargeable.

[80] In the event that an additional nil rate band is available (because the testator had been married before and his spouse had predeceased without making use of her IHT nil rate band), the wording of 'the nil rate sum' will catch both the deceased's and the transferred nil rate band. Amend if this is not desired: see generally **5.29** for the drafting of nil rate band legacies and whether the executors should be obliged to claim any transferred nil rate band which may be available.

(ii) pay transfer or apply the whole or any part or parts of the capital of the Legacy Fund for any purpose whatever which my Legacy Fund Trustees consider to be for the benefit of any one or more of the Beneficiaries for the time being in existence[81] and

(iii) transfer all or any part or parts of the income or capital of the Legacy Fund to the trustees of any Settlement wherever established (whose receipt shall be good discharge to them) to be held free from the trusts of my Will and on the trusts and with and subject to the powers and provisions of that Settlement but only if those trusts powers and provisions are such that (at the time of the transfer) they could themselves have created them under (i) above.

(5) IN default of and subject to any exercise of the powers given them by the preceding provisions:

(i) during the Trust Period my Legacy Fund Trustees shall pay or apply the income of the Legacy Fund to or for the maintenance education support or otherwise for the benefit of such one or more of the Beneficiaries as my Legacy Fund Trustees may in their absolute discretion think fit but with power to accumulate such income or any part or parts of it (with power to apply the accumulations of past years as if they were income of the current year) and with power (during the Trust Period) to resolve to hold the whole or any part or parts of such income as income on trust for any of the Beneficiaries absolutely[82] and

(ii) on the expiry of the Trust Period my Legacy Fund Trustees shall hold the Legacy Fund as to both capital and income on trust absolutely for such of my issue as are then living and if more than one in equal shares through all degrees according to their stocks and so that no issue shall take whose parent is alive and so capable of taking.

(6) ANY other non-residuary gifts made by my Will or any Codicil to it shall have priority to this one.[83]

(7) INSTEAD of satisfying the legacy wholly by the payment of cash (or by the appropriation of property) to the Legacy Fund Trustees my Trustees may:

(i) require the Legacy Fund Trustees to accept in place of all or any part of the Nil Rate Sum a binding promise of payment made by my Trustees as trustees of any residuary property given by this Will or any Codicil hereto

---

[81] This 'advancement type' power can be exercised by trustee resolution: see **2.53**.

[82] As a result of the changes made by PAA 2009, it is possible for trustees to accumulate income throughout the Trust Period: see **2.12**.

[83] This makes it clear that the gift to the Legacy Fund Trustees takes effect after other non-residuary gifts. This ensures that the trustees will only receive what is left of the nil rate band(s): contrast *RSPCA v Sharpe* [2010] STC 975 *revsd* [2011] STC 553, CA.

on trusts under which my [husband/wife] has an interest in possession for the purposes of Inheritance Tax which debt shall be repayable on demand[84]

(ii) charge all or any part of the Nil Rate Sum on any property which is (or but for this clause would be) given by this Will or any Codicil to it on trusts under which my [husband/wife] has an interest in possession for the purposes of Inheritance Tax.[85]

(8) THE Legacy Fund Trustees may lend money currently held by them to my spouse.[86]

(9) IN amplification of the foregoing provisions

(i) if my Trustees exercise their powers under (7)(i) above they shall be under no further liability to see that the Legacy Fund Trustees receive the sum promised and if they exercise their powers under (7)(ii) they shall be under no further liability to see that the Legacy Fund Trustees receive the sum secured[87]

(ii) if my Trustees exercise their powers under (7)(ii) above they may give an assent of the property subject to the charge and no one in whose favour the assent is made shall become personally liable for the sum secured[88]

(iii) the Legacy Fund Trustees may require security to be given for any debt to be created by a promise within (7)(i) above or by a loan within (9) and in relation both to such debts (whether or not secured) and to any debt to be secured by a charge within (7)(ii) (all of which shall be debts payable on demand) they
  (1) may (subject to the foregoing provisions) impose such terms (if any) as they think fit including terms as to interest and the personal liability of the borrower and terms linking the debt to the Index of Retail Prices or otherwise providing for its amount to vary with the passage of time according to a formula and
  (2) may subsequently leave the debt outstanding for as long as they think fit and refrain from exercising their rights in relation to it and waive the payment of all or any part of it or of any interest due in respect of it
  and they shall not be liable if my Trustees are or become unable to pay the debt or a security is or becomes inadequate or for any other loss which may occur through their exercising or choosing not to exercise any power given by this sub-clause.[89]

---

[84] This enables a simple debt trust to be created.

[85] This envisages the creation of a charge over the deceased's property.

[86] This clause is inserted out of abundant caution: a power to make beneficial loans would probably be implied in discretionary trusts of this type.

[87] This is designed to offer protection to the personal representatives in the event of the surviving spouse defaulting on any loan or the charge proving inadequate: see also **Precedent 5.2**.

[88] This confirms that the charge is non-recourse: inter alia this ensures that a stamp duty land tax charge will not be incurred: see **5.07 and 5.08**.

[89] The Legacy Fund Trustees are able to insist on security for any loan/debt and can require the

(iv) the powers given by this clause are without prejudice to any other powers given by this Will or any Codicil to it or by the general law and are exercisable even though my Trustees and the Legacy Fund Trustees may be the same persons and my spouse may be among them (but they are not exercisable while my spouse is the sole Legacy Fund Trustee) and any of the Legacy Fund Trustees may exercise or concur in existing all powers and discretions given to him by this clause or by law notwithstanding that he has a direct or other personal interest in the mode or result of any such exercise.[90]

CL3 *Residue*

[insert provisions leaving residue to surviving spouse either absolutely or on IPDI trusts]

---

debt to carry interest or be index linked. For a consideration of these matters, see **5.07**. It will be necessary for an agreement to be drawn up between the trustees of the estate and the Legacy Fund Trustees confirming what has been agreed in respect of these matters: see **Precedent 5.2**.

[90] All the usual administrative powers in the will are extended to the Legacy Fund Trustees and there is a clause permitting self-dealing (see **1.36**).

Precedent 5.2: Implementing the NRBDT by a charge for the nil rate sum

1. Agreement between the Executors and the Trustees of the Legacy Fund (when a charge being imposed by the Executors).

This letter records the agreement that has been reached between us as to the way in which the Legacy Fund is to be constituted.

Under the Will of [insert details] Deceased he provided that the Legacy Fund should have a value equal to the unused amount of his nil rate band and gave the executors power to require the trustees of that fund to accept in place of cash or other property either a binding promise of payment by the surviving spouse or a charge over any property passing to that surviving spouse. At the same time the Trustees may, inter alia, impose terms as to the payment of interest or linking the sum outstanding to an appropriate index.

It has now been agreed that you as Trustees will be entitled to the nil rate sum (insert amount) which will be charged over property which will pass to his surviving spouse.[91] In line with the provisions in the Will we as executors will have no further liability to ensure that you receive this amount and when the assets comprised in the residue are transferred to the surviving spouse [he/she] will likewise have no personal responsibility to ensure that you receive the relevant property. Your only recourse therefore is against the charged property.

It is also confirmed that the sum outstanding is repayable on a written demand being made by yourselves either to the executors or, once the assets have been transferred to the surviving spouse to that spouse. [You have further agreed that the debt shall not carry interest nor be linked to an index.]

2. Equitable Charge

THIS CHARGE is made the [   ] day of [   ] 20[   ] between [   ] of [   ] ('the Executors') of the one part and [   ] of [   ] ('the Legacy Fund Trustees') of the other part.

SUPPLEMENTAL to the Will ('the Will') of [insert details] Deceased ('the Testator') dated [   ].

WHEREAS

(A)   The Testator died on [   ] and the Will was proved by the Executors in the [insert details].
(B)   The Legacy Fund and the 'Nil Rate Sum' has the same meaning as in the Will and the Nil Rate Sum amounts to [insert amount].

---

[91]   This assumes that the residue passes to the surviving spouse absolutely.

(C)   The Legacy Fund Trustees were appointed trustees of the Legacy Fund by clause [   ] of the Will.

(D)   The Executors hold the property described in the Schedule ('the Property').

(E)   In exercise of the powers given to them by clause [   ] of the Will the Executors have required the Legacy Fund Trustees to accept in place of the Nil Rate Sum a debt to be secured by a charge over the property [and the Legacy Fund Trustees have required this sum to be indexed linked by reference to the RPI at the date of the Testator's death].

NOW THIS DEED WITNESSES:

1.   In this Deed 'the Sum Owing' shall mean the Nil Rate Sum.

2.   The Executors hereby charge the Property[92] with the payment to the trustees of the Sum Owing and the Executors are under no further liability to ensure that the same is paid to the Trustees who accept that their only recourse in respect of the Sum Owing is against the charged property.

3.   It is confirmed that in the event that the Executors vest the property in the residuary beneficiary ('the Beneficiary') of the Testator's estate
     a.   they will serve notice in writing on the Trustees; and
     b.   the Beneficiary shall not be under any personal liability to ensure that the sum owing is paid to the Trustees.

IN WITNESS etc

SCHEDULE

('the Property')

---

[92]   The charge will be over property in the deceased's estate. In many cases the main asset will be a beneficial interest (typically a half share) in the main residence. The charge will accordingly be over this asset and will, of necessity, be equitable. Of course, in cases where the deceased had been sole legal and beneficial owner of the house a standard legal charge may be employed.

CHAPTER 6

USING IMMEDIATE POST-DEATH INTERESTS

1. IHT TREATMENT OF A QUALIFYING INTEREST IN POSSESSION

6.01 FA 2006 introduced the IPDI: the 'immediate post-death interest'.[1] For completeness, the words 'in possession' should be added, since what is involved is the creation on death of an interest in possession in settled property. An IPDI is a 'qualifying' interest in possession for IHT purposes: ie the beneficiary is treated 'as beneficially entitled to the property in which the interest subsists'.[2] The meaning of 'interest in possession' is considered at **6.12**: the main example of such an interest is a life interest but the interest can subsist for a lesser period (eg until the beneficiary marries).

6.02 Section 49(1) provides that:

'a person beneficially entitled to an [qualifying] interest in possession shall be treated for the purposes of this Act as beneficially entitled to the property in which the interest subsists.'

This is, of course, a fiction. In no real sense is an interest in possession beneficiary the owner of the trust capital.

6.03 An IHT charge may arise on the termination of an IPDI,[3] whether this occurs on the death of the beneficiary or during his lifetime.[4] The termination may give rise to an immediate IHT charge (if the settlement continues) or involve the beneficiary making a PET (if the settlement ends during the life of the beneficiary).

---

[1]   IHTA 1984, s 49A inserted by FA 2006. Initially it was proposed that the definition be restricted so that on the termination of the interest in possession the settlement had to come to an end. Hence overriding powers of appointment or advancement given to the trustees would have had to be severely curtailed. In the event this proposed restriction was abandoned.

[2]   IHTA 1984, s 49(1). See further **6.02**.

[3]   Or any other qualifying interest in possession.

[4]   IHTA 1984, s 4 (the charge on death); s 52 (*inter vivos* terminations). The disposal of the interest (eg an assignment of it by the beneficiary) is treated as a termination: see IHTA 1984, s 51.

Example 6.1

Saskia is the life tenant of her family trust which was set up in 2000 which owns 20% of the shares in Rostoff Investments Ltd (the family property investment company). Saskia owns a further 35% of the shares personally.

1.   On Saskia's death her estate will include both her 35% shareholding and the 20% trust shareholding. For valuation purposes this will involve valuing a 55% shareholding.

2.   Contrast the position if Saskia's life interest came to an end before her death (eg by surrender or by termination by the trustees under an overriding power in the settlement). In this case the transfer of value that she is deemed to make on the ending of her interest in possession is limited to the value of the shares in the settlement which are valued without regard to her personal 35% holding.[5]

Example 6.2

1.   The trustees exercise a wide power of advancement to end the qualifying life interest of Sid and transfer the trust fund to his daughter, Sidonia. Sid makes a PET[6] and so IHT will be avoided provided that he survives for 7 years.

2.   Rollo's qualifying interest in possession is replaced by a discretionary trust in favour of his descendants. Unlike (1) above, this is not a PET but an immediately chargeable transfer by Rollo (accordingly after deducting Rollo's nil rate band – if unused – tax at 20% will be payable by the trustees).[7]

3.   On the death of the qualifying life tenant, Sad, the trust fund passes to his son Sam. The value of the trust fund is aggregated with Sad's free estate for the purposes of calculating IHT on Sad's death.

2. THE DEFINITION OF AN IPDI IN SECTION 49A

6.04 This section is drafted on the basis that L is beneficially entitled to an interest in possession in settled property and provides that this will only be an IPDI if four conditions are met. In general, if the conditions are not met the settlement will be taxed under the IHT relevant property regime.

---

[5]   IHTA 1984, s 52(1) which provides that in this case 'tax shall be charged ... as if at that time [Saskia] had made a transfer of value and the value transferred had been equal to the value of the property in the settlement'.

[6]   IHTA 1984, s 3A(1A)(c)(i).

[7]   The trustees of the settlement are primarily liable for the tax that is payable: see IHTA 1984, s 201(1)(a) and for the limitation on liability: s 204(2). On the ending of a trust (resulting from the termination of a qualifying interest in possession) trustees need to be aware of this liability and may need to retain sufficient assets to cover their potential liability (eg if a PET fails or the beneficiary dies within 7 years thereby leading to an increase in the IHT rate from 20% to 40%).

Condition 1

6.05 The settlement must have been effected by will or under the intestacy rules. So far as this requirement is concerned:

(a) a settlement will be 'effected' by will if either the will contains the settlement or if it provides for property to be paid or transferred into an interest in possession trust which has been established during the testator's lifetime;[8]

(b) there is no restriction on the number of IPDI trusts that can be created in a will: for instance, a testator may settle part of his estate on an interest in possession trust for his son and the residue on interest in possession trusts for his daughter;

(c) under the intestacy rules a statutory IPDI may arise if the deceased is survived by his spouse (or civil partner) and children when the spouse (civil partner) is entitled to:
  (i) the personal chattels;
  (ii) the statutory legacy;
  (iii) a life interest (an IPDI) in one-half of the residue.[9]

Condition 2

6.06 L (the person entitled to the interest in possession) must have become beneficially entitled to that interest 'on the death of the testator or intestate'. Accordingly the interest must be 'immediate'.

Example 6.3

1. On Sid's death his will provides for his residuary estate to be held on trust for his surviving spouse Renata 'for life or until remarriage'. Renata is entitled to an IPDI with the result that on Sid's death the spouse exemption will apply to his residuary estate.[10]

2. If Sid's will had included a standard survivorship clause (*viz* that Renata would only become entitled to the interest if she was alive 28 days after his death) then, assuming that she survives for that period, her interest will be an IPDI. At first sight, this might appear not to be the case given that her interest did not 'immediately' arise on Sid's death. However, IHTA 1984, s 92 provides that in the case of survivorship clauses where the period does

---

[8] Note that the definition of 'settlement' in IHTA 1984, s 43 refers to a disposition of property whereby that property is held in trusts for persons in succession. See also **7.25** and, for confirmation that HMRC agree that an IPDI arises in the situation where property is left by will to a trust established during the deceased's lifetime with an interest in possession, see the exchange of correspondence between them and CIOT/STEP (updated in 2008) at question 13.

[9] See AEA 1925, s 46(1)(i). But note that in the case of deaths on or after 1 October 2014 the spouse receives one half of the residue absolutely (see the Inheritance and Trustees' Powers Act 2014): see Chapter 15.

[10] IHTA 1984, s 18(1) which applies because the property becomes comprised in Renata's estate as a result of IHTA 1984, s 49(1): see **6.15**.

not exceed 6 months from the date of death: 'this Act shall apply as if the dispositions taking effect at the end of the period ... had effect from the beginning of the period.'

In effect, the section provides for a reading-back so that Renata's interest in possession is treated as arising at the date of Sid's death.

3.   Charlie's will leaves property to his wife Renee for life, remainder to his daughter, Cherie, for life and thereafter for his grandchildren absolutely. On Charlie's death Renee (assuming that she survives) will be entitled to an IPDI so that the estate will be spouse exempt. On Renee's death, Cherie's interest in possession is *not* an IPDI (since she did not become entitled on the death of the testator, Charlie). Instead, the continuing trust for her will be taxed under the IHT relevant property regime.[11]

4.   Contrast the position in (3) above if, on Charlie's death, Renee had predeceased but Charlie had not altered his will. Now Cherie is entitled to her interest in possession on Charlie's death: ie. it is 'immediate' and so an IPDI.

6.07 In a number of cases the IHT legislation introduces the fiction of 'reading-back'.[12] HMRC accept that this may result in the creation of an IPDI.

Example 6.4

1.   Roger's will leaves everything to his wife, Miranda. Within 2 years of his death she enters into a deed of variation falling within IHTA 1984, s 142(1) establishing a trust of the estate under which she is entitled to a life interest. Reading-back under IHTA 1984, s 142 results in the creation of an IPDI, and the estate remaining exempt from IHT because of the spouse exemption under IHTA 1984, s 18.[13]

2.   Tony's will leaves his estate on discretionary trusts. Within 2 years of his death the trustees appoint his surviving civil partner, Jack, an interest in possession. Reading-back under IHTA 1984, s 144[14] results in Jack having an IPDI, and the estate being exempt from IHT under IHTA 1984, s 18.

Condition 3

6.08 The property is not held in either a bereaved minor trust or a disabled person's trust.

6.09 A bereaved minor trust (BMT) is subject to a special charging regime modelled on that which formerly applied to accumulation and maintenance

---

11   Renee will make a chargeable transfer of value equal to the value of the settled property at the time of her death and is treated as the settlor of the continuing trust: see IHTA 1984, s 80. Note, however, that the 10-year anniversaries of the settlement will run from the date of Charlie's death: see IHTA 1984, s 61(2). For the use of general powers see **6.33**.

12   See, for instance, IHTA 1984, s 92 considered in **Example 6.3(2)**.

13   Instruments of variation are considered in Chapter 12. For the use of flexible IPDIs in estate planning, see **6.27** which explains why a variation onto IPDI trusts may be attractive.

14   For the scope of IHTA 1984, s 144, see Chapter 13.

trusts.[15] There is no IHT charge when the child becomes 18 (when he must become entitled to the capital of the trust) nor if he dies under the age of 18 (whereupon the property will pass under default provisions). In the definition of a BMT[16] it is provided that whilst the bereaved minor is living and under the age of 18 either (a) he must be entitled to all the income from the settled property or (b) 'no such income can be applied for the benefit of any other person'.[17] In the former case where the beneficiary is entitled to the income there is a potential overlap with IPDI trusts which Condition 3 resolves by providing that the BMT takes precedence.

Example 6.5

1. On his death, Candide leaves his residuary estate on trust to pay the income to his minor son who becomes entitled to capital at age 18. The overlap between the BMT and IPDI regimes is resolved in favour of the BMT.

2. The position is the same if the will trust gave the minor son a right to income and capital at 18 and the trustees exercised a power to accelerate his right to income after Candide's death. The trust remains a BMT.

3. Bernstein, more cautious than Candide, left his entire estate to his infant daughter at 25 but with an immediate right to income excluding TA 1925, s 31. Because capital is vesting later than the age of 18 the trust cannot be a BMT but will fall under s 71D (an '18–25 trust'). In this case, however, the IPDI rules take precedence and apply.[18]

6.10 The exclusion of disabled trusts is perhaps less obvious given that these trusts are generally taxed in the same way as IPDIs, ie the disabled person is taxed on the basis that he is deemed to own the capital in the settlement.[19] There are, however, a number of situations in which a 'disabled person's interest' is capable of arising, only some of which overlap with the definition of an IPDI, and the draftsmen doubtless considered it sensible to tax all such occasions together and avoid any overlap with IPDIs.

Example 6.6

Paul leaves his estate on a life interest trust for his daughter Esme. Esme is a disabled person at the time of Paul's death in accordance with the requirements of IHTA 1984, s 89(4)–(6) and so the settlement is a disabled person's trust, not an IPDI.[20]

---

[15] For a consideration of BMTs see Chapter 7.

[16] In IHTA 1984, s 71A.

[17] IHTA 1984, s 71A(3)(c). If the beneficiary is not entitled to the income the trustees should be given the standard TA 1925, s 31 powers to use that income for his maintenance or benefit and to accumulate any balance.

[18] For the overlap between IPDI trusts and 18–25 trusts see 7.20. Section 71D(5)(a)(ii) provides that in this case the IPDI trust takes precedence. For the significant differences that result from the trust being IPDI rather than 18–25, see 7.22.

[19] IHTA 1984, s 49(1A)(b) and for the meaning of a 'disabled person's interest' see s 89B.

[20] There is, however, no significant IHT difference between the two!

Condition 4

6.11 This states that Condition 3 must continue to be met throughout the duration of the interest of L, ie it is possible that an interest which was originally an IPDI may cease to be so if the trust subsequently falls within the definition of a BMT, or if the interest becomes a disabled person's interest.[21]

> *Example 6.7*
>
> Julius' will provides that his 16-year-old son, Mikel, is to have an immediate right to income in the residue of his estate (so excluding TA 1925, s 31) and to receive capital at age 30. The trustees are given an overriding power of appointment which they exercise one year after Julius' death to give Mikel a contingent entitlement to capital at age 18. The analysis is as follows:
>
> 1. Initially Mikel enjoyed an IPDI given that Conditions 1–3 were met;
>
> 2. However, the making of the appointment results in the trust becoming a BMT (because Mikel is now entitled to capital at 18) and so Condition 3 which must be satisfied for there to be an IPDI ceases to be met. As a result, Mikel ceases to be beneficially entitled to the capital of the trust and makes a PET! This is wholly bizarre given that:
>
> (a)   at 18 there is no exit charge on the ending of the BMT;
>
> (b)   were he to die before 18 the PET would be chargeable![22]

3. WHAT IS MEANT BY AN INTEREST IN POSSESSION?

6.12 Sometimes misleadingly used as a synonym for a life interest, the basic meaning is a right to income as it arises[23] (ie a right which is in no way dependent on the exercise of the trustees' discretion). It also encompasses:

(a)   a right to use the trust property (eg the right to occupy a dwelling house or to have possession of trust chattels);[24]

(b)   the situation where there is no income currently produced by the trust but, were there to be, the beneficiary would be entitled to it.

6.13 The existence of overriding powers which, if exercised, would end the beneficiary's income entitlement are ignored in deciding whether an interest in possession exists. Obviously once exercised they may have the effect of ending

---

21   IHTA 1984, s 49A(5).
22   See IHTA 1984, s 49(1A) which provides that the deemed entitlement to capital only applies 'so long as' the interest is an IPDI. Section 3A(1A)(c)(iii) provides for a PET if a gift into a BMT takes effect on the ending of an IPDI. Once Mikel becomes 18 (and entitled to the trust property) double charges on the failed PET and the trust fund which he now owns are prevented by the Inheritance Tax (Double Charges Relief) Regulations 1987, SI 1987/1130.
23   See especially *Pearson* (or *Pilkington*) *v IRC* [1981] AC 753.
24   See IHTA 1984, s 50(5).

that interest and, for instance, replacing it with a discretionary trust. Modern IPDI will trusts depend upon such powers for their flexibility.[25]

6.14 An interest in possession beneficiary is not as such entitled to capital: and the power of advancement given by TA 1925, s 32 applies only to beneficiaries with an interest in capital, albeit that the interest may be conditional on the happening of certain events. Modern settlements will normally give trustees a power to advance capital to the life tenant/interest in possession beneficiary.[26]

> *Example 6.8*

> 1.   The Wilkins' Settlement gives Ray a life interest with remainders to his children at 25. The trustees have an overriding power to appoint capital and income in favour of Ray's children. Until this power is exercised, Ray enjoys an interest in possession.

> 2.   Under the Gullit Settlement, Ruud has a right to income for 2 years after which the income is to be paid to his three siblings in equal shares and to the survivors until the last death. Ruud enjoys an interest in possession (note that it is not a life interest) as will his siblings in due course.

> 3.   Cicely is given a right to occupy a flat in Mitcham in the will of her brother who has recently died. On her death or, if earlier, when she ceases to occupy the flat, it is to be sold and the sale proceeds paid to the brother's children. Cicely has an interest in possession falling short of a life interest (since her right will end if she ceases to occupy the property). Note that she is not given an income interest in the proceeds of sale.[27]

> 4.   Reg is entitled to the income from the family trust fund unless the trustees (within a reasonable time) determine to accumulate it. Because Reg is not entitled to the income as it arises he does not have an interest in possession.

> 5.   The Archer discretionary trust was set up many years ago and there is now one remaining beneficiary, old Dan. As there is no possibility of further beneficiaries being born, the trustees must pay the income to Dan who has an interest in possession.

> 6.   Property is settled on Zoe contingently on her attaining the age of 21. Until the age of 18 the income may be applied for her maintenance and any balance accumulated: from the age of 18 she will be entitled to the income as it arises and hence will enjoy an interest in possession.[28]

---

[25]   See **Precedent 6.1, clause 5.**

[26]   See **Precedent 6.1, clause 4(b).**

[27]   These arrangements are relatively common in practice: care needs to be exercised in determining what it is that the testator wants. Does he, as in the example, want to limit his sister's rights to the occupation of a particular property or would he be happy for her to occupy a replacement property (of her or the trustees' choosing)? If the property is sold, does he want her to have a right to the income from the sale proceeds? If so, then the drafting is simplified since she can be given a 'full blown' life interest in the trust fund currently made up of the property. Other issues that need to be addressed are who determines when Cicely ceases to occupy in the event of any dispute and what, in any event, is meant by 'occupation'.

[28]   TA 1925, s 31. The draftsman may, if he wishes, vary or exclude s 31 and provide, for instance, that Zoe is to have the income even whilst a minor or only on attaining 21.

The meaning of a 'qualifying' interest in possession

6.15 The term a 'qualifying' interest in possession is found in the IHT legislation and determines the IHT treatment of the settlement or will trust.[29] If the interest is 'qualifying' then s 49(1) applies to treat the beneficiary as 'beneficially entitled to the property in which the interest subsists'. By contrast, if the interest is not qualifying then the relevant property regime applies (ie the settlement will be subject to 10-year anniversary and interim exit charges).[30]

6.16 Before the FA 2006 changes in the IHT treatment of settlements, virtually all interests in possession were qualifying. From 22 March 2006, however, the position is quite different and the list of qualifying interests is now as follows:[31]

(a)   a pre-22 March 2006 interest in possession;

(b)   a transitional serial interest;[32]

(c)   a disabled person's interest;[33]

(d)   an IPDI.

4. THE DRAFTING OF IPDIS[34]

6.17 IPDIs will normally be drafted with a view to flexibility. This has two aspects:

(a)   the trustees will be given a power to pay capital to the interest in possession beneficiary. Often it is a surviving spouse who is the beneficiary and this power may be desirable to allow for future emergencies (eg the cost of private hospital treatment). It is rare in such cases to provide for a right to income without the possibility of any recourse to capital should the need arise;[35]

(b)   at the opposite extreme, the trustees will be given power to terminate the interest in possession in whole or in part. Accordingly if the beneficiary no longer needs the income it can be taken from him if the trustees exercise this power. The consequences of so doing are that the beneficiary will then

---

[29]   See IHTA 1984, ss 58(1) and 59.

[30]   For the relevant property regime see IHTA 1984, Part III, Chapter III and 3.60 *et seq.*

[31]   See IHTA 1984, ss 49(1), (1A).

[32]   For the definition of a transitional serial interest, see IHTA 1984, ss 49B–49E.

[33]   For the definition of a disabled person's interest, see IHTA 1984, s 89B.

[34]   See **Precedent 6.1.**

[35]   From the standpoint of the surviving spouse the question may arise as to whether the provision is adequate in terms of the Inheritance (Provision for Family and Dependants) Act 1975. In *Berger v Berger* [2013] EWCA Civ 1305 the Court of Appeal commented on the importance in such applications of considering the provision which would be ordered had the marriage ended not in death but on divorce. Since the House of Lords decision in *White v White* [2001] 1 AC 596 a spouse would normally expect to receive a share of the available capital. If capital is paid to the IPDI beneficiary there is no IHT liability: see IHTA 1984, s 53(2) although a charge to CGT may arise: TCGA 1992, s 71(1).

make either a PET or chargeable transfer.[36] The power may therefore be exercised with an eye to IHT planning for the beneficiary.[37] In the situation where the beneficiary has lost mental capacity the existence of this power enables IHT planning to be carried out for the beneficiary without the need for the consent of the Court of Protection.

6.18 An issue that the draftsmen will need to consider is what (if any) additional safeguards should be built-in for the beneficiary. For instance, should his consent be necessary to the exercise of the power to terminate the interest? Consider the following:

(a) one of the attractions of the overriding power is that it can be used in a case where the beneficiary is no longer mentally capable. Accordingly any consent requirement (if included) should apply only during such time as the beneficiary is mentally capable;

(b) if the beneficiary is one of the trustees (who must act unanimously unless the will provides to the contrary) then the consent requirement becomes redundant;

(c) if a consent is required will this mean that the beneficiary makes a gift, for instance, for the purpose of the reservation of benefit rules? Arguably not since the consent merely permits a decision taken by the trustees (who must first decide to exercise the power) to go ahead. In any event, what is it that has been given away? Presumably the right to income but that interest will have been extinguished by the exercise of the power so that it is difficult to see that there is any property for the reservation of benefit rules to 'bite on'![38]

6.19 A provision that is sometimes found in trust deeds allows the interest in possession beneficiary to call for the capital (eg when he becomes 30). Unless and until the beneficiary calls for the capital the settlement remains in being (eg for CGT purposes he is not absolutely entitled to the property until that happens) but the existence of such a power undermines any attempt to use the trust as an asset protection vehicle.[39] The authors accordingly do not recommend that this provision should be incorporated into standard precedents.

Should such a power be desired it will be necessary to consider whether the beneficiary should be able to call for the whole of the capital of the fund or

---

[36] See **6.03**.

[37] This matter is considered at **6.20** *et seq.*

[38] The forms in this book do not include a consent requirement reflecting the authors' view that this is best avoided. The reservation of benefit issue has been largely resolved by the widened definition of 'gift' adopted by FA 1986, s 102ZA (inserted by FA 2006).

[39] For IPDIs as asset protection vehicles, see **6.30**. It is thought that this right to call for capital would, for instance, vest in a trustee in bankruptcy whilst in cases where the interest in possession was not qualifying a failure to exercise the right might have IHT consequences under IHTA 1984, s 3(3) (failure to exercise a right).

whether the right should be capped at a particular figure allowing the trustees' discretion to extend to the balance of the fund: for instance:

> 'If at any time and from time to time my Spouse wishes my Trustees to raise capital out of any property in which s/he has an interest in possession under [ ] above [even to the extent of exhausting that property] [up to the figure of £ but no further] and to pay it to him/her or apply it for his/her benefit s/he may make a written request to that effect and they shall comply with it.'

5. RESERVATION OF BENEFIT AND THE TERMINATION OF THE INTEREST DURING THE LIFETIME OF THE BENEFICIARY[40]

6.20   Before changes introduced by FA 2006, interests in possession with a power for trustees to terminate (so-called flexible interests in possession) were widely used to circumvent the IHT reservation of benefit rules as illustrated in the following example:

Example 6.9

Under her husband's will (he died in 2004) Suzie was left a flexible life interest in the residue of his estate. The will also includes a nil rate band discretionary trust to use up the husband's nil rate band.[41] In 2005 the trustees terminate Suzie's interest in possession in property worth £285,000 which they appoint onto a continuing discretionary trust under which she could continue to benefit (it was envisaged that she would be the principal beneficiary being paid the income and, if she needed it in the future, the capital).

In 2005 the IHT consequences were as follows:

1.   on the (partial) termination of her interest in possession Suzie was treated as making a chargeable transfer but of an amount which fell within her IHT nil rate band (assuming, of course, that she had not used this up);

2.   it was not thought that Suzie made a 'gift' as is necessary if the reservation of benefit legislation is to apply.[42] Accordingly the fact that she continued to benefit from the property did not have adverse IHT consequences;[43]

3.   at the end of 7 years the chargeable transfer fell out of her cumulative total (so that the exercise could be repeated!).

---

[40]   For an outline of the reservation of benefit rules see **3.04**.

[41]   Rules allowing for the transfer of unused nil rate bands between spouses and civil partners were only introduced in October 2007: see Chapter 5. The nil rate band at this time was £285,000.

[42]   It is thought that even if Suzie's consent was necessary she would still not make a gift for these purposes. So far as the POA rules are concerned Suzie does not dispose of an interest in land so that there is no charge to income tax on her continued occupation.

[43]   Contrast the position if Suzie had been given the residuary estate absolutely and had then created this settlement. Now (unless she entered into a deed of variation within IHTA 1984, s 142(1)) she would make a gift and the reservation of benefit rules would apply.

6.21 A major attraction of the arrangement was that Suzie became the principal beneficiary under two nil rate band discretionary trusts (one in the will of her dead husband, the other created by the appointment) but neither would be taxed on her death as part of her estate. Unsurprisingly, FA 2006 amended the reservation of benefit rules (by inserting a new section, s 102ZA, into the reservation of benefit code in FA 1986) to put a stop to such arrangements.[44]

The scope of FA 1986, s 102ZA

6.22 The change took effect from 22 March 2006: it was neither retrospective nor retroactive, although it does apply when a qualifying interest in possession is terminated on or after that date even if (as will usually be the case) the interest came into being before 22 March 2006. The legislation is narrowly drafted and, as will be seen, may be circumvented in some situations.

6.23 The basic principle in s 102ZA is that on the termination of a qualifying interest in possession during the lifetime of the beneficiary he is deemed to make a gift. (The requirement that the taxpayer makes a gift is an essential prerequisite for the operation of the reservation of benefit rules.) Further, the legislation states that the gift is of 'the no longer possessed property' defined in s 102ZA as:

> 'the property in which the interest in possession subsisted immediately before it came to an end other than any of it to which the individual becomes absolutely and beneficially entitled in possession on the coming to an end of the interest in possession.'

Taking the facts in **Example 6.9**, the consequence is that if Suzie's interest had been terminated on or after 22 March 2006 she would be deemed to make a gift of £285,000 (being 'the no longer possessed property').

6.24 But note that this is all that the legislation does. It does not deem there to be a reservation: that will depend on whether (on the facts) the beneficiary has reserved a benefit in the gifted property. In **Example 6.9** Suzie has reserved a benefit, since she remains capable of benefiting under the terms of the discretionary trust. On her death, therefore, the then value of the discretionary trust fund will be taxed as part of her estate.[45]

---

[44] More aggressive arrangements involved further terminations of Suzie's interest in favour of interest in possession trusts for the children (these terminations then being PETs by Suzie and the children's interests in 2005 being 'qualifying') followed by the termination of the children's interests so that further discretionary trusts arose, thereby resulting in a plethora of nil rate band discretionary trusts under which all the family could benefit.

[45] FA 1986, s 102(3).

Implications of s 102ZA

6.25 When a qualifying interest in possession is terminated during the lifetime of the beneficiary (which will usually be by a deed of appointment made by the trustees)[46] it is important that the beneficiary is excluded from all future benefit in the 'no longer possessed property' (ie in the appointed fund) if reservation of benefit problems are to be avoided.

Limited effect of s 102ZA

6.26 The inserted section is said to apply for the purposes of:

'(a)   Section 102 above; and
(b)   Schedule 20 to this Act.'

Curiously, the section therefore does not apply for the purposes of s 102A–102C (being that part of the reservation of benefit code introduced in 1999 to prevent *Ingram* schemes over land).[47] Section 102A provides that there is a reservation of benefit where an individual disposes of an interest in land by way of gift on or after 9 March 1999 and the donor or his spouse or civil partner enjoys a significant right or interest, or is party to a significant arrangement, in relation to the land. A right, interest or arrangement is not significant if the donor paid full consideration for it;[48] a right or interest is not significant if it was owned for 7 years before the date of the gift.[49]

Tax planning avoiding s 102ZA

6.27 The limitations on the scope of s 102ZA has left open the following IHT planning.

> *Example 6.10*
>
> On his death in 2009, Jasper leaves the residue of his estate on a flexible IPDI trust for his surviving spouse Martha. There are continuing trusts after the IPDI for the children of the marriage. Included in the residue is the family home, 'Westwinds', which was solely owned by Jasper. Martha lives (and intends to go on living) in Westwinds. In 2016 the house is worth around £800,000 and Martha is in her early 70s. Her IHT nil rate band will be needed for her investments and so on her death Westwinds will attract an IHT charge at 40%. The following IHT planning opportunity exists:
>
> 1.   the trustees carve a 20-year lease out of the property. This can be done by granting it to a nominee. No rent will be payable under the lease and its duration should not exceed 21 years because of the enfranchisement rights which would then apply to enhance its value;[50]

---

[46]   See **Precedent 6.2.**
[47]   For *Ingram* schemes and the scope of s 102A–102C see **Example 6.10** and **Precedent 6.6.**
[48]   FA 1986, s 102A(3).
[49]   FA 1986, s 102A(5).
[50]   The length of the lease should be related to Martha's life expectancy (ie to how long she

2.   having carried out Step 1 the trustees retain the lease on the IPDI trust for Martha but use their overriding power to appoint the (encumbered) freehold interest to, say, Martha's children;

3.   Martha continues to occupy Westwinds because of the lease that has been retained in the IPDI trust.

The tax consequences of this arrangement are as follows:

(a)   Martha will make a PET on the termination of her interest in the freehold. Provided that she survives for 7 years, an IHT charge will be avoided. Before the FA 2006 changes in the IHT treatment of settlements, the appointment in favour of the children would usually have been on continuing trusts. However, such trusts are now relevant property settlements and Martha would therefore make not a PET but an immediately chargeable transfer. If the value of the transfer of value arising on the ending of her interest in possession exceeded her available nil rate band, a 20% tax on the excess would result. Hence, it will commonly be desirable to make an outright appointment to the children albeit that this may have a CGT downside (see **6.29**);

(b)   main residence relief will be available to prevent a CGT charge when the freehold is appointed out of the trust to the children;[51]

(c)   so far as reservation of benefit is concerned, Martha is treated by s 102ZA as making a gift of the freehold interest (this is the 'no longer possessed property') but she does not reserve any benefit in this property. Her continued occupation of Westwinds results from her entitlement under the lease which has, of course, been retained in the IPDI trust. The arrangement is modelled on the *Ingram* scheme which was stopped in the case of arrangements made by individuals by the 1999 legislation. However, as already noted, s 102ZA does not apply for the purpose of these sections.[52]

Reversionary leases

6.28 An alternative to the above would be for a reversionary (or deferred) lease to be employed. This would involve the trustees carving out a long (eg 299-year) lease to take effect in, say, 20 years' time.[53] This element of deferral is crucial since it means that until the expiry of that period the freeholder retains the right to occupy the property. As a result, in **Example 6.10**, the trustees could appoint the benefit of the deferred lease to Martha's children, retaining the freehold interest in the IPDI trust thereby ensuring the continued right of occupation of the property by Martha for the next 20 years.

---

anticipates continuing to live in the property). For an older taxpayer, therefore, a shorter lease may be taken. Bear in mind that at the end of the lease term, if Martha is still alive and wishes to continue to occupy the property, she will have to pay a full rent to avoid a reservation of benefit (FA 1986, Sch 20, para 6(1)(a)). See **Precedent 6.6**.

[51]   TCGA 1992, s 225.

[52]   See **6.26**. Because Martha does not dispose of an interest in land it is not thought that the pre-owned asset income tax charge applies.

[53]   See LPA 1925, s 149(3) which some commentators believe means that the deferral period cannot exceed 21 years. Query, however, whether this provision applies if the lease is not granted in consideration for a fine or at a rent. In this arrangement no rent (not even a peppercorn) would be payable.

As a *practical* matter, there is little to choose between the *Ingram* arrangement illustrated in the example and the deferred lease. Arguably the former is the more common arrangement and the deferred lease is very much the creation of a tax planning exercise. The deferred lease, however, has a significant advantage in that it does not fall foul of the reservation of benefit legislation introduced in 1999 to counter *Ingram* schemes,[54] provided that either of the following conditions is met:

(a)   the freehold interest in the property has been owned by the taxpayer for 7 years before the grant of the lease;[55] or

(b)   the freehold interest was acquired for full consideration in money or money's worth.[56]

Accordingly, the use of a reversionary lease means that the arrangement is outside both s 102ZA and s 102A. Hence even if the scope of s 102ZA was in the future to be widened to apply to the 1999 legislation, a reversionary lease arrangement (meeting one of the above conditions) entered into by the trustees would still not be caught unless the 1999 legislation was also amended.

CGT issues

6.29   The arrangement discussed in **Example 6.10** works well in cases where there is no intention that the property will ever be sold – typically where it is the historic family home which will in due course be occupied by a child. In other cases, however, where the house will be sold after the death of the surviving spouse, the sale of the house is likely to lead to a substantial CGT charge given that:

(a)   the freehold interest appointed to the children will be heavily discounted because of the rent-free lease (a discount of 60% would not be unusual which on a current value for the property of £800,000 would value the encumbered freehold at £320,000);

(b)   the children will not be occupying the property as their main residence so that CGT relief under TCGA 1992, s 222 *et seq* will not be available.

This problem may be overcome by taking advantage of the *Crowe v Appleby*[57] decision. Broadly speaking, this case decided that for CGT purposes land remains settled property until one or more beneficiaries is absolutely entitled to

---

[54]   See FA 1986, s 102A–102C.

[55]   FA 1986, s 102A(5). The Appendix to HMRC's Guidance Notes to the Pre-Owned Assets Charge says in relation to reversionary leases: 'HMRC had previously held the view that section 102A Finance Act 1986 would apply to them because the donor's occupation would be a "significant right in relation to the land" ... HMRC now consider that where the freehold interest was acquired more than seven years before the gift, the continued occupation by the donor would not be a significant right.'

[56]   FA 1986, s 102A(3) indicating that an interest is not significant if it was acquired for 'full consideration in money or money's worth'. This get out is no help in **Example 6.10**.

[57]   [1975] 3 All ER 529: see **3.116**.

the entirety. For instance, if land is settled on the four children of the settlor contingently on them attaining the age of 21, then until the youngest attains that age the land remains settled, albeit that the older three children have become entitled to undivided shares in the land. On the facts of **Example 6.10,** were the trustees to appoint (say) 95% of the encumbered freehold interest to the children leaving 5% held on the IPDI trust for Martha then the freehold would remain settled property for CGT purposes and in these circumstances TCGA 1992, s 225 will apply to give main residence relief to the trustees on a sale of the property.

> *Example 6.11*
>
> Assume that in **Example 6.10** Martha's IPDI continued in the leasehold interest and 5% of the freehold (95% of the latter having been appointed to the children).[58] After Martha's death the trustees sell the property. CGT relief under s 225 will be due given that during Martha's life it was her main residence and she was 'a person entitled to occupy it under the terms of the settlement'. Relief is given on the entire property owned by the trustees: it is not limited to the lease occupied by Martha.

6. TYPICAL USES OF THE IPDI

6.30 When drafting wills for spouses or civil partners, there are (non-IHT) advantages in leaving property (often the residue of the estate) on a flexible IPDI trust for the surviving spouse/civil partner. Specifically this will 'ring fence' the capital of the trust against:

(a)   future bankruptcy of the survivor;

(b)   nursing home fees in the event that the survivor has to go into a care home;

(c)   against the claim of any future spouse/civil partner of the survivor.[59]

6.31 The flexible IPDI is also a useful tool in IHT planning for the survivor. Judicious terminations of the interest in possession can be effected by the trustees to take advantage of the beneficiary's annual £3,000 IHT exemption[60] and the normal expenditure out of income exemption.[61] If the consent of the beneficiary is not required then such partial terminations of the interest can take place even if the beneficiary no longer has mental capacity.[62]

---

[58]   In the case of a reversionary lease arrangement retain 5% of the lease in the IPDI trust.

[59]   If the will leaves everything to the survivor then that person can vary it under IHTA 1984, s 142 in order to establish an IPDI trust. However, in the 'real world', this will involve a lifetime gift which may be vulnerable, eg in the event of future bankruptcy/nursing home fees. Better, therefore, to get the will right!

[60]   The beneficiary must elect for his annual exemption to be so used: see IHTA 1984, s 57(3)–(4).

[61]   As happened in *Bennett v IRC* [1995] STC 54.

[62]   For the requirement of consent, see **6.18.**

6.32   An attraction of the IPDI trust is that it can be used with an eye to longer term IHT planning. Assume for instance that a widowed mother wishes to use her estate to provide for her son and his children. If the estate exceeds her available nil rate band then a relevant property trust will be subject to 10 yearly charges. By contrast, if the son is, say, mid-30s, an IPDI trust for him may be the preferred solution. It may be many years before a tax charge arises on his death and in the meanwhile the flexibility of this means that IHT planning can be carried out.

> *Example 6.12*
>
> Paul was left an interest in possession in the residue of his mother's estate. With a view to establishing a fund to educate his children, the trustees terminate his interest in £100,000 which they appoint on interest in possession trusts for those children. These trusts are taxed under the relevant property regime[63] (the children's interests in possession are not 'qualifying') and so Paul makes a chargeable transfer falling within his nil rate band. He is not the settlor and so the income is not taxed on him even if the children are minor.

6.32A   Grandparents may wish to create a settlement on death for the benefit of grandchildren. If they use a discretionary or contingent interest trust, it will be within the relevant property regime and subject to anniversary and exit charges.[64] Bereaved minor and bereaved young person's trusts[65] can only be created by parents, so the IPDI is the only way for grandparents to settle property and avoid ongoing tax charges.

7. CIRCUMVENTING THE IPDI REQUIREMENTS: THE USE OF GENERAL POWERS

6.33   It is not normally possible to create a succession of IPDIs because of the requirement that the beneficiary must have become entitled 'on the death of the testator or intestate'. However, judicious planning can produce this result.

Consider the following example. In her will, Daphne leaves her estate on an IPDI trust for her daughter. Before the 2006 changes it would have been normal to provide for the daughter's surviving spouse to have an interest in possession (doubtless revocable) after the daughter's death. This would secure the spouse exemption. After the 2006 changes, if Daphne's will makes this provision (ie daughter for life and husband for life, etc) the daughter has an IPDI but, as explained above, the husband's successive life interest cannot be an IPDI (it is not 'immediate') and so the trust falls into the relevant property regime with the result that on her death the daughter will make a chargeable transfer.

---

[63]   The rate of tax charged on anniversaries and exits should be considered before embarking on this arrangement.

[64]   See **3.62** *et seq.*

[65]   See **7.05** *et seq.*

If, however, Daphne's will had left her daughter a life interest and also given the daughter a general power of appointment exercisable by will then the daughter could (in her will) exercise the power to appoint a life interest to her husband. The daughter creates the interest in her will and, hence, it qualifies an IPDI and so the spouse exemption applies.[66]

The same strategy can be employed in the following situation.

Example 6.13

Julie wishes to leave her estate on IPDI trusts for her two sons. She is also the life tenant under a family settlement subject to which discretionary trusts arise. She would like the sons (members of the discretionary class) to have similar life interests in the trust fund. Assume that the trustees have a power to advance capital for Julie's benefit. Consider the following alternatives:

1.   the trustees appoint the sons concurrent interests in possession to take effect on Julie's death. These continuing trusts will be taxed under the relevant property regime. Julie will, of course, make a chargeable transfer on her death and there will be the usual CGT death uplift; alternatively

2.   the trustees exercise their power to apply capital to benefit Julie by giving her a general power of appointment exercisable by her will. The trustees' exercise of the power has no immediate tax consequences because Julie is treated as beneficially entitled to the property before and after the exercise of the power.[67] Julie then amends her will to exercise the general power that the trustees have given her by creating a trust giving her sons concurrent life interests. When Julie dies, the consequences are as in (1): ie there is a charge to IHT on the value of the property in the settlement with CGT uplift. But the continuing trusts, having been created by Julie's will, give the sons IPDIs. Accordingly all the property (both Julie's free estate and the settled property) has been settled on the same IPDI trusts.

---

[66]   See **Precedent 6.5**.
[67]   IHTA 1984, s 49(1).

PRECEDENTS

Precedent 6.1: Flexible IPDI trust of residue for a surviving spouse or civil partner[68]

Trusts of Residue

I GIVE DEVISE AND BEQUEATH all my property both movable and immovable of whatever nature and wheresoever situated except property otherwise disposed of by this Will or by any Codicil hereto unto my Trustees UPON TRUST to sell call in and convert the same into money (so far as not already consisting of money) with power to postpone the sale calling in and conversion thereof (even as regards property of a terminable hazardous or wasting nature) in the absolute and uncontrolled discretion of my Trustees without being liable for loss and to hold the net proceeds and my ready money upon the following trusts:

(1)   UPON TRUST to pay thereout (in exoneration of any property which would otherwise be liable for payment of the same) all my funeral and testamentary expenses and debts and any general legacies given by this Will or any Codicil hereto and any tax or duty arising in respect of my death (even if not a testamentary expense) on all gifts in this Will and any Codicil hereto given free of such tax or duty;

(2)   UPON TRUST if necessary to invest the remainder after such payment in or upon any investments hereinafter authorised for the investment of trust funds with power to vary and transpose the same;

(3)   UPON TRUST to stand possessed of such investments and such of my estate as remains for the time being unsold and my ready money and all property from time to time representing the same (hereinafter together called '**my Residuary Trust Fund**') and the income from it upon the following trusts;[69]

(4)   UNTIL SUBJECT to and in default of any appointment under sub-clause (5):
      (a)   The income of the Residuary Trust Fund shall be paid to my surviving spouse during her lifetime;[70]

---

[68]   This form creates a flexible IPDI over the testator's residuary estate. Note especially the overriding power of appointment in clause (5) and the power to apply capital for the benefit of the surviving spouse in clause 4(b). Clause 4 is in the nature of a default provision: it takes effect until the trustees exercise their clause 5 power. Note, therefore, that even after the death of the surviving spouse the children do not become absolutely entitled unless the trustees release their power of appointment or until it ceases to be exercisable (at the end of the Trust Period).

[69]   The first part of the Form establishes the residuary trust fund. It remains commonplace to include a trust for sale. Sometimes a testator will wish to provide for tax on failed PETs to be paid out of his residue: this will involve (in effect) the making of a further gift to the relevant PET beneficiary.

[70]   This creates an IPDI for the surviving spouse so that the residue will benefit from the spouse exemption under IHTA 1984, s 18.

(b) My Trustees may at any time during the Trust Period pay or apply the whole or any part of the Residuary Trust Fund in which my surviving spouse is then entitled to an interest in possession to her or for her advancement or otherwise for her benefit in such manner as my Trustees shall in their discretion think fit and in exercising the powers conferred by this subclause my Trustees shall be entitled to have regard solely to the interests of my surviving spouse and to disregard all other interests or potential interests under my Will;[71]

(c) Subject thereto my Trustees shall hold the capital and income of my Residuary Trust Fund for such of my children as shall survive me and if more than one in equal shares PROVIDED THAT if any child is already dead or predeceases me the share of my Residuary Trust Fund to which such child would have been entitled if he or she had survived me shall be held in trust for such of his or her children and remoter issue (if any) as shall be living at my death and shall reach the age of twenty one [21] years such issue to take through all degrees according to their stocks if more than one in equal shares and so that no issue shall take whose parent is living at my death and so capable of taking.

(5) MY TRUSTEES shall have power to appoint the whole or any part of the capital and/or income of my Residuary Trust Fund upon trust for or for the benefit of such of the Discretionary Beneficiaries[72] at such ages or times in such shares upon such trusts which may include discretionary or protective powers or trusts and in such manner generally as my Trustees shall in their discretion think fit. Any such appointment may include such powers and provisions for the maintenance education or other benefit of the Discretionary Beneficiaries or for the accumulation of income and such administrative powers and provisions as my Trustees think fit.

(6) NO EXERCISE of the power conferred by sub-clause (5) shall invalidate any prior payment or application of all or any part of the capital or income of my Residuary Trust Fund made under any other power conferred by my Will or by law.

(7) ANY TRUSTS and powers created by an appointment under sub-clause (5) may be delegated to any extent to any person whether or not including my Trustees or any of them.

(8) ANY EXERCISE of the power of appointment conferred by sub-clause (5) shall:

(a) be subject to the application if any of the rule against perpetuities; and

(b) be by deed revocable during the Trust Period or irrevocable and executed during the Trust Period.

(9) IN THIS clause:

---

[71] A wide power to apply capital for the 'benefit' of the spouse: it can be exercised by means of a settled advance. Considering giving the surviving spouse a general testamentary power of appointment to enable IPDI trusts to continue after her death: see 6.33.

[72] See the definition below.

(a) 'the Trust Period' shall mean the period of 125 years commencing with the date of my death;

(b) 'the Discretionary Beneficiaries'[73] shall mean my issue (whether children or more remote) together with their spouses, widows and widowers (whether or not remarried) together with such other persons as my Trustees may declare to be Discretionary Beneficiaries.

---

[73] Consider who should be included in 'the Discretionary Class': typically children, grandchildren and spouses but what of civil partners, widows, widowers, etc. Build in some flexibility by giving the trustees the power to add to (and remove from) the class of Discretionary Beneficiaries. Beware including the surviving spouse (the IPDI beneficiary) because of the reservation of benefit dangers of doing so (see **6.25**).

Precedent 6.2: Deed of appointment terminating IPDI and providing for property to be held on discretionary trusts[74]

THIS DEED OF APPOINTMENT is made the [   ] day of [   ] 20[   ] by [   ] of [   ] and [   ] of [   ] ('the Appointors')

SUPPLEMENTAL to the will dated [insert date] ('the Will') of [insert name] ('the Deceased') who died on [insert date] and which will was proved in the [insert registry] by [insert details].

WHEREAS

(A)   The property listed in the Schedule hereto ('the Appointed Fund')[75] is held on the trusts declared by the Will.

(B)   Under the provisions of clause [insert number] of the Will, the Deceased's surviving spouse is currently entitled to the income from the Appointed Fund, inter alia, until such date as the Trustees may by deed appoint and subject thereto the Trustees shall hold the income and capital of the Appointed Fund upon trust for [insert details] upon such trusts and with such powers and provisions as the Trustees may appoint ('the Clause [   ] Power').

(C)   The Appointors are the present trustees of the Will Trusts and are desirous of exercising the Clause [   ] power as set out in this deed.

NOW THIS DEED WITNESSES:

1. Revocation of the surviving spouse's Interest in Possession and New Appointment

In exercise of the Clause [   ] Power and all other relevant powers (if any) the Appointors hereby declare and direct that from and after the date of this deed the surviving spouse's right to income from the Appointed Fund shall be terminated and the Appointed Fund and the income thereof shall be held on the trusts and with and subject to the powers and provisions hereinafter set out.[76]

2. Declaration of Discretionary Trusts

(a)   In this clause:

---

[74]   The effect of this appointment is that the IPDI beneficiary (the surviving spouse) will make an immediately chargeable transfer for IHT purposes. Hence the value of the property appointed ('the Appointed Fund') should be limited to that beneficiary's unused IHT nil rate band. Take care to exclude the IPDI beneficiary from future benefit in the Appointed Fund (see **6.25**).

[75]   Note that in this precedent only part of the property in the will trust is being appointed.

[76]   This clause effects a partial revocation of the IPDI: although the coming into force of the Trusts (Capital and Income) Act 2013 makes it unnecessary to exclude apportionments of income in trusts created on or after 1 October 2013, it is helpful to include a statement that apportionment is not required (see **clause 4**).

(i) 'the Discretionary Beneficiaries' shall mean [   ];[77]

(ii) 'the Trust Period' shall mean the period of 125 years from the date of the Deceased's death.[78]

(b) The Trustees shall stand possessed of the Appointed Fund and the income from it on such trusts and with and subject to such powers and provisions whatever in favour or for the benefit of all or any one or more exclusively of the others or other of the Discretionary Beneficiaries as the Trustees in their absolute discretion shall at any time or times during the Trust Period by any deed or deeds revocable or irrevocable appoint (regard being had to the law relating to remoteness).

(c) In default of and until and subject to any and every appointment made under the power or powers conferred by clause 2(b) above the income of the Appointed Fund shall during the Trust Period be held by the Trustees upon trust to pay or apply or (in the case of a minor) allocate the same to or for the maintenance support or otherwise for the benefit in any manner of all or any one or more exclusively of the others or other of the Discretionary Beneficiaries for the time being living and if more than one in such shares and in such manner in all respects as the Trustees shall in their absolute discretion think fit with power during the Trust Period to accumulate any balance.[79]

(d) The Trustees shall have power exercisable in their absolute discretion at any time or times during the Trust Period to apply the whole or any part or parts of the capital of the Appointed Fund for any purpose whatever which the Trustees may think to be for the benefit of any one or more of the Discretionary Beneficiaries for the time being in existence or to transfer or pay the whole or any part or parts of the capital of the Appointed Fund to any one or more of the Discretionary Beneficiaries for the time being in existence (being of full age) for his, her or their absolute use and benefit.[80]

3. Continuation of Terms of the Will Trust[81]

Subject to all the trusts powers and provisions of this deed the default trusts and administrative and other powers and provisions provided for in clauses [   ] and [   ] of the Will shall continue to apply to the Appointed Fund.

4. Exclusion of Apportionment

---

[77] Exclude the IPDI beneficiary: see **6.25**. Instead of defining the term in the appointment, it may be more satisfactory to refer to the definition in the will: see, eg, **Precedent 6.1, clause 9(b)**.

[78] The mandatory perpetuity period under PAA 2009, assuming that the will was executed after 5 April 2010. Instead of defining the term in the appointment, it may be satisfactory to refer to the definition in the will: see, eg, **Precedent 6.1, clause 9(a)**.

[79] PAA 2009 removed the statutory restrictions on accumulations of income for wills executed after 5 April 2010.

[80] This 'advancement type' power can be exercised by trustee resolution (eg. to deal with outright transfers of money to one of the beneficiaries). Cf the power of appointment in **clause 2(b)** which requires a deed.

[81] The appointment does not create a new CGT settlement: it modifies the existing trusts.

All income of the assets specified in the Schedule received by or on behalf of the Trustees from and after the date of this deed shall be treated as if it had arisen wholly after such date.[82]

IN WITNESS etc

SCHEDULE

('the Appointed Fund')

[Insert details of property comprised in this fund]

---

[82] This clause is no longer necessary after the Trusts (Capital and Income) Act 2013 but may be included to make the position clear.

Precedent 6.3: IPDI trust of residue for (minor) children of the testator with substitution in the case of a pre-deceasing child leaving issue

I GIVE all my property not otherwise disposed of by this Will or any Codicil to my Trustees:

(1)   With power at their discretion to sell all or any of such property when they think fit and to invest the proceeds in any investments hereby authorised and with power from time to time to vary investments for others of an authorised nature.

(2)   To pay all debts funeral and executorship expenses legacies and tax.

(3)   To hold the remainder and the income thereof ('my Residuary Estate') for such of my children as survive me ('my Children') and if more than one in equal shares but if any of them dies before me leaving a child or children [who attain the age of [21]][83] such child or children shall take the share of my Residuary Estate which my deceased child would otherwise have taken and if more than one in equal shares absolutely and PROVIDED ALWAYS that the share in my Residuary Estate of any child of mine ('My Child') shall not vest in him absolutely but shall be retained and invested by my Trustees and held upon the following trusts.

(4)   The provisions of sub-clauses (5) to (7) shall apply to the share of the Trust Fund held upon trust for my Child under sub-clause (3). In these provisions, such share is called 'The Share' and that one of my Children who is primarily interest in the Share is called the 'Life Tenant'.

(5)   The income of the Share shall be paid to the Life Tenant during his lifetime. If and so long as the Life Tenant is under the age of 18, the Trustees may pay or apply any income of the Share to him or for his maintenance or education or otherwise for his benefit as they shall in their discretion think fit. Any balance of the income shall be retained by the Trustees upon trust for the Life Tenant absolutely. Section 31 of the Trustee Act 1925 shall not apply to the Share.[84]

(6)   The Trustees may, at any time or times, during the Trust Period, pay or apply the whole or any part of the Share in which the Life Tenant is then entitled to an interest in possession to him or for his advancement or otherwise for his benefit in such manner as the Trustees shall in their discretion think fit. In exercising the powers conferred by this sub-clause the Trustees shall be entitled to have regard solely to the interests of the Life Tenant and to disregard all other interests or potential interests under this Deed.

(7)   The Life Tenant shall have power to appoint his spouse (or civil partner) a life or lesser interest (including an interest terminable by the Trustees at

---

83   Complete as appropriate.
84   It is essential to exclude the trustees' power to accumulate under TA 1925, s 31 if a minor beneficiary is to enjoy an IPDI. For the problems arising on a failure to do this, see *Fine v Fine* [2012] EWHC 1811 (Ch).

any time) in the income of all or any part of the Share. The Life Tenant may make the commencement of such interest dependent upon conditions as to survivorship or otherwise as he shall in his absolute discretion determine [and he may confer on the Trustees the same power for the benefit of his spouse as they have under sub-clause (6) for his benefit]. No such appointment shall be valid unless, at the date if takes effect, the Life Tenant is entitled to an interest in possession in the Trust Fund or the part of the Trust Fund to which the appointment relates.[85]

(8) Subject as above, the capital and income of the Share shall be held upon trust for such of the children of the Life Tenant as attain the age of 25 before the end of the Trust Period or are living and are under that age at the end of the Trust Period; and if more than one, in equal shares absolutely.[86]

(9) Subject as above, the Share, together with any accrual to it, shall accrue to the other Shares the trusts of which shall not previously have failed or determined (otherwise than by absolute vesting) and, if more than one, equally between them. Each such accrual shall be held upon, with and subject to the same trusts, powers and provisions as the Share to which it accrues.

---

[85] If desired flexible trusts may be adopted: e g the trustees may be given a power of appointment in favour of the Discretionary Beneficiaries (as defined) which could be exercised to terminate the interest in possession of the surviving spouse. A continuing trust for a surviving spouse will not be an IPDI: it will fall into the relevant property regime. Consider giving the child a general power of appointment exercisable by will which he can then exercise to create an IPDI for a surviving spouse: see **6.33** and **Precedent 6.5**.

[86] The continuing trust will, for IHT purposes, be taxed under the relevant property regime.

Precedent 6.4: Revocable appointment of IPDI out of a discretionary will trust[87]

THIS DEED OF APPOINTMENT is made the [   ] day of [   ] 20[   ] by [insert details] of [   ] (together 'the Appointors')

SUPPLEMENTAL TO:

(A)   A will dated [insert date] ('the Will') made by [   ] ('the Deceased') and

(B)   An assent dated [insert date] ('the Assent') under which certain freehold land described in the Schedule to this deed ('the Property') was assented to the Appointors as trustees to hold on the discretionary trusts set out in clause [insert number] of the Will.

WHEREAS:

1.   The Deceased died on [insert date] and the Will was proved on [insert date] at [   ] District Probate Registry.[88]

2.   The Appointors are the present trustees of the residuary estate of the Deceased.

3.   Under clause [insert number] of the Will the residuary estate of the Deceased (therein called 'the Trust Fund') was held on such trusts in favour or for the benefit of all or any one or more of the Discretionary Beneficiaries and in such shares or proportions and with and subject to such powers and provisions for their respective maintenance education or other benefit as the Appointors (being at least two in number) by any deed or deeds revocable during the Trust Period (which period is defined in the Will as the period of 125 years from the date of the Deceased's death)[89] or irrevocable and executed during the Discretionary Period shall appoint.

4.   The Discretionary Beneficiaries include the adult children of the Deceased namely A and B and their respective spouses, widows, widowers, children and remoter issue.

5.   The Appointors have not yet exercised their aforesaid powers of appointment but are now desirous of revocably exercising their powers under the Will and as hereinafter set out.

NOW THIS DEED WITNESSES as follows:

1.   EXPRESSIONS used in this Deed shall where the context admits have the same meanings as set out in the Will and in this deed 'the Appointed Fund' means the Property (as described in the Schedule) the net sale proceeds thereof and the assets from time to time representing the same.

---

[87]   For a consideration of IHTA 1984, s 144 and 'reading-back', see **13.11** *et seq*.

[88]   To come within s 144 it is essential the deceased died within the previous 2 years.

[89]   In some precedents, a 2-year period is specified but this is considered to be undesirable as being unnecessarily restrictive.

2.   IN exercise of their powers contained in clause [insert number] of the Will and of every other power them enabling the Appointors hereby revocably appoint and declare that the Appointed Fund and the income thereof shall from the date of this Deed be held upon trust to divide the same into two equal parts of which the first such equal part and the assets from time to time representing the same ('A's Fund') shall be held upon the trusts declared and contained in clause 3 below and of which the second such equal part and the assets from time to time representing the same ('B's Fund') shall be held upon the trusts declared and contained in clause 5 below.

3.   THE Trustees shall hold A's Fund and the income thereof upon the following trusts and subject to the following powers and provisions:

      (a)   The Trustees shall pay the income of A's Fund to A during his life.[90]

      (b)   The Trustees may, at any time or times pay, transfer or apply to or for the advancement or benefit (whether absolutely or in trust) of A the whole or any part of A's Fund to which A is then entitled to an interest in possession. In exercising the powers conferred by this sub-clause, the Trustees shall be entitled to have regard solely to the interests of A and to disregard all other interests or potential interests in A's Fund.

      (c)   Subject thereto A's Fund and the income thereof shall be held on trust for such of A's children as attain the age of 21 or are living and under that age at the end of the Trust Period and if more than one in equal shares absolutely.[91]

4.   IF the trusts of A's Fund shall fail the Trustees shall hold A's Fund as an accretion to B's Fund and upon the trusts appertaining thereto (including absolute beneficial interests therein) the trusts of which have not failed and as one fund therewith.

5.   THE Trustees shall hold B's Fund and the income thereof upon the trusts contained in clauses 3 and 4 above with the substitution wherever the same appears:

      (a)   For A's Fund of B's Fund
      (b)   For A of B
      (c)   For B's Fund of A's Fund
      (d)   For B of A
      (e)   For A's children of B's children.

6.   THE administrative and other provisions contained in the Will shall continue to apply to the Appointed Fund in so far as those powers and provisions are consistent with the provisions declared by this Deed.

7.   THE Trustees shall have power at any time or times before the end of the Trust Period by deed or deeds wholly or partly to revoke or vary all or any of the trusts powers and provisions which apply to the Appointed Fund by virtue of this deed and if thought fit by the same or similar deed or deeds to make such fresh appointment in exercise of their said powers of

---

[90]   This gives A an IPDI as a result of 'reading-back' under s 144.

[91]   The continuing trust will fall under the relevant property regime.

appointment conferred by the Will as they may in their absolute discretion think fit provided that no exercise of their powers of revocation shall invalidate any prior payment or application of all or any part or parts of the capital or income or deprive a beneficiary of income or capital to which he has already become entitled.

8.   THE Trustees may by deed or deeds executed during the Trust Period release or restrict the future exercise of their power of revocation either wholly or to the extent specified in the relevant deed.

IN WITNESS etc.

SCHEDULE

(Insert details of the Appointed Fund)

Precedent 6.5: Clause giving the IPDI beneficiary a general power of appointment exercisable by will[92]

1.   The income of my Residuary Trust Fund shall be paid to [insert beneficiary, eg my daughter] during [her] lifetime.[93]

2.   My daughter shall have power to appoint by will or codicil my Residuary Trust Fund to such person or persons or for such purpose or purposes in such shares and proportions and upon such terms and in such manner as she shall think fit.[94]

---

[92]   These clauses can be inserted into **Precedent 6.1** to give the surviving spouse the general testamentary power or in **Precedent 6.3** to give each child such a power in respect of his share.

[93]   This creates an IPDI for the daughter: see **Precedent 6.1** for the definition of 'my Residuary Trust Fund'.

[94]   This gives the daughter a general testamentary power of appointment which is akin to absolute ownership. Any such appointment, if on continuing trusts, will involve the creation of a new settlement (eg. the perpetuity period will run from the exercise of the power: it will not be the original period from the will which creates the power). Provided therefore that the daughter exercises the power by will (or codicil) she will be disposing of property comprised in her estate (by virtue of the IPDI) and so may create an IPDI, eg. for her surviving spouse thereby enabling the spouse exemption to apply on her death: see **6.33**.

Precedent 6.6: Appointment of nominees and grant of rent free lease by trustees to nominees[95]

(1) Appointment of Nominees[96]

THIS DECLARATION OF TRUST dated the [   ] day of [   ] 20[   ]

BETWEEN:

(1)   [   ] of [   ] ('the Trustees')
(2)   [   ] of [   ] ('the Nominees')

RECITALS

(A)   The Trustees are the present trustees of a settlement dated [   ] and made between [   ] and [   ].

(B)   The Trustees wish to appoint the Nominees to act in the following manner.

OPERATIVE PROVISIONS

1. Definitions

In this deed the 'Lease' shall mean a lease of even date made between (1) the Trustees (2) the Nominees for a term of 20 years commencing on [   ] 20[   ] and expiring on [   ] in relation to the property known as [   ].

2. Appointment of Nominees

The Trustees hereby appoint the Nominees as nominees to hold the Lease for the Trustees.

3. Indemnity

The Trustees shall indemnify the Nominees jointly and severally and their personal representatives against any claims, demands, losses, liabilities or costs which the Nominees may incur in connection with the Lease or the performance of their obligations under the Lease.

SIGNED as a Deed etc

(2) Grant of Lease[97]

---

95   See **Example 6.10.**
96   This form appoints nominees to act for the trustees in taking a grant of the lease.
97   No rent or premium is payable and the lease is for a term of 20 years (it may be less if it is not expected that the life tenant will live that long). Because of enfranchisement rights it should not exceed that period.

THIS LEASE is made the [   ] day of 20[   ]

(1)   [insert details of trustees] ('the Landlord') acting as trustees of the trusts declared and contained in a Settlement dated [   ]

(2)   [insert details of nominee] ('the Tenant')

OPERATIVE PART

1 Definitions and Interpretations

In this lease:

1.1   'the Property' means the property known as [insert name] which property is registered at HM Land Registry with title number [insert number];

1.2   'the Term' means a term of [20] years commencing on the date hereof;

1.3   'the Landlord' where the context so admits includes the trustees from time to time of the trusts declared in the above recited variation;

1.4   'the Tenant' where the context so admits includes the Tenant's successors in title;

1.5   where any part comprises more than one person the obligations and liabilities under this lease shall be joint and several obligations and liabilities of those persons.

2.   In consideration of the Tenant's covenants the Landlord demises to the Tenant the Property **TO HOLD** to the Tenant for the Term **SUBJECT TO** all rights easements privileges restrictions covenants and stipulations affecting the Property or any part thereof.

3 The Tenant's Covenants

The Tenant covenants with the Landlord:

3.1   to pay (or procure the payment of) all local taxes assessed upon himself or other occupiers of the Property and to pay the Council Tax and all other rates taxes assessments duties charges impositions and outgoings which during the Term are charged assessed or imposed upon or in respect of the Property;

3.2   to repair and keep properly cleaned and in good and tenantable repair and condition the interior and exterior of the Property including the gardens and grounds;

3.3   not to make or to permit to be made any structural alterations or additions to the property nor to cut maim or injure any of the walls or timbers of the Property without the previous written consent of the Landlord except for the purpose of carrying out needful repairs provided always that any alterations or additions which shall be improvements to the Property shall become the property of the Landlord and no compensation shall be payable to the Tenant for such alterations or additions on the termination of this lease;

3.4 to insure the Property against loss or damage by fire and other usual risks in the full cost reinstatement of the Property from time to time together with:

    3.4.1 architects' surveyors, and other professional fees and all other fees payable in connection with reinstatement of the Property;

    3.4.2 the costs of demolition site clearance temporary shoring and other costs which may be incurred in making the Property safe,

and supply a copy of such insurance policy together with an up-to-date Schedule on demand and promptly pay out any monies received from such insurance in repairing rebuilding or reinstating the Property or any part thereof;

3.5 not to do anything or suffer or permit anything to be done as a result of which any policy of insurance on the Property may become void or voidable;

3.6 not to assign underlet or part with or share possession of the Property or any part of the Property;

3.7 to pay all expenses (including solicitors' costs and surveyors' fees) incurred by the Landlord incidental to the preparation and service of a notice under the Law of Property Act 1925 section 146 notwithstanding that forfeiture is avoided otherwise than by relief granted by the Court;

3.8 upon receipt from a competent authority of any notice order direction or other thing affecting or likely to affect the Property whether served directly on the Tenant;

    3.8.1 to comply with the notice order or direction at his own expense so far as he is required to do so by the notice order or direction or the statute regulations or other instrument under which it is used or the provisions of this lease; and

    3.8.2 within 7 days of receipt to deliver to the Landlord a copy of the notice order direction or other thing;

3.9 not to do or permit or suffer to be done any act matter or thing on or in respect of the Property which contravenes the provisions of the Town and Country Planning Act 1990 or any statutory modification or re-enactment of it for the time being in force and to keep the Landlord indemnified against all claims demands and liabilities in respect of any contravention;

3.10 to yield up the Property together with all Landlord's fixtures in good and tenantable repair and condition in accordance with the Tenant's covenants in this lease at the determination of the Term with all locks keys and fastenings complete.

4 The Landlord's Covenants

The Landlord covenants with the Tenant that the Tenant performing and observing the covenants on his part contained in this lease shall peaceably hold and enjoy the Property without any interruption by the Landlord or any person rightfully claiming under or in trust for him.

5 Property and Declarations

5.1 If at any time during the Term any covenant by the Tenant contained in this lease is not performed or observed it shall be lawful for the Landlord at any time after that to re-enter upon the Property or any part of the Property in the name of the whole and upon re-entry this demise shall absolutely determine but without prejudice to the right of action of the Landlord in respect of any breach of any covenant by the Tenant contained in this lease.

5.2 Nothing contained in this lease shall confer on the Tenant any liberty privilege easement right or advantage whatsoever mentioned or referred to in the Law of Property Act 1925 section 62 save as expressly granted.

6 Stamp Duty Certificate

It is hereby certified that there is no agreement for lease or tack to which this lease gives effect and that this transaction does not form part of a larger transaction or series of transactions in respect of which the amount or value of the consideration exceeds [insert amount].

IN WITNESS etc

CHAPTER 7

PROVISION FOR CHILDREN

1. THE FAMILY WILL

In this chapter, for the sake of simplicity, references to 'spouse' include a civil partner.

7.01 In inheritance tax terms, those drafting wills have a greater variety of trusts at their disposal than those drafting lifetime settlements.[1] The following matters are worthy of note when planning the standard family will for spouses and children/grandchildren.

(a) The introduction of the transferable unused nil rate band means that, in general, the first spouse to die does not have to make use of their IHT nil rate band. However, there are still reasons for setting up a nil rate band discretionary trust.[2]

(b) So far as gifts of residue to the surviving spouse are concerned, an immediate post-death interest (IPDI) trust may be more attractive than an absolute gift for the following reasons:

    (i) it offers capital protection and ring fences the capital for the remainder beneficiaries which is useful if the spouse remarries, is declared bankrupt or goes into a nursing home;

    (ii) the trustees can be given overriding powers of appointment to terminate the interest of the surviving spouse in some or all of the trust fund. If the trustees exercise their power to give capital to the remainder beneficiaries absolutely, the surviving spouse will be treated as making a potentially exempt transfer.

        Note, however, that from 22 March 2006 the spouse will only be treated as making a potentially exempt transfer (rather than an immediately chargeable transfer) if the appointment is (i) to another beneficiary absolutely (ii) to a disabled person trust or (iii) into a bereaved minor's trust.[3] And the former advantage – that the spouse could continue to benefit from property that had been appointed

---

[1] For lifetime arrangements for children and issue, see the authors' *A Modern Approach to Lifetime Tax Planning*, Chapter 26.

[2] See **5.30** and **5.31** *et seq.*

[3] For IHT planning using IPDIs, see Chapter 6.

away from her without falling into the IHT reservation of benefit rules – was removed by the FA 2006 in respect of terminations after 21 March 2006.[4]

In the case of cohabiting couples with children the options are more limited because of the absence of the spouse exemption.

2. TRUSTS FOR CHILDREN OF THE TESTATOR

7.02 If minor children of the testator are to benefit then the following trust options are available:

(a) a bereaved minor trust (BMT) which has the attraction of no further IHT charges once set up, but which requires the vesting of capital at age 18 years with only limited flexibility permitted;[5]

(b) a 's 71D trust' (sometimes called an 18–25 trust or a bereaved young person's trust), under which capital must vest no later than age 25 years. There may be an IHT charge after the child attains age 18 years and there is only the same limited flexibility as with the BMT, but testators will commonly prefer to use the s 71D trust instead of the BMT. It is likely that the latter will become something of a dead letter for those making wills;[6]

(c) an IPDI trust for the minor children – this may be an attractive option since the interest in possession can be highly flexible in that there can be overriding powers enabling it both to be enlarged and terminated. Also, of course, it offers the prospect of the property remaining settled without IHT charges for a longer period than is permitted under either the BMT or s 71D trusts. Two points to note are:
  (i)   the Trustee Act 1925, s 31 must be excluded[7] if a minor is to have an interest in possession at the death of the testator which is necessary for an immediate post-death interest trust;
  (ii) if the interest of the minor child were to end (eg on death) the termination would be a transfer of value for IHT purposes resulting in a possible tax liability;

(d) a relevant property trust for the minor – this is the 'fall back' option in cases where the conditions necessary for the earlier options to apply are not met;

---

4   See FA 1986, s 102ZA: considered at **6.22**.
5   The BMT is the nearest equivalent (in terms of IHT treatment) to the old accumulation and maintenance trusts. For the permitted flexibility, see **7.13** *et seq*.
6   The statutory trusts on intestacy for minor children of the intestate satisfy the conditions for a BMT.
7   This is because of the 'divesting effect' of TA 1925, s 31(1)(i) and (2) which gives trustees a discretion as to whether they apply income for a minor's benefit or accumulate it; the minor will only receive the accumulations if he reaches 18 or the trustees choose to apply it earlier: see **2.72** *et seq* and *Fine v Fine* [2012] EWHC 1811 (Ch).

(e) a bare trust for the minor – the property will form part of the minor's estate and he will be entitled to demand it from the trustees when he becomes aged 18 years.[8]

Trusts for adult children/grandchildren

7.03 So far as beneficiaries other than minor children of the testator are concerned (eg grandchildren or adult children) the BMT and s 71D trust is not available and so the options, if a trust is required, are narrowed to:

(a) an IPDI trust;

(b) a relevant property trust; or

(c) a bare trust.

7.04 Testators should remember that if property held on IPDI trusts remains settled on a further interest in possession trust after the death of the IPDI beneficiary, the next beneficiary will not have an IPDI – the settlement will become a relevant property settlement. Similarly, if an IPDI trust is set up for, say, a son, a subsequent interest in possession for the son's spouse or civil partner will not be an IPDI. Hence the settled property does not become comprised in the spouse's estate and so the spouse exemption in IHTA 1984, s 18 is not available. Instead, the continuing trusts will fall into the relevant property regime.[9]

> *Example 7.1*
>
> 1. Tom, a widower, leaves his residuary estate on a life interest trust for his daughter Rosamund and the remainder to her children contingent on attaining 18. There is a chargeable transfer on Tom's death into the IPDI trust for Rosamund. On her death she will make a chargeable transfer of the then settled property. If her children are still minor at that time the continuing trust will be taxed under the relevant property regime.
>
> 2. If in the above example Tom had included a life interest for Rosamund's widower to take effect on her death then at that time Rosamund will make a chargeable transfer of value of the settled property and the continuing trusts for the widower and children will be taxed under the relevant property regime.

3. BEREAVED MINOR TRUSTS (BMTS)

7.05 BMTs are trusts falling within IHTA 1984, s 71A. Such trusts:

(a) can only be set up by will (or on intestacy);[10]

---

[8] See **7.24** *et seq.*

[9] For a way of circumventing this problem by the use of general powers of appointment, see **6.33**.

[10] They can also be set up under the Criminal Injuries Compensation Scheme or under the Victims

(b)   must benefit a minor child of the testator;

(c)   must provide for capital to vest no later than age 18 years;

(d)   the beneficiary must either be entitled to the income, or if it is accumulated, it must be accumulated for his benefit and there must be no power to apply income for the benefit of any other person.

7.06   The requirement that capital must vest by 18 appears problematic for two reasons:

(a)   it is impossible to guarantee that capital will vest by 18 as a child may die without reaching that age. However, as was the case with old style accumulation and maintenance settlements, 'must' is interpreted as 'must, if at all'. It is expressly provided that there is no charge to IHT where a beneficiary dies without reaching 18.[11]

(b)   s 32 of TA 1925 applies to all settlements, unless excluded, and allows trustees to advance a beneficiary's vested or presumptive entitlement for his 'benefit'. Benefit is a wide word and has been held to include settling funds on trusts for the beneficiary *and close family members.*[12] The problem is solved by s 71A(4) which provides that a settlement can still meet the capital requirement even if s 32 applies or the terms of the settlement widen the statutory power to allow the whole of the beneficiary's interest to be advanced.[13]

7.07   The tax treatment of these trusts mirrors that which applied to old style accumulation and maintenance trusts: ie no anniversary or exit charges; no charge upon the minor becoming absolutely entitled to the property, nor when s 71A ceases to apply as a result of the death (under the age of 18 years) of the minor. Capital gains tax hold-over relief is available on the ending of this trust.[14] Unlike IPDI trusts, there is no requirement that s 71A trusts take effect immediately on death. They can, for example, take effect on termination of an IPDI.

Example 7.2

Adam's will leaves the residue of his estate to his son, Julian, contingent on attaining 18 absolutely failing which it is to be divided amongst Adam's siblings.

---

of Overseas Terrorism Compensation Scheme. In the case of an intestacy a bereaved minor's trust can arise for the benefit of issue, and not simply children, where there is a substitution for a deceased beneficiary under AEA 1925, s 47.

11   IHTA 1984, s 71B(2) which also provides that there is no charge where property is advanced to or for the benefit of a minor.

12   A 'settled advance': see **2.47** *et seq.*

13   In the case of settlements arising before 1 October 2014 the statutory power is limited to one half of the vested or presumptive entitlement although it can be, and often is, extended. For trusts arising on or after that date the Inheritance and Trustees' Powers Act 2014 removes the limitation so that whole of the entitlement is available: See **2.44** *et seq.*

14   Under TCGA 1992, s 260(2)(da) inserted by FA 2006, Sch 20, para 32.

Sections 31 and 32 of TA 1925 apply and in the latter case there is power to advance the entire presumptive share of a beneficiary. Julian is aged 10 at the time of Adam's death.

1. The trust for Julian is a BMT. Capital vests at 18; the existence of the modified statutory power of advancement is ignored[15] and during Julian's minority, s 31 ensures that income can only be used for his benefit and that he will become entitled to any accumulations at 18.

2. On the attainment of 18, the BMT will end with Julian becoming absolutely entitled to the trust property. There is no IHT exit charge[16] and CGT hold-over relief is available.[17]

3. If Julian dies under the age of 18, the BMT ends; again there is no exit charge[18] and CGT hold-over relief is available. This is the position whoever takes the property under default trusts that apply if Julian does not survive until the age of 18.

4. If the trustees decide before Julian attains 18 that it will be for his benefit that he does not become entitled to the trust property absolutely, they may exercise their power of advancement so that he becomes entitled to a life interest at 18 with the trustees reserving a power to advance capital to him in the future subject to which the trust fund is held for the benefit of his children.[19] His consent is not required. This exercise of the power has the following results:

    (a) it brings the BMT to an end: however there is no IHT exit charge;[20]

    (b) provided that the power is exercised 'in the narrower form' it will not create a new settlement for CGT purposes so that there will not be a deemed disposal of the property;[21]

    (c) the continuing trusts will be taxed under the relevant property regime for IHT purposes, and so subject to anniversary and exit charges: Julian's interest in possession is not 'qualifying' since it is not an IPDI. There is no base cost uplift to market value on his death[22] and the settled property is not treated as part of his estate for IHT purposes under IHTA 1984, s 49(1). Should the trustees use their powers to give Julian capital, there will be an exit charge from the relevant property settlement.

5. As in 4 above except that the trustees exercise their power to give Julian an interest in possession at 18 and provide for capital to vest in him at 25. The tax consequences are as in 4 above except that the trust now falls within

---

[15] For the flexibility that this provides, see **Example 7.2(4)**.

[16] See IHTA 1984, s 71B(2)(a).

[17] TCGA 1992, s 260(2)(da) inserted by FA 2006, Sch 20, para 32.

[18] IHTA 1984, s 71B(2)(b); TCGA 1992, s 260(2)(da).

[19] Such an exercise of the power is commonly termed a 'settled (or *Pilkington*) advance'.

[20] IHTA 1984, s 71B(2)(c).

[21] For a consideration of powers in the wider and narrower form see *Bond v Pickford* [1983] STC 517 and note that a power in the wider form (such as the power of advancement) can be exercised as a narrow form power so as not to create a new settlement: see *Swires v Renton* [1991] STC 490, **2.60** and the authors' *A Modern Approach to Lifetime Tax Planning*, Chapter 20.

[22] See TCGA 1992, ss 72 and 73 and see **3.105**.

s 71D (18–25 trusts).[23] The material differences from 4 above are that (a) if the beneficiary dies between 18 and 25 so that the s 71D trust ends there is an IHT exit charge, (b) the trust is not subject to anniversary charges and (c) when Julian reaches 25, or takes capital earlier, there will be an IHT exit charge.

4. SECTION 71D TRUSTS

7.08   During the passage of the 2006 Finance Bill the Government responded to criticism that vesting capital at age 18 was often inappropriate by introducing a new regime for age 18–25 trusts ('s 71D trusts'). Broadly speaking, the same conditions have to be met as for BMTs. Accordingly the provisions only apply to trusts set up in the will of a deceased parent, but whereas bereaved minor trusts require absolute vesting no later than age 18, s 71D trusts require capital and income to vest in the beneficiary (a bereaved child) not later than the attainment of age 25. As with s 71A trusts, there is no requirement that s 71D trusts take effect immediately on death. They can, for example, take effect on termination of an IPDI.

7.09   The tax treatment of s 71D trusts is as follows:

(a)   whilst the beneficiary is under the age of 18, as for BMTs (ie old style accumulation and maintenance treatment with no anniversary or exit charges). Accordingly if the trust ends at or before the child becomes 18, IHT charges are avoided. As is the case with s 71A trusts, the trust may end before 18 without a charge to IHT because the beneficiary dies under the age of 18[24] or because the trustees exercise a widened power of advancement to transfer the property to him;

(b)   once the beneficiary attains age 18 a special charging regime laid down in IHTA 1984 s 71F applies, ie in general up to age 18 there is no IHT charge but once the beneficiary attains that age IHT becomes payable until the capital vests (which must, of course, be no later than age 25). For example, if a parent dies when his daughter, Amy, is aged 6 and under the terms of the will capital is to vest at age 25, then when Amy reaches 25 an IHT charge will arise calculated as follows:
(i)   up to age 18 years no charge;
(ii)   from age 18–25 IHT (which is payable on the ending of the s 71D trust) is calculated in accordance with s 71F.[25]

Example 7.3

Adam Kaplan died in 2010. His will created the Kaplan Trust which has an investment portfolio for his twin children, Asa and Cathy, in equal shares. Their interests are contingent on reaching 25 and there is a widened statutory power of

---

[23]   See **7.08** *et seq.*
[24]   IHTA 1984, s 71E(2)(a).
[25]   See **7.10**.

advancement allowing the trustees to advance the whole of a beneficiary's presumptive entitlement to capital. Income can be accumulated until they reach 25. The following events occur:

1.   In 2020 (when the value of the fund is £1m), just before the twins' 24th birthday, the trustees make a settled advance to Asa of his share (£500,000) whereby he is given an interest in possession with remainder over to his wife and children.

2.   In 2021 Cathy becomes 25 and takes her share absolutely.

The position is as follows:

(a)   the Kaplan Trust is a s 71D trust when Adam dies;

(b)   the settled advance brings that trust to an end in respect of Asa's share (because Asa is no longer entitled to capital at 25) and triggers an exit charge under s 71F;

(c)   the continuing trusts for Asa fall outside s 71D; he does not have a qualifying interest in possession and the relevant property rules apply;

(d)   because Asa's trust continues there is no CGT disposal;[26]

(e)   so far as Cathy is concerned her absolute entitlement brings the trust for her to an end; there is an IHT exit charge under s 71F and, because this part of the settlement is ending, a deemed disposal for CGT purposes on which hold-over relief is available.[27]

Calculating the tax charge on s 71D trusts

7.10   The s 71F charge closely resembles charges under the relevant property regime but because it is intended to tax the period between the beneficiary becoming 18 and the ending of the settlement (a period of at most 7 years) it is inappropriate to impose an anniversary charge and instead the charge is in the form of a single exit charge calculated on the length of time the property has remained settled since the beneficiary's 18th birthday.

Take the case of Asa (in **Example 7.3**): his s 71D trust lasted from his 18th birthday until the settled advance was made just before his 24th birthday. Hence the charge is for a period of just under 6 years and is calculated as follows:

(a)   obtain the value of the property ceasing to be comprised in the s 71D trust. Asa's share is worth £500,000 (this is the 'chargeable amount');[28]

(b)   calculate the number of complete quarters (periods of 3 months) in the period beginning with the day on which he became 18[29] and ending with

---

[26]   The settled advance is drafted to modify the terms of the existing settlement, not to create a new settlement: see **Precedent 13.3**.

[27]   Under TCGA 1992, s 260(2)(a).

[28]   See IHTA 1984, s 71F(4): in this case the IHT will be paid out of Asa's share, not out of the property remaining in the settlement for Cathy, and hence grossing-up does not apply.

[29]   If the property only became comprised in the s 71D trust after the beneficiary had become 18, take this later time.

'the day before the occasion of charge'. In this case there are 23 complete quarters.[30] The 'relevant fraction' is then 3/10 multiplied by so many fortieths as there are complete quarters in the period, ie by 23/40;

(c) the 'chargeable transfer' is arrived at by aggregating (i) the value of the property in the settlement immediately after it commenced plus (ii) the value, again immediately after it commenced, of property in a related settlement[31] plus (iii) the value of added property.[32] In this case there is no added property but the value of Cathy's share must be included and hence it is necessary to know the value of the whole fund at the time when Adam died. Assume that this was £750,000. The chargeable transfer is of this amount which is treated as made by a hypothetical transferor who had cumulative transfers equal to the chargeable transfers made by Adam in the 7 years before he died (disregarding any chargeable transfers made by his will). Assume that there were none;

(d) the tax charge is on the basis of lifetime rates in the year in which the property leaves the settlement, in this case 2020;[33]

(e) the 'settlement rate' can now be arrived at, being tax on the chargeable transfer (£750,000) made by a transferor with no cumulative chargeable transfers so that the applicable rate is:

	£
chargeable transfer	750,000
less nil rate band	(325,000)[34]
balance	425,000
tax at 20% on balance equals	£85,000

this produces a settlement rate of 85,000/750,000 × 100 = 11.33%

(f) the amount of tax is calculated as follows:

chargeable amount (£500,000) × [relevant fraction (23/40) × (3/10)] × settlement rate (11.33)

Working through the bracketed calculations produces a rate of charge of 1.95%

So the tax is £500,000 × 1.95% = £9,750

7.11 The top rate of charge that can arise is 4.2% which will apply if the following conditions are met:

---

[30] IHTA 1984, s 71F(5) and compare s 68(2).
[31] A related settlement is one created on the same day so, in the case of will trusts, in the same will: see further **3.63**.
[32] IHTA 1984, s 71F(8).
[33] IHTA 1984, s 71F(8)(c).
[34] Rates in 2020 are unknown. For the purposes of this example, the nil rate band in 2015–16 (£325,000) is used.

(a) the property was held in trust until the beneficiary became 25 and the trust began not later than his 18th birthday. Hence the relevant fraction will be 28/40;

(b) the testator (hypothetical transferor) had exhausted his IHT nil rate band so that the rate applicable is 20%;

(c) the calculation of the tax rate is then $28/40 \times 3/10 \times 20 = 4.2\%$.

Calculating the tax charge on s 71D trusts: proposed changes

7.12 The proposed changes in the IHT taxation of relevant property trusts from 6 April 2015 in relation to 'same day additions' are discussed at **3.71**. So far as s 71D trusts are concerned, although a 'same day addition' cannot be made to that trust, it is possible for the will to add property to a lifetime pilot trust which the testator had set up. In these circumstances, the draft new s 62A(2) will deem there to be a same day addition to the s 71D trust even though the will is not actually adding property to an existing trust (it is a *'transfer of value as a result of which property first becomes comprised in Settlement A'*). As a result, in calculating the s 71D charge the value of the addition and the property in the pilot trust when that trust was set up will be included.

5. DRAFTING BMT AND S 71D TRUSTS[35]

Limited flexibility for BMT and s 71D trusts

7.13 In the case of both BMT and 18–25 trusts, the mere existence of the statutory power of advancement (even widened by the exclusion of the 50% restriction found in TA 1925, s 32(1)(a)) or of an express power 'to the like effect' will not prevent the trust from satisfying the requirements. This power can be used, by making a settled advance, to extend the life of the trust beyond 18 (BMT) or 25 (s 71D trusts): see **Example 7.3**.

Drafting

7.14 There is only limited room for manoeuvre in the drafting of a BMT and the trusts will frequently be straightforward. For instance:

> 'I leave my residue on trust for my daughter Dolly contingently on attaining the age of 18 absolutely and subject thereto (insert default trusts).'

In the case of more than one child:

> 'I leave my residue on trust for such of my children as (shall survive me and) attain the age of 18 and if more than one in equal shares absolutely and subject thereto (insert default trusts).'

---

[35] See **Precedents 7.2** and **7.3**.

If a child dies and the property passes to his minor siblings outright at 18 the share remains subject to the BMT regime.

7.15 Substitutionary clauses may result in part, or all, of the settled property becoming held on a relevant property settlement. Consider the following typical substitutionary clause:

> 'provided that if any child dies before me or before reaching the age of 18 leaving a child or children living at my death or born thereafter who reach the age of 21 then such child or children shall take by substitution and if more than one in equal shares the share of my residue which his her or their parent would have taken had such parent survived me and attained a vested interest.'

Clauses such as this are commonly used in order to preserve equality between the testator's children and their issue. However, the definition of a BMT does not generally allow for substitutionary interests. This has the following consequences:

(a)   if, at the death of the testator, all his children are minors and alive the trust is a BMT. If subsequently a child dies in circumstances when substitution provisions along the lines of the above apply then (i) there will be no IHT exit charge[36] but (ii) that part of the fund will then be held on a relevant property trust;

(b)   if, at the time of the death of the testator, one of his children had already died and the substitutionary provisions apply so the child's issue take that share, it will be held on a relevant property trust and the shares of the surviving minor children of the testator in a BMT.

7.16 In practice, it is unlikely that a child will die under 18 leaving issue, so mixed BMT and relevant property settlements are unlikely to arise. However, they may arise in practice where an adult child predeceases the parent and the parent's will includes a substitutional gift to the child's children.

Example 7.4

Andrew has three adult children Ben, Cara and Dan.[37] They are all married with children. He leaves his property outright to his children with substitutional provisions for grandchildren at 18 if one of the children dies before him. Ben dies before Andrew leaving three young children who under Andrew's will take Ben's share in equal shares if they reach 18. Unless they are given immediate interests in possession (which would be IPDIs)[38] their shares will be held on relevant property trusts.

Despite the creation of a relevant property settlement for the substituted grandchildren, most testators will want to leave property for the benefit of the bereaved grandchildren. They will simply accept that the price of settling the

---

[36]   Because s 71B(2) provides that there is no charge on the death of a minor.

[37]   Note that BMTs are not a possibility in this case.

[38]   For IPDIs, see Chapter 6.

property is anniversary and exit charges. Remember though that when calculating these charges the value of property in the s 71A trust will be included so the charges may be higher than might be first thought.[39]

7.17 Similar comments to those made in connection with the drafting of BMT are appropriate for the drafting of s 71D trusts: specifically, the legislation permits only limited flexibility whilst beneficiaries are under 25.

7.18 Of course, it will be attractive to retain what flexibility is allowed, ie to give the trustees power to vary the shares of beneficiaries whilst they are under the age of 25. At first sight the legislation does not appear to be drafted in a way which permits the trustees to vary the shares of the beneficiaries. Both s 71A and s 71D are drafted by reference to a single beneficiary (in s 71D called 'B' and in s 71A called the bereaved minor) who must become entitled to the settled property held for them.[40] However, HMRC considers that it is possible to pluralise B or the bereaved minor to include all beneficiaries within the relevant class provided they are *alive* at the date the s 71A or s 71D trust takes effect and are under the specified age. It is, therefore, not necessary to fix the shares in which each child takes income and capital while they are all under 18 and it is possible to pay out income and capital to the minor children in unequal shares.

7.19 Care needs to be taken to ensure that any power to vary the shares cannot be exercised so as either to increase or diminish the share of a beneficiary once he has attained 25 as this will breach the statutory requirements. Moreover, HMRC takes the view that if the power has been exercised revocably to exclude a beneficiary it is not possible to 'bring him back in' by revoking the previous exercise of the power. Accordingly, it is important in such cases to leave the beneficiary with a small share which can then be increased (if desired) by the exercise of the power of revocation and reselection.[41] The following clause will not breach the s 71D(6) requirements:

'to such of my children as attain the age of 25 years and if more than one in such shares as the trustees shall from time to time by deed or deeds revocable or irrevocable appoint and in default of such appointment in equal shares absolutely at 25 provided always that no such appointment shall be made and no appointment shall be revoked so as to either diminish or increase the share (or the accumulation of income forming part of the share) of a child who at the date of such appointment or revocation has reached the age of 25 nor benefit a child who has been excluded from benefit as a result of the exercise of the power.'

An interest in possession trust for the testator's child

7.20 Frequently trusts vesting capital at 25 will give the beneficiary a right to income before that age, for example as a result of TA 1925, s 31 when the

---

[39] For the calculation of anniversary and exit charges, see **3. 62** *et seq.*
[40] See HMRC Guidance issued in June 2007 and reproduced in the **Appendix** to this Chapter.
[41] Similar drafting considerations had applied to accumulation and maintenance trusts.

beneficiary becomes 18 or because the accumulation period expires before that age.[42] The existence of such a right to income:

(a)   does not prevent the trust from satisfying the BMT or s 71D conditions;

(b)   is not a qualifying interest in possession for IHT purposes unless it takes effect on the death of the testator and the trust would otherwise be a s 71D trust, not a BMT: ie. the interest in possession must be 'immediate' (an IPDI) and the trust must not meet the s 71A requirements;[43]

(c)   for CGT purposes will result in an uplifted value (but no charge) in the event that the beneficiary dies before the age of 18.[44] Note, however, that if he dies after that age there is no uplift (however, any CGT charge may be avoided by the making of a hold-over election under TCGA 1992, s 260(2)(a)). This distinction defies rational analysis!

Relationship between BMT, IPDIs and s 71D trusts

7.21   Because of the possibility of overlap between on the one hand IPDI trusts and on the other BMTs and 18–25 trusts, the legislation makes provision for a 'pecking order' which is:

(a)   BMT;

(b)   IPDI;

(c)   18–25 (s 71D trusts).

Accordingly, if the will provides for the minor child to have an immediate right to income with capital vesting at 25 this is not a s 71D trust but instead gives the child an IPDI.[45]

Relationship between sections 71D and 144

7.22   Section 71D trusts must be set up under the will of a deceased parent but unlike IPDIs do not have to take effect from death.[46] They can, for example, follow an IPDI.

If they result from the conversion of a discretionary trust within 2 years of death they are read back to the date of death (under s 144) so that no exit charge on the ending of the earlier, relevant property settlement will arise. By contrast, if the 'conversion' of the s 144 trust occurs more than 2 years after the

---

[42]   In rare cases a right to income is given while the child is still a minor: if capital vests at 18 this will be a BMT: even though the interest in possession arises on the testator's death it is not an IPDI.

[43]   See **7.20**. This is because of the 'pecking order' for trusts. But note the 'reading-back' effect of IHTA 1984, s 144: see **7.22** and **13.23** *et seq.*

[44]   TCGA 1992, ss 72(1A)(b) and 73(2A)(b).

[45]   Contrast the position with a BMT which takes precedence: IHTA 1984, ss 49A, 71D(5)(c)(ii).

[46]   This is also true of a BMT.

death, a s 71D trust will still come into being but only at that date and therefore with an IHT exit charge arising on the ending of the relevant property trust.[47]

7.23 Section 144 can operate to destroy what at first sight would appear to be a s 71D Trust.

> *Example 7.5*
>
> Roy dies in 2010. He leaves his entire estate to his three children Alex, Bob and Clare equally at 25. Alex is 19 when Roy dies, Bob is 17 and Clare is 14.
>
> At 18 each child will become entitled to income (as a result of TA 1925, s 31).
>
> *Position of Alex*: he has a right to income when Roy dies which is an IPDI. When he becomes entitled to capital at 25 there will be no IHT charge (IHTA 1984, s 53(2)) and CGT hold-over relief will not be available unless the property is business assets within TCGA 1992, s 165. If he dies before 25 the value of the IPDI fund will be taxed as part of his estate.
>
> *Position of Bob*: he will become 18 within 2 years of Roy's death and when this happens s 144 will apply to 'read-back' his entitlement to income to the time of Roy's death. He too, therefore, will have an IPDI. Of course, if he died before 18 the trust for him will satisfy the s 71D requirements.[48]
>
> *Position of Clare*: the trust for Clare is within s 71D. Accordingly an exit charge may arise in respect of the period from Clare becoming 18–25.[49] At that time CGT hold-over relief will be available.
>
> *Advice*: if Roy had wanted all his children treated the same and had intended the s 71D regime to apply then the will as drafted in this case is a potential disaster. The problem has resulted from the right to income at 18 given by s 31 which should have been excluded. Instead the will draftsman should have provided that until 25 the income from each share can be used for the child's maintenance with any balance being accumulated and added to the share[50] as in **Precedent 7.3(2)**.

6. BARE TRUSTS FOR MINORS

7.24 A bare trust is commonly one in which a single beneficiary has an immediate and absolute title to both income and capital.[51] The beneficiary is entitled to the entire beneficial interest in the trust fund and his entitlement is

---

[47] The same result follows if the property becomes held on trusts which satisfy the requirements for a BMT.

[48] And because he died before 18 there will be no exit charge: in effect, it is treated as a BMT.

[49] For the calculation of the charge, see **7.10**.

[50] It is, of course, possible for income to be used to maintain the other children who are under 25 at the time and for any accumulated income to be added to the general capital then held on s 71D trusts. As a result of the PAA 2009 allowing unlimited accumulations of income, it will not matter that a child is under 4 at the time of death since the old 21-year accumulation period no longer applies.

[51] This will not always be the case: there will be a bare trust if at the conclusion of the administration of an estate property is held for A and B who are jointly absolutely entitled. Insurance companies produce a bare trust (for instance, as part of a discounted gift plan) which

not subject to any contingency. It is sometimes said that the trustee has no discretion in respect of the trust property other than to retain it as nominee on behalf of the beneficiary. However, a bare trustee is a fiduciary so that, for example, the rule against self-dealing, will apply. Further, a trust for a minor or an incapacitated person who is absolutely entitled to the property gives the trustees active duties to perform: for instance in respect of the management and investment of the trust fund. It remains uncertain how far, in the absence of express provision, a trustee is required to give effect to directions given by an absolute beneficiary of full age and capacity other than a direction to transfer the trust property to him or as he directs. A beneficiary of full capacity can direct the retirement of trustees[52] and give directions in relation to the insurance of trust property.[53] If the bare trustee holds shares in a company it is unclear whether he must vote in accordance with the directions of a beneficial owner who is of full capacity.[54]

Tax treatment

7.25   Under IHTA 1984, s 43(2)(a) 'settlement' is defined to include property held in trust for persons in succession or subject to a contingency. If TA 1925, s 31 has not been excluded might this be sufficient to make a bare trust for a minor settled on the basis that the trustees can withhold income or distribute it at their discretion? No, since the accumulations belong to the infant's estate, ie. the retention of income under TA 1925, s 31 in this case is not an accumulation for s 43 purposes because it is in the nature of an administrative power. Hence a gift of property 'on trust for my infant son absolutely' will be an outright gift and so a PET. HMRC have confirmed that it does not regard a bare trust as a settlement for IHT purposes.

7.26   For CGT purposes there is no settlement where assets are held as bare trustee for another.[55] Hence actual disposals will be treated as made by the child. The annual exemption of the child will be available to set against any gains and, assuming the child has limited income, gains are likely to be taxed at the rate of 18% rather than the 28% which applies to trust gains.[56]

7.27   For income tax purposes the income will be treated as that of the child.[57]

---

can be for any number of beneficiaries (who must be given a fixed share of the totality). See **Precedent 7.1** and see the authors' *A Modern Approach to Lifetime Tax Planning*, Chapter 24.

[52]   See TLATA 1996, ss 19, 20.

[53]   TA 1925, s 19(2).

[54]   See *Re Kirkpatrick* [2005] NZHC 469 where it was held that there is no such obligation and compare *Re Castiglione's Will Trusts* [1958] Ch 549 at 558.

[55]   TCGA 1992, s 60: see **3.110**.

[56]   See **3.85**.

[57]   Unless the bare trust is created by lifetime transfer for the settlor's child in which case while the child is under 18 and neither married nor in a civil partnership, the income will be taxed as the settlor's: ITTOIA 2005, s 629. The position was different for bare trusts created before 9 March 1999 when the income was taxed as the child's: see Sch 2, Part 8, para 133.

7.28 On the death of the beneficiary, the trust property (including any accumulations of income) is treated as his so that if the child dies (whether before or after 18) the funds form part of his estate for IHT purposes. If the child dies before the age of 18 the property will pass under the intestacy rules and therefore normally to the child's parents. After the age of 18 the fund will pass according to the will of the child (or on his intestacy if there is no will).

7.29 At 18[58] the child can call for the trust property to be transferred to him. If the child is disabled, the effect of any bare trust on means-tested state benefits should be considered.

Can the beneficiary's absolute entitlement to capital be deferred?

7.30 There would appear to be no reason why the trustees of a bare trust cannot exercise a power of advancement just before a child reaches 18 to make a settled advance postponing vesting of the capital.[59] It will therefore be desirable for the declaration of bare trust to contain an express power of advancement, otherwise the trustees will be relying on the statutory power in TA 1925, s 32 which is limited to one-half of the beneficiary's entitlement for trusts created or arising before 1 October 2014.[60]

If the power of advancement is exercised in this way it will involve a disposal (for CGT purposes) since the property now becomes settled. Capital gains tax charges may arise if the asset shows a gain and it is not thought that hold-over relief is available (see **7.32**).

7.31 Does the settled advance involve a chargeable transfer by the beneficiary for IHT purposes? If the exercise of the power of advancement is not a chargeable transfer then there is no charge on the creation of the continuing trust although that trust will be taxed under the relevant property regime.[61] To be chargeable a transfer must be a transfer of value which IHTA 1984, s 3(1) defines as:

> 'a disposition made by a person as a result of which the value of his estate immediately after the disposition is less than it would be but for the disposition.'

There is no statutory definition of disposition. It is said to be an ordinary English word of wide meaning.[62] In this case the beneficiary has not

---

[58]   16 in Scotland.

[59]   It is thought that the statutory power in TA 1925, s 32 will be implied and that an express power – permitting the advancement of 100% of the child's interest – may be included in the trust document. *Lewin on Trusts* (19th edn, 2015) at 1.04 confirms this but notes that once the child becomes 18 the power is destroyed and so cannot be exercised after that time. See *Pilkington v IRC* [1964] AC 612, at 641.

[60]   The Inheritance and Trustees' Powers Act 2014 removed this limitation for settlements created or arising after that date: see 2.46.

[61]   Unless it creates a disabled person's interest within IHTA 1984, s 89B.

[62]   See *Ward v IRC* [1956] AC 391 and see IHTM 4023 although HMRC do not refer to the need for the transferor to have made the disposition.

intentionally divested himself of his beneficial ownership of the property; this has been done by the trustees. So it might be argued that there is no disposition and therefore no chargeable transfer by the minor. Section 3(3) deems there to be a disposition:

> 'where the value of a person's estate is diminished and the value of ... any settled property is increased by the first-mentioned person's omission to exercise a right.'

However, it is difficult to see that the beneficiary has omitted to exercise a right.

7.32   Do the reservation of benefit provisions apply? The beneficiary has not made a gift so FA 1986, s 102 is not in point. Section 102ZA only applies where (a) there is a termination of an individual's interest in possession in settled property and (b) that interest was 'qualifying'. But the interest that is ended by the trustees exercising the power of advancement in the case of a bare trust is not an interest in *settled property* for IHT purposes. Accordingly it is not thought that the exercise of the power by the trustees gives rise to a reservation of benefit.

Income and CGT consequences

7.33   For CGT and income tax purposes HMRC consider that the minor beneficiary is the settlor of the settled advance. (They take a similar view where the court consents to a variation of trust on behalf of a minor beneficiary.)[63] For CGT this means that the trust is settlor-interested so that if the assets being settled by exercise of the trustees' powers of advancement show a gain, a hold-over claim is not possible because it is a disposal to a settlor-interested trust.

7.34   For income tax purposes the beneficiary will often be entitled under the terms of the settled advance to receive all the income and so will be taxed as life tenant. The main consequence if the beneficiary is treated as the settlor is that no deduction is possible for trust management expenses and the beneficiary is taxed on the gross income whether or not he receives all of it. He will also be taxable on any deemed income such as the proceeds of share buy-backs.

When to use a bare trust

7.35   When is it appropriate to consider the use of a bare trust? Grandparents who wish to give substantial property to young grandchildren may consider a bare trust as an alternative to a relevant property settlement. The advantages are that the creation of the bare trust will be a PET and the property can be held until 18 without incurring IHT exit and anniversary charges, CGT and income tax will be payable at the child's rates instead of the trust rates. The

---

[63]   See CGTM 37902 and also *Mills v IRC* 49 TC 367 where a minor actress (aged 14) had her earnings paid into a trust.

property can then be settled by way of a settled advance at a later stage if it is not appropriate to give the child the property at 18.

7. DISABLED CHILDREN[64]

7.36 Trusts for the disabled and for vulnerable beneficiaries which meet the statutory requirements receive special tax treatment.

Definition of a 'disabled person'[65]

7.37 For property transferred into settlement before 8 April 2013 a disabled person was a person who was:

(a) incapable by reason of mental disorder within the meaning of the Mental Health Act 1983 of administering his property or managing his affairs. This may include persons suffering from Downs Syndrome; depression and bipolar disorders; or

(b) in receipt of an attendance allowance under the Social Security Contributions and Benefits Act 1992, s 64; or

(c) in receipt of a disability living allowance under the Social Security Contributions and Benefits Act 1992, s 71 by virtue of entitlement to the care component at the highest or middle rate.[66]

7.38 For transfers into trust on or after 8 April 2013 the definition was changed and is set out in Sch 1A inserted into the Finance Act 2005.[67] 'Disabled person' now means:

'(a) a person who by reason of mental disorder within the meaning of the Mental Health Act 1983 is incapable of administering his or her property or managing his or her affairs,

(b) a person in receipt of attendance allowance,

(c) a person in receipt of a disability living allowance by virtue of entitlement to—
    (i) the care component at the highest or middle rate, or
    (ii) the mobility component at the higher rate,

(d) a person in receipt of personal independence payment (including persons entitled to the mobility component at either the standard or enhanced rate),

(e) a person in receipt of an increased disablement pension

(f) a person in receipt of constant attendance allowance, or

---

[64] See **Precedent 7.4** and for a complete disabled trust, the authors' *A Modern Approach to Lifetime Tax Planning*, **Precedent 23.1**.

[65] IHTA 1984, s 89(4); FA 2005, s 38(1).

[66] The Welfare Reform Act 2012 provides a framework for the replacement of the disability living allowance with a 'Personal Independence Payment'. This is being phased-in for people aged 16–64 starting in April 2013. The above definition accordingly needed amendment: see HMRC's 'Consultation on Vulnerable Beneficiary Trusts' (August 2012).

[67] From 6 April 2014 the definition was further amended in respect of the mobility components of the Disability Living Allowance and Personal Independence Payment.

(g)   a person in receipt of armed forces independence payment.'

The IHT treatment of a disabled trust

7.39   The disabled person is treated as having a qualifying interest in possession with the result that:

(a)   the value of the settled property is treated as forming part of his estate and will; for instance, be subject to an IHT charge on his death;[68]

(b)   the trust is accordingly outside the relevant property regime and so does not attract 10-yearly charges or interim exit charges;

(c)   the lifetime creation of the trust will be a PET.

7.40   A will trust may qualify as an IHT disabled trust in two situations:

(a)   if it creates an interest in possession to which the disabled person becomes entitled;[69]

Example 7.6

Roy dies in 2014 and by his will:

1.   *leaves his estate to his spouse, Renata*: this creates an IPDI and so the spouse exemption is available on Roy's death;

2.   *subject thereto to his disabled daughter, Sally, for life*: this creates a disabled person's trust. There will be an IHT charge on Renata's death but the continuing trust will fall outside the relevant property regime;[70]

3.   there will then be suitable remainders and note that the trustees may be given power to pay or apply capital for the benefit of each of Renata and Sally.

(b)   if the trust satisfies the requirements of IHTA 1984, s 89(1), *viz* that during the disabled person's lifetime, any capital that is applied is applied for his benefit[71] and, similarly, if any income is applied it is applied for the benefit of the disabled person. For trusts set up before 8 April 2013 the requirements were:

(i)   during the life of the disabled person the trusts do not create an interest in possession; and

(ii)   they secure that not less than half of the settled property which is applied during the disabled person's life is applied for his benefit.[72]

---

[68]   IHTA 1984, s 49(1), (1A)(b).

[69]   IHTA 1984, s 89B(1)(c). Note that this is not an IPDI (see ibid, s 49A(4)(b)) albeit that the IHT consequences are the same!

[70]   There will be the usual CGT uplift in value on the deaths of Renata and Sally.

[71]   There are a number of capital disregards: see IHTA 1984 s 89(3) and see the authors' *A Modern Approach to Lifetime Tax Planning*, Chapter 23.

[72]   The person must be disabled at the time when the trust is set up. The existence of the statutory power of advancement in TA 1925, s 32 is ignored in deciding whether these conditions are met.

Example 7.7

As in **Example 7.6**, save that on Renata's death Roy's estate is held on trust during the life of Sally to apply income for her maintenance (in the trustees' discretion) and to accumulate the balance and to apply capital for her benefit, again in the discretion of the trustees. There is no power to pay income or capital to any other beneficiary.

IHT analysis: the conditions in s 89(1) are met (note in particular that it is not necessary for the disabled person to receive any income or capital!) and so Sally is treated as having a qualifying interest in possession. The IHT consequences are as for Example 7.6 and on Sally's death there is a CGT uplift.[73]

7.41 In choosing between the two types of disabled trust, consider whether the entitlement to income would have an effect on the child's means tested benefits. It is likely that if the second type of trust is chosen (ie. one meeting the s 89(1) conditions) that it will be set up in pilot form during the testator's lifetime so that the will can then add property to it.[74]

Income and capital gains tax reliefs

7.42 These are available in respect of trust for a disabled beneficiary and for a relevant minor (meaning a person who has not attained the age of 18 and one whose parents have died).[75]

7.43 The conditions for obtaining these reliefs are now the same as those which apply for IHT.

7.44 Provided that an election is made, the effect is to treat the trust as transparent: accordingly the income tax is limited to what would have been paid if the income had belonged to the beneficiary and the CGT calculated as if the gains had been realised by the beneficiary (ie with the benefit of his CGT rate – which may be less than the trust rate of 28% – and his annual exemption).

Example 7.8

Take the trust for Sally in **Example 7.7**. Because no other beneficiary can receive either income or capital during Sally's lifetime, the special income tax and CGT rules apply (provided that appropriate elections are made). This means:

1. that income will be taxed at Sally's rate, not the trust rate;

2. that trust gains are taxed on the basis of Sally's rates and £11,000 annual exemption.

---

[73] This was not the case before a change in the law effective for deaths on and after 5 December 2013 because she did not actually have an interest in possession. CGT hold-over relief might have been available.

[74] Make sure (as with all pilot trusts) that the trust is in existence when the will is executed. An attraction of setting up the trust in pilot form is that other family members can then add property to it, ie it can be used as a general receptacle for gifts from the family.

[75] FA 2005, s 39: this will include a BMT.

PRECEDENTS

Precedent 7.1: Bare trust

THIS DECLARATION OF TRUST is made the [   ] day of [   ] 200[   ] by [   ] of [   ] ('the Donor')

WHEREAS:

(A) The Donor is the legal and beneficial owner of the property described in the Second Schedule ('the Property').

(B) The Donor wishes to make provision by way of gift for [insert details of beneficiary] who is under 18 years of age ('the Beneficiary') by declaring himself a trustee of the Property.

NOW THIS DEED WITNESSES as follows:

1. Definitions

In this Deed:

1.1 'the Trust Fund' means the Property and any additions to the Trust Fund by way of further declaration or otherwise and the assets from time to time representing the said property and additions or any part or parts thereof.

1.2 'the Trustees' means the Donor or other the trustees or trustee for the time being of this Declaration.

2. Declaration of Trust

The Donor declares that from the date of this Declaration the Trustees shall hold the Trust Fund and any income thereof upon trusts for the Beneficiary absolutely.[76]

3. Power of Appointment of Trustees

The power of appointing a new or additional trustee or trustees of this Declaration shall be vested in the Donor during his lifetime and thereafter the statutory power of appointment of trustees shall apply.

---

[76] A bare trust can be set up for more than one beneficiary, e g 'for my two children Jack and Jill in equal shares absolutely'.

4. Administrative powers

Until the Beneficiary attains the age of 18 the powers and provisions contained in the First Schedule shall apply to the Trust Fund and the income of it.

5. Power of Maintenance

Section 31 of the Trustee Act 1925 shall not apply to this Declaration to the intent that the Beneficiary shall have the immediate right to the income of the Trust Fund notwithstanding his minority.

6. [Extended] Power of Advancement[77]

Section 32 of the Trustee Act 1925 shall apply [as if the words 'one-half of' were omitted from proviso (a) of subsection (1)].

THE FIRST SCHEDULE

(insert administration provisions)

THE SECOND SCHEDULE

[Insert details of property settled]

IN WITNESS etc.

---

[77] For a consideration of the making of a settled advance before the beneficiary becomes 18: see **7.29** *et seq*. From 1 October 2014 s 32 had been amended to remove the 50% limitation.

Precedent 7.2: Bereaved minor trust

1. A single beneficiary

'To [insert name of child] absolutely contingently on her attaining the age of 18 years and subject thereto to [insert default beneficiary] absolutely'[78]

2. Inflexible trusts for children

'To such of my children as survive me and attain the age of 18 and if more than one in equal shares absolutely'

3. Flexibility when more than one child

'To such of my children as survive me and attain the age of 18 in such shares as my Trustees shall appoint and in default equally provided always that the Trustees' power of appointment shall not be exercised to increase or diminish the share of a child who has attained 18 [nor to benefit a child who has been excluded from all benefit as a result of the exercise of this power of appointment]'[79]

4. A [widened] power of advancement

'Section 32 of the Trustee Act 1925 shall apply [but with the deletion of the words "one-half of" in Section 32(1)(a)]'[80]

---

[78] If desired the child could be given an immediate right to income (TA 1925, s 31 would need to be excluded). The clause would still create a BMT (not an IPDI) and the CGT death uplift would be available in the event of the child dying before the age of 18: see **7.20**.

[79] HMRC accept that limited flexibility is possible in these trusts. Although the wording in the legislation refers to a single bereaved minor beneficiary this must be construed to cover the plural hence a power for trustees to pick and choose between beneficiaries will presumably be acceptable provided that it cannot be exercised in favour of a beneficiary who has already attained 18 or to take away a share from a beneficiary who has attained 18. It is not thought that the words in square brackets are necessary (although HMRC do not agree) and that such a child can be included again provided that he is under the age of 18: see **7.17–7.18** and for HMRC's view the **Appendix** at the end of this Chapter.

[80] The inclusion of a widened power of advancement does not prevent the trusts from satisfying s 71A: see **7.06**. From 1 October 2014 s 32 is amended to remove the 50% limitation.

Precedent 7.3: s 71D trusts

1. Simple Trust

'I leave the residue of my estate to such of my children as shall survive me and attain the age of 25 and if more than one in equal shares absolutely'[81]

2. Modifying the Trustee Act 1925, s 31[82] (see **Example 7.5**)

'The Trustee Act 1925, s 31 (as amended) shall apply to the presumptive shares of my children under the trusts declared in clause [ ] subject to the following modifications:

[(a)   with the substitution in subsection (1)(i) of the words "the trustees in their absolute discretion think fit" for the words "may in all the circumstances be reasonable" and the omission of the proviso to subsection (1)]

(b)   so that in its application to the presumptive shares of any of my children under the trusts declared in clause xx above in relation to whom the Vesting Age (as defined below) exceeds the age of 18 years s 31 (as modified by clause (a) above) shall have effect as if the age of majority were the Vesting Age (the expressions "infant" "infancy" and "minority" therein being construed accordingly) and as if there were substituted the Vesting Age for the words "18 years" wherever the same occur in s 31 (as modified)

(c)   the expression "the Vesting Age" in relation to any of my children shall mean the age of 25 years'

3. Making the s 71D trusts flexible (giving the trustees a power of selection)[83]

'1.1   The Trustees shall stand possessed of the Trust Fund and the income from it upon trust for such of my children as shall attain the age of 25 years and if more than one in such shares as the Trustees shall by any deed or deeds revocable or irrevocable executed so as to comply with clause 1.3 below appoint and until and subject to and in default of any such appointment in equal shares.

1.2   Subject to clause 1.3 below any appointment made in exercise of the power conferred by clause 1.1 above:

1.2.1 may provide for any share or shares in the Trust Fund to be ascertained either by reference to a fraction or fractions of the Trust Fund or by reference

---

[81]   If the trustees subsequently exercise a widened power of advancement to give a minor child an immediate right to income this will not prevent s 71D from continuing to apply although care should be taken not to give a child an interest in possession within 2 years of death because of 'reading-back' under s 144 which will create an IPDI. If a minor child dies under the age of 18 there is no IHT charge and, if he had enjoyed an interest in possession, a CGT uplift: see **7.20**. If a child dies under the age of 25 and his share accrues to his siblings, the IHT position is that if the siblings are under the age of 25 so that their shares are held on 18–25 trusts there is no IHT charge. In other cases if the deceased child is over 18 the normal s 71D exit charge will apply to his share.

[82]   For the 'pecking order' see **7.21**. From 1 October 2014 s 31 has been amended and it is no longer necessary to include the words in square brackets.

[83]   Combine this power of selection with the modification of s 31 above.

to any sum or sums of money or by reference to (or to the value of) any specific assets then forming part of the Trust Fund; and

1.2.2 may (if the Trustees think fit) expressly provide that the whole or any part or parts of the accumulations of income then forming part of the general capital of the Trust Fund or any part of it or then only forming part of the presumptive share of any such child in the Trust Fund shall therefore go and accrue to and form part of only the presumptive share or shares of any of my children in the Trust Fund or form part of the general capital of the Trust Fund or any part of it but in default of any such express provision all such accumulations of income shall continue to belong to and form part of the general capital to which they belong or (as the case may be) to the presumptive share to which they solely belonged immediately prior to such appointment.

1.3   No appointment in exercise of the power conferred by clause 1.1 above shall be made and no such appointment shall be revoked so as either to diminish or to increase the share (or the accumulations of income forming part of the share) of or give a new share (or new accumulations of income) to a child who at the date of such appointment or revocation has attained the age of 25 [nor to benefit a child who has been excluded from benefit as a result of the exercise of the power].'[84]

---

[84]   For HMRC's views on permitted flexibility, see the **Appendix** at the end of this chapter.

Precedent 7.4: Clause establishing a disabled person's trust

Beneficial trusts during the lifetime of the Principal beneficiary[85]

X.1 During the lifetime of the Principal Beneficiary the Trustees may from time to time pay or apply the income of the Trust Fund to or for the benefit of the Principal Beneficiary PROVIDED that:

X.1.1 such payment or application shall from time to time be made in such manner and upon such terms and conditions (if any) as the Trustees in their discretion shall from time to time think proper[86]

X.1.2 the Trustees shall accumulate the whole or any part of the income of the Trust Fund that is not paid out under clause 2.1.1 by investing the same and the resulting income of it in any investments by this settlement authorised and adding the accumulations to the capital of the Trust Fund

X.2 The Trustees shall have power in their absolute discretion to pay transfer or apply in any manner to or for the benefit of the Principal Beneficiary the whole or any part or parts of the capital of the Trust Fund

---

[85] This clause is designed to meet the requirements of IHTA 1984, s 89(1) which are that during the life of the disabled person he is the only person to whom capital or income can be applied. For a complete disabled trust see the authors' *A Modern Approach to Lifetime Tax Planning*, **Precedent 23.1**, which includes the power to pay capital/income to persons other than the disabled person up to an annual limit.

[86] Note that if the disabled beneficiary does not have any entitlement to income his means tested benefits should not be restricted. In fact, the IHT rules would permit all the income to be paid to someone else.

APPENDIX

HMRC Guidance on ss 71A, 71D and accumulation and maintenance trusts (20 June 2007)

This guidance has been agreed with HMRC. It outlines the way in which HMRC interpret s 71 (as amended by FA 2006), s 71A and ss 71D-H IHTA 1984. **It should not be regarded as a comprehensive explanation covering all aspects of these sections.**

There are three particular areas of concern, namely:

1.   the meaning of 'B' in the legislation;
2.   the class closing rules;
3.   the scope of settled powers of advancement.

1. The meaning of 'B' or 'bereaved minor' in the legislation

Both s 71A and s 71D are drafted by reference to a single beneficiary (in s 71D called 'B' and in s 71A called the bereaved minor). However, HMRC consider that it is possible to pluralise B or the bereaved minor to include all beneficiaries within the relevant class provided they are <u>alive</u> at the date the s 71A or s 71D trust takes effect and are under the specified age.

Accordingly a will trust in the following terms can qualify as a s 71A trust:

> 'to such of my children alive at my death as attain the age of 18 years and if more than one in such shares as the trustees shall from time to time by deed or deeds revocable or irrevocable appoint and in default of such appointment in equal shares absolutely at 18 provided that no such appointment shall be made and no such appointment shall be revoked so as to either diminish or to increase the share (or the accumulations of income forming part of the share) of or give a new share (or new accumulations of income) to a child who at the date of such appointment or revocation has reached the age of 18 nor to benefit a child who has been excluded from benefit as a result of the exercise of the power.'

Note the following:

1.1 It is not necessary to fix the shares in which each child takes income and capital while they are all under 18. Hence it is possible to pay out income and capital to the minor children in unequal shares.

1.2 The power of selection must not be capable of being exercised so as to vary the share of a child who has <u>already</u> reached 18. Assume three beneficiaries B1, B2 and B3. It is possible to specify at any time before the eldest (B1) reaches 18 the share he is to take but once he reaches 18 any further power of selection can only be exercised between B2 and B3. B1 ceases to be within the definition of 'B' in these circumstances.

1.3 If the power of selection is exercised revocably then it is not possible by revoking that exercise to benefit someone who has been wholly excluded from benefit albeit revocably. If, for example, the whole relevant share is appointed revocably to B3 (but on terms that the appointment could be revoked to confer benefits on B1 or B2) then even though B1 and B2 are under 18 the trust ceases to qualify for s 71A status. HMRC considers that it is not possible under the s 71A regime for someone who is not currently benefiting to become entitled in the future. Practitioners will therefore need to be careful before exercising any power of appointment revocably.

1.4 HMRC do not consider that s 71A is breached merely because a power of appointment might be exercised in this way. Nor is it a problem if, in the above example, the power of appointment is exercised revocably so as to give B1 5%, B2 5% and B3 90%. Since B1 and B2 are not wholly excluded HMRC take the view that they can still benefit under a future exercise of the power since they remain within 'B'.

1.5 Nor is there a problem if a beneficiary dies under 18 leaving children in whose favour there will be incorporated substitutionary provisions. Hence if B1 dies before 18 leaving children and his presumptive or fixed share passes to those children under the terms of the Will, it is only from that point that the presumptive share of B1 will cease to qualify under s 71A and fall within the relevant property regime. The mere possibility that B1 could die before 18 with children taking his share does not breach the s 71A conditions. Any power of selection though must not be capable of varying the presumptive share of the deceased B1 once he has died – because B1's children are not within the definition of B and their share must not be increased or deceased after B1 has died.

1.6 No overriding powers of appointment can be included so that 'B's' absolute entitlement could be defeated at 18 although the legislation provides that the existence of an extended power of advancement (ie an express or statutory power of advancement that could be used to defer the beneficiary's capital entitlement by, for instance, providing that his share was to be held on life interest trusts beyond the age of 18) will not in itself cause the trust to fail to satisfy the s 71A conditions from the outset. However, if the settled power of advancement is exercised so as to defer vesting of capital at 18 (eg by the making of a settled advance) then although there is no charge under s 71A on the ending of the bereaved minor trust the relevant share from that point falls within the relevant property regime.

1.7 All the points above apply to section 71D trusts set up by Will and to accumulation and maintenance ('A&M') trusts which are converted to fall within s 71D before 6 April 2008 (or before a beneficiary has attained an interest in possession if earlier). Hence it will be necessary to ensure that any powers of appointment that are retained do not permit a beneficiary's absolute share to be altered after he has reached 25 or defeated on reaching that age and if a power of appointment is exercised revocably it must not be capable of benefiting anyone who has been wholly excluded from benefit (even if under 25 and even if the exclusion was revocable).

2. The class closing rules

2.1 Difficult questions arise where an existing A&M trust is converted into a s 71D trust. Existing A&M trusts can become s 71D trusts provided this happens on the earlier of the beneficiary taking an entitlement to income or by 6 April 2008.[87]

2.2 In the case of existing A&M trusts it is possible that the class of potential beneficiaries will not yet have closed. (This is different from s 71A and s 71D trusts set up by Will where by definition the deceased parent cannot have any further children, apart from the case of a child *en ventre sa mère* whose father has died). In the same way that HMRC do not consider 'B' can include a beneficiary who has been excluded from benefit (albeit revocably) HMRC do not consider that B can include any unborn beneficiary, again, apart from a child *en ventre sa mère*.

2.3 So if, for example, an existing A&M trust in favour of the settlor's grandchildren provides that the class closes only when the eldest becomes 25 and the trust currently benefits only B1 and B2 (say grandchildren of a settlor) being the sole living beneficiaries aged 8 and 9, in order to be s 71D compliant, the terms of the trust must be amended to exclude any future born beneficiaries. If B1 and B2's parent has a further child in 2009 that child must not be capable of benefiting from the trust fund (except in the event of the death of either B1 or B2 in which case the relevant portion of the trust will from that point fall within the relevant property regime).

2.4 Hence the power to appoint shares must only be exercisable between all or some of the beneficiaries under 25 who are alive at the date of conversion to s 71D status. HMRC consider this follows from the drafting in s 71D(1)(a),(3)(b)(i) and (6)(a) when taken together.

2.5 This is not the case if an existing A&M trust continues to satisfy the conditions in s 71 beyond April 2008 because it falls within para 3, Sch 20 FA 2006. A trust which provides for all grandchildren to take outright at 18 will continue to have A&M status under s 71, as amended by para 3, Sch 20, beyond April 2008. It will be possible to pay income and capital between them in such shares as the trustees think fit and for future born children to benefit if

---

[87]   It will not be possible to convert an A&M trust into a s 71D trust after the beneficiary has become entitled to income on or after 22 March 2006 because once a beneficiary takes entitlement to income it no longer qualifies as an A&M trust under s 71. Section 71D(3)(b) requires conversion of the trusts immediately before the property ceases to be property to which s 71 applies. Hence it will need to be s 71D-compliant by the time the beneficiary attains an interest in possession. Of course if one beneficiary becomes entitled to income from part of the trust fund the remaining part will remain within the A&M regime and so could have been converted subsequently (but before 6 April 2008).

the trust deed permits this flexibility provided that no child's share can be varied after reaching 18. The class should therefore generally be closed once the eldest child reaches 18.

3. *The scope of settled powers of advancement*

3.1 HMRC accept that the mere possibility of a power of advancement being used to defer entitlement to capital at 18 or 25 does not cause the trust to fail to satisfy the requirements of s 71A or s 71D given the terms of s 71A (4) or s 71D(7) respectively. If the power of advancement is exercised in favour of that person so as to create continuing trusts under which the beneficiary's capital entitlement will be deferred beyond the age of 18 or 25 as appropriate, those trusts will fall within the relevant property regime (with either no exit charge in the case of BMTs or with the usual exit charge under s 71E, computed according to the provisions in s 71F, assuming the proper exercise of the power causes property to be 'paid or applied for the advancement or benefit of B'; otherwise, the computation would be under s 71G).

3.2 HMRC accept that in the case of A&M trusts (including trusts which are modified so that they satisfy the amended s 71 definition after 6 April 2008) the mere inclusion of a wide power of advancement is unobjectionable. The exercise of such a power will not trigger an inheritance tax charge if the beneficiary takes absolutely or an interest in possession (albeit not qualifying) on or before 18 (see s 71(4) IHTA 1984) and his capital entitlement is deferred beyond 18, although in the latter event, the trust for the beneficiary will thenceforth be a relevant property trust unless it can come within s 71D.

CHAPTER 8

PILOT TRUSTS

8.01 Pilot trusts became increasingly popular after the changes in the IHT treatment of settlements introduced by FA 2006. Their attraction lay in reducing (usually eliminating) the IHT anniversary and exit charges payable on settled property held on relevant property trusts.[1] Instead of creating a single large value settlement which attracted 10-year anniversary and exit charges, the settlor divided the property into a number of trusts, all of which benefitted from a nil rate band. Note, however, that pilot trusts did not reduce the tax charged on the transfer of property into the settlements.

Given this popularity, it is not surprising that HMRC has seized the opportunity in the Consultations designed to simplify the tax treatment of relevant property trusts to introduce proposals which would largely take away their advantages.[2] It was intended that the changes would take effect from 6 April 2015 but that anti-forestalling provisions would have effect from 10 December 2014. Trusts already set up and fully constituted before that date were not to be affected by the changes (ie they would retain their IHT benefits). In the event, the changes were not incorporated in FA 2015 but the Revenue have said that they will be included in a future Finance Bill. It is not clear how this delay will affect the proposed implementation date. This chapter should be read in the light of these proposed changes, the general effect of which is summarised in the final section.

1. DEFINITION

8.02 A pilot trust is established by the settlor during his lifetime and will normally be fully discretionary in form.[3] It is called a 'pilot' trust because it is set up with a nominal sum (typically £10) but with the intention that in the future (either during the settlor's lifetime or by his will) further assets will be added to it.

---

[1] See **3.54** *et seq.*
[2] For details, see **3.72** *et seq.*
[3] See **Precedent 8.1**. Once the would-be settlor is dead it is not possible to create pilot trusts for him which are then added to by a deed of variation read-back under IHTA 1984, s 142(1): see further **8.33**.

2. POINTS OF DETAIL IN ESTABLISHING THE TRUST

8.03 It is modern practice to set up the majority of settlements in pilot form and then to add property: for instance, if the settlor intends to settle shares he will normally set up a £10 trust and then transfer the shares to the trustees using the appropriate stock transfer form.

8.04 A trust may be defined as an arrangement that involves trustees holding property (and it can be any form of property) on trust for the benefit of the beneficiaries. Until the trustees have been given property of some description, therefore, a trust has not been created. As will be considered later, if it is important to be able to show that a particular trust was established on the date stated in the trust deed it is essential that the initial trust fund (typically £10) has been received by the trustees on that date. If this has not happened the trust will only come into existence at the time when the substantial assets are added, which may well defeat the intended IHT planning.[4] It is also important that the initial sum settled is not spent before the further assets are added. Otherwise the trust originally established (with the nominal value property) will have ended so that a new settlement will arise when the further assets are transferred to the trustees (thereby nullifying any advantages of the pilot trust).

8.05 With the changes in the IHT treatment of settlements in FA 2006, setting up a lifetime settlement today involves the creation of an IHT relevant property trust (the only exception is a trust for a disabled person) with the result that:

(a) the settlor will make an immediately chargeable transfer of value into the settlement, not a PET;[5]

(b) the settlement itself will be subject to 10-year anniversary charges and interim exit charges.

The consequence is that, from an IHT perspective, the *form* of the trust is irrelevant – it can be discretionary; interest in possession or accumulation and maintenance – the IHT treatment is the same. It was stated above that pilot trusts will normally be discretionary in form but they do not have to be, except if the intention is that the settlor will add property to the trust by his will. In this case, if the trust has been set up as an interest in possession settlement, the addition of funds to it will involve the creation of an IPDI trust with wholly different IHT consequences from what would have been intended.[6]

---

[4] The trust may be established with property of any description and of any value. (The authors do not agree that it is necessary to settle a minimum sum of £100 as has been suggested on the Trust Discussion Forum.) For instance, trusts are sometimes set up with an unused first-class postage stamp or with a debt owed by the settlor to the trustees (provided, of course, that it is enforceable which, if no consideration has been provided, means that it should be contained in a deed).

[5] Of course, it may be that the sum involved is small (eg £10) and so will fall within the settlor's IHT annual exemption or be normal expenditure out of income and so exempt, or it may involve a transfer of business or agricultural property attracting 100% relief.

[6] The matter is not wholly free from doubt: see IHTA 1984, s 49A which defines an IPDI trust as 'a settlement ... effected by will'. Arguably the settlement was effected *inter vivos* by the

8.06 Usually, more than one pilot trust will be set up and the questions which then arise are whether it is important for the trusts to be set up on different days, and whether it matters that each trust is identical. So far as the latter question is concerned, there is no *trust law* objection to creating a series of identical settlements, each one of which will be treated as a separate entity. From an IHT perspective (and it was important for the planning to work for each trust to be taxed as a separate entity) HMRC sought in the *Rysaffe* case to have five settlements treated as a single trust but were unsuccessful.[7] Accordingly, it is not thought to be essential to establish the trusts with different trustees, beneficiaries etc. Remember, however, to distinguish the settlements one from another so that no problems will arise in identifying to which entity property is added, for instance by naming each settlement: 'The [*name of settlor*] 2015 No 1 Discretionary Trust'. Having said this, when a relatively small number of settlements are to be set up the cautious adviser may well feel more comfortable if the trusts are not identical. For instance, there may be differences in the class of beneficiaries (all the trusts will have a standard power to add) and in the case of trusts for (say) grandchildren, each trust may be identified as being earmarked for a particular grandchild (eg 'Debbie's Trust'; 'Jason's Trust' etc).

Related settlements

8.07 The objection to setting up all the trusts on *the same day* is that they are then, for IHT charging purposes, 'related settlements'.[8] Generally this can result in extra charges being incurred but in the case of pilot trusts it is important to note that the only consequence of them being related settlements is that, when taxing any one of the settlements, the IHT rate is calculated by adding the value of property in any related settlement *at the time when it was created*. In the case of four settlements (each of £10) created on the same day, this means adding £30 to the value of the property in any one of those trusts for the purposes of arriving at the appropriate IHT rate of charge, which is, of course, neither here

---

creation of the pilot trust with further property then being added by will. However, it is best to be cautious and avoid any risk of there being an unintended IPDI. IPDI trusts are considered in Chapter 6 and see **5.03**.

[7] *Rysaffe Trustee Co (CI) Ltd v IRC* [2003] EWCA Civ 356, [2003] STC 536 and see also the decision of Park J at *First Instance* [2002] STC 872. In this case, the settlor sequentially made five discretionary settlements each of 6,900 shares. The Revenue contended that the making of the settlements were associated operations so that the settlor had made one composite settlement as a result of the extended meaning of the word 'disposition'. This argument, although accepted by the Special Commissioner, was rejected by both Park J and the Court of Appeal. Mummery J in the Court of Appeal held that the questions 'what is a settlement?' and 'what property is comprised in a settlement?': 'can be determined without asking any additional questions, such as whether the dispositions were "associated operations" ... The inclusion of the "associated operations" in the statutory description of "disposition" is not intended for cases, such as this, where there is no dispute that there was a "disposition" of property falling within s 43(2). They are intended for cases where there is a dispute as to whether there was a relevant "disposition" at all. The Revenue may be entitled to invoke the extended description to catch a case which would not be regarded as a "disposition" of property in its ordinary and natural sense.'

[8] See **3.63**.

nor there. The position would be quite different if each settlement had been established with an initial trust fund of £100,000.[9]

The effect of GAAR

8.08 Pilot trusts were expressly dealt with in the guidance approved by the Interim Advisory Board and published in April 2013.[10] Although pilot trusts were clearly tax arrangements and involve contrived steps HMRC accepted that they would not be challenged under the GAAR provisions even if done on or after 17 July 2013 because they accorded with established practice accepted by HMRC:

> 'The practice was litigated in the case of *Rysaffe Trustee v IRC* [2003] STC 536. HMRC lost the case and having chosen not to change the legislation, must be taken to have accepted the practice.'

Joint settlors

8.09 It is not unusual to find settlements created by joint settlors (typically husband and wife). A pilot trust could be so established and then each could add assets to the trust in the future. In principle, this ought to be effective in IHT planning terms since IHTA 1984, s 44(2) provides that each settlor will be treated as having created a separate settlement when 'the circumstances so require'. Better to avoid relying on this provision, however, and for each to create a separate pilot trust so that there can be no doubt about the position. Otherwise, if the husband (say) adds property to the settlement that he jointly created with his wife, is he adding it to his fund (ie to his separate settlement under s 44(2)) or to his wife's fund or is it treated as being added 50:50 to each? *Avoid the problem: do not have joint settlors!*

3. ADDING PROPERTY TO THE PILOT TRUST

8.10 The settlor may add property either during his lifetime or on death by his will. It was important that in cases where a number of pilot trusts have been created the property is added to all of them *on the same day* (obviously not a problem if the addition is provided for in the settlor's will). This was because where additional funds were added to the settlements *on the same day*, they did not adversely affect the availability of the nil rate band of each settlement.[11] If property was added on different days, however, each such chargeable transfer increased the settlor's cumulative total and, therefore, the rate at which IHT is charged on anniversaries and exits from the settlements to which property is

---

[9]   The limited scope of the related settlement rule is the reason for the proposed new legislation introducing the concept of a 'same day addition': see **3.74**. It is envisaged that the definition of 'related settlements' will be amended and limited to relevant property trusts.

[10]   See the GAAR Guidance (revised January 2015) at D26.

[11]   IHTA 1984, s 67(3)(b)(i). For the limited scope of this section, see **8.44**.

added later. Not surprisingly, FA 2015 attacked the use of pilot trusts by introducing rules which aggregated 'same day additions' made by the same settlor to more than one settlement.

The addition of property will involve a transfer of value for IHT purposes which cannot (in the case of a lifetime transfers) be a PET and may trigger a CGT charge in cases where the settlor is disposing of chargeable assets standing at a gain. In considering the use and advantages of pilot trusts, it was important to bear in mind that there were no special IHT rules governing this addition so that to the extent that the transfer exceeded the settlor's available nil rate band there was an immediate charge to IHT.[12] It could therefore be the case that the initial IHT charge was prohibitive, so making pilot trusts an unattractive proposition.[13]

Checking the settlor's clock

8.11 The IHT attraction of pilot trusts was derived from the availability of the settlor's full IHT nil rate band to each of the pilot trusts created. Hence it was important to check:

(a)   that at the time when the settlor sets up the pilot trust he had made no chargeable transfers in the previous 7 years; *and*

(b)   that the position remained the same at the time when he added property.

If the settlor had made a PET in the 7 years before creating the pilot trust then, provided that he survives that PET by 7 years, it will drop out of charge: on the other hand, death within 7 years of the PET will result in that transfer being chargeable (a 'failed PET') and so may invalidate any planning based on the use of pilot trusts. Ideally, therefore, the settlor would wait until the PET has been exempted before setting up the pilot trusts: to act before that has happened involved an element of risk.[14] When the settlor has made a chargeable transfer in the previous 7 years, any pilot trust that he establishes will not benefit from a full nil rate band. For instance, if the chargeable transfer was of £100,000 then any pilot trust will have (at 2015–16 rates) a nil rate band of only £225,000. To obtain a full nil rate band it is necessary to wait until the chargeable transfer has dropped off the cumulative total of the settlor.

Additions by will

8.12 Where the settlor intends to add to the settlement by will, it is important not to alter the terms of the settlement after the execution of the will. For instance, if the pilot trust had been set up as a discretionary trust for his

---

12   Unless the transfer is exempt, eg under the normal expenditure out of income rules, or benefits from a valuation relief under the BPR/APR provisions.

13   See **8.18** *et seq*.

14   Bear in mind that taper relief (under IHTA 1984, s 7(4)) merely reduces tax charged once the donor has survived his gift by 3 years: it does not reduce the transfer of value (ie what is on the taxpayer's clock).

children, his grandchildren should not be added to the class of beneficiaries once the will adding property to it has been made.[15] If the terms of the trust are altered then a new will should be executed adding property to the (amended) trust. The pilot trust should not create an interest in possession since otherwise the addition of property by will results in an IPDI trust arising.[16]

The s 81 trap

8.13   It is also important to take care in adding the property: the addition should be directly into the relevant pilot trusts and not, for instance, via a discretionary trust set up in the will. This is because of IHTA 1984, s 81 which provides:

> 'Where property which ceases to be comprised in one settlement becomes comprised in another then, unless in the meantime any person becomes beneficially entitled to the property (and not merely to an interest in possession in the property), it shall for the purposes of this Chapter be treated as remaining comprised in the first settlement.'[17]

Example 8.1

During his lifetime, Jim set up four pilot trusts. On his death he leaves his residuary estate on discretionary trusts giving the trustees power to pay or transfer the property into any lifetime trust that he had created. The trustees duly transfer the assets into the four pilot trusts. For the purposes of the IHT relevant property charging regime the effect of IHTA 1984, s 81 is that the property is treated as remaining comprised in the will trust and hence the multiple nil rate bands of the pilot trusts have been wasted.[18]

---

[15]   See **1.11** and *Re Jones* [1942] Ch 328. The will must refer to a trust document existing at that time. If the terms of the trust document have changed between the execution of the will and death, the changes cannot be incorporated. If the testator refers in the will to 'such trusts as he should declare or such directions as he should give by any memorandum under his hand' this would be a reference to a future document which could not be incorporated: *Re Edwards* [1947] 2 All ER 521 at 526 and confirmed on this point by the Court of Appeal in [1948] Ch 440.

[16]   See further **8.05**.

[17]   This section is an anti-avoidance measure designed to prevent property being switched from a trust with a 10-year anniversary looming into a new settlement with the intention of avoiding the 10-year charge.

[18]   Section 81 is considered further at **8.22**. It may be possible to correct the mistake if the trustees appoint the property to a beneficiary absolutely (taking advantage of IHTA 1984, s 144) who then (still within 2 years of Jim's death) varies the will to provide for the property to be put into the four pilot trusts. By using a combination of IHTA 1984, ss 144 and 142, double reading back is obtained.

4. THE IHT TREATMENT OF PILOT TRUSTS

8.14   The legislation dealing with the IHT treatment of relevant property trusts is in IHTA 1984, Part III, Chapter III (ss 58–85). The settlement is taxed as a separate entity (distinct from both the settlor and the beneficiaries) and charges are levied on two occasions:

(a)   on property in the settlement on 10-year anniversaries running from the date of its creation ('the anniversary charge');[19]

(b)   on property which ceases to be comprised in the settlement, eg by outright appointment to a beneficiary ('the exit charge').[20]

8.15   In arriving at the rate of IHT, the legislation attributes to the trust the chargeable transfers made by the settlor in the period of 7 years ending with the day on which the settlement commenced.[21] Such chargeable transfers never drop out of account, ie they remain on the settlement clock forever. Assume, for instance, that the settlor had made chargeable transfers of £500,000 in this 7-year period. As this exceeds the IHT nil rate band the result is that the settlement will suffer IHT charges even if the value of the settled property itself is no more than the IHT nil rate band. Of course, the converse is also true: *viz* that if the settlor has made no chargeable transfers in this period then if the value of the settled property falls within the nil rate band the tax charge on the settlement will be nil.

---

[19]   For 10-year anniversary charges, see s 64 and for the rate of such charges see s 66. See further **3.60** *et seq*. Section 60 provides that a settlement commences when property first becomes comprised in it (in the case of a pilot trust when the trustees receive the initial sum settled, eg £10). Section 61 provides that a 10-year anniversary means the 10th anniversary of the date on which the settlement commenced (so for a settlement set up on 1 July 2010 the first 10-year anniversary will be on 1 July 2020 and so on). The charge is on the value of the property in the settlement immediately before the anniversary: s 64.

[20]   For the exit charge, see s 65. For the rate which applies before the first 10-year anniversary, see s 68; for the rate thereafter see s 69. See further **3.60** *et seq*. The charge is on property which ceases to be relevant property and does not include payments of costs or expenses nor payments which are income in the hands of the recipient beneficiary. Nor is there a tax charge on sales of trust property (since there is no fall in the value of the relevant property in the settlement) but depreciatory transactions are caught.

[21]   IHTA 1984, s 66(5)(a). See further **3.62**.

Diagram 1: calculating the IHT rate on a 10-year anniversary (before the 2015 changes – see Diagram 2)

| *The amount of the chargeable transfer* | Value of any property in a related settlement when it commenced | Note 1 |
| | Value of the property in the settlement immediately before the 10-year anniversary | Note 2 |

| *What is on the clock? The settlement's cumulative total* | Value subject to an exit charge in the last 10 years | Note 3 |
| | Previous transfers of the settlor in the 7 years before creating the settlement | Note 4 |

Notes

1   For the definition of a related settlement, see IHTA 1984, s 62.[22] Note carefully that it is only the value of the settled property when the related settlement began that is taken into account. Hence pilot trusts may be set up on the same day without an adverse IHT result.[23] Also included in the chargeable transfer is property comprised in the settlement which has never become relevant property (for instance, if the settlement was established with two funds, one, eg, for a disabled beneficiary which creates a qualifying interest in possession and the other of relevant property). As with related settlements it is the value of this property at the date when the settlement commenced that is taken into account: IHTA 1984, s 66(4)(b). This property is not itself taxed (it is not relevant property in the settlement) but its inclusion in the tax computation may increase the rate of charge on the relevant property.

2   This is the property which is taxed. It may, of course, be the only property taken into account in calculating the tax rate (for instance if the settlor had not made previous chargeable transfers: there was no related settlement and no payments out of the settlement in the last 10 years).

3   As with the case of an individual, account is taken of previous transfers out of the settlement. In this case, a 10-year period is taken and, of course, this total falls out of account (being replaced by any transfers out in the following decade) on the next anniversary charge.

4   Ideally the settlor created the settlement when his cumulative total was zero: see **8.09**.

---

22   See **3.62** and **8.07**.
23   See **8.06**.

Example 8.2

On 1 January 2014 Tobias establishes four pilot discretionary trusts each of £10. He adds £325,000 to each trust on 10 January 2014. Tobias had made no previous chargeable transfers. Note the following:

1.   in arriving at the tax charge on the four settlements in 2024 (the first 10-year anniversary) the related settlement rules apply which means that, in each case, £30 must be added to the chargeable transfer (being the property in the three related settlements when they commenced);

2.   as Tobias had made no previous chargeable transfers there is nothing on the settlement 'clock'. Note that if he had established the four trusts over four consecutive days by the time he reached the fourth trust he would have settled £30 on the three earlier settlements: however, such transfers will fall within his IHT annual exemption (see IHTA 1984, s 19) and so will not be 'chargeable' transfers (see IHTA 1984, s 2(1)). Hence there will still be nothing on the settlement 'clock';

3.   in calculating the rate of tax for each of the four settlements the only significant element in the chargeable transfer is the value of the settled property at the time (the value of the related settlements is *de minimis*) and so provided that this has not increased in value by more than rises in the IHT nil rate band the tax charge will be nil. *Each settlement will accordingly benefit from a full IHT nil rate band*;

4.   additions of property to the pilot trusts are considered at **8.10** but it should be noted that no special rules apply: ie the addition will be a chargeable transfer by the settlor.

Suppose that in this example, Tobias made a lifetime transfer of £1.3m on 20 January to the four settlements. After deducting his nil rate band of £325,000 the tax liability will be 20% × £975,000 = £195,000. Given this liability, it was highly unlikely that he could choose to set up the trust with such a substantial cash sum (for illustrations of when pilot trusts could be used without an entry charge, see **8.23** *et seq*).

8.16 Just because the sum added to the pilot trust falls within the IHT nil rate band, it does not follow that the settlement will never attract IHT charges. This will depend on:

(a)   future rates of IHT; and

(b)   the value of the relevant property at the time of the 10-year charges.

Example 8.3

A pilot trust was set up on 1 August 2013. On the death of the settlor the following December, £300,000 was added to it. The first 10-year anniversary falls on 1 August 2023 and if, at that time, the value of the settled property is £500,000 but the nil rate band has remained frozen at £325,000, then IHT will be charged on the £175,000 excess above the nil rate band (at 2014–15 rates tax will be £10,500).

8.17   With this in mind, it was suggested:

(a)   that it was sensible, given that there was no restriction on the number of pilot trusts that may be created, not to add property up to the full value of the nil rate band but to 'leave room' for the value of the trust fund to grow: in the above example, for instance, if £150,000 had been put into the pilot trusts then the trust fund would have had to more than double in value before there would be any risk of a charge;[24]

(b)   because property is only revalued for the purpose of the IHT charge every 10 years on the anniversary occasion, it follows that if the property settled did not exceed the IHT nil rate band then distributions out of the trust in the first 10 years will be tax free. The trustees should always review the tax position of the trust (say) 3 months before a 10-year anniversary.

Example 8.4

In **Example 8.3**, just before the 2023 anniversary, the trustees distribute the entire fund. Because the value originally settled falls within the then nil rate band there is no IHT exit charge.[25]

IHT consequences of the addition of property to a pilot trust

8.18   In the case of relevant property settlements (eg discretionary trusts) the position is dealt with by IHTA 1984, s 67 from which it is clear:

(a)   that the addition does not involve the creation of a new settlement;[26]

(b)   for the purpose of future IHT charges, chargeable transfers of the settlor in the 7 years immediately before he made the addition of property will be taken into account (instead of the settlor's transfers in the 7 years before creating the pilot trusts) if the total is greater (see IHTA 1984, s 67(4)). It is for this reason that pilot trusts will only benefit from a full IHT nil rate band if in both the 7-year periods immediately before creating the

---

[24]   Assuming, of course, that the nil rate band was not reduced from its current £325,000!

[25]   It might be tempting to distribute just the excess above the nil rate band (£175,000) thereby reducing the value of the relevant property to £325,000 (the nil rate band) on the anniversary. This will not, however, achieve a tax saving since distributions in the first 10 years of the trust are taken into account in calculating the rate of the anniversary charge: see **8.15**, Note 3. For the calculation of exit charges in the first 10 years, see IHTA 1984, s 68 noting especially s 68(5)(a) which defines the amount to be taxed as 'the value, immediately after the settlement commenced of the property then comprised in it' (£10) together with (s 68(5)(c)) 'the value, immediately after it became comprised in the settlement, of any property which became so comprised' (in the example £300,000). See **3.58**. Difficulties can arise where property qualifying for business or agricultural property relief was settled; is sold by the trustees and the proceeds distributed before the first 10-year anniversary: see **3.70**.

[26]   When FA 2006 made major changes in the IHT treatment of settlements, HMRC indicated that additions to existing settlements would create a new settlement (which would be outside the transitional rules applicable to existing settlements). Whatever the position in relation to interest in possession and accumulation and maintenance trusts, this view cannot have been correct for discretionary (relevant property) trusts. Note that s 67 only applies to an addition by chargeable transfer. Accordingly if the settlor adds property by an exempt transfer (eg normal expenditure out of income) the section does not apply.

settlement and before adding the property the settlor had made no chargeable transfers (see **8.11** above);

(c) transfers made on the same day as the additions are, however, ignored.

Example 8.5

1. On 1 September 2013 Sid adds £300,000 to each of four pilot trusts created when his cumulative total was zero. In taxing each of these trusts account is taken of chargeable transfers made by Sid in the 7 years before the additions but the addition of property to the other pilot trusts as it happens on the same day is ignored. Provided Sid has made no chargeable transfers in the 7 years before adding the property, each settlement will have a full nil rate band available to it.

2. Frankie has made no lifetime chargeable transfers when he dies in August 2014. His will (a) adds £325,000 to a discretionary trust that he had set up a few weeks before his death, and (b) sets up a £325,000 discretionary trust. Because transfers made on the same day are ignored under the relevant property regime both trusts will benefit from a full IHT nil rate band when calculating anniversary and exit charges.

The proposed changes

8.19 As can be seen from the above discussion, the IHT benefits of pilot trusts depend on:

(a) the settlor having an unused IHT nil rate band both when setting up the trust and when adding the property to it;

(b) property subsequently being added to all the trusts on the same day or in order to avoid the related settlement rules and the s 67 provisions dealing with additions.

8.20 The proposed attack on pilot trusts accordingly will remove the benefits of same day additions by providing that in taxing each of the settlements, account is to be taken (in working out the rate of tax) of the value of property added by the same settlor on the same day to another relevant property settlement (as well as to the settlement being taxed).

As a result the calculation becomes:

Diagram 2: calculating the IHT rate on a 10 year anniversary after the FA 2015 changes

The amount of the chargeable transfer	Value of any property in a related settlement when it commenced
	Value of the property in the settlement immediately before the 10-year anniversary
	Value of a same day addition (and if not to a related settlement, also the value of the property originally in that settlement)
What is on the clock? The settlement's cumulative total	Value subject to an exit charge in the last 10 years
	Previous transfers of the settlor in the 7 years before creating the settlement

8.21 It will be appreciated that:

(a) the result is not to aggregate the value of the property in the various relevant property settlements but only to include the value at commencement (eg under the related settlement rules) and the value added by a same day addition. There may still be a benefit from the use of a multiplicity of settlements (over a single settlement) if the values of the settled property rise;[27]

(b) the new rules are only concerned with same day additions and so if the additions are on different days it is s 67 which needs to be watched. Provided, therefore, that no chargeable transfer is involved, an IHT advantage may be obtained';[28]

(c) there will be limited transitional rules for additions by will[29] and the new rules will not apply to same day additions before the commencement date (which was intended to be 10 December 2014).

Merging the pilot trusts

8.22 A practical objection to the creation of a number of pilot trusts is that, whilst there is an IHT advantage in that each benefits from a full nil rate band, it is expensive and inconvenient to run a number of relatively small trusts. One solution is to merge the trusts: any well drafted discretionary trust will give the trustees power to transfer the property to another settlement under which all or

---

27   See **8.42**.
28   See **8.44**.
29   See **3.79**.

at least some of the same beneficiaries can benefit.[30] For the purpose of the IHT relevant property regime, IHTA 1984, s 81 provides that:[31]

> '(1) Where property which ceases to be comprised in one settlement becomes comprised in another then, unless in the meantime any person becomes beneficially entitled to the property (and not merely to an interest in possession in the property), it shall for the purposes of this Chapter be treated as remaining comprised in the first settlement.'

Example 8.6

Assume that four settlements originally created on 1 December 2013 are merged. On the 10-year anniversary in 2023 the value of the merged trust fund is £1.6m. For IHT charging purposes, s 81 requires four tax returns to be submitted (one for each of the four discretionary trusts originally created) with the fund being divided amongst them. Assuming that, at the time of the merger, the four funds were of equal value, the result is that each of the settlements will have attributed to it £400,000. A full nil rate band can then be deducted in the case of each of the trusts.

It might be thought that if a number of pilot trusts were to be merged soon after creation this could give rise to the argument that there was, in reality, only ever a single settlement. In the *Rysaffe* case the five settlements were not merged and the case itself involved the calculation of the 10-year anniversary charge. Delaying merger beyond the first 10-year anniversary might accordingly be considered prudent. An alternative strategy would be for the trustees to pursue a common investment policy, ie they might agree that they would pool their trust funds for investment purposes. The trusts would remain separate entities but there would then be administrative benefits.[32]

5. WHEN ARE PILOT TRUSTS USED?

8.23 As already discussed, the addition of property to a pilot trust normally involved the settlor making an immediately chargeable transfer for IHT purposes with the result that an IHT charge was incurred (see, for instance, **Example 8.2(4)**). Pilot trusts are accordingly particularly attractive if they could be set up in situations where this charge was avoided. The following illustrate situations where pilot trusts have been regularly used. In general, whenever the taxpayer wishes to establish a long-term settlement (ie one which involved

---

[30] See **Precedent 8.1, clause 2(c)**. Theoretically the perpetuity rule can pose a problem: there is a potential breach of that rule if property passes into a settlement with a different period from that of the transferor trust: for instance, if the first settlement's perpetuity period was 125 years from 1 August 2010 and the recipient settlement had a 125-year period from 1 September 2010. In practice, such a transfer is not void *ab initio* because of the 'wait and see' rule. Of course, there would be no problem if the transfer was to a settlement created earlier (eg. if the above order had been reversed).

[31] Section 81 is an anti-avoidance provision designed to prevent benefits being obtained by moving property out of a relevant property trust into another trust just before a 10-year anniversary.

[32] See the authors' *A Modern Approach to Lifetime Tax Planning*, **Precedent 22.1**.

10-year anniversary occasions) he would consider whether fragmenting his gift into a number of settlements was advantageous.[33]

First case: using up two IHT nil rate bands on death

8.24   Fred (see **Example 5.8**) is a widower with substantial assets and (on his death) will benefit from the unused IHT nil rate band of his deceased first wife. He wishes to leave his estate to his second wife, Flossie, who is a widow and whose estate will also benefit (on her death) from two IHT nil rate bands because of her pre-deceasing first husband. Ideal IHT planning advice is for Fred (and Flossie) to make wills which use up their two available IHT nil rate bands.[34] In Fred's case he may do this by setting up a discretionary trust to which he leaves assets worth twice the nil rate band under which Flossie and the children from his first marriage will be beneficiaries. If he were to set the trust up by his will then no IHT will be payable on its creation (because of the availability of the two nil rate bands) but on a 10-year anniversary the IHT charge will only take into account the availability of the settlor (Fred's) nil rate band. Hence at current rates and values a tax charge of 3% will arise. He ought instead:

(a)   to establish (say) two pilot discretionary trusts;
(b)   then make a will leaving the benefit of a single nil rate band to each of the two trusts.

As a result, the IHT position on Fred's death will be unaltered but the availability of a nil rate band for both trusts may ensure that there are no 10-year anniversary charges.[35] Should Fred wish he could establish a single lifetime pilot trust (to which he adds property by his will) and set up the other trust in the will itself (see **Example 8.5(2)**). This planning falls within the proposed changes since it involves a same day addition to the pilot trusts.

Second case: the substantial relevant property settlement

8.25   Sid is a widower and wishes to leave his £5m estate on trusts for his collection of grandchildren and great-grandchildren. He accepts that a substantial IHT liability will arise on his death. He envisages that trust being kept in being for many years to provide a long-term family fund to be used for beneficiaries as the need arises.[36] To avoid substantial 10-year charges on this

---

[33]   Note the CGT consequences of creating a multiplicity of settlements: in general, the annual exemption will be divided amongst them: see TCGA 1992, Sch 1. This was, however, considered 'small beer'.

[34]   This is because no one can benefit from more than one transferred nil rate band (see **5.23**) and Flossie's estate will benefit from her first husband's nil rate band.

[35]   See **Precedent 8.2** for clauses adding property to a pilot trust by will. Consider whether Fred would be best advised to have more than two (perhaps four) pilot trusts: see **8.14**.

[36]   A settlor like Sid benefits from the PAA 2009 which enables settlements to be set up with an extended 125-year perpetuity period and for income to be accumulated (if so desired) throughout this period.

family fund, Sid might establish (say) 20 lifetime pilot trusts between which he could then divide his estate at death. Given that the usual conditions were met,[37] each would benefit from a full IHT nil rate band and, for administrative convenience, they might subsequently be merged into a single settlement.[38] Again, the proposed changes will apply to nullify this planning.

Third case: using 100% business or agricultural property relief

8.26 The availability of relief prevents any IHT entry charge. Putting the property into pilot trusts is particularly attractive if it was envisaged that the business will be sold as in the following example.[39]

Example 8.7

Denis Wideboy owned all 100 issued shares in Jalopy Ltd which dealt in second hand cars. He has received an offer to sell the business for £5m which he was minded to accept and envisaged settling the proceeds on trust for his 'dodgy crew of relatives'. He did not need any of the monies (he owns a number of football clubs).

His proposal had unattractive tax consequences. As soon as a binding contract for sale of the business is concluded, Denis ceased to enjoy the benefit of business property relief.[40] The settlement of the cash was accordingly a chargeable transfer by Denis giving rise to a substantial IHT charge. The resultant settlement will suffer 10-year charges.

The following was a more tax efficient alternative:

Settling the shares into pilot trusts: Denis created (say) 20 pilot trusts to which he then transferred his shares (5 per trust). That transfer benefitted from business property relief. The sale then went ahead (the trustees entering into the sale contract) and cash was received by the settlements. Accordingly the IHT entry charge was avoided and, provided that the usual conditions were met,[41] each settlement will benefit from a full IHT nil rate band.[42]

8.27 A number of points of detail should be noted about the above example:

(a)   an IHT clawback charge would arise in the event that Denis dies within 7 years of having transferred the shares to the trustees assuming that the trustees have by then sold the shares and not purchased qualifying replacement property.[43] Were this to happen the transfers became chargeable (so that the advantage of avoiding an IHT entry charge was lost). However, the benefit of the pilot trusts (each having a full IHT nil

---

[37]   See **8.09**.
[38]   See **8.17**.
[39]   For the availability of business and agricultural property relief, see Chapter 10.
[40]   IHTA 1984, s 113 but note the replacement property provisions in s 107. For a consideration of the duties of professional advisers when a client is about to lose a valuable IHT relief, see *Swain Mason v Mills Reeve (a firm)* [2012] EWCA Civ 498.
[41]   See **8.11**.
[42]   For the merger of pilot trusts, see **8.22**.
[43]   For the clawback rules, see IHTA 1984, s 113A.

rate band) remained and, because of a lacuna in the clawback rules, it did not matter whether or not the shares were put into the pilot trusts on the same day;[44]

(b)   consideration needed to be given to the CGT position. The transfer of the shares involved a chargeable disposal by Denis but he might elect for the resultant gain to be held-over.[45] However, the position regarding entrepreneur's relief also needed to be taken into account and Denis may wish to incur the charge if he would benefit from entrepreneur's relief. Bear in mind that the trusts would not benefit from that relief unless they retained the shares for 12 months on an interest in possession trust;[46]

(c)   it was obviously easier to fragment ownership of a business which is operated through a limited company. Difficulties arise if the business is run by a sole trader or through a partnership;

(d)   in *Reynaud v IRC*[47] shares were settled into a number of pilot trusts and immediately sold by the trustees. The Revenue failed in an argument that what was, in reality, settled, was the sale proceeds. It is, of course, important that there is no binding contract for the sale of shares in existence at the time when they are settled.

For the effect of the proposed changes on this planning, see **8.44**.

Fourth case: taking advantage of the normal expenditure out of income exemption

8.28   This exemption is available for gifts out of the income of the taxpayer provided that such gifts are 'normal' (ie represent an established pattern of payments) and do not have the effect of reducing his standard of living.[48] It should be stressed that, provided that the conditions are met, the gifts are exempt when made: ie it is not the case that the donor has to survive by a specified period (contrast the position with PETs).

Example 8.8

Rich has surplus income of £600,000 each year. To take advantage of the s 21 exemption he determines to settle £200,000 each year into each of three pilot trusts. Note:

1.   the entry charge is avoided because of the availability of the exemption;

---

44   This is because, although the rules impose a charge on the transfer of the shares into the trust, they do not operate to increase the cumulative total of chargeable transfers made by the settlor: ie they do not go onto his 'clock': see s 113A(2). For the continued use of such arrangements, see **8.44**.

45   Under TCGA 1992, s 260 given that the trust is not 'settlor-interested': see **3.102**.

46   For entrepreneur's relief, see TCGA 1992, ss 169H–169R and **3.86**. It is not obvious from the legislation that the interest in possession must be in existence for 12 months before relief is available, but this is the strongly held view of HMRC.

47   [1999] STC (SCD) 185.

48   See IHTA 1984, s 21 and the leading cases of *Bennett v IRC* [1995] STC 54 and *McDowall v IRC* [2004] STC (SCD) 22. For HMRC guidance, see IHTM 14231 *et seq*. See also the authors' *A Modern Approach to Lifetime Tax Planning*, Chapter 38.

2.   given that the normal conditions are met, each trust will benefit from a full IHT nil rate band;

3.   given that the payments are exempt from IHT, it does not matter that the sums are paid into the trusts on different days: ie this is not the classic pilot trust arrangement where the additions must be made to all the trusts on the same day. In fact, it is unnecessary to use pilot trusts: the sums could be settled directly into the three trusts.

8.29   Note carefully the following matters:

(a)   to ensure that the gifts conform to a pattern (ie are 'normal') it is common for the donor to make a written declaration of intent (eg 'I declare that I will each year settle my surplus income (or stated amount) on trusts for the benefit of my issue');

(b)   because the gifts are exempt it is not necessary to first establish pilot trusts: in the above example, Rich could simply settle £200,000 on consecutive days into three settlements. It is, of course, important in such a case to ensure that the settlements are not related: ie they must be set up on different days. This is because it is the size of the initial trust fund which is taken into account under the related settlements rule: contrast the position with pilot trusts generally (see 8.07);

(c)   when advantage is to be taken of the exemption by making settled (as opposed to outright) gifts, HMRC consider that (as the sum settled exceeds the annual exemption of the settlor) the transfer has to be reported.[49] As the obligation is to report chargeable transfers,[50] which excludes exempt transfers, it may be doubted if this view is correct. However, there may be attractions in submitting the IHT100 to force HMRC to confirm the availability of the exemption.

For the continued use of this planning, see 8.44.

Fifth case: providing for cohabitees and children

8.30   This is a problem, particularly where the children are from a different relationship. The taxpayer usually wants to provide for the cohabitee while making sure that some funds are available to the children and will want to minimise IHT.

There is, of course, no spouse exemption and so IHT is a particular issue. It will be payable on all non-relievable property in excess of the taxpayer's available nil rate band.

---

[49] IHTM 10652.
[50] IHTA 1984, s 216(1)(a).

Option 1

The taxpayer can leave the estate to the cohabitee for life (an IPDI), remainder to the children. The taxpayer kept control over the devolution of the property by ensuring that the children will get the capital but there are downsides:

(a)   the children have to wait till the cohabitee's death to benefit from their parent's estate;

(b)   for IHT purposes the deceased's property will be aggregated with the cohabitee's own property producing an increased IHT burden on the cohabitee's death. The IHT payable will be apportioned between the IPDI trust and the cohabitee's free estate.

Option 2

The deceased can leave a legacy equal to his available nil rate band to a discretionary trust for the cohabitee and children. The advantages are that there is no aggregation of the settled property with the cohabitee's IHT estate and funds can be made available to the children, if necessary. Because the sum settled is within the deceased's available nil rate band, there will be no charges in the first 10 years.

But what should the deceased do with the balance of the estate? From the point of view of guaranteeing the assets for the children, the obvious solution is to leave the residue on IPDI trusts to the cohabitee. However, the IHT consequence would be two related settlements resulting in anniversary and exit charges on the discretionary trust. This option is, therefore, unattractive when the value of the estate makes IHT an issue.[51]

Option 3

If the deceased sets up a lifetime pilot trust in discretionary form, the nil rate sum can be left to the pilot trust, residue on IPDI trusts to the cohabitee for life. The related settlement rules do not apply.

The result was that the deceased had guaranteed that assets will pass to the children, made sure that funds equal to the nil rate band were not aggregated with the cohabitee's estate and ensured that there were no IHT charges on the relevant property settlement in the first 10 years. This planning involves a same day addition to the two trusts and so will be caught by the proposed changes.

Option 4

The deceased sets up a number of pilot trusts in discretionary form for the benefit of his cohabitee and children and then by will divided his estate between

---

51   The proposed changes will amend the definition of a related settlement so that IPDI trusts will cease to be related to relevant property trusts.

the trusts. Given that all trusts benefit from a nil rate band, IHT was avoided on the cohabitee's death (contrast the position if the cohabitee is given an IPDI). Note:

(a)   it was important that a letter of wishes was left making it clear that during the lifetime of the cohabitee (s)he is to be the main beneficiary;

(b)   after 2 years from the deceased's death the cohabitee can be given an interest in possession in all or some of the trusts without this being treated as an IPDI.

This planning involves a same day addition.

Sixth case: using a pilot trust to receive a death in service benefit (spousal by-pass trust)

8.31   In cases where a taxpayer would be entitled to a substantial death in service benefit under the terms of his pension arrangements were he to die prematurely, he should consider giving the trustees a letter of wishes (a non–binding nomination) indicating to whom he would like it to be paid.[52] Frequently he will wish the sum to be paid to his spouse or civil partner but if it is substantial then the consequence is likely to be an IHT charge on the death of that person. An alternative strategy, therefore, involves the use of a spousal by-pass trust.[53] This is a pilot trust established during the member's lifetime to which he requests the pension trustees to pay the death benefit.

8.32   If the sum involved is large (say £900,000) was it attractive to establish three pilot trusts and then request the pension trustees to pay £300,000 into each? Given that the death benefit is already held in trust, the answer is that this did not produce any IHT advantage since this is a situation where s 81[54] operates to deem the £900,000 to remain comprised in the original (pension) trust.[55]

8.33   It may be the case that the taxpayer has taken out more than one pension so that death benefits may be payable out of more than one pension trust. In this case, there is already a fragmentation of the total sum into different trusts and, provided that the member had not used up his nil rate band at the time when he took out the relevant pension, each may benefit from an IHT nil rate band.

---

[52]   The terms of the pension should, of course, be checked but most provide for death benefits to be paid amongst a class of beneficiaries to be selected by the trustees. The class will normally include a trust established by the member for his family. Contract based arrangements (such as retirement annuity contracts) do not involve a pension trust.

[53]   The term is a misnomer in that the surviving spouse will commonly be the main intended beneficiary. For the perpetuity issues involved, see **2.15** *et seq*.

[54]   See **8.13**.

[55]   See further the ABI's technical guidance available at http://wingatefp.com/uploads/2011.06.20_abi_pensions_q_and_a_paper_2.pdf.

8.34 The use of spousal by-pass trusts will not be affected by the proposed changes.

6. PRACTICAL ISSUES

Unscrambling an unwanted pilot trust

8.35 Assume that property was added to a number of pilot trusts on the death of the taxpayer and that, for whatever reason, the trusts are unwanted and the family/trustees want to amend the will to redirect the gifts that have been made. In such a case, IHTA 1984, s 144 offers a solution to the problem.[56] The section is widely drafted: it applies:

> 'when property comprised in a person's estate immediately before his death is settled by his will … '

Note, in particular that the will has to 'settle' the property but this can be done by providing for it to be paid into a pilot trust. The settlement itself does not have to be established by the will.[57]

8.36 The effect of the section applying is that if within the period of 2 years following the death of the testator, an 'event' occurs that would normally involve an exit charge out of a relevant property trust then:

(a)   there is no exit charge; and

(b)   'this Act shall have effect as if the will had provided that on the testator's death the property should be held as it is held after the event'.

In effect, a reading-back occurs.

> *Example 8.9*
>
> 1.   Roland, by his will, added £200,000 to a pilot trust which he had set up before his death. The trustees appoint that sum to Roland's surviving civil partner, Ted, within 2 years of Roland's death. Under s 144 that appointment is read back so that the gift to Ted is exempt under IHTA 1984, s 18.
>
> 2.   Peter, by his will, added £200,000 to a discretionary trust which he had set up with £300,000 more than 7 years ago. The result of the addition is that the trust will suffer 10-year charges given that its value will exceed the IHT nil rate band. Accordingly within 2 years of Peter's death the trustees appoint the added £200,000 on an IPDI trust for Peter's daughter. This will be read back under s 144 and treated as a separate settlement with a qualifying interest in possession.[58]

---

[56]   For a full discussion of s 144 see **13.15** *et seq.*

[57]   Contrast the slightly different wording in s 49A(2) relating to IPDIs: see **8.05**.

[58]   IPDIs are discussed in Chapter 6. An appointment on separate discretionary trusts would not be effective because of IHTA 1984, s 81: see **8.22**.

The s 80 trap

8.37 The taxpayer, having set up lifetime pilot trusts, might wish to provide first in his will for a surviving spouse or civil partner and then, after that person's death, put the property into the pilot trusts. In effect, what was envisaged was an IPDI for the spouse/civil partner followed by a gift over into the trusts. Unfortunately, as a result of the operation of IHTA 1984, s 80, this arrangement did not achieve what the taxpayer wanted.

8.38 Section 80 applies in the situation where a settlor creates a settlement with an initial 'postponing interest',[59] being a qualifying interest in possession for either the settlor or his spouse (or civil partner). The section provides that 'for the purposes of this Chapter' (*viz* Part III, Chapter III dealing with the taxation of relevant property settlements) the property shall be treated as becoming comprised in the relevant property settlement on the termination of that postponing interest with that settlement being treated as made by the beneficiary whose interest in possession has ended.

Example 8.10

Jake established two lifetime pilot trusts and, in his will, left his estate on an IPDI trust for his wife, Julie, with the remainder gift into the two trusts. On Jake's death:

1. the IPDI trust for Julie takes effect and the estate is spouse exempt;

2. on Julie's death, the property passes into the two relevant property settlements created by Jake. For IHT purposes s 80 applies and Julie is treated as making the two relevant property settlements. The normal consequences of a settlor adding to his pilot trust therefore do not apply: instead it is Julie (a separate settlor) who is to be treated as having made the settlements. The two settlements will be related to each other and if Julie creates any further settlements in her will, they will be related to the two settlements.

3. Julie could, of course, either disclaim her IPDI interest or effect a deed of variation within 2 years of Jake's death which would, as a result of reading-back, result in Jake adding property to his pilot trusts.

4. To avoid the problem, Julie needed to establish the pilot trusts during her lifetime (as well as Jake) and once that had been done Jake's will could leave his estate on an IPDI trust for Julie remainder to the pilot trusts that she has created. In the event of Julie predeceasing Jake his will would leave the estate to the pilot trusts that he has created.

5. This planning involves the same day addition of property to a number of settlements and so will be caught by the proposed changes.

---

[59] A 'postponing interest' is defined in s 80(4)(b) as an immediate post-death interest (an IPDI) or a disabled person's interest. This reflects the FA 2006 changes in the IHT taxation of settlements which limited the occasions when a 'qualifying' interest in possession can arise. The postponing interests as defined are qualifying interests in possession.

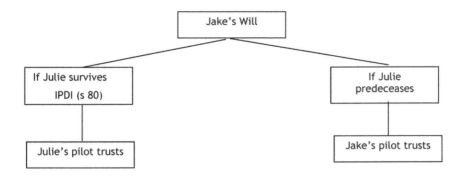

The limits of deeds of variation[60]

8.39 A deed of variation is employed 'to vary the dispositions ... of the property comprised (in the deceased's) estate immediately before his death'. As illustrated in **Example 8.10,** it can therefore be used to redirect property into a pilot trust which the deceased had set up during his lifetime. If, however, the deceased had not created the pilot trust then it was not possible, by a variation, to create such a trust into which property was then directed.

> *Example 8.11*
>
> 1.   On Jane's death, her entire estate passes to her husband, James. He settles a sum equal to her IHT nil rate band onto discretionary trusts by a deed of variation which is read back into Jane's will.
>
> 2.   If, however, instead of a simple variation setting up a discretionary trust in Jane's will, James set up two pilot trusts and then, by a variation, redirected Jane's estate into these trusts then the normal pilot trust analysis does not apply because James is the settlor of the trusts and, by the variation which deems Jane to add property to them, she becomes a separate settlor (ie it is a simple case of adding property to another's settlement). Hence she would be treated as establishing both trusts at the time of her death and they would therefore be related settlements. If James had set up the trusts in the variation then they would not be trusts created before Jane's death so that the result would be that both trusts would be created by her will and again would be related settlements.[61]

8.40 It is not thought that the transitional protected settlement rules to be introduced by a future Finance Bill apply if a will is varied to add property to a pre-10 December 2014[62] pilot trust: see **3.67.**

---

[60]   For variations, see IHTA 1984, s 142 and for disclaimers, s 93.

[61]   It is not thought that the position would be altered if the variation was worded to say that Jane is to be treated as having created two lifetime trusts with the will being varied to provide for property to be added to each. See *PRs of Glowacki v RCC* [2007] STC (SCD) 188 for a discussion of the limitations of what can be achieved by a post-death variation.

[62]   Or whatever may be the commencement date.

7. WILL THERE STILL BE SCOPE FOR USING MULTIPLE TRUSTS IF THE PROPOSED CHANGES GO AHEAD?

First case: create a settlement every 7 years

8.41 There will be no change in the rules concerning the use of the settlor's nil rate band, ie it remains possible for a settlor to establish a number of settlements each with a nil rate band.

> *Example 8.12*
>
> On 3 January 2015 Sam settles £325,000 into a relevant property trust. On 3 January 2022 this chargeable transfer falls out of cumulation (ie his 'clock' is reset to nil) and he can therefore create a further relevant property trust benefitting from a full nil rate band.[63]

Second case: the same day addition and related settlement rules do not result in settlements being taxed as one

8.42 It is important to appreciate that the effect of the 'same day addition' and related settlement rules is limited. Assume that were are concerned with taxing a settlement (Settlement A) and that the settlor created a related settlement (Settlement B) with an initial fund of £10 and made a same day addition of £100,000 to a third settlement (Settlement C). If the value of each of the three settlements is now £500,000, then in taxing Settlement A include:

(a) the value of the property in the related settlement when set up. This is £10 and the fact that this settlement is now worth £500,000 is ignored.

(b) the value of any same day addition: this involves the sum of £100,000 added to Settlement C (together with the initial value of that settlement assuming that this was not caught under the related settlement rules). Again, the current value of £500,000 is not taken into account.

8.43 If the legislation had provided for the aggregation of Settlements B and C with Settlement A then, of course, the tax charge on Settlement A would take account of the full value (in each case £500,000) of those other settlements. For an example showing the relevant calculations, see **3.80**.

Third case: exploiting the limitations of s 67

8.44 Because same day additions will fall foul of the proposed legislation, consider adding property to pilot trusts on different days. Of course, this will normally involve the aggregation under s 67 of the earlier additions, but note the limitations of this section:

---

[63] The example assumes that Sam does not make other chargeable transfers or PETs between 2015 and 2022.

(a)   it only applies to additions made by a chargeable transfer. Accordingly an addition which involves the normal expenditure out of income exemption is not affected, hence the planning noted at **8.28** above can still be employed;

(b)   under s 67 what is aggregated is 'the values transferred by any chargeable transfers of the settlor'. Business property relief and agricultural property relief operate to reduce the value transferred[64] and accordingly the planning noted at **8.26** above can still be employed provided that the shares are settled on different days.

---

[64]   They are 'valuation reliefs': see Chapter 10.

PRECEDENTS

Precedent 8.1: Pilot discretionary trust

THIS SETTLEMENT is made the [   ] day of [   ] 20[   ] between [   ] ('the Settlor') and [   ] and [   ] ('the Original Trustees')

WHEREAS

(A) The Settlor has paid to the Original Trustees the sum of £10[65] and envisages adding further property to the settlement in the future.

(B) This settlement is irrevocable and shall be known as [*select name, eg Wilmington No 1 Discretionary Trust*].

(C) The Original Trustees have agreed to act as the first trustees of the settlement.

NOW THIS DEED WITNESSES:

1. Definitions

(a) In this trust document:
'Beneficiary'[66] means:
   (i) any widow or widower or surviving Civil Partner of the Settlor whether or not remarried or in a civil partnership;
   (ii) any child or grandchild of the Settlor whenever born;
   (iii) anyone (other than the Settlor) descended from the father or mother of the Settlor;
   (iv) anyone who is or has been married to or who is the Civil Partner or former Civil Partner of anyone falling within (ii) or (iii) above;
   (v) after the death of the Settlor anyone who may be entitled to inherit all or any part of the Settlor's estate if the Settlor died intestate or under the Settlor's will;
   (vi) any person (other than the Settlor) notified in writing by the Settlor during his lifetime to the Trustees;
   (vii) any body of persons or trust established for charitable purposes only in accordance with the law of England and Wales, notified in writing by the Settlor during his lifetime to the Trustees; and
'Civil Partner' means civil partner as defined in the Civil Partnership Act 2004.
'Trustees' mean the Original Trustees and any other trustees for the time being of this trust.
'Trust Fund' means the sum of £10 and all property transferred to the Trustees by any person or persons, at any time held by the Trustees whether by way of accumulation of income, capital appreciation, further

---

[65] For the requirement that property, albeit of a nominal value, must be put into the pilot trust, see **8.04**.

[66] A wide class of beneficiaries will normally be chosen.

settlement or otherwise and all monies, investments, income and other property for the time being representing or arising from the whole or any part of the same.[67]

'Trust Period' shall mean the period of 125 years from the date of this deed.[68]

(b)   Words describing relationships include adopted and stepchildren and those tracing their descent through them.

(c)   Words importing the singular shall include plural and vice versa. Words importing a gender include every gender.

2. The Trust Provisions

(a)   During the Trust Period the Trustees (being at least one corporate trustee or two individual trustees) may by deed or deeds appoint that they shall hold the Trust Fund for the benefit of any of the Beneficiaries on such terms as the Trustees think fit.

(b)   An appointment may create any provisions including discretionary trusts and dispositive and administrative powers exercisable by the Trustees or any other person. An appointment may be revocable during the Trust Period or irrevocable.

(c)   The Trustees may pay, transfer or apply any part or all of the Trust Fund to or for the advancement or benefit of any Beneficiary or to any fund or settlement in which one or more Beneficiaries is capable of benefiting.[69]

(d)   Subject to the exercise of the powers in clauses 2(a) to 2(c), the Trustees may accumulate the whole or part of the income of the Trust Fund which income shall be added to the Trust Fund. The Trustees shall pay or apply the remainder of the income to or for the benefit of any Beneficiaries as the trustees think fit during the Trust Period.[70]

3. Ultimate trusts
[insert a default beneficiary/beneficiaries][71]

---

[67]   Note that the definition envisages that further property may be transferred to the trustees in the future.

[68]   This is the mandatory period laid down by PAA 2009. Note, however, that if desired, a shorter Trust Period can be selected (in this case the draftsman must take care to distinguish it from the perpetuity period).

[69]   This is a power 'in the wider form' and enables the trust fund to be resettled. Note the width of the power: some settlors would limit the recipient trust to one in which *all* the Beneficiaries can benefit or one which the trustees themselves could have set up in exercise of their powers of appointment: see **Precedent 4.13**.

[70]   As a result of PAA 2009 all the statutory restrictions on accumulations of income have been removed and it is possible to accumulate throughout the perpetuity period.

[71]   This 'long-stop' provision is designed to prevent a resulting trust to the settlor. Select one or more living beneficiaries.

4. Trustees' powers[72]

In addition to any other powers conferred on the Trustees by this deed, the Trustees shall have the widest possible powers of administration and management of the Trust Fund as if they were absolute owners of the Trust Fund and beneficially entitled to it. In particular, and without prejudice for the foregoing:

(a) The Trustees may (with due regard to any required investment criteria and subject to obtaining advice, if required by law) make any kind of investment they could make if they were absolute beneficial owners (and in particular (i) may invest in and retain non-income producing assets situated anywhere in the world and (ii) need not have regard to any rule of law requiring them to consider diversifying the investments).

(b) The Trustees may make any disposition they could make if they were absolute beneficial owners.

(c) The Trustees may lend all or any part of the Trust Fund to any Beneficiary on such terms (whether or not including provision for the payment of interest and with or without security) as the Trustees in their absolute discretion think fit.

(d) The Trustees may borrow on the security of all or any part of the Trust Fund or without giving any security and on such terms as to interest as the Trustees in their absolute discretion think fit.

(e) The Trustees may pay or transfer capital or income to the parent or guardian of any Minor who is beneficially entitled to it and the receipt of such parent or guardian shall be a full discharge to the Trustees.

(f) The receipt of the treasurer or other proper office in respect of capital or income paid to a charity shall be a full discharge to the Trustees.

(g) The Trustees may apply all or part of the Trust Fund in purchasing or maintaining any policy of assurance on the life of any person and shall have all the powers of an absolute beneficial owner in relation to any such policy.

(h) The receipt of the Trustees for any money payable under or deriving from any dealing with any policy of life assurance shall be a full and sufficient discharge to the company issuing such policy, which company shall not be concerned in the application of any such monies.

(i) In so far as the governing law of this trust permits, the Trustees may delegate in any way the exercise of any of the powers of investment and management of the Trust Fund and may employ agents, discretionary investment managers, nominees and custodians on such terms as the Trustees in their absolute discretion think fit.

---

[72] Draftsmen frequently use the STEP Standard Administrative provisions in place of this list of powers.

(j)   The Trustees may appropriate all or any part of the Trust Fund as they think fit in or towards satisfaction of the interest of any Beneficiary and may for that purpose place such value on any property as they think fit.[73]

(k)   Any Trustee (other than the Settlor or any spouse or Civil Partner for the time being of the Settlor) who is a solicitor or other person engaged in a profession or business or any corporate trustee, may charge all usual reasonable professional charges in relation to work carried out in connection with this trust and shall have the power to resign from office as a Trustee.[74]

(l)   No Trustee shall be precluded from joining in the exercise of any of the powers conferred upon them notwithstanding that he will or may benefit from such exercise or by reason of the fact that he is or may become a Beneficiary provided that at least one other Trustee who takes no benefit is also a party to the exercise.[75]

(m)   The Trustees may by deed (and so as to bind their successors) release or restrict the future exercise of all or any of the powers conferred on them by this trust document or by law.

5. Trustees liability
No Trustee shall be liable for any loss to the Trust Fund or part of the Trust Fund at any time unless that loss is caused by his own knowing breach of trust.[76]

6. Excluded persons

(a)   During the lifetime of the Settlor, no part of the capital or income of the Trust Fund shall be capable of being paid or lent or applied to or for the direct or indirect benefit of the Settlor or any spouse or Civil Partner for the time being of the Settlor in any circumstances whatsoever.

(b)   The prohibition of this clause 6 shall apply notwithstanding anything else contained in or implied by the provisions of this trust document.

7. The Settlor's power to appoint and remove Trustees[77]

(a)   During his lifetime and whilst he has capacity, the Settlor shall have power to appoint new and additional trustees and to remove any trustee as long as there shall be at least one corporate trustee or two individual trustees acting after such appointment and/or removal.

---

[73]   The statutory power of appropriation in AEA 1925, s 41 does not apply to trustees. It is therefore important that they are given an express power.

[74]   The settlor should be made aware of this clause and agree its terms.

[75]   For difficulties that may be caused by the 'self-dealing' rule, see *Kane v Radley Kane* [1999] Ch 274 and *Breakspear v Ackland* [2008] EWHC 220 (Ch).

[76]   Ensure that the settlor is made aware of and agrees this clause: see **1.42**.

[77]   It is common for the settlor to have power to appoint trustees: less common for him to have a power of removal.

(b) After the Settlor's death or after he loses capacity, the Settlor's powers in clause 7(a) shall vest in the Trustees.

IN WITNESS etc

Precedent 8.2: Clauses to use the double nil rate band by settling property in two (or four) pilot trusts set up during the lifetime of the testator before his will was made[78]

1. I GIVE a sum equal to the upper limit of the nil rate percent band in the table of rates (applicable at my death) in Schedule 1 to the Inheritance Tax Act 1984 to the trustees of the [*insert name*] Discretionary Settlement 2009 to be held by those trustees on the trusts set out in a deed of settlement dated [*insert date*] and made by me as settlor and the Original Trustees (as therein defined).[79]

2. I GIVE a sum equal to 50% of the upper limit of the nil rate per cent band in the table of rates (applicable at my death) in Schedule 1 to the Inheritance Tax Act 1984 to the trustees of the [*insert name*] Discretionary Settlement 2009 to be held by those trustees on the trusts set out in a deed of settlement dated [*insert date*] and made by me as settlor and the Original Trustees (as therein defined).[80]

---

[78] These clauses assume that the deceased makes no chargeable transfer *inter vivos* or in the will which will eat into the nil rate band.

[79] This clause is appropriate to transfer a single nil rate band (for 2015–16, £325,000).

[80] This clause may be used when the nil rate is to be split into two pilot trusts: each will receive, at 2015–16 rates, £162,500.

CHAPTER 9

REDUCED RATE OF INHERITANCE TAX WHEN 10 PER CENT OF THE NET ESTATE LEFT TO CHARITY

1. TAX RELIEF TO ENCOURAGE CHARITABLE GIVING

9.01 In the 2011 Budget, the Chancellor set out a proposal to reduce the inheritance tax rate by 10% for taxpayers leaving 10% or more of their net estate to charity. After a consultation, legislation was enacted in the 2012 Finance Act.[1] This measure applies to estates where death occurs on or after 6 April 2012. The lower rate can only apply if part of the estate would otherwise be chargeable to inheritance tax at a rate other than 0%: in practice at 40%.[2]

9.02 It is not possible to identify whether or not the relief has encouraged additional charitable giving. The *UK Charity Tax Relief Statistics 1990-91 to 2013-14* published by HMRC on 27 Jun 2014 stated at page 12 that: '*IHT relief has increased by about 4% in 2012-13 and is expected to increase by a further 6% in 2013-14*'. However this change probably simply reflects the general rise caused by increased asset values following the slump in 2007 and the long term freeze in the nil rate band. One might expect the following:

(a) if the taxpayer is a higher or additional rate taxpayer, lifetime gifts obtaining relief under the gift aid scheme will be more attractive;

(b) in other cases, there may be a temptation to postpone the making of charitable gifts until death in order to secure the reduced IHT rate on the chargeable estate.

2. THE COMPOSITION OF AN INHERITANCE TAX ESTATE

9.03 The estate of a taxpayer for inheritance tax purposes at the time of his death may contain:

(a) his free estate: ie property passing under his will;

---

[1] See FA 2012, s 209 and Sch 33. This involved the insertion of a new Sch 1A into IHTA 1984. References are to paragraphs of that Schedule. See also IHTM 45000.

[2] The legislation refers to the part of the value transferred that is chargeable to inheritance tax at a rate other than 0% as 'TP': see para 1(2).

(b)   joint property passing by survivorship (the so-called *'ius accrescendi'*);[3]

(c)   settled property in which he had enjoyed a qualifying interest in possession (under IHTA 1984, s 49(1): see **3.05**);

(d)   it may also include property which the deceased had given away but in which he had reserved a benefit. This property is different from the three cases above in that it is owned by the donee of the gift or his successor. Its inclusion in the deceased's estate is therefore a fiction since ownership of the property does not change on his death.

Allocating the nil rate band[4]

9.04   On death, the deceased's available inheritance tax nil rate band is allocated *pro rata* between the different elements of the estate. Accordingly, if the estate comprises all four elements listed above and the value of each is £500,000 with the available nil rate band being £300,000, it follows that:

(a)   the total estate is worth £2 million;

(b)   the nil rate band is allocated equally between the four elements (each therefore benefitting from £75,000); and

(c)   in the absence of any reduced rate relief for inheritance tax, each element is taxed on £425,000 at 40% = £170,000.[5]

3. THE STATUTORY COMPONENTS

9.05   Paragraph 3 divides the taxpayer's estate into three 'components' as follows:

(a)   *The survivorship component:*[6] 'all the property comprised in the estate that, immediately before D's death, was joint (or common) property liable to pass on D's death ... by survivorship ...'[7]

---

3   The deceased's share as a tenant in common falls into his free estate.

4   Including any transferable nil rate band from a pre-deceasing spouse or civil partner.

5   A curious situation can arise when there is reservation of benefit property. It may be that the original gift involved a failed PET in which case there is a potential double charge to IHT: once on the gift and, again, because by virtue of FA 1986, s 102(3) the property is included in the donor's estate at death. Relief is afforded by the Inheritance Tax (Double Charges Relief) Regulations 1987, SI 1987/1130, reg 5 as a result of which the Revenue will tax either the failed PET or the property at death but not both and they will obviously take whichever value is the higher. Assume in the example in the text that at the time of the gift the property was worth £600,000, whereas it had fallen to £500,000 at death. Because HMRC will tax the failed PET this will use up the deceased's IHT nil rate band (so the donee will be taxed on £600,000 – £300,000 = £300,000 x 40% = £112,000) and the estate taxed at death (£1.5m ignoring the reservation property) will not benefit from any nil rate band so that tax will be at 40%. But if the property had risen in value (from £400,000 at the date of the gift) the Revenue will ignore the PET; include the £500,000 as part of the death estate which will benefit from the nil rate band which is now unused so that the calculation will be as set out above.

6   Paragraph 3(2).

7   The categorisation is not altered by a deed of variation which might operate to 'sever' the joint

It is unlikely that property in this component will pass to charity on the taxpayer's death: this will only happen if:

(i)   the charity was a joint tenant with the deceased; or

(ii) the joint tenancy is 'severed' by a post-death deed of variation and the share of the deceased redirected to charity.[8]

This component applies to all joint property owned by the deceased: for instance, he may jointly own a seaside cottage with his brother and an investment property in Spain with his son. The value of his interest in these two properties is comprised in the survivorship component.

9.06

(b)   *The settled property component*: this is made up of the value of all the settled property in which he was entitled to an interest in possession. Since the 2006 changes in the IHT treatment of settlements it is only 'qualifying' interests in possession which result in the beneficiary being deemed to own the settled property under IHTA 1984, s 49(1).

A deceased may, of course, have been entitled to an interest in more than one settlement. If so, the values will be aggregated to form the settled property component.

Family settlements sometimes provide for a charity to benefit: for instance, the trusts may be to A for life then equally between his niece and a named charity. Reduced rate relief may then be due. This will not be the case, however, if on the deceased's death there is a discretionary trust in favour of a class of beneficiaries including one or more charities even if an appointment in favour of charity is made soon after this death. This is because the relief requires the charitable gift to be comprised in the value transferred by the 'relevant transfer' which means the transfer of value that the deceased is treated as making immediately before his death.[9]

9.07

(c)   *The general component*: this is made up of all the property comprised in the estate other than property in the other two components (*viz* joint and settled property) and reservation of benefit property. Reservation of benefit property forms part of none of the components although, as will be discussed below, it may (if a merger election is made) benefit from the reduced IHT rate. The general component is therefore made up of what is often called the 'free estate': ie property capable of passing under the deceased's will.

---

tenancy thereby providing for the property to pass under the deceased's will. This is because IHTA 1984, Sched 1A, para 3(2) says that the survivorship component includes all the property comprised in the deceased's estate that, immediately *before* death was liable to pass by survivorship: see IHTM 45004.

[8]   For post-death variations, see generally Chapter 12.

[9]   Paragraphs 2(2); 4 and 10.

4. HOW THE INHERITANCE TAX RELIEF OPERATES

9.08 If the 10% test is met for any one of the three statutory components of the estate, that component is taxed at the reduced rate. The test is 'all or nothing' so that a gift of 9% of the component to charity will not give rise to any relief. It is most likely that the test will be met in respect of the free estate, but as already noted:

(a) in the case of settled property, the terms of the settlement might provide on the deceased's death for all or part of the settled fund to pass to charity (so that the 10% test is met for this component);

(b) exceptionally, property may be jointly owned by an individual and charity. In other cases, the surviving joint tenant(s) may by deed of variation (falling within IHTA 1984, s 142(1)) 'sever' the joint tenancy and redirect all or an appropriate part of the deceased's severed share to charity (so that, again, the 10% test may be met); or

(c) in the case of the free estate, the will may leave property on discretionary trusts for a class of beneficiaries including charities. If the trustees make an appointment in favour of charity within 2 years of death which is read back under IHTA 1984, s 144, the 10% test may then be met for this component.[10]

9.09 The division of the estate into the three components makes it easier for the relief to be obtained since:

(a) if all the components were to be treated as one, the 10% test would have to be met in respect of the total value;

(b) it is unlikely that any charitable giving will occur in the survivorship and settled property components;

(c) reservation of benefit property does not belong to the deceased (albeit that it is deemed to form part of his estate) so there is no question of it meeting the charitable giving condition.

5. WHEN THE INHERITANCE TAX RELIEF IS AVAILABLE

9.10 In the case of each component, first calculate 'the donated amount': that is, the value of the property gifted to charity. There is no restriction on the type of assets that can be so gifted, but it will be necessary to value the assets that are given.

Next, calculate the net value of the assets in that component ('the baseline amount'). This involves determining the part of the value transferred by the chargeable transfer on death that is attributable to the property in that component. This will involve deducting liabilities in the usual way together with:

---

[10]   See **13.11** *et seq* for a consideration of s 144.

(a)   any available inheritance tax nil rate band (including any transferred nil rate band from a pre-deceasing spouse or civil partner);

(b)   any exemptions (for example, the spouse and charity exemption); and

(c)   agricultural and business property relief which operates to reduce the value of assets in the component.

9.11   The value of property passing to charity (exempt under IHTA 1984, s 23(1)) is then added back in to give the baseline amount. Note therefore that this is made up of the value of the component that would attract tax at rates in excess of the nil rate band (since this is deducted) plus the charitable gift. Which makes sense, given that the charitable gift must be 10% in value of the total baseline amount.

Example 9.1

The deceased's free estate (i e the general component) comprises:

1.   private company shares attracting business property relief and worth £10 million, which are left to his son;

2.   a share as tenant in common in his main residence, which he leaves to his wife (valued at £250,000);

3.   a legacy of £50,000, which is left to charity;

4.   the residue of the estate comprising works of art, cash reserves and investments worth £600,000 in total, which he leaves to his daughter.

A full nil rate band is available. In determining the rate of inheritance tax that applies:

(a)   ignore the business property relief property and the spouse exempt gift;

(b)   accordingly, the baseline amount is £650,000 less his nil rate band of £325,000; that is, £325,000;

(c)   the charitable gift (of £50,000) is more than 10% of this amount (which is £32,500) and accordingly the chargeable estate for inheritance tax purposes (which will be £325,000 – £50,000 = £275,000) is taxed at the reduced rate of 36%, giving a tax liability of £99,000 (instead of being taxed at 40% which would have been £110,000 so giving a tax saving of £11,000).

9.12   The same exercise is then repeated for each of the other components when relevant (i e when the estate includes survivorship or settled property). It is of course possible for relief to become available because of events taking place after death: for instance:

(a)   if beneficiaries make a deed of variation in favour of charity which is 'read-back' into the will under IHTA 1984, s 142(1);

(b)   if loss on sale relief applies: i e if certain assets are sold after death for less than the market value at death.[11]

---

[11]   See generally **14.25** *et seq* for loss on sale relief.

The calculations involved can be arithmetically challenging. However, on the HMRC website at http://www.hmrc.gov.uk/inheritancetax/pass-money-property/charity-reduce.htm#4 there is a helpful calculator which can calculate the size of legacy required to obtain the rate reduction.

9.13 It is important to bear in mind that relief is only available (and needed) when all or part of the deceased's estate would otherwise suffer IHT: ie is taxed at rates in excess of the nil rate. At present, that means taxed at 40%. Remember also that the relief is limited to the chargeable transfer made on death: it cannot be used to reduce the tax payable on a failed PET because of the deceased's death within 7 years. This will have become a chargeable lifetime transfer.

6. ELECTING TO MERGE COMPONENTS[12]

9.14 Electing to merge components may be attractive if, for example, a substantial charitable gift is made by the deceased's will which exceeds 10% of the baseline amount for the general component and the deceased had also enjoyed either a qualifying life interest in settled property (the settled property component) or had owned joint property (the survivorship component). The effect of the election is to treat the merged components as one so that the 10% test is then applied to the merged components. This election can also be made in respect of reservation of benefit property which forms part of the deceased's estate but does not come within any of the three components.[13]

The election must be made by the 'appropriate persons', who are the personal representatives (for the free estate), the surviving joint owners (for the joint property component) the trustees (for the settled property component) and the donee (owner) of the reservation of benefit property.[14] The election must be made by notice in writing to HM Revenue and Customs within 2 years after the death of the deceased. It can be withdrawn by the same parties within the period of 2 years and one month of the deceased's death. (HM Revenue and Customs has a discretion to extend these time limits if, for example, asset values cannot be agreed.)[15]

Example 9.2

Marcus' will provides as follows:

1.   pecuniary legacies totalling £500,000 to godchildren;

2.   a gift of his dwelling house (a small 15th century manor house) to the National Trust (arrangements have been made for them to take this property);

---

[12]   Paragraph 7.
[13]   Paragraph 7(5)(b); 7(d).
[14]   Paragraph 7(6).
[15]   Paragraph 9.

3.   residue totalling £8m to be held on discretionary trusts for his family and charities.

In addition, Marcus had been the life tenant of a settlement established in 1980 by his grandfather which contains shares in the family go-carting business (valued at £2m) and artworks worth £2m. The settled property passes to his eldest son.

There is no joint property nor reservation of benefit property. Marcus' wife died some years ago leaving him all her assets so that there is an additional nil rate band available.

Does the reduced rate apply?

(a)   The estate comprises two components: the general and the settled property which must be considered separately.

(b)   In the *general component* it is first necessary to value the gift to charity: assume that the property is worth £3m. Deduct the value of the charitable gift and the general component's share of the nil rate band available on Marcus' death. For this purpose, the value of the general component is £8.5m (pecuniary legacies plus residue).

(c)   In the *settled property component* assume that 100% business property relief is available in respect of the shares which leaves the value of this component at £2m.

(d)   Accordingly the available nil rate band (£650,000) is divided as to 8.5/10.5 to the general component (£526,190) and 2/10.5 to the settled property component (£123,810).

(e)   Looking again at the general component the baseline amount is:

	£
Chargeable transfer	8,500,000.00
Deduct share of NRB	526,190.00
	£7,973,810.00
Add back charitable gift	3,000,000.00
Baseline amount	£10,973,810.00

10% of that is £1,097,381 and so, because the charitable gift of £3m is in excess of this sum the reduced IHT rate applies to the chargeable estate to produce tax of:

£7,973,810 x 36% =	2,870,571.60
instead of tax of	
£7,973,810 x 40% =	3,189,524.00

so producing a tax saving of £318,952.40.

(f)   So far as the settled property component is concerned, the tax position is as follows:

	£
Chargeable transfer	2,000,000.00

Deduct share of NRB	<u>123,810.00</u>
	£1,876,190.00
Tax at 40% =	750,476.00

(g)   However if the executors and the trustees agreed to merge the two components, the baseline amount would then become:

	£
General component	10,973,810.00
Settled component	<u>1,876,190.00</u>
	£12,850,000.00

10% of that is £1,285,000 and because the charitable gift exceeds that the reduced rate is available. Accordingly tax on the settled property becomes:

£1,876,190 x 36% =	675,428.40
	(a saving of £75,047.60)

7. ELECTING TO OPT OUT OF LOWER INHERITANCE TAX RATE[16]

9.15   The lower rate of inheritance tax will apply to any component where the 10% test is met, unless an election to opt out is made. The appropriate person and time limits are the same as for the merger election. It appears that the reason for this opt-out election is that the costs of valuing certain assets left to charity may outweigh any benefit from the inheritance tax rate reduction. However, it is questionable how often this will be the case: an opt out is most likely when private company shares not attracting business property relief are left to charity, which rarely happens.

8. MISCELLANEOUS TECHNICAL PROVISIONS

9.16   If a grossing-up calculation is required (for instance, where the will leaves the residue to charity and there are chargeable specific gifts), this is first done at the 36% rate of inheritance tax. As a result, it is easier to meet the 10% test.[17]

Example 9.3 (taken from IHT 45030)

Stephen died on 11 September 2012 leaving an estate valued at £1,000,000 after deduction of liabilities. The will left pecuniary legacies of £245,000 free of tax to his children and 10% of the residue to the RSPCA. To qualify for the reduced rate of tax, the amount passing to charity must be at least £67,500 (£1,000,000 – £325,000 = £675,000 x 10%).

---

[16]   Paragraph 8.
[17]   See para 6(1). For grossing up calculations, see **3.41** *et seq.*

Ignoring grossing up, the residue of the estate is £1,000,000 – £245,000 = £755,000. The donated amount would be £75,500 and so, initially, the estate appears to qualify for the reduced rate. But as there are legacies that are left free of tax, they must be grossed up to reflect the fact that in reality, the residue and so the share passing to charity will be reduced by the tax paid.

If the estate is grossed up at 40%, the calculations are as follows:

Initial residue (£1,000,000 – £245,000)	£755,000.00
less initial exempt residue (£755,000@10%)	£75,500.00
Initial chargeable residue	£679,500.00
Initial chargeable estate (£245,000 + £679,500)	£924,500.00
Tax on initial estate (£924,500 – £325,000) @ 40%	£239,800.00
Gross up gifts at estate rate (£245,000 x (£924,500 ÷ (£924,500 – £239,800))	£330,805.00
Final residue (£1,000,000 – £330,805)	£669,195.00
Donated amount (£669,195@10%)	£66,919.00

Grossing up the pecuniary legacies at full rate has increased their value for tax to £330,805. This must be fed into the calculation to determine the baseline amount as follows:

Estate on death	£1,000,000.00	
Legacy to charity (donated amount)	£66,919.00	
Chargeable transfer	£933,081.00	
		(step 1)
Less nil-rate band	£325,000.00	
	£608,081.00	
		(step 2)
Add back legacy to charity	£66,919.00	
Baseline amount	£675,000.00	
		(step 3)

The donated amount (£66,919) is less than 10% of the baseline (£67,500) so the estate does not qualify for the reduced rate when the legacy is grossed up at the full rate.

If the estate is grossed up at 36%, however, the calculations are as follows:

Initial chargeable estate – as above (£245,000 + £679,500)	£924,500.00
Tax on initial estate (£924,500 – £325,000)@36%	£215,820.00
Gross up gifts at estate rate (£245,000 x (£924,500 ÷ (£924,500 – £215,820))	£319,611.00
Final residue (£1,000,000 – £319,611)	£680,389.00
Donated amount (£680,389@10%)	£68,039.00

Here, the value of the legacies is grossed up to £319,611. The value of the residue is not reduced by quite so much as when the legacies are grossed up at 40%, so the donated amount is slightly higher. The baseline calculation is as follows:

Estate on death	£1,000,000.00
Legacy to charity (donated amount)	£68,039.00
Chargeable transfer	£931,96.00
	(step 1)
Less nil-rate band	£325,000.00
	£606,961.00
	(step 2)
Add back legacy to charity	£68,039.00
Baseline amount	£675,000.00
	(step 3)

The donated amount (£68,039) is now greater than 10% of the baseline (£67,500) so the estate qualifies for the reduced rate. The grossed up value of the legacies and the chargeable estate must be calculated using the 36% rate grossing calculator.

9.17 When it is necessary to allocate agricultural property relief or business property relief (for instance, where the relevant business or agricultural property is not specifically gifted and the estate is to be divided between charity and chargeable beneficiaries), the normal allocation rule contained in IHTA 1984, s 39A does not apply in calculating the amount given to charity. Again, this may make it easier to meet the 10% requirement.[18]

9.18 There are also specific provisions dealing with the situation where there are deferred inheritance tax charges (assets that attract conditional exemption from inheritance tax are ignored), but any recapture charge cannot benefit from the reduced rate. Successive charges relief (under IHTA 1984, s 141) has been appropriately amended by the insertion of a new s 141A.

9. PRACTICAL IMPLICATIONS

9.19 The practical implications of the reduced rate provisions are as follows:

(a) The legislation is complex and imposes burdens on personal representatives and will draftsmen. Whether the 10% test is met depends on factors at the time of the deceased's death: notably on the value of the assets then in the estate.[19] The draftsman may therefore use a discretionary trust so that account can be taken of the position at the time of death, with the trustees making an appointment of the requisite size in favour of

---

[18] Paragraph 6(2). For the allocation of the relief, see **10.55** *et seq.*

[19] And, of course, values may change during the administration, eg if land is sold for less than its value at the time of death so that although the reduced rate had not originally applied it may, as a result of the reduced value, come to apply.

charity to obtain reading-back under IHTA 1984, s 144. It is more likely, however, that a formula will be used to ensure that the conditions for the relief are met and the drafting involved is considered at **9.20** *et seq.*[20]

(b)   After a death beneficiaries may be able to achieve a tax saving by varying the dispositions of the estate to give more to charity thereby obtaining the benefit of the reduced rate.

If the deceased left 4% of his net estate to charity, the gift can be increased to 10% (by the use of a deed of variation) without the chargeable beneficiaries suffering any reduction in the value of the benefits that they receive; that is, the cost of the increase is wholly borne by HM Revenue and Customs. When the gift falls in the range of 5% to 9% and is increased to 10%, the beneficiaries will also receive more as the following table illustrates.

Example 9.4

Assume baseline amount = 100

Gift to charity (%)	3	4	9	10
Inheritance tax rate on rest of estate (%)	40	40	40	36
Other beneficiaries receive (%)	58.2	57.6	54.6	57.6

9.20   Assume that the gift to charity amounts to 9% of the baseline amount. To increase that gift by a further 1% will:

(a)   mean that the charity gets slightly more;

(b)   increase the entitlement of the chargeable beneficiaries by 3%.

Are the PRs under any duty to point this out to the beneficiaries? It is thought not (although obviously if the matter is raised it should be considered) because:

(i)   the job of the PRs is to administer the estate in accordance with the terms of the deceased's will, not to come up with suggested variations to the will;

(ii)   this finds support in the case of *Cancer Research Campaign v Ernest Brown*[21] in which the deceased left property to his sister who died soon afterwards leaving her estate to charities. The charities sued the solicitors for negligence in that they should have advised the sister to vary the gift from her brother in favour of the charities. The action failed on the basis that the sister was perfectly entitled to retain the inherited assets.[22] Further, the sister's executors were under no duty to take steps to reduce

---

[20]   In their guidance, HMRC include a draft will clause which is closely modelled on one produced by the Society of Trust and Estate Practitioners – www.step.org. See IHTM 45008.

[21]   [1997] STC 1425.

[22]   Harman J commented that the sister might have considered that 'tax avoidance was something rather unattractive, to be indulged in by sharp people with connections with the City of London who use various arcane devices to get out of their proper obligations to the Crown'.

the tax burden on the charities since 'the duties imposed by law' did not include a duty to advise on 'the entry into a scheme of tax avoidance'.[23]

9.21   There is no point in discussing the reduced rate with a client if:

- the whole estate is going to charity;
- no IHT is payable either because the estate is below the limit of the nil rate band or because the rest of the estate is eligible for 100% relief or going to a spouse or civil partner;
- only a token amount is going to charity;
- the client does not want to make a gift to charity.

10. DRAFTING WILLS TO TAKE ADVANTAGE OF THE REDUCED INHERITANCE TAX RATE WHEN CHARITABLE GIFTS ARE TO BE MADE

Drafting basics

9.22   It is, of course, possible to leave a stated sum (or property eg stocks and shares) to charity, but it will then be necessary to ensure that it meets the 10% test and this will be determined at the date of death. Consequently there is a risk that if a fixed sum or assets are given to charity and the other assets in the estate rise in value after the date of the will that the test will not be met. Accordingly there would be a need to monitor the property values and, if necessary, to revise the size of the charitable legacy. To avoid such complications the draftsman may prefer to employ a formula to ensure that – whatever the value of the estate – the legacy to charity will always meet the 10% test.

This will involve using terms from the legislation which should be defined as such in the will.

The basic formula gift

9.23

> '1.1   I give to [insert name of charity] such a sum as shall be equal to 10% of the baseline amount in relation to the general component of my estate.
> 1.2   In this clause "baseline amount" and "general component" have the meanings given to those terms in Schedule 1A of the Inheritance Tax Act 1984.'

---

23   For variations made on behalf of a deceased beneficiary, see Chapter 12.

Merging components?

9.24 The testator may wish to provide in his will for the charitable gift to be large enough to satisfy the 10% test in respect of components[24] in addition to the general component to ensure that other parts of his IHT estate will benefit from a 36% IHT rate.

The above clause may accordingly be modified as follows:

> '... 10% of the baseline amount in relation to the aggregate of the general component and [insert other component(s)/reservation of benefit property] of my estate.'

Then amend the definition clause to include other terms used (eg the survivorship component) or in the case of reservation of benefit property define it as:

> 'property treated as part of my estate as a result of section 102(3) of the Finance Act 1986.'

The election to merge components

9.25 In appropriate cases, it will be desirable to give the PRs an express power to make the election provided for in para 7. In cases where the will is to provide for the baseline amount to be calculated by including the general and other component(s) then the will should *require* the PRs to make the election. Cases may arise where PRs have to decide which of two components to merge with and the will may therefore provide that the trustees may exercise their power 'as they shall in their absolute discretion think fit'. Of course this situation will only arise if the charity gift does not depend upon the above formula so that there may be a 'surplus' because the size of the gift exceeds 10% of the baseline amount for the general component.

Specifying a maximum and/or a minimum

9.26 With any sum calculated by reference to a formula, an issue is that the amount payable cannot be known until the death of the testator (which is when the value of the general component, and hence the baseline amount, will be known). A testator may feel that he wants the charity to have a certain amount even if that exceeds 10%: alternatively, he may be concerned to ensure that the gift to the charity does not exceed a certain figure. A clause could be inserted to deal with these concerns: for instance:

> 'Provided always that the legacy given by clause 1.1 shall:
>
> (a)   not be less than £X; and

---

[24]   Including reservation of benefit property: see **9.14**.

(b)   shall not exceed £Y even if the result is that the lower rate of tax will not apply.'[25]

Similar issues have always been faced when a nil rate band gift (eg to the testator's children) is to be made since the amount of the nil rate band will be unknown at the time when the will is executed.[26] Occasionally a ceiling is placed on the amount (especially if the nil rate gift is, say, to children and will deplete the estate passing to a surviving spouse). However, in general the evidence suggests that this has not happened and it seems likely that testators will be comfortable with a 10% gift to charity and will not feel the need to include a maximum.[27]

Other clauses

9.27   It is not felt that giving the trustees power to opt out of the IHT lower rate (by making the election under para 8) is appropriate when a formula gift of this type is involved. The rationale for including the election in the legislation is that there may be some cases when valuing the gift to charity (presumably if it is of, say, private company shares) is likely to exceed the benefit of any tax saved.

Any well-drafted will is likely to include a standard charity receipts clause and a clause allowing the PRs to appropriate assets to satisfy the legacy so repeating these clauses is not necessary.

Conclusion

9.28   It is suggested that the basic drafting will involve one of the following precedents.

---

[25]   It is only in respect of a maximum ceiling on the gift that the benefit of the reduced IHT rate may be lost. Define 'the lower rate of tax' in the definition clause.

[26]   Dramatic increases in the nil rate band have occurred in the past: for instance, on 6 April 1996 it went up from £154,000 to £200,000.

[27]   Especially when it is remembered that the 10% amount is of the estate after deducting the nil rate band.

PRECEDENTS

Precedent 9.1: Formula gift (general component only)

1.1   I give to [insert name of charity or charities[28]] such a sum as shall be equal to 10% of the baseline amount in relation to the general component of my estate.

1.2   In this clause 'baseline amount' and 'general component' have the meanings given to those terms in Schedule 1A of the Inheritance Tax Act 1984.

(It is not thought that other clauses are needed.)

---

[28]   If more than one charity then specify the shares in which they are to take.

Precedent 9.2: Formula gift (merging components)

1.1 I give to [insert name of charity or charities] such a sum as shall be equal to 10% of the baseline amount in relation to the general component and survivorship component[29] of my estate.

1.2 In this clause 'baseline amount' 'general component' and 'survivorship component' shall have the meanings given to those terms in Schedule 1A of the Inheritance Tax Act 1984.

2. My trustees shall make the election under paragraph 7 of Schedule 1A of the Inheritance Tax Act 1984 to merge the general and survivorship components of my estate.[30]

---

[29] Or as the case may be. For instance, it might be 'the settled property component' or 'the reservation of benefit property' or all four! Remember to revise the definition clause accordingly.

[30] Of course surviving joint tenants would need to join in this merger election: see para 7.

Precedent 9.3: Gift of specific sum or other property to charity

1. I give [specify property] to [identify charity].
2. My trustees shall have power to make the election under paragraph 7 of Schedule 1A of the Inheritance Tax Act 1984 as they shall in their absolute discretion think fit.

CHAPTER 10

AGRICULTURAL AND BUSINESS PROPERTY

This chapter looks at two main areas:

(a) general matters those drafting wills should consider when the testator has a family business or company, such as who is to inherit the business but (and especially in the short term) how the business is to be run;

(b) the scope and use of the two IHT valuation reliefs: business property relief (BPR) and agricultural property relief (APR).

1. SUCCESSION PLANNING

10.01   When taking instructions for a will from someone who owns a business or an interest in a business, it is important to discuss the testator's plans for the business after his death. In the case of a sole trader there may be an heir apparent to whom the business can be left; if so, it will usually be convenient to make the donee a special executor of that part of the estate.[1] If the donee is one of the testator's children, there may be difficulties achieving a distribution which satisfies all the children. Where the other assets are limited, it may be possible to make some provision for the others by giving one child an option to purchase the business at a reduced price, and using the proceeds to fund legacies for the other children.[2]

10.02   Where the testator is a partner in a business, any partnership deed or agreement should be consulted before drafting any gift of the interest in the business. Such a document may provide that on the death of any partner, the surviving partners may buy the testator's interest in the partnership from his estate. From an IHT perspective it is important that the deceased is not regarded as dying with a binding contract in place to sell the partnership interest to the surviving partners. This would result in a loss of business property relief as the testator would be treated as dying entitled to the proceeds of sale rather than the business.[3] HMRC have accepted that options to buy and even automatic accruer clauses do not constitute binding contracts for sale.[4] To avoid arguments after the death, the partnership agreement should deal with the basis of valuation of partnership assets. This may be the current market

---

[1]   See **Precedent 10.2.**
[2]   See **Precedent 10.5.**
[3]   IHTA 1984, s 113.
[4]   See *Law Society's Gazette,* 4 September 1996.

value at the date of the death (likely to be the most beneficial for the deceased's estate), or the historic value at which assets are carried in the partnership's accounts (likely to benefit the continuing partners). There is no presumption as to the basis. It is simply a matter of evidence of intention. Failure to clarify the basis before death may lead to prolonged and expensive argument between beneficiaries and the surviving partners.[5]

Where there is no partnership deed or agreement, or where there is such a document but it contains no provisions for the death of a partner, then the death of any partner causes the dissolution of the partnership,[6] and the amount due to the deceased partner for his interest must be paid to his personal representatives. This is not normally what the parties would want.

10.03   In all cases involving an unincorporated business, it is important to identify what assets comprise business property. For instance, in the case of a sole trader which bank accounts and other assets are comprised in the business? In the case of a partnership which assets are partnership property, and which are merely used by the partnership?

10.04   If the business in question is incorporated, the testator can leave his shareholding to whoever he chooses, subject to any pre-emption rights contained in the articles of association. Accordingly it is important to consider the articles when taking instructions for the will. If the client does not want to comply with the pre-emption rights, it may be possible to alter the articles. This requires a 75% majority in general meeting. If the testator has a sufficiently large shareholding, he can do this alone. In other cases he will need the support of other shareholders. Failure to alter the articles will mean that the testator's beneficiary will take the shares subject to the pre-emption rights.[7]

It may be that the articles provide for the appointment by will of a permanent director to succeed the testator if he himself was a permanent director.

Precedents 10.1–10.6 should be considered in the light of the trustees' powers to appoint agents and nominees under the Trustee Act 2000, s 11.

2. APR AND BPR GENERAL ASPECTS

10.05   These two reliefs are amongst the most valuable in the IHT legislation: they are valuation reliefs which can reduce the value of the relevant property by 100%. We will first consider the requirements to be satisfied if the reliefs are to be available and then the best way to draft wills to ensure that relief is not wasted.

---

[5]   See *Re White, deceased, White v Minnis* [2001] Ch 393, [2000] 3 All ER 618, [2000] WTLR 755 (CA) and *Drake v Harvey* [2010] EWHC 1446 (Ch).
[6]   PA 1890, s 33.
[7]   See *Cottrell v King* [2004] EWHC 397 (Ch), [2005] WTLR 63.

10.06 The two reliefs are similar (in that both are concerned with businesses[8]) and overlap but the following distinctions are worthy of note:

(a) APR is given in priority to BPR;[9]

(b) differences exist in the treatment of woodlands, crops, livestock, deadstock, plant and machinery, and farmhouses, etc. When APR does not apply, consider whether BPR is available (it can apply to any part of the value transferred which is not relieved under APR: for instance on the hope value of agricultural land);

(c) at one time APR was only available on property situated in the UK, Channel Islands and Isle of Man whereas BPR was not so restricted. After an ECJ decision, FA 2009 changed this, allowing APR and woodlands relief for property in the EEA. This change was significant in respect of:
   (i) let farmland in the EEA;
   (ii) a farmhouse situated in the EEA.
   In both situations BPR (which has always applied to a business anywhere in the world) would not have applied to make good the absence of APR.

Where agricultural property is replaced by business property and vice versa, relief may continue to be available (without the need to satisfy the minimum ownership period) despite the change. In 1994,[10] the Revenue commented that:

> 'Where agricultural property which is a farming business is replaced by a non-agricultural business property, the period of ownership of the original property will be relevant for applying the minimum ownership condition to the replacement property. Business property relief will be available on the replacement if all the conditions for that relief were satisfied. Where non-agricultural business property is replaced by a farming business and the latter is not eligible for agricultural property relief, s 114(1) does not exclude business property relief if the conditions for that relief are satisfied.
>
> Where the donee of the PET of a farming business sells the business and replaces it with a non-agricultural business the effect of s 124A(1) is to deny agricultural property relief on the value transferred by the PET. Consequently s 114(1) does not exclude business property relief if the conditions for that relief are satisfied: and, in the reverse situation, the farming business acquired by the donee can be "relevant business property" for the purposes of s 113B(3)(c).'

Example 10.1

Rufus has for many years farmed at Little Wallop. In all, some 200 acres is under cultivation and Rufus lives in the Grade II listed farmhouse, Wallop Hall. The farm

---

[8] In the case of APR see *Dixon v IRC* [2002] STC (SCD) 53. APR was not available because there was no history of agricultural production (certainly no commercial activity was undertaken) and the evidence was that the property was merely occupied for the purposes of a private residence. Even for APR (in the case of BPR it is required that the business be carried on for gain: see s 103(s)) it is therefore thought that there needs to be a business (*viz* the intention to make a profit).

[9] IHTA 1984, s 114(1).

[10] *Tax Bulletin* 1994, p 182: see now RI 95.

machinery is stored in a magnificent barn and two farm cottages are occupied by farm workers (one has recently retired). Other cottages have been renovated and are now run as furnished holiday lettings. A small area of the land, adjacent to the proposed Dorset expressway, has development potential. In considering the reliefs available to Rufus:

1.   first consider APR which will be available on the agricultural value of the land.[11] It may also be given on the farm cottages (including the one occupied by the retired farm worker) and the farmhouse, provided that it is of a 'character appropriate' to the property;[12]

2.   business property relief may then be available on the farm machinery and on the 'hope' value of the land adjacent to the expressway. It is unlikely to be given on the let cottages because furnished holiday lettings is generally an investment activity (in the light of the *Pawson* decision). However, relief may be given on the business looked at 'in the round' because the mixed business carried on by Rufus is not 'mainly' that of holding investments.[13]

10.07   In the case of both reliefs, a minimum ownership period has to be satisfied before relief is available: in the case of BPR, a 2-year period is required.[14] So far as APR is concerned, s 117 imposes a minimum period of ownership or occupation which is 2 years when the agricultural property is occupied by the transferor and 7 years when occupied by the owner or another (eg when the land is let).[15]

3. AGRICULTURAL PROPERTY RELIEF

10.08   APR is given on the agricultural value of 'agricultural property'. Agricultural property is defined by s 115(2) which, for convenience, may be divided into three limbs:

(a)   'agricultural land or pasture' ('*Limb 1*');

(b)   'and includes woodland and any building used in connection with the intensive rearing of livestock or fish if the woodland or building is occupied with agricultural land or pasture and the occupation is ancillary to that of agricultural land or pasture' ('*Limb 2*');

(c)   'and also includes such cottages, farm buildings and farmhouses, together with the land occupied with them, as are of a character appropriate to the property' ('*Limb 3*').

---

[11]   See **10.10**.

[12]   See **10.11**.

[13]   See the discussion of *Brander v RCC* [2009] SFTD 374 *affd* [2010] STC 2666 at **10.24**. The *Pawson* decision is discussed at **10.40** *et seq*.

[14]   In recent years investment in AIM portfolios has become popular for taxpayers who are likely to survive 2 but not 7 years. Beware that not all AIM shares qualify and that such investments carry a substantial risk element.

[15]   In BPR there are rules dealing with replacement property (in s 107 which deals, inter alia, with the incorporation of a business and the formation of a partnership) which were considered in the *Brander* case (see **10.26**) and with successions (in s 108). In the case of APR, equivalent provisions are in s 118 (replacements) and s 120 (successions).

It is important to appreciate that it is the agricultural land which is the dominant property: the property in Limbs 2 and 3 is essentially ancillary to the land.

10.09 The critical issues that arise in connection with APR are:

(a) the limitation of the relief to the 'agricultural value' of the agricultural property;

(b) in Limb 3, the 'character appropriate' test (including the meaning in Limb 3 of 'the property');

(c) the meaning of 'a farmhouse' in Limb 3;

(d) the meaning of 'occupied for agricultural purposes';

(e) getting relief at 100% instead of 50%.

We will consider each of these issues in turn.

Relief is given on the 'agricultural value'

10.10 APR is given only on the 'agricultural value' of agricultural property. 'Agricultural value' is defined in s 115(3) as follows:

> 'For the purposes of this Chapter the agricultural value of any agricultural property shall be taken to be the value which would be the value of the property if the property were subject to a perpetual covenant prohibiting its use otherwise than as agricultural property.'

In the *Antrobus* case[16] before the Land Tribunal, it was agreed that the market value of Cookhill Priory[17] was £608,475 but the Tribunal decided that the agricultural value was only £425,932.50 (ie a discount of some 30% on the market value). The taxpayers argued that the property would remain a farmhouse if purchased by someone who carried on a farming business on the land even though he might spend little time in the business.[18] Thus they would have been unaffected by the s 115(3) covenant since they would have complied with it and as they will be the highest bidders in the market the agricultural

---

[16] See in the matter of a notice of reference between *Lloyds TSB Private Banking plc (as PRs of Antrobus deceased)* and *Peter Twiddy* (IR Capital Taxes) decision dated 10 October 2005.

[17] It was accepted by HMRC that this property was a farmhouse: see further **10.18**.

[18] The so-called 'lifestyle farmer'. Giving expert evidence for the taxpayers Mr Clive Beer commented that: 'There were at least three ways in which a lifestyle buyer could carry on a farming business without prior experience and without spending much time at the farm. Firstly, the land could be farmed with the assistance of one or more employees, for example a farm manager, or through a contract farming arrangement. Secondly, the land could be farmed in partnership with an active local farmer. Thirdly, the new owner could come to a share-farming arrangement, whereby the landowner would grow grass or other crops for sale to a local livestock farmer, whose cattle or sheep would eat down the crop which he had bought in situ. Whichever of these methods was adopted by the lifestyle farmer, the farmhouse would continue to be occupied by him and used as agricultural property.'

value would therefore be equal to the amount which the highest bidder would pay.[19] This was rejected by the Tribunal in the following terms:

'A farmhouse is the chief dwelling-house attached to a farm, the house in which the farmer of the land lives. There is, we think, no dispute about the definition when it is expressed in this way. The question is: who is the farmer of the land for the purpose of the definition in section 115(2)? In our view it is the person who lives in the farmhouse in order to farm the land comprised in the farm and who farms the land on a day to day basis. It is likely, although it may not necessarily always be the case, that his principal occupation will consist of farming the land comprised in the farm. We do not think that a house occupied with a farm is a farmhouse simply because the person living there is in overall control of the agricultural business conducted on the land; and in particular we think that the lifestyle farmer, the person whose bid for the land is treated by the appellant as establishing the agricultural value of the land, is not the farmer for the purposes of the provisions.'[20]

The 'character appropriate' test

10.11 In the *Antrobus* case[21] the Special Commissioner identified the following factors as being relevant:

'the principles which have been established for deciding whether a farmhouse is of a character appropriate to the property may be summarised as: first, one should consider whether the house is appropriate by reference to its size, content and layout, with the farm buildings and the particular area of farmland being framed (see *IRC v Korner*[22]); secondly, one should consider whether the house is proportionate in size and nature to the requirements of the farming activities conducted on the agricultural land or pasture in question (see *Starke v IRC*[23]); thirdly, that although one cannot describe a farmhouse which satisfies the "character appropriate" test one knows one when one sees it (see *Dixon v IRC*[24]); fourthly, one should ask whether the educated rural layman would regard the property as a house with land or a farm (see *Dixon*); and, finally, one should consider the historical dimension and ask how long the house in question has been associated with the agricultural property and whether there was a history of agricultural production (see *Dixon*).'

In *McKenna*,[25] the Special Commissioner added a further factor: the relationship between the value of the land and the profitability of the land.[26] In

---

[19] Mr Beer accepted that the open market value would have to be discounted for any actual or potential non-agricultural uses of the property to which additional value might be attributable (eg any value attributable to sporting rights; development potential or mineral rights). It appears that there were no such factors present in this case.

[20] See further the *McKenna* case at **10.18** below.

[21] *Lloyds TSB (PRs of Antrobus dec'd) v IRC* [2002] STC (SCD) 468.

[22] [1969] SC (HL) 13.

[23] [1994] STC 295, [1994] 1 WLR 888.

[24] [2002] STC (SCD) 53.

[25] *Arnander & Ors (Exors of McKenna dec'd) v RCC* [2006] STC (SCD) 800. See **10.16**.

[26] From the evidence of comparables it was clear that Rosteague House was at the 'top end' of the size of a Cornish farmhouse and that a house of that size would generally have more land. It

that case she concluded that the return from agriculture (a profit of £6,820 in 1998 falling to a loss of £7,975 in 1994) 'would not provide a living income for a person who paid over £3m for the whole estate and so would not attract demand from a commercial farmer'.[27]

10.12 In the *Golding* case[28] the taxpayer owned a farmhouse with 16.29 acres. He died aged 81 and in the years before his death he had scaled down his farming operations[29] to the extent that at the time of death he owned 70 hens laying free range eggs and had some 15–20 customers who would buy the eggs at the farm gate. Despite this the First-tier Tribunal commented 'We are satisfied, however, that in a very limited way he was still working on the farm when he died'. His income from the farming was just over £1,000 pa which was less than 25% of his total income. The farmhouse and buildings were in a poor condition.

10.13 The Revenue accepted that the house was a farmhouse[30] but did not accept that it was of a character appropriate to the farm. They argued that:

'the relevant factors in deciding whether the dwelling house is character appropriate, are the level of farming activity and the functional requirement or otherwise of the dwelling house … in the case of small areas of land the market did not consider it necessary to retain the house in the same ownership because the land could be sold separately … the level of activity being conducted on the subject land did not give rise to a functional requirement for a dwelling house to serve the farming of that land.'

The Tribunal rejected these arguments deciding that the fact that the farm made only a small profit did not affect the position (in the *Antrobus* case the farm consistently made losses):

'It seems to us that the question to be asked is "was the deceased farming?". At 80 years of age, it would be unreasonable to expect that to be an extensive activity. In fact if one did, there would be very few farms which would qualify as "character appropriate" … We suspect that as farming is very much a vocational activity, farmers are prepared to forego luxuries.'[31]

---

only came into use as a farmhouse in 1984 (so the historical association was weak) whilst lack of repair went, she considered, to value rather than character.

[27] At para 113.

[28] *Golding v RCC* [2011] UKFTT 351 (TC).

[29] At one time he had 600 free range chickens; 7–10 cattle; harvested fruit off the fruit trees and grew vegetables.

[30] Although they seem to have had some doubts about this – in the event they were not allowed to reopen this question.

[31] See IHTM24053 where the significance of the case is played down:
'each case is judged on its own particular facts. It is unlikely that the facts will be the same as those of *Golding* in many cases … in assessing whether or not property is proportionate to the farming activities undertaken, it remains HMRC's view that the income or profit of a farmer is a useful indicator of the activities undertaken, particularly in extreme cases.'

The nexus required

10.14 The character appropriate test must be satisfied in relation to 'the property'. The *Rosser* case considered what was meant by 'the property' and concluded that:[32]

> 'the nexus between the farm buildings and the property in s 115(2) is that the farm buildings and the property must be in the estate of the person at the time of making the deemed disposition under s 4(1) of the 1984 Act. The alternative view that the farm buildings are in the estate but the property to which they refer is not is untenable. This view would seriously undermine the structure for inheritance tax and create considerable uncertainty about when tax is chargeable and the amount of the value transferred. I would add, however, that estate is defined in the 1984 Act as the aggregate of all property to which the person is beneficially entitled. Property is widely defined in the 1984 Act to include rights and interests of any description. It will therefore cover not only tangible property but also equitable rights, debts and other choses in action, and indeed any rights capable of being reduced to money value.'

The *Hanson*[33] case

10.15 At the time of his death the Deceased was tenant for life of a farmhouse occupied by his son from which the son farmed 128 acres of land, which he owned together with a smaller area owned by the Deceased and 20 acres rented from a third party. It was agreed:

(a) that the house in question was a farmhouse (even on the Revenue view that the necessary nexus was common ownership, the house was still a farmhouse by reference to the farming activities of the son in relation to the land owned by the Deceased);[34]

(b) that if the 128 acres were to be taken into account the character appropriate test was met but if it was not to be included then the farmhouse would fail that test and so no relief would be available.

The case therefore turned on whether the necessary nexus was common ownership or common occupation. If the former, as the Revenue contended, then the 128 acres must be excluded whereas if the latter they must be included.[35]

10.16 The Tribunal decided that:

(a) the definition of 'agricultural property' in s 115(2) must be construed as a whole: the division into three limbs was for convenience with 'each limb

---

[32] *Rosser v RCC* [2003] STC (SCD) 311 at para 55.

[33] *Hanson v RCC* [2012] UKFTT 95 (TC) *aff'd* [2013] UKUT 0224 (TCC).

[34] See para 48.

[35] It was accepted that there had to be some nexus between the property in Limb 3 and the agricultural land: a house cannot be a farmhouse merely because of the existence of adjoining land. See para 46.

informing the meaning of the others'. It was not helpful to delve back into the history of the definition since 1894 ('an exercise of legislative archaeology');[36]

(b) in considering what agricultural property is capable of attracting relief, in addition to a freehold or leasehold interest in land, 'anything which the law recognises as an interest in land and which would give rise to an inheritance tax charge on death as an asset of the deceased's estate ought, in principle, to be capable of attracting relief';[37]

(c) in terms of the required nexus, occupation is not the only possible alternative to ownership: 'a different nexus might be established by seeing what agricultural land the ... farmhouse actually services';[38]

Example 10.2

F owns and occupies a farmhouse which serves farmland owned and occupied by a family company in which F is Managing Director and a minority shareholder.[39] On these facts, the Tribunal commented that 'it is at least arguable that there is a sufficient nexus'.

(a) the common ownership test as accepted by the Special Commissioner in *Rosser* is rejected 'whether or not the actual result is correct';[40]

(b) Limb 2 provides for a nexus based on common occupation and it would be 'odd' if the Limb 3 nexus was different;

(c) the common occupation test may result in relief being due on a farmhouse even though the taxpayer owned no agricultural land (ie where the farmhouse was occupied by another with land in his ownership);[41]

(d) it is not correct to see the sole purpose of APR as being 'to facilitate the continuance of farming after the death of the farmer': that is merely one purpose;[42]

Example 10.3

A owns a farm and appropriate farmhouse which has been let for many years. On A's death, APR will be available although it has nothing to do with the continuance of the farming business by the tenant.

(e) the Tribunal gave a number of examples to illustrate the difficulties and anomalies that could arise if the nexus was based on common ownership;

---

[36] Paragraphs 11–12.
[37] Paragraph 15.
[38] Paragraph 19.
[39] Contrast the position if he had been a majority shareholder when IHTA 1984, s 119(1) treats him as occupying the land.
[40] Paragraph 23.
[41] See also the example of a lifetime gift of the farmhouse divorced from the land in para 61.
[42] Paragraphs 40–41.

Example 10.4 (para 51)

Working farmer (F) occupies a farm including the farmhouse under a tenancy. Just before his death he acquires the freehold interest in the farmhouse. Relief is available since he has occupied the agricultural property for many years (ie the requirement in s 117(a) is met) and the necessary nexus derives from the tenancy over the land (even if the tenancy was at market rent with no capital value). The Tribunal commented that '*the nexus is relevant only to ascertaining the relevant agricultural property as a physical piece of land*'.

Example 10.5 (para 54)

F gives most of the farmland to son A. He moves out of the farmhouse (which he continues to own along with some land). A lives in the farmhouse from which he operates the same business as F. On F's death the house attracts no relief on the Revenue's approach since there is no ownership nexus with the land given away. But the position would be different if A had been given a 999 year lease at a peppercorn rent since F would then have retained the freehold interest (albeit it would be of little value).

Example 10.6 (para 55 et seq)

A owns a farm including the farmhouse which is let to T. On the death of both A and T relief will be due. But if the freehold in the land was owned by A's brother B, then on the death of T and B relief would be due but on the death of A, on the Revenue view, because of no land ownership no relief would be due.

Example 10.7 (para 60)

F owns a farm including a farmhouse. He lets the greater part of the land to a neighbour, retaining the farmhouse and a small area of land. On the common occupation test, the farmhouse does not attract relief but on the common ownership test (which includes the freehold interest in the let land) it does.

10.17 The common occupation test would not have affected the result in *Rosser* where the farmhouse was not occupied with the 39 acres of land given away. In cases where the taxpayer farms in a partnership with the land being partnership property but the farmhouse being owned by him, the common occupation test (given that the taxpayer occupies the land *qua* partner) will be met whatever his partnership share. When the farming in such a case is through the family company, IHTA 1984, s 119 attributes occupation by the company to a controlling shareholder: in other cases, the common occupation nexus will not be met.

What is a farmhouse?

10.18 In the leading case[43] Mr McKenna died on 29 January 2003 and his wife, Lady Cecilia, on 16 June 2003. From 1997 they had been the joint owners of the Rosteague Estate. This comprised a substantial Grade II* house (Rosteague House); some 187 acres (of which around 52 were foreshore and

---

[43]   *Arnander & Ors (Exors of McKenna dec'd) v RCC* [2006] STC (SCD) 800.

110 agricultural land); various farm outbuildings and a cottage, stable flat and lodge. The estate had originally been purchased by Mr McKenna in 1945 as a second home and only occupied as the main home on his retirement in 1984. Initially the land was tenanted but in 1984 the tenancy was surrendered and thereafter it was contract farmed under a succession of agreements with different contractors. A land agent, acting for the McKennas, was responsible for the management of the land, the farming activities and dealing with the contractors. He purchased a property on the estate and hence was on the spot to supervise and manage the farming operation. At the date of death, Mr McKenna was aged 91 and had suffered from ill health since 1997. After his death Lady Cecilia, who was aged 92 and who had suffered from ill health since a heart seizure in 1998, entered a nursing home. The Special Commissioner decided that Rosteague House was not a farmhouse.[44]

10.19 The Special Commissioner made the following general comments on the meaning of 'farmhouse' in IHTA 1984, s 115(2):

(a) the wording of the legislation makes it clear that the agricultural land is paramount: other things must be either ancillary or of a character appropriate to the land;

(b) there is nothing to suggest that every farm must have a farmhouse: the reference in s 115(2) is to farmhouses generally;

(c) she adopted the definition given in the *Rosser* case[45] as 'a dwelling for the farmer from which the farm is managed' and accepted that the Land Tribunal conclusion in *Antrobus II* that 'the farmer of the land is the person who farms it on a day to day basis rather than the person who is in overall control of the agricultural business conducted on the land' was a 'helpful principle';

(d) the status of the occupier of the property is not the test: rather it is the purpose of the occupation which is relevant;

(e) whether a building is a farmhouse is a matter of fact to be decided on the circumstances of each case and according to ordinary ideas of what is appropriate in terms of size, content and layout in the context of the particular farm buildings and the area of land farmed.

It was the land agent who was responsible for the management of the farming operation (albeit as agent for the McKennas). Hence:[46]

'the purpose of Mr McKenna's occupation of Rosteague House was not to undertake the day to day farming activities. In any even ... Rosteague House was

---

[44] The sale particulars (the estate was sold for in excess of £3m after the McKennas' deaths) described the house as follows: 'long hall, dining room, library, study, drawing room, flower room, main foyer and stairs, cloakroom, rear hall, kitchen, staff sitting room, back kitchen, seven bedrooms, three bathrooms, sewing room, laundry room, staff flat, detached lodge, cottage, music room, garage, gardens, range of outbuildings.' There was no mention of it being a farmhouse!

[45] [2002] STC (SCD) 311 at para 53.

[46] At para 92.

larger, grander, more elaborate and more expensive than was required for the reduced farming purposes for which it was in fact used. Its size, content and layout, taken in conjunction with the farm buildings and the particular area of farm being farmed points to the conclusion that it was primarily a rich man's residence rather than a farmhouse.'

10.20 Perhaps inevitably, the above statements give rise to unresolved queries: for instance:

(a)   does it matter that there is a farm office which is separate from the farmer's house (typically it may be in a converted barn)? That will leave the house as the dwelling for the farmer but not the place from which the farm is managed. However, given that the farmer is living in the property because he is farming the land, this should not matter;

(b)   is the condition of the property a significant factor? In some of the cases the run down condition of the property has been commented on – consider the following from *Golding*:

> 'From the photographs provided by the experts, it seems to us that the state and condition of the farm is such that it would be acceptable as a farmhouse. The kitchen is spartan at best; we have been told that apples were stored in one of the bedrooms; there was no electricity in any of the bedrooms upstairs so that they could only have been functional for sleeping and it appears storage of farm produce; the bathroom was downstairs, which would have been very convenient for Mr Golding, when coming in having worked on the farm.'

In principle it is difficult to see why this should be determinative: there is no reason why a farmhouse cannot be (say) a new modernist construction which has replaced the old property;

(c)   suggestions that the occupier of the farmhouse should farm the land on a day to day basis may also be doubted. Whilst the farming business has to be run by the farmer, that may be via a contract farming arrangement. The Land Tribunal in the *Antrobus* case further commented that:

> 'it is likely, although it may not necessarily always be the case, that his principal occupation will consist of farming the land comprised in the farm.'

This also seems too restrictive.

When is agricultural property 'occupied for the purpose of agriculture'?[47]

10.21 The legislation requires the property to be occupied for the purposes of agriculture throughout the period of 2[48] (or 7)[49] years ending with the death of the owner (or lifetime gift as the case may be). In the *McKenna* case, the Special Commissioner commented that:

> 'it is clear that neither Mr McKenna nor Lady Cecilia were able to engage in farming matters throughout the period of two years ending with the relevant dates of death.'

This raises the spectre of the aged farmer ending his days in a nursing home with his farmhouse unoccupied. In the *Atkinson* case,[50] the deceased owned farmland including his bungalow which was let to a farming partnership. He lived in the bungalow[51] until he became ill some 4 years before his death. Thereafter he was in hospital and a nursing home. No one lived in the bungalow which remained furnished and contained Mr Atkinson's belongings. During this time the other partners visited the bungalow two or three times a week to collect post, etc. Mr Atkinson remained a partner until his death and took part in discussions relating to the farm at least once a week: he occasionally visited the bungalow. It was exempt from council tax because he was residing elsewhere. It appears that Mr Atkinson's partnership share was a small one (eg his share of profits was £2,305 out of £77,957 and his partnership interest was worth £42,771 out of £491,138). The First-tier Tribunal decided that APR was available on the bungalow since it was occupied for agricultural purposes.

> '16. "Occupied" is qualified by the requirement that it be "for the purposes of agriculture". But "for the purposes of agriculture" is not further qualified. This no doubt reflects the wide range of activities that can constitute agriculture. It also recognises that the class of properties defined as agricultural property by section 115(2) includes those that are directly used in the functioning of the agricultural activity, such as land and farm buildings, as well as those that are less directly employed but nonetheless provide the structure within which the agricultural activities are conducted. Farm cottages are an example of the latter. Their function is to accommodate people engaged in the relevant agricultural activities. The farm cottages (such as the bungalow in the present case) must perform that function throughout the seven year period; but there is nothing in the Act that prescribes that the accommodation of such people is to be continuous. Nor does the Act provide in what right the person in question (ie the person engaged in the agricultural activities) is accommodated in the cottage; it could be the farm owner occupying as such, it could be an employee accommodated under a licence or it could be a partner in the farming business accommodated by

---

[47] See IHTA 1984, s 117.
[48] IHTA 1984, s 117(a).
[49] IHTA 1984, s 117(b).
[50] *Atkinson v Anor (Exors of Atkinson dec'd) v RCC* [2010] UKFTT 108 (TC); *revsd* [2012] STC 289, UT.
[51] This was not the farmhouse but was considered to be a farm cottage within Limb 3.

agreement between the partners. The reference in subsection (b) of section 117 to the property in question being occupied "by him or another" indicates as much.

17. In the present circumstances the occupation referred to in section 117(b) is the occupation of the three partners in the William M Atkinson & Son partnership as tenant under the agricultural tenancy of the Farm holding. Throughout the period of the partnership the entire holding, the bungalow included, was occupied for the purposes of the partnership's farming activities. The residential buildings, ie. Abbotson's Farmhouse and the bungalow were used by the partnership to accommodate the partners. For twenty-two years from the time the bungalow was built it housed Mr Atkinson. For the last four years of Mr Atkinson's life the impact of his illness reduced the likelihood of Mr Atkinson being able to return and live in the bungalow until it appears to have become necessary for him to stay permanently in the care home. But he continued to participate in partnership matters and his possessions remained in the bungalow; and from time to time he visited the bungalow. The partners chose to notify the local council that the bungalow was not lived in. Otherwise they did nothing with the bungalow to alter the state of affairs that had subsisted throughout the partnership.

18. Occupation by the partnership continued until Mr Atkinson's death; it was occupation for the purposes of agriculture in the relevant sense because the bungalow was still used to accommodate the diminishing needs of the senior partner.'

On appeal this decision was (perhaps unsurprisingly) reversed by the Upper Tier Tribunal[52] in the following terms:

'The correct approach is to identify what does and what does not amount to a sufficient connection between the use and occupation of the property in question (the Bungalow in the present case) and the agricultural activities being carried on on the agricultural property (the Farm in the present case); and to ask whether the facts give rise to a sufficient connection. If the Tribunal had adopted that approach it could, in our judgment, have come to only one conclusion, namely that the Bungalow was not immediately before Mr Atkinson's death, occupied for the purposes of agriculture and had not been so occupied since, at latest, it had become apparent that he would never be able to return there to live. In particular, neither the occasional attendance of Margaret and Gary at the Bungalow to deal with post or frost, nor the fact that some of Mr Atkinson's belongings and furniture remained at the Bungalow, can be said to constitute occupation for the purposes of agriculture throughout the seven years prior to Mr Atkinson's death.'

The facts of this case are all too common, given that many farmers are aged whilst continuing to farm from the farmhouse. In the event of illness and relocation to a nursing home, when will relief on the farmhouse be lost and how can it be preserved? The suggestion from the Tribunal is that relief will be lost 'at the latest (from when) it had become apparent that he would never be able to return to live there'. In a case such as this, to preserve relief consider arranging for another person to take over the occupation of the farmhouse to run the farm (for instance, it may always have been envisaged that one day the

---

52 Note that the taxpayer was not represented at the appeal.

son would move into the farmhouse and continue to run the business from there). If that is not feasible (say that as in *Atkinson* the property is not the farmhouse but a 'farm cottage') then consider letting it commercially with a view to claiming business property relief on the basis that, as in *Brander*,[53] this does not affect the basic trading nature of the farming business.

It may be clear that a farmer is not retired and is actively managing the land but there may be an issue as to whether the use of the land can be regarded as agricultural. The Inheritance Tax Act does not contain a definition of agriculture'. Paragraph 24062 of the Inheritance Tax Manual says that the position has to be considered carefully where land is used other than for arable or pastoral farming. An example of non-agricultural use is the cutting of reeds for thatching on the basis that there is no tilling, sowing or cultivating. The reeds are simply cut. The grazing of land by horses other than those connected with agriculture is not occupation of land for an agricultural purpose.[54] The breeding and grazing of racehorses on a stud farm is made an agricultural purpose for the purposes of agricultural relief by IHTA 1984, s 115(4).

Paragraph 24061 of the Inheritance Tax Manual says that land which is normally used for agricultural purposes can occasionally be used for other purposes without compromising its status. Provided those other purposes are not the primary reason for the occupation of the land, the land continues to be regarded as occupied 'for the purposes of agriculture'. One example is a working farm over which an annual point-to-point race is run.

Getting 100% relief on let property

10.22 Relief at 100% is available for land let on farm business tenancies and succession 1986 Act tenancies granted on or after 1 September 1995. Land let on Agricultural Holding Act tenancies granted before 1 September 1995, however, attracts APR at only 50% for the landowner. As a result of the TRIG Reforms[55] of 2006 it may be possible to 'convert' a pre-1995 tenancy into a new tenancy thereby securing relief at 100% for the landowner. The mechanics are outside the scope of this book but given the substantial benefits that may accrue to the landlord this is something which should be considered.

4. BUSINESS PROPERTY RELIEF

10.23 Relief is given when the whole or any part of the value transferred by a transfer of value is attributable to the value of 'any relevant business property'.[56] Relevant business property is then defined[57] to include a business;

---

[53] See **10.26**.
[54] See *Executors of the Will of Walter Wheatley Deceased v IRC* [1998] STC (SCD) 60 and *Hemens v Whitsbury Farm Ltd* [1987] 1All ER 430 (a rating valuation case).
[55] See Regulatory Reform (Agricultural Tenancies) (England and Wales) Order 2006, SI 2006/2805.
[56] IHTA 1984, s 104.

an interest in a business and any unquoted shares in a company. Generally, subject to satisfying a 2-year ownership period,[58] relief is at 100%.[59]

The 'wholly or mainly' test

10.24 In general, BPR is given on trading businesses but not on investment businesses (such as property investment). The 'wholly or mainly' test in IHTA 1984, s 105(3) determines whether relief is due on a 'mixed' business (the two leading cases are the Special Commissioner's decision in *Farmer*[60] and the Court of Appeal decision in *Stedman*).[61]

A business will not obtain relief if it is *mainly* one of holding investments. Because the relief is 'all or nothing' a business involving the holding of investments may attract relief (even on those investments) provided that this is not the *main* activity. Conversely, a business which is *mainly* one of holding investments will not benefit from relief even on any trading element.[62]

Not surprisingly, the 'wholly or mainly' test has spawned voluminous litigation and some of the more significant cases are considered in the following paragraphs.[63] Although the question is one of fact[64] to be determined by a consideration of the matter in the round by an intelligent businessman,[65] certain factors have been identified as relevant.

The factors

10.25 A number of factors have been identified in determining whether the business is mainly one of holding investments:

(a)   the overall context of the business (in *Farmer* the business involved a landed estate with the bulk of the land being used for farming);

(b)   the capital employed: was this mainly in the trading activity or the investment part of the business?[66]

(c)   the time spent by the employees;

(d)   the turnover; and

---

57   In IHTA 1984, s 105.
58   IHTA 1984, s 106.
59   Exceptionally only 50% relief is due: see for instance IHTA 1984, s 105(1)(cc), (d) and (e).
60   *Farmer v IRC* [1999] STC (SCD) 321.
61   *IRC v George (Exors of Stedman dec'd)* [2004] STC 147 (CA).
62   The issue of whether one business or two was being carried on was considered in the *Brander* case: see **10.26**.
63   There is also a line of cases on caravan parks/mobile homes including *Hall (Exors of Hall dec'd) v IRC* [1997] STC (SCD) 126; *Powell (PR of Pearce dec'd) v IRC* [1997] STC (SCD) 181; and *IRC v George (Exors of Stedman dec'd)* [2004] STC 147, CA.
64   *IRC v George (Exors of Stedman dec'd)* [2004] STC 147.
65   *McCall v RCC* [2009] STC 990, Girvan LJ at para 11.
66   Note that in *Brander* [2010] STC 2666 (see **10.26**) the Upper Tier Tribunal accepted that this was to be ignored given that there was no intention to sell the estate.

(e)   the profit.

Having identified these factors, the Special Commissioner in *Farmer* commented:[67]

> 'When these factors have been considered it will then be necessary to stand back and consider in the round whether the business consisted mainly of making or holding investments.'

The *Brander* case[68]

10.26   Lord Balfour held his interest in Whittingehame Estate as a life-renter. (HMRC had argued unsuccessfully that his father's will had not created a life-rent.) The business was the typical mix of a traditional Scottish landed estate consisting of a blend of agricultural (in-hand and let farms), woodland and forestry management and related sporting interests and the letting of cottages and other properties within the estate either to estate workers or others.

On 6 November 2002 the House of Lords released the estate from the life-rent with the effect that from that date until his death Lord Balfour owned the estate absolutely. He formed a farming partnership with his heir and died in 2003.

HMRC took various points unsuccessfully. The final point was whether the business was wholly or mainly one of holding investments. Both at first instance and on appeal they lost.

The Upper Tribunal summarised the case law on this question as follows:

(a)   In deciding what the term 'the business of holding investments' means, the test which the decision-maker applies is that of an intelligent businessman who would be concerned with the use to which the asset was being put and the way it was being turned to account.[69]

(b)   The question whether a business consists wholly or mainly of making or holding investments is a question of fact for the decision-maker.[70]

(c)   The decision-maker is required to look at the business in the round and, in the light of the overall picture, to form a view as to the relative importance to the business as a whole of the investment and non-investment activities in that business.[71]

(d)   This exercise involves looking at the business over a period of time as the First-tier Tribunal did in this case.[72]

---

[67]   [1999] STC (SCD) 321 at para 53.
[68]   *Brander v Revenue and Customs Commissioners* [2009] SFTD 374 *affd* [2010] STC 2666.
[69]   *McCall v RCC* [2009] STC 990, Girvan LJ at para 11.
[70]   *IRC v George* [2004] STC 147.
[71]   *IRC v George*, Carnwath LJ at paras 13, 51, 52 and 60.
[72]   See, for example, *Farmer's Executors v IRC* [1999] STC (SCD) 321.

In so doing, the decision-maker can have regard to various factors, such as the overall context of the business, the turnover and profitability of various activities, the activities of employees and other persons engaged to assist the business, the acreage of the land dedicated to each activity and the capital value of that acreage. Not one of these factors is conclusive as the exercise involves looking at the business in the round: *Farmer's Executors v IRC*, Dr A N Brice at para 53; *IRC v George*, Carnwath LJ at para 52. While the decision-maker must consider all relevant factors in relation to a particular business, there will be circumstances in which a factor, which is relevant to one business, is not relevant to another.

(a)   The fact that the owner of an investment engages in activities to manage and maintain his investment does not of itself take the business out of the investment category.[73]

(b)   In looking at the question in the round it is not appropriate in every case to compartmentalise the business and attribute management and maintenance activity either to investment or to non-investment as an ancillary activity.[74]

(c)   Because the question is one of fact, the Upper Tribunal can interfere with the decision of the First-tier Tribunal only if an error of law has been demonstrated.[75]

The question therefore was whether Judge Reid reached a view which was open to him on the evidence. Looking at that evidence, it was clear that it was:

(i)   *Use of the land*:

The in hand farms and woodlands fell to be treated as non-investment activity throughout. Judge Reid had made an error in his calculation but this was not significant. The Tribunal accepted that sporting activities generated little income but they were combined with vermin control throughout the estate and were to be considered on the non-investment side of the business.

The use of land was split between non-investment and investment activities approximately equally. As a result the acreage used was not a weighty factor in one or other direction.

(ii)   *Overall context*:

Looking at the overall context of Lord Balfour's business in operating a unitary landed estate with in hand farming, forestry/woodland, and sporting activities as well as the letting of farms and surplus dwelling-houses, Judge Reid was entitled to treat that context as a factor which pointed towards a business which was mainly a trading business.

(iii)   *Turnover and net profit*:

---

[73]   *Martin (Executors of Moore) v IRC* [1995] STC 5, Sir Stephen Oliver QC at paras 20-23; *Burkinyoung's Executor v IRC* [1995] STC (SCD) 29; *IRC v George*, Carnwath LJ at para 18.

[74]   *IRC v George*, Carnwath LJ at paras 51 and 60.

[75]   *Edwards v Bairstow* [1956] AC 14; *IRC v George* (above).

Judge Reid was entitled to conclude that those factors strongly supported the conclusion that the management of the estate was mainly a trading activity.

Period	Trading Turnover (£)	Letting Turnover (£)	Net Trading Profit (£)	Net Letting Profit (£)
1996	166,285	49,622	39,369	2,231
1997	184,935	56,219	50,237	1,035
1998	123,527	57,583	22,999	9,682
1999	141,601	68,068	23,040	21,354
2000	121,546	67,009	(15,617)	31,825
2001	119,804	82,027	11,181	8,342
2002	101,966	95,266	25,452	(22,551)
To Nov 2002	119,364	96,248	14,249	43,484

(iv) *Time spent*:

Again this pointed to the predominance of the trading activity. In 2001 79% of time was trading related and 21% related to letting. In 2002 the percentages were 78% and 22%.

(v) *Capital value*:

Using the agreed property values at the date of Lord Balfour's death on 23 June 2003, the capital value of the let properties (£4,357,500) exceeded the value of the other properties (£2,313,065) in the ratio of 1.88:1. Other things being equal, this factor pointed to some degree towards investment activity. However Judge Reid had been invited by counsel to ignore, or at least attach little weight to, capital value as the long-term policy of the estate was to retain land so that market values were generally immaterial to Lord Balfour's business decisions.

The Upper Tribunal agreed that he was entitled to share that view.

On the evidence before him, Judge Reid was entitled to conclude that s 105(3) did not apply because Lord Balfour's business at Whittingehame Estate did not consist mainly of holding investments.

Implications

10.27 Taxpayers with mixed businesses need to watch the make-up of the business. What they choose to do will depend on their attitude to risk. While an investment/letting element can be sheltered within a business which is eligible for relief, once it exceeds 50% it will result in total loss of relief. The risk of complete loss of relief should be clearly explained and may be too great for some taxpayers.

The cautious approach is to transfer non-eligible assets[76] out of the business before the tipping point is reached sacrificing relief on those elements in order to maintain relief on the rest of the business. But be careful to ascertain the CGT position first.

The *Conacre* case[77]

10.28   The deceased let 33 acres of farmland which she had inherited from her husband in 1983 under grazing agreements to local farmers.[78] The land was zoned for development and when the deceased died, although the agricultural value was only £165,000, its market value was £5.8m. Two preliminary matters should be noted:

(a)   there was no doubt that APR was available in respect of the agricultural value of the land. The issue concerned the availability of business property relief on the enhanced value (ie on the difference between the market value and the agricultural value);

(b)   the letting arrangements were arranged on behalf of the deceased (whose mind rapidly deteriorated after the death of her husband) by her son-in-law. The Special Commissioner accepted that it remained her business.

10.29   So far as the availability of business property relief was concerned, he decided (and the NI Court of Appeal agreed) that:

(a)   the activity of tending the land undertaken by the son-in-law coupled with the annual letting of the land was just enough to constitute a business. Around 100 hours per annum was spent in weed control; fence maintenance; litter and damage control and drainage and water works;

(b)   but the business consisted wholly or mainly of the holding of investments so that (as a result of IHTA 1984, s 105(3)) business property relief was not available. He concluded:

---

76   After *HMRC v Trustees of Nelson Dance* [2009] EWHC 71 (Ch) it is possible to obtain relief on the transfer of individual assets from a business. It is not necessary to transfer a business or part of a business: see **10.33**.

77   *McCall and Keenan (PRs of McClean Deceased) v RCC* [2008] STC (SCD) 782; *aff'd* [2009] STC 990.

78   Although there was much discussion of local letting arrangements in Northern Ireland (especially 'conacre' or 'agistment' arrangements) the agreements in this case were essentially the same as those employed in England and Wales: for instance, the lettings were for the period during which grass was growing, 1 April to 1 November. Hence the case is of general significance.

'The activities of the business do not involve the cutting of the grass and the feeding of it to the cattle but simply making the asset available so that the cattle may live and eat there: the income arises substantially from the making available of the asset not from the other activity associated with it or from selling separately the fruits of the asset: that is the business of holding an investment, and it was the main activity of this business. It was not like a "pick your own" fruit farm where after months of weeding, fertilising, spraying and pruning, customers are licensed to enter to take the produce and pay by the pound for what they take away: in the business of letting the fields there was less in preparatory work, the fields were let for the accommodation of the cattle as well as for the grazing and the rent was paid by the acre rather than by the ton of grass eaten: it was not a business consisting of the provision of the grass but of the provision of the (non-exclusive) use of the land.'

The courts did not accept the taxpayer's argument that the correct analysis of a grazing licence was that it involved the business of selling a grass crop.

10.30 It is thought that the decision is significant in relation to grazing arrangements in England and Wales. These take a variety of forms: for instance, the grazing licence which may if it grants exclusive possession amount to a short-term business tenancy. An alternative, for which the CLA provide a precedent, is a *profit à prendre* under which the grazier is allowed to put cattle on the land to take the grass. What precisely was the arrangement in this case? Girvan LJ explained the nature of the agistment arrangement as follows:[79]

'The use by Northern Ireland landowners of conacre and agistment arrangements with other farmers is common even though such arrangements have been criticised as unsatisfactory arrangements which do not assist in good land management practices. The fact that such arrangements are common is in part due to their traditional use in Northern Ireland, in part due to a fear on the part of both landowners and graziers and conacre tenants of creating agricultural tenancies with potential adverse legal consequences and in part due to the desire of landowners to retain a degree of control over the land during the period of the contract. What appears clear from the old Irish authorities is that an agistment contract confers on the grazier only a right to graze and not possession of the land in law. They do not create a tenancy. Such an arrangement partakes of the quality of the profit à prendre but one which by way of exception to the normal rules does not require to be created by deed. Such an arrangement bears a close comparison to a contractual licence.'

He further commented that the absence of a full and exclusive right of occupation of the land for the grazier and the existence of a right by the owner to enter the land during the period of the agistment did not prevent the business being regarded as the holding of an investment.

10.31 The fact that the deceased did not qualify for business property relief is important when, as in this case, the land has hope value. It will also be significant, however, in deciding whether any house can be a farmhouse: if the

---

[79] At para 16.

correct analysis is that the grazing agreement involves the holding of an investment, then it is difficult to see how the property occupied by the landowner can be a farmhouse.[80]

10.32 If only a part of the farmland is subject to a grazing agreement and the bulk of the farm is farmed in hand, then on the basis of the 'wholly or mainly' test in s 105(3) it is thought that business property relief will be available on all the land.

What must be transferred?

10.33 It had been thought that BPR was only available in the case of unincorporated businesses on a transfer of either the whole business or a part of the business. Whilst this would not present difficulties on the death of the owner, it could present problems in the case of lifetime gifts. In 2002, Nelson Dance[81] settled property forming part of his farming business on discretionary trusts. This transfer did not involve either the transfer of his entire business or any part of that business (ie it amounted to a transfer of mere assets). He died within 7 years of the transfer. The Special Commissioner had to decide whether the original transfer into the discretionary trust qualified for business property relief.[82] He decided, contrary to the unanimous views of the textbook writers on the subject, that it did and his decision was upheld in the High Court. The relevant arguments are as follows:

(a)   business property relief is given when the whole or part of the value transferred by a transfer of value is attributable to the value of any relevant business property;[83]

(b)   in the IHT legislation value transferred means the fall in value of the transferor's estate;

(c)   in the context of business property relief, IHTA 1984, s 110 requires liabilities incurred for the purposes of the business to be deducted in arriving at the net value of that business;

(d)   but there is nothing to say that the value transferred must be attributable to the transfer of the whole business or indeed a part of the business;

(e)   that is only relevant to the definitions in s 105 which lists property capable of being 'relevant business property' (for instance, s 105(1)(a) is dealing with the situation where a taxpayer is a sole trader or a partner in a partnership).

10.34 The decision is significant in allowing individual assets to be stripped out of a business: for instance, in the case of a mixed business where there is

---

[80]   For a consideration of the meaning of farmhouse, see the *McKenna* case at **10.18**.

[81]   *RCC v The Trustees of the Nelson Dance Family Settlement* [2008] STC (SCD) 792 *aff'd* [2009] STC 802.

[82]   The transfer attracted agricultural property relief but only on the agricultural value of the relevant land which had substantial development potential.

[83]   IHTA 1984, s 104(1).

concern that the investment aspect may become predominant, it will be possible to remove sufficient of the investment assets to ensure that the 'wholly or mainly' test in s 105(3) continues to be met. Suppose that a business is predominantly one of house building but has, over the years, acquired a number of tenanted properties. These properties may be transferred out while the business is still 'mainly' a trading business. The transfer will attract relief and the remaining business will be in less danger of losing relief in the future. Likewise if a business has accumulated a substantial cash reserve which it has been keeping for business purposes (as in the *Brown* case[84]) then this may be distributed with the benefit of relief.

Property development companies

10.35 In the *Piercy* case,[85] the company had been established for property development and had large holdings of land for which it received substantial amounts of rent. Although, for corporation tax purposes, it was generally classified as trading, HMRC considered this to be irrelevant, contending that the receipt of substantial rents meant that business property relief was not available since the activities of the company fell foul of s 105(3) in involving mainly the holding of investments.

10.36 The Special Commissioner concluded, however, that the business of the company involved marshalling sites for development with a view to selling the finished developments. Accordingly, land was held as trading stock and even though it produced a rental income, there was no evidence that it had been appropriated as an investment. Note:

(a)   the reference in s 105(3) to a land dealing company (the shares in which do not qualify for business property relief) does not affect building companies:

> 'the only type of land dealing company whose shares fail to qualify for the relief is some sort of dealing or speculative trader that does not actually develop or actually build on land';

(b)   a company can only conduct the business of holding investments if it has got some investments! In *Piercy*, whilst the company had retained land, it had not appropriated it as an investment. For instance, the company had acquired land in Islington for residential development but could not proceed because of planning delays. As an interim measure, it had built poor quality limited life industrial workshops on this land (let on short-term leases) but with the continuing intention of knocking down these units once residential development became possible. The Special Commissioner concluded that this land had never become appropriated as an investment (incidentally, had it been so appropriated the corporation tax returns of the company over a number of years should have been quite

---

[84]   *Brown's Exors v IRC* [1996] STC (SCD) 277.
[85]   *Executors of Piercy Deceased v RCC* [2008] STC (SCD) 858.

different and, contrary to the arguments of HMRC, the Special Commissioner decided that this was a case where the two taxes 'go hand in hand').

Furnished holiday lettings

10.37   There had been uncertainty over whether business relief was available in the case of a furnished holiday lettings business. Specifically the question was whether the business is mainly that of receiving income from an investment; if that was the case, no relief was due. A commercial landlord, for example, is treated as receiving income from the properties which is an investment activity, whereas a person running a hotel or bed–and–breakfast business is treated as running a non-investment business which attracts relief.

Although a number of factors have been identified as relevant to the question whether the business is mainly one of holding investments,[86] ultimately the matter is a question of fact which has to be decided by looking at the matter 'in the round'.

It is thought that whether or not relief is due depends on the particular facts: in one case the landlord will do little more than receive a rent for the letting of the property (and furniture): in another, substantial services will be provided which means that from the tenant's point of view he is receiving benefits not dissimilar from staying in a hotel or B&B.

Old HMRC view

10.38   Some of the difficulties inherent in this area can be seen from the entries in the HMRC IHT Manual. Formerly it contained the statement that:

> 'in some instances the distinction between a business of furnished holiday lettings and, say, a business of running a hotel or motel may be so minimal that the Courts would not regard such a business as one of "wholly or mainly holding investments" … you should therefore normally allow relief where:
>
> - the lettings are short term (eg weekly or fortnightly), and
> - the owner – either himself or via an agent such as a relative or housekeeper – was substantially involved with the holidaymaker in terms of their activities on and from the premises.' (IHTM 25278)

Subsequent view of HMRC

10.39   In November 2008 this part of the manual was withdrawn (doubtless because of the reference to the personal involvement of the taxpayer in the lettings which are irrelevant to relief). The subsequent approach of HMRC was expressed in correspondence as follows:

---

[86]   See 10.25.

'our starting point in cases involving holiday lettings is that the short term letting of furnished accommodation is the exploitation of property rights, and, as such, will be a business of mainly holding investments ... We then look at the nature and level of the services provided by the particular business to see if that status is inappropriate.'

Obviously service levels will differ but a holiday letting business may offer some or all of the following which would not normally be available to a tenant who simply rents property:

(a)   a fully furnished property complete with a Sky TV contract;

(b)   the provision of towels, linens, etc;

(c)   a 'welcome pack';

(d)   a meet and greet service;

(e)   detailed information of things to do/places to visit/local restaurants etc;

(f)   the provision of a parking permit;

(g)   the availability of a cleaning service;

(h)   problems arising during the stay are dealt with by either the letting agent or by the owner.

Unfortunately for taxpayers the Upper Tribunal decision in *Pawson*[87] emphasized the fact that in the case of a property letting business additional services or facilities provided to the occupants are unlikely to be material. They will not be enough to prevent the business remaining 'mainly' that of holding the property as an investment. This point was also made in the later decisions considered below.[88]

THE *PAWSON* CASE

10.40   The deceased owned a 25% share in a bungalow on the Suffolk coast (the remaining 75% share was owned by her children). Normal lettings were for 2 weeks at most but many were for shorter periods, eg. long weekends. It could accommodate up to 11 people, had direct access to the sea and grounds of 0.4 acres. The financial return was:

	Income (£)	Profit (£)
2003/04	4,342.99	680.27
2004/05	6,072.51	802.32
2005/06	8,120	(2,071.61)
2006/07	16,589.67	4,449.66

---

[87]   *Revenue and Customs Commissioners v Lockyer and another (personal representatives of Pawson, deceased)* [2013] UKUT 50 (TCC) discussed at **10.40**.

[88]   At **10.44** *et seq.*

The family occupied the property for 3 weeks during the summer, paying the sum prescribed by HMRC for private use. In 2005–06 the loss was caused by substantial decorating/improvement works. The services provided for holidaymakers comprised:

(a)   telephone/television;

(b)   cleaning between each letting;

(c)   clean bedclothes (but only after the deceased's death);

(d)   fully furnished: night storage heaters, hot water etc; and

(e)   regular inspection of the property by the cleaner/caretaker.

The family advertised for lettings and visited the property in an emergency.

10.41   The First-tier Tribunal decided that BPR was available. The key passage in the decision commented:

> 'We have no doubt that an intelligent businessman would not regard the ownership of a holiday letting property as an investment as such and would regard it as involving far too active an operation for it to come under that heading. The need constantly to find new occupants and to provide services unconnected with and over and above those needed for the bare upkeep of the property as a property lead us to conclude that no postulated intelligent businessman would consider such a property as Fairhaven to be correctly characterised as an investment. He would consider it to be a business asset to be exploited as part of the provision of services going well beyond an investment as such.'

10.42   That decision was, however, reversed on appeal by Henderson J. He made the following points:

(a)   whether a property right is an 'investment' is to be considered in its context and given the same meaning as a businessman would give it (quoting Lawrence Collins in the *Weston*[89] case);

(b)   there is no distinction between an 'active' and 'passive' property investment business (quoting Stephen Oliver QC in the *Martin*[90] case);

(c)   activities can be divided into:

    (i)   'making' the investment: finding and negotiating with tenants; grant of leases;

    (ii)   'compliance' activities laid on the landowner in accordance with the lease; and

    (iii)   'management' activities: repairs; dealing with tenants' complaints; lease covenants.

    All are necessary incidents of a business of holding investments;

---

[89]   *Weston (exors of Weston dec'd v IRC* [2000] STC 1064.
[90]   *Martin (exors of Moore decd) v IRC* [1995] STC (SCD) 5.

(d) there is a spectrum ranging from exploiting land by granting a tenancy (an investment), to 'while land is still being exploited the element of services means that there is a trade, such as running a hotel, or a shop from premises owned by the trader';[91]

(e) matters must be looked at in the round: the fact that additional services are provided for in the lease does not make them mere incidents of the letting.

10.43 In the crucial passage of the judgment he commented:

'... when the business is one of letting a building, the provision of additional services or facilities to the occupants is "unlikely to be material" because they will not be enough to prevent the business remaining "mainly" one of holding the property as an investment ... in any normal property letting business the provision of additional services or facilities of a non-investment nature will either be incidental to the business of holding the property as an investment, or at least will not predominate to such an extent that the business ceases to be mainly one of holding property as an investment ... the owning and holding of land in order to obtain an income from it is generally to be characterised as an investment activity.'[92]

After *Pawson*: the *Zetland*[93] case

10.44 The taxpayer was a successful entrepreneur who transferred company shares into a discretionary settlement. He contended that no anniversary charge was due because the business of the company (an actively managed office block, Zetland House) qualified for BPR. HMRC said relief was not available because the business of the company was holding investments.

Zetland House was originally a multistory factory occupied by a few firms of printers. The property had outlived its original purpose. Leases were for very long periods and there were large parts of the property which were empty. By 1997, one-quarter of the building was empty. The gross rent was about £510,000.

The taxpayer acquired the premises and transformed them. His business model was to offer flexible office space for computer, media and high technology businesses. This required major changes to the property, both physically and in terms of use and type of occupant. He made office space more available and offered short leases, which made rentals more attractive. He made the offices smaller and in reconfiguring the business lost approximately 15,000 sq ft of letting area. The gross rent and service charges in the year 5 April 2007 was slightly under £2.4m.

---

[91] *Stedman's Exors v IRC* [2002] STC (SCD) 358.

[92] It may be thought that the final sentence is too general: what of the farmer who owns land to produce an income farming it?

[93] *Trustees of David Zetland Settlement v HMRC* [2013] UKFTT 284 (TC).

In order to assist with the running of the building he hired more staff to provide services and facilities to tenants. The building had a restaurant, gym, cycle arch, WiFi, portage, 24-hour access, meeting rooms, media events, outdoor screens for viewing football matches and film shows as well as an art gallery area. It was run on the basis of a community with regular barbeques and socials. The taxpayer listed the services provided as follows:

(a)   conference rooms;

(b)   mail room, reception and porters;

(c)   seven to eight full-time and four part-time staff working on Zetland House business (general administration, dealing with tenants, organising events, marketing and branding of the building, including web design, Twitter and Facebook, security property management, legal matters, taking conference room bookings and approximately 40% of her time was spent on Zetland House matters);

(d)   cafe;

(e)   communal events (barbeques in summer, Brazilian lunch, computer course, carol singing and Christmas parties);

(f)   internet services;

(g)   bicycle stands;

(h)   project management;

(i)   cleaning services;

(j)   24-hour security;

(k)   gym and hair salon.

10.45 The taxpayer claimed that these services to the tenants of Zetland House meant that it ought not to be classified as an investment business. The services provided went beyond the normal incidents of letting property (maintenance, finding tenants etc) and took the business into a different area. The services provided would certainly 'tip the balance' when compared with the services offered in the *Pawson* case. HMRC said that the purpose of the additional services was to increase occupancy and increase the rent collected under the lease. The services were incidental to their core business of collecting rent and service charges.

10.46 The Tribunal referred to the passage of Carnwarth LJ quoted in *Pawson* that in the case of a business of letting a building, the provision of such services is 'unlikely to be material' because it will not be enough to prevent the business remaining mainly one of property investments. The implication it said is that in any normal case an actively managed property letting business will fall within the exception in s 105 because the 'mainly' condition will still be satisfied.

It looked at the income of the various activities.

	Rent and service charges	Other activities
2006	£2,174,483	£47,920
2007	£2,343,951	£61,415

The breakdown of the figures to 2007 showed that the rental income was the main income. The area of the building given to tenants (104,000 square feet of the 140,000 square feet) was also substantial and was more than that allocated to other activities. In any event, the gym, cafe and hair salon were run by tenants and not the company. While a quantitative assessment is not determinative, the analysis of the figures pointed to an investment business. Qualitatively, the business had to be looked at in the round without giving predominance to any one factor in determining whether the business consisted mainly of investments.

10.47 The activities were predominantly investment activities or related to investment. The services provided were mainly of a standard nature aimed at maximising income through the use of short-term tenancies. The non-investment side was incidental to the core business and the services were insufficient to make the business one that was mainly non–investment. The purpose of the activities was largely to improve the building and its fabric, to keep the tenants there and to keep the occupancy rates high. The Tribunal said:

> 'the reality is that most of these activities generate rental income. The income from the cycle rack and gallery as well as the coffee shop, hairdressing salon and gym is all rental income. The tenants rent office space in a large building. They are some services which are provided over and above that which is required to be provided. This includes cleaning of the common parts, post sorting and delivery, reception, free food and drink at socials and gift vouchers. It would be difficult to classify security as something which is over and above a landlord's responsibility especially in London and where a building is open late at night and early morning. However, these do not tip the balance in favour the Settlement nor are they sufficient to rebut the "mainly" investments argument.'

After *Pawson*: the *Best* case[94]

10.48 The deceased owned shares in an unquoted company which managed a Business Centre letting office space (15% of income), warehouses and light industrial units.

The site included car parking space available to occupiers, their employees and customers. There was a reception area with a receptionist employed by the Company. The occupiers of industrial units and most of the offices did not have their own telephone landline but did have extensions. The receptionist operated a switchboard and put calls through to the extension, or to the occupier's mobile phone number. Outgoing calls were re-charged to users. The company provided site security. Entrance to the site was via a manned security barrier.

---

[94] *Best (executor of Buller, decd) v Revenue and Customs Comrs* [2014] UKFTT 077 (TC).

There was a full time site maintenance worker. In total there were three full time employees and two part-time employees. There were also three security guards employed. The deceased spent much of his time at the Business Centre dealing with the everyday matters that might arise with occupiers. On his death the company employed a full time replacement as a '*site administrator*'.

Services were provided and charged for by way of service charge for items such as grass cutting, pest control, cleaning of the common areas, site security 5pm–9am Monday to Friday and 24-hour security at weekends and holidays, site maintenance and repairs were accepted by all parties as the types of services a landlord would commonly provide to occupiers. The taxpayer argued that the provision of a receptionist to answer telephone calls, sort incoming and outgoing mail and take delivery of parcels, together with general reception duties for visitors and guests was an additional service which might be a non-investment activity. There were the following additional services that could be provided by the company if required at an additional fee:

(a)   provision of telephone services, calls and line rental;

(b)   provision of forklift driver, if required;

(c)   provision of secretarial services;

(d)   provision of photocopying and postage facilities;

(e)   acquisition of stationery, if required;

(f)   provision of fax facilities for both incoming and outgoing correspondence;

(g)   hire of boardroom;

(h)   additional car parking for extra vehicles, if required;

(i)   for industrial occupants – metered electrical supply, if required.

The layout and physical limitations of the Business Centre meant that many of the industrial units were accessible only by small vans. For example, some internal units occupied the ground floor in circumstances where height restrictions prevented larger lorries gaining access. The taxpayers argued that some units with restricted access would be unlettable without the provision of a forklift truck service which made the provision of this additional service particularly important. The tribunal did not accept that units would be unlettable without the provision of a forklift truck service. A significant number of units were occupied by small businesses which would have no need for large deliveries. Even if this had been true, it amounted to a 'but for' test which was not supported by the authorities.

The income of the company generated in the year ending 31 December 2007 was as follows:

	£
Licence Fees	447,068

	£
Service Charges	53,335
Sundry	4,517
Hire of Fork Lift Truck	4,452
Heat and Light	31,284
Telephone	45,568
Postage	20,056
Car Parking	5,192

Unsurprisingly the tribunal found that the business was mainly an investment business. It listed the following principles to be applied in deciding whether or not a business consists wholly or mainly of holding investments:

(i) the various activities involved in operating a business relating to the exploitation of land may be allocated between '*investment*' and '*non-investment*' activities;

(ii) in the light of that allocation the question is whether the investment element of the business is predominant (see *George* at [11]);

(iii) the ultimate issue concerns the relative importance of non-investment activities to the business as a whole (see *George* at [51]);

(iv) there is a wide spectrum involved in such businesses. At one end is the granting of a tenancy together with activities sufficient to make it a business. At the other end is the running of a hotel or shop on the land. The holding of land as an investment may be the very business carried on or it may be merely incidental to the business. It may also be one of a number of principal components of a composite business (see *George* at [12] and [16]);

(v) it is necessary to look at the business in the round. The relative income and profitability of the various activities is relevant but not determinative (see *George* at [13]);

(vi) the exception in s 105(3) IHTA 1984 is not confined to purely passive property investment (see *George* at [18]);

(vii) property '*management*' is part of the business of holding property as an investment, including finding occupiers and maintaining the property as an investment. However that term does not extend to additional services or facilities provided to occupiers and it is irrelevant whether the provision of such additional services is included in the lease. The characterisation of such services depends on the nature and purpose of the activity and not on the terms of the lease (see *George* at [27] and [28]);

(viii) the test to be applied is that of an intelligent businessman, concerned with the use to which the asset was being put and the way in which it was being turned to account (see *McCall* at [11]);

(ix) the test involves a question of fact and degree as to where a particular business falls within the spectrum (see *McCall* at [18]).

As in the *Zetland* case,[95] HMRC suggested there was 'a working presumption' that in any normal property letting business, the provision of additional services or facilities of a non-investment nature will either be incidental to the business of holding the property as an investment, or at least will not predominate to such an extent that the business ceases to be mainly one of holding the property as an investment. The tribunal said at [39] that it preferred not to use the term 'presumption'.

The tribunal rejected the argument that units were unlettable without the additional services and, even if it had been established on the facts, it would not have led to a conclusion that the forklift truck service predominated. The fact that some units could not be let without the provision of a forklift truck service would tend to suggest that the service is part of the investment activity. It was an element of sensible property management, not generally but certainly in the context of this particular property.

Looking at the business in the round, the non-investment services were subsidiary. Most of the income from them related to re-charges for electricity, telephone and postage. The income from the other additional services was modest.

Considering the facts by reference to the nature of the activities and the income produced by those activities, the Business Centre was well towards the investment end of the spectrum.

The future

10.49 In the light of their success in *Pawson*, it seems clear that the Revenue will look to deny business relief for all businesses when exploiting the ownership of land is a major factor. It is thought that in the future the following businesses will come under increasing scrutiny:

(a) the provision of accommodation for asylum seekers and the vulnerable;

(b) the budget hotel industry;

(c) car parks;

(d) moorings;

(e) DIY livery.

---

[95] At **10.44**.

EXCEPTED ASSETS

10.50 Even if a business qualifies for relief, no relief is given on the value of excepted assets which are defined in s 112(2) of IHTA 1984 as follows:

> 'An asset is an excepted asset in relation to any relevant business property if it was neither—
>
> (a) used wholly or mainly for the purposes of the business concerned throughout the whole or the last two years of the relevant period defined in subsection (5) below, nor
> (b) required at the time of the transfer for future use for those purposes;
>
> but where the business concerned is carried on by a company which is a member of a group, the use of an asset for the purposes of a business carried on by another company which at the time of the use and immediately before the transfer was also a member of that group shall be treated as use for the purposes of the business concerned, unless that other company's membership of the group falls to be disregarded under section 111 above.'

The purpose of this provision is to prevent assets being held in the business structure which have no connection with that business in an attempt to secure relief on them. The problem typically arises when the business is holding large cash reserves: are these required for business purposes or are they simply a sum that has built up out of retained profits year on year? The question is one of fact but 'required' is a strong word so compelling evidence of intended business use will be needed.[96]

The *Barclays Bank* case[97]

10.51 The one reported decision on the provision is not wholly satisfactory but is much relied on by HMRC. In this case the business involved selling bathroom and kitchen fittings. The following matters should be noted:

(a) the company had small overheads: its sales were to trade and it occupied rent free rather cramped premises;

(b) it built up a strong cash position: taking trade discounts for prompt payment;

(c) it did not hold substantial stock in trade;

(d) cash at the relevant time was of £450,000 which was invested for periods of up to 30 days;

(e) turnover was around £600,000.

---

[96] In the Manual (IHTM 25352) HMRC comment that: 'Whether this test is satisfied is a question of evidence in the circumstances of the particular case. Have regard to the nature and previous history of the business and such evidence as may be produced . . . as to prospective development and capital outlay.'

[97] *Barclays Bank Trust Co v IRC* [1998] STC S(CD) 125.

The cash had built up over the years as follows:

	£
1986/87	188,084
1987/88	254,589
1988/89	341,789
1989/90	413,195
1990/91	459,130

It will be noted that year on year the cash surplus grew.

10.52 The taxpayer argued that:

(a) the cash was required for future business opportunities;

(b) in 1990 there was the possibility of purchasing properties of a liquidating business. But apart from an exploratory letter, the matter was not pursued; and

(c) in 1997 over £300,000 was used in connection with the Euro Plumbing venture. Whilst this was some 7 years after the date of death, the taxpayer argued that no time was imposed by the section.

10.53 The Special Commissioner (DA Shirley) agreed with the Revenue that £150,000 was needed for the business but £300,000 was an excepted asset. He commented:

(a) the question of whether the cash was needed is one of fact and he was not persuaded on the evidence before him;

(b) '"required" involves some imperative that the money will fall to be used on a given project or for some palpable business purpose'. 'Future' does not mean at any time in the future and 'required' does not mean that there is a possibility.

10.54 Three key issues are therefore:

(a) the evidence of how the cash balance has fluctuated: ie has it *in fact* been used for business ventures in, say, the last 5 years or, as in the *Barclays* case, has the cash balance grown year on year;

(b) evidence that the directors monitor the position annually and record the business justification for retaining that amount of cash (in *Barclays* there was an unsatisfactory undated statement made by the sole director that they needed the cash deposit at the relevant time);

(c)   in practice, taxpayers may be advised to invest the cash and argue that they are carrying out predominantly non-investment activities so that the 'wholly or mainly' restriction is not infringed.

5. ISSUES FOR THE WILL DRAFTSMAN

The need for a specific gift of qualifying property

10.55   Where property attracting BPR or APR is left specifically to a legatee that legatee alone benefits from the relief.[98]

> *Example 10.8*
>
> T, who has exhausted his nil rate band, leaves £1m of business property attracting 100% relief to his wife, residue of £1m to his son.
>
> The benefit of the BPR goes exclusively to the property passing to the wife. The property passing to the son is taxed at 40%: ie £400,000 in tax.
>
> *Compare*
>
> T leaves the property attracting BPR to his son and the residue to his wife. The gift to the son attracts BPR. The property passing to the wife is spouse exempt so there is no IHT payable.

It is desirable from an IHT perspective that the property eligible for relief is given to the non-exempt beneficiary. However, the testator may object that the surviving spouse (or civil partner) is the one who is to take over the business. In this case, consider the 'two bites of the cherry' arrangement: see **10.66**.

10.56   An appropriation of assets is not a specific gift for this purpose. If therefore a cash legacy is left, for instance, to nil rate band trustees, the appropriation by the executors of business/agricultural property to satisfy that legacy will not lead to full relief being due under s 39A(2) since the property was not the subject matter of a specific gift.

Property attracting relief not specifically bequeathed

10.57   The position here is different. The rules can be a trap for the unwary personal representative but can also produce an unexpected tax saving. This is because s 39A(3) provides that, where property attracting relief is not specifically bequeathed, the benefit of the relief is apportioned amongst the rest of the assets (ie amongst specific, pecuniary legacies and residue).

---

[98]   IHTA 1984, s 39A(2).

Example 10.9

A will leaves legacies of £200,000 to A and to B and the residue of the estate (which includes property eligible for BPR) to C. The benefit of the BPR is apportioned through the estate so that the pecuniary legatees benefit as well as the residuary legatee.

10.58   The apportioning requires the use of the formula:

$$\frac{R}{U}$$

Where R is the value of the estate as reduced by agricultural and business relief less the value of any specific gifts qualifying for relief and U is the unreduced value of the estate less the value of any specific gifts qualifying for relief.

Example 10.10

Tom, who has exhausted his nil rate band, dies with an estate of £2m which includes property attracting 100% BPR of £800,000.

He leaves a pecuniary legacy of £600,000 to his son, residue to his wife.

The BPR of £800,000 must be apportioned.

R is £2m less £800,000 = £1,200,000.

U is £2m

The son's legacy must be multiplied by R/U.

$$£600,000 \; x \; \frac{1,200,000 \; R}{2,000,000 \; U} = £360,000$$

The value attributed to the residue is

$$£1,400,000 \; x \; \frac{1,200,000 \; R}{2,000,000 \; U} = £840,000$$

Accordingly IHT is chargeable on only £360,000 of the son's legacy.

If the legacy is given tax free and the residue to an exempt beneficiary, it will be necessary to gross up the tax free legacy.[99]

Problems with 'nil rate band' legacies

10.59   Section 39A can create problems in relation to the amount passing under 'nil rate band' legacies where property attracting relief is not specifically bequeathed.

---

[99]   For grossing-up, see **3.41** *et seq.*

Example 10.11

T dies in March 2012 leaving a NRB legacy to his son. His estate is worth £1m and includes assets qualifying for BPR at 100% valued at £500,000. He has a nil cumulative total and his will leaves:

'the largest sum that can be given without any IHT being payable'

to his son and the residue to his wife.

T expected his son to take the amount of the nil rate band at his death less any lifetime chargeable transfers he made. However, this is not the case. The assets eligible for relief have not been specifically bequeathed and so s 39A(3) requires that the relief be apportioned between the residue and the pecuniary legacy. This increases the amount that the son can take without payment of IHT. The calculation is complex because you are working backwards to find the sum which after allowing the appropriate proportion of relief equals the nil rate band.

$$\frac{R}{U} = \frac{500,000}{1,000,000} = \frac{1}{2}$$

The son will take a legacy with *an IHT value* of £325,000. Allowing for BPR this is:

$$£650,000 \times \frac{1}{2} = £325,000$$

So instead of taking only £325,000 (the value of the nil rate band in 2012–13) the son will take £650,000.

If the proportion of property attracting BPR is greater, the size of the son's legacy will be proportionately greater.

Solution?

10.60 If the problem is recognised at the will drafting stage, and the testator does not want to give such a large legacy, the solution is either to leave the property attracting relief specifically to his spouse or civil partner or to amend the gift to the son as follows:

'a sum which is the smaller of:

(i)   the largest amount that can be given without any IHT being payable, or
(ii) the upper limit of the nil rate band applicable on my death.'

If the problem is not recognised until after the death, consider a post-death variation.[100]

---

[100] Variations are considered in Chapter 12.

Difficulty in assessing the extent to which relief will be available on death

10.61   There may be uncertainty as to whether relief will be available on death. Not only is there the possibility of the relief in the future being withdrawn by the government or reduced but also the nature of the business may change between the date when the will is executed and death (typically what was a trading company may become so infected with investment activities that the 'mainly' test is failed).

Because of this uncertainty as to the availability of relief on death, testators may suggest leaving the business to my daughter 'if it qualifies for 100% BPR, otherwise to my wife'. This is not advisable as HMRC will only consider whether relief is available if IHT is at stake. Here, whichever answer they come up with no tax will be payable. If the will has been so drafted it may leave the executors in some uncertainty when it comes to administering the estate!

10.62   Even if relief is available, it may not be available at 100% of the full value as there are situations where BPR is given at a reduced percentage or only on part of the value of the business property. For instance:

(a)   the relief is at 50% on certain assets (land and buildings, plant and machinery) used by a partnership in which the deceased was a partner at death or by a company which he then controlled;[101]

(b)   relief is at 50% on a controlling shareholding in a listed company;[102]

(c)   the value of a business qualifying for relief is reduced by the value of excepted assets[103] (eg cash reserves not needed for business purposes);

(d)   the value of a shareholding is reduced when there is a non-qualifying subsidiary company.[104]

In the case of agricultural property, the agricultural value may be less than the open market value. In such cases, the difference will not be relieved unless it attracts BPR as it may do, for instance, in the case of 'hope' value attached to farmland but not when the market value of a farmhouse exceeds its agricultural value.[105]

10.63   In the above situations while some relief may be due, the unrelieved value may attract an IHT charge. The taxpayer may therefore be faced with paying some IHT in order to obtain relief on the qualifying portion of the property or giving the whole property to an exempt beneficiary thus foregoing the relief completely. In some cases it may be possible to limit the chargeable gift, eg. in the **10.62**(b) situation to give chargeable persons shares in the listed

---

[101]   See IHTA 1984, s 105(1)(d).
[102]   IHTA 1984, s 105(1)(cc).
[103]   IHTA 1984, s 112 and see **10.50**.
[104]   IHTA 1984, s 111.
[105]   See **10.10**.

company to a value not exceeding £650,000 thereby ensuring that, after 50% relief, the transfer falls within the nil rate band of the testator. It may be difficult to assess the situation at the date the will is drafted with sufficient accuracy to allow for precise drafting of this type. For a solution see **10.64**.

Obtaining a ruling from HMRC on the availability of relief

10.64 Assume that the testator wants to leave his business property to his son if it attracts relief but otherwise to his wife. Taking into account the various uncertainties concerning the availability of relief (see **10.61** above); the possibility of only obtaining relief on part of the value transferred (see **10.62**) and the desirability of ensuring that the relief is considered and agreed by HMRC,[106] the solution for the will draftsman is to:

(a)   establish a discretionary trust;

(b)   put into that trust the relevant business or agricultural property without a qualification along the lines of 'provided that it shall qualify for IHT relief'. This will constitute a specific gift of the property within s 39A(2) and, because tax will be at stake (the gift is not spouse exempt and will, see below, in all cases exceed the available nil rate band of the testator) HMRC must then rule on the availability of the relief; and

(c)   add a cash gift of an amount equal to the testator's available nil rate band (taking care not to define this as such sum as would not attract an IHT charge but ignoring for this purpose the gift of the business/agricultural property) to ensure that even if the business/agricultural property is worth no more than £325,000 the issue of relief still will be determined by HMRC.

See **Precedent 10.7**.

10.65 The advantage of employing a discretionary trust is that appointments out of the trust (falling within IHTA 1984, s 144)[107] will be read-back into the will. It is, therefore, possible, once the position of APR/BPR has been agreed with HMRC, to take a view on the future of the trust. For instance, if full relief is given then either the trust may continue or property could be appointed to chargeable persons outright (eg to children/grandchildren). By contrast, if relief is not available then an appointment to the surviving spouse may be made to obtain the benefit of spouse relief. Note:

(a)   whilst APR/BPR disputes can drag on with HMRC over a long period, the majority are settled within 2 years of death. Of course the existence of this deadline should operate to concentrate minds and make sure that this happens;

---

[106] Note especially that if the testator left the business property to his son 'if it attracts relief' but otherwise to his wife, then HMRC will not consider whether relief is due given that no tax is at stake.

[107] Section 144 is considered at **13.11**.

(b)   bear in mind the CGT position if the trust is to be broken up within 2 years of death with IHT reading-back. The usual hold-over relief under TCGA 1992, s 260 will not be available but this should not matter if the estate is still in the course of administration when the beneficiaries will take qua legatees at probate value;[108]

(c)   if the testator wishes to use up his nil rate band then in the past it was not uncommon for the testator to make two gifts and, for example adding the nil rate band sum to a pilot discretionary trust established during the testator's lifetime. This will mean that both trusts will then benefit from a full nil rate which was attractive if the business property was sold so that that trust becomes a cash vehicle. The FA 2015 changes in the IHT treatment of settlements, however, have largely destroyed the use of pilot trusts.[109]

Maximising the relief in the case of married couples[110]

10.66   Assume that H owns the business property (eg shares in the family trading company) and is survived by his wife. The couple have a daughter who is not involved in the business which will be continued by the wife. If H were to gift the shares to her the spouse exemption would apply and BPR would be wasted.

What is sometimes called the 'two bites at the cherry' scheme involves the same business property attracting relief on the deaths of both husband and wife. This takes advantage of the fact that BPR is available if, at the date of death, the taxpayer owned assets which qualified for the relief. The fact that the assets are sold soon after the death does not result in any 'clawback' of the relief.[111] The main risk involved in the arrangement is that the surviving spouse will not survive the sale by 2 years. Failure to do so will mean that BPR will not be available on the purchased business property. This will mean that the expense of implementing the scheme (including stamp duty and any CGT payable on the sale) will have been wasted.

The first death: the discretionary trust

10.67   It is important that the shares are left in a discretionary trust since this will force HMRC to address the availability of BPR (see **10.64**). The key provisions to be included in the discretionary trust are:

---

[108]   See, for instance, *Cochrane's Executors v IRC* [1974] STC 335; *IRC v Matthew's Executors* [1984] STC 386 and CGTM para 31432.

[109]   For pilot trusts, see Chapter 8.

[110]   Similar planning is available for registered civil partners.

[111]   By contrast, clawback rules do exist in the case of lifetime gifts of such property: see IHTA 1984, ss 113A and 113B.

(a) the trustees must be allowed to exercise their power of appointment even if the administration of the estate is incomplete;[112]

(b) in the case of an unincorporated business, there must be a power for the surviving spouse to run it or to act as a partner in the business;

(c) the rule against 'self-dealing' should be excluded given that the surviving spouse is likely to be one of the trustees.[113]

10.68 If HMRC accept that the assets attract full relief then the trustees may consider selling the property to the surviving spouse. Note that this may give rise to:

(a) stamp duty (if shares) at 0.5% or SDLT if land involved;

(b) CGT if values have risen since death and bear in mind that the value for IHT purposes will not be ascertained at death if HMRC conclude that relief is due.

10.69 If the spouse purchases the business property she may obtain full BPR in the future. As the spouse will not take by succession, the normal 2 years qualifying period applies so, as explained at **10.66**, there is a risk of IHT on the business if the spouse does not survive the necessary 2 years.

---

[112] It is thought that this provision is inserted 'out of abundant caution' since the will trust is constituted at death: see **Precedent 4.1, clause 12.**

[113] See **Precedent 10.6(d).**

PRECEDENTS

Precedent 10.1: Gift of shares

Gift of shares

(a) I give to [   ] [provided he/she survives me by 28 days] all my shares in [   ] Ltd.

[(b) Any charge on the shares existing at my death shall be paid out of my Residuary Estate.[114]]

[(c) If any of the shares referred to in the gift in paragraph (a) above are as a result of any takeover amalgamation or reconstruction represented by a different holding at the time of my death paragraph (a) above shall take effect as a gift of that holding.[115]]

---

[114] See **1.48**(c).
[115] This may prevent ademption from applying: see **1.48**(d) and **Precedent 4.6**.

Precedent 10.2: Gift of a small business[116]

(a) I GIVE to [*name*] all my business of ... trading as [*name of business*] from the premises at [*address[es]*] to include [*the said premises and*] all plant machinery stocks vehicles tools and all other things employed or used in carrying on the said business together with the goodwill of the same and the benefits of all contracts entered into and all book debts due to the said business and together also with any cash at bank and cash in hand but subject in all respects to the liabilities of the said business.

(b) In the event of any premises from which my business trades being held under a lease or tenancy agreement at the time of my death then the said [*name*] shall pay the rent due from time to time in respect of those premises and shall observe and perform the lessee's covenants under the said lease or tenancy agreement and shall keep my estate indemnified against all liability under the said lease or tenancy including any liability that may have arisen in my lifetime or from acts or omissions done or arising in my lifetime.

(c) I APPOINT the said [*name*] as special executor of this my will to act only in respect of the business and other property bequeathed to him and I direct that the inheritance tax attributed to the above gift (allowing for any reduction in value for inheritance tax purposes) and the expenses of obtaining a grant limited to such property shall be paid by the said [*name*].[117]

---

[116] Where a gift is of a 'business', it is normally taken to include all the testator's interest in all the assets of the business, including business premises: *Re Rhagg* [1938] Ch 828.

[117] See 10.01.

Precedent 10.3: Gift to trustees of a business to carry on the business for a limited period[118]

I GIVE to my trustees all my business of ... trading as [*name of business*] from the premises at [*address[es]*] to include [*the said premises and*] all plant machinery stocks vehicles tools and all other things employed or used in carrying on the said business together with the goodwill of the same and the benefits of all contracts entered into and all book debts due to the said business and together also with any cash at bank and cash in hand but subject in all respects to the liabilities of the said business upon the following trusts:

(a) TO CARRY ON the said business and/or any other business on the said premises or any other suitable premises for so long and in such manner and on such terms as they in their sole discretion may think fit and subject thereto without being liable to my estate for any loss arising therefrom.

(b) UPON TRUST to sell the said business including any premises used in connection with the said business as a going concern together with the goodwill thereof and all the then existing assets thereof or such of them as my trustees think fit but subject to the liabilities thereof or such of them as my trustees think fit upon such terms as they may in their sole discretion think proper [and thereafter the proceeds of sale of the said business shall fall into and become part of my residuary estate].

---

[118] For a general power for PRs to run a business, see **Precedent 4.1, clause 9(7)**.

Precedent 10.4: Trusts of net profits of business until sale and of net proceeds of sale

I DECLARE that my trustees shall stand possessed of the said business and the net annual profits thereof after payment of all the expenses and liabilities of the same until sale of the said business as aforesaid and after the said sale shall also stand possessed of the net proceeds of sale thereof and of any other monies arising therefrom or in connection therewith and of the income of such proceeds of sale and other moneys UPON TRUST to pay such annual profits or income as the case may be to my wife [*name*] during her life and after her death as to the said business and the said annual profits or (as the case may be) the said proceeds of sale and other moneys and the income thereof respectively UPON TRUST etc.[119]

---

[119] Bear in mind that if the business is left to the testator's wife on an IPDI trust, the spouse exemption will apply and BPR will accordingly be wasted.

Precedent 10.5: Provision for child of testator to take on business on payment to trustees[120]

(a)   I DECLARE that if any child of mine shall give notice to my trustees within [3] months of my death of his or her wish to carry on my said business and shall pay to my trustees the sum of £[   ] such sum if not paid at once to be paid within a period not exceeding [2] years from the date of my death and to bear interest at the rate of [5] per cent per annum then my trustees shall transfer the business as aforesaid including any premises but subject to all liabilities of the business to my said child and my trustees shall stand possessed of the said sum of £[   ] and any interest thereon as and when the same shall be received upon the following trusts ...

(b)   I FURTHER DECLARE that where more than one of my children wish to carry on my business and give notice to my trustees as hereinbefore prescribed then the eldest of such children shall be entitled to the transfer of the business to his or her name on the making of the payments as aforesaid and in priority to and to the exclusion of my other children.

---

[120] See **10.01.**

Precedent 10.6: Trustees' powers

(a) Power for trustees to carry on business where there is a trust for sale

I DECLARE that my trustees shall have full power to carry on my business of [ ] at [ ] and to postpone the sale and conversion thereof into money for so long as they shall think fit until such time as the same may be sold either as a going concern or otherwise and that during any period when the business is being carried on by my trustees they shall be free from control or interference from any person or persons beneficially entitled to the said business or the proceeds of sale thereof under this my will.

(b) Power for willing trustees to carry on testator's business where other trustees refuse

I DECLARE that should any one or more of my trustees be unwilling to carry on my business then the other or others of my trustees may carry on such business and may exercise alone all powers authorities and discretions hereby conferred on my trustees in relation to carrying on the said business or the winding up or sale of the said business.

(c) Provision of salary for trustees managing business

I DECLARE that any one or more of my trustees who act as manager or manageress of my business aforesaid shall be entitled to [a salary of £ ... per annum] [such salary as may be agreed upon by my trustees for the time being] throughout the period during which he she or they shall so act without being liable to account to my estate in respect thereof.

(d) Provision for exercise of powers though trustees interested in business

All or any of the above powers hereinbefore granted to my trustees shall be exercisable and may be exercised by any of my trustees notwithstanding that he or she may be interested as a partner in the said business or as a beneficiary under this my will.

(e) Indemnity to trustees carrying on business

I DIRECT that each and every one of my trustees concerned in the running of my business shall be fully and effectively indemnified from my estate in respect of any personal loss or liability arising from the carrying on of the said business and I DECLARE that none of my trustees shall be liable to my estate or any part thereof for any loss arising from the carrying on of the said business.

Precedent 10.7: Clauses for NRB legacy including business property[121]

Nil rate-band legacy

1 Definitions

In this Clause:

1.1 'the Discretionary Beneficiaries' means such of the following as are alive at my death or born during the Trust Period: my [wife/husband/civil partner] children and remoter issue and the spouses widows and widowers and civil partners (whether or not remarried) of such children and remoter issue

1.2 'the Trust Period' means the period expiring 125 years from my death which period shall be the perpetuity period applicable to the trusts set out in this Clause

1.3 'the Legacy Fund' means:
1.3.1 the Specified Sum and my Business Property (as hereinafter defined);
1.3.2 all accumulations (if any) of income directed to be held as an accretion to capital; and
1.3.3 the money investments and other property from time to time representing the above

1.4 'the Legacy Fund Trustees' means [   ] and the trustees for the time being of the Legacy Fund

1.5 'my Business Property'[122] means all my interest in the business known as (*name of business*) ('the Business') including:
1.5.1 all goodwill stock vehicles machinery plant and other equipment;
1.5.2 all book debts money standing to the credit of the Business at any bank or elsewhere and the benefit of all contracts;
1.5.3 any freehold or leasehold premises used at the date of my death by the Business;
1.5.4 any property of mine used wholly and exclusively in the Business;
and if at the date of my death the name of the Business has changed or if as a result of any amalgamation restructuring rearrangement or sale of the Business my interest is represented by substituted capital holdings or interests in a new business whether as a sole trader or partner or in a company not being a public limited company then this gift shall not fail but shall take effect as a gift of such newly named business holdings or interests

1.6 'the Specified Sum'[123] means a pecuniary legacy of the maximum amount which can be given under this Clause without inheritance tax being payable in respect of my death but subject to the following:

---

[121] See **10.59.**

[122] This definition will require amendment in the event that the testator owns shares in the family business rather than an interest in an unincorporated business.

[123] It is only necessary to include a gift of 'the Specified Sum' in addition to a gift of the business

1.6.1 the Specified Sum shall not exceed the upper limit of the nil per cent rate band (applicable on my death) in the table of rates of tax in Schedule 1 to the Inheritance Tax Act 1984 (or any statutory re-enactment thereof);[124]

1.6.2 any other legacy given by my Will or any codicil shall be paid in priority to the Specified Sum; and

1.6.3 no account shall be taken of the value transferred by the gifts of my Business Property in calculating the Specified Sum.

2   Gift of the Legacy Fund

If my [wife/husband/civil partner] survives me by 30 days I give to the Legacy Fund Trustees the Legacy Fund subject to the payment of inheritance tax (if any).

---

property when the value of the latter (before relief) will fall below the testator's available nil rate band so that, in the absence of other chargeable transfers, no tax would be at stake and HMRC would not need to consider the availability of relief.

[124] Hence the amount will be limited to one unused NRB not two in a case where there would otherwise be a transferred nil rate band (see Chapter 5).

Section C

ADMINISTERING THE ESTATE (INCLUDING ESTABLISHING AND RUNNING WILL TRUSTS)

CHAPTER 11

OBTAINING THE GRANT

1. THE STEPS TO BE TAKEN

11.01 In order to obtain a grant of representation, it is necessary to make an application to either the Principal Registry of the Family Division or to a district probate registry. Applications can be made in person by those entitled to act as personal representatives using PA1 available on the Probate Registry section of the Justice website.[1] Personal applicants attend an interview at the appropriate registry where they identify themselves and swear or affirm that the information provided is correct. Where an application is made by a solicitor or other professional, a PA1 is not used. Instead the professional submits an oath sworn or affirmed by those entitled to act as personal representatives.

In both cases the original will and any codicils together with two A4 copies must be sent together with a probate fee.

11.02 In addition the personal representatives must complete an IHT 400 and whichever of the supporting Schedules 401–423 are relevant to the estate (unless the estate qualifies as an excepted estate, in which case the shorter IHT 205 can be completed).

The personal representatives submit the forms to HMRC together with any IHT due. They will receive back a receipted Form 421 confirming the payment of IHT which should be submitted along with the other papers to the probate registry in order to obtain the grant of representation.

2. FIRST STEPS

11.03 The personal representatives will have to determine the size of the estate in order to decide whether they need to complete a full IHT 400 or the smaller IHT 205 which can be submitted where the estate fulfils the requirements to be 'excepted'.

The estate on death[2] comprises all property to which the deceased was beneficially entitled[3] at the moment before death other than excluded property.[4]

---

[1] http://www.justice.gov.uk/courts/probate/obtain-probate.
[2] See IHTA 1984, s 5 as amended and 3.05 for the definition of 'estate'.
[3] See **3.14** *et seq* for a discussion of valuation issues.

It therefore includes the value of beneficial joint tenancies and trust property in which the deceased had an interest in possession created before 22 March 2006, an immediate post-death interest, a disabled person's interest and a transitional serial interest.[5]

Liabilities of the deceased and reasonable funeral expenses may be deducted when determining the value of the taxable estate.[6]

Where exemptions and reliefs are available, the personal representatives claim them on the appropriate schedule.

ELECTED DOMICILE FOR SPOUSES AND CIVIL PARTNERS

11.04   Until 6 April 2013 there was a limit of £55,000 on the IHT exemption[7] for transfers made by UK-domiciled individuals to non-UK-domiciled spouses or civil partners. In October 2012, the European Commission formally requested the UK to review the limit on the ground that it was discriminatory.

In response Finance Act 2013 amended IHTA 1984, s 18 to increase the limit of the spouse exemption to the level of the nil rate band for transfers on or after 6 April 2013. This was helpful but did not deal with the discrimination point.

In addition, therefore, the Finance Act 2013 introduced a new s 267ZA and s 267ZB into IHTA 1984 which allows spouses and civil partners to elect to be domiciled in England and Wales for IHT purposes, thereby obtaining an unrestricted exemption. The power to elect is not restricted to EU nationals; it is available to any non-domiciled individual.

As explained at **11.08** below the election is most likely to be made after the death of a domiciled spouse or civil partner and should be considered when dealing with the administration of an estate.

> *Example 11.01*
>
> Mary (UK-domiciled) is married to Jean-Pierre (not domiciled in the UK). She dies in 2015/16.
>
> She can pass to Jean-Pierre free of IHT assets to the value of £325,000 (using the limited spouse exemption) plus another £325,000 if she has an unused nil rate band plus another £325,000 if she has the benefit of an unused nil rate band from an earlier spouse who pre-deceased.

11.05   In the case of estates with more substantial assets, the surviving spouse will need to consider making an election to be treated as domiciled here. However, it is not necessarily beneficial in tax terms to make the election. The

---

[4]   IHTA 1984, s 5 as amended.
[5]   IHTA 1984, s 5(1A) and s 49(1A).
[6]   For liabilities see further 3.07 *et seq.*
[7]   IHTA 1984, s 18.

downside of an election is that the worldwide estate of the previously non-domiciled spouse is brought into the IHT net. Not only does this mean that IHT will be payable if they die whilst the election remains in force, but also, because the election can be backdated, earlier gifts are potentially bought within the IHT charge.

HMRC gives this example at IHTM 13047.

Example 11.02

> David, who is domiciled in the UK transfers property worth £1m in 2014 to his spouse, Birgit who is not domiciled in the UK. Subsequently, in 2016, Birgit transfers some German shares to the trustees of an offshore trust. David dies in 2019.
>
> At the time of David's transfer, the value transferred is exempt to the extent of £325,000 and a PET to the extent of £675,000. Following his death, the failed PET is chargeable and after deducting the nil-rate band, £350,000 is subject to tax.
>
> Birgit's transfer was a transfer of excluded property: see IHTA 1984, s 6(1). Following David's death, Birgit has the choice of electing to be treated as domiciled in the UK. If she does so, the gift from David in 2014 will become fully exempt as a transfer where both spouses are domiciled in the UK.
>
> However, Birgit will then be treated as domiciled in the UK from 2014 for all IHT purposes. This means that her transfer to the trustees is no longer one of excluded property and will be subject to IHT. As a transfer to a trust, it will be immediately chargeable to tax.[8]
>
> Birgit will need to consider all the consequences of making an election. Should she decide to go ahead with the election, the requirements to deliver an account in respect of the transfer and the changes to the due dates for tax and interest are set out at IHTM13048.

As a result great care needs to be exercised in determining whether the election will be advantageous.

It is not possible to revoke an election although there are circumstances in which it will lapse. See **11.09**.

Making the election

11.06 There is extensive guidance in the IHT Manual.[9] The election must be made by notice in writing, although there is no prescribed form. IHTM13043 says for HMRC to keep meaningful records the notice must contain:

---

[8] The legislation provides for extended dates for accounting and payment. HMRC concedes at IHTM13048 that in such a case it would 'not be reasonable for the original due dates for delivery of an account and for the payment of tax and interest to apply'. IHTA 1984, s 267ZB(8) provides that the due date for the delivery of an account is 12 months from the end of the month in which the election is made. For the payment of the tax and the date from which interest is charged, the transfer is treated as if it was made at the date of the election.

[9] IHTM13040 – 13049.

- the full name and address of the person making the election, or for whom the personal representatives are making an election;
- their date of birth and, if appropriate, their date of death;
- the full name of their spouse or civil partner who is domiciled in the UK; and
- the date the election is to take effect from.

The HMRC Technical Note of 11 December 2012 comments that 'HMRC will keep a record of elections and will, if requested by the personal representatives of any individual who has died, confirm whether or not, and when, an election has been made by the deceased person'.

Two types of election

11.07 A lifetime election is made by the non-domiciled spouse or civil partner during the lifetime of the other partner.[10] At the time of the election the person making it does not need to be:

(a) married or in a civil partnership;

(b) resident in the UK; nor

(c) domiciled outside the UK.

The only requirement is that during the period of 7 years ending with the date on which the election is made, the person had a spouse or civil partner who was domiciled in the UK.[11]

A death election is made either by a surviving non-domiciled spouse or civil partner following the death of the UK-domiciled partner, or by the personal representatives of the non-UK-domiciled partner.[12] Again the only requirement is that the person making the election, or on whose behalf the election was made, had a spouse or civil partner who was domiciled in the UK during the period of 7 years ending with the date on which the election is made. Again, the person making the election does not need to be resident in the UK nor domiciled outside the UK.

Time limits

11.08 The first opportunity to make an election was on 17 July 2013 (the date when the 2013 Finance Act received Royal Assent). Both types of elections take effect on a 'date specified'.[13] The date specified must:

(a) be no earlier than 6 April 2013,

---

[10] IHTA 1984, s 267ZA(3).
[11] IHTA 1984, s 267ZA(3).
[12] IHTA 1984, s 267ZA(4).
[13] IHTA 1984, s 267ZB(3).

(b) be within the period of 7 years ending with –
- (i) in the case of a lifetime election, the date on which the election is made, or
- (ii) in the case of a death election, the date of the deceased's death

The lifetime election can be made at any time. The death election must be made within 2 years of the death of the spouse or such longer period as an officer of the Revenue may in the particular case allow.[14]

In the case of a potentially exempt transfer, it makes sense for the non-domiciled spouse to wait and see whether it is necessary to make an election. If the transferor survives 7 years, the election is unnecessary.

> *Example 11.03*
>
> In May 2014 Mary (domiciled in the UK) gives Jean-Pierre (not domiciled in the UK) £1m. There is no point in Jean-Pierre making an election at that point because if Mary survives 7 years IHT is not an issue. If she dies (say in March 2015) he can elect and backdate the election to a date immediately before the transfer.

Because the election cannot be backdated before 6 April 2013 earlier gifts may be chargeable to tax despite an election.

> *Example 11.04*
>
> In May 2012, Jane, who was domiciled in the UK transferred £400,000 to her civil partner Kate, who was not domiciled in the UK. Of this transfer, £55,000 was exempt under the unamended IHTA 1984, s 18 and £345,000 was a potentially exempt transfer. If Jane dies in 2017, the potentially exempt transfer becomes chargeable and after deduction of the nil rate band, £20,000 will be subject to tax. An election cannot change this.

When the election ceases to have effect

11.09 The election cannot be revoked but, if the person making it is not UK-resident 'for the purposes of income tax for a period of 4 successive tax years beginning at any time after the election is made, the election ceases to have effect at the end of that period'.[15]

> *Example 11.05*
>
> 1. Following Mary's death Jean-Pierre makes an election in tax year 2015–16. He ceased to be UK resident on April 5, 2016. The election will remain in force until the end of tax year 2019–20. This is because there must be non-residence throughout 4 successive tax years beginning after the election is made. The 4-year period begins with 2015–16. Non-residence is required throughout that year and 2016–17; 2017–18 and 2018–19.
>
> 2. Once the election has ceased to have effect, it is not revived. If Jean-Pierre

---

[14] IHTA 1984 s 267ZB(6).
[15] IHTA 1984, s 267ZB(10).

becomes UK-resident in tax year 2016–17, the election remains in force. However, if having remained non-UK-resident for 4 tax years, he returns and becomes resident for the first time in 2019–20 the election remains lapsed.

Problems for personal representatives

11.10 Personal representatives may not know whether the deceased made a lifetime election. However, they will need to check because it could have a significant impact on the tax liability that arises following their death. If they cannot trace any information amongst the deceased's papers, they may contact HMRC to see whether there is any record of an election.

IHTM 13045 says that HMRC will not disclose any information about the existence of an election over the phone. Instead, executors should make their request in writing and provide evidence that they are the people entitled to apply for a grant of representation.

If the executors can demonstrate that they are appointed by sending a copy of the Will, the information will be provided. Administrators will need to demonstrate that they are applying for letters of administration, or that they are entitled to apply.

3. IS THE ESTATE EXCEPTED?

11.11 For deaths on or after 6 April 2004 there are three categories of excepted estate.[16]

11.12 *Category 1* – low value estates

An estate is excepted where the deceased died domiciled in the UK and the gross value of the estate for IHT purposes, plus the chargeable value of any specified transfers in the 7 years prior to death, does not exceed the current IHT threshold (for 2015–16, £325,000). The nil rate band threshold is increased where the deceased inherited one full nil rate band from one spouse or civil partner.[17]

---

[16] Inheritance Tax (Delivery of Accounts) (Excepted Estates) Regulations 2004, SI 2004/2543 as amended by the Inheritance Tax (Delivery of Accounts) (Excepted Estates) (Amendment) Regulations 2006, SI 2006/2141 for deaths on or after 1 September 2006 (which increased the financial limits), the Inheritance Tax (Delivery of Accounts) (Excepted Estates) (Amendment) Regulations 2011, SI 2011/214 which came into force on 1 March 2011 and made further amendments principally to allow the nil rate band to be increased in certain cases where the estate benefitted from a transferred nil rate band and the Inheritance Tax (Delivery of Accounts) (Excepted Estates) (Amendment) Regulations 2014, SI 2014/488 which came into force on 1 April 2014 and amended the rules on 'liabilities' to take account of the restrictions on the deductibility of certain liabilities introduced by Finance Act 2013.

[17] See **11.16**.

In full, the requirements are as follows:[18]

> '(a) the person died on or after 6 April 2004, domiciled in the United Kingdom;
> (b) the value of that person's estate is attributable wholly to property passing:
>> (i) under his will or intestacy;
>> (ii) under a nomination of an asset taking effect on death;
>> (iii) under a single settlement in which he was entitled to an interest in possession; or
>> (iv) by survivorship in a beneficial joint tenancy;
> (c) of that property:
>> (i) not more than £150,000[19] represented value attributable to property which, immediately before that person's death, was settled property;[20] and
>> (ii) not more than £100,000[21] represented value attributable to property which, immediately before that person's death, was situated outside the United Kingdom;
> (c)(a) that person was not a person by reason of whose death one of the alternatively secured pension fund provisions applies;[22]
> (d) that person died without having made any chargeable transfers[23] in the seven years before his death other than specified transfers[24] where the aggregate value transferred before deduction of business or agricultural relief[25] did not exceed £150,000;[26] and
> (e) the aggregate of:
>> (i) the gross value of that person's estate;
>> (ii) the value transferred by any specified transfers made by that person; and
>> (iii) the value transferred by any specified exempt transfers[27] made by that person,

---

[18] Inheritance Tax (Delivery of Accounts) (Excepted Estates) Regulations 2004, reg 4(2).

[19] £100,000 for deaths before 1 September 2006.

[20] Property which was settled property immediately before the person's death is not settled for this purpose to the extent that the property is transferred on that person's death to a spouse, civil partner or charity: Inheritance Tax (Delivery of Accounts) (Excepted Estates) Regulations 2004, reg 4(8).

[21] £75,000 for deaths before 1 September 2006.

[22] 'Alternatively secured pension fund provisions' means IHTA 1984, s 151A–151C (person dying with alternatively secured pension fund). Note, however, that this provision does not apply in relation to deaths occurring on or after 6 April 2011: Inheritance Tax (Delivery of Accounts) (Excepted Estates) Regulations 2004, reg 4(9).

[23] For this purpose 'chargeable transfer' includes transfers made within 7 years of death which are exempt as normal expenditure out of income (IHTA 1984, s 21) and exceed £3,000 in the tax year: Inheritance Tax (Delivery of Accounts) (Excepted Estates) Regulations 2004, reg 4(7A).

[24] 'Specified transfers' means chargeable transfers made within 7 years of death where the value transferred is attributable to (a) cash, (b) personal chattels or corporeal moveable property, (c) quoted shares or securities, or (d) an interest in or over land, save to the extent that sections 102 and 102A(2) of FA 1986 apply to that transfer or the land became settled property on that transfer: Inheritance Tax (Delivery of Accounts) (Excepted Estates) Regulations 2004, reg 4(6).

[25] Inheritance Tax (Delivery of Accounts) (Excepted Estates) Regulations 2004, reg 4(7).

[26] £100,000 for deaths before 1 September 2006.

[27] Specified exempt transfers means transfers of value made within 7 years of death which are exempt transfers only by reason of IHTA 1984, s 18 (transfers between spouses or civil partners), s 23 (gifts to charities), s 24 (gifts to political parties), s 24A (gifts to housing

did not exceed the IHT threshold.'[28]

Example 11.06

Eric, who is domiciled in England and Wales, dies. His will leaves his estate to his wife and daughter in equal shares. He gave his daughter £50,000 in cash 2 years before he died.

His estate consists of:

	£
Half share in house owned jointly with his wife	80,000
Cash in UK Banks	50,000
Cash in offshore account	50,000
Personal chattels	20,000
Life Interest in trust fund established in his father's will	
Value of trust assets	30,000
Credit card debts	(5,000)

The estate is excepted because it fulfils the requirements to be a category 1 low value estate:

- Eric was domiciled in the UK.

- His whole estate passes by will and under the single settlement in which he had a life interest.

- His settled property does not exceed £150,000.

- His non-UK property does not exceed £100,000.

- He made a specified transfer to his daughter but it does not exceed £150,000.

The combined value of his gross estate (before exemptions and reliefs) and chargeable lifetime transfer is £280,000, which is below the nil rate threshold.

11.13   *Category 2 – exempt estates*

An estate is excepted where the gross value of the estate plus certain lifetime transfers does not exceed £1,000,000 and the net chargeable estate after deduction of spouse and/or charity exemption does not exceed the IHT

---

associations), s 27 (maintenance funds for historic buildings, etc), or s 28 (employee trusts): Inheritance Tax (Delivery of Accounts) (Excepted Estates) Regulations 2004, reg 4(6).

[28] For applications between 6 April and 1 August each year the threshold is the threshold for the previous tax year. In the case of deaths occurring on or after 6 April 2010 the threshold is increased by 100% where certain criteria are satisfied. Broadly, one whole nil rate band must have been transferred to the deceased from one deceased spouse or civil partner. The threshold is not increased if only a proportion of a nil rate band is transferred or if the deceased had whole additional nil rate band made up of portions transferred from more than one deceased spouse/civil partner: Inheritance Tax (Delivery of Accounts) (Excepted Estates) Regulations 2004, reg 5A(3) and 4.

threshold. As was the case for small estates for deaths on or after 6 April 2011 the nil rate threshold is increased by 100% where the deceased had the benefit of one full nil rate band transferred from a predeceased spouse or civil partner.[29]

In full, the 2004 Regulations for this category provide as follows:[30]

'(a) the person died on or after 6 April 2004, domiciled in the United Kingdom;

(b) the value of that person's estate is attributable wholly to property passing:

    (i) under his will or intestacy;

    (ii) under a nomination of an asset taking effect on death;

    (iii) under a single settlement in which he was entitled to an interest in possession; or

    (iv) by survivorship in a beneficial joint tenancy;

(c) of that property:

    (i) not more than £150,000[31] represented value attributable to property which, immediately before that person's death, was settled property;[32] and

    (ii) not more than £100,000[33] represented value attributable to property which, immediately before that person's death, was situated outside the United Kingdom;

(c)(a) that person was not a person by reason of whose death one of the alternatively secured pension fund provisions applies;[34]

(d) that person died without having made any chargeable transfers[35] during the period of seven years ending with his death other than specified transfers[36] where before deduction of business or agricultural relief,[37] the aggregate value transferred did not exceed £150,000:[38]

---

[29] Inheritance Tax (Delivery of Accounts) (Excepted Estates) (Amendment) Regulations 2011, SI 2011/214.

[30] Inheritance Tax (Delivery of Accounts) (Excepted Estates) Regulations 2004, reg 4(2).

[31] £100,000 for deaths before 1 September 2006.

[32] Property which was settled property immediately before the person's death is not settled for this purpose to the extent that the property is transferred on that person's death by a spouse, civil partner or charity: Inheritance Tax (Delivery of Accounts) (Excepted Estates) Regulations 2004, reg 4(8).

[33] £75,000 for deaths before 1 September 2006.

[34] 'Alternatively secured pension fund provisions' means IHTA 1984, s 151A–151C (person dying with alternatively secured pension fund). Note, however, that this provision does not apply in relation to deaths occurring on or after 6 April 2011: Inheritance Tax (Delivery of Accounts) (Excepted Estates) Regulations 2004, reg 4(9). This is because FA 2011 removed the requirement to buy an annuity by age 75 and the charges that applied where a scheme member failed to take their entitlement no longer apply.

[35] For this purpose 'chargeable transfer' includes transfers made within 7 years of death which are exempt as normal expenditure out of income (IHTA 1984, s 21) and exceed £3,000 in the tax year: Inheritance Tax (Delivery of Accounts) (Excepted Estates) Regulations 2004, reg 4(7A).

[36] 'Specified transfers' means chargeable transfers made within 7 years of death where the value transferred is attributable to (a) cash, (b) personal chattels or corporeal moveable property, (c) quoted shares or securities, or (d) an interest in or over land, save to the extent that sections 102 and 102A(2) of FA 1986 apply to that transfer or the land became settled property on that transfer: Inheritance Tax (Delivery of Accounts) (Excepted Estates) Regulations 2004, reg 4(6).

[37] Inheritance Tax (Delivery of Accounts) (Excepted Estates) Regulations 2004, reg 4(7).

[38] £100,000 for deaths before 1 September 2006.

(e) the aggregate of:
    (i)   the gross value of that person's estate,
    (ii) the value transferred by any specified transfers made by that person, and
    (iii) the value transferred by any specified exempt transfers made by that person,
    did not exceed £1,000,000;
(e)(a) in the case of deaths occurring on or after 1 March 2011 the total value transferred on that person's death by a spouse, civil partner or charity transfer is greater than nil;[39] and
(f) the aggregate of A – (B + C) does not exceed the IHT threshold,[40] where:
    A is the aggregate of the values in sub-paragraph (e);
    B, subject to paragraph (4) of reg 4, is the total value transferred on that person's death by a spouse, civil partner or charity transfer; and
    C is the total liabilities[41] of the estate.'

Example 11.07

Elsie, who is domiciled in England and Wales, has just died. Her will leaves £50,000 to her son and the residue to her husband. She gave £50,000 in cash to her son one year before she died and £50,000 to her husband.

Her estate consists of:

	£
Half share in house owned jointly with her husband	400,000
Cash in UK Banks and UK investments	150,000
Cash in offshore account	50,000
Personal chattels	20,000
Life Interest in trust fund established in her father's will	
Value of trust assets	30,000
Credit card debts	(15,000)

The estate is excepted because it fulfils the requirements to be a category 2 exempt estate:

- Elsie was domiciled in the UK.

---

[39] Inheritance Tax (Delivery of Accounts) (Excepted Estates) (Amendment) Regulations 2011.

[40] For applications between 6 April and 1 August each year the threshold is the threshold for the previous tax year. In the case of deaths occurring on or after 6 April 2010 the threshold is increased by 100% where certain criteria are satisfied. See **11.16**. Broadly, one whole nil rate band must have been transferred to the deceased from one pre-deceasing spouse or civil partner.

[41] For deaths occurring on or after 1 April 2014 'total liabilities of the estate' do not include liabilities of the estate to the extent that they (a) are not discharged as required by s 175A(1)(a) of the 1984 Act (discharge of liabilities after death); (b) are prevented from being taken into account as mentioned in s 175A(1)(b) of the 1984 Act (discharge of liabilities after death); or (c) are attributable as mentioned in s 162A(1)(a) or (b), or s 162A(5), of the 1984 Act (liabilities attributable to financing excluded property): Inheritance Tax (Delivery of Accounts) (Excepted Estates) (Amendment) Regulations 2014, SI 2014/488, reg 2(1), (3).

- Her whole estate passes by will and under the single settlement in which she had a life interest.

- Her settled property does not exceed £150,000.

- Her non-UK property does not exceed £100,000.

- She made a specified transfer to her son but it does not exceed £150,000.

- Property is actually passing to her spouse.

- The combined value of her gross estate (before exemptions and reliefs) and chargeable and exempt lifetime transfers is £750,000 which is below £1m.

- After deducting the spouse exemption and liabilities the combined value of the death estate and lifetime transfers is £85,000 which does not exceed the nil rate threshold. The credit card debts will only be deductible to the extent that they are discharged from the estate.[42]

11.14 *Category 3* – foreign domiciliaries

The third category is where the deceased was never domiciled or treated as domiciled in the United Kingdom and his estate in the United Kingdom consists only of cash or quoted shares or securities with a gross value not exceeding £100,000.

In full, the 2004 Regulations for this category provide as follows:

'(a) the person died on or after 6 April 2004;
(b) that person was never domiciled in the United Kingdom or treated as domiciled in the United Kingdom by IHTA 1984, s 267;
(c) that person was not a person by reason of whose death one of the alternatively secured pension fund provisions applies;[43] and
(d) the value of that person's estate situated in the United Kingdom is wholly attributable to cash or quoted shares or securities passing under his will or intestacy or by survivorship in a beneficial joint tenancy, the gross value of which does not exceed £150,000.'[44]

Example 11.08

Eduardo is an Italian who has never been domiciled in the UK. He dies with £100,000 in a UK bank account. The estate is excepted because it fulfils the requirements to be a category 3 foreign domiciliary estate.

11.15 In relation to deaths occurring on or after 1 March 2011 any transfers of value made by the deceased person in any tax year which exceed £3,000 and which are exempt transfers by virtue of IHTA 1984, s 21 (normal expenditure out of income) are treated as chargeable transfers.[45]

---

[42] Required by Inheritance Tax (Delivery of Accounts) (Excepted Estates) Regulations 2004, reg 4(7B) inserted by Inheritance Tax (Delivery of Accounts) (Excepted Estates) (Amendment) Regulations 2011 (SI 2011/214).

[43] See footnote 34 above.

[44] £100,000 for deaths before 1 September 2006.

[45] Inheritance Tax (Delivery of Accounts) (Excepted Estates) Regulations 2004, reg 7A.

11.16 The IHT threshold was originally defined as the lower limit shown in the Table in IHTA 1984, Sch 1 for the year of death unless the deceased died on or after 6 April and the application for probate or confirmation was made before 6 August in that tax year, in which case it was the limit for the previous tax year. The threshold did not take account of any transferred nil rate band available to the deceased. In the case of deaths occurring on or after 6 April 2010, reg 5A[46] provides that the threshold will be increased by 100% for a surviving spouse or civil partner where the following criteria[47] are satisfied.

In relation to the surviving spouse or civil partner:

(a) either:
  (i) in a case where the first deceased person was the spouse of the survivor, the first deceased person died on or after 13 November 1974, or
  (ii) in a case where the first deceased person was the civil partner of the survivor, the first deceased person died on or after 5 December 2005; and

(b) a claim is made pursuant to s 8A of the 1984 Act:
  (i) by virtue of which the nil-rate band maximum at the time of the survivor's death is treated, for the purpose of the charge to tax on the death of the survivor, as increased by 100%, and
  (ii) which is made in respect of not more than one first deceased person.

(c) the first deceased person died domiciled in the United Kingdom;

(d) the value of the first deceased person's estate is attributable wholly to property passing:
  (i) under the first deceased person's will or intestacy, or
  (ii) by survivorship in a beneficial joint tenancy or, in Scotland, by survivorship in a special destination;

(e) of that property, not more than £100,000 represented value attributable to property which immediately before the first deceased person's death was situated outside the United Kingdom;

(f) the first deceased person was not a person by reason of whose death one of the alternatively secured pension fund provisions applies[48] but note that this provision does not apply in relation to deaths occurring on or after 6 April 2011;

(g) the first deceased person died without having made any chargeable transfers during the period of 7 years ending with the first deceased

---

[46] Inserted by the Inheritance Tax (Delivery of Accounts) (Excepted Estates) (Amendment) Regulations 2011.

[47] Set out in Inheritance Tax (Delivery of Accounts) (Excepted Estates) Regulations 2004, reg 5A(3) and (4).

[48] For deaths on or after 6 April 2010 'alternatively secured pension fund provisions' means the following sections of the 1984 Act: s 151A (person dying with alternatively secured pension fund); s 151B (relevant dependant with pension fund inherited from member over 75); and s 151C (dependant dying with other pension fund).

person's death (business and agricultural property relief shall not apply in determining whether the first deceased person has made a chargeable transfer); and

(h) the value transferred by any chargeable transfer made on the death of the first deceased person was not reduced by virtue of s 104 (business property relief) or s 116 (agricultural property relief) of the 1984 Act.

The increase in the nil rate threshold is limited to the simple situation where the **whole** of a nil rate band is transferred from **one** person which means that it will often be unavailable even though the value of the deceased person's estate is substantially below the enhanced nil rate threshold.

> *Example 11.09*
>
> Ernest, who is domiciled in England and Wales, has just died leaving everything to his son, Sam. His estate consists of a house and UK investments and bank accounts and its gross value is £500,000. His wife, Wendy, died a year ago leaving £65,000 to Sam and everything else to Ernest. The gift to Sam used 20% of Wendy's nil rate band and an additional 80% of the current nil rate band (which is £260,000) is therefore available to Ernest's estate.
>
> Ernest's nil rate band is increased by £260,000 to £585,000 but the additional £260,000 is ignored for the purpose of the excepted estates regulations as Ernest did not inherit the whole of Wendy's nil rate band. His estate is, therefore, not excepted.

11.17 In its Newsletters HMRC regularly makes the point that it is not necessary to inform it of all changes in the value of excepted estates.[49] There is no need to report an adjustment to the value of an excepted estate unless the estate no longer qualifies as an excepted estate and either:

- the changes mean Inheritance Tax will be due, or

- the estate, before deducting reliefs, is more than the nil rate band – for example, where relievable property, such as a farm, that was exempt because passing to the surviving spouse is redirected to children (this allows HMRC to consider whether in its view relief is actually available).

Where the estate remains non-taxpaying because 100 per cent transferable nil rate band is available, it is necessary to send HMRC Trusts and Estates Nottingham a copy of the form IHT205, a form C4 *Corrective Account* showing the amendments and form IHT217 *Claim to transfer unused nil rate band for excepted estates* in order to claim the TNRB, This must be done within 2 years from the end of the month when the deceased died, or a form IHT400 will be required. More guidance can be found in the guidance notes for the form IHT205.

---

[49] See *IHT & Trusts Newsletter* for August 2007 and April 2008 and *Trusts and Estates Newsletter* for December 2012.

In the December 2007 IHT and Trusts Newsletter, HMRC said that where it transpires that an estate no longer qualifies as an excepted estate, the personal representatives must deliver an account of the estate. However, it will accept a Corrective Account (C4) provided it is accompanied by a copy of IHT205 as delivery of an account. It is, therefore, important to keep a copy of form IHT205/C5 on file. Without it, taxpayers will have to deliver a full IHT400. If the change in status results from the execution of a deed of variation, a copy should be attached.

> *Example 11.10*
>
> Ralph died in 2001 leaving a widow, Rita. All of Ralph's estate valued at £300,000 passed to Rita under the terms of Ralph's will. As a result, Ralph's entire nil rate band is available to transfer to Rita's estate when she dies.
>
> Rita leaves everything to her daughter. The gross value of her estate was originally £300,000. No IHT was payable and the estate qualified as an excepted estate. One year after Rita's death, her PRs discover an additional asset worth £50,000. No IHT is payable as the estate is within Rita's enhanced nil rate band and the estate can continue to qualify as excepted, since Ralph's entire nil rate band was transferred to Rita. However, the PRs must send Forms C4 and IHT217 to HMRC together with a copy of the IHT205.

11.18   To counter the risk of abuse of excepted estates status, in England and Wales and Northern Ireland all applications for probate must be accompanied by either:

- an IHT205 (or 207 for those domiciled abroad) for excepted estates, or
- an IHT421 in all other cases (even where no IHT is payable); the Probate Registry will not issue a grant unless the IHT421 bears HMRC's authorisation, so in all cases the IHT 421 will have to be submitted to HMRC Inheritance Tax before making the probate application.

IHT 206 contains guidance on completing IHT205 and is available from HMRC Inheritance Tax.

There is an automatic discharge system so that unless HMRC Inheritance Tax contacts personal representatives within 35 days (60 days in Scotland) asking for more detailed information, those liable for tax will be discharged.

HMRC selects a random sample of excepted estates to review. It also compares the data provided on death with lifetime data provided by the deceased to HMRC and information from other sources. If it turns out that an estate does not meet the criteria for an excepted estate, the statutory clearance will not apply (as the estate was not within the excepted estate regulations at the outset).

11.19   The April 2011 *Trusts and Estates Newsletter* said that HMRC has noticed an increase in cases where an application for a grant is made as an excepted estate, but the discovery of undervaluation or omissions leads to tax being payable. It reminded practitioners that Form IHT205/C5 is a 'document' for the purposes of FA 2007, Sch 24, para 1(1)(a) and where it is shown that personal representatives have failed to take reasonable care (or worse), HMRC will require payment of the appropriate penalty.

11.20 While it is possible to vary the estate of a deceased beneficiary to redirect inherited property elsewhere so that for IHT purposes the assets no longer form part of the deceased beneficiary's estate, the reading back applies only for the purposes of IHT and TCGA 1992, s 62. The variation has no effect for probate purposes. The estate for which the grant of probate is required is the 'combined' estate and the assets from both estates must be taken into account to establish the gross value of the estate on the second death. Where this gross value exceeds the IHT nil rate band, the second death cannot qualify as an excepted estate. The correct process is to complete Form IHT400 for the 'combined' estate, so the correct values are carried forward for probate and then deduct the assets that are being redirected away from the second estate as a relief. This way, the correct position is reported for probate purposes and the impact of the variation is correctly applied for tax purposes only.

4. COMPLETING THE IHT205

11.21 The IHT205 is a short form (updated in September 2006) based on the form completed by personal applicants. IHT206 provides guidance on completing IHT205. The guidance notes have been rewritten and are extremely helpful, particularly in relation to pensions.

Question 1 requires details about the deceased. The rest of the form requires details of the estate.

Questions 2–12 require information about the estate and are designed to establish whether or not the estate fulfils the requirements for excepted status. For example, Question 3 asks whether the deceased made any lifetime transfers or made a gift from which he continued to benefit. The instructions on the form are that applicants should stop completing the form if there were any gifts from which the deceased continued to benefit or if lifetime transfers exceeded £150,0000 or did not qualify as 'specified transfers'. Question 4 asks whether the deceased was a beneficiary of a trust the assets of which were treated as part of his estate for inheritance tax purposes. The instructions on the form are that applicants should stop completing the form if there are trust assets which exceed £150,000 or if there is more than one trust.

Questions 6–8 require information in relation to insurance policies and pension schemes.

Question 9 establishes the extent of lifetime gifts, trust assets and of joint and nominated assets forming part of the estate on death which do not require a grant. Question 10 identifies debts and other liabilities attributable to such assets.

Question 11 elicits details of all the deceased's assets which require a grant. Question 12 identifies debts, other liabilities and funeral expenses attributable to such assets.

Question 14 allows the deduction of exemptions.

The form concludes with an instruction that if the value exceeds the excepted estates limit, the applicant must complete Form IHT400.

5. THE REDUCED IHT400

11.22   If part of an estate is exempt from inheritance tax, HMRC accepts that it does not need precise values for property that passes to an exempt beneficiary. The reduced account in intended to reduce the burden on personal representatives where because of exemptions part or all of an estate is free from tax. What this means in practice is that provided certain conditions are met the personal representatives only have to complete some of the supplementary pages.

When an estate is not excepted, it is possible to deliver a reduced IHT Account where:

- the deceased died domiciled in the UK; and
- assets are passing under will or intestacy to a spouse or civil partner domiciled in the UK (either absolutely or through an interest in possession trust) or pass immediately to a charity or similar body; and
- the gross value (*before* liabilities, reliefs or exemptions) of other property chargeable on death plus chargeable gifts (*after* deducting liabilities, reliefs or exemptions) made in the 7 years before death does not exceed the IHT threshold.

The IHT threshold for this purpose will be increased if the deceased had the benefit of any transferred nil rate band.

Where a percentage or fractional share of residue is left to an exempt beneficiary a full account must still be delivered as all the assets should be divided between the residuary beneficiaries. On the other hand if the Will bequeaths a nil-rate band legacy to chargeable beneficiaries with the residue left to an exempt beneficiary, a reduced account may be delivered for the assets that devolve upon the exempt beneficiary[50].

---

[50]   See IHTM10473.

A reduced account can also be delivered if the deceased's estate qualifies for exemption from inheritance tax under the death of members of the armed forces/emergency service personnel (IHTA 1984, ss 153A-155A).[51]

11.23 Where a reduced account is appropriate, only the following parts of the form need to be completed:

- Boxes 1–28 must be completed in full.

- Boxes 29–48 must be completed in full but it may not be necessary to answer all the questions on the accompanying schedules. If the answer is 'yes' to questions 29–31, 35, 36, 44, 45 or 47, the appropriate supporting schedule must be completed. If an asset included in the schedule passes to an exempt beneficiary, an estimate of open market value (but not a nominal value) can be included. If the answer to any other question is 'yes', the supporting schedule need not be completed at all provided all the assets concerned pass to an exempt beneficiary. Instead the totals of the assets are written directly on to IHT 400 at the relevant boxes on pages 6 and 7.

- The boxes on pages 6–10 must be completed although an estimate of market value (but not a nominal value) can be given for any assets passing to an exempt beneficiary.

- All assets passing to exempt beneficiaries must be included in boxes 92 and 93.

- Boxes 109 and 110 can be left out as there will be no tax to pay. However, boxes 111–117 should be completed.

- Box 118 can be left out but the declaration at box 119 must be completed.

Estimates of open market value for assets passing to an exempt beneficiary do not need to be listed in the Declaration on page 12 and it is not necessary to enclose supporting valuations of assets passing to exempt beneficiaries.

11.24 There are two other circumstances where the IHT 400 does not need to be completed in full:

(i) *Proposed grant limited to certain assets*
    The assets to be covered by the grant should be entered on pages 6–10 of the IHT400. Assets to be excluded from the grant should be included at box 76. Only the schedules that apply to the assets for which the grant is required should be completed. Full details of the procedure are to be found at page 4 of IHT400 Notes.

(ii) *Settled Land Act grant*
    A Settled Land Act grant is required where land continues to be settled after the death of the tenant for life. IHT400 and IHT405 should be completed to give details of the settled land and the declaration on page 12

---

[51] IHTA 1984, s 154 and see **5.17**.

should be amended to state that the grant is to be 'limited to the settled land of which true particulars and value are given'. The other property in the deceased's estate should be entered at box 105 on the IHT400. The IHT418 (Assets held in trust) should not be completed. Full details of the procedure are to be found at page 4 of IHT400 Notes.

6. COMPLETING THE IHT400

11.25   Where an estate is not excepted and the requirements for a reduced IHT400 are not satisfied, the personal representatives must complete Form IHT400 in full. The purpose of Form IHT400 is to determine the tax payable on death. Hence, it must include details of all the assets[52] and all the deductible liabilities[53] of the estate.

Exemptions and reliefs are claimed and IHT is calculated on the value of the chargeable estate at the appropriate rate.

11.26   The bulk of the form seeks to elicit the relevant information to enable the tax liability to be determined. Supporting information of values is provided on the relevant schedules (IHT401–IHT420) so that only totals appear on the IHT400 itself. All boxes on the relevant schedules must be completed. There is a probate summary (IHT421) which has to be receipted and sent to the Probate Registry (unless the estate is excepted) as proof that any tax due has been paid.

In a simple case where none of the tax is being paid by instalments and no interest is due, the calculation of IHT can be made on page 11 of IHT400. In other cases the tax is calculated by following the working sheet on 'IHT400 Calculation'.

If IHT is payable, personal representatives will need an IHT reference number and should complete IHT422, unless the deceased had a National Insurance number in which case they can apply online. If they want to make use of the IHT direct payment scheme,[54] they will need to complete an IHT423 for each paying institution.

11.27   HMRC has supplied comprehensive instructions on the completion of the forms (IHT400 Notes). This is a relatively user-friendly guide. It is important to have this guidance available when completing the forms as failure to follow guidance may lead HMRC to impose penalties if inaccuracies result.[55]

---

[52]   See **3.05** for a discussion of what is included in the estate and **3.14** *et seq* for valuation issues.

[53]   See **3.07** *et seq*.

[54]   Banks and building societies may agree to make funds available to HMRC from the deceased's accounts on an informal basis. The more formal Direct Payment Scheme was introduced on 1 April 2003: see the *IHT Newsletter* (April 2003). Personal representatives apply to HMRC for an IHT reference number and complete a form IHT423 for each institution that will be transferring funds. A completed form IHT423, which includes the IHT reference number, is sent to each institution. The institution then releases funds to HMRC.

[55]   See **11.82** *et seq*.

The IHT Toolkit

11.28 HMRC has also produced an IHT Toolkit aimed primarily at professional advisers who do not prepare IHT 400s on a regular basis. It identifies the main areas of risk associated with the IHT400. This toolkit identifies errors which are seen in many forms IHT400 received. It does not deal with errors associated with claims for Business Property or Agricultural Property Relief and reliefs associated with works of art and other National Heritage Assets on the basis that claims for these reliefs are not made in the majority of forms IHT400 completed and received.

The Toolkit starts by identifying what HMRC see as the main risk areas. According to HMRC these fall into four categories.

- *Omissions*

    HMRC say that because lay people do not understand what makes up the IHT estate, it is important to ask the right questions, not simply 'what assets did the deceased have?' Specific questions should be asked about whether the deceased had an interest in jointly held property or under a trust. Questions should also be asked about gifts made by the deceased as they may increase the IHT payable on the death estate.

- *Valuations*

    According to the Toolkit valuations are the biggest single area of risk. HMRC say

    > 'it is important to instruct a qualified independent valuer, to make sure the valuation is made for the purposes of the relevant legislation, and for houses, land and buildings meets Royal Institution of Chartered Surveyors (RICS) or equivalent, standards.

    > Some issues are easily overlooked when instructions are given. For example, the potential for the development of the land, the existence of tenancies or occupancy by people other than the deceased. Copies of relevant agreements, or full details where only an oral agreement exists, are often not given to the valuer so misunderstandings arise. Where we are satisfied that all the relevant information has been considered by the valuer, we are less likely to challenge the valuation.'

- *Applying the correct legislation, rules and practices*

    HMRC complains that it regularly receives form IHT400 in estates where it is clear that the information submitted does not meet current requirements. It is clearly important to keep up-to-date with changes in legislation and guidance.

- *Record keeping*

    Good record keeping is important. However, in the case of inheritance tax, the personal representatives have to rely on the deceased's records. HMRC suggest that practitioners advise clients about the importance of lifetime records when they visit for other issues, eg to have a will drafted.

The type of records which HMRC considers it would be helpful for clients to retain include, for example, gifts made and circumstances that affect the amount of nil rate band available for transfer to the surviving spouse or civil partner.

In the main body of the Toolkit HMRC highlights particular risks.

These include errors in relation to the transferable nil rate band such as failure to appreciate that there was no spouse exemption for estate duty until 22 March 1972 and, even then, that it was limited to £15,000 until 12 March 1974. HMRC also reminds practitioners that, if the deceased was UK-domiciled but the surviving spouse is not, the spouse exemption is limited.[56]

HMRC Guidance

11.29 The guidance issued by HMRC is full: note the following points which are of particular importance.

(a) Instalment and non-instalment option property

11.30 Pages 6–10 of form IHT400 are divided into two columns, column A for non-instalment option property and column B for instalment option property. This is so that the deceased's assets can be listed in a logical order with joint assets first, followed by the most common assets of house, bank accounts, cash and so on. Each asset can be placed in only one box with the exception of traded unlisted shares and unlisted shares which should be put into box 65 unless they qualify for the instalment payment option when they should be put into box 66.

(b) Transfer of unused nil rate band

11.31 Transferable nil rate band is claimed using schedule IHT402 with a clause in the declaration on page 12 of the IHT400 relating to the claim.

(c) Joint property

11.32 The deceased's share of co-owned assets, whether held as beneficial joint tenant or tenant in common, are listed on schedule IHT404 with separate totals for instalment and non-instalment property. Assets passing by survivorship and, therefore, not relevant for probate purposes are deducted from the probate summary (IHT421).

---

[56]   To £55,000 for deaths before 6 April 2013 and to the level of the nil rate band for deaths on or after that date unless the survivor elects to be treated as domiciled in England and Wales. See **11.08** for matters to consider in relation to this election.

(d) Household and personal goods

11.33 The only items which need to be listed individually are:

- items of jewellery valued at over £500;
- vehicles, boats and aircraft; and
- antiques, works of art and collections.

All other items such as general furniture, white goods and jewellery valued at less than £500 should be totalled and the total value entered at box 4 of IHT407.

(e) Pensions

11.34 Lump sum benefits payable on death are only included on IHT409 if:

- payable to the deceased's personal representative, either by right or because there is no one else who qualifies for the payment, or
- the deceased could, right up until their death, have signed a binding 'nomination' (either for the first time or after having revoked an existing 'nomination') that obliged the trustees of the pension scheme to make the payment to the person named by the deceased.

Most (if not all) pension schemes will pay lump sum death benefits if a person dies before drawing any pension benefits. Some will also pay lump sum death benefits in the form of unused funds if a person dies whilst in drawdown. That means they are drawing or entitled to income from a pension arrangement where the funds have not been used to secure an income for life. Many lump sum death benefit payments will be subject to an income tax charge if they are made from a UK registered scheme. The charge is:

> 35% before 6 April 2011,
>   55% from 6 April 2011 to 5 April 2015, and
>   45% from 6 April 2015.

If the deceased made changes to the benefits to be taken and the date at which they were to be taken, this may amount to a transfer of value which will have to be reported on IHT409 under the heading 'Transfers to or changes to pension benefits'. HMRC will look at the changes made and decide whether they amount to a transfer of value.

11.35 Examples given in the guidance notes of changes which may amount to transfers of value and which should therefore be included are:

- where the deceased reached pension age and decided not to take the payment of their pension at that time or chose to take income drawdown;[57]
- where the deceased, having got to pension age and chosen to take 'income drawdown' decided at a later date (and whilst in ill health) to reduce the level of income taken; or
- where the deceased, having got to pension age and chosen to take 'phased retirement',[58] decides at a later date (and whilst in ill health) to reduce the number of segments taken.

If the personal representatives accept that there was a transfer of value, they can include the value of the transfer on IHT403 (Gifts and other transfers of value) instead of on IHT409. However, they must provide information as to how they arrived at the figure for the value transferred. Value will depend on the deceased's health and life expectancy at the date of the change so evidence such as a doctor's letter or report should be supplied.

Contributions to a pension scheme may be a transfer of value if made within 2 years of death at a time when the deceased was in ill health.

The notes also deal with alternatively secured pension schemes where death occurred before 6 April 2011.[59]

(f) Stocks and shares

11.36   There are two schedules for stocks and shares:

- IHT411 for listed stocks and shares, including UK Government and municipal securities;
- IHT412 for unlisted, traded unlisted and control holdings of stocks and shares.

If business relief is being deducted from qualifying holdings of unlisted, traded unlisted and control holdings of stocks and shares, this should be shown on IHT412 and not on IHT413 which deals with business and partnership interests and assets.

(g) Assets mentioned in the will and not included in the estate

11.37   It is necessary to explain at box 26 of IHT400 what happened to property named as the main residence in the will. However, the guidance to the

---

[57]   Income drawdown arises where a person reaches pensionable age and, instead of buying an annuity, draws a certain level of income with a view to buying an annuity at a later date. For changes to the provisions requiring purchase of an annuity see footnote 34 above.

[58]   Phased retirement occurs where a person divides their pension entitlement into segments and agrees with the pension provider to take a certain number of segments each year.

[59]   For changes to the provisions relating to annuity purchases see footnote 34 above.

question states that if the deceased sold the property but used all the sale proceeds to buy another main residence and this happened more than once, it is not necessary to give details of all the events. It is sufficient to say that the residence was replaced by the current property. In all other cases, it is necessary to give details of exactly what happened with dates. At box 28 it is necessary to give details of any items referred to in the will and not owned at death.

It is easy to imagine circumstances in which it will be difficult or impossible to provide all the information requested.

7. CONSIDERATIONS RELEVANT TO COMPLETING THE IHT400

The instalment option

11.38   To obtain a grant of representation, personal representatives must pay all the inheritance tax for which they are liable when they deliver their account to HMRC.

In the case of certain property the tax may, at the option of the personal representatives, be paid in 10 equal yearly instalments with the first instalment falling due 6 months after the end of the month of death. The object of this facility is to prevent the particular assets from having to be sold by the personal representatives in order to raise the necessary inheritance tax.

The instalment option is available on the following assets:[60]

(a)   land, freehold or leasehold, wherever situated;

(b)   shares or securities in a company which gave the deceased control of that company ('control' is defined as voting control on all questions affecting the company as a whole[61]);

(c)   a non-controlling holding of unquoted shares or securities in a company (ie shares or securities which are not listed on a recognised stock exchange) where the tax on the shares or securities, and on other property carrying the instalment option, comprises at least 20% of the tax due from that particular person (in the same capacity);

(d)   a non-controlling holding where HMRC is satisfied that payment of the tax in one lump sum would cause 'undue hardship';

(e)   other non-controlling shareholdings in unquoted companies, where the value of the shares exceeds £20,000 and either their nominal value is at least 10% of the nominal value of all the issued shares in the company, or

---

[60]   IHTA 1984, ss 227, 228 as amended.
[61]   IHTA 1984, s 269. Surprisingly s 269 (which treats the voting power as belonging to the interest in possession beneficiary in the case of an interest in possession trust) was not amended after the FA 2006 changes.

the shares are ordinary shares whose nominal value is at least 10% of the nominal value of all ordinary shares in the company;[62] and

(f)   a business or a share in a business, for example, a partnership share.[63]

An added attraction of paying by instalments is that, generally, no interest is charged so long as each instalment is paid on the due date. In the event of late payment the interest charge is merely on the outstanding instalment. Interest is, however, charged on the total outstanding inheritance tax liability (even if the instalments are paid on time) in the case of land which is not a business asset and shares in investment companies. If the asset subject to the instalment option is sold, the outstanding instalments of inheritance tax become payable at once. It should be noted that the definition of 'qualifying property' for these purposes is not subject to the same limitations as business property relief with regard to investment businesses and excepted assets.[64]

Exercising the instalment option: cashflow benefit

11.39 If the instalment option is exercised, the first instalment of tax is payable 6 months after the end of the month of death. Hence, personal representatives normally exercise the option in order to pay as little inheritance tax as possible before obtaining the grant. Once the grant has been obtained they may then discharge the inheritance tax on the instalment property in one lump sum.

Personal representatives should, however, bear in mind that some inheritance tax is usually payable before the grant. The necessary cash may be obtained from the deceased's account at either a bank or a building society (building societies, in particular, commonly issue cheques to cover the initial inheritance tax payable);[65] from the sale of property for which a grant is not necessary; or by means of a personal loan from a beneficiary.

11.40 If a loan has to be raised commercially, the interest qualifies for income tax relief for 12 months from the making of the loan so long as it is on a loan account (not by way of overdraft) and is used to pay the tax attributable to personal property (including leaseholds).[66]

11.41 Personal representatives should, therefore, be advised to exercise the instalment option to defer inheritance tax until after obtaining the grant. Where the inheritance tax is a testamentary expense, the tax can then be paid in one lump sum. If the residuary legatee objects (it may, for instance, be necessary to

---

[62]   For the meaning of 'ordinary shares' for these purposes see IHTA 1984, s 228(4).

[63]   It may be that the value of the property in such cases is reduced by 100% business or agricultural property relief with the result that no tax is payable on the death.

[64]   See **10.50**.

[65]   See HMRC *IHT Newsletter* (April 2003).The scheme is voluntary so personal representatives should check that the particular bank or building society is part of the scheme and complete a form IHT423 for each institution.

[66]   ITA 2007, ss 383, 403–405.

sell an asset to pay the inheritance tax), the personal representatives could arrange to vest the residue in that beneficiary and for him to discharge the future instalments. Adequate security should, however, be taken in such cases because if the beneficiary defaults, the personal representatives remain liable for the outstanding inheritance tax.[67] In the case of a specific gift which bears its own inheritance tax and which qualifies for the instalment option, the decision whether to discharge the entire inheritance tax bill once probate has been obtained should be left to the legatee. Personal representatives should not make a unilateral decision.

Once the personal representatives have paid all the outstanding inheritance tax they are entitled to a certificate of discharge[68]

11.42 Sometimes personal representatives may encounter great difficulties in raising the cash to pay inheritance tax. In exceptional cases HMRC may allow a grant to be obtained before paying tax if the personal representatives 'can demonstrate that it is impossible to raise the money before obtaining the grant'.[69]

The extent of the deceased's interest in assets

11.43 When assessing the size of a deceased's estate it can be difficult to determine the extent of their interest in certain assets, in particular:

(a)   co-owned land;

(b)   joint bank accounts;

(c)   land subject to a proprietary estoppel claim.

The extent of a co-owner's interest in land

11.44 The courts have produced a number of rules which may apply to establish the extent of a person's interest in co-owned land, but the answer in any particular case will depend on the facts. Written declarations as to beneficial interest are conclusive unless varied by subsequent agreement or affected by proprietary estoppel.[70] Unfortunately there are many cases where no express declaration is made.[71]

---

[67]   See *Howarth's Executors v IRC* [1997] STC (SCD) 162 for a salutary tale of the dangers of not securing payment.

[68]   IHTA 1984, s 239(2).

[69]   IHTM para 05071. HMRC will ask for written undertakings to pay the tax within a specified period before allowing the grant.

[70]   See *Goodman v Gallant* [1986] 1 All ER 311; *Pankhania v Chandegra* [2012] EWCA Civ 1438 [2013]. There may be an agreement which is held not to apply because the circumstances envisaged by the agreement have not occurred: see *Gallarotti v Sebastianelli* [2012] EWCA Civ 865.

[71]   See *Goodman v Carlton* [2002] 2 FLR 259 where Ward LJ urged conveyancers to do this as a matter of course.

11.45 In the absence of a written declaration the presumptions of resulting trust or advancement[72] may apply although the House of Lords decision in *Stack v Dowden*[73] has affected the presumption in the case of co-ownership in the domestic consumer context.

11.46 In *Stack v Dowden* the House of Lords held (Lord Neuberger dissenting) that in the domestic consumer context the presumption is that beneficial title follows legal title irrespective of the way in which the parties contributed to the purchase price and on-going costs. Hence, a person who claims that the beneficial ownership is different from the legal ownership must produce evidence to prove this. Baroness Hale of Richmond, who gave the leading judgment, commented that:[74]

> 'The burden will therefore be on the person seeking to show that the parties did intend their beneficial interests to be different from their legal interests, and in what way. This is not a task to be lightly embarked upon.'

11.47 'Domestic consumer context' is not limited to cohabiting couples living together in a platonic or sexual relationship. In *Adekunle v Ritchie*,[75] the court followed the *Stack v Dowden* approach in a case where property had been purchased by a mother and son. In the case of a purchase by friends the Court of Appeal agreed with the comment of the trial judge that in the light of the close relationship between the parties when the property was purchased the analysis to be carried out was 'to be seen more in the domestic than in the commercial context'.[76] The court held that the principles were the same.

Family members may, of course, purchase property together as an investment in which case the principle of *Stack v Dowden* will not apply. For an illustration see *Laskar v Laskar*,[77] in which the Court of Appeal held that where property was purchased jointly as an investment, albeit by a mother and daughter, it was not appropriate to apply the presumption of joint ownership. Despite the familial relationship between the parties, it was clear that the purchase was nothing more than a business venture. Both parties led separate and distinct lives and maintained separate and distinct finances. The relationship was one between investors, and the presumption of joint ownership did not apply in such circumstances. Accordingly, there was nothing more than a resulting trust, and each party was entitled to the value of her own contribution.

---

[72] The Equality Act 2010, s 199 abolishes the presumption of advancement but only in relation to acts done after its commencement. At the time of writing the section had not been brought into force.

[73] [2007] UKHL 17.

[74] At para 68.

[75] [2007] WTLR 1505. See also *Gibson v Revenue and Customs Prosecution Office* [2008] EWCA Civ 645.

[76] *Gallarotti v Sebastianelli* [2012] EWCA Civ 865.

[77] [2008] All ER (D) 104 (Feb).

11.48 HMRC were quick to recognise the significance of the decision in relation to inheritance tax. This appeared in the December 2007 *IHT and Trusts Newsletter*:

> 'We have noted an increasing number of claims that real or leasehold property in an estate should be valued at less, often substantially less, than the full open market value. Many of these claims are based on the assertion that someone, usually a family member, has a beneficial interest in the property where their name is not on the legal title.'

HMRC went on to say that in the light of Baroness Hale's comments in *Stack v Dowden* practitioners should consider all the facts carefully before claiming that beneficial interests differed from the legal title.

> 'If, having done this, practitioners wish to contend that there is a valid claim in law; we would expect to receive a full and detailed account of those facts together with all the relevant evidence, as if the claimant were presenting the claim ... unless there is a case that we consider sufficiently strong that it would be upheld by the courts, the claim will be rejected.'

11.49 The Supreme Court reconsidered the issue in *Jones v Kernott*[78] another cohabitation case where there was no written declaration of the beneficial interests. The Supreme Court largely confirmed the *Stack* approach. At para 51 Lord Walker gave this summary of the principles to be applied:

'(1) The starting point is that equity follows the law and they are joint tenants both in law and in equity.

(2) That presumption can be displaced by showing (a) that the parties had a different common intention at the time when they acquired the home, or (b) that they later formed the common intention that their respective shares would change.

(3) Their common intention is to be deduced objectively from their conduct: "the relevant intention of each party is the intention which was reasonably understood by the other party to be manifested by that party's words and conduct notwithstanding that he did not consciously formulate that intention in his own mind or even acted with some different intention which he did not communicate to the other party" (Lord Diplock in *Gissing v Gissing* [1971] AC 886, 906). Examples of the sort of evidence which might be relevant to drawing such inferences are given in *Stack v Dowden*, at para 69.

(4) In those cases where it is clear either (a) that the parties did not intend joint tenancy at the outset, or (b) had changed their original intention, but it is not possible to ascertain by direct evidence or by inference what their actual intention was as to the shares in which they would own the property, "the answer is that each is entitled to that share which the court considers fair having regard to the whole course of dealing between them in relation to the property": Chadwick LJ in *Oxley v Hiscock* [2005] Fam 211, para 69. In our judgment, "the whole course of dealing ... in relation to the property"

---

[78] [2011] UKSC 53.

should be given a broad meaning, enabling a similar range of factors to be taken into account as may be relevant to ascertaining the parties' actual intentions.

(5)   Each case will turn on its own facts. Financial contributions are relevant but there are many other factors which may enable the court to decide what shares were either intended (as in case (3)) or fair (as in case (4)).'

The significance of *Jones v Kernott* is the recognition that, even where there is an agreement between the parties as to how the beneficial interests are to be held, intentions may change over time.[79]

11.50 Similar problems arise where legal title is in one person and another person claims to have a beneficial interest. At para 52 Lord Walker noted that the starting point is different.

'The first issue is whether it was intended that the other party have any beneficial interest in the property at all. If he does, the second issue is what that interest is. There is no presumption of joint beneficial ownership. But their common intention has once again to be deduced objectively from their conduct. If the evidence shows a common intention to share beneficial ownership but does not show what shares were intended, the court will have to proceed as at para 51(4) and (5) above.'

For an example where the court decided that the other party did have an interest in a property in the sole name of another, see *Aspden v Elvy*.[80] The court accepted that, although the evidence was conflicting, the claimant had carried out substantial work converting a barn and had contributed substantial funds on the basis that he would share the beneficial ownership. See also *Graham-York v York and others*[81] where, rather surprisingly, the trial judge found that a longstanding female cohabitee had a 25% beneficial interest in the home, despite the fact that her financial contribution 'did not amount to much'. She had, however, made 'domestic contributions'. The judge described her evaluation of the interest as 'generous'. The Court of Appeal declined to increase the amount of the interest saying that the trial judge had directed herself properly and had fallen into no legal or analytical error. Tomlinson LJ said[82] that had the judge evaluated the claimant's interest at 33%, her decision would 'have been equally unassailable', but to increase the award in that way would have been 'tinkering', and would simply encourage appeals, raising false expectations and leading to the further erosion of modest estates.

Parties may have reached an agreement that is to apply in particular circumstances, but if those circumstances do not occur, the agreement will not apply. This was the case in *Gallarotti v Sebastianelli*[83] where two friends had agreed that although the property was bought in the name of one, the beneficial

---

[79]   See also *Quaintance v Tandan* (unreported) 24 July 2012.
[80]   [2012] EWHC 1387 (Ch).
[81]   [2015] EWCA Civ 72.
[82]   Ibid at para 28.
[83]   [2012] EWCA Civ 865.

interests would be held equally because they would share outgoings equally. In the event one paid more than the other and was awarded a larger beneficial interest by the Court of Appeal.

Ownership of joint bank accounts

11.51 Again ownership is a matter of intention. The elderly may put an account into joint names with an adult child for the sake of convenience in which case the entire account will remain in their beneficial ownership. Others may intend the account to be genuinely joint so that both parties can draw on the account freely and the survivor takes the balance. Alternatively, the intention may be that only the donor is to be entitled to draw on it during the donor's lifetime but that the balance will pass to the joint owner on death.

11.52 In the absence of evidence as to beneficial entitlement the presumptions of resulting trust and advancement[84] may apply.

11.53 In *Re Northall deceased*,[85] Mrs Northall had bought her council house with help from one of her six sons. The property was sold and she received a cheque for £54,836 but did not have a bank account. One of her other sons, Christopher, opened a joint account in her name and his own. Between opening the account and Mrs Northall's death a month later payments amounting to £28,625 were paid out by Christopher. On 24 January 2007 he caused the whole of the remaining balance in the estate to be transferred to his own joint account with his wife. The following principles were applied:

(a) When one person puts money into joint names there is a presumption of a resulting trust to the provider. The presumption can be rebutted:
   (i) if the circumstances give rise to the presumption of advancement which was not the case here;[86] or
   (ii) by evidence that the provider intended to transfer the beneficial interest.

(b) The burden of proof of such an intention is on the person alleging it.

The court held that there was no evidence that the money had been intended as a gift to Christopher. Mrs Northall had intended it to remain hers to spend as she wished. There was insufficient evidence to establish that she intended any balance remaining to pass to Christopher. Admittedly the account opening form provided for survivorship but the judge found that this was insufficient, particularly since there was nothing to show that it was ever drawn to her attention. He therefore ordered that Christopher should account for the amount remaining in the account at the date of Mrs Northall's death and for the lifetime withdrawals apart from those where there was evidence to show that they were made on Mrs Northall's instructions.

---

[84] See footnote 72 above.
[85] [2010] EWHC 1448 (Ch).
[86] See footnote 72 above.

11.54   *Sillett v Meek*[87] is another decision where the evidence was insufficient to rebut the presumption of a resulting trust.

11.55   The decisions show how important evidence is as to the intentions of the parties when the account is opened. In *Aroso v Coutts*,[88] the deceased had transferred substantial amounts into an account in the joint names of himself and a nephew. The evidence showed that the terms of the bank mandate were clear and had been drawn to the deceased's attention by the bank. The effect was that the presumption of resulting trust was displaced and the balance in the account passed by survivorship to the joint account holder.[89]

11.56   Frequently, while one party does intend to make a gift, it is not intended to be an immediate gift but is limited to what is in the account at the date of death. In effect an immediate gift of a fluctuating balance.[90]

Tax treatment of joint accounts

11.57   HMRC may argue that the whole of an account in joint names is to be included in the estate of the deceased. They did so successfully in *Sillars v IRC*[91] where a mother had put a bank account into joint names with her two daughters. The mother had provided all the funds for the account and was the only one of the three to draw it. However, each of the daughters had included one-third of the interest earned on the account in their income tax returns. HMRC advanced two arguments:

(a)   IHTA 1984, s 5(2) provides that a person's estate for IHT includes property over which he has a general power. A general power for this purpose is 'a power or authority enabling the person by whom it is exercisable to appoint or dispose of property as he sees fit';

(b)   the deceased had reserved a benefit in the account because she had access to the entire account.

The Special Commissioner agreed with both arguments.[92]

Section 5(2) was applied in the same way in *Perry v RCC*[93] where a deceased property developer had put a bank account containing £1m into joint names with the appellant; in *Taylor v RCC*[94] where the deceased had put a bank

---

[87]   [2007] EWHC 1169 (Ch).
[88]   [2002] 1 All ER (Comm) 241.
[89]   See also *Taylor v RCC* [2008] STC (SCD) 1159.
[90]   For examples see *Young v Sealey* [1949] Ch 278; *In re Figgis* [1969] 1 Ch 123; *Sillars v IRC* [2004] STC (SCD) 180; *Drakeford v Cotton* [2012] EWHC 1414 (Ch).
[91]   [2004] STC (SCD) 180.
[92]   Although on these facts the daughters had no interests for IHT as they had no rights to draw on the accounts during the mother's life, it would be possible for HMRC to argue in a suitable case that all parties were to be treated as beneficially entitled to the whole account under IHTA 1984, s 5(2).
[93]   [2005] WTLR 1077.
[94]   [2008] STC (SCD) 1159.

account into joint names with her brother-in-law intending that the accounts would pass to his grandchildren on her death and in *Mathews v RCC*[95] where a mother had put an account into joint names with her son. In all cases the accounts were to be included in the deceased's estate.

Proprietary estoppel claims

11.58 The House of Lords in *Thorner v Curtis*[96] reversed the Court of Appeal decision and confirmed that proprietary estoppel can be available in relation to promises to leave property by will. The issue in broad terms is whether one person (A) has acted to his detriment in reliance on a belief which was known to and encouraged by another person (B) that he either has or will be given a right over B's property. If so, B cannot insist on his strict legal rights. The necessary elements of a claim for proprietary estoppel are therefore:

(a) assurance;

(b) reliance; and

(c) detriment.

If these elements are established sufficiently so that it is unconscionable for the court not to give relief, the court will grant relief but it will be the minimum necessary to achieve equity. There are several cases where individuals were promised 'everything' or 'the house' but where the courts have decided that this would be disproportionate to the detriment and have awarded lesser amounts.[97]

> *Example 11.11*
>
> Minnie, a wealthy but mean widow, tells Handy that if he works for her for no wages, she will leave him her entire estate. When she dies over 10 years later, he discovers that she has left everything to charity. Clearly Handy acted to his detriment in reliance on an assurance given to him by Minnie and it would be unconscionable not to grant relief. However, the court will not necessarily order that Handy receives the entire estate. It will consider what is proportionate to the detriment suffered.

Proprietary estoppel and IHT

11.59 Where it can be shown that a third party has a claim to an interest in assets of the estate, one would expect the value of those assets to be reduced (depending on the strength of that claim). HMRC is becoming more difficult about agreeing such reductions. It is certainly true that a claimant cannot easily

---

[95] [2012] UKFTT 658 (TC).

[96] [2009] UKHL 18.

[97] See *Jennings v Rice* [2002] EWCA Civ 159, *Campbell v Griffin* [2001] EWCA Civ 990. But see *Bradbury v Taylor & Burkinshaw* [2012] EWCA Civ 1208 where the court found that it was not disproportionate for the promisees to receive the entire house. Similarly *Lothian v Dixon and Webb* [2014] where the court ruled that the degree of detriment suffered was such that the promisee should receive what she had been promised.

quantify a claim because the court will award only the minimum necessary to do equity. Depending on the facts, it may be difficult to argue that no part of the value of the promised property should be included in the promisor's estate.[98]

However, where a case of proprietary estoppel can be established a promisor is not free to deal with his own property. The promisee has enforceable rights against the property. See, for example, *Gillett v Holt*[99] where the court intervened during the promisor's lifetime to order that the promisee should receive a farm and £100,000.[100] Therefore, there will be a reduction in the value of the property in the promisor's estate.

In *Fielden v Christie-Miller*[101] the court said that it was possible for a representation made by trustees to give rise to a proprietary estoppel claim. However, because trustees have to act unanimously unless the trust document authorises them to act otherwise, a claimant must show that a representation made by only one trustee is authorised by all the other trustees, or that the other trustees acquiesced in the representations or caused the trustee to appear to be authorised to act on their behalf.

8. VALUATIONS

11.60 Once the extent of a person's assets is determined, it is necessary to value the various assets and interests. Valuations are a particularly fertile ground for penalties[102] so great care should be taken to follow HMRC guidance.[103]

Estimates

11.61 HMRC dislikes the use of estimates. Their advice is that if it is necessary to use an estimate because there is a difficulty in obtaining the actual figures, the taxpayer should let them know what the problem is:[104]

---

[98] Note that the issue may arise in two cases: (1) where the deceased has failed to honour his assurance; and (2) where the will carries out that assurance.

[99] [2001] Ch 210. For other examples of lifetime claims (both unsuccessful) see *Cook v Thomas* [2010] EWCA Civ 227 and *Clarke v Meadus* [2010] EWHC 3117 (Ch). For successful examples see *Bradbury v Taylor* [2012] EWCA Civ 1208 and *Lothian v Dixon and Webb* 28 November 2014 (unreported, transcript available on Lawtel, Westlaw).

[100] It might be thought that the promisor will have made a lifetime transfer of value at the time of the reduction of his estate. However, the promise must have led to detriment suffered by the promisee so it may be argued that there was no gratuitous intent and so no transfer of value: IHTA 1984, s 10.

[101] [2015] EWHC 87 (Ch).

[102] For penalties see **11.82** *et seq*.

[103] See **11.62** *et seq*. Also see **3.14** *et seq* for a discussion of valuation issues.

[104] *IHT & Trusts Newsletter*, August 2009. See also IHT400 Toolkit which says in relation to information gathering: 'To enable you to gather all the necessary information and valuations and to submit as complete a form IHT400 as possible, use as much of the allowable time for submission of the form as necessary. If there is still a problem and, for example, you are unable

'Having this information at an early stage helps to demonstrate that you are doing everything reasonable to produce the actual figures.'

Basis of valuation

11.62 The value of property comprised in the estate at death is the price which the property might reasonably be expected to fetch if sold on the open market at that time, provided that such price is not assumed to be reduced on the ground that the whole property is to be placed on the market at the same time.[105] In other words, the value will be the open market value of the property immediately before the death. There is no deduction for the costs of the notional sale.[106] Two types of property which often cause valuation problems are personal chattels and land.

Personal chattels

11.63 In the April 2006 *IHT Newsletter* HMRC gave the following advice to practitioners when valuing household and personal goods:

(a)   if there are such goods but the personal representatives consider that they are valueless, it is still necessary to report that such goods exist;

(b)   where items are valueless, explain why they are considered to have no value;

(c)   do not simply give a value without explanation; attach a valuer's report if one was obtained; if the valuation was an estimate by the personal representatives, explain how the estimate was arrived at and what comparisons were made;

(d)   a valuer's report must state that it was made on an open market basis;

(e)   if there is a car, state its value separately and give details of its make, model, year of registration and registration number;

(f)   if the deceased owned a holiday home, separate details of the contents must be provided even if the personal representatives consider them to be valueless;

(g)   when taking an inventory, be sure not to overlook items which are not in the house; check garden sheds and garages; ascertain whether there is a car parked in the street and whether any items have been placed with friends or relatives for safekeeping.

---

to get exact values, you can enter a reasonable estimate of value. But you must tell us which figures are estimates. Tell us how you have arrived at the values and why you had to use them, preferably on pages 15–16 in form IHT400, or in a covering letter or note. You should only use estimates on form IHT400 if you have no other option. To mitigate interest charges, it is possible to make a payment on account if Inheritance Tax is due on the estate.'

[105]   IHTA 1984, s 160 and see generally Chapter 3.

[106]   *Duke of Buccleuch v IRC* [1967] 1 AC 506. This was an estate duty decision but the principle applies to IHT: see *Price v RCC* [2010] UKFTT 474 (TC). See generally **3.15** *et seq.*

Land

11.64   When obtaining valuations of land, it is important to instruct the valuer to provide an open market valuation and to have a written record of the basis of valuation. Development value and 'hope' value must be included. HMRC recommends using a qualified valuer. Its online guidance 'How to value land and buildings for Inheritance Tax' says this:

> 'Professionals like property valuers and chartered surveyors specialise in valuing land and buildings for people's estates. HM Revenue & Customs (HMRC) strongly recommend that you use a professional valuer because they'll make sure the valuation is as accurate as possible.'

Similarly the IHT400 Toolkit says in relation to valuations:

> 'For assets with a material value you are strongly advised to instruct a qualified independent valuer, to make sure the valuation is made for the purposes of the relevant legislation, and for houses, land and buildings, it meets Royal Institution of Chartered Surveyors (RICS) or equivalent standards.'

11.65   Obtaining a professional valuation is not necessarily sufficient. HMRCs online guidance on how to value land and buildings makes it clear that taxpayers should look critically at a valuer's report and, when completing the Account, take into account events occurring after receipt of the valuation.[107] The guidance says:

> 'Sometimes it may become clear before you apply for probate that the valuation was wrong.
>
> For example, if the property was worth £400,000, but you then got several offers of £450,000 for it, it may mean that this amount is a more realistic market value.
>
> If you think the original valuation may have been too low you should ask the valuer to reconsider it. They should take into account the length of time since the person died and what has happened to the property market during that time.
>
> If the property has been under-valued you must write to HMRC to tell them the new value.'

The August 2010 *Newsletter for Estates and Trusts Practitioners* published the guidance with the following commentary:

> 'In these circumstances, HMRC recommends that the taxpayer should ask the valuer to reconsider and, if appropriate, amend the date of death value, taking into account such things as the length of time since the death and movements in the property market.

---

[107] Online guidance: *How to value land and buildings for Inheritance Tax.*

HMRC hopes that this will make it clearer to both practitioners and personal applicants that it is important to instruct a properly qualified person on the correct basis and to reconsider the initial valuation if any offers received suggest the property may be worth more. Valuing the property in this way will help prevent the risk of substantial undervaluation and HMRC charging penalties as a result.'

This advice from HMRC requires taxpayers to take a proactive approach to valuations to be sure of avoiding a penalty. However, if faced with a penalty claim it is worth remembering that HMRC lost in two recent cases[108] where taxpayers challenged the imposition of penalties.

Valuation of an interest in co-owned land

11.66 The value of the deceased's undivided interest in land will be discounted because of the difficulties of selling an interest (unless the other joint owner is the deceased's spouse when the related property rules will apply).[109]

In the case of residential property occupied by the co-owners it is usually possible to argue for a discount of 15% on the basis of *Wight v IRC*[110] where the Lands Tribunal agreed with the Revenue that a discount of 10% was customary in the case of commercial property but said that a bigger discount was appropriate for residential property:

> 'The position in the case of such a half share as has to be valued here is unusual in the sense that the purchaser would have the right to occupy the property jointly with the other owner and that is a factor which in my judgment on the evidence is one which also points to a larger percentage than 10%.'

In *St Clair-Ford v Ryder*[111] the Lands Tribunal considered the value of a 50% share owned by the deceased as tenant in common in a rented investment property and concluded that, in the case of non-residential property where the deceased was simply receiving rent, the correct discount would normally be 10%. The tribunal did allow for the possibility of a greater discount where the interest was less than 50% or where there were complicating factors.

Shares and securities

11.67 The value of listed shares and securities is taken as the smaller of the 'quarter-up' and 'mid-price' calculation. The valuation of unquoted shares and securities is a complex topic. A number of factors are taken into account, for example the company's profit record, its prospects, its assets and its liabilities. The percentage of shares being valued is a major factor. A majority shareholding of ordinary voting shares carries certain powers to control the affairs of the company (it will, for instance, give the owner the power to pass an

---

[108] See **11.91**. But note that the two cases were decided on the basis of the old legislation.
[109] See **3.16** and **11.68**.
[110] (1984) 264 EG 935.
[111] [2006] WTLR 1647.

ordinary resolution). A shareholding representing more than 75% confers greater powers, notably the power to pass special resolutions. Correspondingly, a shareholder who owns 50% or less of the voting power (and, even more so, a shareholding of 25% or less) has far fewer powers (he is a minority shareholder). In valuing majority and substantial minority holdings HM Revenue and Customs takes a net asset valuation as the starting point and then applies a discount (between 10–15%) in the case of minority holdings.

When shares are subject to a restriction on their transfer (for example pre-emption rights) they are valued on the assumption of a sale on the open market with the purchaser being permitted to purchase the shares, but then being subject to the restrictions.[112]

Related property

11.68 Inheritance tax savings could be engineered by splitting the ownership of certain assets (typically shares, sets of chattels, and interests in land) amongst two or more taxpayers. The saving would occur when the total value of the individual assets resulting from the split was less than the value of the original (undivided) asset. A pair of Ming vases, for instance, would be worth more as a pair than the combined values of the two individual vases. When it is desired to split the ownership of such assets, however, the transfer needed to achieve this result will normally be potentially chargeable and, as any tax will be charged on the entire fall in value of the transferor's estate, no tax saving will result. Inter-spouse or civil partner transfers are, however, free of inheritance tax and hence, were it not for the related property provisions, could be used to achieve substantial savings by asset splitting. To frustrate such schemes, the related property rules[113] provide that, in appropriate circumstances, an asset must be valued together with other related property, and a proportion of that total value is then attributed to the asset.

Inter-spouse or civil partner transfers are the main instance of transfers which attract the related property provisions. However, the rules also catch other exempt transfers (for example transfers to a charity or political party) in circumstances where the transferor could otherwise obtain a similar tax advantage.

When property in a deceased's estate is valued on the basis of these rules, relief is provided if the property is sold within 3 years after the death for a price lower than the related property valuation. In such circumstances the property is revalued on death ignoring the related property rules.

---

[112] *IRC v Crossman* [1937] AC 26, [1936] 1 All ER 762, HL: see 11.61.
[113] See IHTA 1984, s 161 as amended by FA 1989, s 171(4), by FA 1998, s 143(6) and by SI 2005/3229.

Property subject to restrictions on transfer

11.69 In *IRC v Crossman*[114] the testator owned shares in a private company the articles of which imposed restrictions on alienation and transfer. By a bare majority the House of Lords held that in valuing those shares for estate duty purposes the basis to be taken was the price which they would fetch on the open market on the terms that a purchaser would be registered as the owner of the shares but would in turn be subject to the restrictions contained in the company's articles of association. As was recognised by Lord Hailsham in the case, the view contended for by the executors would have the result that property which could not be sold in the open market would escape the tax net altogether.

The case of *IRC v Crossman* was subsequently followed by the House of Lords[115] and has been adopted in a series of cases concerning inheritance tax. For instance, in *Alexander v IRC*[116] a flat was purchased under the 'right to buy' provisions of the Housing Act 1980. All or part of the discount under that legislation had to be repaid if the flat was sold within 5 years of its purchase. The taxpayer died in the first year. The Court of Appeal (following *IRC v Crossman*) held that for valuation purposes an open market value must be taken and the flat was to be valued on the basis of what a purchaser would pay to stand in the deceased's shoes: ie taking over the liability to repay the discount should he sell the property within the prescribed period. It is inherent in this approach that the valuation thereby obtained may result in a higher figure than would actually be the case if the property was sold by the executors, and it appears that such a sale, even if occurring within 4 years of death, will not result in revaluation relief under IHTA 1984, s 191.

Lotting and *IRC v Gray*[117]

11.70 In valuing an estate at death, 'lotting' requires a valuation on the basis that 'the vendor must be supposed to have' taken the course which would get the largest price for the combined holding 'subject to the caveat ... that it does not entail undue expenditure of time and effort'.[118] For instance, if a taxpayer dies possessed of a valuable collection of lead toy soldiers they would not be valued individually but rather as a collection.[119]

In *IRC v Gray* the deceased had farmed in partnership with two others and the land was subject to tenancies which the deceased, as freeholder, had granted to the partnership. The Inland Revenue (now HM Revenue and Customs) sought to aggregate (or lot) the freehold in the land with the deceased's partnership share as a single unit of property so that the value of the deceased's freehold

---

[114] *IRC v Crossman* [1937] AC 26, [1936] 1 All ER 762, HL.
[115] See *Lynall v IRC* [1972] AC 680, [1971] 3 All ER 914, HL.
[116] *Alexander v IRC* [1991] STC 112, CA.
[117] *IRC v Gray* [1994] STC 360, CA.
[118] See *IRC v Gray* [1994] STC 360 at 373, CA.
[119] See *Duke of Buccleuch v IRC* [1967] 1 AC 506, [1967] 1 All ER 129, HL.

reversion was an appropriate proportion of the aggregate value of that reversion and the deceased's partnership interest, treated as a single item of property. In effect therefore the reversion was being valued on a vacant possession basis with an allowance for the partnership interests of the other partners. It may be noted that under the partnership deed the deceased was entitled to 92.5% of profits (and bore virtually all the losses). The Court of Appeal reversed the Lands Tribunal, holding that lotting was appropriate because that was the course which a prudent hypothetical vendor would take to obtain the best price. The fact that the two interests could not be described as forming a 'natural unit of property' was irrelevant. Hoffmann LJ commented[120] that:

> 'The principle is that the hypothetical vendor must be supposed to have "taken the course which would get the largest price" provided that this does not entail "undue expenditure of time and effort". In some cases this may involve the sale of an aggregate which could not reasonably be described as a "natural unit". ... The share in the farming partnership, with or without other property, was plainly not a "natural" item of commerce. Few people would want to buy the right to farm in partnership with strangers. Nevertheless [Section 160] requires one to suppose that it was sold. The question for the tribunal was whether, on this assumption, it would have been more advantageous to sell it with the land.'

In many ways this was not a typical case involving the fragmentation of farm land within a family and therefore it should not be assumed that this decision will apply in all such cases.[121]

Property subject to an option etc

11.71 Where the deceased entered into a contract as a result of which the right to dispose of property was excluded or restricted, then in valuing that property that exclusion or restriction is taken into account in so far as money or money's worth was given for it.[122] The precise ambit of this provision is far from clear: it would for instance catch an option to purchase the property granted for less than full consideration, but would not, it is thought, catch the standard accruer clause which is included in many professional partnership agreements.[123]

Liabilities

11.72 Liabilities only reduce the value of an estate if incurred for consideration in money or money's worth, eg an outstanding mortgage and the deceased's unpaid tax liability.[124] This means that if the deceased simply granted an IOU

---

[120] See *IRC v Gray* [1994] STC 360 at 377, 378, CA.
[121] See *Private Client Business* (1994) p 210.
[122] IHTA 1984, s 163.
[123] This is because either the restriction is inherent in the partnership share owned by the deceased or because it results from an agreement made for full consideration.
[124] IHTA 1984, s 5(5) and see 3.07 on liabilities generally.

(or entered into a deed of covenant) in favour of a member of his family or friend without receiving consideration, it would not be deductible for IHT purposes.

11.73 FA 1986, s 103 introduced further restrictions on the deductibility from an estate at death of debts and incumbrances created by the deceased.[125] These provisions supplement s 5(5) in relation to debts or incumbrances created after 17 March 1986. Broadly, their aim is to prevent the deduction of 'artificial' debts, where the deceased gives assets away and then buys them back leaving the price outstanding. A deduction is denied to the extent that any value given for the debt was 'derived from the deceased'.

> *Example 11.12*
>
> Berta gives a picture to her daughter Bertina in 2014. In 2015 she buys it back, leaving the purchase price outstanding until the date of her death.
>
> 1. The gift is a PET and escapes IHT if Berta survives 7 years.
>
> 2. The debt owed to Bertina is incurred for full consideration (the picture) and hence satisfies the requirements of IHTA 1984, s 5(5). Deduction is, however, prevented by FA 1986, s 103 as the consideration given for the debt, the picture, derived from the deceased.

Section 103(1) provides that debts must be abated in whole or in part if any portion of the consideration for the debt was *either* derived from the deceased *or* was given by *any* person to whose resources the deceased had contributed. In the latter case contributions of the deceased are ignored, however, if it is shown (ie by the taxpayer) that the contribution was not made with reference to or to enable or facilitate the giving of that consideration.

Accordingly, unless property derived from the deceased furnished the consideration for the debt, a causal link is necessary between the property of the deceased and the subsequent debt transaction.

Finance Act 2013 introduced further restrictions on the deductibility of liabilities. See **3.09** *et seq*.

9. LIFETIME TRANSFERS MADE WITHIN 7 YEARS OF DEATH

11.74 Personal representatives need to establish what non-exempt lifetime gifts the deceased made during the 7 years before death. Such gifts reduce the nil rate band available to the death estate. Personal representatives should make enquiries of relatives and associates of the deceased as to what lifetime gifts have been made.

---

[125] See further **3.07**.

11.75   The IHT Toolkit suggests that personal representatives put in some hard work. It says in relation to lifetime gifts:

> 'It is strongly recommended that you check all bank and building society statements for the seven years prior to death to see what transactions have taken place which may be regarded as 'gifting'. We would suggest initially checking at least the previous three years statements; this will provide you with a good indication of the gifting history of the deceased. If you find any withdrawals and transfers which seem unusual in their amount or regularity then you should consider a review of the bank statements for the full seven years.'

It also suggests checking:

(a)   what gifts family members have received including gifts for birthdays, Christmas or other religious festivals, and on marriage;

(b)   whether the deceased paid for anything on someone else's behalf, eg holidays, bills, or made loans which have been waived;

(c)   whether the deceased disposed of any property within 7 years of death for less than full market value or without receiving the full sale proceeds.

The existence of property in apparent co-ownership may reveal lifetime gifts made by the deceased to the co-owner(s) which need to be disclosed. The Toolkit, therefore, suggests checking:

(i)   whether the co-owners' contributions to the purchase and other costs matches their respective interests in the property;

(ii)   how the joint owners funded their shares of the purchase price – parents may give their children money to fund the children's shares;

(iii)   whether the co-owners paid proportionately any ancillary costs of the purchase of a joint asset, for example, fees and stamp duty were not paid in the same shares then a gift will have been made.

Failure to make sufficiently careful investigations may give rise to a penalty if tax is underpaid as a result.[126]

11.76   To the extent that the value of the gifts exceeds the nil rate band, tax will be payable on the gifts themselves. The primary liability for the tax on lifetime gifts falls on the transferee but if the tax remains unpaid for 12 months after the death, the personal representatives will become liable.[127]

Calculating tax on chargeable lifetime transfers

11.77   Inheritance tax on lifetime chargeable transfers will have been charged, at half the then death rate,[128] at the time when the transfer was made. In

---

[126]   See discussion in *Hutchings v HMRC* [2015] UKFTT 9 (TC) and **11.93**.
[127]   IHTA 1984, s 204(6). See **3.29** *et seq*.
[128]   IHTA 1984, s 7(2) as substituted by FA 1986, s 101(1), (3), Sch 19, para 2.

computing that tax, transfers in the 7 preceding years will have been included in the cumulative total of the transferor. As a result of the transferor's death within the following 7 years, inheritance tax must be recalculated on the original value transferred at the full rate of inheritance tax in force at the date of death (unless rates have increased in which case the rate at the date of transfer[129]). After deducting the tax originally paid, extra tax may be payable.

Taper relief

11.78 If death occurs more than 3 years after the gift, taper relief ensures that only a percentage of the death rate is charged. The tapering percentages are as follows:[130]

(a) where the transfer is made more than 3 but not more than 4 years before the death, 80%;

(b) where the transfer is made more than 4 but not more than 5 years before the death, 60%;

(c) where the transfer is made more than 5 but not more than 6 years before the death, 40%; and

(d) where the transfer is made more than 6 but not more than 7 years before the death, 20%.

Example 11.13

David settles £350,000 on discretionary trusts in July 2007 (inheritance tax is paid by the trustees). Consider the situation if he dies: (i) on 1 January 2009; (ii) on 1 January 2013; or (iii) on 1 January 2015.

The original transfer in 2007 was subject to inheritance tax at one half of the rates in force for 2007–08.

1. In (i) David dies within 3 years of the gift; accordingly, a charge at the full tax rates for 2008–09 must be calculated, tax paid in 2007 deducted, and any balance is then payable.

2. In (ii) David dies more than 5 but less than 6 years after the gift: therefore only 40% of the full amount of tax on death is to be calculated, the tax paid in 2007 deducted, and the balance (if any) is then payable.

3. In (iii) death occurs more than 7 years after the transfer and therefore no supplementary tax is payable.

If it is assumed that the 2007–08 rates of inheritance tax apply throughout this period when the nil rate band was £300,000,[131] the actual tax computations are as follows (assuming that the 2007 transfer was the first chargeable transfer of David):

---

[129] IHTA 1984, Sch 2, para 2 as amended by FA 1986, ss 101(1), (3), 114(6), Sch 19, para 37, Sch 23, Pt X.

[130] IHTA 1984, s 7(4) as inserted by FA 1986, s 101(3), Sch 19, para 2.

[131] In fact, the nil rate band was £312,000 for 2008–09 and £325,000 for 2009–10 and subsequent years (it is frozen until the end of tax year 2017–18). Note that from 6 April 2015

4.   Inheritance tax on the 2007 chargeable transfer is as follows:

  (a)   first £300,000 = nil;

  (b)   remaining £50,000 at 20% = £10,000;

  (c)   total inheritance tax payable by the trustees = £10,000.

5.   If death occurs within 3 years, tax on a transfer of £350,000 at the then death rates is:

  (a)   first £300,000 = nil;

  (b)   remaining £50,000 at 40% = £20,000;

  (c)   total inheritance tax is therefore £20,000 which, after deducting the sum paid in 2007 (£10,000), leaves a further £10,000 to be paid.

6.   If death occurs in 2013, the calculation is as follows:

  (a)   full inheritance tax at death rates: £20,000 (as in (5) above);

  (b)   take 40% (taper relief) of that tax: £20,000 x 40% = £8,000;

  (c)   as that sum is less than the tax actually paid in 2007 there is no extra inheritance tax to pay.

Note that in the above example that even though the result of taper relief may be to ensure that extra inheritance tax is not payable because of the death, it does not lead to any refund of the original inheritance tax paid when the chargeable transfer was made.[132] Taper relief is moreover of no benefit if the gift falls within the donor's nil rate band because, although the gift used up all or part of that band, no tax is actually paid and taper relief operates by reducing the tax payable.

Fall in value of gifted property

11.79 If the property given falls in value by the date of death, the extra inheritance tax is calculated on that reduced value.[133] This relief is not available in the case of tangible movables which are wasting assets and there are special rules for leases with less than 50 years unexpired.

Example 11.14

In May 2015 Don gave a drawing worth £375,000 to his discretionary trustees (who paid the inheritance tax). He died in June 2017 when the drawing was worth only £335,000.

1.   Assuming it was Don's first chargeable transfer, inheritance tax paid on the 2015 gift was £375,000 – £325,000 = £50,000 @ 20% = £10,000.

---

the nil rate band will rise (if ever!) in line with the Consumer Prices Index ('CPI') although this will be subject to an override if Parliament determines that a different amount shall apply: see FA 2012, s 208.

[132] IHTA 1984, s 7(5) as inserted by FA 1986, s 101(3), Sch 19, para 2.

[133] IHTA 1984, s 131 as amended by FA 1986, s 101, Sch 19, para 23.

2.   Inheritance tax on death (assume rates unchanged) is calculated on £335,000 – £325,000 = £10,000 @ 40% = £2,000.

Hence extra inheritance tax payable is nil.

Had the property been sold by the trustees before Don's death for £40,000 less than its value when given away by Don, the inheritance tax payable on death within 7 years would be charged on the sale proceeds with the same result as above. If, however, the property had been given away by the trustees before Don's death, even though its value might at that time have fallen by £40,000 since Don's original gift, no relief is given, with the result that the extra charge caused by Don's death will be levied on the full £375,000.

The value of a chargeable lifetime transfer for cumulation purposes is not reduced in the 7-year period because IHTA 1984, s 131 merely reduces the value that is taxed (not the value cumulated) whilst taper relief is given in terms of the rate of inheritance tax to be charged on that transfer. Hence the full value of the lifetime transfer remains in the cumulative total of the transferor and there is no reduction in the tax charged on his death estate. Further, as already noted, in cases where the transfer fell within the transferor's nil rate band, taper relief does not assist because it takes effect as a reduction in the tax charge.

PETs made within 7 years of death

11.80 A potentially exempt transfer made within 7 years of death becomes a chargeable transfer on the death and is subject to inheritance tax in accordance with the taxpayer's cumulative total at the date when it was made (ie taking into account chargeable transfers in the preceding 7 years). The value transferred is frozen at the date of transfer, unless the property has fallen in value by the date of death, in which case the lower value is charged. Despite these provisions, which look back to the actual date of the transfer of value, the inheritance tax is calculated by reference to the rates in force at the date of death, unless rates have increased, in which case the rates at the time of the transfer are taken (subject to taper relief, as above).

Example 11.15

In October 2014 Doris gave a unique doll then worth £380,000 to her granddaughter Grace. Doris died in July 2015 when the value of the doll was £330,000. Assuming that Doris had made no other transfer of value during her life, ignoring exemptions and reliefs, the inheritance tax consequences are that:

1.   the 2010 transfer was potentially exempt. However, as Doris died within 7 years it is made chargeable;

2.   as the asset had fallen in value by the date of death, inheritance tax is charged on the reduced value, ie on £330,000;

3.   inheritance tax at the rates current when Doris died are:

      (a)   first £325,000 = nil;

      (b)   next £5,000 at 40% = £2,000;

4.   total inheritance tax = £2,000. Doris died more than 3 but less than 4 years after the gift. Therefore tax is £2,000 x 80% = £1,600.

Note that although inheritance tax is calculated by reference to the reduced value of the asset, for cumulation purposes (and for capital gains tax purposes) the original value transferred (£380,000) is retained.

Combination of PETs and chargeable transfers made within 7 years of death

11.81   Potentially exempt transfers are treated as exempt transfers unless the transferor dies within the following 7-year period. Accordingly, they are not cumulated in calculating inheritance tax on subsequent lifetime chargeable transfers. Consider the following example:

Example 11.16

In July 2010, Derek gives shares worth £327,000 to his son. In April 2014, Derek settles land worth £335,000 on discretionary trusts and pays the inheritance tax himself (so that grossing-up applies).[134] He dies in February 2015. (Assume that no other transfers of value were made by Derek and that 2014–15 inheritance tax rates apply throughout; ignore exemptions and reliefs).

1.   The transfer in 2010 was a potentially exempt transfer.

2.   In calculating the inheritance tax on the chargeable transfer in 2014, the potentially exempt transfer is ignored so there will be a full nil rate band available leaving £10,000 in excess of the nil rate band. As Derek is paying the tax the £10,000 must be grossed up at 20% giving a gross transfer of £12,500 on which IHT of £2,5000 must be paid. The chargeable transfer in 2014 is therefore £337,500 (£335,000 + £2,500).

3.   As a result of Derek's death within 7 years, the potentially exempt transfer is made chargeable and the inheritance tax calculation is as follows:

(a)   *On the 2010 transfer:* inheritance tax at the rates when Derek died is subject to 40% taper relief (gifts more than 4, less than 5 years before death). Hence inheritance tax at death rates is:

(i)   first £325,000 = nil;

(ii)   next, £2,000 at 40% = £800;

(iii) taper relief at 40%: £800 x 60% = £480 (tax due on 2010 transfer).

Note: Primary liability for this tax falls upon the donee. Grossing-up does not apply when inheritance tax is charged, or additional tax is payable, because of death.

(b)   *On the 2014 transfer:* inheritance tax must be recalculated on this transfer because the transferor has died within 7 years, and the former

---

[134] When chargeable lifetime transfers are made and the inheritance tax paid by the donor, tax must be calculated on the basis that he made a net gift. This process is known as 'grossing up': see **3.41** *et seq.*

potentially exempt transfer must be included in the cumulative total of Derek at the time when this transfer was made. Hence:

(i)   cumulative transfers of Derek in 2010 = £327,000;

(ii)   value transferred in 2010 = £337,500;

(iii)   inheritance tax at death rates on transfers between £327,000 and £664,500 is £337,500 x 40% = £135,000.

Taper relief is not available on this transfer as Derek died within 3 years. Therefore deduct inheritance tax paid in 2014: £135,000 − £2,500 = £132,500 additional inheritance tax payable on the 2014 transfer.

Note: The cumulative total of transfers made by Derek at his death (which will affect the inheritance tax payable on his death estate) is £664,500.

When a potentially exempt transfer is made after an earlier chargeable transfer and the transferor dies in the following 7 years, tax on that potentially exempt transfer is calculated by including the earlier transfer in his cumulative total. In this sense the making of the potentially exempt transfer means that there is no reduction in his cumulative total for a further 7 years and the result is that inheritance tax could eventually turn out to be higher than if the potentially exempt transfer had never been made ('the PET trap').

Example 11.17 (the 'PET trap')

Cara made a chargeable transfer of £325,000 on 1 May 2008 and on 1 May 2014 made a gift of £300,000 to take advantage of the potentially exempt transfer regime. Unfortunately, she dies after 1 May 2015 (when the 2008 transfer drops out of cumulation) but before 1 May 2017 (when taper relief begins to operate on the potentially exempt transfer).

1.   Inheritance tax on the former potentially exempt transfer (at 2014–15 rates) is £120,000 as the 2008 transfer forms part of Cara's cumulative total in 2014. Tax on the death estate is then calculated by including the 2014 transfer (the former potentially exempt transfer) in Cara's cumulative total.

2.   Had Cara not made the 2014 potentially exempt transfer so that £300,000 formed part of her death estate, tax thereon (ignoring the 2008 transfer which has dropped out of cumulation) would be nil.

10. PENALTIES

11.82   HMRC has developed one consistent penalty regime for inaccuracies in tax returns and other tax documents to apply across all the taxes and duties they administer. FA 2007, Sch 24 introduced this new regime for, *inter alia*, income tax and CGT. FA 2008, Sch 40 extended it to other taxes including IHT and it applies to IHT for all chargeable events that occur on or after 1 April 2009.[135]

---

[135] See SI 2009/571, Art 2.

11.83   The provisions of s 247(1) and (2) of IHTA 1984 continue to apply to events before that date under which there is a penalty liability where a person 'fraudulently' or 'negligently' furnishes an incorrect account.

11.84   Schedule 24, para 1(2) provides that a penalty is payable where a document contains a 'relevant inaccuracy'. This is one which amounts to, or leads to:

(a)   an understatement of a liability to tax;

(b)   a false or inflated statement of a loss; or

(c)   a false or inflated claim to repayment of tax,

and the inaccuracy was careless or deliberate.

11.85   In relation to inheritance tax inaccuracies commonly arise in relation to:

- properties sold for more than their initial valuation where HMRC considers that the initial valuation was careless; and
- claims for the transfer of a nil rate band in circumstances where HMRC considers that it should have been plain that no nil rate band was available, for example because the first spouse died in estate duty days when there was no spouse exemption available;
- failure to make appropriate efforts to identify lifetime gifts;
- claiming reliefs in circumstances where it is wholly inappropriate, for example claiming agricultural relief on land used for grazing a couple of ponies or claiming business property relief on the whole value of a business when it is apparent that the business is holding cash which is far in excess of anything that could be required for future business purposes.

11.86   Penalties are chargeable under Sch 24, para 1(1) on the person ('P') who gives the account to HMRC. In the case of IHT, this is the PR (though HMRC does also have power under para 1A to impose a penalty on anyone who deliberately gives the PR false information).

11.87   There were initially concerns that a professional agent might also be regarded as 'giving' documents to HMRC. However, in an exchange of correspondence with CIOT in 2009,[136] HMRC agreed that professionals who were merely advising would not be liable to penalties under para 1 'because the clear intention of the legislation is that the person becoming liable to a penalty under this penalty is the taxpayer'. HMRC went on to say that 'we would not usually expect agents to become liable to penalties under Paragraph 1A of Schedule 24, since we would not normally expect an agent to cause an inaccuracy in a return by deliberately supplying false information to the person making the return'.

---

[136]   http://www.tax.org.uk/tax-policy/newsdesk/2009/the-finance-act-2007-penalties-regime-penalties-on-advisers.

11.88 HMRC also has power under Sch 24, para 1A to charge a penalty on a third party ('T') where:

'(a) another person (P) gives HMRC a document of a kind listed in the table in paragraph 1,
(b) the document contains a relevant inaccuracy, and
(c) the inaccuracy was attributable to T deliberately supplying false information to P (whether directly or indirectly), or to T deliberately withholding information from P, with the intention of the document containing the inaccuracy.'

This power is particularly likely to be used in inheritance tax cases where personal representatives may depend on information provided by others. However, HMRC has always made it clear that, although it may impose a penalty on a third party, this will not mean that the person submitting the return is safe. For example the *Inheritance Tax and Trusts Newsletter April 2009* included the following:

'The new regime also contains a provision that allows a penalty to be charged where an inaccuracy in the liable person's document was attributable to another person. This is particularly relevant to Inheritance Tax where the personal representatives will inevitably be relying on other people to provide them with information about the deceased's estate.

Where it can be shown that the other person deliberately withheld information or supplied false information to the liable person, with the intention that the Inheritance Tax account or return would contain an inaccuracy, a penalty may be charged on that other person. But that will not necessarily mean that the personal representative themselves may not also be chargeable to a penalty. If the withheld or false information gave rise to inconsistencies in the information they had received about the estate and they did not question those inconsistencies; the liable person may still be charged a penalty for failing to take reasonable care as well.'

Personal representatives who submit an incorrect IHT Account on the basis of information provided by family members will need to show that they took all reasonable steps or they may face their own penalty under para 1 of the Schedule. The recent case of *Hutchings v HMRC*[137] is a good illustration of HMRC's approach.

11.89 There are three categories of error:[138]

(a) 'careless' if the inaccuracy is due to failure by the person submitting the document (P) to take reasonable care;
(b) 'deliberate but not concealed' if the inaccuracy is deliberate on P's part but P does not make arrangements to conceal it; and

---

[137] [2015] UKFTT 9 (TC) discussed below at **11.93**.
[138] See FA 2007, Sch 24, para 3.

(c)   'deliberate and concealed' if the inaccuracy is deliberate on P's part and P makes arrangements to conceal it (eg by submitting false evidence in support of an inaccurate figure).

Penalties are graded depending on the category into which they fall and on whether disclosure was prompted or unprompted. So, for example, in the case of careless errors they range from 0% to 30% of the tax underpaid and in the case of deliberate and concealed errors from 30% to 100%.[139]

11.90   It is crucial that taxpayers take 'reasonable care' if they are to avoid a penalty. The *IHT and Trusts Newsletter* for April 2009 had this to say:

'HMRC considers the PRs will have taken reasonable care where they

- follow the guidance provided about filling in forms such as the IHT400 and IHT205/207/C5
- make suitable enquiries of asset holders and other people (as suggested in the guidance) to establish the extent of the deceased's estate
- ensure correct instructions are given to valuers when valuing assets
- seek advice about anything they are unsure of
- follow up inconsistencies in information they receive from asset holders, valuers and other people
- identify any estimated values included on the form.'

Cases

Robertson v IRC[140]

11.91   A Special Commissioner quashed the imposition of a £9,000 penalty imposed on a Scottish solicitor, awarding costs against the Revenue. The solicitor had valued an English cottage at an estimated £50,000. The formal valuation was £315,000. The original figure had been described as an estimate. The corrective account was submitted within 6 months of the end of the month of death and all the tax was paid within that period. There had been an urgent need to obtain the grant quickly as the executors had wanted to sell a Scottish house included in the estate before winter set in. Death was in October, the inventory was submitted in November and the grant obtained in December. The valuation was obtained in January and the additional tax paid in January. Special Commissioner Gordon Reid said:

'the Revenue wholly failed to satisfy me that Mr Robertson did not make the fullest inquiries that were reasonably practicable in the circumstances, and thus, in some way negligently delivered, furnished or produced to the Revenue an incorrect account, information or document.'

---

[139] See Sch 24, Part 2.
[140] [2002] STC (SCD) 182.

In *Robertson (No 2) v IRC*,[141] Mr Robertson successfully applied for costs against the Revenue. Mr Reid said:

> 'I can find no logical or rational basis in the evidence presented by the Revenue or the agreed statement of facts for bringing proceedings.'

Cairns v RCC[142]

11.92 The same Special Commissioner disagreed with the imposition of a penalty in a second case. He had two grounds for dismissing the penalty.

(a) *The summons issued by the Revenue was insufficiently specific*: apart from attaching extracts from the relevant legislation, the summons, which the Commissioner described as having 'the flavour of a summary criminal complaint', contained no further specification whatsoever of how or in what respect Mr Cairns had acted fraudulently or negligently. The account or document to which these allegations related was not even identified.

It was irrelevant that the notice had been preceded by lengthy correspondence. An initiating document, be it summons, summary complaint or indictment must set out the parameters of the enquiry, and the essential facts and basis in law upon which a public authority relies. If it does not do so, there is bound to be significant prejudice or the risk of such prejudice.

(b) *The penalty was unjustified on the facts*: in this case, the deceased became unable to manage his own property and affairs. Mr Cairns was asked by Midlothian Council to act as the deceased's guardian. At that time the deceased was residing in Roslynlee Hospital, but was anxious to return home to Stonefield, which he owned. The property was in a terrible condition suffering from wet rot, dry rot, rising damp and structural defects in the roof. Mr Cairns obtained a valuation of Stonefield in January 2004 of £400,000 but this was stated to be an 'arbitrary figure pending investigations as to costs involved in upgrading'. Mr Cairns spent some money making one room habitable and the deceased did return home but died in October 2004. Mr Cairns submitted an IHT 200 in which he valued Stonefield at £400,000 and paid the tax due at that point. He was uncertain of the true value of Stonefield but considered that the sale price would probably be agreed in due course with the District Valuer to be value at the date of death. He considered it unnecessary to go to the expense of obtaining a further valuation which would probably be heavily qualified and not necessarily any more accurate than the existing valuation. There was no evidence of any significant increase in the value of properties in the locality between January 2004 and October 2004. He did not describe the value attributed to Stonefield as a 'provisional estimate', something which the Commissioner described as 'in the circumstances, careless'.

---

[141] [2002] STC (SCD) 242.
[142] [2009] UKFTT 67 (TC).

Stonefield was subsequently sold for £600,000. Mr Cairns sent a cheque for the tax based on an HMRC estimate of the tax due. There was still some doubt as to the full extent of the deceased's estate and, in the event, some tax was refunded.

HMRC argued that Mr Cairns should have obtained another professional valuation before submitting his account. However, the Special Commissioner described this as bare assertion. The mere failure to obtain another valuation when it had not been established that a second valuation would have led to a different figure being inserted in the statutory form did not constitute negligent delivery of an incorrect account. It could not be suggested that a prudent personal representative should have foreseen, when completing the statutory form, that Stonefield was likely to sell for £600,000.

The Special Commissioner said:

> 'Negligent conduct amounts to more than just being wrong or taking a different view from HMRC.'

Although the Special Commissioner had said that the failure to describe the value as a provisional estimate, was a careless error, he said that it was 'minor, technical and of no consequence whatsoever'. It had no effect on the dealings between HMRC and Mr Cairns as executor. HMRC were kept informed of the intention to sell the property. They, in effect, reserved their position as to whether they would regard the sale price as the date of death value. The tax was duly paid, indeed overpaid and a refund eventually paid to the deceased's estate.

Hutchings v RCC[143]

11.93 Mr Hutchings, the residuary beneficiary of his late father's will, appealed to the First-tier Tribunal against a penalty imposed on him personally under para 1A of Schedule 24 to the Finance Act 2007. The penalty had been imposed on the basis that Mr Hutchings, a beneficiary of his father's estate, had deliberately withheld information about a gift received from his father in the year before his death from the executors of the will. The executors were a retired solicitor and a land agent. The bulk of the work was done by a former partner of the retired solicitor.

11.94 The deceased, who died on 14 October 2009, transferred the balance (£443,669) of an undeclared Swiss bank account into the name of Mr Hutchings 7 months before he died. This was a PET which became chargeable and the failure to disclose it led to a substantial understatement of tax.

The executors had held a meeting on 29 October 2009, attended by Mr Hutchings and other family members, at which they explained that any gifts

---

[143] [2015] UKFTT 9 (TC).

made by the deceased would be relevant to the calculation of IHT. On 19 November 2009 (just over a month after the death) the executors wrote to various members of deceased's family, including Mr Hutchings, asking for details of any lifetime gifts.

Mr Hutchings did not reply to this letter and the executors submitted the IHT 400 on 25 March 2010. It made no mention of the gift of the money in the account because they were not aware of it.

On or around July 2011 HMRC received anonymous information that Mr Hutchings had an offshore bank account. Mr Hutchings denied deliberately withholding information and challenged the legal basis of the penalty.

The case was the first to consider the new penalty regime. The Tribunal held that the burden of proof was on HMRC who had to prove on the balance of probabilities that 'T' had deliberately withheld information in relation to third parties.

The taxpayer presented a number of arguments all of which were rejected. They included the following:

(a)   The executors had not made it clear that lifetime gifts were to be disclosed
      The Tribunal accepted that lifetime gifts had been discussed at the meeting. There was a contemporaneous attendance note made by the solicitor acting for the executors which recorded 'I mentioned lifetime gifts'. The Tribunal discounted a statement made by him in later letter to HMRC that he 'read the Riot Act' to the family in relation to lifetime gifts; it considered that the contemporaneous note was likely to be more accurate.
      Mr Hutchings described the letter written by the executors asking about gifts as 'complete gibberish' and said a reasonable reading of the letter was that it was only referring to birthday gifts worth less than £250, and failed to refer to cash or bank accounts. The Tribunal disagreed, describing the letter as 'very clear'. The letter said that, in compliance with the executors' duty to HMRC to investigate lifetime gifts for the purpose of paying IHT, the executors needed to know 'what the gift was and when it was made'. It said that they needed to know of 'any' gift in last 7 years, although they did not need details if the total value of gifts within a tax year was less than £250. It concluded

> 'Please can you let me know about any gifts whether to you or to your family. It may well be that the gifts are not taxable but we still need to know about them.'

      The letter did not specifically refer to gifts of cash nor did it refer to a gift of a bank account but it used 'gift' in a general sense and was clearly referring to any gift worth more than £250.

(b)   The omission of the gift from IHT 400 was the fault of the executors

Mr Hutchings alleged that the executors had been negligent in failing to discover the account themselves and/or failing to chase a reply to the letter asking about gifts' and that this broke the chain of causation. In particular he criticised the executors for:

(i)   not writing to a sufficient number of banks to investigate whether the deceased had any accounts;

(ii)   not thoroughly searching the deceased's home for relevant documents, which might have disclosed the gift to them; and

(iii) for submitting the IHT400 form earlier than it need have been.

The Tribunal rejected these criticisms. The suggestion that the executors should have raised queries with banks including those with whom they had no reason to suspect the deceased had kept an account was 'utterly unreasonable'. Executors cannot write to every bank in the world on the off chance a deceased person might have had an account with them unknown to his advisers.

It is not reasonable (unless perhaps there are specific indications that something was hidden) for executors to conduct a thorough search of a deceased's house where the family and advisers were present to inform the executors about the deceased's affairs and the executors themselves had had a pre-existing relationship with the deceased. Moreover, such a search would probably not have revealed the account as it was paperless.

The executors had submitted the IHT 400 before they had to but it is good practice to do so in order to obtain the grant and to prevent unnecessary interest becoming payable on the tax due.

(c)   The withholding was not 'deliberate'

All parties accepted that mere inadvertence or oversight would not amount to deliberate conduct. Mr Hutchings claimed that the withholding was not culpable because he did not know that the Swiss bank account had tax implications. The Tribunal did not agree for a number of reasons.

Firstly, the executors had made it clear that they wanted to know of all gifts and not just those subject to tax. Secondly, and more importantly, Mr Hutchings did know the money had tax implication. In particular, he had inadvertently revealed the existence of the account to his own solicitor but failed to act on her advice to disclose it to HMRC.

(d)   Mr Hutchings did not 'intend' the IHT 400 would be inaccurate

HMRC had to show that Mr Hutchings must have intended the IHT 400 to contain the inaccuracy. The Tribunal accepted that this must require foreknowledge that the executors would be making a tax return to HMRC.

The Tribunal found that he did know this. He might well not have known the name of the form and he probably did not know the date on which it was due to be filed, but that was irrelevant. He knew that the executors were making an inheritance tax return on which gifts should be recorded and he deliberately failed to tell them about the gift to him of the Swiss account with the intention that the return would not contain this information in order to evade tax.

11.95 HMRC raised a penalty enquiry with the executors but having inspected the file relating to the administration were satisfied that the executors had acted properly and in particular had made reasonable enquiries of financial institutions. HMRC were also satisfied that the executors had had no knowledge of an offshore bank account. Hence condition 2 was not fulfilled: in other words, while the return filed by the executors did contain an inaccuracy, HMRC considered that the inaccuracy was not due to carelessness or deliberate behaviour of the executors and, therefore, did not impose a penalty on the executors for the inaccurate IHT 400.

The case is an illustration of the importance of making appropriate enquiries and having records available to show HMRC in case of later investigation.

Avoiding a penalty

11.96 Fighting a battle with HMRC is never a pleasant prospect so it is important to do everything possible to avoid facing a penalty investigation. The advice has to be:

Valuations

(a) tell HMRC why you are using an estimated value and describe it as such on the IHT account;

(b) instruct valuers to give an open market valuation and make sure to include any development or hope value;

(c) draw the valuer's attention to any matters which may be relevant to hope value;

(d) unless the valuation is totally straightforward it will normally be preferable to instruct a qualified valuer rather than to rely on an estate agent's figure. The valuer will produce a reasoned valuation and will be able to justify the figure if a dispute arises at a later stage;

(e) if using an estate agent, give the instructions on the same basis and obtain more than one valuation. If the values are spread, do not take the lowest;

(f) if offers are received in excess of the valuation before the application for the grant is made, inform the valuer and ask whether the valuation should be increased;

(g) check that exemptions and reliefs are available before claiming them.

Lifetime gifts

(a) inspect bank and building society statements for at least 3 years;

(b) provide family members and associates with clear written instructions as to the information they have to provide and preserve the instructions in case of investigation by HMRC;

(c) follow up inconsistencies.

What to do if facing a penalty

11.97 The decision of *Hanson v RCC*[144] is helpful to lay personal representatives. The taxpayer's accountants had wrongly advised the taxpayer that he was entitled to capital gains tax loss relief and HMRC had imposed a penalty on the taxpayer.

The First-tier Tribunal held that the taxpayer was protected by para 18 of Sch 24 to FA 2007 which provides that 'P is not liable to a penalty in respect of anything done or omitted by P's agent where P satisfies HMRC that P took reasonable care to avoid inaccuracy'.

Cannan J said 'In my view, if a taxpayer reasonably relies on a reputable accountant for advice in relation to the content of his tax return then he will not be liable to a penalty under Schedule 24'.

The key is of course that the reliance must be reasonable. A person cannot abrogate responsibility. Cannan J referred to the Compliance Handbook at CH84540 and said that he agreed with its general thrust – in particular that a taxpayer cannot simply leave everything to his agent:

'However, in matters that would not be straightforward to a reasonable taxpayer and where advice from an agent has been sought, which is ostensibly within the agent's area of competence, the taxpayer is entitled to rely on that advice.'

Obviously what is reasonable care in any particular case will depend on all the circumstances:

'In my view this will include the nature of the matters being dealt with in the return, the identity and experience of the agent, the experience of the taxpayer and the nature of the professional relationship between the taxpayer and the agent.'

What if the PR is a professional?

11.98 Here *Hanson* is of no assistance. However, it may be possible to persuade HMRC to suspend the penalty.

According to the Compliance Handbook:[145]

'The penalty provisions in Finance Act 2007 seek to influence behaviour by encouraging and supporting those who try to meet their obligations and penalising those who do not.'

To this end HMRC has power, under FA 2007, Sch 24, para 14 to suspend all or part of a penalty for a careless inaccuracy for a period of 2 years.

---

[144] [2012] UKFTT 314 (TC).
[145] http://www.hmrc.gov.uk/manuals/chmanual/CH83110.htm.

HMRC will set 'suspension conditions' which are designed to help a person to avoid becoming liable to a further careless inaccuracy under para 1. A suspended penalty will become payable if, during the period of suspension, the person becomes liable for a further penalty for an inaccuracy in a return or document. At the end of the suspension period HMRC will cancel the penalty if satisfied that the suspension conditions have been met. If not, the penalty becomes payable.

According to the Compliance Handbook HMRC 'must consider suspension for every penalty for a careless inaccuracy'. In the same paragraph it says '[w]e should discuss the suspension with the person and give them factsheet CC/FS10'.

Hence, if HMRC does not suggest suspension, the issue should be raised as it could save a significant sum.

CHAPTER 12

INSTRUMENTS OF VARIATION AND DISCLAIMER

1. 'READING-BACK' GENERALLY

12.01 Beneficiaries of an estate may want to pass on property which they have been left to others: sometimes out of generosity but often with the intention of distributing the estate in a more tax efficient manner. Beneficiaries are always free to make lifetime gifts of property but unless they take advantage of a specific statutory provision, the gifts will be transfers of value for IHT purposes and disposals for CGT. Normally the beneficiaries will not want this result and will prefer their redirection of the property to be read-back and treated as the deceased's disposition.[1]

12.02 There are a number of 'reading-back' provisions by which a redirection of property can be treated as made by the deceased for tax purposes. Some are effective for both IHT and CGT: some only for IHT. These are:

(a) post-death variations and disclaimers (IHTA 1984, s 142 and TCGA 1992, s 62(6));

(b) precatory trusts (IHTA 1984, s 143);[2]

(c) property ceasing to be comprised in a discretionary will trust (IHTA 1984, s 144);[3]

(d) the settlement of a claim under the Inheritance (Provision for Family and Dependants) Act 1975 (IHTA 1984, s 145).[4]

12.03 Deeming provisions invariably give rise to logistical problems. In the case of variations, for instance, in the 'real world' the varying beneficiary is making a gift and so what matters is that:[5]

---

[1] But see **12.44** *et seq* for cases where reading-back is not beneficial. In the 2015 Budget the Chancellor announced a consultation into the operation of the provisions dealing with variations and disclaimers.

[2] See **12.51** *et seq* and **Precedent 4.1, clause 4**.

[3] See **13.11** *et seq*.

[4] See generally **14.70 and Chapter 17**.

[5] For a discussion of 'deeming' under s 142 see *Russell v IRC* [1988] STC 195. See **2.14** for the perpetuity rule when a variation creates a settlement.

(a) the gifted property is identified with property passing by a disposition of the deceased. It does not matter that the property left by the deceased was sold after death provided that the gift is of the proceeds of sale or other property representing the property left by the deceased;

(b) if the gift is on trust, the trust was either set up by the deceased (for instance a pilot trust established during his lifetime) or is in existence at the date of the variation (it may be created by the variation);

(c) the person making the variation was alive to inherit on the death of the deceased – note, however, that it is not necessary for the beneficiary of the variation to have been alive at the date of death of the deceased and that the personal representatives of a beneficiary dying after the deceased can make a variation on his behalf.[6]

2. TAX TREATMENT OF VARIATIONS AND DISCLAIMERS

12.04 IHTA 1984, s 142 provides as follows:

'(1) Where within the period of two years after a person's death –

(a) any of the dispositions (whether effected by will, under the law relating to intestacy or otherwise) of the property comprised in his estate immediately before his death are varied, or

(b) the benefit conferred by any of those dispositions is disclaimed,[7]

by an instrument in writing[8] made by the persons or any of the persons who benefit or would benefit under the dispositions, this Act shall apply[9] as if the variation had been effected by the deceased or, as the case may be, the disclaimed benefit had never been conferred.

(2) Subsection (1) above shall not apply to a variation unless the instrument contains a statement, made by all the relevant persons, to the effect that they intend the subsection to apply to the variation.[10]

(2A) For the purposes of subsection (2) above the relevant persons are –

(a) the person or persons making the instrument, and

(b) where the variation results in additional tax being payable, the personal representatives.

---

6   See **12.36**.
7   See **12.13** *et seq*.
8   See **12.21**.
9   For different treatment of variations and disclaimers for IHT and CGT purposes as a result of the wording of s 142 and s 62 see **12.06**.
10   See **12.21**.

Personal representatives may decline to make a statement under subsection (2) above only if no, or no sufficient, assets are held by them in that capacity for discharging the additional tax.[11]

(3)   Subsection (1) above shall not apply to a variation or disclaimer made for any consideration in money or money's worth other than consideration consisting of the making, in respect of another of the dispositions, of a variation or disclaimer to which that subsection applies.[12]

(3A) Subsection (1) does not apply to a variation by virtue of which any property comprised in the estate immediate before the person's death becomes property in relation to which section 23(1) applies unless it is shown that the appropriate person has been notified of the existence of the instrument of variation.

(3B) For the purposes of subsection (3A) "the appropriate person" is –

(a)   the charity or registered club to which the property is given, or
(b)   if the property is to be held on trust for charitable purposes or for the purposes of registered clubs, the trustees in question.[13]

(4)   Where a variation to which subsection (1) above applies results in property being held in trust for a person for a period which ends not more than two years after the death, this Act shall apply as if the disposition of the property that takes effect at the end of the period had had effect from the beginning of the period; but this subsection shall not affect the application of this Act in relation to any distribution or application of property occurring before that disposition takes effect.[14]

(5)   For the purposes of subsection (1) above the property comprised in a person's estate includes any excluded property but not any property to which he is treated as entitled by virtue of section 49(1) above or section 102 of the Finance Act 1986.[15]

(6)   Subsection (1) above applies whether or not the administration of the estate is complete or the property concerned has been distributed in accordance with the original dispositions.'

12.05   TCGA 1992, s 62(6)–(8) provide:

'(6) Subject to subsections (7) and (8) below, where within the period of 2 years after a person's death any of the dispositions (whether effected by will, under the law relating to intestacy or otherwise) of the property of which he was competent to dispose are varied, or the benefit conferred by any of those dispositions is disclaimed, by an instrument in writing made by the persons or any of the persons who benefit or would benefit under the dispositions –

---

[11]   See **12.19**.
[12]   See **12.25**.
[13]   Subsections (3A) and (3B) inserted by FA 2012 in respect of deaths on or after 6 April 2012.
[14]   See **12.28**.
[15]   See **12.32**.

(a)   the variation or disclaimer shall not constitute a disposal for the purposes of this Act, and

(b)   this section shall apply as if the variation had been effected by the deceased or, as the case may be, the disclaimed benefit had never been conferred.

(7) Subsection (6) above does not apply to a variation [unless the instrument contains a statement by the persons making the instrument to the effect that they intend the subsection to apply to the variation].

(8) Subsection (6) above does not apply to a variation or disclaimer made for any consideration in money or money's worth other than consideration consisting of the making of a variation or disclaimer in respect of another of the dispositions.'

Different treatment for IHT and CGT

12.06   There is an important distinction between the two provisions. IHTA 1984, s 142 provides that a variation or disclaimer of the disposition of a deceased's property will be treated as if the deceased had left his property on the varied terms for *all IHT purposes*.[16] By contrast, TCGA 1992 is more limited, providing merely that the deceased will be treated as leaving his property in that way *for the purposes of s 62* of the Act. Section 62 is the section which deals with dispositions on death. Hence, variations and disclaimers are not treated as made by the deceased for other CGT purposes. For example, if a variation creates a settlement, the settlor for CGT purposes will be the person making the variation which will determine whether the settlement is to be treated as created by a non-resident settlor.[17]

Example 12.1

Bela, domiciled in France, leaves his villa in Tuscany and moneys in his Swiss bank account to his son Gerard, a UK resident. By a variation of the terms of his will made within 2 years of Bela's death, Gerrard settles the property on discretionary Jersey trusts for the benefit of Gerard's family. For IHT, reading-back ensures that the settlement is excluded property. For CGT purposes, Gerard is treated as the settlor.

Income tax consequences

12.07   There is no specific income tax relief for post-death variations (or disclaimers) so normal income tax rules apply and there is no reading-back effect. The actual treatment will depend on the nature of the gift as discussed at **12.08–12.10**.

---

[16]   This includes the reservation of benefit rules in FA 1986, ss 102, 102ZA, 102A–C and Sch 20.

[17]   TCGA 1992, s 68C and *Marshall v Kerr* [1995] 1 AC 148, [1994] STC 638.

Pecuniary legacies

12.08 These carry interest from one year after the date of death.[18] If the variation takes place before that date, there is no interest to worry about. After 12 months, interest is payable but legatees are not charged to tax on interest which is neither claimed nor paid (*Dewar v IRC*).[19] Accordingly, if it is paid after the variation to the 'new' beneficiary, he is taxed on it.

Specific legacies

12.09 The legatee is entitled to income produced between death and variation. Subsequent income will be taxed as the new beneficiary's unless the settlor-interested trust rules apply.[20]

Residuary beneficiaries

12.10 Where there are successive limited interests, the effect of ITTOIA 2005, ss 674 and 675 is that each beneficiary is taxed on the income he receives in the relevant tax year (except for the final year of the administration when the beneficiary is taxed on all undistributed income even if not received until later). In the case of successive absolute interests each beneficiary will be taxed on what he receives. In the final year of the administration for the purposes of calculating the residuary beneficiary's assumed income entitlement[21] his share of the residuary income is treated as including sums paid to previous beneficiaries.[22]

Settlor-interested trusts and income tax

12.11 ITTOIA 2005, s 620 defines a settlement as including 'any disposition, trust, covenant, agreement, arrangement or transfer of assets'. A post-death variation may be a 'settlement' for the purposes of the income tax legislation. Hence, a beneficiary who disposes of his interest by way of post-death variation will remain liable to income tax on post-variation income if payments are made to his minor children or stepchildren who are neither married nor in a civil partnership.[23]

12.12 In the case of a disclaimer it is thought that the disclaiming beneficiary is not caught by the 'settlement' provisions as HMRC accept that a disclaimer prevents the gift from taking effect at all.

---

[18] Subject to a contrary provision in the will.
[19] [1935] 2 KB 351.
[20] See **12.11**.
[21] This determines how much of the final distribution is treated as income and how much as capital.
[22] ITTOIA 2005, ss 671–672.
[23] ITTOIA 2005, s 629.

3. DISTINCTION BETWEEN A VARIATION AND A DISCLAIMER

12.13   A disclaimer is a refusal to accept property left on death. In this case, the only formalities required for reading back under s 142 are that the disclaimer must be made in writing within 2 years of death.[24] There is no requirement for any separate statement within the disclaimer as there is with a variation.

12.14   Disclaimers are not common as they are inflexible and can only be made if the beneficiary has not benefited from the gift. The person disclaiming cannot direct where the property is to go; the property disclaimed passes automatically to the person next entitled under the will or intestacy rules.[25]

Because it is a refusal to accept property, it is usually all or nothing so that the person disclaiming cannot refuse part of a single gift nor can he disclaim once he has accepted a benefit from the property.

However, a disclaimer is not always 'all or nothing'. Whilst this is generally true for English law, other systems of law (eg Scotland; New York; California) permit partial disclaimers. Further an English will may allow a partial disclaimer.[26]

> *Example 12.2*
>
> Sid's will leaves his residuary estate to his daughter Sally who purports to disclaim half of it (so that it passes to her children) but to retain the other half. This is ineffective under English law (but see **Precedent 12.7(b)**).
>
> *Contrast:*
>
> Sally is left a half share of residue and a specific legacy of Sid's investments. She disclaims the half share of residue (within s 142(1)) but retains the legacy.

In the two situations set out at 12.15 and 12.16 disclaimers have advantages over a variation.

To avoid the income tax settlor-interested trust provisions[27]

12.15   A person making a post-death variation will be treated as making a disposition for income tax purposes with the result, as noted above, that income paid or applied for the benefit of his minor child will be taxed as his

---

[24]   For succession purposes a disclaimer can be inferred from conduct: *Re Cook* [2002] STC (SCD) 318.

[25]   There was some uncertainty as to the effect of a disclaimer on future entitlements. Was the person disclaiming to be treated as if he had died at the date of the disclaimer, thus accelerating later entitlements? See Law Commission Report: *The Forfeiture Rule and Law of Succession* (Law Com No 295). The Estates of Deceased Persons (*Forfeiture Rule and Law of Succession*) Act 2011 provides that in the case of deaths on or after 1 February 2012 the person disclaiming is to be treated as having predeceased unless the will provides otherwise.

[26]   *Guthrie v Walrond* [1883] LR 22 Ch D 573 and SP E18. See **Precedent 12.7(b)**.

[27]   ITTOIA 2005, Part 5, Chapter 5.

and not as the child's. HMRC accepts that, because a disclaimer prevents the gift taking effect, a disclaiming beneficiary is not a 'settlor'.

To disclaim a life interest after the life tenant has died

12.16 Where a person with an IPDI[28] dies within 2 years of the testator, there may be an IHT advantage if the interest is disclaimed as this will prevent the value of the trust property being aggregated with his free estate. HMRC accepts that it is possible for the dead life tenant's personal representatives to disclaim the life interest on behalf of the life tenant (but only if the life tenant had received no benefit from the interest): see IHTM para 35165.

> *Example 12.3*
>
> Ted dies when the IHT nil rate band is £325,000 leaving his £325,000 estate to his sister, Sarah, for life remainder to her son, Nick. Sarah dies shortly after Ted, also with an estate of £325,000 and leaving everything to Nick. Both Ted and Sarah have a full single nil rate band available.
>
> Because the value of the trust fund is included in Sarah's estate, there will be a charge to IHT on £325,000.[29]
>
> By contrast, if Sarah's personal representatives disclaim the interest in possession (which they can do provided she received no benefit from it during her lifetime) then her estate will be reduced to £325,000 so that no IHT is payable and Ted's estate will pass to Nick under the terms of his will (Ted's estate is, of course, covered by his available IHT nil rate band).

12.17 HMRC do not accept that it is possible to vary a life interest once the life tenant has died, taking the view that once the interest has terminated there is no property left to vary. That view was confirmed in *Soutter's Executry v IRC*[30] in relation to a right to occupy property. However, it is far from certain that this is an end of the matter. First, it may be said that the HMRC view fails to take account of the fact that a variation according to s 142(1) of 'any of the dispositions of the property comprised in (the deceased's) estate' and of course the life interest did involve the disposition of such property. Secondly, if income has been produced by the settlement during the life of the now dead life tenant and which is redirected by the variation that view would not hold good given that the variation is redirecting that property: see **Precedent 12.4**.

4. PITFALLS AND PROBLEMS

12.18 There are a number of pitfalls to be avoided when using variations and disclaimers.

---

[28] For the meaning of an IPDI, see **6.04** *et seq.*
[29] See IHTA 1984, s 49(1) providing for the value of the property in a qualifying interest in possession trust such as an IPDI to be treated as part of the beneficiary's estate. Sarah's interest is an IPDI (a qualifying interest in possession: see generally Chapter 6).
[30] [2002] STC (SCD) 385.

Time-limit

12.19   The instrument must be made within 2 years from death. There is no discretion on the part of HMRC to extend the period.

Parties

The parties must include the person varying the disposition (the original beneficiary). It is usual to make any new beneficiary a party to show acceptance of the gift. However, this is not necessary. If more IHT is payable as a result of the variation or disclaimer, the personal representatives must be parties. They cannot refuse to join in so long as they have funds available to meet the IHT. In other cases they do not need to be parties.[31]

Charities

12.20   In the case of deaths on or after 6 April 2012, FA 2012 inserted new subsections (3A) and (3B) into IHTA 1984, s 142. These provide that a variation made in favour of a charity (and designed to take advantage of the charity relief in IHTA 1984, s 23) will not be read-back unless 'it is shown that the appropriate person has been notified of the existence of the instrument of variation'. The 'appropriate person' is either the charity or, if there is a trust for charitable purposes, the trustees.[32] It is thought that this requirement can be met in two ways:

(a)   by making the charity a party to the deed of variation. In practice it is unlikely that this will prove popular although if trustees are involved this may be attractive;

(b)   by an exchange of correspondence: ie by letter sent to the charity enclosing a copy of the variation which is acknowledged by the charity and then sent to HMRC along with the instrument of variation.[33]

Writing

12.21   Although it is usual to use a deed, the legislative provisions only *require* writing. However, as there must be no consideration,[34] it is prudent to use a deed to ensure that the gift is validly made and that all parties are legally bound. IHTM para 35025 says that it is necessary for the original disposition to be identified. A document such as a deed of assignment which merely transfers property which had been received by A under the will of X to B without mention of the gift made by X's will would not satisfy this requirement.

---

[31]   In the case of a variation in favour of charity, consider joining the recipient charity: see **12.20**.

[32]   It is understood that this change resulted from pressure by the charitable lobby which was concerned to monitor gifts by deed of variation in the same way that it can monitor gifts by will. Reading-back under s 143 and s 144 is not affected.

[33]   See IHTM 35124 and **Precedent 12.8**.

[34]   See s 142(3) and **12.25**.

However, all that is required is a document which recites that property was received as a result of X's death and then disposes of all or part of that property to a new beneficiary.

Statement that disposition is to be treated as deceased's[35]

The instrument must contain a statement that the beneficiaries intend the variation to be treated as having been made by the deceased for IHT and/or CGT purposes (sometimes called 'reading-back'). For instance:

'The provisions of TCGA 1992, s 62(6) and IHTA 1984, s 142(1) apply to this variation.'

It is no longer possible (as it was before 1 August 2002) to make the election for reading-back in a separate document. An accidental failure to include the statement cannot be corrected unless the court can be persuaded to rectify of the document.[36]

Need to send variation to HMRC

HMRC only require sight of the variation if additional tax is due as a result. However, in the more common case where less tax is payable as a result of the making of the variation, the taxpayer will have to produce it to justify his claim for a refund or the payment of a reduced sum.

Multiple variations of same property not possible

12.22 While it is possible to make more than one variation or disclaimer in respect of *the same estate*, it is not possible to vary *a disposition* that has already been varied and have the second disposition treated as the deceased's.[37] It is, therefore, important to be sure that the instrument of variation is correct before it is executed.

Example 12.4

On his father's death Jed enters into a deed of variation whereby instead of receiving the residuary estate it is redirected to his daughter Fenella. Reading-back under s 142(1) is claimed. Still within 2 years of the father's death, Fenella further varies the residue in favour of her son Philip. This further variation cannot be read-back for IHT purposes and will take effect as a PET by Fenella (see *Russell v IRC* [1988] STC 195).

Note, however, that it is possible to combine a disclaimer with a variation and to combine variations with reading-back under s 144.

---

[35] A statement is not necessary in the case of a disclaimer: see **12.13**.
[36] For the rectification of instruments of variation, see **12.47**. For when it will be desirable to 'read-back' for one tax but not the other see **12.44**.
[37] *Russell v IRC* [1988] STC 195.

Not possible for parents or guardians to give up property on behalf of a minor

12.23   According to HMRC[38] a parent or guardian cannot make a variation on behalf of a minor which adversely affects the interests of a minor or unborn. A parent's signature on behalf of a minor is not sufficient. In their view an application to the court under its inherent jurisdiction or the Variation of Trusts Act 1958 is required. The important question is whether or not a variation 'adversely' affects the minor's interests. There are often situations where a variation giving up property on behalf of a minor is beneficial, for example where the varied property would reach the minor by a different route and with a saving in tax. Some practitioners include a clause in wills authorising personal representatives to vary on behalf of minor beneficiaries: see **Precedent 12.7(a)**.

Not possible to vary a discretionary trust unless all beneficiaries join in

12.24   A disposition to a trust can only be varied if all the beneficiaries are of full age and capacity and join together to consent.[39] In the case of a discretionary trust this is usually impossible as the class is likely to include minors, unborn and unascertained beneficiaries. Accordingly there would have to be an application to the court under the Variation of Trusts Act 1958 and the court will need to be satisfied that the variation is for the benefit of any minor, unborn, or unascertained beneficiaries.

However, in a case where beneficiaries and trustees of the trust are agreed that a variation of the terms of the trust is appropriate, it will be possible to get round this problem by combining an appointment from the trust under IHTA 1984, s 144 with a post-death variation.[40] HMRC accepts that the two sections can both apply to the same property to achieve (in effect) double reading-back.[41] This can be useful in a variety of circumstances. For example the terms of the trust may require the trustees to distribute within 2 years of death or the class of beneficiaries may be very restricted.

Example 12.5

The terms of a discretionary trust created in a will for the deceased's wife, Sonia, and children are unsatisfactory. They require that the trust be wound up within 2 years of death while the trustees would prefer it to continue.

---

38   IHTM para 35045.
39   *Saunders v Vautier* (1841) 4 Beav 115.
40   IHTA 1984, s 144 is considered at **13.15**. In cases where a nil rate band discretionary trust is unwanted, some practitioners have sought to use s 142 to 'get rid' of the trust. The easiest (and normally only) way of dealing with this problem is to make a s 144 appointment (usually to the surviving spouse or civil partner) within 2 years of death.
41   IHTM para 35085.

The trustees appoint the trust fund absolutely to Sonia. As a result of IHTA 1984, s 144 the appointment is read back into the will and Sonia is treated as absolutely entitled.[42]

Sonia can then makes a post-death variation under IHTA 1984, s 142 within 2 years of her husband's death to create a new discretionary trust and elect for reading-back.[43]

No consideration

12.25   A variation or disclaimer must not be made for any consideration (other than the making of another variation or disclaimer of the same estate). The consideration does not have to be adequate nor does it have to come from the person benefiting from the variation. For example, an agreement that the person making the variation is to have his legal costs paid is sufficient. Problems *may* arise where the person receiving the benefit of a variation wishes to make a gift to the person making the variation.

Example 12.6

Harry dies leaving legacies of £600,000 to each of his three daughters from his first marriage. He leaves the rest of his £7m estate to his second wife, Wanda. The legacies to the daughters are free of tax and have to be grossed up producing a substantial IHT bill which will greatly reduce Wanda's benefit from the estate.

It will be mutually beneficial for Wanda and the daughters to agree that in return for the daughters' varying the will to give the whole estate (save Harry's nil rate band) to Wanda (thus obtaining the benefit of the spouse exemption), Wanda will make potentially exempt transfers to the daughters of an amount equal to or in excess of their entitlement under the will. Sadly for the family the effect of the agreement is to make the variation ineffective for tax purposes under s 142(3) so the benefit of the spouse exemption is not obtained.[44]

12.26   In the case of a united family the children may make a variation in favour of the surviving spouse relying on the surviving spouse to 'see them right'. Unsurprisingly HMRC take a keen interest in such arrangements. IHTM para 35094 says that:

'where a chargeable beneficiary makes a variation in favour of the deceased's spouse or civil partner or to a trust with a life interest for the spouse or civil partner we will ask whether there had been any discussion between the parties

---

[42]   Note the '*Frankland* trap': see **13.13**.

[43]   Note that she will be the settlor for income tax purposes and so, if she can benefit under the trust that she has created, she will be taxed on any income arising.

[44]   See *Lau v RCC* [2009] STC (SCD) 352 for a case involving similar facts. Note, however, that in the absence of any agreement the position is different. For instance, if Wanda could have retained the property, the fact that she makes gifts to the daughters will not give rise to a problem. Often the variation in favour of Wanda is made on interest in possession trusts which can be terminated in favour of the daughters (and usually will be once 2 years have expired from Harry's death: see **12.28**).

about how the benefit redirected to the spouse or civil partner should be dealt with, and whether after the variation any transfers in favour of the original beneficiaries are contemplated.'

Taxpayers making such a variation should therefore be prepared for questioning on the intentions of the surviving spouse or, in a case where an IPDI trust for the spouse is involved, the trustees.

'Buy-in' from the surviving spouse

12.27 The creation of a life interest for the surviving spouse means that the trust property is aggregated with the surviving spouse's own property.[45] If the trust continues until the spouse's death, the rate of IHT may be increased by the aggregation.

If, as is more likely, the life interest is terminated in whole or in part before the spouse's death, the spouse will be treated as making a potentially exempt transfer[46] with a consequent reduction in the nil rate band available to the spouse's estate should death occur within the 7 years following the termination.[47] When the spouse is (say) a second wife and the termination is in favour of children of the first marriage, in fairness to the spouse, funds should be made available to cover the cost of insuring against the risk of an increased IHT liability on her death.

In addition the spouse should be involved in the tax planning exercise. Particularly in the case of second spouses where there may be underlying tensions, it is important to avoid any impression of high handedness or presenting the spouse with a 'fait accompli'. A spouse who is sufficiently annoyed by the way the arrangement is presented could decide to disclaim the immediate post-death interest, completely destroying the beneficial tax planning.[48]

The dangers of IHTA 1984, s 142(4)

12.28 This subsection provides that where a variation results in property being held in trust for a period which ends within 2 years of death, the disposition taking effect at the end of the period will be treated as if it had taken effect on death. Thus, if children entitled to their father's estate create by variation made within one year of his death a life interest in favour of their mother, which automatically terminates after one year there will be no spouse exemption available to the father's estate. Instead the property will be treated as having

---

[45] See IHTA 1984, s 49(1).
[46] Provided that the settlement then ends. If trusts continue after the termination of the IPDI then the surviving spouse will make an immediately chargeable transfer (taxed at 20% once the nil rate band is exhausted).
[47] Sometimes referred to as 'stealing the nil rate band'.
[48] Or make a claim on the estate under the Inheritance (Provision for Family and Dependants) Act 1975. And see *Berger v Berger* [2013] EWCA Civ 1305.

been left directly to the children. However, HMRC accept that if a spouse is given a life interest by variation and happens to *die* within 2 years, it is the death not the variation that results in the trust being of a short duration so s 142(4) does not apply.

Example 12.7

After the death of their father (H), the children enter into a deed of variation in favour of W (H's surviving spouse) under which she is given an interest in possession. The intention is that this should be read back under s 142 so that the spouse exemption will apply on H's death. However, the interest in possession is subject to an overriding power of appointment which the trustees exercise within 2 years of H's death to appoint the property to the children. They intended this to be a PET by W but does s 142(4) apply to nullify the arrangement (by providing that tax shall be charged as if H had left his estate to his children so that we are back where we started!)? On the strict wording of the legislation, it may be said that it is not the variation which results in the property becoming held in trust for a period which ends not more than 2 years after the death but that this is the result of the exercise of the trustees' power (this argument being on all fours with the HMRC view that the death of the spouse within 2 years does not fall within this provision). However, it is far from certain that this view will succeed and, to avoid that risk, it is important that the trustees make no appointments until the end of the 2-year period.

Care should be taken when drafting to avoid any possibility of falling foul of the sub-section. In *Kevern v Ayres*[49] the parties had varied the effect of the intestacy rules to give the deceased's surviving spouse a short term life interest in the bulk of the estate to benefit from the IHT spouse exemption.

The variation said that the income from the trust property would be paid to the surviving spouse 'for the period of 24 months from the date of the death of the [deceased]'. HMRC's refused to allow reading back, contending that a period of 24 months is the same as, not more than, a period of 2 years, so the trust created by the variation was short by 24 hours. At the time of writing the taxpayer was involved in litigation to establish whether HMRC's view was correct and, if so, whether rectification would be available.

The 'double dip'

12.29 Taxpayers who make gifts to charity can obtain relief against income and CGT liabilities if they come within the 'gift aid' provisions.[50] Gift aid relief was introduced in October 1990 to provide income tax relief similar to that given to payments under deeds of covenant in respect of one-off gifts to charity. The donor has to make a declaration which is made or confirmed in writing. A person making a gift aid payment is treated as having deducted tax at basic rate. The charity can then reclaim the tax deducted. A donor who is a higher (or additional) rate taxpayer is entitled to higher (or additional) rate tax relief

---

[49] *Kevern v Ayres* [2014] EWHC 165 (Ch).
[50] On gifts to charity, see generally the authors' *A Modern Approach to Lifetime Tax Planning*, Chapter 39.

on the gross amount of the gift. It is a condition of the relief[51] that in the case of a gift of cash, neither the donor nor any person connected with him[52] receives a benefit in consequence of making the gift which exceeds the permitted limits. The maximum benefit which can be taken is £250. (The benefit of admission rights to, for example, National Trust properties etc, is disregarded for this purpose.) As from 2000–01 a taxpayer has been able to claim relief against either income tax or CGT.

It would obviously be beneficial for a beneficiary of an estate who varies a disposition in favour of a charity to obtain gift aid relief as well as a reduction in IHT, the so-called 'double dip'. Unfortunately this is not generally possible. In *Harris v RCC*,[53] taxpayers lost a claim for gift aid relief against their income tax liability in relation to charitable gifts made via a deed of variation.

In *Harris*, the executors, who were also residuary beneficiaries, executed a deed of variation to give substantial amounts to a charitable trust. For IHT purposes the gifts to charity were exempt and the effect of the variation was to reduce IHT on the estate. The issue was whether this reduction in IHT consequent on the variation disqualified the payments from gift aid relief. This question had been decided before, against the taxpayer, by a Special Commissioner in *St Dunstan's v Major (Inspector of Taxes)*.[54] In *Harris*, the Tribunal said that while it should pay due regard to decisions of the Special Commissioners, it was not bound by them. Accordingly, it would make its own determination by reference to its own construction of s 25. There were a number of separate elements to be considered in determining whether or not gift aid was available:

(a)   *Was there a benefit?* Yes. There had been a liability to IHT which was reduced by the deeming effect of the deed of variation. That was a benefit.

(b)   *If so, had the donor (or a person connected with the donor) received that benefit?* The taxpayers had argued that the use of the word 'receives' is deliberate and imports the concept of the prohibited benefit being provided to or accepted by the donor by or from another person. As such it is not apt to describe changes in the donor's fiscal position taking effect by operation of law without any provision of property by a third party. That construction was consistent with the perceived mischief of the legislation, namely to prevent the donor clawing back or securing from the charity or some other person a financial benefit in consequence of making the payment. They gave the analogy of a lifetime gift of cash to a charity attracting the IHT exemption. The exemption allows the donor to make a higher payment than he otherwise would have done, but no one suggests that the donor is enjoying a prohibited benefit.

The Tribunal dismissed this argument. It said there is a qualitative difference between the IHT exemption afforded on a lifetime gift to charity and a reduction in IHT by means of a deed of variation of a

---

[51]   FA 1990, s 25.
[52]   For definition of 'connected person', see ITA 2007, ss 993–994.
[53]   [2010] UKFTT 385 (TC).
[54]   [1997] STC (SCD) 212.

deceased's estate. In the case of the variation, the benefit is the removal of the IHT liability that has arisen on death. In the case of the lifetime gift, there never is such a liability requiring removal, and consequently the IHT exemption on a lifetime gift to charity is not a benefit within s 25(2)(e).

(c) *If so had the donor (or the connected person) received that benefit in consequence of making the gift?* The 'making of the gift' encompasses the whole process whereby the gift is made and all the arrangements for the making of it. Hence the IHT benefit was a consequence of the variation and the subsequent payment of cash.

12.30 Different circumstances may produce a different result. Suppose it is not the residuary beneficiaries who make the variation.

Example 12.8

Tom is left a tax free pecuniary legacy of £100,000 which he varies in favour of charity. He is not connected with the residuary beneficiaries. In this situation is gift aid available? As Tom has not received any IHT benefit (nor has a connected person) relief is available.

Share and Land Aid

12.31 Also, different rules apply if Qualifying Investment Donation Relief ('Share Aid') or Gifts of Real Property Relief ('Land Aid') is used instead of Gift Aid. The Income Tax Act 2007, s 431 provides that relief is available to an individual who disposes of the whole beneficial interest in a qualifying investment (defined to include listed shares, units in an authorised unit trust, shares in an OEIC) or a qualifying interest in land. Income tax relief remains available even if a benefit is obtained although the relief is reduced by the value of any benefits received in consequence of making the disposal (by the individual making the disposal or a connected person). Hence if IHT relief at 40% is obtained which benefits the donor, 60% of the value of the gifted property is still capable of attracting income tax relief.

No redirection of reservation of benefit or settled property

12.32 Not all property comprised in the deceased's estate at death can be redirected. Section 142(5) specifically excludes property included in the estate as a result of the reservation of benefit rules[55] and settled property in which the deceased had enjoyed a qualifying interest in possession.

Example 12.9

Sid had been the life tenant of a will trust set up by his father. On Sid's death the value of the settled property is aggregated with his free estate and the settled property becomes held in trust for his wife for life. She cannot use s 142 to vary her entitlement but IHTA 1984, s 93 permits a beneficiary to disclaim an interest

---

[55] See FA 1986, ss 102ZA; 102; 102A–C; Sch 20 and generally the authors' *A Modern Approach to Lifetime Tax Planning*, Chapter 12.

in settled property without that disclaimer being subject to IHT. She could therefore disclaim that interest without an IHT charge.

It should be noted that the position of trustees can be adversely affected by a variation.

Example 12.10

Mort had been life tenant of a trust fund and on his death the settled property passed to his sister, Mildred, absolutely. He left his free estate equally to his widow and daughter. By a post-death variation the widow gave her half-share in his estate to the daughter. Assuming that this variation is read back for IHT purposes extra tax will be charged on Mort's death as a result of the lost spouse exemption. This will increase the tax for which the trustees are liable yet they not required to consent to the reading-back statement and are not protected by a deed of discharge (IHTA 1984, s 239(4)).

General powers

12.33 A person with a general power of appointment[56] is for most purposes treated as the outright owner of the property subject to the power. However for the purposes of a post-death variation HMRC takes a rather more restricted view.

The Revenue Manual comments as follows:[57]

'Settled property (IHTM16000) in which the deceased had an interest in possession (IIP) (IHTM16061) is excluded from the death estate for the purposes of IHTA84/S 142 (1) by IHTA84/S 142 (5). However we do not apply that exclusion to settled property

- in which the deceased had a beneficial IIP, if
- the deceased had *and exercised by Will* a general power of appointment over it.

Where both these conditions are satisfied, you should treat the settled property as part of the death estate for the purposes of IHTA84/S 142 (1).

The taxpayers may seek to extend this treatment, to cases where the deceased

- had exercised the general power of appointment by deed
- had a general power but had not exercised it, or
- had a general power but not a beneficial IIP in the trust property.

---

[56]   For definition see **2.56.**
[57]   IHTM 35072.

Where this occurs, you should ask them to demonstrate the grounds on which they consider the particular situation falls within the scope of the legislation. Then, if they press, or if they appear to have a persuasive argument, you should refer the case to TG.'[58]

Interest on gifts made by deed of variation

12.34 Pecuniary legatees are entitled to interest in certain circumstances[59] and specific legatees are entitled to income produced by the property from the date of death.

What, if any, entitlement does the beneficiary of a redirected legacy have?

STEP[60] issued a technical note in the following terms:

'The right, or otherwise, to interest on a cash sum gifted by an Instrument of Variation is not clearly defined.

Often, neither the person making the IoV thinks of the point, nor does their adviser raise it, instead concentrating on the inheritance tax aspects.

Where a cash gift is clearly defined as a "legacy", either by the notional incorporation of an additional clause in the will, or by the setting out of a fictional will within the IoV, in the absence of any direction to the contrary, that gift may well carry the right to interest as though it were a general legacy. However, as the gift cannot be paid before it arises under the IoV, any right to interest can only run from the date of the IoV, if at all.[61]

Where the gift is not given the character of a "legacy" then it is likely it will be treated as a simple cash gift, not carrying any right to income before payment.

When discussing an IoV, the original beneficiary and their advisers should also consider if interest should be paid on any gift made by the IoV and the instrument drafted to reflect the beneficiary's intentions. This could take the form of "Provided that no such sum shall carry the right to interest or income before its actual date of payment".'

It is a little difficult to follow the logic in the statement on legacies when it is remembered that a variation is a lifetime gift and is not, in the real world, part of the will. Calling the gift a legacy in the variation does not make it a legacy! It is therefore suggested that the position is that, as a cash gift, no interest in payable unless the terms of the gift so provide.

---

[58] For the use of general powers to create a succession of IPDIs, see **6.33.**
[59] See **1.52.**
[60] The Society of Trust and Estate Practitioners: www.step.org.
[61] Applying *Re Scadding* (1902) 4 OLR 632.

5. USES OF SECTION 142

12.35   There are a number of ways to use the section as an IHT planning tool. The following are illustrations of some of the most useful.

Variation in favour of a person already dead

Example 12.11

Anna dies at a time when the nil rate band is £325,000 leaving her estate of £525,000 to her son, Sam. George, her husband, dies 18 months later (when the nil rate band is still £325,000) leaving his estate of £125,000 to Sam. Both Anna and George had a full single nil rate band available on death.

Sam can redirect £200,000 of Anna's estate to George to utilise his nil rate band. There will then be an IHT saving on the redirected £200,000 (of £80,000).

Original position

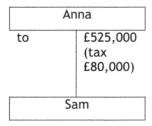
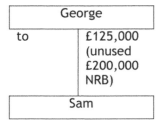

After the variation

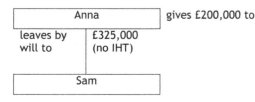
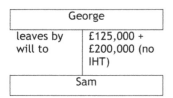

Variation on behalf of person already dead

12.36   Fred dies leaving his estate of £325,000 to his nephew, Neil, who has an estate of £325,000 of his own. Neil dies within 2 years of Fred leaving everything to his daughter, Danuta. Both Fred and Neil have a full single nil rate band of £325,000 available. It will be beneficial for the disposition of Fred's estate to be varied to leave all Fred's property to Danuta instead of to Neil, thereby saving the IHT that would otherwise be payable on Fred's property once it became comprised in Neil's estate.

Who should make the variation on behalf of Neil? According to HMRC it is the beneficiaries. IHTM para 35042 says:

'The beneficiaries of a person who has died may make a variation redirecting that person's entitlement on an earlier death. The variation must be within the two-year period following that earlier death ... It is not essential that a grant of representation has been obtained to either estate.'

In principle, however, it should be the personal representatives of the deceased beneficiary and HMRC have accepted variations made by personal representatives in cases where there have been logistical difficulties getting all the beneficiaries to sign in time. Interestingly, *Tax Bulletin* Issue 74 (dated around the same time as the manual guidance) refers to the variation being made by the personal representatives:

'VARIATION OF INHERITANCES FOLLOWING THE DEATH OF AN ORIGINAL BENEFICIARY WITHIN THE STATUTORY TWO-YEAR PERIOD

... for Section 142 IHTA 1984 to apply, all the beneficiaries affected by the variation must join in a written **instrument effecting the variation.** We have been asked how this requirement should be interpreted when one of the beneficiaries dies before a variation is made.

Our view is that the legal personal representatives of a beneficiary (the second deceased) may enter into a variation.

If the variation will reduce the entitlements of the beneficiaries of the second deceased then they, as well as the legal personal representatives of the second deceased, must agree to the variation. The Revenue will require evidence of the consent of the beneficiaries of the second deceased to the variation. If they are not themselves parties to the variation, other written evidence of their consent will be sought.'

Variation to remove survivorship clause

12.37 Since the introduction of the transferable nil rate band,[62] there are occasions where as between husband and wife (or civil partners) a survivorship clause is not desirable.

Example 12.12

Horace leaves his estate to his wife Wilhelmina provided she survives for 28 days and, if not, to his adult children. Wilhelmina dies 2 days after Horace. Horace's estate is valued at £400,000 and Wilhelmina's £200,000. Both have full nil rate bands of £325,000 available.

From an IHT point of view the survivorship clause is not beneficial, since Horace's £400,000 passes to the children and tax will be payable on £75,000. Wilhelmina has unused nil rate band.

Without the survivorship clause Horace's property passes to Wilhelmina and attracts the spouse exemption. Wilhelmina's estate benefits from Horace's

---

[62] See generally Chapter 5.

transferred nil rate band so the combined estate of £600,000 passes from Wilhelmina to the children without a tax liability.

If the children who take Horace's estate are of full age, they should vary his will to leave some or all of his estate to Wilhelmina.

If the children are minors HMRC may not accept a variation as their view is that a variation giving up property on behalf of minors needs court approval under the Variation of Trusts Act 1958.[63] In this case, it is arguable that a variation on behalf of the children would be effective on the basis that the children are not, in fact, giving up a benefit as the property will return to them from Wilhelmina's estate. However, the position is not clear cut; what if a huge liability emerged in relation to Wilhelmina's estate, swallowing up her assets?

Severing a beneficial joint tenancy to redirect property passing by survivorship

12.38 The reference to property passing 'otherwise' in s 142(1)(a) allows (in effect) the severance of a beneficial joint tenancy after death.[64] The deceased's share can, therefore, be redirected by the surviving joint tenant declaring that the property is to be treated as if he had severed the joint tenancy before the death and the deceased had then left his share to the desired new beneficiary. Watch the wording of a variation which is intended to vary the destination of both assets owned wholly by the deceased and joint property passing by survivorship. If the wording of the variation refers only to property passing under the deceased's will, payments or transfers of the joint property will not attract the protection of s 142 and will therefore involve a potentially exempt transfer.

See **Precedent 12.6.**

Severance of beneficial joint tenancy to obtain benefit of co-ownership discount

12.39 Where husband and wife (or civil partners) own land jointly, there is no co-ownership discount because of the IHT related property rules.[65] In other cases there is normally a discount on the full valuation of between 10% and 15% to reflect the difficulty of selling a part share in property. Where spouses or civil partners die within 2 years of each other owning land as beneficial joint tenants, it may be worth varying the disposition of the interest of the first to die to enable it to pass elsewhere, thus gaining the benefit of the discount for the survivor's estate.

---

[63] See **12.23** and **Precedent 12.7(a).**
[64] IHTM para 35092.
[65] See IHTA 1984, s 161 and **3.16** *et seq.*

Example 12.13

Bill and Beth own 'The Willows' as beneficial joint tenants. The property is valued at £1m when Bill dies. Beth dies 6 months later leaving everything to her son, Max. Max can vary the disposition of Bill's estate on behalf of Beth to pass Bill's interest in 'The Willows' to himself. On Beth's death, a discount on the value of her interest will then be available.

HMRC may argue that the market value of Beth's interest immediately before her death would not have been discounted because of the existence of a special purchaser, Max. However, it ought to be possible to resist this argument or agree on a reduced level of discount.[66]

Passing the benefit of assets which have been sold

12.40   It is possible to vary a will to redirect property representing assets which have already been sold.

Example 12.14

Trevor leaves his quoted shares to Margaret, who sells them for £200,000 and now wants to give the cash to her daughter, Dorothea, and have the disposition treated as Trevor's.

The variation should recite that the Will left the shares to Margaret and that the shares having been sold, they are now represented by the sum of £200,000.

See **Precedent 12.3.**

Avoiding the rules on reservation of benefit and pre-owned assets

12.41   As noted above, IHTA 1984, s 142 states reading-back is effective for all IHT purposes. Hence a redirection of property will not be caught by the reservation of benefit rules even if the beneficiary continues to derive a benefit from the property.

Example 12.15

On her mother's death Wanda is left a seaside cottage worth £300,000. By a deed of variation falling within s 142(1) she transfers this property to her son. Wanda continues to use the cottage on a regular basis.

The variation is read back into her mother's will. Although Wanda derives a benefit from the use of the property she is not within the reservation of benefit rules since, because of the reading-back effect, she has never made a gift of the property.

Additionally, there is no pre-owned assets charge since FA 2004, Sch 15, para 16 provides that a disposition is disregarded for the purposes of this charge if it is not treated as a transfer of value by the chargeable person.

---

[66]   See *St Clair-Ford v Ryder* [2006] WTLR 1647 and 11.66.

The same principle applies if a beneficiary creates a discretionary trust by variation and is one of the class of beneficiaries. For IHT purposes the testator is treated as creating the settlement not the person making the variation.

'Freezer legacies'

12.42   The rules on attribution of value[67] can sometimes be used to achieve an IHT saving. The effect of s 38 and s 39 of IHTA 1984 is that the value of the estate is attributed to specific gifts before residue.

> *Example 12.16*
>
> T (who has used up his nil rate band) leaves the residue of his estate (worth £300,000) to his widow. The estate increases in value within 2 years of his death to £500,000. The widow could execute a deed of variation under which she retains a specific legacy of £300,000 and leaves the residue to her daughter. Under IHTA 1984, s 38 the death estate of £300,000 is attributed to the spouse exempt legacy.

Appointments/advancements followed by a variation

12.43   We saw at **12.22** that it is possible to combine s 142 (variations) with s 144 (appointments out of discretionary trusts) to obtain, in effect, a double reading-back. HMRC also accept that the following falls within s 142.

> *Example 12.17*
>
> Tiberius leaves property to Adonis contingent on his attaining the age of 25. There is a wide power of advancement. At the date of Tiberius' death, Adonis is over 18 and the trustees exercise their power of advancement so that he becomes absolutely entitled to the property.
>
> Adonis then redirects the property to his son and opts for reading-back under s 142(1). Assuming that the 2-year time-limit is met, HMRC accept that this is an effective variation and the gift to the son is made by Tiberius not Adonis even though Adonis was not absolutely entitled to the property at the date of death.

6. WHEN IS IT PREFERABLE NOT TO HAVE A DISPOSITION READ-BACK?

12.44   Property redirected by a post-death variation is only treated as passing from the deceased for IHT and CGT purposes if a statement to that effect is included in the instrument (and the other formalities are complied with). Without such a statement the person making the variation is treated as making a lifetime gift. There are circumstances where it will be more tax efficient for a beneficiary to make a lifetime gift rather than electing that the disposition be treated as the deceased's. Sometimes it is beneficial to elect to read-back for one tax but not the other.

---

[67]   IHTA 1984, ss 38–42.

For IHT purposes

12.45 It is normally desirable to make the election for IHT purposes if the variation:

(a) will attract the spouse or charity exemption for the estate, for example where the estate is passing to non-exempt beneficiaries one of whom wants to make a gift to charity; or

(b) if it is being made by one non-exempt beneficiary (A) to another (B) and A wants to avoid making a PET for IHT purposes. The amount of IHT payable by the estate remains the same; A is replaced by B and drops out of the picture completely.

The election should not normally be made where:

(a) the deceased has already used up his nil rate band and the estate is passing to a surviving spouse or civil partner. Anything passing from the deceased to non-exempt beneficiaries will attract IHT. It will be better for the surviving spouse to make a potentially exempt transfer and hope to survive for 7 years;[68]

(b) the deceased had an unused nil rate band available, and the surviving spouse wishes to pass property to, for example, children, it may not matter whether the election is made or not as the survivor will normally benefit from any unused nil rate band of the deceased. If, however, the surviving spouse or civil partner already has the benefit of an additional nil rate band inherited from a previous spouse or civil partner, the additional nil rate band will be wasted unless the election is made.[69]

For CGT purposes

12.46 Depending on the facts it may be beneficial not to have the disposition treated as the deceased's for CGT purposes. Consider the following cases:

(a) the variation is of an asset which has increased in value since death by less than the annual exemption and the person varying the disposition is making no other disposals in the relevant tax year or has losses available to set against gains.

 If the original beneficiary makes a lifetime disposal of the asset, the new beneficiary will acquire the asset at its current value and so will have a higher acquisition cost. The original beneficiary will avoid CGT because the increase in value is covered by the annual exemption or by the available losses.

---

[68] Unless the surviving spouse is anxious to conserve his nil rate band for the benefit of his own beneficiaries.

[69] See the discussion of the transferable nil rate band in Chapter 5. If the nil rate band remains frozen (as is envisaged until the end of tax year 2017–18) then there is an argument that it should be used sooner rather than later.

(b)   the variation is of an asset which has fallen in value since the date of death. If the original beneficiary makes a lifetime disposal of the asset, the loss will be available to the original beneficiary to offset against any gains. But if the original beneficiary has no chargeable gains and the new beneficiary does, the election should be made. The new beneficiary will then acquire the asset with a higher (probate) acquisition cost and will be able to use his loss when the asset is eventually sold.

7. WHEN IT ALL GOES WRONG: CURING DEFECTIVE VARIATIONS

12.47   It is not unknown for deeds of variation to contain errors. Practitioners may be able to take advantage of the equitable remedy of rectification to correct the error. Rectification is one aspect of a wider equitable jurisdiction to relieve parties from the consequences of their mistakes. Its function is to enable the parties to correct the way in which their transaction has been recorded. It is not limited to bilateral agreements and the court has power to rectify a voluntary disposition.[70] Rimer J commented in *Allnutt v Wilding*:[71]

> 'Rectification is a discretionary equitable remedy. Its function is to enable parties to a transaction to correct mistakes in the way their transaction has been recorded. It is no part of its function to enable parties to change the substance of the transaction they have entered into. Thus, at the simplest level, if V agrees to sell his house to P for £300,000, and the sale and purchase contract mistakenly records the price as £30,000, V will in principle have a right to have the contract figure corrected to £300,000. The remedy of rectification is also available to achieve the correction of a voluntary settlement so as to enable any mistakes in the settlement as executed to accord with the settlor's true intention when he executed it. Thus, again at the simplest level, if the settlor's instructions were to create a discretionary settlement for the benefit of A, B, C and D, and them alone, and the settlement as executed mistakenly included E as a discretionary beneficiary, the settlor would in principle be entitled to have the settlement rectified so as to exclude E from benefit.

In the Court of Appeal Mummery LJ said:[72]

> 'rectification is about putting the record straight. In the case of a voluntary settlement, rectification involves bringing the trust document into line with the true intentions of the settlor as held by him at the date when he executed the document. This can be done by the court when, owing to a mistake in the drafting of the document, it fails to record the settlor's true intentions. The mistake may, for example, consist of leaving out words that were intended to be put into the document; or putting in words that were not intended to be in the document; or through a misunderstanding by those involved about the meanings of the words or expressions that were used in the document. Mistakes of this kind have the effect that the document, as executed, is not a true record of the settlor's intentions.'

---

[70]   *Re Butlin's Settlement* [1976] Ch 251.
[71]   [2006] EWHC 1905 (Ch). For a recent illustration involving the rectification of a deed of appointment, see *Fine v Fine* [2012] EWHC 1811.
[72]   [2007] EWCA Civ 412.

12.48 Thus, those seeking rectification must be able to show that they understood what the transaction was intended to achieve but that, as a result of a mistake in the form of the document, the desired result was not achieved. The remedy is not available where the parties' error is as to the consequences of the deed. The particular attraction of rectification and what makes it unique is that, unlike other remedies, it does not undo the document, it modifies it. The rectified document can take effect as intended as opposed to the whole transaction being nullified as may happen in mistake cases. Unsurprisingly several of the reported cases on rectification involve post-death variations where there is a strict time-limit and where it is not possible to 're-vary' to deal with an error in the original.[73]

In *Allnutt*, the deceased had made a transfer to a settlement for the benefit of his children more than 7 years before his death believing that the transfer was potentially exempt. However, because the settlement was discretionary in form, the transfer was, in fact, chargeable. Setting aside the transaction for mistake would not have helped as the property would simply have returned to the estate of the settlor and attracted IHT. The trustees wanted to rectify the settlement deed so that it gave the children interests in possession. The transfer would then have been a PET and achieved the desired tax saving result.

12.49 The Court of Appeal did not accept that rectification was available. The settlor intended to execute the settlement which he in fact executed, conferring benefits on his three children. The settlement correctly recorded his intention to benefit them through the medium of a trust rather than the alternative of making direct gifts in their favour. There was no mistake in the recording of his intentions in the settlement. The mistake of the settlor and his advisers was in believing that the nature of the trusts declared in the settlement for the three children created a situation in which the subsequent transfer of funds by him to the trustees would qualify as a PET and could, if he survived long enough, result in the saving of IHT. The advice he received was negligent and rectification was not available to cure the problem.

12.50 Compare *Allnutt* with cases where rectification was available.

Summers v Kitson[74]

The deceased had interests and powers of appointment under two trusts that had been set up in the 1960s. Throughout the period 1994–2000, the deceased had, by the terms of variously executed wills, altered the appointments under the terms of the trust. During 2001, the deceased's solicitors prepared a new will, and, in relation to the trusts, two separate deeds of appointment in favour of the deceased's grandchildren. The two deeds of appointment did not contain any words rendering the appointments revocable and:

---

[73] See *Lake v Lake* [1989] STC 865; *Martin v Nicholson* [2004] EWHC 2135 (Ch); *Ashcroft v Barnsdale* [2010] EWHC 1948 (Ch).

[74] [2006] EWHC 3655 (Ch).

'as a matter of law the default setting is that absent words rendering the appointment revocable it is irrevocable.'

The documents were sent to the deceased under the cover of a letter which explained that the deeds of appointment had been drafted separately from the will to enable the terms of the trust to remain confidential once the will became a public document, and to enable any further changes to the appointments to be made without the need to alter the terms of the deceased's will. Subsequently, the deceased purported to vary the terms of the appointments by the execution of two further wills in 2002 and 2003. Could the deeds of appointment be rectified or set aside for mistake? David Donaldson QC held that they could. The deceased had never intended to execute irrevocable documents. She had intended when executing the two deeds that they should be revocable but, unknown and unappreciated by her, the wording amounted to an irrevocable appointment.

Wills v Gibbs[75]

A deed of variation accidentally omitted the required statements that the gifts were to be treated as the deceased's for the purposes of IHT and CGT. The solicitor who had prepared the document gave evidence that he was aware of the need to include such statements and his firm's standard precedent in use at the time incorporated them. He believed that the statements had been accidentally deleted.

Ashcroft v Barnsdale[76]

The parties rearranged the disposition of the estate so that the surviving spouse took residue instead of specific gifts and the children took specific gifts instead of residue. The deed did not mention the burden of IHT on the specific gifts to the children (which exceeded the available nil rate band); the tax would, therefore, have to be paid from residue and would have to be calculated after grossing up. The court accepted that this had not been the intention of the parties and granted rectification. The judge stated that the distinction between 'effects' and 'consequences' of a transaction applies to rectification of both *voluntary* transactions, and deeds (such as this one) which were the product of an agreement between the parties. He was prepared to grant rectification because on the facts the deed of variation had failed to give effect to the parties' true agreement. It was not merely a mistake as to the fiscal consequences. The effect of the rectification was that the document continued in effect but with the inclusion of words putting the burden of IHT on the children.

---

[75]   [2007] EWHC 3361 (Ch).
[76]   [2010] STC 2544.

Giles v RNIB and Others[77]

The deceased, Hilda, left a valuable flat and a small amount of residue to her sister, Elsie, who died 18 months later leaving her estate to four named charities.

The solicitor, acting as PR for both estates, realised that a substantial IHT saving could be made by varying the terms of Hilda's will on behalf of the beneficiaries of Elsie's will to redirect the assets directly to the four charities.[78] Unfortunately the variation, as drafted, redirected only the residuary gift not the specific gift of the flat.

By the time the error was spotted it was too late to make a further variation to redirect the gift of the flat. Fortunately the court agreed to use its equitable powers of rectification to amend the document so that it carried out the parties' clear intention.

8. PRECATORY TRUSTS[79]

12.51 It is common for testators to leave their personal chattels to one person (or the personal representatives) with a request that they should be distributed in accordance with the testator's wishes. This is often referred to as a 'precatory trust'. There is no obligation to comply with the request but if it is complied with within 2 years of death, the IHT treatment is governed by IHTA 1984, s 143 which provides as follows:

> 'Where a testator expresses a wish that property bequeathed by his will should be transferred by the legatee to other persons, and the legatee transfers any of the property in accordance with that wish within the period of two years after the death of the testator, this Act shall have effect as if the property transferred had been bequeathed by the will to the transferee.'

The reading-back occurs automatically and there may be cases where it is disadvantageous, for example where valuable chattels are left initially to a spouse and the subsequent transfer will lose the benefit of the spouse exemption. Obviously the legatee can delay the distribution until the 2 years has elapsed. If the distribution has already been made, there is no reason why the recipient should not make a post-death variation to return the property to the spouse.

12.52 There is no corresponding CGT provision so the distribution will be treated as a disposal by the original legatee. The legatee could make a post-death variation with a statement that the disposition is to be treated for CGT purposes as the deceased's.

---

[77] [2014] EWHC 1373 (Ch).

[78] An example of a variation made on behalf of someone who is already dead, see **12.36** above.

[79] See **Precedent 4.1, clause 4**.

PRECEDENTS

General drafting hints

1. When drafting always have a copy of the will (and, if relevant, any codicil) and full details of the assets comprised in the estate and of any lifetime transfers made by the deceased. It is very easy to make an error in a clause number as occurred in *Giles v RNIB and Others*.[80]

2. The beneficiary wishing to make the variation needs to be fully informed of the consequences: remember the restrictions in s 142(3) and s 142(4).

3. It is common to include as parties: (a) the donee and (b) the personal representatives. In the case of the former so that he is made aware of and accepts the gift; in the latter case, so that the estate can be duly administered (if the administration is not complete) in the light of the variation. As noted at **12.19** there are some cases where the personal representatives must be joined and if the purpose of the variation is to secure a refund of IHT it is the personal representatives who must claim this (by sending HMRC a copy of the variation).

4. Be careful to identify the disposition of the property in the estate that is being redirected precisely, particularly if the beneficiary is only making the variation in respect of part of his entitlement under the will. For instance, he may wish to redirect only the pecuniary legacy that he was left, retaining a share of residue. Alternatively he may wish to retain 50% of the residue redirecting the other 50%.

5. In cases where the variation is not simply using up the nil rate band or utilising the spouse exemption, consider where the burden of the tax should be placed: for instance if the redirection is of a legacy should that legacy be free of tax (so that it is borne by residue which, if spouse exempt, will involve grossing up) or be subject to the payment of tax?

---

[80] See **12.50**.

Precedent 12.1: Variation whereby father varies legacy in favour of daughter[81]

THIS DEED OF VARIATION is made the [ ] day of [ ] 20[ ] between (1) [ ] of [ ] ('the Son') (2) [ ] of [ ] ('the Grandson') and (3) [ ] of [ ] and [ ] of [ ] ('the Executors')

SUPPLEMENTAL to the will dated [ ] ('the Will') of [ ] late of [ ] ('the Testator') who died on [ ]

WHEREAS:

(A) By clause [ ] of the Will [and in the events which have happened][82] the Son is entitled to a pecuniary legacy of £100,000 ('the Legacy').

(B) The Son desires to redirect the legacy to the Grandson.

(C) The Executors are the executors and trustees named in the Will and obtained a grant of probate to the estate out of the [ ] Registry on [ ].

NOW THIS DEED WITNESSES:

1. Variation of the Legacy
   The Testator shall be deemed to have left the Legacy to the Grandson.[83]

2. Reading-back statement
   The provisions of the Inheritance Act 1984, s 142(1) and of the Taxation of Chargeable Gains Act 1992, s 62(6) shall apply to the disposition of property effected by this deed.

IN WITNESS etc

---

[81] This is a simple variation with a father (the Testator's son) redirecting the legacy to his son (the Testator's Grandson). The attraction of the variation is that the father avoids making a PET: instead the IHT paid on the testator's death will cover the redirected gift.

[82] Insert words in square brackets if, for example, the legacy was subject to a survivorship period – hence the entitlement of the son is derived from the will coupled with survival.

[83] Consider the burden of IHT on the legacy. Commonly it will be payable out of the residue. Often the legacies will fall within the IHT nil rate band with the residue being exempt. For an illustration of when a specific gift was intended to bear its own IHT see *Ashcroft v Barnsdale* discussed at 12.50.

Precedent 12.2: Variation creating terminable/short-lived IPDI for the surviving spouse/civil partner[84]

THIS DEED OF VARIATION is made the [   ] day of [   ] 20[   ] between (1) [   ] of [   ] ('the Daughter') and (2) [   ] of [   ] ('the Trustees')

SUPPLEMENTAL to the will dated [   ] ('the Will') of [   ] late of [   ] ('the Testator') who died on [   ]

WHEREAS

(A)   By clause [   ] of the Will the Testator left his residuary estate (defined in the Will as 'my Trust Fund') on trust for the Daughter absolutely.

(B)   The Daughter wishes to vary the Will by settling the Trust Fund on the trusts set out in this instrument.

(C)   The Trustees are the present trustees of the Will.

NOW THIS DEED WITNESSES:

In variation of the dispositions of property made by the Will the following clauses[85] shall be deemed to be inserted into the Will in place of the existing clauses [*insert numbers*].

NEW CL1   Definitions

In this Will where the context so permits the following expressions shall have the following meanings:

(a)   'the Beneficiaries'[86] shall mean:
    (i)   my children and remoter issue
    (ii)   the spouses widows and widowers of the persons mentioned in (i)
    (iii) and 'Beneficiary' shall have a corresponding meaning;

(b)   'the Trust Period' shall mean the period commencing with the date of my death and ending 125 years thereafter and such period of 125 years shall be the perpetuity period applicable to the dispositions made by my Will;[87]

---

[84]   This Precedent may be used when the deceased has left his residuary estate to (say) his daughter (a chargeable transfer for IHT purposes) and she redirects this to the deceased's surviving spouse (so that the IHT spouse exemption will be available with the result that the residue will not attract IHT on the deceased's death: see generally **12.25** *et seq*). For CGT and income tax purposes the daughter is the settlor: see **12.06**.

[85]   The clauses in the Will leaving the residuary estate to the daughter are replaced by these new clauses ('NEW CL1, 2, 3'). Normally these will follow the numbering of the Will. NEW CL1 provides definitions used in the other two clauses: note that the definition of 'the Beneficiaries' excludes the surviving spouse since it is considered that she is fully catered for in NEW CL2 by being given a life interest together with the trustees having power to advance her capital.

[86]   If desired, greater flexibility can be obtained by including a power to add further members to the class of beneficiaries: see for instance the definition in **Precedent 4.1**.

[87]   For the 125-year perpetuity period see **2.05**.

(c)   'my Trustees' shall mean the trustees from time to time being of my Trust Fund;

(d)   'my Trust Fund' shall have the meaning given by clause [   ] of the Will.

NEW CL2   Trusts for surviving spouse and child

The provisions of this clause shall apply in default of until and subject to any exercise of the powers conferred by clause NEW CL3.[88]

(a)   THE income of my Trust Fund shall be paid to my [*Husband/Wife*] during [*his/her*] lifetime.[89]

(b)   THE Trustees may, at any time during the Trust Period, pay or apply the whole or any part of the Trust Fund in which my [*Husband/Wife*] is then entitled to an interest in possession to [*him/her*] or for [*his/her*] advancement or otherwise for [*his/her*] benefit in such manner as the Trustees shall in their discretion think fit. In exercising the powers conferred by this subclause, the Trustees shall be entitled to have regard solely to the interests of my [*Husband/Wife*] and to disregard all other interests or potential interests under my Will.

(c)   Subject thereto the Trustees shall hold the capital and income of my Residuary Trust Fund for my Daughter absolutely.

NEW CL3   Overriding powers[90]

My Trustees shall have the following powers exercisable during the Trust Period:

(a)   My Trustees shall hold the capital and income of my Trust Fund in favour or for the benefit of all or such one or more of the Beneficiaries at such ages or times exclusive of the other or others of them in such shares or proportions if more than one and with and subject to such powers trusts and provisions for their respective maintenance education or other benefit or for the accumulation of income (including administrative powers and provisions and discretionary or protective trusts and powers to be executed or exercised by any person or persons whether or not being or including my Trustees or any of them and including powers or trusts to accumulate the whole or any part of the income of my Trust Fund) and in such manner generally as my Trustees (subject to the application (if any) of the rule against perpetuities) by any deed or deeds revocable during the Trust Period or irrevocable and executed during the Trust Period shall

---

[88]   Note that the trusts in NEW CL2 are subject to the overriding power of appointment given to the trustees in NEW CL3. Accordingly the life interest for the spouse can be terminated and the remainder interest of the daughter taken away.

[89]   This, as a result of reading-back under s 142(1), creates an IPDI and hence results in the spouse exemption applying.

[90]   The overriding powers are in familiar format (see **Precedent 4.1**) comprising the usual wide power of appointment together with a power to transfer the property to a new settlement (a 'resettlement' power: see **2.60** *et seq*).

appoint **PROVIDED ALWAYS** that such power may only be exercised by the Trustees during the lifetime of my spouse and provided further that no exercise of this power shall deprive the spouse of any income to which s/he was entitled at the time when it arose or otherwise invalidate any prior payment or application of all or any part or parts of the capital or income of the Trust Fund made under any other power or powers conferred by my Will or by law.

(b)   My Trustees may transfer pay or apply any part of the capital and income of my Trust Fund to the trustees for the time being of any settlement wherever established (whose receipt shall be a good discharge to them) to be held free from the trusts of the Will and on the trusts and with and subject to the powers and provisions of that settlement but only if those trusts powers and provisions are such that at the time of the transfer they could themselves have created them under clause NEW CL3(a) above.

[*Include other clauses, eg reading-back statement and exclude apportionments of income*]

Alternative

Frequently the intention behind the variation is that having obtained the benefit of the IHT spouse exemption by creating the IPDI that interest will be terminated, for example in favour of the daughter so that the spouse makes a PET. In cases where it is desired to ensure that this happens, consider giving the spouse an interest in possession for a limited period at the end of which time the property reverts to the daughter or becomes held on a discretionary trust. For instance, NEW CL2 might be amended to provide:

'(a)   The income of my Trust Fund shall be paid to my [husband/wife] during his/her lifetime or until the expiry of the period of 2 years and 6 months from the date of my death if he/she shall then be living.'

The period of the IPDI must exceed 2 years or the effect of s 142(4) is that the IPDI will be disregarded: see **12.28**.

Precedent 12.3: Variation of the proceeds of sale of property which has been sold[91]

Recital

By clause [ ] of the Will the Testator left his property 'Greengages' to the Beneficiary absolutely. That property has since the date of death been sold and is now represented by the sum of [£1m] being the net proceeds of sale ('the Property').

Operative part

In variation of the dispositions of the Will the Deceased shall be treated as having left the Property to [*insert name of recipient*].

---

[91]   See **12.40**.

Precedent 12.4: Variation by personal representatives of deceased life tenant of the benefit of his life interest in certain shares[92]

THIS DEED OF VARIATION is made the [   ] day of [   ] 20[   ] between:

(1)   [   ] of [   ] and [   ] of [   ] ('the Beneficiary's Trustees')
(2)   [   ] of [   ] and [   ] of [   ] ('the Children')
(3)   [   ] of [   ] and [   ] of [   ] ('the Deceased's Trustees')

SUPPLEMENTAL to the will dated [   ] ('the Will') of [   ] who died on [   ] ('the Deceased')

WHEREAS:

(A)   By the Will the Deceased settled his residuary estate on trust for the Beneficiary for life and subject thereto to the Children in equal shares absolutely.

(B)   The Beneficiary died on [   ] leaving her residuary estate to the Children[93] and the Beneficiary's Trustees are the executors and trustees appointed by her will.

(C)   It has been agreed by the Beneficiary's Trustees and the Children that the Will shall be varied in accordance with the terms of this deed and the Deceased's Trustees (who are the present trustees of the trusts created by the Will) have agreed to administer the estate of the Deceased in accordance with its terms.

NOW THIS DEED WITNESSES:

1.   The Will of the Deceased shall be varied by the inclusion of the following legacy:

> 'Clause 2A I BEQUEATH to my children [   ] shares in [   ] together with all dividends paid from and after my death (subject to the payment of Inheritance Tax)'[94]

---

[92]   HMRC have expressed the view that it is not possible to vary a life interest after the death of the life tenant. However, the writers believe that this is not correct where, as here, there is income which can be redirected: see **12.17**. HMRC accepts that it is possible to disclaim a life interest on behalf of a deceased life tenant where the life tenant has taken no benefit from the trust property and, when possible, this is obviously a safer course of action: see **Precedent 12.5**.

[93]   HMRC consider the children's consent to be important: see **12.36**.

[94]   Note that the property being varied is shares which have produced dividend income after the date of death. This income is being varied.

2. The Inheritance Tax Act 1984, s 142(1) and s 62(6) of the Taxation of Chargeable Gains Act 1992 shall apply to the variation effected by this deed.

IN WITNESS etc

Precedent 12.5: Disclaimer of life interest when the life tenant has died[95]

THIS DEED OF DISCLAIMER is made the [   ] day of [   ] 20[   ] BY [*insert details*] of [   ] ('*the Executors*') acting in their capacity as personal representatives of [*insert details of the life tenant*] ('*the Life Tenant*') who died on [   ].

WHEREAS:

(A)   [   ] ('*the Testatrix*') died on [   ]

(B)   Under clause [*insert number*] of the Will of the Testatrix dated [*insert date*] ('*the Will*') her residuary estate (which property is set out in the Schedule hereto and is called in this deed '*the Trust Assets*') was left upon trust to pay the income therefrom to the Life Tenant during his lifetime or until his remarriage and thereafter for her children [*insert details*] in equal shares absolutely.

(C)   The Life Tenant died within 2 years of the death of the Testatrix and the children of the Testatrix are entitled to take the Trust Assets in equal shares absolutely.

(D)   The Life Tenant had not done any act or thing which could constitute an acceptance of any part of the income and the Executors wish to disclaim on his behalf his interest in the Trust Assets.

NOW THIS DEED WITNESSES:

1.   THE Executors hereby irrevocably disclaim and renounce all the rights, interest and entitlement of the Life Tenant in the Trust Assets and all other rights, interest and entitlement (if any) that he may have arising under the Will.

2.   THE Executors declare and confirm that the Life Tenant did not accept his interest in the Trust Assets and received no benefit from the same.[96]

IN WITNESS etc.

THE SCHEDULE
[*insert details of Trust Assets disclaimed*]

---

[95]   See **12.16**. For variations of life interests after the death of the life tenant, see **12.17** and **Precedent 12.4**.

[96]   A disclaimer is only possible if the beneficiary has not received a benefit (ie accepted the interest). In the case of a disclaimer no reading-back statement is required.

Precedent 12.6: Variation providing for (a) severance of beneficial joint tenancy (b) settlement of severed half share in land (c) gift of severed half share in building plot (d) reading-back for CGT only[97]

THIS DEED OF VARIATION is made the [   ] day of [   ] 20[   ] by [   ] of [   ] ('Mrs A')

SUPPLEMENTAL to the will dated [   ] ('the Will') of [   ] of [   ] who died on [   ] ('the Deceased').

WHEREAS

(A)   Mrs A is the sole executrix of the estate of the Deceased.

(B)   The property listed in the First Schedule of this deed was owned by the Deceased and Mrs A as beneficial joint tenants and accordingly passed on the Deceased's death to Mrs A by right of survivorship.

(C)   Mrs A is absolutely entitled to the Residuary Estate of the Deceased in accordance with the provisions of clause [   ] of the Will.

(D)   Mrs A is desirous of varying the dispositions of the property comprised in the estate of the Deceased as set out in this deed.

NOW THIS DEED WITNESSES

Severance of joint tenancy[98]

1.   Mrs A shall be deemed to have severed the beneficial joint tenancy in the property listed in the First Schedule immediately before the death of the Deceased so that the Deceased owned a 50% share in that property as a beneficial tenant in common at the date of his death.

Settlement of the Deceased's beneficial interest in Property X[99]

2.   The Will shall be varied by the inclusion of a settled gift of the Deceased's beneficial share in Property X onto the trusts set out in the Second Schedule to this deed.

---

[97]   This variation is for use when a beneficiary wishes to give away the deceased's share in joint property. That property has risen in value since the date of death so that CGT reading-back is needed: however, because the deceased had used up his IHT nil rate band the beneficiary will not elect for reading-back under s 142(1) but will instead make a PET (in the case of the outright gift of the building plot) or an immediately chargeable transfer (in the case of the settled gift).

[98]   For the post-death severance of joint tenancies see **12.38**.

[99]   Mrs A is the settlor of this property for IHT purposes in the absence of a reading-back election and, because of the limitation on CGT reading-back (see **12.06**), is also the settlor for CGT purposes.

Gift of Deceased's beneficial interest in the building plot[100]

3.   The Deceased's Will shall be varied to gift the Deceased's beneficial interest in the building plot to his three children in equal shares absolutely.

Reading-back statement

4.   Section 62(6) of the Taxation of Chargeable Gains Act 1992 shall apply to dispositions of property effected by this instrument.

Continuance of other terms in the Will

5.   Save as aforesaid the other dispositions of property in the Deceased's estate shall remain governed by the Will.

IN WITNESS etc

FIRST SCHEDULE
(Property passing by survivorship)

1.   Bank of [   ] Account Number [   ] jointly owned with Mrs A. Value at the date of the Deceased's death £[   ] (value of the Deceased's severed share £[   ]).
2.   Property X. Market value at the date of death £[   ] (value of Deceased's severed share £[   ]).
3.   The building plot. Market value at death £[   ] (value of Deceased's severed share £[   ]).

SECOND SCHEDULE
(Trusts of Deceased share in Property X)

1.   **Definitions**

In this Schedule the following expressions shall have where the context admits the following meanings:

(a)   'the Trustees' means [*insert details*] or other the trustee or trustees for the time being;
(b)   'the Trust Fund' shall mean the Deceased's 50% beneficial interest in Property X further property added to the trust in the future and any accumulations of income and all property from time to time representing the same;

---

[100] This will result in the building plot being held in the shares Mrs A half; the three children one-sixth each.

(c) 'the Beneficiaries' shall mean the Deceased's three children and his grandchildren whether born at the date of the Deceased's death or at any time during the Trust Period;

(d) 'the Trust Period' shall mean the period of 125 years beginning with the date of this deed.

2. Powers of appointment

DURING the Trust Period the Trustees (being at least two in number or a trust corporation) may at any time or times:

(a) by deed or deeds revocable during the Trust Period or irrevocable appoint that all or any part or parts of the income or capital of the Trust Fund shall be held on such trusts (including discretionary and protective ones) in favour or for the benefit of all or any one or more of the Beneficiaries and with and subject to such powers (including dispositive and administrative powers exercisable by the Trustees or any other person) and other provisions as the Trustees think fit; and

(b) transfer all or any part or parts of the income or capital of the Legacy Fund to the trustees of any Settlement wherever established (whose receipt shall be a good discharge to them) to be held free from the trusts of this Schedule and on the trusts and with and subject to the powers and provisions of that Settlement but only if those trusts powers and provisions are such that (at the time of the transfer) they could themselves have created them under (a) above

3. Default trusts

IN DEFAULT of and subject to any exercise of the clause 2 power of appointment:

(a) during the Trust Period the Trustees shall pay or apply the income of the Trust Fund to or for the maintenance education support or otherwise for the benefit of such one or more of the Beneficiaries as the Trustees may in their absolute discretion think fit BUT with power to accumulate and add to capital such income or any part or parts of it (and to apply the accumulations of past years as income of the current year) AND with power (during the Trust Period) to resolve to hold the whole or any part or parts of such income as income on trust for any of the Beneficiaries absolutely; and

(b) on the expiry of the Trust Period the Trustees shall hold the Trust Fund as to both capital and income ON TRUST for the Beneficiaries as are then living and if more than one in equal shares through all degrees according to their stocks and so that no issue shall take whose parent is alive and so capable of taking.

Precedent 12.7: Clauses providing for (a) personal representatives to consent to a variation on behalf of minors (b) a partial disclaimer

(a) The trustees shall have power to execute any Deed of Variation for the purpose of altering any of the dispositions of this Will on behalf of any person having an interest, whether vested or contingent, under the said disposition who by reason of infancy or other incapacity is incapable of assenting.[101]

(b) I declare that any adult beneficiary may within 2 years after my death execute a deed to disclaim all or part (including a fraction or percentage) of his or her entitlements in this Will in which event what is disclaimed shall devolve under this Will as if he or she had died before me.[102]

---

[101] See **12.23**.
[102] See **12.14**.

Precedent 12.8: Variation in favour of charity (with notification evidence)

THIS DEED OF VARIATION is made the [   ] day of [   ] 20[   ] by [   ] of [   ] ('the Beneficiary')

SUPPLEMENTAL to the will dated [   ] ('the Will') of [   ] of [   ] who died on [   ] ('the Deceased').

WHEREAS

(A)   The Beneficiary is the sole executor of the estate of the Deceased and is absolutely entitled to the residuary estate of the Deceased in accordance with the provisions of clause [ ] of the Will.

(B)   The Beneficiary is desirous of varying the disposition of certain property comprised in the estate of the Deceased as set out in this deed.

NOW THIS DEED WITNESSES

1.   The Will shall be varied by the inclusion of a pecuniary legacy of [*insert amount*] to [*insert details of charity*] ('the Charity').

2.   Save as aforesaid the other dispositions of property shall remained governed by the Will.

3.   The Inheritance Tax Act 1984, s 142(1) shall apply to the variation effected by this deed and the Beneficiary declares that in accordance with the requirements of s 142(3A) the charity as the 'Appropriate Person' has been notified of the existence of his instrument of variation.[103]

IN WITNESS etc

---

[103] For the notification requirement, see **12.20**. This statement in the variation is not sufficient: proof has to be supplied of the notification. This may be done by writing to the charity enclosing a copy of the deed and indicating that under its terms they are to receive (indicate the benefit eg a cash legacy of £X) and requesting the charity to sign a copy of the letter to confirm the receipt of notice. This copy letter should then be sent to HMRC along with the instrument of variation.

CHAPTER 13

CONSTITUTING AND ADMINISTERING WILL TRUSTS

This chapter considers a number of problem areas that arise in practice in connection with will trusts.

1. TRANSITION FROM ADMINISTRATION TO TRUST

13.01 There are a number of situations where it is important to know whether or not the administration period has terminated and the personal representatives hold the property on trust. For example:

(a) personal representatives have joint and several authority in relation to personalty (joint in relation to land)[1] whereas trustees must act jointly unless the trust instrument provides otherwise;

(b) a sole personal representative can give a good receipt for the proceeds of sale of land whereas a sole trustee cannot unless a trust corporation;

(c) on the death of a sole personal representative, a grant *de bonis non* is required unless the chain of executorship[2] applies. On the death of a sole or surviving trustee, new trustees are appointed under Trustee Act 1925, s 36(1)[3] or under the trust instrument;

(d) the limitation period is 12 years for claims against personal representatives[4] but 6 for claims against trustees[5] (with an exception for both trustees and personal representatives in the case of fraud or property converted to their own use where there is no limit);[6]

(e) so far as CGT is concerned, personal representatives are entitled to a full annual exemption in the tax year of death and the 2 following tax years but thereafter nothing.[7] Trustees generally have half an annual exemption.[8] Gains made by bare trustees are taxed as gains made by the

---

[1] See AEA 1925, s 2(2) as amended.
[2] See AEA 1925, s 7: the executor of a sole or last surviving proving executor (E) automatically becomes executor of any estates of which E was the executor.
[3] By the personal representatives of the last surviving or continuing trustee: Trustee Act 1925, s 36(1)(b).
[4] Limitation Act 1980, s 22(1).
[5] Limitation Act 1980, s 21(1).
[6] See Limitation Act 1980, s 21(1) and (2).
[7] TCGA 1992, s 3(7).
[8] TCGA 1992, s 3(8). See further **3.88**.

beneficiaries on whose behalf they hold the property.[9] According to the Scottish case of *Cochrane's Executors v IRC*,[10] where there is doubt, disposals will be deemed to have been made by personal representatives acting as personal representatives rather than as bare trustees;

(f)   for income tax, personal representative are liable to basic rate tax. When they transfer income to trustees it will be received with the appropriate tax credit but may become liable to the additional rate applicable to trusts;[11]

(g)   IHT loss relief on the sale of land or qualifying investments is restricted where the person claiming the relief purchases other assets of the same type within certain periods. However, a change from personal representative to trustee between the sale and purchase may mean that there is no restriction, for example where the sale is made as personal representative and the purchase is made as trustee: see **14.28**.

13.02 So when does the change take place? It is necessary to consider individual assets. For example where particular assets have been left on trust, the trust will commence as soon as those assets are assented[12] or appropriated to the trustees even if the personal representatives are still dealing as personal representatives with other assets. Where the residue is left on trust and the same people are both personal representatives and trustees there may be a lack of clarity. An assent or written appropriation will be proof positive that the trust has commenced. Without a formal document taxpayers may argue one way or the other depending on what is most beneficial – and HMRC may argue the converse!

HMRC regards completion of administration as occurring on the date when residue is 'ascertained', ie when the PRs have established the net worth of the estate and have liquid funds to pay liabilities and pecuniary legacies: see CGTM30810.

13.03 Where there is no assent, then if personal representatives are appointed as trustees in the will, they will become trustees when they complete the administration:

> 'The question which I am asked to decide is whether the administrators of the estate, having cleared the estate and completed the administration in the ordinary way (the testator having been dead for about 10 years) are in a position to appoint new trustees of the will, and whether those new trustees, when so appointed by them, will continue to exercise the powers which are conferred by the will upon the trustees for the time being of the will. I feel no doubt about the matter at all. Whether persons are executors or administrators, once they have completed the

---

[9]   TCGA 1992, s 60. See further **3.110**.
[10]   (1974) 49 TC 299.
[11]   If it is an accumulation or discretionary trust where beneficiaries have no right to income: see **3.134**.
[12]   In the case of land.

administration in due course, they become trustees holding for the beneficiaries either on an intestacy or under the terms of the will, and are bound to carry out the duties of trustees.'[13]

According to *Snell's Equity*[14] there is a presumption that trusteeship begins when personal representatives produce their accounts[15] or exercise a power of appropriation.[16] According to Williams, Sunnucks & Mortimer:[17] 'Once the administration is complete the representative becomes a trustee of the net residue for the persons beneficially entitled' and 'It would seem that failure to execute an assent in his own favour could not prevent the trusts arising'. Note, however, *Re King's Will Trusts*[18] which requires a written assent to vest legal title to land.

2. CONSTITUTING THE TRUST

The assets settled

13.04   A will may leave specific items on trust. If it does, the trustees, like any other specific legatees, cannot insist on taking possession of the item until the personal representatives are satisfied that the asset is not required for payment of debts. The trustees have a *chose in action* until the executors assent the item. When the item is assented the trustees will become entitled to any income produced by the asset since the date of death.

Commonly the trust will be of residue or of a pecuniary legacy equal to the deceased's available nil rate band.

Residuary legatees have no right to any assets until the residue is ascertained. They do, however, have a *chose in action* to compel due administration of the estate.[19]

Pecuniary legatees are normally general legatees and are entitled to cash or to an appropriation of assets equal to the value given or, if the estate is insufficient to pay legacies in full, an abated sum. They cannot insist on receiving anything until the personal representatives are satisfied that the estate is sufficient to make payment. They will be entitled to interest to compensate for late payment from 12 months after the date of death or the date, if any, fixed for payment.

---

[13]   *Re Cockburn's Will Trusts* [1957] Ch 438.
[14]   33rd edn, 2015, para 21.055.
[15]   *Re Claremont* [1923] 2 KB 718.
[16]   *Phillipo v Munnings* (1837) 2 My & Cr 309.
[17]   *Executors, Administrators and Probate* (20th edn, 2013), 81.02.
[18]   [1964] Ch 542.
[19]   *Commissioners of Stamp Duties (Queensland) v Livingston* [1965] AC 694.

Using a debt or charge to satisfy a legacy

13.05 Problems often arise in relation to trusts of nil rate band legacies where there are insufficient liquid assets to constitute the trust, too much of the estate being locked up in the matrimonial home. It is possible to appropriate all or part of the deceased's interest in the matrimonial home but this is often unpopular with the surviving spouse or civil partner and may have other disadvantages.[20]

13.06 Before the introduction of the transferable nil rate band,[21] nil rate band discretionary trusts were widely used as an instrument of inheritance tax planning and it was common to constitute the trust with a debt[22] or charge.[23] This had the advantage of allowing the surviving spouse to have ownership of all the assets during his or her lifetime. The trustees would simply hold the debt or charge as an asset of the trust.[24]

On the death of the surviving spouse the trustees become entitled to payment of the nil rate sum with interest or indexation if this was provided for in the original arrangement.

Interest on the sum owed

13.07 The trustees have to pay income tax on interest received at the trust rate which is 45% on everything in excess of the first £1,000.[25] However, they may be able to appoint the income to a beneficiary liable to income tax at a lower rate in which case the tax can be recovered. Alternatively they can disclaim the interest in which case income tax is not payable.[26]

Indexation of the sum owed

13.08 A payment resulting from the indexation of the sum owed is, in the view of HMRC, also liable to income tax. Many practitioners dispute this[27] but HMRC is adamant and unless and until a test case goes to trial, taxpayers will

---

[20] See discussion at **5.04**.
[21] See generally Chapter 5.
[22] In the simplest version this would be an IOU from the surviving spouse to the discretionary trustees.
[23] The executors would charge the assets transferred to the surviving spouse.
[24] For documentation for debt charge arrangements see **Precedents 5.1** and **5.2**.
[25] ITA 2007, s 479.
[26] *Dewar v IRC* [1935] 2 KB 351. The IHT deduction from the survivor's estate will be smaller if interest is disclaimed.
[27] In *National Westminster Ltd v Riches* (1945) 28 TC 159 Lord Wright (at 189) said: 'the essence of interest is that it is a payment which becomes due because the creditor has not had his money at the due date. It may be regarded either as representing the profit he might have made if he had had the use of the money, or conversely the loss he suffered because he had not that use. The general idea is that he is entitled to compensation for the deprivation.' Indexation is simply aimed at preserving the value of the money outstanding. Appendix 4 of *Drafting Trusts and Wills Trusts* (12th edn, 2015) by Kessler, provides convincing arguments for treating the index linking element as capital. The Revenue have been most reluctant to bring a test case!

be invited to pay the income tax demanded or delay the administration of the estate until the outcome of the test case is known.

Inadequate paperwork

13.09 It is not uncommon to discover on the death of the surviving spouse that no steps were ever taken to constitute the nil rate band discretionary trust. Instead the surviving spouse took all the assets and continued to live in the matrimonial home. The discretionary trust was simply ignored. What should the personal representatives do on the death of the surviving spouse?

13.10 There are two possibilities:

(1) The trustees may be taken to have decided that the trust was unnecessary and that the nil rate sum should be given to the spouse. If this took place within 2 years of death, there would have been reading back under IHTA 1984, s 144.[28] The trust would have disappeared and the whole estate could be treated as left to the surviving spouse. The benefit is that the nil rate band of the first spouse will be unused and, therefore, available for transfer to the survivor.

　　The problem is that there is no deed of appointment or evidence of any advancement to the surviving spouse. However, most discretionary trusts have two powers for trustees in relation to capital: a power of appointment which normally has to be exercised by deed and a power of advancement which requires no particular formalities. If nothing whatever has been done to suggest that the trust continued, HMRC may accept that there was an advancement.

(2) The alternative is that the trust still exists and the PRs misdistributed the estate by failing to transfer assets to the trustees. The survivor's estate received too much and is in possession of trust assets. The trustees are entitled to recover the nil rate sum.[29]

3. READING-BACK AND IHTA 1984, S 144

13.11 In Chapter 12 we looked at rearranging estates by use of post-death variations and disclaimers. Here we will look at ways to rearrange certain will trusts. Where the will creates a settlement without an interest in possession, the trustees of the settlement can make use of IHTA 1984, s 144 to give the settled

---

[28] See **13.11** *et seq* below.

[29] Perhaps with interest from 12 months after death until payment. Pecuniary legacies normally carry the right to interest at the basic rate payable on money held in court: see CPR, Part 40, Practice Direction: Accounts, Inquiries etc, para 15 and **Appendix I**. However, interest is payable to compensate for late payment and the will may indicate that it is not payable at all or is payable from a later date. The inclusion of debt charge provisions in the will authorising the personal representatives to delay payment may be taken as an indication that interest is not to be payable. Of course, the debt may have become statute barred.

property to individuals and have the rearrangement treated as the deceased's for IHT purposes. Section 144 provides as follows:

'(1) Subsection (2) below applies where property comprised in a person's estate immediately before his death is settled by his will and, within the period of two years after his death and before any interest in possession has subsisted in the property, there occurs—

(a)   an event on which tax would [(apart from subsection (2) below)] be chargeable under any provision, other than section 64 or 79, of Chapter III of Part III of this Act, or

(b)   an event on which tax would be so chargeable but for sections [65(4)],[30] 75, 75A or 76 above or paragraph 16(1) of Schedule 4 to this Act.

(1A)   Where the testator dies on or after 22 March 2006, subsection (1) above shall have effect as if the reference to any interest in possession were a reference to any interest in possession that is:

(a)   an immediate post-death interest, or
(b)   a disabled person's interest.

(2)   Where this subsection applies by virtue of an event within paragraph (a) of subsection (1) above, tax shall not be charged under the provision in question on that event; and in every case in which [this subsection] applies in relation to an event, this Act shall have effect as if the will had provided that on the testator's death the property should be held as it is held after the event.

(3)   Subsection (4) below applies where:

(a)   a person dies on or after 22 March 2006,
(b)   property comprised in the person's estate immediately before his death is settled by his will, and
(c)   within the period of two years after his death, but before an immediate post-death interest or a disabled person's interest has subsisted in the property, there occurs an event that involves causing the property to be held on trusts that would, if they had in fact been established by the testator's will, have resulted in:
(i)   an immediate post-death interest subsisting in the property, or
(ii)   section 71A or 71D above applying to the property.

(4)   Where this subsection applies by virtue of an event:

(a)   this Act shall have effect as if the will had provided that on the testator's death the property should be held as it is held after the event, but

---

[30]   The addition in square brackets (of s 65(4)) was to have been made by FA 2015 in respect of deaths on or after 10 December 2014 in order to remove the *Frankland* trap: see **13.13** *et seq*. Due to the haste with which the Finance Act 2015 proceeded through parliament, all the changes to the taxation of relevant property settlements which had been announced on 10 December 2014 were dropped. HMRC has said that they will be included in a future Finance Bill.

(b)   tax shall not be charged on that event under any provision of Chapter 3 of Part 3 of this Act.

(5)   Subsection (4) above also applies where—

(a)   a person dies before 22 March 2006,
(b)   property comprised in the person's estate immediately before his death is settled by his will,
(c)   an event occurs:
      (i)   on or after 22 March 2006, and
      (ii)   within the period of two years after the testator's death,
      that involves causing the property to be held on trusts within subsection (6) below,
(d)   no immediate post-death interest, and no disabled person's interest, subsisted in the property at any time in the period beginning with the testator's death and ending immediately before the event, and
(e)   no other interest in possession subsisted in the property at any time in the period beginning with the testator's death and ending immediately before 22 March 2006.

(6)   Trusts are within this subsection if they would, had they in fact been established by the testator's will and had the testator died at the time of the event mentioned in subsection (5)(c) above, have resulted in—

(a)   an immediate post-death interest subsisting in the property, or
(b)   section 71A or 71D above applying to the property.'

13.12   The section allows an appointment from a settlement to be read-back into the will so that the deceased is treated as having left his property in accordance with the appointment.[31]

Example 13.1

Trevor leaves a sum equal to his available nil rate band on discretionary trusts for the benefit of his wife and family, residue to his wife. Eight months after his death the trustees appoint the nil rate sum to his wife.

The discretionary trust will disappear and the whole estate will be treated as left to his wife by Trevor's will and so will attract the spouse exemption.[32]

The appointment must be made before any interest in possession has subsisted in the property and so is of no assistance where property is left to persons in succession. For example, if property was left 'to mother for life and then to my husband', s 144 could not be used to rearrange the disposition of the estate.[33] Although triggered most often by an express appointment, the section is not so limited. Section 1(1) refers to the occurrence of 'an event' on which tax would

---

[31]   Note that the section applies more widely: it is triggered by 'an event' within the prescribed period of which an appointment is merely one illustration.
[32]   For a suitable deed of appointment, see **Precedent 13.1**.
[33]   The life tenant and remainderman could, however, use a post-death variation to vary their own interests: see Chapter 12.

otherwise be chargeable. The event could be an advancement of capital by trustees or an entitlement to income arising at age 18.[34]

Timing issues and the *Frankland* trap

13.13 When property leaves a discretionary trust within 3 months of creation,[35] no IHT is payable. Therefore, under the original wording of s 144(1)(a) if an outright appointment was made within the first 3 months of death, there could be no reading-back because there was no event on which tax would otherwise be chargeable. If this was not appreciated, the consequences could be devastating. See, for example, *Frankland v IRC*[36] where a substantial estate was left on discretionary trusts. The trustees made an appointment to the surviving spouse just short of the required 3 months. While agreeing with the taxpayers that it was difficult to see a rational reason for the denial of read-back, the Court of Appeal held that it followed from the clear and unambiguous wording of the legislation that it was not available.

13.14 Subsections (3)–(6) were introduced by FA 2006 to allow for reading-back where property is appointed to create an IPDI or on bereaved minor or s 71D trusts. Different wording was used allowing appointments to be made within 3 months of death.

> *Example 13.2*
>
> 1.   Ted leaves his substantial estate on discretionary trusts. Two months after his death on 9 December 2014 the trustees appoint the estate to his wife Sally outright. There is no charge to IHT when the property leaves the settlement but there is no reading-back either and the spouse exemption is not available so that on Ted's death the estate is subject to IHT. (This is the so-called 'Frankland trap'.)
>
> 2.   If the trustees make the appointment to Sally 2 months after Ted's death but on life interest trusts, there is reading-back and the spouse exemption is available.

When the testator dies on or after 10 December 2014, it is envisaged that the wording of s 144(1)(b) will be amended to remove the *Frankland* trap. Accordingly if Ted in **Example 13.2** dies one day later then the appointment to Sally may be read-back and so the spouse exemption will be available.

---

[34]   For example, as a result of the vesting effect of TA 1925, s 31: see further **2.72**.

[35]   The same is true when property leaves a settlement within 3 months of a 10-year anniversary. IHTA 1984, s 65(4) provides that s 65(1) (ie the provision which charges tax where property ceases to be property in which no interest in possession subsists) does not apply if the event in question occurs in a quarter beginning with the day on which the relevant settlement commenced or with a 10-year anniversary of the commencement of the settlement: see **3.68**.

[36]   *Frankland v IRC* [1996] STC 735 aff'd [1997] STC 1450, CA. It was possible, in the event of such a mistake occurring, for the spouse to make a variation on life interest trusts for herself which would be 'read-back' as a spouse exempt IPDI. But, of course, 2 years must not have elapsed since death.

Unscrambling unwanted nil rate band discretionary trusts

13.15 Section 144 allows trustees to dismantle unwanted nil rate band trusts in order to take advantage of the transferable nil rate band on the death of a first spouse. Many families take the view that the complexity of a trust is no longer justified.[37] Of course, in the case of a death more than 2 years ago 'unscrambling' is not possible and the trusts will need to be kept in being.

> *Example 13.3*
>
> 1.   Tom leaves his substantial estate to his wife, Sian, apart from a nil rate band discretionary trust for the benefit of Sian and his children. Eight months after his death the trustees appoint the nil rate sum to Sian. As a result of s 144, the whole estate will be treated as left to his wife and so will attract the spouse exemption.
>
> 2.   If the trustees make the appointment to Sian 3 years after his death, there is no reading-back under s 144. Tom will have used his nil rate band so no nil rate band is available for transfer to Sian's estate and as a result of the appointment, the property is now part of Sian's estate. This is not a happy result!

Appointment before assets vested in trustees

13.16 If it is obvious from an early stage that the trust is going to be dismantled, it is pointless for the personal representatives to vest assets in the trustees and it is not necessary for them to do so. The trustees of the settlement, like any beneficiary of the estate have a *chose in action* from the date of death (the right to receive the property left to them unless it is required for the purposes of the administration).[38] They can, therefore, make an appointment of their rights under the will.[39] Many settlements specifically authorise trustees to exercise their powers before the completion of the administration of the estate. Although this is probably unnecessary (because the trustees always have the *chose in action*), it is sensible to include it since HMRC appear to attach importance to it. See, for example, CG Manual 31432.

It is often administratively convenient to make an early appointment and there are CGT considerations which may make an early appointment desirable.[40]

Form of appointment

13.17 The section does not impose any requirements as to the form of appointment and indeed talks in terms of 'events' so an informal advancement

---

[37]   For the introduction of the transferable nil rate band and its effects on will drafting, see Chapter 5.

[38]   *Commissioners of Stamp Duties (Queensland) v Livingston* [1965] AC 694; see also *Re Hayes WT* [1971] 2 All ER 341 at 347. See also **13.04** above.

[39]   They should word it as an appointment of their rights under the will: see **Precedent 13.1**.

[40]   See **13.22**. Some wills expressly permit an appointment before the estate is administered: see **Precedent 4.1, clause 12**.

of capital will suffice. However, if trustees are exercising a power of appointment, the trust instrument will normally require the use of a deed and it is important to comply with those requirements to ensure that the appointment is valid. The appointment should either identify the assets appointed expressly or if, as is often the case, the appointment is being made before the personal representatives have transferred specific assets to the trust, the trustees will simply appoint their rights to whatever they are entitled to under the deceased's will.[41]

Who makes the appointment?

13.18   It is the trustees of the will trust who must make the appointment and it is, therefore, important to ensure that they are:

(a)   correctly identified; and

(b)   have power to make the appointment.

Trustees and personal representatives may be different

13.19   Normally executors and the trustees will be the same people but, quite often, only some of the named executors will have proved the will. The others may have renounced or had power reserved to prove at a later stage.

Any appointment must be by all the trustees named in the will unless they have disclaimed their trusteeship. Disclaimer is normally done by deed although it can be inferred from conduct:[42]

> 'It is most prudent that a deed of disclaimer should be executed by a person named trustee, who refuses to accept the trust, because such deed is clear evidence of the disclaimer, and admits of no ambiguity; but there may be conduct which amounts to a clear disclaimer.'

Inaction may suffice but within the s 144 time frame, this is unlikely to be useful. Note that a renunciation of probate is not sufficient to disclaim trusteeship, though it is of evidential value. The two offices are different.[43] Some draftsmen like to define the trustees as 'the persons entitled for the time being to administer the estate'. This allows all named to act as trustees before the grant is taken but once the grant is taken, only those who have proved can act as trustees unless and until they are appointed as trustees by those who took the grant.

Appointment of 'partners in firm'

13.20   In the case of the appointment of the partners in a solicitor's firm as executors and trustees, wholesale disclaimers may be an unattractive prospect.

---

[41]   See **Precedent 13.1**.
[42]   *Stacey v Elph* (1833) 1 My & K 195.
[43]   *Re Gordon* (1877) 6 Ch D 531.

The problem is discussed in *Williams on Wills*[44] which says that *prima facie* all partners are trustees not just the ones who took the grant. However, it suggests that it should be possible to argue that only those who accept office become trustees so that the others can be taken to have disclaimed. The usual wording of 'I express the wish that only two partners shall prove my will and act in its trusts' may be sufficient to avoid the problem.

In relation to s 144 appointments be careful about using precedents such as 'As trustees I appoint the persons who take out a grant of probate to my estate' as this will make it impossible to make an appointment before a grant has been taken.

A neat way to deal with the drafting is to define the trustees as the personal representatives but provide that, once a grant of representation is obtained, only those taking a grant are to be trustees. This means that there are trustees pre-grant in case of need but post-grant it is obvious who the trustees are.

Can the trustees act?

13.21 Beneficiaries are often appointed as trustees. There can then be problems if they wish to exercise powers in their own favour. The role of a trustee is fiduciary and without express authority in the trust instrument, trustees may fall foul of the rule against self-dealing. Infringing the self-dealing rule means that beneficiaries can have trustees' actions declared void irrespective of the fairness or otherwise of the transaction. See, for example, *Kane v Radley-Kane.*[45]

It is important to look at the terms of the trust instrument. There will usually be provisions allowing trustee/beneficiaries to exercise powers in their own favour but the extent of such clauses varies. The STEP standard provisions provide that a trustee can exercise powers to benefit himself provided:

(a)   the trustees consist of or include all the trustees originally appointed under the Principal Document; or

(b)   there is an independent trustee.

'Independent trustee' is defined to exclude spouses, civil partners and close relatives.

This means there would have to be an independent trustee if any of the original trustees appointed had died or disclaimed. Other precedents usually allow a trustee to exercise powers even though beneficially interested sometimes requiring there to be at least one other trustee.[46]

---

[44]   (9th edn, 2007) paras 203.15–203.19.
[45]   *Kane v Radley-Kane* [1999] Ch 274. See 14.08.
[46]   See **Precedent 4.1, clause 13.**

It is desirable for a trust instrument to include express provision for self-dealing as this will provide clarity. However, there is some authority that a settlor who has chosen to appoint a beneficiary as trustee is to be taken to have impliedly authorized the trustee to exercise powers in his own favour.[47]

CGT considerations

13.22 Section 144 deals only with IHT and there is no corresponding provision for CGT so normal CGT principles apply. An absolute appointment from the trust gives rise to a deemed disposal which may result in a charge to CGT to the extent that the assets have increased in value since death. However, provided the appointment is made before the personal representatives have vested the assets in the trustees, HMRC accepts that the appointment is to a person who takes *as legatee* rather than as a beneficiary of a trust. This means that CGT is not payable. See CGTM para 31432:

> 'Where the trustees exercise their powers of appointment before the assets have vested in them then the assets are still in the hands of the personal representatives at the time of the exercise. Even though these may be the same individuals as the trustees they are different bodies of persons for CGT purposes, see CG31110–CG31123. If, in these circumstances, the trustees make an appointment under the specific powers given to them in the will, then when the asset(s) vest they should be treated as passing direct to the appointee.
>
> The asset(s) appointed should be treated as never becoming subject to the trust. In effect, the appointment is read back into the will. It is treated as though the deceased had intended the assets concerned to pass directly to the legatee rather than into trust. The appointee then takes those asset(s) as legatee and therefore acquires the asset(s) at probate value by reason of Section 62(4) TCGA 1992, see CG31140+.'

In a case where CGT is likely to be an issue, it is important that the trustees make the appointment before the assets are vested in them.

The scope of s 144

13.23 The section is widely drafted and can apply in the following situations:

(a) in combination with IHTA 1984, s 142 (instruments of variation). For instance, the trustees may make an outright s 144 appointment to a beneficiary (B) who may then (still within 2 years of the death) vary the gift to him which has been read-back into the will;

(b) to convert an 18-25 trust into an IPDI as a result of 'an event' (typically the beneficiary becoming entitled to income at 18 under TA 1925, s 31) happening within 2 years of death;[48]

---

[47] See *Sargeant v National Westminster Bank plc* (1990) 61 P & CR 518; *Brudenell-Bruce, Earl of Cardigan v Moore* [2012] EWHC 1024 (Ch).

[48] See **7.22**.

(c)   to unscramble the addition of property into a lifetime trust: the section does not require the will to set up the trust, merely that property is 'settled by the will'.

Example 13.4

Tom set up a discretionary trust in 1999 which has funds worth £300,000 at the time of his death. By his will he adds a further £300,000 to the 1999 trust. This is undesirable as it causes the trust to suffer 10-year charges in the future (given that its assets will be well in excess of the nil rate band).

The trustees of the 1999 trust can appoint the additional £300,000 settled by will to a beneficiary absolutely and the appointment will be read back into the will.

Alternatively, it may be attractive for the appointment to be made on IPDI trusts which, under s 144, are read-back into the testator's will.

PRECEDENTS

Precedent 13.1: A deed of appointment made within 2 years of death and vesting the trust property in the surviving spouse absolutely: variants depending the assets in the trust

THIS DEED OF APPOINTMENT is made the [ ] day of [ ] 20[ ] by [*insert name*] of [*insert address*] and [*insert name*] of [*insert address*] ('the Appointors')

SUPPLEMENTAL to the will dated [*insert date*] ('the Will') of [*insert name*] ('the Deceased') who died on [*insert date*][49]

WHEREAS

1. By clause [*insert number*] the Will established a nil rate band discretionary trust ('the Trust').

2. [*Insert name of the Deceased's surviving spouse*] ('the Beneficiary')[50] is a member of the class of Beneficiaries as defined in the Will.

3. The Appointors are the present trustees of the Will Trust and are desirous of appointing the property comprised in the Will Trust (listed in the Schedule to this Deed) to the Beneficiary absolutely.

NOW THIS DEED WITNESSES:

1. In exercise of their power under clause [*insert number*] and all other relevant powers, the Appointors hereby irrevocably appoint that the property set out in the Schedule[51] shall from the date of this Deed be held upon trust as to both capital and income for the Beneficiary absolutely.[52]

2. All income received by or on behalf of the Trustees or Trustee for the time being of the Trust from and after the date of this Deed shall be treated as if it had arisen wholly after such date.

3. [It is hereby agreed between the Appointors and the Beneficiary that the charge over property details of which are set out in the Schedule shall be removed and that all sums payable thereunder are hereby released].[53]

IN WITNESS etc.

---

[49] 'Reading-back' under IHTA 1984, s 144 only applies if the appointment takes effect within 2 years of death.

[50] The Beneficiary is the surviving spouse (or civil partner) of the Deceased and as a result of s 144 (reading-back) the trust fund will be spouse exempt (see IHTA 1984, s 18) with the result that (assuming that no other chargeable transfers had been made by the Deceased) his IHT nil rate band will be unused and so may be claimed on the death of the surviving spouse.

[51] Or 'the debt details of which are set out in the Schedule'.

[52] In the case of a *debt* include the words 'to the intent that the debt and all sums payable thereunder shall be released'.

[53] Consider inserting this clause when the NRBDT was set up by a charge over property subsequently assented to the surviving spouse.

SCHEDULE

- Identify property held in the Will Trust[54]
    Or

- A **debt** evidenced by an agreement dated [*insert date*] and made between the Appointors and the Beneficiary[55]
    Or

- The benefit of the **charge** over [the Deceased's share in] [*identify the property*][56]
    Or

- The Nil Rate Sum gifted to the Appointor by clause [*insert number*] of the Will of the Deceased.

---

[54] Use when the executors have appropriated specific assets out of the estate to the trustees.
[55] Consider including in the deed the additional wording in footnote 51 above.
[56] Consider including clause 3 into the deed to deal with the lifting of the charge.

Precedent 13.2: Declaration of 100–year perpetuity period[57]

THIS DECLARATION is made the [   ] day of [   ] 20[   ] by [   ] of [   ] and [   ] of [   ] ('the Trustees')

SUPPLEMENTAL to [*insert details of the settlement*] ('the Settlement')

WHEREAS

A.   By clause [*insert number*] of the Settlement the applicable perpetuity period was defined by reference to the lives of persons in being at the time when the Settlement was created.

B.   The Trustees are of the opinion that it is difficult and not reasonably practicable[58] to ascertain whether the lives have ended and so whether the perpetuity period has ended.

C.   They are therefore entering into this deed to take advantage of the 100 year perpetuity period provided for in s 12 of the Perpetuities and Accumulations Act 2009.

NOW THIS DEED WITNESSES

The Trustees hereby declare they believe that it is difficult and not reasonably practicable for them to ascertain whether the lives in being referred to in the definition of the perpetuity period in the Settlement have ended and so to determine whether the perpetuity period has ended and accordingly declare that s 12(2)[59] of the Perpetuities and Accumulations Act 2009 shall apply to the Settlement.

IN WITNESS etc.

---

[57]   This declaration has only been possible from 6 April 2010 when the PAA 2009 came into force. The declaration is irrevocable. See 2.07.

[58]   Contrast the wording of the legislation which is 'difficult or not reasonably practicable'.

[59]   This provides for a 100-year period taking effect from the date when the settlement was created: for instance, in the case of a settlement set up on 1 April 1960 the period will run until 1 April 2060.

Precedent 13.3: Settled advance not creating a new settlement[60]

THIS DEED OF APPLICATION is made the [ ] day of [ ] 200[ ] by [insert details of trustees] ('the Trustees')

SUPPLEMENTAL TO a Settlement dated [insert date] and made between [ ] as Settlor and [ ] as the Original Trustees ('the Settlement') and to the other instruments listed in the First Schedule to this Deed

WHEREAS

1. The Trust Fund (as defined in the Settlement) is held upon trusts, *inter alia*, under which B is entitled to income and under which he will become absolutely entitled to the assets contained in that Fund on attaining the age of 25 years.

2. By clause [*insert number*] of the Settlement the trustees for the time being are entitled at any time or times before B becomes 25 to apply the whole or any part or parts of the capital of the Trust Fund for his advancement maintenance education or benefit.

3. The Trustees are the present trustees of the Settlement and are desirous of exercising the said power in modification[61] of the existing trusts affecting the Trust Fund for B's benefit in the manner set out in this Deed.

NOW THIS DEED WITNESSES:

Definitions

1. In this Deed the following expressions shall where the context permits have the following meanings:
    (i)   'B' shall mean [ ] who was born on [ ].
    (ii) 'the Trustees' shall mean the Trustees and the survivor of them or other the trustees or trustee for the time being of the Settlement.
    (iii) 'the Perpetuity Date' shall mean the day on which shall expire the period of twenty-one years after the death of the issue of the Settlor [ ] who were alive on [*insert date of settlement*][62]

Application of capital and income

2. The Trustees as trustees for the time being of the Trust Fund in exercise of their above-recited power and of any and every other power them enabling **HEREBY RESOLVE DETERMINE AND DIRECT** that the Trust Fund

---

60 See **2.60** *et seq.*
61 It is not intended to resettle the trust fund: the power is being exercised 'narrowly' to modify the existing trusts: see *Swires v Renton* [1991] STC 490.
62 It may be that no perpetuity period had been set out in the original settlement: in this situation a subsequent exercise of the trustees' dispositive powers may select an appropriate period by reference to the date when the settlement was created. In this case it is assumed that the 'old rules' apply: see **2.03**.

and the income thereof shall now be and hereby is applied for the benefit of B by henceforth being held by the Trustees upon the trusts and with and subject to the powers and provisions hereinafter declared and contained in respect of the same.

3.   As from the date hereof the Trustees shall stand possessed of the Trust Fund and the income thereof on the following trusts and with and subject to the following powers and provisions namely:

(1)   The Trustees shall continue to pay the income to B during his life.[63]

(2)   The Trustees shall have power by deed or deeds revocable before the Perpetuity Date or irrevocable to appoint to [   ] or to any spouse of B who shall survive him a life or lesser interest in the income of all or any part of the Trust Fund.[64]

(3)   Subject as aforesaid the Trustees shall hold the Trust Fund upon trust for all or such one or more exclusively of the others or other of the children of B at such ages or times and if more than one in such shares and with such provisions for their respective maintenance education and benefit generally at the discretion of the Trustees or of any other person or persons as the Trustees shall by any deed or deeds revocable before the Perpetuity Date or irrevocable appoint and in default of and until and subject to any and every such appointment upon trust for all or any of the children of B who shall attain the age of 21 years on or before the Perpetuity Date or shall be living and under that age on the Perpetuity Date and if more than one in equal shares absolutely and so that such interests shall carry the intermediate income.

(4)   Subject thereto the Trust Fund and the income thereof shall be held on trust for [*insert details*] absolutely.

(5)   Notwithstanding the foregoing the Trustees shall have power at any time or times before the Perpetuity Date to pay or apply the whole or any part of the Trust Fund to B during his lifetime or for his advancement or otherwise for his benefit in such manner as the Trustees in their discretion shall think fit and after the death of B shall have a like power exercisable in favour of any person appointed an interest in possession under clause 3(2) above.

---

[63]   It is assumed that B became entitled to the income at 18 as a result of TA 1925, s 31 (see **2.72**). If this happened before 22 March 2006 that right to income will be a qualifying interest in possession which the trustees will not wish to disturb by this settled advance. Hence the wording of clause 3(1) which is intended to show that B's income entitlement remains unchanged. If, however, it could be shown to have ended and been replaced by a 'new' interest under the settled advance, then (bizarre though it seems!) B would make an immediately chargeable transfer and the trusts created by the settled advance would be taxed under IHT (the relevant property regime). If B's income entitlement only arose after 21 March 2006 then this issue does not arise and the settlement will, in any event, be taxed under the relevant property regime.

[64]   If B's interest is a qualifying interest in possession then it will be attractive for this power to be exercised since the spouse will on B's death take a transitional serial interest: see **3.59**.

[(6) Section 32 of the Trustee Act 1925 shall apply to the trusts hereinbefore contained with the omission of the words 'one-half' from proviso (a) of subsection (1) and the omission of subsection (2)].[65]

Continuance of Settlement terms[66]

4.   It is hereby confirmed that the administrative powers and provisions of the Settlement contained in clauses [insert numbers] inclusive shall continue to apply to the Trust Fund and the income thereof

IN WITNESS etc.

FIRST SCHEDULE (details of settlement instruments)

---

[65]   This clause has been unnecessary from 1 October 2014 when the Inheritance and Trustees' Powers Act 2014 became law since it removes the one-half restriction in this section.

[66]   There is no intention to create a new settlement for CGT purposes: the instrument modifies the existing trusts.

Precedent 13.4: Exercise of a power of appointment to convert a discretionary trust into an interest in possession[67]

THIS DEED OF APPOINTMENT is made the [ ] day of [ ] 20[ ] by [ ] ('the Appointors').

SUPPLEMENTAL to a deed of settlement dated [ ] and made between [ ] ('the Settlement')

WHEREAS

A. By clause [ ] of the Settlement the Trustees have power to appoint capital and income of the Trust Fund amongst such of the Beneficiaries as they may see fit. The power is exercisable and any exercise may be made revocable during the Trust Period.

B. B is a member of the class of Beneficiaries.

C. The Appointors are the present Trustees of the Settlement and the Trust Period has not expired.

NOW THIS DEED WITNESSES

1. **Definitions**
    In this Deed 'the Trustees', 'the Trust Period', 'the Trust Fund' and 'the Beneficiaries' shall have the meaning given to these terms in the Settlement.

2. **Exercise of power of appointment**
    In exercise of the power of appointment conferred on them by clause [ ] of the Settlement and of all other relevant powers the Appointors hereby appoint that from and after the date hereof the Trust Fund shall be held on trust to pay the income thereof to B for his life.

3. **Power of revocation reserved[68]**
    The Trustees may at any time or times during the Trust Period by deed or deeds revoke or vary either wholly or in part the appointment contained in clause 2 above.

---

[67] The deed may be used to convert a discretionary trust into an interest in possession trust. The interest so created is not 'qualifying' for IHT and so for the purposes of this tax the deed is a 'nothing'. However, it will change the income tax treatment of the trust: see **3.134** *et seq*. The appointment may be over the entire trust fund or selected assets (eg 'all stocks and shares' or 'shares in X plc'). It is common in the latter case to refer to an Appointed Fund and list the assets in a Schedule. The appointment has no CGT consequences: it has the effect of modifying the existing settlement, not creating a new one. Whilst the trust is interest in possession, the 'tax pool' cannot be used: ie it is in abeyance. However, if in the future the trust becomes discretionary it can then be used to 'frank' distributions in the usual way. Whilst the interest in possession subsists, the trustees suffer only basic rate income tax (or equivalent) leaving the beneficiary to pay any higher or additional rate tax for which he is liable: see **3.137**.

[68] The deed is revocable during the Trust Period. This enables the Trustees to switch the income to another beneficiary. Note that if nothing is said about the power being exercised revocably then it is irrevocable. For a deed of revocation and new appointment see **Precedent 13.5**.

4. Exclusion of apportionment of income[69]

All income of the Trust Fund received by or on behalf of the Trustees from and after the date of this Deed shall be treated as if it had arisen wholly after such date and no apportionment of income shall be required.

IN WITNESS etc.

---

[69] The Trusts (Capital and Income) Act 2013 makes this clause unnecessary for trusts created on or after 1 October 2013 as it disapplies the apportionment rules: see **14.62** *et seq*. However, it is sensible to include a general statement that apportionments are not required in the interests of clarity.

Precedent 13.5: Exercise of a power of revocation and new appointment to change the interest in possession beneficiary[70]

THIS DEED OF REVOCATION AND APPOINTMENT is made the [   ] day of [   ] 20[   ] by [   ] ('the Appointors').

SUPPLEMENTAL to:

1.   a deed of settlement dated [   ] and made between [   ] ('the Settlement')

2.   a revocable deed of appointment dated [   ] and made by the Appointors ('the Revocable Deed').

WHEREAS

A.   By clause [   ] of the Settlement the Trustees have power to appoint capital and income of the Trust Fund amongst such of the Beneficiaries as they may see fit. The power is exercisable and any exercise may be made revocable during the Trust Period.

B.   By the Revocable Deed B a member of the class of Beneficiaries was appointed a life interest in the income of the Trust Fund.

C.   The Appointors are the present Trustees of the Settlement and are desirous of revoking the Revocable Deed and making such new appointment as is set out below.

D.   The Trust Period has not expired.

NOW THIS DEED WITNESSES

1.   **Definitions**
      In this Deed 'the Trustees', 'the Trust Period', 'the Trust Fund' and 'the Beneficiaries' shall have the meaning given to these terms in the Settlement.

2.   **Revocation of Revocable Deed**
      In exercise of the power reserved to them the Appointors hereby revoke in its entirety the Revocable Deed.

3.   **Exercise of power of appointment**
      In exercise of the power of appointment conferred on them by clause [   ] of the Settlement and of all other relevant powers the Appointors hereby appoint that from and after the date hereof the Trust Fund shall be held on trust to pay the income thereof to C for his life.

4.   **Power of revocation reserved**

---

[70]   Similar comments to those made in relation to **Precedent 13.4** apply to this deed: for IHT purposes it is a 'nothing' and, for CGT, does not lead to a deemed disposal of the trust property. Retain flexibility by making the appointment revocable and, to avoid mathematical calculations, exclude apportionment.

The Trustees may at any time or times during the Trust Period by deed or deeds revoke or vary either wholly or in part the appointment contained in clause 3 above.

5. **No apportionment of income**

All income of the Trust Fund received by or on behalf of the Trustees from and after the date of this Deed shall be treated as if it had arisen wholly after such date.

IN WITNESS etc.

Precedent 13.6: Resolution to transfer assets to a beneficiary pursuant to an express power in the trust deed

We [   ] of [   ] and [   ] of [   ] being the present trustees of the settlement ('the Settlement') dated [   ] and made between [   ] resolve as follows:

1. To transfer and pay immediately the investments and cash sum described in the schedule to [B] for his absolute use and benefit freed and discharged from the trusts powers and provisions contained in the Settlement.

2. Until the date of such transfer and payment to hold such investments and sum of cash for [B] absolutely subject to any lien vested in us as such trustees for any costs or taxes payable in respect of such investments and cash sum.[71]

Dated

SCHEDULE

Investments and Cash Sum

[describe]

Signed

---

[71] For CGT purposes it may be important to establish when the beneficiary is entitled to the property. If this is to be from the date of the resolution, the trustees should declare that they hold the assets for him absolutely (a bare trust) pending a formal transfer since otherwise HMRC may argue that the settlement of the assets continues until they are actually transferred to the beneficiary.

Precedent 13.7: Memorandum of Appropriation

Estate of [*Testator*] deceased

[*Testator*] of [*Address*] died on [*Date*].

His will dated [*Date*] was proved by [*Names of Executors*] at the [*Name*] Registry on [*Date*].

Under the terms of the will, the residuary estate is to be divided between the three charities named below in the percentage shares there set out.

We, [*names*], as Executors of [*Testator*] deceased hereby give notice to ABC, DEF and GHI Charities that we have today appropriated the stocks and shares set out in the Schedule hereto in part satisfaction of each charity's share of the residuary estate of the Testator.

As from the date hereof, we the Executors declare that we shall hold the shares set out in the Schedule hereto as bare Trustees for the three charities and not as Executors of [*Testator*].

SCHEDULE

Charity	% entitlement	Number of shares appropriated
ABC	50	100
DEF	25	50
GHI	25	50

....
Signed   Dated

Precedent 13.8: Definition of Trustees

The expression 'my trustees' means my executors and the trustees of this will from time to time (whether original or substituted) but after there has been a grant of probate or letters of administration in respect of my estate it shall not include, by virtue of the foregoing appointment of executors, any person appointed an executor who for the time being has not proved this will.

CHAPTER 14

TAX EFFICIENT ADMINISTRATION

1. APPROPRIATIONS

14.01 The Administration of Estates Act 1925, s 41 gives personal representatives power to appropriate any of the deceased's real or personal property in or towards satisfaction of any legacy or other interest or share in the deceased's estate. The personal representatives can make the appropriation in such a way as seems just and reasonable according to the respective rights of the persons interested in the deceased's property but must not prejudice a specific gift. The section requires the personal representatives to obtain the consent of the person in whose favour the appropriation is made.

Example 14.01

William leaves shares in X Co to Ann, £20,000 to Ben and residue to Cadfael. The estate also includes shares in Y Co and Z Co.

William's personal representatives can appropriate the Y or Z Co shares in or towards satisfaction of Ben's legacy so long as Ben consents. They cannot appropriate the shares in X Co.

If the beneficiary is absolutely and beneficially entitled to the legacy the consent required is that of the beneficiary or, if the beneficiary is a minor or mentally incapable of managing his own affairs, the consent is that of the beneficiary's parent or guardian, receiver or deputy.

If the legacy is settled the consent is that of the trustees (provided they are not also the personal representatives) or of the person for the time being entitled to the income provided such a person is of full age and capacity. If the personal representatives are the only trustees and there is no person of full age or capacity for the time being entitled to the income no consents are required. However, in this case the appropriation must be of an investment authorised by law or by the will. This limitation as to the type of property appropriated does not exist in other cases.[1]

The requirement for consent is frequently varied by will to allow the personal representatives to appropriate without a formal consent. This used to be done

---

[1]　AEA 1925, s 41(1).

to prevent a charge to stamp duty as an appropriation with consent was treated as a sale. It is no longer necessary for this purpose.[2]

Appropriation at the value at the date of appropriation

14.02   The appropriation is made at value *at the date of the appropriation* not at the value at the date of death.[3] Personal representatives need to be aware of this, particularly in relation to partly exempt and non-exempt beneficiaries, since it can make a great difference to the amount that a legatee will take. HMRC are aware of the legal position and will challenge excessive appropriations.

Example 14.02

Unwin died owning a house worth £325,000 at a time when the nil rate band was £325,000. He had other assets and his will provided for a nil rate band legacy to his nephew, Nathan, with residue to charity. The house is now worth £360,000. The administration of the estate is not complete and nothing has been done in relation to the house or the nil rate band legacy. The executors wish to appropriate the house to Nathan. However, it is too late as the value now exceeds the available nil rate band.

The following points should be considered:

1.   Can Nathan pay the difference between the current value of the property and £325,000? The power of appropriation only allows an appropriation in or towards satisfaction of a legacy so an appropriation is not possible[4] but the personal representatives can exercise their power of sale[5] to sell the asset to Nathan in consideration of a part payment of cash and the satisfaction of the legacy.

2.   Is a post-death variation possible? Nathan and the charity would have to agree to vary the disposition of William's estate to leave the house to Nathan as a specific gift. The charity may, of course, feel unable to enter into a variation which will reduce its share of the estate.

3.   What happens if the personal representatives do appropriate the deceased interest in the house without appreciating the problem? The charity, if it realises what has happened may attempt to recover the excess from Nathan, or, more likely, from the personal representatives on the basis of a devastavit.

---

[2]   From 1 May 1987 when the Stamp Duty (Exempt Instruments) Regulations 1987, SI 1987/516 exempted from duty all instruments giving effect to an appropriation in or towards satisfaction of a general legacy. It may now be preferable to retain the need for consent, as an appropriation of land or quoted shares for less than the value at the date of death can form the basis of a claim for IHT loss relief: see **14.25**. For a consideration of the requirements for an effective appropriation of shares, see *Hughes v Bourne* [2012] EWHC 2232 (Ch).

[3]   See *Re Collins* [1975] 1 WLR 309 and *Re Charteris* [1917] 2 Ch 379.

[4]   *Re Phelps* [1980] Ch 275.

[5]   Under AEA 1925, s 39.

Directions in the will as to date of valuation

14.03 HMRC has accepted that personal representatives can value at the date of the appropriation death when the will included a direction that the personal representatives should have a discretion as to whether to appropriate at death value rather than at the date of the appropriation.

> 'I declare that in exercise of the power conferred by this clause my Trustees shall within the period of 2 years after my death be entitled to exercise such power by valuing the property to be allotted appropriated partitioned or apportioned either as at the date of my death or as at the date of such allotment appropriation partition or apportionment as they shall in their absolute discretion think fit.'[6]

This is a standard precedent but it does raise some problems.

(a) Why a period of 2 years? What is the logic? Why not the executors' year?

(b) On what basis would the personal representatives exercise their discretion? In a family will, the more assets appropriated to the nil rate band legacy, the less is available for the surviving spouse. It may be helpful to include a letter of wishes from the testator indicating the matters the personal representatives should take into account.

Implications of differential CGT rates

14.04 In the case of disposals on or after 23 June 2010 personal representatives pay CGT at 28%. For individuals the rate remains at 18% where total taxable gains *and income* are less than the upper limit of the income tax basic rate band (£31,785 in 2015–16) and is only 28% to the extent that the gain, when aggregated with income, exceeds that limit.[7]

This means that if personal representatives are planning to sell an asset which will realise a gain at a time when they have no annual exemption,[8] they should consider appropriating the asset to a beneficiary and letting the beneficiary make the disposal. A CGT saving will be achieved in any of the following situations:

(a) the beneficiary has part or all of his annual exemption available;

(b) the beneficiary will pay at 18% on any part of the gain;

(c) the beneficiary has losses available to offset the gain.

Personal representatives should also consider appropriating assets to a beneficiary where the sale will realise a loss and it is apparent that the personal representatives will not be making further disposals producing gains to make use of the losses.

---

[6] See also the STEP Standard Provisions, 2nd edn, which provide for a 3-year period.

[7] See **3.85**.

[8] The PRs exemption is the same as that of an individual but is available only in the tax year of death and the 2 following tax years.

Appropriations where there are outstanding liabilities

14.05 Personal representatives may find they have an outstanding liability and no liquid funds but that the assets in the estate are all showing gains. Section 36(10) of the Administration of Estates Act 1925 allows them to transfer an asset to a beneficiary charged with a debt.

More than one beneficiary entitled

14.06 A simple appropriation is not possible where more than one beneficiary is involved. Assume, for instance, that included in the estate is the deceased's house which is to be sold and the proceeds distributed amongst a number of beneficiaries. Appropriations of undivided shares in the land can most easily be achieved by the personal representatives declaring:

(a)   that the property is appropriated to the beneficiaries in accordance with their respective shares; and

(b)   that legal title is accordingly held by the personal representatives (now as bare trustees) for the beneficiaries.

The consequences of this are:

(i)   that for CGT purposes the beneficiaries are absolutely entitled as against the trustees so that any disposal will be treated as a disposal by the beneficiaries;

(ii) the trustees, having retained the title to the property, have a lien over it for expenses, etc.[9]

Charities as residuary beneficiaries

14.07 Charities benefit from a CGT exemption in respect of gains realised on the disposal of assets if the gains are applicable and applied for charitable purposes.[10] However, the exemption will only apply if the relevant property is beneficially owned by the charity. If, during the administration of an estate, an asset has increased in value since the date of death and is to be sold with the proceeds distributed to charity, it will be attractive either for the assets to be vested in the name of the charity prior to the sale, or for the executors to execute an assent declaring that they hold the asset for the charity absolutely. Failure to take these steps will mean that the gain will be realised by the executors and not by the charity and HMRC will claim CGT on the gain realised, even if the benefit of the sale proceeds pass to the charity. The need to consider appropriation before sale is a good reason for consulting charities early in the administration.

---

[9]   And note that the existence of the lien does not affect the CGT position: see TCGA 1992, s 60(2) and see *McLaughlin v RCC* [2012] UKFTT 174 (TC) and *Tarlochan Singh v RCC* [2011] UKFTT 584 (TC).

[10] TCGA 1992, s 256: see **Precedent 13.7**.

Many of the major charities have helpful notes advising executors on the correct procedure. See, for example, the note issued by the Guide Dogs for the Blind Association:

> 'May we please draw the attention of the executors and their advisers to the fact that as a national charity we are exempt, under the provisions of TCGA 1992, s 256(1), from payment of capital gains tax on the sale of any securities made on our behalf.
>
> The exemption relates to any sale made on our behalf in respect of the residue or shares of the residue of the estate to which we are entitled.
>
> The procedure to be followed to comply with HMRC requirements is that the securities should be appropriated to our account by a simple but clear designation in your books, or by a memorandum or resolution signed by the PRs in your files. Any sales subsequently made by you are made as bare trustee on our behalf under TCGA 1992, s 60.
>
> Executors should be careful if they require an indemnity from the charity for the payment of administration expenses in return for the transfer of assets to the charity. The Revenue may argue that such an indemnity is to be construed as a payment for the asset and accordingly a sale by the executors, or alternatively that the gain realised by the charity is not fully applicable and applied for charitable purposes.'

Appropriations and self-dealing

14.08 A disposition of trust property to a trustee is automatically voidable at the suit of a beneficiary (the rule against self-dealing), unless authorised by the trust instrument.[11] The rule also applies to personal representatives and is something of a trap since nothing in s 41 exempts personal representatives from the rule. *Kane v Radley-Kane*[12] is a good illustration of the effects of the rule.

The deceased had died intestate married to a second wife and with adult children from his first marriage. The estate (which included a number of shares in an unquoted company) had been valued at £93,000 with the shares valued at £50,000. The widow was entitled to the statutory widow's legacy which at the time was £125,000 and to a life interest in one-half of any residuary estate after payment out of that sum. In view of the size of the estate the widow was appointed sole personal representative. She treated herself as being absolutely entitled to all the assets of the estate in part satisfaction of her statutory legacy and registered the shares in her name without obtaining the consent of the other beneficiaries. She subsequently sold the shares for £1,131,438. One of the sons applied for a declaration that the appropriation was invalid and that the proceeds of the sale of the shares formed part of the assets of the estate. The court granted the declaration. It said such an appropriation is voidable unless:

---

[11] For reasons of clarity the authorisation should be express although it may be implied from the terms of the trust instrument: see **2.68** and **13.21**.

[12] [1999] Ch 274.

(a) the will authorises beneficiaries who are personal representatives to 'self-deal';[13]

(b) the appropriations are of cash or assets which are equivalent to cash, such as government stock or quoted securities.

Where neither of these exceptions apply, personal representatives who wish to appropriate assets to themselves must either obtain the consent of the other beneficiaries or the sanction of the court.

Retaining a power to re-appropriate

14.09 All too often, assets are appropriated into different funds and subsequently it is desired to switch those assets. For instance, assume that a will creates two trust funds, one for the testator's son and his family and the other for his daughter and her family. The trustees appropriate land to the son's fund and stocks and shares to the daughter's. Subsequently the daughter marries a farmer and the son determines to train for the church. Accordingly the daughter would like the land switched to her fund and son would like the stocks and shares switched to his fund. To allow for the possibility of switching between funds, the original appropriation should reserve an appropriate power.

See **Precedent 14.1**.

2. PROBLEMS ARISING FROM LOW INTEREST RATES AND LOW INFLATION

14.10 Low interest rates and asset values pose particular difficulties for executors and trustees.

Power to apply capital for impoverished life tenant

14.11 Trustees may be under pressure to increase payments to a life tenant whose income has fallen. Many modern settlements and will trusts give a power to pay capital to a life tenant and this power may be used to top-up income (in the absence of such a power, such a beneficiary will have no entitlement to capital).

14.12 The trustees should ensure that such top-up payments do not become income in the hands of the beneficiary (thereby attracting an income tax charge). In general, provided that the beneficiary has no 'right' to have his income maintained at a particular level and that the trustees can be shown to be exercising their discretionary powers over capital, it is thought that the additional payment will retain its capital nature.[14]

---

13   See **Precedent 4.1, clause 13**.
14   See generally *Brodie's WT v IRC* (1933) 17 TC 432 and *Cunard's Trustees v IRC* [1946] 1 All ER 159.

Is it permissible to invest for income at the expense of capital?

14.13 Trustees must act impartially and it is often said that they must hold the scales equally between tenant for life and remainderman. However, in *Nestle v National Westminster Bank*,[15] Hoffmann J said that he did not like the traditional image of the scales and preferred to express the duty in the following way:

> 'the trustee must act fairly in making investment decisions which may have different consequences for different classes of beneficiaries.'

He had two reasons for disliking the image of the scales:

(a) it suggests a weighing of known quantities whereas investment decisions are concerned with expectations and predictions which may not be met;

(b) it suggests a more mechanistic process than the law requires. The trustees have a wide discretion. They are entitled to take into account the income needs of the tenant for life or the fact that the tenant for life was a primary object of the trust whereas the remainderman was a remoter relative or a stranger:

> 'Of course these cannot be allowed to become the overriding considerations but the concept of fairness between classes of beneficiaries does not require them to be excluded. It would be an inhuman law which required trustees to adhere to some mechanical rule for preserving the real value of the capital when the tenant for life was the testator's widow who had fallen upon hard times and the remainderman was young and well off.'

14.14 On appeal to the Court of Appeal this aspect of the judgment did not attract much attention but Staughton LJ said:

> 'The obligation of a trustee is to administer the trust fund impartially, or fairly (I can see no significant difference), having regard to the different interests of beneficiaries. Wilberforce J said in *Re Pauling's Settlement, Younghusband v Coutts & Co (No 2)* [1963] 1 All ER 857 at 862, [1963] Ch 576 at 586:
>
> > "The new trustees would be under the normal duty of preserving an equitable balance, and if at any time it was shown that they were inclining one way or the other, it would not be a difficult matter to bring them to account."
>
> At times it will not be easy to decide what is an equitable balance. A life tenant may be anxious to receive the highest possible income, whilst the remainderman will wish the real value of the trust fund to be preserved. If the life tenant is living in penury and the remainderman already has ample wealth, common sense suggests that a trustee should be able to take that into account, not necessarily by seeking the highest possible income at the expense of capital but by inclining in that direction. However, before adopting that course a trustee should, I think,

---

[15] [2000] WTLR 795.

require some verification of the facts. In this case the trustees did not, so far as I am aware, have any reliable information as to the relative wealth of the life tenants and [the remainderman].'[16]

Trustees and modern portfolio theory

14.15 Increasingly, trust funds are administered in accordance with 'modern portfolio theory'. This theory, developed by economists and financial analysts, may be expressed in the following propositions:

(a) investment decisions must be based upon the two extremes of risk and return;

(b) from this, it follows that the greater the risk the greater the return;

(c) this balance between risk and return has to be taken into account in the overall management of a portfolio and because diversification is fundamental to managing risk is a basic consideration in all prudent investment management.

14.16 From these factors, it can be seen that the making of a particular investment cannot be characterised as *in itself* prudent or imprudent: rather it must be considered as part of the overall composition of the portfolio. It may therefore be concluded that:

(a) there is no such thing as a speculative investment *per se*; and

(b) low risk investment may be judged imprudent.

It may be said under the tenets of modern portfolio theory that trustees should invest the trust fund, in the light of the particular circumstances of the trust (which determines the investment strategy to be pursued), with a view to the proper management of risk: a wholly different approach from the nineteenth-century view that the paramount duty of a trustee was to maintain the value of the trust fund.[17]

To what extent should trustees embrace modern portfolio theory and, specifically, how will it affect actions for breach of trust brought against trustees? Hoffmann J, at first instance, in the *Nestle* case, commented:

---

[16] The Law Commission consulted on the relevance of personal circumstances to investment decisions. Its Report said: 'We note that a narrow majority of the consultees who addressed the Consultation Paper's questions supported the approach advocated by Mr Justice Hoffmann at first instance in *Nestle* and by Lord Justice Staughton in the Court of Appeal.' Nevertheless, the Report made no recommendations.

[17] 'Preservation of real value can be no more than an aspiration which some trustees may have the good fortune to achieve': Hoffmann J in *Nestle v National Westminster Bank plc* [2000] WTLR 795, at 803.

'Modern trustees acting within their investment powers are entitled to be judged by the standards of current portfolio theory, which emphasises the risk level of the entire portfolio rather than the risk attaching to each investment taken in isolation.'

14.17   Extra judicially, Lord Nicholls of Birkenhead commented as follows:[18]

'(Investment) policy is aimed at producing a portfolio of investments which is balanced overall and suited to the needs of the particular trust ... Such a strategy falls to be judged likewise, that is overall. Different investments are accompanied by different degrees of risk, which are reflected in the expected rate of return. A large fund with a widely diversified portfolio of securities might justifiably include modest holdings of high risk strategies which will be altogether imprudent and out of place in a smaller fund.

In such a case it would be inappropriate to isolate one particular investment out of a vast portfolio and enquire whether that can be justified as a trust investment. Such a "line by line" approach is misplaced. The enquiry, rather, should be to look at a particular investment and enquire whether that is justified in a holding in the context of the overall portfolio. Traditional warnings against the need for trustees to avoid speculative or hazardous investments are not to be read as inhibiting trustees from maintaining portfolios of investments which contain a prudent and sensible mixture of low risk and higher risk securities. They are not to be so read, because they were not directed at a portfolio which is a balanced exercise in risk management.'

14.18   Much will obviously depend on the strategy that is appropriate for a particular trust fund and, as made clear in Lord Nicholls' article, the size of the fund is a crucial factor. So too will be evidence that the settlor wished the life tenant to be viewed as the principal beneficiary so that trustees may be justified in investing with a view to the production of greater income, albeit at the expense of capital growth, than would otherwise have been the case.[19]

14.19   The portfolio theory also predicates that investment should not be dictated by the need to produce a certain income return. Ideally on this theory, income may be viewed as a maximum amount that an individual can consume

---

18   In 'Trustees and their broader community: where duty, morality and ethics converge' (1995) 9 Trusts Law International 71.

19   Commenting on the observations of Megarry VC in *Cowan v Scargill* [1985] Ch 270 that trustees have a duty 'to exercise their powers in the best interests in the present and future beneficiaries of the trust, holding the scales impartially between the different classes of beneficiaries', Hoffmann J in the *Nestle* case noted that 'a trustee must act fairly in making investment decisions which may have different consequences for different classes of beneficiaries ... the trustees have a wide discretion. They are, for example, entitled to take into account the income needs of the tenant for life or the fact that the tenant for life was a person known to the settlor and a primary object of the trust whereas the remainderman is a remoter relative or stranger. Of course, these cannot be allowed to become overriding considerations but the concept of fairness between classes of beneficiaries does not require them to be excluded. It would be an inhuman rule which required trustees to adhere to some mechanical rule for preserving the real value of capital when a tenant for life was the testator's widow who had fallen upon hard times and the remainderman was young and well off.'

in a week and still expect to be as well off at the end of the week as he was at the beginning, treating capital gains as if they were income available for distribution.[20]

Often, however, the legal distinction between income and capital is crucial and will affect the investment strategy of the trustees: for instance, in the case of the standard life interest trust. However, even in this situation trustees may find that they have a power to pay capital to the life tenant thereby enabling the income return to be supplemented if appropriate.[21]

Reviewing debt/providing fresh security

14.20 Falling asset values may lead to lenders reviewing their outstanding loans and, if not calling them in, seeking greater security. Trustees should avoid giving security over trust assets attracting business and agricultural property at 100%. The general IHT rule is that 'a liability which is an incumbrance on any property shall, so far as possible, be taken to reduce the value of that property'.[22] If existing debts are charged over, for example, a farm, it is desirable to switch them to non-relievable assets (such as the trust's investment portfolio).

The recent limitations on deductibility of debts restrict deduction for IHT purposes where borrowing is charged on non-relievable assets and used to acquire relievable assets.[23] However, it does not affect the restructuring of existing borrowing in this way.

It is also important to remember that personal debts of a deceased which exceed his personal estate cannot be deducted from property which is deemed to be included in his estate because he has a qualifying interest in possession or as a result of the reservation of benefit rules.[24]

Delay in selling an investment

14.21 The Trustee Act 2000, s 4(2) puts trustees (and personal representatives) under a duty to review the investments of the trust and to consider whether they should be varied. In the past, annual reviews were the norm but in the present volatile state of the markets more regular reviews are likely to be desirable.

---

[20]   See JR Hicks, *Value and Capital* (1938), p 177.
[21]   With care, capital used for this purpose will not be taxed as income: contrast *Brodie's Will Trustees v IRC* (1933) 17 TC 432 and *Cunard, Trustees v IRC* [1946] 1 All ER 159, 27 TC 122, CA (illustrating that trustees should not be required to make the income of the life tenant up to a prescribed level out of the capital if it would otherwise suffer a deficiency) with regular payments made in the trustees discretion in *Stevenson v Wishart* [1987] 2 All ER 428, CA.
[22]   See IHTA 1984, s 162(4).
[23]   IHTA 1984, s 162B Introduced by Finance Act 2013 for borrowings made on or after 6 April 2013. See **3.12**.
[24]   *St Barbe Green v IRC* [2005] STC 288. See **3.07**.

14.22 If the trust owns a substantial shareholding in the family business, given that the business may be a major source of the family wealth, the trustees will commonly be under pressure not to 'rock the boat' which may include desisting from disposing of their shares or seeking a winding-up of the company and, in other cases, to provide additional funding. Commonly, some protection for trustees is afforded by anti-*Bartlett* clauses[25] and by trustee exoneration clauses. In general, however, trustees should be careful about investing further funds in a business which is showing signs of failing.

14.23 The trust instrument may include a direction that shares are to be retained and the trustees may use such a direction as a defence, arguing that this sets aside more general obligations to invest prudently or to diversify. It has been held that specific trust directions may oust the trustees' investment discretion altogether.[26] Of course, in appropriate cases the trustees may wish to apply to court under the Trustee Act 1925, s 57 to have such a direction removed.

14.24 *Gregson v HAE Trustees Ltd*[27] sheds some light on the relationship between the Trustee Act 2000 duties and the trust instrument. The family that owned the furniture company Courts plc created a trust company, HAE Ltd which was appointed trustee of a number of family settlements. The claimant was a beneficiary of one of those settlements. Substantially the whole of the property of the settlement consisted of shares in Courts which the settlor transferred to HAE shortly after the settlement was created. None of the Courts shares represented later purchases by HAE. Courts eventually went into administration and it became insolvent (with an estimated deficit of £70m), making the shares which constituted the property of the trust worthless. The claimant alleged that HAE had a duty to consider the need to diversify the assets of the settlement[28] when reviewing the trust investments[29] and had breached that duty. If it had considered the need for diversification and taken appropriate professional advice, it would have diversified and avoided the

---

[25] *Re Lucking's Will Trusts* [1967] 3 All ER 726 and *Bartlett v Barclays Bank* [1980] Ch 515 both suggest that a shareholding in a private company large enough to confer some measure of control brings special responsibilities. It is not enough for trustees to leave the conduct of the business to the directors. They are under a duty to keep themselves informed about the company's affairs and the directors' plans. They must be willing to act on the information and will be liable for a breach of trust if they fail to take steps to prevent the dissipation of the company's assets in a speculative and ill-considered venture. However, unless specially chosen for their expertise, trustees will not normally have the expertise to satisfy themselves that a trading company is being managed prudently. It is, therefore, common to include so-called anti-*Bartlett* clauses which limit the obligations of trustees in relation to such shareholdings. Clauses vary widely some may simply remove the obligation to supervise, others may prohibit trustees from using the votes attached to the trust's shares. There is a discussion of types of anti-*Bartlett* clause in *Lewin on Trusts* (19th edn, 2015), at **34.50**.

[26] *Re Hurst* [1890] 63 LT 665.

[27] [2009] 1 All ER (Comm) 457.

[28] Part of the standard investment criteria contained in TA 2000, s 4(3).

[29] As required by TA 2000, s 4(2).

losses suffered. Since HAE had no assets, the real targets were the directors of HAE (mostly members of the family that owned Courts), a so-called 'dog-leg' claim.

Although the dog-leg claim was rejected, the court was asked to rule on whether HAE, as trustee, had a duty to consider diversification when reviewing the trust fund.

Section 4 provides:

> '(1) In exercising any power of investment, whether arising under this Part or otherwise, a trustee must have regard to the standard investment criteria.
>
> (2) A trustee must from time to time review the investments of the trust and consider whether, having regard to the standard investment criteria, they should be varied.
>
> (3) The standard investment criteria, in relation to a trust, are:
>
> (a)   the suitability to the trust of investments of the same kind as any particular investment proposed to be made or retained and of that particular investment as an investment of that kind, and
> (b)   the need for diversification of investments of the trust, in so far as is appropriate to the circumstances of the trust.'

The court made the following points:

(a)   the subsection 1 duty to have regard to the standard investment criteria applies to the retention of original assets as well as to new investments made by the trustees;

(b)   there is no requirement to diversify. Section 4(3)(b), which deals with diversification, contains the qualification 'in so far as is appropriate to the circumstances of the trust'. Hence, trustees can properly take into account matters such as the nature and purposes of the settlement, the terms of the trust instrument, any letter of wishes and the shareholdings of other family members.

3. LOSS ON SALE RELIEF

14.25   IHT is charged on the market value of property at the date of death.[30] In general, changes in value after death are ignored. Accordingly if shares in the family investment company are worth £1m at death but within 6 months the letting market collapses and they become valueless, there is no relief against the IHT charge on the probate value. IHTA 1984, s 171(2) provides only a limited exception in allowing the value at death to be revised where that value has been changed 'by reason of the death'. This can result in the value being increased

---

[30]   IHTA 1984, s 160.

(eg where a life insurance policy on the deceased's life is included in the estate) or reduced (eg when there is a business resulting from the death of a charismatic proprietor).

Loss on sale relief enables the probate value to be revised but only in respect of certain property (land and quoted shares) and only if that property is sold within a prescribed period of the death. A fall in value of retained property does not attract any relief.

14.26 IHT loss on sale relief may be claimed where land or interests in land or qualifying investments are sold within 4 years or 12 months respectively of death for less than their probate value by 'the appropriate person'.[31]

One problem, particularly in the case of land, is that a sale may not take place for some considerable time after the death. Until sale, personal representatives will have to pay IHT on the district valuer's assessment of the value. Exercising the instalment option will reduce the need for cash in the short term, although interest is payable on the unpaid tax. In relation to qualifying investments personal representatives may have difficulty in deciding whether to sell or to retain them in the hope of a rise in the market.

It is the date of 'sale' which is relevant. In the case of land, s 198 provides that this is the date on which a contract to sell is entered into.[32]

Sale must be by the 'appropriate person'

14.27 The 'appropriate person' is the person liable for the IHT or, if there is more than one such person, the person actually paying.[33] This will normally be the personal representatives but could include others, for example, a surviving joint tenant. Beneficiaries who sell assets transferred to them cannot make claims unless they are actually paying the tax. A claim must state the capacity of the claimant.[34] Hence, if the personal representatives assent assets to a beneficiary and the beneficiary sells, this will normally mean the relief is not available. However:

(a) HMRC accepts that where the personal representatives and the beneficiaries are identical, relief can be claimed;

(b) the beneficiary may be the appropriate person, for example, in the case of land the beneficiary may be paying the instalments. Note, however, that it is unwise for personal representatives to release all the assets to beneficiaries relying on them to pay the IHT instalments. The personal

---

[31] The provisions dealing with the sale of quoted investments are contained in IHTA 1984, ss 178–189 and those dealing with the sale of land in ss 190–198.

[32] The contract must result in completion of the sale (whether or not within the 4-year period). A contract which is rescinded without ever being completed does not count as a sale for the purposes of the relief: see *Jones (Balls' Administrators) v IRC* [1997] STC 358.

[33] IHTA 1984, ss 178 and 190.

[34] IHTA 1984, ss 179(3) and 199(1)(b).

representatives remain liable for the IHT and this can produce real problems if the beneficiaries do not pay.[35]

Restrictions on relief

14.28 Loss on sale relief is intended to help those who have to sell for administration purposes not for those who are simply selling to reinvest the proceeds in similar assets. Hence the relief is restricted if the appropriate person buys:

(a)   new qualifying investments within the period starting with death and ending 2 months after the date of the last sale;[36] or

(b)   new land or an interest in land within the period starting with death and ending 4 months after the last sale.[37]

The amount of the relief is reduced by the proportion that the gross purchase price bears to the gross sale value. Of course a personal representative may also be a beneficiary or a trustee. A purchase in the capacity of beneficiary or trustee as opposed to personal representative does not restrict the relief provided the change in capacity is clear. IHTM para 34213 says:

'In general the major change in capacity from PR to trustee/legatee will only occur when the estate has been fully administered and the residue is ascertained

However, a change of capacity will occur if an irrevocable appropriation of assets – including cash from the proceeds of shares – is made under either

•   specific powers included in the will, or
•   the general authority of s 41 Administration of Estates Act 1925.

So for example, if

•   the PRs appropriate investments to the trustees of an existing trust, and
•   the trustees then make purchases of qualifying investments using the proceeds from the sale of these investments

then the purchases are not taken into account by the appropriate person when considering an application for a loss on sale relief and the restrictions imposed by IHTA84/s 180.

If, however, the trust was established by the Will of the deceased and the executors were also the trustees, in the absence of an assent to the trustees, it is likely that the purchases will be by the appropriate persons in the same capacity. In this case, s 180 will apply.'

---

[35]   See *Howarth's Executors v CIR* [1997] STI 640 for a horrid example of the problems the personal representative can face where the beneficiary does not pay.
[36]   IHTA 1984, s 180 where relief is claimed in relation to qualifying investments.
[37]   IHTA 1984, s 192 where relief is claimed in relation to land.

Beneficiaries want to retain assets and benefit from relief

14.29 A common problem is that beneficiaries may not want the personal representatives to sell assets at a loss but still want the IHT reduction. In the case of qualifying investments there is nothing to stop a beneficiary buying the same investments the PRs have just sold. However, a neater solution may be for the personal representatives to appropriate the investments to the beneficiary. HMRC accepts that an appropriation made by the personal representatives to a pecuniary legatee[38] is a sale for this purpose if it is made:

(a)   in satisfaction of a pecuniary legacy;

(b)   with the consent of the legatee under AEA 1925, s 41; and

(c)   there is no power of appropriation without that consent.

IHTM para 34153 says:

> 'where the Will allows appropriation of assets in satisfaction of a pecuniary legacy without consent, such appropriation, even if made with consent, should not be treated as a sale.
>
> If it is claimed that the PRs do not need the legatee's consent to the appropriation, provided they can confirm that the legatee falls within s 41 Administration of Estates Act 1925 then the appropriation can be accepted. (Legatees falling within the scope of the act include unborn children, untraced beneficiaries, a mentally disordered person without a receiver.) In all other cases you should refer the claim to Technical Group. You should also refer your case to Technical Group if it is claimed that the appropriation was in favour of a residuary beneficiary.'

In the case of land the relief is not available if the sale is to a beneficiary or close relative:[39] see **14.36**.

Qualifying investments – how does the relief work?

14.30 Qualifying investments are holdings in authorised unit trusts and shares quoted on a recognised stock exchange.[40] This includes NASDAQ but not shares traded on AIM. The appropriate person has to make the claim in relation to the aggregate proceeds of all the qualifying investments he has sold in the period of 12 months following the death.[41] It is not possible to limit the claim to only those qualifying investments that have fallen in value.

Example 14.03

An estate includes holdings in A Co, B Co and C Co, each worth £20,000 at the date of death. The personal representatives sell the A shares for £10,000, the B

---

[38]   But not, apparently, to a residuary beneficiary.
[39]   IHTA 1984, s 191(3).
[40]   IHTA 1984, s 178 and IHTM para 34131.
[41]   IHTA 1984, s 179.

shares for £5,000 giving a claim for loss on sale relief of £25,000. If they then sell the C shares within 12 months of death for £40,000, the aggregate loss is reduced by that £20,000 profit to only £5,000.

To maximise relief personal representatives should aim to sell 'loss' shares within the 12-month period and to postpone sales of 'gain' shares beyond that period. If this is not possible, they could consider transferring 'gain' shares to beneficiaries and letting them make the sale.

If the aggregate sale proceeds exceed the value at death, the personal representatives do not have to increase the IHT value of the qualifying investments. So in the above example had the C shares increased to £50,000, the total aggregate sale proceeds would have increased to £65,000 but the personal representatives would not have been required to pay more tax. They would simply be denied relief.

The relief must be claimed using Form IHT35 and within 4 years of the end of the 12 month qualifying period. Special rules apply if there are changes in shareholdings between the date of death and the date of sale, for example, where there is a company re-organisation (eg a rights or bonus issue).[42]

Value reduced for CGT

14.31 If the personal representatives claim the relief, the value of the shares is also reduced for CGT purposes.[43] It is, therefore, not possible to claim both an IHT reduction and a CGT loss (save for any incidental expenses incurred on the disposal). Normally the IHT saving is preferable but not if the estate is exempt or only just exceeds the nil rate band threshold. However, the CGT loss is of no use to the personal representatives unless they have gains against which to set it.[44]

Unsaleable investments

14.32 Relief is available if a share is suspended and remains suspended 12 months after the date of death. The shares are treated as having been sold immediately before the end of the period of 12 months following the date of death for a price equal to their value at that time.[45] Shares which are cancelled without replacement within 12 months of the death are treated as having been sold immediately before cancellation for £1.[46]

---

[42] IHTA 1984, s 183 and see IHTM para 34181.
[43] IHTA 1984, s 187.
[44] See also **14.39**.
[45] IHTA 1984, s 186B.
[46] IHTA 1984, s 186A. Special arrangements were made to treat shares in Northern Rock as cancelled where the owner died in the period 22 February 2007 to 21 February 2008 (inclusive), and the PRs still held the shares when they were taken into public ownership on 22 February 2008. See *IHT Newsletter*, August 2008 (similar arrangements were made for shares in *Bradford and Bingley* where the owner died in the period 29 September 2007 to 28 September 2008).

Land or interests in land – how does the relief work?

14.33 Where an interest in land is sold within 3 years of death, the personal representatives can claim that the sale price be substituted for the probate value of that interest. Once the relief is claimed the sale price of all interests in land sold within the 3-year period must be substituted for their date of death value.[47]

Land sold in the fourth year following death will be treated as sold within the 3-year period if it is sold for *less* than probate value but not if it is sold for more.[48] Where the claim for relief relates to a lease of less than 50 years duration the sale price is adjusted.[49]

The relief is claimed using Form IHT38. The claim must be made within 4 years of the end of the 3–year period during which qualifying sales can be made.[50]

Claims in relation to land may be disadvantageous

14.34 In the case of land (unlike qualifying investments) values can be increased as well as reduced as a result of making a claim. This could be disadvantageous for the estate and result in an increased IHT bill. It is, therefore, best to postpone making a claim until it is certain that there will be no further sales. There is no procedure for withdrawing a disadvantageous claim.[51]

> *Example 14.04*
>
> Plot A and Plot B are both worth £100,000 at death. Plot A is sold for £60,000 and Plot B is sold for £200,000.
>
> If relief is claimed on Plot A, the value of Plot B must be increased.

De minimis losses

14.35 De minimis losses, defined as the lower of £1,000 or 5% of the value of the land at death are ignored.[52]

Artificial sales

14.36 The relief is not available if the sale is to a person beneficially entitled to the property sold or to the spouse, civil partner or issue of such a person.[53] However HMRC interprets the section in a way which is helpful for taxpayers. IHTM para 33082 says:

---

[47] IHTA 1984, s 191.
[48] IHTA 1984, s 197A.
[49] IHTA 1984, s 194.
[50] IHTA 1984, s 191(1A). This time limit came into effect on 1 April 2011. Before this date the claim period was 6 years from the date of the last payment or repayment.
[51] See IHTM para 33013.
[52] IHTA 1984, s 191(2).
[53] IHTA 1984, s 191(3).

'Essentially, the interest sold must be exactly the same as the beneficiary's interest in order for relief not to be available.'

The following examples are taken from the IHT Manual at para 33082.

Example 14.05

'1. A house is left to Angela, Brian and Carol. Angela buys the house from the executors. The property 'comprising' the interest sold is the whole house. Angela's beneficial interest was in a 1/3 share only. Her beneficial entitlement was included in the interest sold but was not the interest sold, which was the whole. As a result the sale qualifies for relief.

2. A house is left to Aarif and Basheera. Basheera's half share of the house is sold to Aarif's son. The relief is allowed because the sale is to the child of a beneficiary of a different share.

3. A house is left to Chandra as sole beneficiary. The house is sold to Chandra's daughter. IHTA 1984 s 191 (3) (a)(ii) will prevent the relief from applying, as the sale is of the same interest (the whole) to the child of the original beneficiary of the interest.'

Para 33082 continues:

'If relief is available, it should be allowed **in full**. The relief should **not** be split pro-rata and restricted to reflect the interest of any original beneficiary's share. For example, if a whole house is sold for £70,000 (valued at death at £100,000) to a person who had an interest in a 1/3 share as a beneficiary, the relief allowable would be £30,000. Any cases which cause difficulty should be referred to Technical Group.

You must take care to determine in allowable cases that the agreed sale price is the best consideration for the property at the date of the sale.'

Where family members wish to retain land until prices improve but want to crystallise a claim for loss relief, consider selling to a company or family trust within the 4-year window. There is, however, a downside to such an arrangement. The sale will cause the loss of the instalment option so that all the outstanding IHT on the property will become payable.[54]

Co-ownership discount

14.37 Where the deceased was a co-owner of land, there will normally be a discount of 10%–15% allowed on the value of the deceased's interest to reflect the difficulty of selling a share in a property. If the land is sold for less than probate value, the loss relief substitutes the sale price for the probate value. One-half of the sale price may be *more* than one-half of the discounted value at

---

[54]   The sale may also produce an SDLT liability.

the date of death. Remember that the election cannot be withdrawn if it proves to be disadvantageous. The following example is taken from the IHT Manual.[55]

Example 14.06

'The deceased owned a half-share of "The Gallops".

At the date of death "The Gallops" was valued at £200,000 for the whole, £90,000 for the deceased's half share.

A year after the death, the whole property was sold for £190,000.

The sale value of the property for the purposes of IHTA 1984, s 191 is an arithmetic half share of the gross proceeds of sale, which is £95,000.

So, any claim would not be in the taxpayer's favour as additional Inheritance Tax would be payable as a result of the claim.'

Changes to the interest in or to the underlying land

14.38 The sale price has to be adjusted if the interest in land or the land itself changes between death and sale.[56] Where the revaluation of the interest results in a revised date of death value that is greater, the sale price is reduced to what it would have been if the changes had not occurred.

Example 14.07

At the time of death the market value of land is £100,000. Within the 4-year period a house is built on the land. The market value at the date of sale of the land with the house is £250,000 but without the house the value of the land would have been £80,000. Had the house been on the land at the time of death its value would have exceeded £100,000 (the value of the land at the date of death). For relief purposes the sale value is taken to be £80,000.

If this revised value is less than the actual date of death value, an addition must be made to the sale price of the interest in land. The amount of the addition is equal to the difference between:

(a) the value on death of the interest; and

(b) what the value would have been if the circumstances prevailing at the date of sale had prevailed immediately before the death.

Example 14.08

At the time of death the market value of land is £120,000. Within the 4-year period a depreciatory lease is granted. Had this been in existence at the date of death the land would have been worth £70,000.

The sale price subject to the lease is £60,000.

For relief purposes the sale price of £60,000 is increased by £50,000 (£120,000 – £70,000) to £110,000.

---

[55] IHTM para 33182.
[56] IHTA 1984, s 193. See also IHTM paras 33122 and 33123.

The relief on land and CGT

14.39   There is no provision which specifically states that the changed value becomes the CGT acquisition value. However, TCGA 1992, s 274 provides that where IHT is chargeable on an estate and the value of an asset has been *ascertained* for the purposes of IHT, that value shall be taken as the acquisition value for CGT. In *Stonor v IRC*,[57] personal representatives unsuccessfully claimed the relief where no IHT was payable simply to increase the acquisition value for CGT purposes. The Special Commissioner agreed with the Revenue that this was impossible. The claim has to be made by the appropriate person, that is the person paying the tax. If there is no tax payable, there is no appropriate person.

4. TRUST CAPITAL OR INCOME?

14.40   Trustees need to distinguish income receipts from capital receipts for tax and distribution purposes.[58] Often the distinction is clear but not always.

Many of the cases concern distributions by companies to trustee shareholders. The directors of a company which makes a profit (whether a trading profit or a capital profit) and who want to pass the benefit to their shareholders generally have two courses of action available to them. They may choose to distribute the profit to the company's shareholders in the form of a dividend. Alternatively they may capitalise the profit by issuing more shares to the shareholders.

The rule in *Bouch v Sproule*[59]

14.41   The rule in *Bouch v Sproule* is that generally profits of a company that are distributed by the company by way of dividend are received by trustees as trust income. If there is an interest in possession in the trust, such income belongs to the beneficiary. Payments made by the company as capital, or which are appropriated to the capital of the company, are capital and belong to the trust as such. The essence of the rule is encapsulated in the following passage from the judgment of Fry LJ in the Court of Appeal, which was cited with approval by Lord Herschell:[60]

---

[57]   [2001] STC (SCD) 199. In this case the residuary estate was left to charity and so exempt and the non-residuary estate was within the deceased's nil rate band. It would seem that a similar conclusion would be reached if property benefitted from 100% APR on death and was later sold at a profit. Again, no one would be liable for the tax to make the claim. Further, the values would not (as the Revenue successfully argued in *Stonor*) in any event be 'ascertained' for CGT purposes (as required by TCGA 1992, s 274). See IHTM33026. The position might be different if the relief was restricted because the market value of the land exceeded its agricultural value with the result that some IHT was payable.

[58]   Likewise trust expenses need to be correctly classified.

[59]   (1885) 12 App Cas 385.

[60]   At 397–398.

'When a testator or settlor directs or permits the subject of his disposition to remain as shares or stocks in a company which has the power either of distributing its profits as dividend or of converting them into capital, and the company validly exercises this power, such exercise of its power is binding on all persons interested under the testator or settlor in the shares, and consequently what is paid by the company as dividend goes to the tenant for life, and what is paid by the company to the shareholder as capital, or appropriated as an increase in the capital stock in the concern, enures to the benefit of all who are interested in the capital.'

14.42 When a company capitalises its profits, the classification produced by the rule in *Bouch v Sproule* does reflect reality as far as the company is concerned. The capitalised profits remain within the company so that the sum total of the company's assets remains unchanged. As the overall number of issued shares increases so the value of each individual share decreases. In these circumstances it would be unfair on the beneficiary interested in capital to attribute the additional allotted shares to income. It is similarly self-evident that current trading profits, distributed to shareholders as dividends, should be considered income; what the company received as income is distributed as income.

The result may be less appropriate where a company is deemed to have distributed accumulated profits to shareholders by way of dividend. The rule in *Bouch v Sproule* classifies these dividends as income in the hands of trustee/shareholders. This is the case even though the capital value of the company has fallen as a result of the distribution, to the detriment of beneficiaries with an interest in the trust capital. Sometimes, the accumulated trading profits represent a large proportion of the value of a company and the distribution of these profits can drastically reduce the value of the trust's capital holding.

14.43 Where the distribution is of capital profits, rigid application of *Bouch v Sproule* has the potential to cause even greater unfairness. This difficulty is illustrated by *Re Sechiari*.[61] A testatrix had bequeathed shares in Tilling Ltd to her children for life, with remainder to her children's issue. Under the Transport Act 1947, Tilling Ltd was obliged to sell its road transport interests to the British Transport Commission in return for British Transport stock. The company distributed this stock among its shareholders as a capital profits dividend. Each shareholder received £5 of British Transport stock for each £1 of ordinary stock they held in Tilling Ltd. As a result of this distribution the value of shares fell by over 75% but the distribution was held to be income.

14.44 In *Re Bates*,[62] a testator bequeathed shares in a company which owned and operated steam trawlers to his wife for life with remainder to a third party. The company sold some of its vessels for sums in excess of their balance sheet values thereby realising a capital profit. After the testator's death the company's directors resolved to distribute these profits to shareholders as cash dividends

[61] [1950] 1 All ER 417.
[62] [1928] Ch 682.

and sent a circular to shareholders explaining that the payments were made out of capital and were not in the nature of a dividend or bonus upon the shares. Eve J held that on the facts the capital profits had not been capitalised and so remained distributable. Applying the rule in *Bouch v Sproule*, any payment made to shareholders from that profit was, for trust purposes, income notwithstanding that the profits themselves were of a capital (rather than trading) nature.

14.45 Companies' statements that distributions are not to be treated as dividends are therefore irrelevant to their proper classification. The court looks to the intention of the company as manifested by its actions (ie resolutions) rather than its words. As Lord Russell of Killowen said in *Hill v Permanent Trustee Company of New South Wales Ltd*[63] the essence of the case was what the company showed 'not by its statements, but by its acts'.

14.46 In *Hill* a corporate trustee held shares in a farming company. The company sold almost all of its land, livestock and other assets, and ceased to carry on business. Subsequently the company declared a dividend of these capital profits and stated that 'the dividend is being paid out of profits arising from the sale of breeding stock, being assets of the company not required for resale at a profit, and that is free of income tax'. The company's express intention in making this statement was to protect the shareholders from liability for income tax.

The Supreme Court of New South Wales held that the dividend should be treated as capital of the trust.

On appeal the Privy Council reversed this decision and held that the dividend should be treated as income of the trust. Lord Russell set out five principles as a fundamental restatement of the rules governing the classification of corporate receipts:

> '(1) A limited company when it parts with moneys available for distribution among its shareholders is not concerned with the fate of those moneys in the hands of any shareholder. The company does not know and does not care whether a shareholder is a trustee of his shares or not. It is of no concern to a company which is parting with moneys to a shareholder whether that shareholder (if he be a trustee) will hold them as trustee for A, absolutely or as trustee for A, for life only.
>
> (2) A limited company not in liquidation can make no payment by way of return of capital to its shareholders except as a step in an authorized reduction of capital. Any other payment made by it by means of which it parts with moneys to its shareholders must and can only be made by way of dividing profits. Whether the payment is called "dividend" or "bonus", or any other name, it still must remain a payment on division of profits.

---

[63]   [1930] AC 720 (PC).

(3) Monies so paid to a shareholder will (if he be a trustee) prima facie belong to the person beneficially entitled to the income of the trust estate. If such monies or any part thereof are to be treated as part of the corpus of the trust estate there must be some provision in the trust deed which brings about that result. No statement by the company or its officers that moneys which are being paid away to shareholders out of profits are capital, or are to be treated as capital, can have any effect upon the rights of the beneficiaries under a trust instrument which comprises shares in the company.

(4) Other considerations arise when a limited company with power to increase its capital and possessing a fund of undivided profits, so deals with it that no part of it leaves the possession of the company, but the whole is applied in paying up new shares which are issued and allotted proportionately to the shareholders, who would have been entitled to receive the fund had it been, in fact, divided and paid away as dividend.

(5) The result of such a dealing is obviously wholly different from the result of paying away the profits to the shareholders. In the latter case the amount of cash distributed disappears on both sides of the company's balance sheet. It is lost to the company. The fund of undistributed profits which has been divided ceases to figure among the company's liabilities; the cash necessary to provide the dividend is raised and paid away, the company's assets being reduced by that amount. In the former case the assets of the company remain undiminished, but on the liabilities' side of the balance sheet (although the total remains unchanged) the item representing undivided profits disappears, its place being taken by a corresponding increase of liability in respect of issued share capital. In other words, moneys which had been capable of division by the company as profits among its shareholders have ceased for all time to be so divisible, and can never be paid to the shareholders except upon a reduction of capital or in a winding up. The fully paid shares representing them and received by the trustees are therefore received by them as corpus and not as income.'

14.47 The principles of *Hill* were expressly approved and applied by the Court of Appeal in *Re Doughty, Burridge v Doughty*[64] where the company's articles of association authorised the distribution of capital profits by capital distribution. It was held that the article did not purport to fix the character of the distributed profits as between life tenant and remainderman.

According to Sir David Nicholls VC in *Sinclair v Lee*, the rationale for the general principles of *Hill* is an endeavour by the law to give effect to the presumed intention of the settlor. If a settlor intends to use the word 'income' in some special sense, he should make this clear.[65] In general therefore the court will not seek to enquire as to what the settlor would have intended in any given circumstance; the gap created by the absence of stated intention is filled by the principles established for that purpose by the law.[66]

---

[64] [1947] Ch 263.
[65] Note, however, that a direction allowing trustees to determine that a receipt which would otherwise be treated as income is to be treated as capital is likely to mean that beneficiaries do not have a 'right' to income with potentially adverse income tax consequences.
[66] Given that the purpose of the general rule is to give effect to the presumed intention of the

14.48 Most recently these principles were applied in *Taube Discretionary Settlements v RCC*[67] where trustees of two family settlements wished to extract capital from a family company to finance a new house purchase for the benefit of the beneficiaries. A simple buy back of shares by the company would have triggered a charge to income tax.[68] Instead the shares held by the trustees were reclassified as A shares and a special dividend was paid on those shares to leave only the nominal value of the shares.

The taxpayers argued that the distribution could validly be treated by the trustees as capital, submitting that the special dividends were a division of part of the capital value of the company on a par with a reduction of capital or a purchase of own shares, as a matter of effect, if not of company law. Those dividends reduced the capital value of the shares by dint of materially diminishing the capital participation rights following the declaration and payment of the dividend. It would be manifestly absurd and unfair as a matter of general principle if the trustees were to treat the receipt as income for trust purposes. It was self-evident that the presumed intention of the settlor in such a case was that the special dividend should belong to the capital beneficiaries.

The court disagreed. There was nothing in the circumstances of this case to take it outside the normal position where dividends are paid on shares out of accumulated profits. The special dividend was trust income. The conversion of the ordinary shares of the trusts into A shares, and the effect of the special dividend upon the future rights attaching to those shares, did not result in the transaction being treated otherwise than as a distribution. Although there was a very substantial diminution in the value of the A shares as a consequence, there was no reduction or return of capital. It was not possible to argue that the transaction could be regarded as equivalent to a purchase by the company of its own shares, and thus as a sale of capital assets by the trustees:[69]

> 'Economic equivalence requires more than that the same amount of money is received and that the value of a share, having regard to its future rights, is substantially diminished. An own-share purchase involves both a sale and purchase of shares as a matter of substance, and necessarily entails a cancellation of the shares, and an elimination of all rights including rights to share capital itself.'

---

settlor as regards the interests of income and capital beneficiaries, it should not be applied in such a way as to defeat that objective. This formulation allowed the Vice-Chancellor to avoid an 'absurd' result in *Sinclair v Lee* [1993] Ch 497: see **14.54**.

[67] [2010] UKFTT 473 (TC).
[68] Under Income and Corporation Taxes Act 1988, s 686A (rewritten as ITA 2007, s 482).
[69] Per Judge Roger Berners at para 48.

Distributions treated as capital

14.49   The following distributions have been held to be capital:

(a)   A distribution will be treated as capital when the life tenant assented to the purchase of the original shares *as a capital investment* in the knowledge that the investment was motivated by the contemplated distribution.[70]

(b)   When a distribution is made after the testator's death but relates to a transaction completed before the testator's death, income must be treated as accruing before death.[71] Accordingly the distribution of a dividend relating to a period which ended before the testator's death should be treated as trust capital.[72]

(c)   Where a company purports to accumulate profits as capital although it has no power to increase its capital, such profits when distributed by way of dividend are received by trustee-shareholders as capital.[73]

Judicial discretion to apportion

14.50   In *Re Sechiari*,[74] Romer J suggested that there might be cases where the court has a 'jurisdiction to apportion the dividend on equitable principles between income and capital'. In *Re Kleinwort's Settlements*,[75] Vaisey J held that while there was no general rule requiring apportionment of distributed profits for the benefit of capital, the court may, in 'suitable special circumstances', have jurisdiction to order apportionment. This jurisdiction was, however, limited to cases where there had been a breach of trust. If, for example, a trustee had acquired the shares on the initiative of the life tenant, or with the object of benefiting the life tenant, apportionment to capital might be appropriate.[76]

Demergers

14.51   A demerger involves the transfer by a company ('Company A') of part of its business to a new company ('Company B'). The shareholders of Company A receive shares in Company B. The mechanism of demerger can take two forms:

(a)   direct demerger;

(b)   indirect demerger.

---

[70]   *Re Maclaren's Settlement Trusts* [1951] 2 All ER 414.
[71]   *Re Winder's Will Trust* [1951] Ch 916.
[72]   The same principle would apply to a lifetime trust.
[73]   *Irving v Houston* (1803) 4 Paton Sc App 521 (HL), distinguished in *Bouch v Sproule* on the basis that the company in *Irving* had no power to increase its capital.
[74]   [1950] 1 All ER 417.
[75]   [1951] Ch 860.
[76]   *Re Maclaren's Settlement Trusts* [1951] 2 All ER 414 suggests a broader interpretation of special circumstances which might allow apportionment where there was a 'glaring error'. But the requirement of a breach of trust was reaffirmed by *Re Rudd's Will Trusts* [1952] 1 All ER 254.

In each case the original company transfers the appropriate parts of its business to a new subsidiary company (wholly owned by it at the time of the transfer) and then declares a dividend to its shareholders. The difference between the two types of demerger lies in the way that the dividend is satisfied.

Direct demergers

14.52 In a direct demerger the dividend is satisfied by Company A issuing to its shareholders the entire share capital of Company B. It is well settled that these shares are received by shareholders as income.[77] This rule applies notwithstanding the fact that a demerger inevitably results in a fall in the value of the trust's shares in Company A. The operation of the rule in *Bouch v Sproule* therefore adversely affects the capital beneficiary.

Indirect demergers

14.53 An indirect demerger includes a further step absent from a direct demerger; at the same time as declaring a dividend, Company A transfers all its shares in Company B to another (wholly separate) holding company ('Company C'). In consideration for this transfer of shares Company C satisfies Company A's dividend by issuing its own shares to the shareholders of Company A.

14.54 The classification of shares received by shareholders as a result of an indirect demerger was the subject of litigation in *Sinclair v Lee*.[78] In that case a testatrix bequeathed shares in ICI plc ('ICI') to her husband for life with the remainder to her son. After her death, ICI resolved to demerge its bioscience activities. In preparation it consolidated its bioscience activities into a wholly owned subsidiary company. ICI proposed to transfer the shares of this subsidiary company to a newly created holding company called Zeneca Group plc ('Zeneca'). Zeneca was then to issue its own paid up shares to ICI shareholders.

14.55 The 'instinctive reaction' of Sir Donald Nicholls VC when asked to consider the nature of the Zeneca shares in the hands of the trustees, was that the shares were received as trust capital. This result would accord with the economic realities of the situation, as after the demerger the combined values of the ICI and Zeneca shares would be approximately equal to the pre-demerger value of the ICI shares. He said:

> 'I venture to think that no one, unversed in the arcane mysteries I shall be mentioning shortly, would have any doubt over the answer to these questions. The ICI shares form part of the capital of the fund. For the future the ICI undertaking will be divided up, with one part belonging to ICI and the other to Zeneca Group. To compensate for this loss of part of the ICI undertaking, the ICI shareholders

---

[77]   *Re Sechiari* [1950] 1 All ER 417.
[78]   [1993] Ch 497.

will be receiving a corresponding number of shares in Zeneca Group. No one would imagine that the Zeneca Group shares could sensibly be regarded as income.'

14.56 Sir Donald Nicholls VC conceded that the line of cases developing the rule in *Bouch v Sproule* ran directly against his instincts. These authorities suggested that the Zeneca shares should be treated as income but none of them dealt with the precise situation of an indirect demerger. The Vice-Chancellor therefore felt able to distinguish *Bouch v Sproule* on the basis that the ICI transaction was to be characterised, not as a distribution at all (which, whether in cash or in specie, he would have been bound to hold was income), but as a company reconstruction resulting in a single capital asset in the trustees' hands being replaced by two such assets.

He said:

'It is unsatisfactory to treat all accumulated profits as earmarked as income to the extent that any distribution of such profits, regardless of the amount or the circumstances, will belong to the tenant for life.'

The Law Commission said of the decision in its Report[79] that, while helpful, it had:

'given rise to an unprincipled distinction between direct and indirect demergers. The formalistic ground for distinction adopted by the Vice-Chancellor enabled him to avoid what he considered to be an "absurd" result, but did not affect the equally absurd result that arises from direct demergers.'

14.57 The tax treatment of shares received on a demerger depends on whether or not the demerger fulfils the requirements of CTA 2010, Part 23, Chapter 5[80] to qualify as an exempt demerger. An exempt demerger is not a distribution for the purposes of corporation tax and does not give rise to income tax liabilities for the recipient.[81] Companies may seek advance clearance under CTA 2010, s 1091 that proposed transactions will be an exempt demerger.

Where the demerger is not exempt, the position is as follows:

(a) On a direct demerger, the demerged shares are received as income of the trust, the life tenant is immediately entitled to those shares, subject to the right of trustees to meet their expenses. The demerged shares are therefore never settled property for Capital Gains Tax purposes, and there is no disposal for Capital Gains Tax purposes from the trustees to the life tenant. There is, therefore, no charge under TCGA 1992, s 71 (beneficiary

---

[79] *Capital and Income in Trusts: Classification and Apportionment*, Law Com No 315 (TSO, 2009).
[80] Formerly Income and Corporation Taxes Act 1988, ss 213–218.
[81] CTA 2010, s 1075.

becoming absolutely entitled). Their base value is the market value at the time of the demerger.[82] The income beneficiaries will not be assessed to income tax.

If the personal representatives or trustees retain the new shares on a direct demerger then they will purchase them from the income beneficiaries. Unless the gain made by the beneficiaries exceeds their annual exemption, etc there will be no tax consequences. This may well mean that, in most cases, this is what happens.

(b)   On an indirect demerger, the income beneficiaries get nothing and all that happens is that the personal representatives, etc have to split their base value for the original holding between the holdings which emerge.[83]

Scrip dividends

14.58   Scrip dividends are dividends which offer shareholders the choice of being paid in the form of cash or shares. When a company declares a conventional scrip dividend each shareholder has the option to take the dividend in cash or in additional shares of equal value. Such dividends will almost always be treated as income in the hands of the shareholder whichever option is chosen.[84]

14.59   The situation is more complicated when the company declares an 'enhanced' scrip dividend. Enhanced scrip dividends give shareholders the option of taking the distribution either in cash or in additional shares of greater value than the cash alternative. If (unusually) the shareholder opts for cash the receipt will clearly be income under the rule in *Bouch v Sproule*.

14.60   The trustee will usually opt to take the more valuable bonus shares. In this case, the classification of the bonus shares will depend on whether the company intended to capitalise its profits or intended to make a distribution. In the majority of cases, especially where (as is common practice) the company arranges for a third party to offer to purchase the new shares at market value to enable shareholders to realise their cash value immediately, the substance of the arrangement will be such that the shares will be received as income.

14.61   However, where the bonus shares are received as capital, it has in some cases been held that the income beneficiary is entitled to a lien over the amount of the cash dividend foregone; in effect, an apportionment of the receipt

---

[82]   TCGA 1992, s 17.
[83]   The Revenue view is fully explained in CGTM 33900–33936.
[84]   This treatment appears to be widely accepted whether the option to take cash or shares is given before or after the dividend has been declared: *Underhill and Hayton: Law of Trusts and Trustees* (18th edn, 2010), at 44.33 and J Mowbray QC et al (eds), *Lewin on Trusts* (19th edn, 2015), para 25–038. HMRC considers scrip dividends to be received as income in trust law and are therefore within the income tax provisions for stock dividends: Income and Corporation Taxes Act 1988, s 249 (rewritten as CTA 2010, ss 1049 and 1051) and s 409 of ITTOIA 2005.

between income and capital.[85] HMRC's position, set out in Statement of Practice 4/94, is that it currently follows the trustees' decision as to the classification of enhanced scrip dividends for tax purposes, provided that their conclusion is supportable on the facts of their particular case. However, on occasion, the courts have retreated from the strict dichotomy of the general rule and ordered an apportionment of receipts from scrip dividends between income and capital.

The Trusts (Capital and Income) Act 2013

14.62 The Law Commission in its Report[86] was critical of the current law on the basis of its inappropriate and unpredictable results, complexity and its uncertainty in application to novel arrangements.

14.63 It recommended that trustees should have a power of allocation. This power would allow trustees, taking the trust's receipts over a given period, to allocate all or part of one or more trust receipts as necessary in order to ensure that a balance was kept between classes of beneficiaries entitled to capital and to income.

This would be coupled with a statutory requirement to balance investment returns arising under a power of allocation, applying solely in the context of the exercise of the power of allocation.

14.64 It also recommended that shares distributed in a tax-exempt demerger[87] should be classified as capital for trust law purposes. This would classify as capital shares received as a result both of direct and indirect demergers. It recommended that when such a distribution is made, trustees should have a power to make a payment of capital to beneficiaries interested in income where otherwise there would be prejudice to those beneficiaries.

14.65 The Trusts (Capital and Income) Act 2013, based on the draft attached to the Law Commission's report,[88] with minor modifications arising from responses to the Ministry of Justice's public consultation on the Bill, came into force on 1 October 2013.

The Act made three changes:

---

[85] See *Rowley v Unwin* (1855) 2 K & J 138; *Re Tindal (Deceased)* (1892) 9 TLR 24; *Re Malam* [1894] 3 Ch 578.

[86] *Capital and Income in Trusts: Classification and Apportionment*, Law Com No 315 (TSO, 2009).

[87] The Law Commission would have preferred to make a recommendation in relation to all demergers but was unable to do so because the introduction of flexibility in treatment of receipts would have impacted on the tax treatment of interests in possession and might have caused an interest in possession trust to lose its status as such for both income tax and, where relevant, IHT purposes.

[88] See footnote 86 above.

(a) disapplication, for new trusts, of certain technical rules requiring the apportionment of receipts and outgoings between income and capital, so that they only apply where the creator of the trust has specifically incorporated them (s 1);[89]

(b) rationalisation of the trust law classification of receipts from tax-exempt corporate demergers by ensuring that all such receipts are treated as capital, together with a power for trustees to redress an income beneficiary's position in appropriate circumstances (s 2 and s 3);

(c) simplification of the procedure for the trustees of charities with permanent endowment to adopt a total return approach to investment within a framework determined by the Charity Commission, so that the amounts retained for further investment and applied for immediate spending are determined by looking across the whole investment return rather than the technical trust law classification of receipts as capital or income.

Time apportionments

14.66 The general duty of trustees not to favour one beneficiary or class of beneficiaries over another resulted in the development of rules of apportionment. In these cases the rules are derived from case law and were invariably specifically excluded by the will draftsman.[90]

All are abolished in respect of 'new' trusts.[91] The legislation defines a 'new trust' as one 'created or arising' after commencement (eg a new lifetime settlement or the death of a testator who establishes a will trust irrespective of when he executed his will). But it also includes a trust arising or created 'under a power conferred before that day'. Presumably, therefore, a new trust can arise for these purposes as a result of the exercise of a dispositive power.

14.67 More generally, s 2 of the Apportionment Act 1870 was a statutory rule of the apportionment whereby income beneficiaries were entitled only to the proportion of income that was deemed to have accrued during their period of entitlement. For instance, if income (typically corporate dividends) accrued over a 6-month period and the interest in possession beneficiary died 3 months into that period, then his estate would receive half of the accruing income with the other half belonging to the beneficiary who next became entitled to income (or, it may be, becoming held on discretionary trusts of income). In practice, whilst this provision could be excluded by the trust and will draftsman, this was

---

[89] See **14.66**.

[90] The three rules are: (a) *Howe v Earl of Dartmouth* (1802) 7 Ves Jr 137 requiring the sale and reinvestment of particular assets (eg wasting and hazardous); (b) *Re Earl of Chesterfield's Trusts* (1803) 24 Ch D 643 designed to compensate an income beneficiary when non-income producing assets are retained by trustees; (c) *Allhusen v Whittell* (1867) LR 4 Eq 295 apportioning debts, legacies, etc between income and capital.

[91] Trusts (Capital and Income) Act 2013, s 1(5).

frequently overlooked. Section 2 has now been abolished for new trusts coming into existence after the commencement of the Trusts (Capital and Income) Act 2013.[92]

5. PRECAUTIONS BEFORE DISTRIBUTION

Dealing with houses: the limits of CGT main residence relief

14.68 Main residence relief[93] is one of the most valuable capital gains tax reliefs for individuals. It is available to personal representatives[94] and trustees[95] but only to a limited extent.

In the case of personal representatives the relief is particularly restrictive being available only if the following conditions are satisfied:

(1) one or more persons must be in occupation of a dwelling-house or part of it as their only or main residence both before and after the deceased's death; and

(2) those individuals must have a 'relevant entitlement' which amounts to at least 75% of the net proceeds of disposal.

A 'relevant entitlement' is entitlement as legatee to, or to an interest in possession in, the whole or any part of the net proceeds of disposal.

Remember, though, that personal representatives are treated as acquiring assets at market value at the date of death so capital gains tax will only be an issue to the extent that the property increases in value between death and disposal. However, in a case where tax is an issue, the limited nature of the relief for personal representatives means that it will often be desirable for them to assent the property to the legatee so that the legatee can make the sale.

Relief for trustees, by contrast, is generous. They are given relief if during their period of ownership the house 'has been the only or main residence of a person entitled to occupy it under the terms of the settlement'. A beneficiary of a discretionary trust who is given a license to occupy by the trustees is 'entitled to occupy it under the terms of the settlement'.[96]

In *Wagstaff v Revenue and Customs Commissioners*[97] the First-tier Tribunal accepted that a trust had been created where Mr and Mrs Wagstaffe bought the house belonging to Mr Wagstaffe's mother and entered into an agreement with her (1) allowing her to live there and (2) agreeing that the property would not

---

[92]   See previous footnote.
[93]   TCGA 1992, ss 222–224.
[94]   TCGA 1992, s 225A.
[95]   TCGA 1992, s 225.
[96]   *Sansom v Peay* [1976] STC 494.
[97]   [2014] UKFTT 43 (TC).

be sold without her consent. The word 'trust' did not appear in the agreement but the Tribunal was satisfied that the parties had intended to create a trust relationship.

Advertising for claimants

14.69 Trustees and personal representatives who distribute the estate incorrectly will be liable to the disappointed beneficiaries unless they have protected themselves. Trustee Act 1925, s 27 protects them provided they:

(a)   advertise for claimants;

(b)   in the *London Gazette*, and in a newspaper circulating in the district in which any land is situated;

(c)   anywhere else that a court would have directed in an administration action;

(d)   wait at least 2 months before distributing; and

(e)   distribute property to all the claimants of whom they have notice.

If the trustees or personal representatives then distribute without notice of a claim, they have no liability in their representative capacity but the disappointed claimant has a claim against the beneficiaries of the estate. Unsurprisingly a person who has been informed of a claim but has forgotten it has been held to have notice for this purpose.[98]

Section 27 only offers protection to a personal representative in the capacity of personal representative. A claimant retains rights to claim from beneficiaries. In any event s 27 only protects against unknown claimants. It offers no protection where the existence of claimants is known but their whereabouts are unknown. Personal representatives can employ professional genealogists to trace missing beneficiaries or seek guidance from the court. The best known order in cases of uncertainty is one permitting the estate to be administered on the basis that a beneficiary who cannot be traced has died.[99] Alternatively, the court may order that known beneficiaries are entitled to their share of the estate immediately. The practical effect is that the cost of further investigations falls on those who have yet to be traced.[100]

Claims under Inheritance (Provision for Family and Dependants) Act 1975

14.70 Close family members and dependents[101] have a right to apply to court under this Act if the deceased did not make reasonable financial provision for

---

[98]   *Aon Pension Trustees v MCP Pension Trustees* [2010] EWCA Civ 377.

[99]   *Re Benjamin* [1902] 1 Ch 723.

[100]   See CPR PD40A, para 7.

[101]   The categories of applicant are set out in the Inheritance (Provision for Family and Dependants) Act 1975 (I(PFD)A 1975), s 1(1). See Chapter 17 for a full discussion of the statute.

their maintenance.[102] If satisfied that reasonable financial provision was not made the court can reorder the disposition of the estate to make reasonable provision.[103] Claims must be made within 6 months of the date of the grant or representation, although the court has power to allow an out of time application.[104] The personal representatives are required to distribute the estate in accordance with the court's order and will be liable to the claimant if they have already distributed the estate. The court can order recipients of assets to return them (however, courts are reluctant to interfere once assets have been distributed).

Provided the personal representatives wait 6 months, they are protected by s 20 from liability in respect of any distributions they have made if the court does allow an out of time application.

14.71 The protection of s 20 is only available where an *out of time* application is granted. There is no statutory protection for personal representatives who wait 6 months from the date of grant, then distribute the assets and are then served with a claim form issued within the 6-month period and served within the 4 months allowed for service under the CPR. Some practitioners, therefore, advocate waiting 10 months from the date of the grant. However, this is a long time for beneficiaries to wait. The chances of personal representatives receiving a claim form with no prior warning are remote. Unless there is particular reason to suspect a claim most personal representatives will feel able to make at least some distributions.

6. INHERITING ISAS: THE 2015 CHANGES

14.72 The Individual Savings Account Regulations 1998[105] have been amended to allow a spouse or civil partner (S) of a deceased ISA saver, where death occurs on or after 3 December 2014, to save additional sums in an ISA, outside the normal subscription limit if certain conditions are satisfied.[106] S will have to make declarations that the conditions are met. The additional amount cannot exceed the value of the ISA investments of the deceased at the time of his death. Slightly different rules apply to cash and non-cash ISAs. HMRC guidance[107] clarifies some points which are not clear in the Regulations themselves.

---

[102] I(PFD)A 1975, s 1(2). In the case of applications by surviving spouses and civil partners the claim is not limited to maintenance. It is such financial provision as it would be reasonable in all the circumstances for spouse or civil partner to receive, whether or not that provision is required for his or her maintenance.

[103] I(PFD)A 1975, s 2.

[104] I(PFD)A 1975, s 4.

[105] SI 1998/1870.

[106] The Individual Savings Account (Amendment No 2) Regulations 2015 (SI 2015/869) came into force on 6 April 2015.

[107] HMRC: ISAs: Additional permitted subscriptions following the death of account holder (12 March 2015) available on the Gov.uk website.

Conditions applying to cash and non-cash ISAs

14.73

(a) S and the deceased were living together at the date of the deceased's death;

(b) the subscription must be made by S to an account held by S;

(c) the subscription must be made within the permitted period which is
  (i) in the case of a subscription comprising non-cash assets inherited by S and invested with the deceased's account manager the period beginning with distribution to S by the deceased's estate and ending no more than 180 days thereafter – where death occurs between 3 December 2014 and 5 April 2015, the deceased is treated as dying on either 6th April 2015, or, the actual date of distribution, whichever is the later;
  (ii) in all other cases 3 years from death or no more than 180 days after administration of the estate is complete, whichever is the later – where death occurs between 3 December 2014 and 5 April 2015, the deceased is treated as dying on 6 April 2015.

Cash ISAs held by the deceased

14.74   S does not need to inherit the deceased's cash ISA

(a) Cash can be invested in one or more accounts with any single account manager. It does not have to the deceased's account manager.

(b) Where the deceased held ISAs with more than one account manager, the surviving spouse will have separate additional subscription limits in relation to the ISAs held with each manager.[108]

Non-cash ISAs held by the deceased

14.75

(a) S can make a subscription comprising those assets or any part thereof if:
  (i) S inherits[109] all or part of those assets; and
  (ii) title to the assets is vested, and has continuously since the deceased's death been vested, in the account manager (unless HMRC gives permission for a different ISA manager).

(b) If S chooses to subscribe non-cash assets *in specie*, the maximum additional allowance for subscription to accounts with a particular ISA

---

[108] Individual Savings Account Regulations 1998, reg 5DDA(3)(b), and see HMRC: ISAs: Additional permitted subscriptions following the death of account holder (12 March 2015), paragraph 6A.3(i).

[109] For these purposes, 'inherit' is defined as including inheriting under a will trust or as the result of a deed of variation. Presumably this will apply if assets are appropriated to the survivor in satisfaction of an entitlement under the intestacy rules. HMRC has confirmed informally that the term includes inheritance by way of intestacy as well as inheritance by will.

manager is the value of the deceased's accounts with that manager at the date of death, but it is the value of the non-cash assets at the date of the spouse's subscription that counts towards the additional allowance.[110] Therefore, if the value of the non-cash assets has:

(i) risen since the death of the deceased, the spouse can subscribe all the assets only if the deceased also had a cash ISA with the same manager and its value at the deceased's death (or that of any cash in the stocks and shares ISA itself) is enough to cover the difference; or

(ii) fallen since the death of the deceased, the spouse can subscribe the balance in cash.

(c) S can subscribe cash up to the value of a non-cash ISA held by the deceased as an alternative to subscribing the non-cash assets held in the ISA *in specie*, or if the requirements for subscribing non-cash assets are not met (for example, if the spouse did not inherit the assets from the deceased).[111] Cash can be invested in one or more accounts with any single account manager. It does not have to the deceased's account manager.

14.76 ISA managers can choose whether to accept subscriptions from S using the additional allowance[112] and whether to allow S to make a subscription using the additional allowance in instalments or to insist on a single payment. A manager who insists on a single payment must make clear to S that if that payment is less than the maximum additional allowance available, the rest of the allowance will be lost (because S cannot use it to make a subscription to a different manager).[113]

14.77 These new provisions, while helpful for taxpayers, introduce additional complications for PRs administering estates. In particular, PRs should as a matter of good practice:

(a) Inform surviving spouses and civil partners of the value of ISAs in the estate and the fact that there is an investment opportunity;

(b) before realising non-cash ISAs left to S, check whether S wants to use the additional allowance to subscribe non-cash *in specie* (once the assets are sold this opportunity is lost although S be able to subscribe an equivalent amount of cash).

There are practical problems. For example if S does not inherit assets there may not be enough cash to take advantage of the full additional allowance within the time limits. There is a particular risk that S will lose part of the allowance by making a subscription of less than the full allowance to an ISA provider who does not accept subscriptions in instalments.

---

[110] Individual Savings Account Regulations 1998, reg 5DDA(3) and (11)(c).
[111] HMRC: ISAs: Additional permitted subscriptions following the death of account holder (12 March 2015), para 6A.10.
[112] Paragraph 6A.1, HMRC draft guidance.
[113] HMRC: ISAs: Additional permitted subscriptions following the death of account holder (12 March 2015).paras 6A.1, 3 and 5.

14.78 Individuals may wish to review wills and consider whether to leave their non-cash ISAs to their spouse outright, rather than, for example, to an IPDI trust. Although, in such a case, the trustees could use an express power of advancement to distribute the assets to S, it is clearly simpler to leave the assets directly to S.

PRECEDENTS

Precedent 14.1: Memorandum of appropriation reserving a power to re-appropriate[114]

We being the trustees of [   ] Will Trust exercise the power of appropriation conferred on us by clause [   ] of the Will to appropriate the assets set out in the Schedule to the fund which is specified in that Schedule and pending transfer of the assets we will hold them on bare trust for the relevant fund PROVIDED ALWAYS that we retain the power in the future to exchange assets appropriated to one fund for assets appropriated to another fund which have an equivalent open market value.

SCHEDULE

Asset	*Appropriated Fund*
[ ] shares in XYZ Ltd	The Children's Fund established by clause [ ] of the Will.
Land at Chiddingfold	The Grandchildren's Fund established by clause [ ] of the Will.

---

[114] See **14.09**.

Section D

MISCELLANEOUS

CHAPTER 15

THE INTESTACY RULES

CONTENTS

15.01 The devolution of certain assets is fixed irrespective of whether there is a will. For instance, property held as beneficial joint tenants passes by the right of survivorship. The intestacy rules apply to those assets which are capable of passing by will but which have not been successfully disposed of by will. This may be because there is no valid will or because the will fails to deal with all of the assets.

15.02 The intestacy rules are in Part IV of the Administration of Estates Act 1925, as amended.

If cohabitants, relatives or dependants feel that the intestacy rules do not make adequate financial provision for them, they may bring a claim under the Inheritance (Provisions for Family and Dependants) Act 1975, s 1(1) which provides that the court is not bound to assume that the intestacy rules make reasonable provision for the next-of-kin.

Where property passes as *bona vacantia*, a deserving claimant may obtain a payment from the Crown, Duchy of Lancaster or Duke of Cornwall.[1]

1. UNDISPOSED OF PROPERTY IS HELD ON A STATUTORY TRUST

The statutory trust

15.03 Undisposed of property is held by the personal representatives on a statutory trust. The Administration of Estates Act 1925, s 33(1) provides:

> 'on the death of a person intestate as to any real or personal estate, such estate shall be held on trust by his personal representatives with the power to sell it.'

Section 33(2) states that:

> 'The personal representatives shall pay out of:

---

[1]   See **15.35**.

(a)   the ready money of the deceased (so far as not disposed of by his will, if any); and

(b)   any net money arising from disposing of any other part of his estate (after payment of costs),

... funeral, testamentary and administration expenses, debts and other liabilities ... and out of the residue of the said money the personal representatives shall set aside a fund sufficient to provide for any pecuniary legacies bequeathed by the will (if any) of the deceased.'

Any balance remaining after the payment of debts and reservation of a fund for any pecuniary legacies is held for the relatives as set out in Administration of Estates Act 1925, s 46.

Order of entitlement under s 46

15.04   Section 46 sets out an order of priority for the relatives specified. To come within s 46, apart from the surviving spouse or civil partner of the intestate, there must be a blood relationship, an adoptive relationship or a relationship under the Human Fertilisation and Embryology Act 2008.[2] Persons related by marriage to a person within one of these categories have no right to share in the estate; nor do step-children of the intestate.

15.05   First, where there is a surviving spouse or civil partner he or she takes everything unless the intestate also left issue (that is children, grandchildren and remoter lineal descendants). Where there are issue, the spouse or civil partner shares the estate with the issue provided the issue satisfy the requirements of the statutory trusts.[3]

If the death occurred before 1 October 2014[4] the surviving spouse or civil partner may have to share the undisposed of property with the intestate's surviving parents or, if there are none, with the surviving brothers and sisters of the whole blood (or their issue) provided that they satisfy the requirements of the statutory trusts. For deaths on or after that date the surviving spouse or civil partner takes all the undisposed of property if there are no issue.

15.06   If the intestate left no surviving spouse or civil partner, the estate is distributed as follows:

(a)   to issue on the statutory trusts, but if none, then to,

(b)   parents absolutely (and equally if both are alive), but if none, then to,

(c)   brothers and sisters of the whole blood (ie the children of the same parents as the deceased) on the statutory trusts, but if none, then to,

---

2   See **15.32** *et seq.*
3   For the statutory trusts see **15.27**.
4   The date on which the Inheritance and Trustees' Powers Act 2014 came into force.

(d)   brothers and sisters of the half blood (ie those who share one parent with the deceased) on the statutory trusts, but if none, then to,

(e)   grandparents absolutely and equally if more than one, but if none, then to,

(f)   uncles and aunts of the whole blood (ie brothers and sisters of the whole blood of one of the parents of the deceased) on the statutory trusts, but if none, then to,

(g)   uncles and aunts of the half blood (ie those with one parent in common with one of the parents of the deceased) on the statutory trusts, but if none, then to,

(h)   the Crown, Duchy of Lancaster or the Duke of Cornwall as '*bona vacantia*'.

15.07   Each category must be considered in the order listed above and only if there is *no one* in a particular category is it necessary to consider the next category. Matters relevant to the particular categories are considered below.

2. ENTITLEMENT OF SPOUSES AND CIVIL PARTNERS

Who is a spouse?

15.08   Same sex spouses and civil partners are treated in the same way as opposite sex spouses under the intestacy rules. In the case of polygamous marriages there can be more than one spouse for the purpose of intestacy rules.[5]

15.09   A divorced spouse has no rights in the intestate's estate and for deaths occurring on or after 1 January 1970, neither has a judicially separated spouse, since they are treated as already being dead provided that the separation is still continuing.[6] A civil partner has no inheritance rights after dissolution of the civil partnership nor after a separation order has been made.[7]

Clients who seek professional advice with a view to obtaining a divorce, judicial separation, dissolution of a civil partnership or separation order, should always be advised to make a will if they have not already done so. If they die

---

5   *Official Solicitor to the Senior Courts v Yemoh* [2010] EWHC 3727 Ch. The deceased had left eight wives and the court held that together they constituted the surviving 'spouse'. The statutory legacy would, therefore, be divided amongst the various widows. As there were surviving issue one half of the residue was held for the 'spouse' for life (see **15.13** below). The court held that the various wives were to be treated as beneficial joint tenants so that the property subject to life interest was to be held until the death of the last, at which point that half of residue would pass to the issue.

6   Matrimonial Causes Act 1973, s 18(2). This is not the case, however, if there is a magistrates' court separation order in effect (see s 18(3)) although no such separation order may be made after the Domestic Proceedings and Magistrates' Courts Act 1978.

7   See Civil Partnership Act 2004, s 57.

intestate before the final order (the decree absolute in the case of a divorce and the final order in the case of a dissolution of a civil partnership), property will pass under the intestacy rules to the spouse or civil partner. Clients who have existing wills, should review them in the light of the changed circumstances.

Survivorship requirement

15.10 The Law Reform (Succession) Act 1995, s 1 introduced a statutory survivorship period for spouses and civil partners of intestates dying on or after 1 January, 1996. In order to take an interest on intestacy a spouse or civil partner must survive the intestate for 28 days before taking an interest.

Entitlement varies

15.11 The precise entitlement of a spouse to the deceased's undisposed-of 'residuary estate' depends on the date of death and whether any other close relatives survived the intestate.

Spouse or civil partner alone surviving

15.12 If the intestate left a surviving spouse or civil partner but no issue, parents or brothers or sisters of the whole blood (or their issue), the personal representatives hold *the whole of the estate* on trust for the spouse or civil partner *absolutely*. Remoter relatives such as grandparents or uncles and aunts have no rights to share in the estate.

Spouse or civil partner and issue surviving

15.13 The estate of an intestate who leaves a surviving spouse or civil partner and issue is divided between the spouse or civil partner and the issue. The details of the division vary depending whether the intestate died before 1 October 2014.[8]

15.14 Where the intestate died before 1 October 2014 the surviving spouse or civil partner received:

(a)   The deceased's 'personal chattels' absolutely. 'Personal chattels' are defined in Administration of Estates Act 1925, s 55(1)(x) as:

> 'carriages, horses, stable furniture and effects (not used for business purposes), motor cars and accessories (not used for business purposes), garden effects, domestic animals, plate, plated articles, linen, china, glass, books, pictures, prints, furniture, jewellery, articles of household or personal use or ornament, musical and scientific instruments and apparatus, wines, liquors and consumable stores, but do not include any chattels used at the death of the intestate for business purposes nor money or securities for money.'

---

8   The date on which the Inheritance and Trustees' Powers Act 2014 came into force.

In essence, personal chattels are items of personal and domestic use and ornament. This has been held to cover a yacht[9] and a collection of watches.[10] In the latter case Russell LJ said that 'cherishing ... by eye and hand [could bring the watches] within the definition of articles of personal use'. The exclusion of assets 'used' for business purposes appears to mean that an asset which is used to any extent for such purposes is not a personal chattel.

(b) A 'statutory legacy' of £250,000 where death occurs on or after 1 February, 2009. The legacy is payable free of tax and costs, together with interest at 6 per cent per annum from death until payment. The costs and interest come from the residue of the estate. In the case of deaths occurring prior to 1 February, 2009 lower levels of statutory legacy were payable.

(c) if there is anything left in the estate after (a) and (b), the spouse or civil partner receives a life interest (ie a right to the income until death) in one-half of the residue.

The other half of the residue and the interest in remainder in the trust created for the spouse or civil partner go to the issue on the statutory trusts.[11]

15.15 Where the intestate dies on or after 1 October 2014 the surviving spouse or civil partner receives:

(a) The deceased's 'personal chattels' absolutely. The definition of 'personal chattels' contained in section 55(1)(x) was amended by the Inheritance and Trustees' Powers Act 2014. The new definition is:

> 'tangible movable property, other than any such property which –
>> consists of money or securities for money, or
>> was used at the death of the intestate solely or mainly for business purposes, or
>> was held at the death of the intestate solely as an investment.'

The first exception for money and securities for money, was found in the old statutory definition. The second exception is similar to the exclusion in the old definition but limits the exclusion to assets used *solely or mainly* for business purposes to make clear that it is only where a chattel was used primarily for business purposes that it should not pass to the surviving spouse or civil partner. The third exception is intended as a narrow exception for property held *solely* as an investment which had no personal use at the date of the deceased's death so it would not include property which had some personal use but which the deceased also hoped might maintain or increase its value.

---

[9] *Re Chaplin* [1950] Ch 507, [1950] 2 All ER 155.
[10] *Re Crispin's Will Trusts* [1974] 3 All ER 772, [1975] Ch 245.
[11] For statutory trusts see **15.27** below.

(b)　A 'statutory legacy' of £250,000 payable free of tax and costs, together with interest from death until payment at the Bank of England rate that had effect at the end of the day on which the intestate died.[12]

(c)　If there is anything left in the estate after (a) and (b), the spouse or civil partner receives one-half of the residue absolutely instead of taking merely a life interest.

The other half of the residue passes to the issue on the statutory trusts.[13]

Although the amount of the statutory legacy is unchanged, provision is made for regular review of the amount.[14]

Spouse or civil partner and parent or brother and sister (or their issue) surviving

15.16　Where the intestate leaves a spouse or civil partner but no issue, parents or, if none, siblings of the whole blood or their issue may be entitled to a share in the undisposed of property depending on the date of death.

15.17　Where the intestate died before 1 October 2014 the surviving spouse or civil partner received:

(a)　the 'personal chattels' (as defined in **15.14** above) absolutely;

(b)　a statutory legacy of £450,000 where death occurred on or after 1 February 2009. Again the legacy is payable free of tax and costs plus 6 per cent per annum interest. In the case of deaths occurring prior to 1 February 2009 lower levels of statutory legacy were payable;

(c)　one-half of the residue absolutely.

The rest of the estate (that is, the other half of any residue) goes to the parent or parents in equal shares absolutely or, if none, to the brothers and sisters of the whole blood or their issue on the statutory trusts (see below).

---

[12]　Unless the Lord Chancellor orders otherwise.

[13]　For statutory trusts see **15.27** below.

[14]　Inheritance and Trustees' Powers Act 2014, inserted a new Schedule 1A into the Administration of Estates Act 1925. Paragraph 4 of the Schedule requires the Lord Chancellor to make an order setting the statutory legacy at least every 5 years – the first order to be made within 5 years of the date on which the new Schedule comes into force. Subsequent orders must be made within 5 years of the previous order. Paragraph 5 provides that, unless the Lord Chancellor otherwise determines, the statutory legacy will be 'index-linked' by reference to the consumer prices index. The procedure operates on an 'upwards only' basis; if there has been no inflation or there has been deflation in the economy, the amount of the fixed net sum will not change. The Lord Chancellor will be obliged to make an order increasing the amount of the statutory legacy between 5-year review dates if the Consumer Prices Index rises to 15% or more, in any month, over its base amount. The rate of increase will be at the discretion of the Lord Chancellor. When this mechanism is triggered, the 5-year period will be reset to commence from the date of such an order.

15.18 Where the intestate dies on or after 1 October 2014 the surviving spouse or civil partner receives the whole of the undisposed of property absolutely. Parents and siblings have no rights to anything.

Two special rules applying to spouses and civil partners

15.19 Spouses and civil partners have two special rights which they can exercise within one year of the death of the intestate, though in both cases the court has power to extend the time limit.

Right to redeem the life interest

15.20 Where the spouse or civil partner is entitled to a life interest in one-half of the residue of the estate, they can elect to convert the life interest into a capital sum.

A complex formula for determining the capital value of the interest is laid down in statutory instruments, the latest of which is the Intestate Succession (Interest and Capitalisation) (Amendment) Order 2008 which came into force on 1 February 2009.

Provided the issue are *sui juris* the life interest can be valued by agreement between the spouse or civil partner and issue, thus removing the necessity of complying with the statutory provisions.

The election must be made in writing to the personal representatives.[15] If the sole personal representative is the surviving spouse or civil partner, the election is made to the Senior Registrar of the Family Division of the High Court.

The effect of the provision can be seen in the following example.

> *Example 15.1*
>
> The deceased died intestate in 2013 leaving a spouse and issue. The residue of the estate, after deducting personal chattels and the statutory legacy, is £50,000, and the spouse or civil partner is entitled to a life interest in £25,000. Instead of receiving the income from this, the spouse or civil partner can capitalise the interest using the formula and receive, say, £10,000 in cash. The rest of the estate, after deducting the costs of the capitalisation is held on the statutory trusts for the issue. See **15.21**.

A spouse or civil partner who makes the election is treated as having always been entitled to the capital sum; they are not treated as making a transfer of value for the purposes of inheritance tax.[16] However, since less of the deceased's estate is treated as passing to the spouse or civil partner, less of the estate is

---

[15]   Administration of Estates Act 1925, s 47A(6).
[16]   Inheritance Tax Act 1984, s 145.

exempt under Inheritance Act 1984, s 18 with the result that more inheritance tax may become payable on the deceased's estate.

15.21   In the case of deaths on or after 1 October 2014 surviving spouses and civil partners will not take a life interest so this right will cease to be relevant.

Right to acquire the matrimonial home

15.22   If the intestate and the surviving spouse or civil partner were joint beneficial tenants of the dwelling-house in which the surviving spouse was resident at the deceased's death, the property will pass by survivorship to the surviving spouse or civil partner.

If, however, the intestate was the sole owner or held a share as a tenant-in-common, the house or the interest as tenant-in-common in the house may be part of the undisposed of property for the purpose of the intestacy rules. And, of course, the surviving spouse or civil partner may wish to acquire the house.

In this case, the Second Schedule to the Intestates' Estates Act 1952 gives a surviving spouse or civil partner the right to *require* the personal representatives to appropriate 'any dwelling-house in which the surviving spouse was resident at the time of the intestate's death' in total or partial satisfaction of an absolute and/or capitalised interest in the estate.

If the dwelling-house is worth more than the absolute entitlement of the spouse or civil partner, the personal representative can still be required to appropriate the dwelling-house but the spouse or civil partner must then pay 'equality money' from his or her own resources to make up the difference.[17]

The property is valued at the value at the date of appropriation, not death.[18] If it is a time of rising property values, it is important to advise the spouse to make such an election quickly.

As with capitalising a life interest, the surviving spouse or civil partner must exercise the right by notice in writing to the personal representatives. The surviving spouse or civil partner will frequently be a personal representative of the deceased. If the spouse is one of two or more personal representatives then notice must be given to the other(s).[19]

15.23   A personal representative is in a fiduciary position as regards the estate and like a trustee must not profit from that fiduciary position. The Schedule provides[20] that where the spouse is one of two or more personal representatives the rule that a trustee should not purchase trust property is not to prevent the

---

[17]   Intestates' Estates Act 1952, Sch 2, para 5(2).
[18]   *Robinson v Collins* [1975] 1 All ER 321.
[19]   Intestates' Estates Act 1952, Sch 2, para 3(1).
[20]   Intestates' Estates Act 1952, Sch 2, para 5(1).

purchase of a dwelling-house from the estate. The Schedule says nothing of the position where a spouse is a sole personal representative. A spouse who is a sole personal representative and who wishes to exercise the right to take a dwelling-house ought to do one of the following:

(a)   secure the appointment of a second personal representative;

(b)   obtain the consent of the other beneficiaries (but this is only appropriate if they are of full age and capacity); or

(c)   obtain the consent of the court.[21]

15.24   When a surviving spouse or civil partner chooses to exercise this right, it does not matter whether the deceased owned the freehold or merely a leasehold interest in the house (except where the lease has less than 2 years to run). However, in certain circumstances,[22] the consent of the court is required before the spouse or civil partner can exercise the right. The court must be satisfied that the exercise of the right will not diminish the value of the other residuary assets nor make them more difficult to sell.

3. THE RIGHTS OF ISSUE

15.25   Issue take their entitlement on the statutory trusts. They may be sharing with a surviving spouse or civil partner or they may be taking the whole of the undisposed of property.

The statutory trusts

15.26   The 'statutory trusts' are set out in the Administration of Estates Act 1925, s 47 under which the property is held equally for the children of the intestate who are either alive or *en ventre sa mere* at the date of the intestate's death. The children who satisfy this requirement have a contingent interest until they reach 18 or marry under that age.

---

[21]   The need for such steps is confirmed by the case of *Kane v Radley-Kane* [1999] Ch 274 which concerned an appropriation by a surviving spouse of shares under Administration of Estates Act 1925, s 41 rather than an election to take a dwelling house. However, the court referred to the right of election under the 1952 Act. It emphasised the fact that the right only exists where the spouse is one of two or more personal representatives and that a sole personal representative would have to take additional steps.

[22]   Set out in the Intestates' Estates Act 1952, Sch 2, paras 2 and 4(2). Such consent is required if the house: (a) forms part of a building, the whole of which is comprised in the residuary estate; (b) is held with agricultural land similarly comprised; (c) as to the whole or part was used as an hotel or lodging house at the death of the intestate; or (d) as to part was used for non-domestic purposes at the death of the intestate (which would be the case if, for example, part of the house was used as a shop). If a surviving spouse or civil partner wishes to avoid an application to the court or if the right of election is unavailable for any other reason (for example, expiry of the 12 months' time limit) it is possible for the personal representatives to make use of the ordinary power of appropriation contained in s 41 of the Administration of Estates Act 1925. However, the spouse or civil partner has no right to insist on such an appropriation and so must seek the agreement of the personal representatives.

If a child dies under 18 and without marrying or forming a civil partnership, their contingent interest ends and the assets are dealt with as if that child had never existed.

However, if a child predeceases the intestate leaving issue alive at the intestate's death, those grandchildren or their issue take *per stirpes* the share which their parent would have taken provided those issue reach 18 or marry or form a civil partnership under that age. No child can take whose parent is living (subject to s 46A of the Administration of Estates Act 1925[23]).

Example 15.2

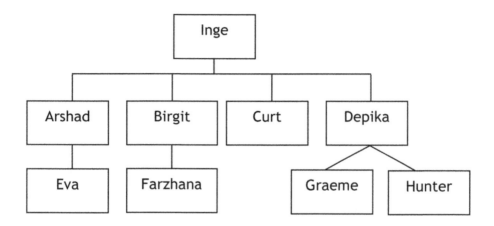

Curt and Depika predeceased Inge who died intestate. Arshad, Birgit and all the grandchildren are over 18. The estate will be divided into three parts. Arshad and Birgit each have vested interests in one-third of the estate. Curt has predeceased the intestate without leaving issue and has no entitlement. Depika has predeceased the intestate but has left issue. Depika's issue divide her share equally between them so that Graeme and Hunter take one-sixth of the estate each. If Graeme or Hunter had also predeceased Inge but were survived by children, the children would have shared the property that would have passed to their parent provided they satisfied the statutory trusts.

Note that Eva and Farzhana have no entitlement because their parents are alive.

---

[23]   See **15.28** below.

Example 15.3

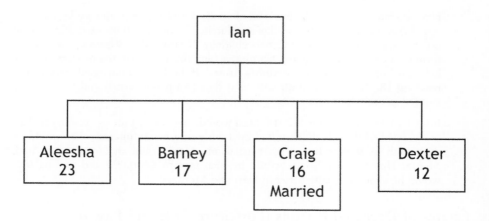

Ian died intestate; all the children survived him. Aleesha and Craig have vested interests immediately on the death of the intestate. If they die before receiving their share of the deceased's property, their share will pass to their estates. Barney and Dexter have only contingent interests and, therefore, if either dies without attaining the age of 18 or marrying, or forming a civil partnership, his share of the estate will be divided amongst Ian's other children.

Example 15.4

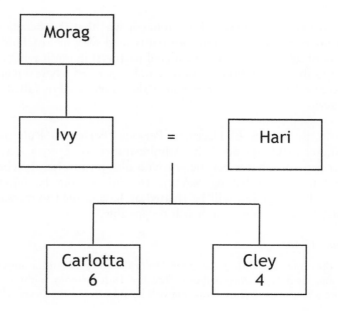

Ivy dies intestate in November 2014, survived by her husband Hari, her two children and her mother, Morag.

Hari, therefore, receives the personal chattels, the £250,000 statutory legacy (plus interest) and one half of the residue absolutely. The other half of the residue is held on the statutory trusts for the two children. If either dies without marrying or forming a civil partnership and before reaching the age of 18, the property will be held for the other on the statutory trusts. If both die unmarried and before reaching 18, the estate is dealt with as if they had never existed and Hari will be entitled to the whole estate.

If Ivy had died in September 2014, Hari would have taken a life interest in one half of the residue. If both children had died without a vested interest, they would be dealt with as if they had never existed and Hari would share the estate with Morag. His statutory legacy would be increased to £450,000 and any balance would be divided equally between Hari and Morag.

Estates of Deceased Persons (Forfeiture Rule and Law of Succession) Act 2011

15.27   The rule that no one can take under the statutory trusts whose parent is living was modified by s 46A of the Administration of Estates Act 1925 which was inserted by the Estates of Deceased Persons (Forfeiture Rule and Law of Succession) Act 2011 with effect from 1 February 2011. It provides that a person who disclaims an interest in the estate of an intestate or forfeits it by killing the intestate is to be treated as having predeceased the intestate. The result is that the issue of such a person can be substituted under the statutory trusts

15.28   The reason for the second amendment was that if a beneficiary with a contingent interest under the statutory trusts died without reaching the age of 18 and without marrying or forming a civil partnership but leaving a child then the statutory substitution did not apply. It only operated where a member of the class predeceased the intestate not where they survived but failed to attain a vested interest.

Section 3 of the Estates of Deceased Persons (Forfeiture Rule and Law of Succession) Act 2011 amended the Administration of Estates Act 1925. The amendment provides that a beneficiary who dies on or after 1 February 2012 with issue but without having reached 18 and without having married or forming a civil partnership will be treated as having died immediately before the intestate. Hence a substitution will be possible.

Example 15.5

Ivana dies intestate with a daughter Devora who is 16 and a single mother of Graziana, aged 1. If Devora dies before her 18th birthday without marrying or forming a civil partnership, Graziana will be substituted for Devora.[24]

---

[24]   Slightly oddly sub-section 1 of s 47 was not amended and this refers to the substitution of issue 'living at the death of the intestate'. It would, therefore, appear that a grandchild of the

4. ADOPTED CHILDREN

15.29 Under an intestacy arising on or after 1 January 1976, s 39 of the Adoption Act 1976 provides that an adopted child is the legitimate child of its adoptive parent or parents and of no one else. (This rule applies if the adoption order was made by a court in the UK, the Isle of Man or the Channel Islands. The same rule applies to certain foreign adoptions.) The child is thus debarred from claiming on the intestacy of its natural parents and is treated as a child of the adopting parents. Such a child may therefore be entitled to take on the intestacy of adoptive grandparents and brothers and sisters.

5. LEGITIMATED CHILDREN

15.30 Sections 5(1)–(4) and 10(1) of the Legitimacy Act 1976 provide that a legitimated child is entitled to share in a deceased's intestacy as if it had been born legitimate.

Children whose parents were not married at the time of their birth

15.31 In the case of deaths occurring before the coming into force of the Family Law Reform Act 1987, an illegitimate relationship was not generally recognised for the purposes of distribution of property on intestacy subject to two limited exceptions.

In respect of deaths occurring after 4 April 1988, the distribution of assets on intestacy (and otherwise) is to be determined without regard to whether or not the parents of a particular person were married to each other.[25]

---

intestate born after the death of the intestate would not be substituted. In **Example 15.5**, therefore, if on Ivana's death, Devora was 12 and gave birth to Graziana when she was 16 and then died without attaining a vested interest, Graziana would not be substituted.

[25] Section 18(2) of the Family Law Reform Act 1987 operates where a person dies intestate and his or her parents were not married to each other at the time of his or her birth. It contains a presumption that the intestate is deemed to have been predeceased by an unmarried father and by any other person to whom the intestate was related only through his or her father. Section 43 of the Human Fertilisation and Embryology Act 2008 allows a child to have a second female parent. The s 18(2) presumption also applies to second female parents (see the Family Law Reform Act 1987, s 18(2A)). The presumption assists personal representatives of an intestate child to distribute the estate where nothing is known of the father. Note, however, that the Inheritance and Trustees' Powers Act 2014 disapplies the presumption for deaths on or after 1 October 2014 where the father or other female parent is registered as the child's parent. The presumption does not apply to children who are legitimated.

6. HUMAN FERTILISATION AND EMBRYOLOGY ACT 2008

15.32 This Act makes significant changes to the legal definition of the term 'parent' with important implications for the application of the above rules in a number of cases:

(a) under s 33, where a woman has carried a child as a result of the placing in her of an embryo or of sperm and eggs she, and she alone, is treated as the mother of that child unless the child is subsequently adopted or another person obtains a parental order.[26] Under s 33 the husband of the mother is treated as the child's father unless it is shown that he did not consent to the procedure. Similarly where a woman is artificially inseminated with donor sperm, her husband is the father of the child unless it is shown that he did not consent;[27]

(b) where a woman is not married or where her husband is shown not to have consented, another man may, in certain cases, be treated as the father of the child. The main requirements are that the procedures involved are conducted in the UK by persons licensed to provide them and both parties have given written notice of consent to the man being treated as the father;[28]

(c) where a woman is a party to a civil partnership and bears a child as a result of the placing in her of an embryo or of sperm and eggs or as a result of artificial insemination, her civil partner is treated as the other parent of the child unless she is shown not to have consented to the procedure.[29] Another woman may be treated as the second parent subject to the same conditions, mutatis mutandis, as apply to a man.[30]

A person treated as the mother, father or parent of the child under these provisions is treated as the mother, father or parent *for all purposes* and 'reference to any relationship between two people in any enactment, deed or other instrument or document (whenever passed or made) are to be read accordingly'.[31] As far as intestacy is concerned this means that the effect of parenthood stretches beyond the child and its parents. For example, a child who is treated as a child of the mother's civil partner will also be treated as the brother or sister of the half blood of the civil partner's other children and the grandchild of the civil partner's parents.

15.33 The act also provides for parenthood in cases of surrogacy.[32] This requires an application to the court for a 'parental order' within 6 months of the birth. The child has to have been carried by a woman who is not one of the

---

26 See **15.33**.
27 Human Fertilisation and Embryology Act 2008, s 35.
28 Human Fertilisation and Embryology Act 2008, ss 36-38.
29 Human Fertilisation and Embryology Act 2008, s 42.
30 Human Fertilisation and Embryology Act 2008, ss 43-45.
31 Human Fertilisation and Embryology Act 2008, s 48.
32 Human Fertilisation and Embryology Act 2008, ss 54-56.

applicants. The embryo must have been created with the gametes of at least one of the applicants, the applicants must be a married couple, civil partners or living as partners in 'an enduring family relationship', they must be both over 18 and at least one of them must be domiciled in the UK, Channel Islands or Isle of Man. The child must be living with the applicants. The woman who bore the child and any other parent of the child (under this Act or otherwise) must consent. The surrogate mother must not have received payment other than for reasonable expenses. Once the order is made the child is effectively treated as adopted by the couple in whose favour the order is made.

7. THE RIGHTS OF OTHERS

15.34 Where there is no spouse or civil partner and no issue, the other relatives take in the order set out in Administration of Estates Act 1925, s 46.[33]

It should be noted that the relatives who take on the statutory trusts (that is brothers and sisters of the whole and half blood and uncles and aunts of the whole or half blood) must fulfil the same requirements as issue; that is, they must be living at the intestate's death and reach 18 or marry earlier. A person who predeceases the intestate can be replaced *per stirpes* by their own issue provided they reach the age of 18 marry or enter a civil partnership earlier.

8. *BONA VACANTIA*

15.35 In the case of property passing as *bona vacantia* s 46(1)(vi) of the Administration of Estates Act 1925 gives the Crown a discretion to make provision for dependants of the intestate whether they are related to the deceased or not. Similarly the Crown may provide for 'other persons for whom the intestate might reasonably have been expected to make provision'.[34]

However, it is rare for estates to be *bona vacantia*. Genealogists are so skilled that they will normally be able to trace next of kin.

---

[33] See **15.06** above.
[34] If the intestate died resident within the Duchy of Lancaster or in Cornwall, the Duchy or the Duke of Cornwall respectively take the assets as *bona vacantia* subject to the same discretions. The policy and the criteria applied by the Treasury Solicitor in making discretionary grants have been published since December 2002. (See The Treasury Solicitor *Bona Vacantia* Division, *Guide to discretionary grants in estates cases* (2005), para 31(a).) The criteria are similar to, but not the same as, the considerations to which the court must have regard in exercising its jurisdiction under the Inheritance (Provision for Family and Dependants) Act 1975. There may be circumstances where it is advantageous to claim under *bona vacantia* rather than under the 1975 Act. For example, cohabitants who claim reasonable financial provision under the 1975 Act, can only receive what is reasonable for their maintenance. There is no such restriction on claims under the *bona vacantia* jurisdiction.

CHAPTER 16

DONATIO MORTIS CAUSA

16.01 A Donatio Mortis Causa ('DMC') is an anomalous exception to the requirements of the Wills Acts. Its continued existence as a legal principle was confirmed by the Court of Appeal in *Sen v Headley*[1] in which Nourse LJ giving the judgment of the Court set out the conditions which are essential for a valid DMC as follows:

(a) the gift must be made in contemplation, although not necessarily in expectation, of impending death;

(b) the gift must be made upon the condition that it is to be absolute and perfected only on the donor's death, being revocable until that event occurs and ineffective if it does not;

(c) there must be a delivery of the subject matter of the gift, or the essential indicia of title thereto, which amounts to a parting with dominion and not mere physical possession over the subject matter of the gift.

16.02 Because of its peculiar characteristics the courts will examine any case of alleged donatio mortis causa and reject it if, in truth, what is alleged to be a donatio is an attempt to make a will not complying with the requirements of the Wills Act.

The elements required for a valid DMC have been considered in several recent decisions.

1. A GIFT CONDITIONAL ON DEATH

16.03 In *King v Dubrey*[2] the deceased over a 5-month period leading up to her death had signed documents purporting to give her house to her nephew (who was acting as an unpaid carer) after her death. Unfortunately they were all invalid as wills as they were not correctly witnessed. The nephew's evidence was that about 4–6 months before she died, his aunt presented him with the deeds to the house and said 'this will be yours when I go'. The nephew was living with his aunt at the time but said that he had put the deeds in his wardrobe in a part of the house his aunt did not enter.

---

[1]   [1991] Ch 425.
[2]   [2014] EWHC 2083 (Ch).

16.04 The residuary beneficiaries of an earlier valid will argued that there was no sufficiently clear and unequivocal evidence of a gift, whether conditional on death or at all. She had made wills which purported to leave the house to her nephew. The proper characterisation of the alleged conversation relating to the title documents was that she was giving him the documents as a matter of administrative convenience, rather than as an act of gift. The words used were not 'If I die, the house is yours', but 'this [the deeds] will be yours when I go'. She did not refer to a gift of the house at all.

Charles Hollander QC sitting as a deputy judge did not accept this.

> 'In my judgment the words used, in context, were indeed suggestive of a gift conditional on death and not consistent with any other interpretation. In particular, I reject the suggestion that the purpose of handing him the deeds was to facilitate his position as executor.'

2. CONTEMPLATION OF DEATH

16.05 In *Vallee v Birchwood*[3] the residuary beneficiaries of the will argued that there was nothing to suggest that the deceased was contemplating impending death. It was necessary for there to be some identifiable event that might cause the donor's death or some identifiable, if not precisely defined, period in which the donor expects his death to occur, and on which the gift is conditional. There was nothing of that nature in this case. The deceased was simply elderly and frail.

The judge found that the gift was made expressly in contemplation of death at a time when the deceased was was increasingly preoccupied with her impending death, as evidenced by the failed wills.

3. HOW IMPENDING MUST DEATH BE?

16.06 It had been thought that the gift must be made in contemplation of death 'within the near future'.[4] However, in *Vallee v Birchwood*[5] the gap between gift and death was 4 months and the deceased had not been diagnosed with any life threatening illness at the time of the gift. The facts were that in August he was visited by his daughter who lived in France. He was not well and coughing badly. When his daughter said that she would visit him again before Christmas, he replied that he did not expect to live very much longer and might not be alive by then. He said that he wanted her to have the house when he died. He went into another room and returned with the deeds to the house and a key, all of which he gave to her. He died on 11 December.

---

3   [2013] EWHC 1449 (Ch).
4   See *Re Craven's Estate (No 1)* [1937] Ch 423. Death occurred within 5 days.
5   [2013] EWHC 1449 (Ch).

16.07 Jonathan Gaunt QC sitting as a deputy judge held that the gift was made in contemplation of his impending death. Counsel had submitted that there was no evidence that the deceased was suffering from an illness likely to prove terminal and that an actual interval of 4 months between gift and death was too long to count as 'impending'. However, Judge Gaunt held that this was not the point. The question is not whether the donor had good grounds to anticipate his imminent demise or whether his demise proved to be as speedy as he may have feared but whether the motive for the gift was that he subjectively contemplated the possibility of death in the near future. It appears that the deceased did contemplate the possibility that he would die before Christmas when his daughter was next to visit him. In that context that was the near future. The fact that the case-law requires only that the gift be made in the *contemplation* and not necessarily the *expectation* of death supports this view.

4. DELIVERY OF SUBJECT MATTER OR SUFFICIENT INDICIA OF TITLE

16.08 Mere symbolic delivery, for example a locked box to which the donor retains the key, will not suffice.[6] There must be something to show that the deceased was parting with dominion and putting it out of his power to deal unilaterally with the asset.

16.09 It might, therefore, be supposed that there could be a valid DMC only of such property as is capable of actual manual delivery. But this is not the case. In *Birch v Treasury Solicitor*[7] the Court of Appeal held that delivery of a Post Office Savings Book and Bank Deposit Pass Books with words indicating that the money in the accounts should belong to the recipients was sufficient. The books were indicia or evidence of title.

16.10 Until 1990, textbook writers were virtually unanimous that there could not be a DMC of land. This view was based in part on the view that there could not be appropriate delivery. However, this was held to be wrong by the Court of Appeal in *Sen v Headley*.[8] The facts were that the deceased, a Mr Hewett, was dying in hospital from inoperable cancer; he was visited daily by his long term friend Mrs Sen who was looking after his house, to which she had always had her own set of keys. He asked her to bring to the hospital a bunch of keys kept in a drawer of the sideboard. Three days before his death Mrs Sen asked Mr Hewett what she should do about the house if anything should happen to him. Mr Hewett replied, 'The house is yours, Margaret. You have the keys. They are in your bag. The deeds are in the steel box.' After Mr Hewett's death, Mrs Sen found in her handbag the bunch of keys which she had brought to the hospital at his request; it appeared that he must have slipped them into her handbag without her noticing. One of them was the key to a locked steel box in which the title deeds to the house were kept; another was the key to a cupboard

---

6   *Ward v Turner* (1752) 28 ER 275, 2 Ves Sen 431.
7   [1951] Ch 298.
8   [1991] Ch 425.

in which Mrs Sen found the box. Mr Hewitt had kept his own set of keys but, as the Court of Appeal observed, the benefits which thereby accrued to him were wholly theoretical. He had uttered the words of gift 2 days after his admission to hospital when he knew that he did not have long to live and when there could have been no practical possibility of his ever returning home. The Court of Appeal, reversing the trial judge, held that land could, in principle, be made the subject of a DMC. So far as delivery was concerned in the case of a chose in action parting with dominion over the essential indicia of title will usually be enough. Here Mr Hewitt had parted with dominion over the title deeds and Mrs Sen had her own set of keys to the house and was in effective control of it.

16.11 In *Vallee v Birchwood*[9] the deceased had remained living in the house after delivering the title deeds to his daughter. Was delivery to the donee of exclusive physical possession or control over the land a crucial element for a valid DMC?

Judge Gaunt QC held that this was not required. A DMC does not become effective until the death of the donor, so until then the property remains both in law and in equity the donor's property. There was no reason why acts of continued enjoyment of his own property should be regarded as incompatible with an intention to make a gift effective on death. Had the subject matter of the gift been land already subject to a tenancy, the donor could have continued to enjoy the rent. This was no different in principle from the donor continuing to enjoy his own house by living in it.[10] The delivery of the deeds would have put it out of his power to transfer it and the handing over of the key as well would give the donee access to the house and diminish to some extent the donor's control.

16.12 In *King v Dubrey*[11] the residuary beneficiaries argued that there had been no sufficient delivery because the deceased remained in possession of the house and the title deeds remained there too, albeit that the donee claimed he had placed them in a wardrobe. They argued that it cannot be said that a person has parted with dominion over a property when the indicia of title continue to be available to them in their own home and thus within their control. Indeed, they contended that the words used by the deceased did not suggest that she parted with dominion over the documents themselves: she simply stated that they would be her nephew's 'when I go'.

Charles Hollander QC held that there had been sufficient delivery. Firstly, the nephew placed the deeds in a wardrobe in his room in the house, in a place which was known to him and which was part of the house used, in practice, exclusively by him. Secondly, the terms of the conversation of which the nephew gave evidence indicated that the deceased did indeed intend to part

---

9   [2013] EWHC 1449 (Ch).
10   In the later case of *King v Dubrey* [2014] EWHC 2083 (Ch) the donor also continued to occupy the house which, it was held, was subject to a valid DMC.
11   [2014] EWHC 2083 (Ch).

with dominion over the property, but that was to be conditional on her death. *Vallee v Birchwood*[12] had made it clear that the continued enjoyment of the property during the life of the donor was not incompatible with an intention to make a gift which was effective on the donor's death.

16.13 Although the requirements of a valid DMC appear to be difficult to establish, recent decisions suggest that courts are prepared to take a general view of the deceased's intentions.

5. INHERITANCE TAX TREATMENT OF A DMC

16.14 Because a DMC is only perfected on death, the property is comprised in the estate of the deceased 'immediately before' his death (like jointly owned property) and so is taxed as part of his death estate under IHTA 1984, s 4. Note, in particular, that it is not a failed PET so that the IHT lifetime exemptions are not capable of applying: it is valued at the date of death and will be taxed at the estate rate. Liability for tax is on the PRs and donee although, like a specific gift in the will, it may be assumed that the tax is to be borne out of the residue.

---

[12] [2013] EWHC 1449 (Ch).

CHAPTER 17

THE INHERITANCE (PROVISION FOR FAMILY AND DEPENDANTS) ACT 1975

INTRODUCTION

17.01 A testator is free to leave property in whatever way he pleases; no relative has a right to receive property under the will. However, this principle of testamentary freedom is to some extent restricted by the Inheritance (Provision for Family and Dependants) Act 1975.[1] This Act gives the court limited powers to order financial provision to be made from the net estate of a deceased person for the benefit of certain categories of applicant. Applications under the Act can also be made when a person dies intestate.

It is, of course, particularly distressing if careful will drafting and tax planning is upset by applications under the Act and so it is desirable to consider whether any such application is likely to be made.

1. WHAT THE APPLICANT MUST ESTABLISH

17.02 To bring a successful claim an applicant must establish that certain preliminary requirements are satisfied, *viz*:

(a) that the application is made within the time limit;

(b) that the applicant falls into one of the five possible categories of applicant; and

(c) that the will or intestacy rules have not made reasonable provision for the applicant.

If these matters are established the court must then decide whether and in what manner to order financial provision for the applicant from the net estate of the deceased (to help the court in its decision there are certain statutory guidelines to be taken into account).

The Act contains anti-avoidance provisions under which orders may, in limited circumstances, be made against people who have received property from the deceased before his death.[2]

---

[1] And its predecessor the Inheritance (Family Provision) Act 1938.
[2] See **17.46** below.

17.03 Significant amendments to the existing legislation were made by the Inheritance and Trustees' Powers Act 2014 for deaths occurring on or after 1 October 2014. It is therefore necessary to deal separately with the provisions applying before and after that date.

2. PRELIMINARY REQUIREMENTS

Domicile

17.04 The Act applies only in the case of a deceased who dies domiciled in England and Wales after 31 March 1976 (s 1(1)); earlier legislation (which was narrower in its scope) applies to deaths before that date).

Questions of domicile frequently arise[3] and often have to be dealt with as a preliminary issue in applications under the Act.

Time limit

17.05 Section 4 of the Act originally provided that applications must be made within 6 months of the date of the first full and effective grant of representation.[4]

In *Re McBroom*[5] Eastham J held that it is necessary for a grant of representation to have been taken out to the deceased's estate before an application can be made. However, the earlier case of *Re Searle*[6] was not cited. In *Re Searle* Roxburghe J said that the time limit was concerned with applications being too late and not too early.

The Inheritance and Trustees' Powers Act 2014 amended s 4 to provide that nothing prevents the making of an application before such representation is first taken out.

It would be difficult to proceed to a substantive hearing of the claim until the assets and liabilities of the estate are reasonably clear. In most cases, this will not be possible without the appointment of personal representatives.

---

3   For examples, see *Cyganik v Agulian* [2006] EWCA Civ 129; *Holliday v Musa* [2010] EWCA Civ 335.

4   Inheritance (Provision for Family and Dependants) Act 1975, s 23 excluded for this purpose a grant limited to settled land or to trust property together with a grant limited to real estate or to personal estate unless a grant limited to the remainder of the estate had previously been made or was made at the same time. For deaths on or after 1 October 2014 the Inheritance and Trustees' Powers Act 2014, Sch 3 amended s 23 to add to the exclusions any other grant that does not permit any of the estate to be distributed and a grant, or its equivalent, made outside the United Kingdom (a grant sealed under the Colonial Probates Act 1892, s 2 counts as a grant made in the United Kingdom for the purposes of this section, to be taken as dated at the date of sealing).

5   *Re McBroom* [1992] 2 FLR 49.

6   *Re Searle* [1949] Ch 73.

CPR 57.16 has been amended to include a new (3A) and (3B) as follows:

'(3A) Where no grant has been obtained, the claimant may make a claim without naming a defendant and may apply for directions as to the representation of the estate. The written evidence must –

(a)   explain the reasons why it has not been possible for a grant to be obtained;

(b)   be accompanied by the original or a copy (if either is available) of the will or other testamentary document in respect of which probate or letters of administration are to be granted; and

(c)   contain the following information, so far as known to the claimant –

(i)   brief details of the property comprised in the estate, with an approximate estimate of its capital value and any income that is received from it;

(ii)   brief details of the liabilities of the estate;

(iii)   the names and addresses of the persons who are in possession of the documents relating to the estate; and

(iv)   the names of the beneficiaries and their respective interests in the estate.

(3B) Where a claim is made in accordance with paragraph (3A), the court may give directions as to the parties to the claim and as to the representation of the estate either on the claimant's application or on its own initiative.'

17.06   The court has always had a discretion to extend the time limit. This discretion is unfettered[7] and the Act itself contains no guidance as to how the court should exercise it. However, in *Re Salmon (Deceased)*[8] Megarry V–C suggested six guidelines. These were concisely summarised in *Re Dennis*[9] as follows:

'First, the discretion of the court, though judicial, is unfettered. Second, the onus is on the applicant to show special reasons for taking the matter out of the general six month time limit; ... this is not a mere triviality but a substantial requirement. Third, the court has to consider how promptly and in what circumstances the application has been made after the time has expired; one has to look at all the circumstances surrounding the delay. Fourth, the court has to see whether negotiations have started within the six month period. Fifth, one has to consider whether or not the estate has been distributed before the claim has been notified. Sixth, the court has to consider whether refusal of leave to bring proceedings out of time will leave the applicant without recourse against anyone else ...'

(An example of a person against whom an applicant might have recourse would be a negligent solicitor.)

---

7   There was a special restriction in relation to interests which had passed by survivorship but this has been removed by an amendment inserted by the Inheritance and Trustees' Powers Act 2014. See **17.43**.

8   *Coard v National Westminster Bank* [1981] Ch 167.

9   *Dennis v Lloyds Bank* [1981] 2 All ER 140.

The list was not intended to be exhaustive and *Re Dennis* itself added a further guideline, 'by analogy with applications for leave to defend in summary judgment proceedings, the applicant must show that he has an arguable case, a case fit to go to trial'.

In *Berger v Berger*[10] the Court of Appeal refused leave despite the appellant's strong arguable case because of the length of the delay (6½ years from the date of the grant). In other cases of lengthy delay where applications had been allowed, there had been a change in circumstance to 'trigger' the application. Here there was no such trigger. The widow had simply come to the conclusion that the provision made for her was inadequate.[11]

Practical considerations

17.07 The reason for having a short time limit is to enable personal representatives to distribute assets without fear of personal liability if a successful application is later made. The Act provides therefore that a personal representative can distribute after the expiry of 6 months from the date of grant without personal liability even if the court does later extend the time limit.[12] Where an out of time application is allowed there is power to recover any part of the estate already distributed to the beneficiaries by the personal representatives.

Obviously a cautious personal representative would wait 6 months before distributing assets; a very cautious personal representative would wait even longer since a claimant, having issued a claim has 4 months in which to serve it.[13] Yet in most cases such caution will be unnecessary and may even cause hardship if a beneficiary is in urgent need of finance. A personal representative should therefore carefully consider the circumstances before deciding whether or not to wait for the expiry of the 6-month period. The following matters are relevant:

(a)   since an order for financial provision is made against the *net* estate of the deceased (see **17.42**) there can be no objection to paying funeral, testamentary and administration expenses, debts and liabilities before the expiry of the 6-month period;

(b)   it will normally be safe to pay a legacy to a beneficiary who is intending to make an application to obtain more (unless there is a risk of applications from other people);

(c)   since it is unlikely that the court would order provision to be financed out of a very small legacy when the estate is large such a legacy can safely be paid;

---

10   *Berger v Berger* [2013] EWCA Civ 1305.
11   For cases where leave was granted see *McNulty v McNulty* [2002] EWHC 123 (Ch); *Stock v Brown* [1994] 1 FLR 840.
12   Inheritance (Provision for Family and Dependants Act 1975, s 20.
13   CPR 7.5.

(d)   similarly it will often be safe to distribute assets to a beneficiary who has a strong moral claim, particularly if in urgent need.

3. THE CATEGORIES OF APPLICANT

17.08   The following persons may apply to the court (under s 1(1) as amended) for an order in their favour on the ground that the deceased's will or the intestacy rules have not made reasonable provision for them.

The spouse or civil partner of the deceased

17.09   The applicant must show that there was a subsisting marriage or civil partnership at the time of the deceased's death. This category includes the wife of a polygamous marriage: *Re Sehota, Surjit Kaur v Gian Kaur*.[14] This category includes a party to a voidable marriage which has not been annulled prior to death.[15]

A judicially separated spouse or a civil partner where a separation order is in place comes into this category but may be barred from making an application by a court order under ss 15 or 15ZA of the Act.[16]

A former spouse or civil partner

17.10   A former spouse or civil partner is a person whose marriage or civil partnership with the deceased was dissolved or annulled during the deceased's lifetime by a decree made under the law of any part of the British Islands (the UK, Channel Islands and Isle of Man) or in any country or territory outside the British Islands by a divorce or annulment 'which is entitled to be recognised as valid by the law of England and Wales'.[17]

The Act provides, however, in the interests of finality that a former spouse or civil partner may be barred from applying for financial provision by a court order on the granting of a decree of divorce, nullity, or judicial separation,[18] or dissolution, nullity or separation order.[19] Moreover, the Court of Appeal

---

[14]   [1978] 3 All ER 385.
[15]   Unusually a person will be regarded as a surviving spouse or civil partner even though the marriage or civil partnership was void, provided the applicant entered into the marriage or civil partnership in good faith, unless in the lifetime of the deceased:
(i) the marriage or civil partnership has been dissolved or annulled; or
(ii) the applicant entered into a later marriage or civil partnership.
However, a ceremony which does not purport to be of the kind contemplated by the Marriage Acts, produces a non-marriage rather than a void marriage and the parties will not be eligible to make an application. See *A v A* [2012] EWHC 2219 (Fam) and *Gandhi v Patel* [2002] 1 FLR 603.
[16]   See **17.10** below.
[17]   Inheritance (Provision for Family and Dependants) Act 1975, s 25.
[18]   I(PFD)A 1975, s 15.
[19]   I(PFD)A 1975, s 15ZA.

observed in *Re Fullard*[20] that in view of the wide powers of the court to make financial arrangements on divorce, the number of cases in which it would be appropriate for a former spouse to apply under the family provision legislation would be small. An example of such a case might be where the estate received the proceeds of a large insurance policy on the deceased's death or where the applicant had been provided for in the divorce proceedings by means of periodical payments rather than by a lump sum.[21]

A person who has lived with the deceased in the same household as husband or wife for 2 years

17.11   To be eligible the applicant must not be included in either of the two preceding categories. The deceased must have died on or after 1 January 1996 and during the whole of the period of 2 years ending immediately before the death of the deceased the applicant must have been living:

(a)   in the same household as the deceased; and

(b)   as the husband or wife of the deceased.

As a result of the wording of the subsection an application is bound to fail if there is any interruption in the 2-year period of cohabitation prior to death. For example, where an applicant ceases living with the deceased, then resumes but fails to 'clock up' a full 2-year period before the death. Separations brought about by external circumstances, eg illness necessitating a stay in hospital or hospice care are irrelevant.[22] Similarly temporary absences which do not put an end to the relationship are ignored. In *Gully v Dix*[23] the Court of Appeal held that the trial judge was correct in finding that a 3-month absence did not prevent the claimant being a person who had lived with the deceased as his wife for a period of 2 years ending with his death. It is necessary to look at the settled state of affairs that existed between the parties before the date of death and not any de facto separation between the couple.

It may be difficult to determine whether a couple are living together as husband and wife. In *Re Watson (Deceased)* the applicant and the deceased had known each other since 1964. She moved into the deceased's house in 1985. They had no sexual relationship after she moved in although they had had one before. Mr Watson worked and provided most of the funds for the household. The applicant paid her share of the cost of utilities and was responsible for shopping, cooking and gardening. The court decided that they had lived together as husband and wife.

---

[20]   *Re Fullard* [1982] Fam 4.
[21]   For unsuccessful applications by former spouses, see also *Barrass v Harding* [2001] 1 FLR 138 and *Cameron v Treasury Solicitor* [1996] 2 FLR 716.
[22]   See *Re Watson (Deceased)* [1999] 3 FCR 595.
[23]   *Gully v Dix* [2004] 1 WLR 1399. For an even more striking example, see *Kaur v Dhaliwal* [2014] EWHC 1991 (Ch).

Neuberger J, as he then was, said that it is necessary to ask whether, in the opinion of a reasonable person with normal perceptions, it could be said that the two people in question were living together as husband and wife. However, 'one should not ignore the multifarious nature of marital relationships'.[24] The fact that the couple had an agreement as to who paid for what and who did which jobs did not prevent the arrangement being a marital one. It was also irrelevant that the claimant had another property available to her.

Importantly, there must be an element of public recognition in the relationship. A marriage and a civil partnership are publicly acknowledged relationships. It is not possible for two persons to live together as civil partners unless their relationship as a couple is an acknowledged one: see *Baynes v Hedger*.[25]

A person who has lived with the deceased in the same household as civil partner for 2 years

17.12   During the whole period of 2 years ending immediately before the death of the deceased the person must have been living:

(a)   in the same household as the deceased; and

(b)   as the civil partner of the deceased.

The same points are relevant as for applications under s 1(1A).

A child of the deceased

17.13   This category includes a child of a non-marital relationship, a legitimated or adopted child and a child *en ventre sa mere*. A child who has been adopted is no longer eligible to make a claim as a child of the natural parent.

There is no distinction between sons and daughters and neither age nor marriage are automatic disqualifications.

It was sometimes said that adult able-bodied children had to show an additional 'threshold' requirement of a special obligation owed to them by the deceased. However, the Court of Appeal has expressly rejected this in a number of cases stating that it is not permissible to apply any 'gloss' to the words of the statute.[26] Section 3 contains a list of factors the court should take into account when deciding whether or not provision is reasonable and it is not permissible to add additional requirements.

---

[24]   *Re Watson (Deceased)* [1999] 3 FCR 595 at 601.
[25]   See *Baynes v Hedger* [2008] EWHC 1587 (Ch). In *Lindop v Agus* [2009] EWHC 1795 (Ch) the court found that there was sufficient public recognition to justify a claim.
[26]   See *Re Hancock* [1998] 2 FLR 346; *Re Pearce* [1998] 2 FLR 705; *Espinosa v Bourke* [1999] 1 FLR 747; and *Ilott v Mitson* [2011] EWCA Civ 346.

Accordingly, the approach now is that the court will consider all the circumstances in reaching its decision and try to balance all factors. An adult able-bodied child who cannot produce an argument to buttress his claim beyond being badly off is still unlikely to be successful.

A person (not being a child of the deceased) who is treated by the deceased as a child of the family

17.14 The concept of 'a child of the family' is imported from family law (Matrimonial Causes Act 1973, s 52(1) although under that Act the child must have been treated as a child of the family by *both* parties to the marriage). Applicants can be children of the family even though they were adult when the deceased married their parent.[27]

For deaths before 1 October 2014 the child must have been treated as a child of the family 'in connection with a marriage or civil partnership to which the deceased was a party'.

For deaths on or after 1 October 2014 the Inheritance and Trustees' Powers Act 2014 removed the requirement for a marriage or civil partnership. The child can be treated as a child of the family in relation to 'any marriage or civil partnership to which the deceased was at any time a party, or otherwise in relation to any family in which the deceased at any time stood in the role of a parent, was treated by the deceased as a child of the family ...'. The reference to a 'family' includes a family of which the deceased was the only member (apart from the applicant). So a single parent family is included within the scope of s 1(1)(d) as amended.

Any person (not being a person included in the above paragraphs) who immediately before the death of the deceased was being maintained wholly or partly by the deceased

17.15 To decide whether a person is being maintained the starting point is s 1(3) which as originally enacted provided that:

> '... a person shall be treated as being maintained by the deceased, either wholly or partly ... if the deceased was making a substantial contribution in money or money's worth towards the reasonable needs of that person.'

For deaths before 1 October 2014, s 1(1)(e) required that the contribution had to be 'otherwise than for full valuable consideration'. These words caused problems where there was inter-dependency: for example where one party provided funds and the other provided care or where both parties provide a mixture of funds and services. The courts accepted that such services were

---

[27]   See *Re Callaghan* [1985] Fam 1; *Re Leach (Deceased)* [1986] Ch 226.

capable of amounting to full valuable consideration.[28] However, it is a question of fact in each case. The court will normally allow an application to proceed to the later stages of trial unless it is absolutely clear that the services made by the applicant outweigh the contributions made by the deceased to the applicant's maintenance. If, however, it is clear that the services amounted to full valuable consideration the application should be struck out at a preliminary stage in order to avoid the costs of further proceedings. In *Bishop v Plumley*[29] the Court of Appeal stated that a common sense approach should be adopted 'avoiding fine balancing computations involving the value of normal exchanges of support in the domestic sense'.

17.16 For deaths on or after 1 October 2014 the Inheritance and Trustees' Powers Act 2014 amended s 1(3). It provided that the words 'otherwise than for full valuable consideration' were to be omitted. Instead, there is a narrower exception for any contribution that was made for full valuable consideration pursuant to an arrangement of a commercial nature. This means that contributions made between people in a domestic context of interdependancy are no longer to be weighed against one another for these purposes.

It is for the applicant to demonstrate that he is within the terms of the subsection.

A 'substantial contribution'

17.17 It is obviously difficult to state definitely what amounts to a 'substantial contribution' but in *Jelley v Iliffe* the Court of Appeal regarded the provision of rent free accommodation as substantial.

The meaning of 'immediately before the death'

17.18 Problems have arisen in connection with this phrase. For example, in *Re Beaumont*[30] the deceased had habitually maintained the applicant but had been unable to do so in the few weeks immediately before her death when she was ill in hospital. Megarry V–C accepted that the court must look at 'the settled basis or ... general arrangement between the parties' not at 'the actual, perhaps fluctuating, variation of it which exists immediately before ... death'.

---

[28] See *Re Wilkinson* [1978] Fam 22; *Re Beaumont* [1980] Ch 444; *Jelley v Iliffe* [1981] Fam. 128, King v *Dubrey* [2014] EWHC 2083 (Ch).
[29] *Bishop v Plumley* [1991] 1 WLR 582 and for a recent example, see *King v Dubrey* [2014] EWHC 2083 (Ch).
[30] *Re Beaumont* [1980] Ch 444.

4. REASONABLE PROVISION

Two standards

17.19 Section 1(2) of the Act sets out two standards for judging whether or not provision is reasonable, one to be applied in the case of a surviving spouse or civil partner (not including a judicially separated spouse or a civil partner where a separation order was in force) and one to be applied in other cases.

The standard for surviving spouses and civil partners

17.20 The standard is such financial provision as it would be reasonable in all the circumstances for a spouse or civil partner to receive 'whether or not that provision is required for his or her maintenance'.[31]

The court has a discretion to apply this standard where a decree of judicial separation, nullity or divorce has been made within 12 months of death and no order for financial provision has been made (or refused) in the matrimonial proceedings.[32]

The ordinary standard

17.21 This is 'such financial provision as it would be reasonable in all the circumstances of the case for the applicant to receive for his maintenance'.[33] It is difficult to give a precise meaning to the word 'maintenance' in this context. It does not mean just enough to enable a person to get by (ie mere subsistence) but on the other hand it does not extend to everything which may be regarded as reasonably desirable for their general benefit or welfare. Buckley LJ suggested in *Re Coventry*[34] that it could be regarded as 'such financial provision as would be reasonable in all the circumstances of the case to enable the applicant to maintain himself in a manner suitable to these circumstances.'

The restriction of provision to that required for maintenance is often fatal to applications by non-spouses.[35]

It is not the purpose of the Act to provide legacies for disappointed beneficiaries but this does not mean that provision for maintenance is limited to income payments. Provision could be by way of a lump sum, for example, to buy a house in which the applicant could be housed, thereby removing one expense from the applicant.[36]

---

[31] Inheritance (Provision for Family and Dependants) Act 1975, s 1(2)(a).
[32] Inheritance (Provision for Family and Dependants) Act 1975, s 14.
[33] Inheritance (Provision for Family and Dependants) Act 1975, s 1(2)(b).
[34] *Re Coventry deceased* [1980] Ch 461.
[35] See, for example, *Re Jennings deceased* [1994] Ch 286.
[36] *Re Dennis* (1981) 2 All ER 140.

An objective standard

17.22   The court is to decide whether the provision made for an applicant is reasonable. This is very much a matter for the first instance tribunal and, as Goff LJ said in *Re Coventry*[37] 'ought not to be interfered with by us unless we are satisfied that it was plainly wrong'. The same view was taken by the Court of Appeal in *Ilott v Mitson*[38] where Sir Nicholas Wall P said that the trial judge's conclusion on the evidence 'should not be lightly disturbed' unless the conclusion reached is 'plainly wrong'.

Under s 3(5) of the Act the court is allowed to consider changes in the position of beneficiaries and applicants arising after the death of the deceased. The court is concerned therefore with the facts of the case rather than merely with the facts known to the deceased.

Where a testator has reasons for making no provision for a relative or dependant it is desirable that they should leave a record of those reasons with the will. The court will not necessarily agree with the reasons[39] but it will consider them.

Reasonable provision may be nothing. So, for example, the court refused to order any provision: in *Re Coventry*[40] for an adult child; in *Rhodes v Dean*[41] for a cohabitee; and in *Parish v Sharman*[42] for a surviving spouse.

5. MATTERS THE COURT MUST CONSIDER (S 3)

17.23   When deciding whether the provision made is reasonable, and, if not, what provision to order, the court is required to consider the matters set out in s 3 of the Act. Some are common to all applicants while some are limited to a particular category. Changes were introduced by the Inheritance and Trustees' Powers Act 2014.

6. MATTERS COMMON TO ALL CATEGORIES

17.24   Under s 3(1) the court will have regard to the following matters:

(a)   *the financial resources and needs of the applicant, any other applicant and any beneficiary.* Earning capacity and social security benefits are relevant.[43] The court must balance the resources and needs of all the

---

37   *Re Coventry deceased* [1980] Ch 461.
38   *Ilott v Mitson* [2011] EWCA Civ 346.
39   See *Singer v Isaac* [2001] WTLR 1045 where the court described the deceased's statement of reasons as 'self-serving'.
40   *Re Coventry deceased* [1980] Ch 461.
41   *Rhodes v Dean* [1996] CLY 555.
42   *Parish v Sharman* [2001] WTLR 593.
43   *Re E* [1966] 2 All ER 44, [1966] 1 WLR 709.

persons with a claim on the estate. It should take into account any needs which are reasonably likely to arise. Those needs do not need to be more likely than not but the degree of probability should be taken into account. In *Challinor v Challinor*[44] the applicant was an adult suffering from Down's syndrome – future increased needs for personal care and physiotherapy were taken into account. In *Barron v Woodhead*[45] provision of living accommodation for an applicant who would otherwise be homeless was considered particularly relevant. Similarly, in *Moore v Holdsworth*[46] an award was increased to enable a chronically ill surviving spouse to return to the home she had shared with the deceased during their long marriage. Poor financial circumstances do not guarantee an order (*Garland v Morris*[47]);

(b) *any obligations and responsibilities of the deceased towards the applicant or any beneficiary.* The Court of Appeal made it clear in *Re Jennings*[48] that the obligations and responsibilities must still be operating on the deceased at the date of death. In that case, the deceased had abandoned his wife and son (the claimant) when the son was 2. He had had no further contact with him and made no provision for him. When the father died, he left nothing to the son, the bulk of the estate going to charity. At first instance the judge construed s 3(1)(d) so as to include legal obligations and responsibilities which the deceased had, but had failed to discharge during the child's minority even though they were long spent and would have been incapable of founding a claim against him immediately before his death. The Court of Appeal said that was a wrong approach. The Act does not 'revive defunct obligations and responsibilities'. However, in *Myers v Myers*[49] and *Gold v Curtis*[50] the court seemed to accept the idea of continuing obligations and responsibilities;

(c) *the size and nature of the estate.* If an estate is large it is frequently relatively easy for the court to make adequate provision for applicants; where the estate is very small, however, it is often impossible to provide adequately for all beneficiaries and applicants. Moreover since the costs of an action normally come out of the estate the action may exhaust a large part of the assets. The courts, therefore, discourage applications in such cases (*Re Coventry;*[51] *Jelley v Iliffe*[52]). The costs of an unsuccessful application are likely to fall on the applicant. Solicitors should always bear in mind the question of costs when advising clients who wish to make a claim, especially one against a small estate.

The source of the deceased's assets is often an important consideration. For example, the court is likely to be sympathetic to an application by a

44 *Challinor v Challinor* [2009] EWHC 180 (Ch).
45 *Barron v Woodhead* [2008] EWHC 810 (Ch).
46 *Moore v Holdsworth* [2010] EWHC 683 (Ch).
47 *Garland v Morris* [2007] EWHC 2 (Ch).
48 *Re Jennings* [1994] Ch 286.
49 *Myers v Myers* [2004] EWHC 1944.
50 *Gold v Curtis* [2005] WTLR 673.
51 *Re Coventry (Deceased)* [1980] Ch 461.
52 *Jelley v Iliffe* [1981] Fam 128.

child when the deceased parent inherited a large part of their estate from the other parent (as in *Espinosa v Bourke*[53]);

(d) *any physical or mental disability of any applicant or any beneficiary*. The availability of state aid, hospital accommodation and social security benefits may be considered (*Re Watkins*[54]);

(e) *any other matter*, including the conduct of the applicant or any other person which the court may consider relevant. This gives the court a great deal of freedom. In *Re Snoek (Deceased)*[55] an award to a spouse was set at a much lower amount than it would otherwise have been as a result of a history of assaults and other abuses in the years before the deceased's death. However, *Barron v Woodhead*[56] suggests that only quite extreme conduct by a surviving spouse should lead to a reduced award. In *Espinosa v Bourke*[57] the applicant's conduct in abandoning her father while she went on extended holidays counted against her as did the applicant's 15-year separation from her father in *Garland v Morris*. In *Re Goodchild*[58] the applicant's mother had died believing that there was an agreement between herself and her husband to leave their combined estates to their son after the death. The agreement was not enforceable but was regarded as relevant to the application. In *Wright v Waters*[59] the applicant's conduct counted strongly against her.

7. MATTERS FOR PARTICULAR CATEGORIES

17.25 Under s 3(2) without prejudice to the common guidelines the court will also consider additional guidelines in relation to each category.

A surviving spouse or civil partner

17.26 Section 3(2) provides that the court will consider:

(a) the age of the applicant and the duration of the marriage or civil partnership;

(b) the contribution made by the applicant to the welfare of the family of the deceased, including any contribution made by looking after the home or caring for the family; and

(c) the provision the applicant might reasonably have expected to receive if on the day on which the deceased died the marriage or civil partnership (instead of being terminated by death) had ended in divorce or dissolution.

---

[53] *Espinosa v Bourke* [1999] 1 FLR 747.
[54] *Re Watkins* [1949] 1 All ER 695.
[55] *Re Snoek (Deceased)* (1983) 13 Fam Law 19.
[56] *Barron v Woodhead* [2008] EWHC 810 (Ch), [2009] 1 FLR 747, [2008] Fam Law 844.
[57] *Espinosa v Bourke* [1999] 1 FLR 747.
[58] *Re Goodchild* [1997] 2 FLR 644.
[59] [2014] EWHC 3614 (Ch).

For deaths on or after 1 October 2014 the Inheritance and Trustees' Powers Act 2014 amended s 3(2) to state expressly that the court is not required to treat the provision likely to be obtained on death or dissolution as setting an upper or lower limit on the provision that can be awarded to applicants. There had been some conflicting case law although in *P v G (family provision: relevance of divorce provision)*[60] the court said that it was permissible to take into account the fact that it was assessing the reasonable needs of one person, not two. Thus the court could decide to make greater provision under the Act than it would have done in determining an ancillary relief application without offending the principle of testamentary freedom.

17.27   Although the provision the applicant might reasonably have expected to receive on divorce or dissolution is only one of the factors to be considered, it is extremely significant and is likely to result in a surviving spouse or civil partner receiving a substantial part of the estate. The House of Lords in *White v White*[61] said there should be no bias in favour of a money earning spouse and that a judge would be well advised to 'check his tentative views against the yardstick of equality of division'. As a general guide, equality should be departed from only if, and to the extent that, there was good reason for doing so.

17.28   In *Adams*[62] the deceased had been married to the claimant for 54 years and they had had 12 children. The deceased left her the household goods, his personal effects and a legacy of £10,000. The claimant contended that this was not reasonable and wanted to receive the family home. Three of her daughters opposed this. They accepted that the provision made was not reasonable but argued that the house was too large for her. Behrens J said there was no reason to depart from the *White v White* principle of equality and held that the question of her needs was irrelevant. She was entitled to receive the family home.

17.29   In *Cunliffe v Fielden*[63] Lord Justice Wall said that in family provision applications caution was necessary when carrying out the *White* cross check with the provision available on divorce:

> 'Divorce involves two living former spouses, to each of whom the provisions of section 25(2) of the Matrimonial Causes Act 1973 apply. In cases under the 1975 Act, a deceased spouse who leaves a widow is entitled to bequeath his estate to whomsoever he pleases: his only statutory obligation is to make reasonable financial provision for his widow. In such a case, depending on the value of the estate, the concept of equality may bear little relation to such provision.'

---

[60]   *P v G (family provision: relevance of divorce provision)* [2004] EWHC 2944 (Fam).
[61]   *White v White* [2001] 1 AC 596.
[62]   *Adams v Lewis* [2001] All ER (D) 274 (Jan).
[63]   *Cunliffe v Fielden* [2006] Ch 361.

17.30 *Berger v Berger*[64] is a particularly important case from an estate planning point of view. The deceased husband left his wife a life interest in the substantial estate. The marriage had been a long one. The trial judge had taken the view that a life interest for an elderly widow was reasonable, bearing in mind her age and health. The Court of Appeal disagreed. Since *White* the claimant's financial needs or reasonable requirements were not to be regarded as determinative in arriving at the amount of an award. A divorce court would not have limited its ancillary relief order for the appellant to provision for her various financial needs for the rest of her life even if the almost inevitable result of giving her more would be that there would remain a balance at her death which would simply be transmitted to the next generation as part of her estate. It was at least arguable that the starting point for an ancillary relief order in this case, given the very long period during which the appellant and the deceased had been together, would have been a 50:50 division of their assets.

17.31 Clients should be advised that if the survivor is unhappy with a mere income entitlement and chooses to make an application under the Act, a court is likely to make a capital order. In *Grattan v McNaughton*[65] a husband left his whole estate to his two children subject to the right of his second wife to occupy the matrimonial home for as long as she remained a widow and did not cohabit. The court found that this was not reasonable provision. It widened the right of occupation by striking out the restrictions on cohabitation and remarriage and permitting her a right of occupation in any substitute property. She also took the residue absolutely subject to legacies of £5,000 to each of the children. In the light of this decision, it is probably necessary to warn a client who wants to include a restriction on cohabitation or remarriage that the restriction may be removed in an Inheritance Act claim.

17.32 In *Aston v Aston*[66] the court accepted that in a case where a marriage had effectively come to an end before the deceased's death, the divorce fiction would play a large part in determining what provision was reasonable. The applicant wife had received a substantial sum as the survivor under a joint life policy and had a half interest in the former matrimonial home. In the court's view, she was better off after her husband's death than she would have been on a divorce and it declined to order any further provision. The court took the same approach in *Goenka v Goenka*[67] refusing to award more than the surviving spouse would have received on divorce.

17.33 In *Cunliffe v Fielden*[68] the court had to consider the effect on an award of a brief marriage. It said that there is a clear distinction between brief marriages which end with divorce and those which end with death. A divorce involves a conscious decision by one or both of the spouses to bring the marriage to an end. The premature termination of the marriage is likely to be

---

[64]   *Berger v Berger* [2013] EWCA Civ 1305.
[65]   *Grattan v McNaughton* [2001] WTLR 1305.
[66]   *Aston v Aston* [2007] WTLR 1349.
[67]   [2014] EWHC 2966 (Ch).
[68]   *Cunliffe v Fielden* [2006] Ch 361.

less important than it would be in the case of a divorce. However, this does not mean that the length of the marriage is irrelevant or that the survivor is entitled to one half of the estate. The brevity of the marriage is an argument against equality of division. It is particularly important in the context of assessing housing needs. There is a clear difference between a widow who had been married for many years and who had made an equal contribution to the family of the deceased and a person who had been married for only just over a year and who had made little contribution to the family wealth. While any surviving spouse (or civil partner) is entitled to have 'a reasonable expectation that her life once again as a single woman need not revert to what it was before her marriage'[69]), it may, depending on the length of the marriage and other factors, be inappropriate for her to continue living in the former matrimonial home.

A former spouse or civil partner

17.34   Guidelines (a) and (b) of the surviving spouse/civil partner guidelines also apply in the case of an application by a former spouse. Guideline (c) does not apply unless the court has exercised its limited discretion to apply the surviving spouse standard (see **17.25** above).

Unless there is some special reason, an application by a former spouse who has already received financial provision on the termination of the marriage with a view to a 'clean break' will rarely be successful.[70]

A person who has cohabited with the deceased for 2 years under either s 1(1A) or (1B)

17.35   Section 3(2A) directs the court to consider:

(a)   the age of the applicant and the length of the period during which the applicant lived as the husband or wife of the deceased and in the same household as the deceased; and

(b)   the contribution made by the applicant to the welfare of the family of the deceased, including any contribution made by looking after the home or caring for the family.

As in the case of a spouse, a cohabitee is entitled to have the standard of living enjoyed with the deceased taken into account.[71]

A child of the deceased

17.36   Section 3(3) requires the court to consider the manner in which the applicant was being or in which they might expect to be educated or trained.

---

[69]   *Miller v Miller* [2006] UKHL 24.
[70]   *Re Fullard deceased* [1982] Fam 42.
[71]   See *Negus v Bahouse* [2008] EWCA Civ 1002; *Webster v Webster* [2008] EWHC 31 (Ch).

A person treated by the deceased as a child of the family

17.37   In addition to the education guideline set out above, s 3(3) requires the court consider:

'(a)   whether the deceased maintained the applicant and, if so, to the length of time for which and basis on which the deceased did so, and to the extent of the contribution made by way of maintenance;

(aa)   whether and, if so, to what extent the deceased assumed responsibility for the maintenance of the applicant;

(b)   whether in maintaining or assuming responsibility for maintaining the applicant the deceased did so knowing that the applicant was not his own child;

(c)   to the liability of any other person to maintain the applicant.'

A person maintained by the deceased

17.38   Section 3(4) requires the court to have regard:

'(a)   to the length of time for which and basis on which the deceased maintained the applicant, and to the extent of the contribution made by way of maintenance;

(b)   to whether and, if so, to what extent the deceased assumed responsibility for the maintenance of the applicant.'

This guideline was reworded by the Inheritance and Trustees' Powers Act 2014 because there had been uncertainty as to whether it was a pre-requisite for an application that the deceased had assumed responsibility for the applicant. The new wording clarifies the position. However, while an assumption of responsibility is not a pre-requisite, it is clear that an application is unlikely to succeed without such an assumption.

There is nothing to prevent a testator leaving a statement to the effect that they assumed no responsibility for the applicant or did so only during their lifetime and not after death.

8. THE ORDERS THAT MAY BE MADE

The types

17.39   Section 2 sets out the types of order the court may make.

(a)   *Periodical payments.* Periodical payments are for the term specified in the order. In the case of a former spouse the Act expressly provides that an order shall cease to have effect on the remarriage of the former spouse (s 19(2)). In any other case, however, the court must decide the date of termination when it makes the order.

Periodical payments are unpopular because they are expensive to provide (requiring trust machinery to operate them) and lack finality. It is more common for the court to order a lump sum.

(b) *Lump sum payment.* A lump sum may be made payable by instalments in which case the number, amounts and dates for payments of the instalments can be varied; apart from that a lump sum order cannot be varied (s 7). A lump sum is appropriate in the case of an application by a surviving spouse but it can also be ordered in the case of other applicants even though they are only entitled to maintenance. Where an estate is very small a lump sum order is particularly useful; indeed it may be the only type of provision which can realistically be made.

(c) *Transfer of property.* The court may order the transfer of a particular asset to an applicant. This may be advisable where a lump sum order would require an improvident sale of assets. Such an order once made cannot be varied.

(d) *Settlement of property.* An order for settlement of property is particularly likely in the case of a minor or a person who is in need of protection. Such a settlement should be drafted with an eye to tax and trust law. Such an order, once made, cannot be varied.

(e) *Acquisition of property for transfer or settlement.* The court may order that assets from the net estate of the deceased be used to acquire a specified item (for example, a house) which will either be transferred to or settled on an applicant. Such an order, once made, cannot be varied.

(f) *Variation of marriage settlements.* An ante- or post-nuptial settlement may be varied by the court for the benefit of the surviving spouse of the marriage or the children of the marriage or any person who was treated by the deceased as a child of that marriage. Such an order for variation, once made, cannot be varied.

A provision in a pension scheme allowing an employee to direct benefits to a spouse may be a settlement for this purpose.[72] Even where not directly available as a settlement, pension benefits may still be important as they may increase the resources of other people interested in the estate.

(g) *Variation of any settlement made during the subsistence of, or in anticipation of a civil partnership formed by the deceased.* Such a settlement may be varied for the benefit of the surviving civil partner, or any child of both the civil partners, or any person who was treated by the deceased as a child of the family in relation to that civil partnership.

The Inheritance and Trustees' Powers Act 2014 added power for the court to vary, for the applicant's benefit, the trusts on which the deceased's estate is held (whether these are trusts arising on intestacy or under a will or both). This provides a more direct way of achieving a result that previously required the creation of a new trust or trusts to replace the existing trust or trusts under which the estate is held.

---

[72] *Brooks v Brooks* [1996] AC 375.

The burden of an order

17.40 Any order made by the court may contain such consequential and supplemental provisions as the court thinks necessary or expedient for the purpose of securing that it operates fairly as between one beneficiary of the estate and another. For example, if the court makes a periodical payments order or a lump sum order it may direct which part of the estate is to bear the burden; if the court orders that an asset which had been specifically left to a beneficiary is to be transferred to the applicant the court may vary the disposition of the estate to make alternative provision for the disappointed beneficiary.

'Beneficiary' in this context includes the donee of a statutory nomination or a donatio mortis causa or a surviving joint tenant.

Inheritance tax

17.41 The court order alters the disposition of the estate of the deceased and is deemed to have done so from the date of the death of the deceased for all purposes including the payment of inheritance tax (Inheritance Tax Act 1984, s 146). So, for example, if an order increases the amount passing to a surviving spouse the chargeable value of the estate for inheritance tax purposes will be reduced whereas if less property passes to a surviving spouse the chargeable value will be increased.

In *Re Goodchild*[73] the court used its variation powers to order that the testator's will was to be treated as if it had always left £185,000 to trustees to pay the income to the deceased's second wife for a very short period and, subject thereto, for the applicant absolutely. The purpose of the order was to get the benefit of the spouse exemption and avoid the inheritance tax which would have been payable had the property been left directly to the applicant. The parties took the risk of an inheritance tax liability arising on the death of the second wife if she died within 7 years of the termination of the interest in possession.

The Court of Appeal expressed some reservations about the use of variation orders under s 1(4) to obtain a tax benefit. However, Morritt LJ admitted that 'if the order made is properly within the jurisdiction of the court the fact that it was sought with the motive of seeking to achieve a better tax position is usually irrelevant'. He went on to say that in future, if such an order was sought 'the grounds on which it is thought to be authorised by s 1(4) should be clearly demonstrated for the consents and wishes of the parties are not enough'.

Interim payments

17.42 Under s 5 the court has power to make an interim order in favour of an applicant who is in immediate need of financial assistance.

---

[73] *Re Goodchild* [1997] 1 WLR 1216.

9. PROPERTY AVAILABLE FOR FINANCIAL PROVISION

The net estate

17.43   If the court decides to order provision to be made for an applicant such an order is made against the 'net estate' of the deceased. The net estate is defined[74] as:

(a) 'All property of which the deceased had power to dispose by his will (otherwise than by virtue of a special power of appointment) less the amount of his funeral, testamentary and administration expenses, debts and liabilities including any inheritance tax payable out of his estate on death'. This will obviously not include insurance policies where the proceeds are payable direct to a beneficiary rather than to the estate of the policyholder as the deceased has no power to dispose of such property.

(b) 'Any property in respect of which the deceased held a general power of appointment (not being a power exercisable by will) which has not been exercised'. If the power was exercisable by will the property subject to the power falls into (a) above whether or not the deceased actually exercised it.

(c) Any property nominated by the deceased to any person under a statutory nomination or received by any person as a result of a donatio mortis causa less any inheritance tax payable in respect of such property and borne by the nominee or done.[75]

(d) The deceased's severable share of a joint tenancy, but only if the court so orders.[76]

(e) Any property which the court orders shall be available as a result of its anti-avoidance powers.[77]

Life assurance policies written in trust for others are not part of the net estate (though settling the benefit of the policy in trust may fall within the court's anti-avoidance powers).

Joint property

17.44   As a result of the right of survivorship a deceased has no power to dispose of the interest under a joint tenancy by will. However, under s 9 where the deceased was a joint tenant of any property immediately before death the court may, for the purpose of facilitating the making of financial provision, order that the deceased's severable share of the shall to such extent as appears to the court to be just in all the circumstances (and after allowing for any inheritance tax payable) be treated as part of the net estate.

---

[74]   I(PFD)A 1975, s 25.

[75]   I(PFD)A 1975, s 8. See *Goenka v Goenka* [2014] EWHC 2966 (Ch) for the availability of death benefits nominated under National Health Service (Injury Benefits) Regulations 1995 of death benefits.

[76]   I(PFD)A 1985, s 9. See **17.44** below.

[77]   See **17.46** below.

As originally drafted the discretion existed only in respect of applications made within 6 months from the date of the grant; there was no power to make such an order in connection with an out-of-time application. This could present a trap for unwary applicants and for deaths on or after 1 October 2014 the Inheritance and Trustees' Powers Act 2014 has removed this limitation.

As originally drafted s 9 referred to the value of the deceased's interest *immediately before death*. If the grant is not taken promptly, an application under s 9 may in fact be made many years after the date of death by which time the value of the deceased's interest may have risen significantly. This problem arose in *Dingmar v Dingmar*.[78] As a result, the Inheritance and Trustees' Powers Act 2014 inserted a new sub-section 1A into s 9 providing that the value of the deceased's severable share of property is taken to be the value that the share would have had at the date of the hearing of the application for an order under s 2 had the share been severed immediately before the deceased's death, unless the court orders that the share is to be valued at a different date.

17.45 Section 9(4) provides, for the avoidance of doubt, that for the purposes of this section there may be a joint tenancy of a chose in action, for example, the asset represented by a credit balance in a joint bank account. Whether or not the proceeds of a life assurance policy taken out by a couple jointly, form part of the deceased's estate or pass directly to the survivor can be a difficult issue. The proceeds of such a policy may be the only real assets of the estate. The position will depend on the terms of the policy but where a lump sum is payable only to the survivor and has no surrender value, it cannot form part of the deceased estate.[79]

10. ANTI-AVOIDANCE PROVISIONS

Introduction

17.46 A deceased might seek to evade the provisions of the Act either by making lifetime gifts of property so that the net estate on death is substantially reduced or by entering into a binding contract to leave property by will; the effect of such a contract would be to give the other party to the contract a right to enforce it against the personal representatives, thus reducing the net estate available for family provision. Sections 10 and 11 of the Act enable the court to prevent such evasion; they give power to order a person to satisfy a claim for family provision if they have benefited under a lifetime disposition or a contract to provide money or other property.

---

[78] *Dingmar v Dingmar* [2006] EWCA Civ 942 where the Court of Appeal criticised the wording of the section as unclear and 2:1 held that it could be interpreted as referring to the extent of the deceased's interest at the date of death.

[79] See *Powell v Osbourne* [1993] 1 FLR 1001; *Murphy v Murphy* [2003] EWCA Civ 1862; *Lim v Walia* [2014] EWCA Civ 1076.

The court's power is discretionary and it will not use its anti-avoidance powers unless satisfied that to do so will facilitate the making of financial provision.

Lifetime Gifts

17.47   A disposition is covered by s 10 if it was made:

(a)   after 31 March 1976 and less than 6 years before the date of death of the deceased;

(b)   with the intention of defeating an application under the Act; and

(c)   for less than full valuable consideration.

A 'disposition' for this purpose includes any payment of money (including insurance premiums) and any conveyance of property whether or not made by instrument. It does not, however, include any statutory nomination, donatio mortis causa or appointment of property under a special power of appointment.

Contracts

17.48   A contract is covered by s 11 of the Act if:

(a)   entered into after 31 March 1976;

(b)   the deceased agreed to leave money or other property by will or agreed that money or other property would be paid or transferred to any person from his estate;

(c)   this will obviously not include insurance policies where the proceeds are payable direct to a beneficiary rather than to the estate of the policyholder as the deceased has no power to dispose of such property;

(d)   the deceased made the contract with the intention of defeating an application under the Act; and

(e)   when the contract was made full valuable consideration was not given or promised.

In the case of a contract there is no time limit as there is in the case of lifetime dispositions.

The intention of defeating an application

17.49   The deceased must have made a disposition or contract with the intention of defeating an application. Section 12 provides that this requirement is satisfied if the court is of the opinion on a balance of probabilities that the deceased's intention (though not necessarily the sole intention) in making the disposition or contract was to prevent an order for financial provision being made or to reduce the amount of the provision which might otherwise be ordered.

In the case of a contract, s 12(2) provides that, if a contract is made for no valuable consideration (ie by way of a deed), there will be a presumption that the deceased's intention was to defeat the application.

Illustration of the use of the power

17.50 *Hanbury v Hanbury*[80] is a good illustration of the court using its anti-avoidance powers. The deceased had had no contact with his mentally and physically disabled daughter from the date of the breakdown of his marriage to her mother save that he paid £900 per annum for her maintenance. After legal advice and with the intention of defeating any claim brought on behalf of the daughter he transferred assets into either the joint names of himself and his second wife or into her name alone. When he died he left his daughter £10,000 from his estate of £11,981 (apparently calculating that this would be sufficient to prevent a claim).

Sections 9 and 10 were used to recover more than £50,000 of assets from the second wife. Shares in investment trusts (worth £100,000 at the date of death) had been bought in the second wife's name from a joint bank account fed by both parties.

Alternative claim under the Insolvency Act

17.51 As an alternative to a s 10 claim, it is possible to bring an application under Insolvency Act 1986, s 423. This allows the court, if satisfied that a donor entered into a transaction at an undervalue for the purpose:

(a)   of putting assets beyond the reach of a person who is making, or may at some time make, a claim against him; or

(b)   of otherwise prejudicing the interests of such a person in relation to the claim which he is making or may make,

to make such order as it sees fit to restore the position to what it would have been if the transaction had not been entered into, and to protect the interests of persons who are victims of the transaction as it sees fit.

17.52 In *B v IB*[81] Parker J held that the Insolvency Act remedy is not confined to applications where the transferor is insolvent, nor need there be insolvency proceedings. The remedy is meant to be a wide-ranging anti-avoidance provision. It is not the existence of insolvency but the existence of debt which triggers the remedy. The existence of a 'tailor made' remedy for I(PFD)A claims does not preclude reliance on s 423. The s 423 test is wider than the s 10 test and the remedy different. There are the following important distinctions between the two remedies:

---

[80]   *Hanbury v Hanbury* [1999] 2 FLR 255. See also *Re Dawkins (Deceased)* [1986] 2 FLR 360 for another example of s 10 in operation.

[81]   *B v IB* [2013] EWHC 3755 (Fam).

(a)   under I(PFD)A 1975, s 10 the applicant must prove that the disposition was made with intention of defeating an application for financial provision;

(b)   under s 423 the applicant must prove that a purpose is to put assets beyond reach or prejudice interests, a more general purpose;

(c)   under the I(PFD)A the court can order the provision of 'such sum of money or other property as may be specified in the order'. Under s 423 the transaction is set aside;

(d)   under the I(PFD)A 1975 the court has to balance various factors such as the circumstances of the disposition made, any valuable consideration given, the relationship of the donee to the deceased, the conduct and financial resources of the donee;

(e)   s 423 contains no such provision. It requires the court to make an order which, so far as is practicable, will restore the position to what it would have been if the transaction had not been entered into and will protect the interests of the victims of it, although there is a general discretion in that it states that the court 'may' make an order.

11. TAX EFFICIENT ORDERS

17.53   It is important to structure the order in as tax efficient a manner as possible. The important points in relation to IHT are:

(a)   court orders are treated as having effect from the date of death;[82]

(b)   court orders staying or dismissing proceedings on terms set out in the order, referred to as Tomlin Orders are treated as full orders. This is important because many claims under the Act are settled by consent without a trial and the reading back effect of s 146 would not otherwise apply to such orders;

(c)   the order may have the effect of increasing IHT if, for example, property in excess of the IHT nil rate band is diverted from an exempt to a non-exempt beneficiary;

(d)   including a short term interest in possession for a spouse retains the spouse exemption for the estate (on the ending of the interest the spouse will generally be treated as making a PET which will become fully exempt if

---

[82]   IHTA 1984, s 146 which provides that where an order is made under I(PFD)A 1975, s 2 in relation to any property forming part of the net estate of a deceased person, then the property shall for the purposes of IHTA 1984 be treated as if it had on the death devolved subject to the provisions of the order.
I(PFD)A 1975, s 19 provides that where an order is made under s 2 then for all purposes, including the purposes of enactments relating to IHT, the will and/or the law relating to intestacy shall have effect and be deemed to have effect as from the deceased's death subject to the provisions of the order.
IHTA 1984 s 146, though similar to I(PFD)A 1975, s 19 is wider. I(PFD)A 1975, s 19 only provides for *the deceased's will and/or the law relating to intestacy* to be deemed to have effect as from the deceased's death – not, for example, the deceased's severable share of joint property or property which was subject to a nomination.

the spouse survives 7 years); however the court may not be willing to agree[83] and HMRC will query any interest in possession of less than 5 years; see Inheritance Tax Manual para 35202 which comments:

> 'If the order creates a short-term (not exceeding five years) interest in possession for the benefit of the deceased's spouse or civil partner you should refer the file to TG with a summary of the deceased's will or intestacy and of the order.'

(e)   if an order results in property being settled or for the variation of a settlement, there shall be no charge under IHTA 1984 s 52(1) which deals with the *inter vivos* termination of interests in possession. For instance, if an IPDI for a spouse is varied in favour of a child, that spouse will make neither a PET nor a chargeable transfer;

(f)   there is no IHT advantage in an exempt beneficiary settling the claim from his/her own resources as IHTA 1984, s 29A provides that the spouse exemption will be lost to the extent that an exempt beneficiary settles a claim against the estate from their own resources;

Example 17.1

A dies leaving everything to Mrs A. Dependant B has a claim against A's estate but is 'bought off' by Mrs A making a payment (out of her own resources) of £150,000.

(1)   In the absence of specific legislation: the arrangement would probably be a PET by Mrs A to B and so free from IHT provided that Mrs A survived by 7 years. Alternatively it could be argued that there was no transfer of value since the compromise was a commercial arrangement under IHTA 1984, s 10. No IHT was, of course, charged on A's death.

(2)   Position under s 29A: A's will is deemed amended to include a specific gift of £150,000 to B with the remainder (only) passing to Mrs A. Accordingly a recalculation will be necessary and an immediate IHT charge will arise.

(g)   in the case of a settlement without a court order if the parties want to achieve backdating, they may be able to use a post-death variation to obtain it. At first sight there would seem to be a problem as a variation is not effective for backdating if there is extraneous consideration. Settling a claim would appear to be consideration. However HMRC accepts that such a variation is not caught by s 142(3) (unless the deceased dies domiciled outside the UK);[84]

(h)   although CGT is not expressly mentioned in I(PFD)A 1975, s 19, its wide wording means that for CGT purposes where an order is made under I(PFD)A 1975, s 2 the will and/or the law relating to intestacy will have effect and be deemed to have effect as from the deceased's death subject to the provisions of the order. Accordingly, neither a beneficiary nor the

---

[83]   See *Re Goodchild* [1997] 1 WLR 1216.
[84]   See Inheritance Tax Manual para 35100. A different view may, however, be taken for CGT purposes.

personal representatives can be treated as making a disposal for CGT purposes as a consequence of any order under I(PFD)A 1975, s 2. Further, a claimant who takes any asset from the estate as a result of an order will take as a legatee for CGT purposes, so there will be no disposal when the asset is vested in him by the personal representatives and he will take the asset with the personal representatives' acquisition cost, ie its market value. But as noted above, I(PFD)A 1975, s 2 does not embrace orders affecting the devolution of property outside the deceased's will or intestacy, eg property which was subject to a nomination and severable shares in joint property, so there may be disposals in respect of these;

(i)   no express provision is made in the CGT legislation for the CGT consequences of a Tomlin Order. HMRC's view appears to depend on the precise form of order made by the judge, see the *Capital Gains Tax Manual* 31800-31813. If the terms of the Tomlin Order are merely that the parties are *at liberty* to carry out the terms of compromise, HMRC will not accept this as an order under I(PFD)A 1975, s 2 but if there is the added requirement that the parties *do* carry out those terms, HMRC will accept this as an order under I(PFD)A 1975, s 2 so that for CGT purposes the will and/or the law relating to intestacy will have effect and be deemed to have effect as from the deceased's death subject to the provisions of the Order (see *Capital Gains Manual CG31813*). But as a fairly new practice, HMRC apparently accepts that a Tomlin Order may be a variation to which TCGA 1992, s 62(6) is capable of applying, see *Capital Gains Manual* 31820.

17.54   Be careful when structuring settlements with post-death variations to achieve a tax efficient result.

An obvious route might seem to be for the variation to create a short (or terminable) life interest for a surviving spouse or civil partner. However IHTA 1984, s 142(4) provides that where a variation results in property being held in trust for a period which ends not more than 2 years after the death, the trust interest is ignored and the estate is taxed as if the disposition which takes effect on the termination of the trust interest had taken effect on death.

Example 17.2

The parties agree that the post-death variation will give the surviving spouse a 6-month interest in possession, after which the property will pass to the claimant absolutely. Because of s 142(4) the spouse exemption will not apply and IHT will be charged as if the property had passed directly to the claimant. The section does not apply if the interest comes to an end as a result of the death of the surviving spouse because then it is not the variation that causes the interest to end within 2 years of the death.

Appendices

APPENDIX I

INTEREST RATES PAYABLE ON FUNDS IN COURT

The current rate is a derisory 0.3% but it has been significantly higher.

Basic Interest rate

Date	Rate of interest (%)
1.10.65	2.50
1.4.71	3.50
1.4.73	4.00
1.2.77	5.00
1.4.83	9.50
1.4.84	8.00
1.8.86	7.50
1.1.87	8.50
1.12.87	8.00
1.5.88	7.50
1.8.88	9.00
1.11.88	10.25
1.1.89	10.75
1.11.89	11.25
1.4.91	9.50
1.10.91	8.00
1.2.93	6.00
1.8.99	5.25
1.2.02	4.00
1.2.09	2.00
1.6.09	1.00
1.7.09	0.30

APPENDIX II

NIL RATE BAND TABLES

Inheritance Tax thresholds – present day back to 18 March 1986

From	To	Threshold/nil rate band
6 April 2009		£325,000
6 April 2008	5 April 2009	£312,000
6 April 2007	5 April 2008	£300,000
6 April 2006	5 April 2007	£285,000
6 April 2005	5 April 2006	£275,000
6 April 2004	5 April 2005	£263,000
6 April 2003	5 April 2004	£255,000
6 April 2002	5 April 2003	£250,000
6 April 2001	5 April 2002	£242,000
6 April 2000	5 April 2001	£234,000
6 April 1999	5 April 2000	£231,000
6 April 1998	5 April 1999	£223,000
6 April 1997	5 April 1998	£215,000
6 April 1996	5 April 1997	£200,000
6 April 1995	5 April 1996	£154,000
10 March 1992	5 April 1995	£150,000
6 April 1991	9 March 1992	£140,000
6 April 1990	5 April 1991	£128,000
6 April 1989	5 April 1990	£118,000
15 March 1988	5 April 1989	£110,000
17 March 1987	14 March 1988	£90,000
18 March 1986	16 March 1987	£71,000

'Capital Transfer Tax' (Inheritance Tax thresholds) – 17 March 1986 back to 13 March 1975 for England, Wales, Scotland and Northern Ireland

From	To	Threshold/nil rate band
6 April 1985	17 March 1986	£67,000
13 March 1984	5 April 1985	£64,000
15 March 1983	12 March 1984	£60,000
9 March 1982	14 March 1983	£55,000
26 March 1980	8 March 1982	£50,000
27 October 1977	25 March 1980	£25,000
13 March 1975	26 October 1977	£15,000

'Estate Duty' (Inheritance Tax thresholds) – 12 March 1975 back to 16 August 1914 for England, Wales and Scotland

From	To	Threshold/nil rate band
22 March 1972	12 March 1975	£15,000
31 March 1971	21 March 1972	£12,500
16 April 1969	30 March 1971	£10,000
4 April 1963	15 April 1969	£5,000
9 April 1962	3 April 1963	£4,000
30 July 1954	8 April 1962	£3,000
10 April 1946	29 July 1954	£2,000
16 August 1914	9 April 1946	£100

'Estate Duty' (Inheritance Tax thresholds) – 12 March 1975 back to 16 August 1914 for Northern Ireland only

From	To	Threshold/nil rate band
22 March 1972	12 March 1975	£15,000
5 May 1971	21 March 1972	£12,500
4 June 1969	4 May 1971	£10,000
22 May 1963	3 June 1969	£5,000
4 July 1962	21 May 1963	£4,000
1 November 1954	3 July 1962	£3,000
29 August 1946	31 October 1954	£2,000
16 August 1914	28 August 1946	£100

INDEX

References are to paragraph numbers.